## TAXONOMY OF INSTRUCTIONAL DESIGN FUNCTIONS

| Design Functions | Components | Description |
| --- | --- | --- |
| Identifying instructional problems | Needs assessment | Normative, comparative, felt, expressed, future, critical incident needs |
| | Goal analysis | Aim, goals, refinement, rank, refinement, final rank |
| | Performance assessment | Knowledge or skills, motivation or incentive, environmental, management, interpersonal |

| Design Functions | Components | Description |
| --- | --- | --- |
| Learner analysis | General characteristics | Age, grade level |
| | Specific entry competencies | Ability to understand abstract information |
| Contextual analysis | Orienting context | Learner's perspective |
| | Instructional context | Lighting, noise, seating |
| | Transfer context | On-the-job support |

| Design Functions | Components | Description |
| --- | --- | --- |
| Task analysis | Topic analysis | Knowledge, concepts, principles |
| | Procedural analysis | Steps and knowledge, concepts, principles |
| | Critical incident method | Interpersonal communication |

| Design Functions | Components | Description |
| --- | --- | --- |
| Objectives | Behavioral | Verb, criterion, condition |
| | Cognitive | General instructional objective, samples of performance |
| Expanded performance-content matrix | Content | Fact, concept, principle or rules, procedure, interpersonal, attitude |
| | Performance | Recall, application |

| Design Functions | Components | Description |
| --- | --- | --- |
| Sequencing | Learning related | Identifiable prerequisites, familiarity, difficulty, interest, and development |
| | World related | Spatial, temporal, physical |
| | Concept related | Class, propositional, sophistication, logical prerequisites |

| | Content expertise | Conceptual sequence, theoretical sequence |
| --- | --- | --- |
| | Task expertise | Simplifying conditions |

| Design Functions | Components | Description |
| --- | --- | --- |
| Strategies | Recall | Rehearsal, mnemonics |
| | Integration | Paraphrasing, generating questions |
| | Organizational | Outlining, categorization |
| | Elaboration | Mental images, diagrams, sentence elaborations |

| Design Functions | Components | Description |
| --- | --- | --- |
| Preinstructional strategies | Pretest | Alerts learner |
| | Objectives | Precisely inform learner |
| | Overview | Prepares learner |
| | Advance organizer | Clarifies content |
| Message design | Signals | Explicit, typographical |
| | Pictures | Decoration, representation, organization, interpretation, transformation |

| Design Functions | Components | Description |
| --- | --- | --- |
| Development | Concrete | Pictures/images |
| | Step size | Terminology, references |
| | Pacing | Examples and elaborations |
| | Consistency | Terminology used |
| | Cues | Highlighting points |

| Design Functions | Components | Description |
| --- | --- | --- |
| Formative Evaluation | Planning | Purpose, audience, issues, resources, evidence, data-gathering techniques, analysis, reporting |
| | Techniques | Connoisseur-based, decision-oriented, objectives-based, public relations–inspired studies |
| Summative Evaluation | Planning | Specify objectives |
| | Techniques | Determine evaluation design for each objective |
| | | Develop data collection instruments |
| | | Carry out evaluation |
| | | Analyze results |
| | | Interpret results |

| Confirmative evaluation | Educational programs | Appropriateness of courses, competencies, benefits |
|---|---|---|
| | Training programs | Appropriateness of training, competencies, benefits |
| Assessment | Standards of achievement | Relative and absolute standards |
| Student self-evaluation | Pretesting | Testing for prerequisites, improved performance |

| **Design Functions** | **Components** | **Description** |
|---|---|---|
| Testing for knowledge items | Objective tests | Multiple choice, true/false, matching, constructed-response items |
| Testing for skills and behavior | Direct, analysis of naturally occurring results | |
| | Ratings of performance | |
| | Rubrics | |
| | Anecdotal records | |
| | Indirect checklist | |
| | Portfolio assessment | |
| | Exhibitions | |
| Testing for attitudes | Observation/anecdotal records | Rating scale |
| | Assessment of behavior | Observation, questionnaire/survey, interview |

| **Design Functions** | **Components** | **Description** |
|---|---|---|
| Proposal preparation | Purpose | Each proposal should include this information. If no format is provided by the funding group, these tools can also serve as the headings |
| | Plan of work | |
| | Milestones and deliverables | |
| | Budget | |
| | Schedule | |
| | Staffing | |
| Project planning | Scope of work | Prepared prior to beginning the work |
| | Scheduling | |
| | Budgeting | |
| Management | Managing resources | Used to monitor, report, and revise the project planning materials |
| | Tracking | |
| | Reporting | |

| Design Functions | Components | Description |
| --- | --- | --- |
| Project team | Instructional designer | Designs the instruction |
| | Media production | Graphic artist, scriptwriter, video production staff, still photographers, programmers, network administrator |
| | Evaluator | Develops evaluation plan |
| | Performance consultant | Helps with nontraining interventions |
| | Subject-matter expert | Provides content information |

| Design Functions | Components | Description |
| --- | --- | --- |
| Implementation plan | CLER model | Configurations, linkages, environment, resources |
| | Development/Information Decision-Making models | Awareness, information-seeking, visualization, tryout, and acceptance |
| Implementation decisions | Instructional delivery | Classroom facilities, media equipment, other equipment, transportation, housing, and food |
| | Materials | Packaging, duplicating, warehousing, and shipping |
| | Instructors | Scheduling, training |

# Designing
# Effective
# Instruction

# Designing Effective Instruction

## Sixth Edition

Gary R. Morrison
*Old Dominion University*

Steven M. Ross
*Johns Hopkins University*

Howard K. Kalman
*Ithaca College*

Jerrold E. Kemp
*Professor Emeritus*
*San Jose State University*

**WILEY**

**JOHN WILEY & SONS, INC.**

| | |
|---|---|
| VP & Executive Publisher | *Jay O'Callaghan* |
| Acquisitions Editor | *Robert Johnston* |
| Marketing Manager | *Danielle Torio* |
| Production Manager | *Dorothy Sinclair* |
| Senior Production Editor | *Sandra Dumas* |
| Creative Director | *Harry Nolan* |
| Cover Designer | *Wendy Lai* |
| Media Editor | *Lynn Pearlman* |
| Editorial Assistant | *Mariah Maguire-Fong* |
| Production Management Services | *LaserWords Maine* |

This book was typeset in New Baskerville by Laserwords Private Limited, Chennai, India and printed and bound by Malloy Lithographics. The Cover was printed by Malloy Lithographics.

The paper in this book was manufactured by a mill whose forest management programs include sustained yield harvesting of its timberlands. Sustained yield harvesting principles ensure that the number of trees cut each year does not exceed the amount of new growth.

This book is printed on acid-free paper.∞

Morrison, Gary R., Ed. D.
  Designing effective instruction / Gary R. Morrison, Steven M. Ross, Howard K. Kalman,
    Jerrold E. Kemp—6th Edition

ISBN 13    978-0-470-52282-0

Printed in the United States of America

10 9 8 7 6 5 4 3 2 1

*We would like to dedicate this book to our mentors:*

I would like to express my appreciation in the memory of Denny Pett, my advisor and chairman at Indiana University, for providing the opportunities and challenges that made graduate school an important part of my career.

—Gary Morrison

I thank Frank Di Vesta, who was my advisor and chairman at Pennsylvania State University, for the training and mentoring that so well prepared me for writing, research, and teaching.

—Steven Ross

I would like to thank Thomas M. Schwen and Ivor K. Davies, who served as advisors and mentors at Indiana University, for providing me valuable learning opportunities and for their guidance.

—Howard K. Kalman

I would like to express my appreciation in the memory of Dick Lewis, who was director of audiovisual services at San Jose State University, as my career started in instructional technology.

—Jerry Kemp

# PREFACE

The sixth edition of Designing Effective Instruction has evolved from one of Jerry's early textbooks. In 1971, *Instructional Design: A Plan for Unit and Course Development* was published by Fearon Publishers. In the preface Jerry wrote, ''Planning for student learning should be a challenging, exciting, and gratifying activity.'' Almost 40 years later, experienced instructional designers would agree with Jerry's statement. We believe that this edition of our textbook will help instructional designers accept the challenge of designing effective and efficient instruction that is exciting and interesting, to find the process is stimulating, and to believe that there is a great deal of satisfaction to gain from completing an instructional design project.

## CONCEPTUAL FRAMEWORK

The model presented in this book is eclectic in that it borrows ideas from many different disciplines and approaches to instructional design. We believe that there is never one perfect approach to solving an instructional design problem. As a result, we have incorporated both behavioral and cognitive approaches into the model so that we can reap the benefits of each.

An effective instructional design model is both flexible and adaptable. No two designers will approach a problem in the same manner, and no two problems are exactly alike. The model in this book is circular rather than a more traditional linear flowchart. Our experience has shown that projects start and end at different places in the design process. Often, designers are not able to complete each and every step because of external constraints. Other times, it is not efficient or necessary to complete each step. The design model must be flexible to accommodate the demands of the job, yet maintain the logic to produce an effective product. A design model must grow with the instructional designer. We have approached instructional design as the application of heuristics that one can apply to a variety of instructional problems. These heuristics are modified and embellished based on each instructional designer's experiences, observations, and interpretations of the literature. This approach to instructional design allows designers to both modify and add to our list of heuristics. We continue to provide a strong emphasis on designing instruction in a business setting. Our approach in this text is one that is applicable to designers in business, military, medical, and government settings as well as to higher education and P–12 classrooms. Designers in each of the environments will take different approaches because of the opportunities created and the constraints imposed by each situation. However, instructional designers will have the common goal of using the instructional design model to guide them in the development of effective instruction.

## INTRODUCTION TO THE SIXTH EDITION

With each of our editions, several of our colleagues strongly encouraged us to maintain the integrity of our model. With each edition, there is always the consideration of how and where to expand the book. We have carefully considered various options and suggestions. Our focus in this book is on the basics of instructional design that will help a student develop a solid foundation in the design process. Students and designers can then use and adapt these basic skills in a variety of settings such as multimedia, classroom, and distance-education instruction.

The organization of this book allows the instructor to adapt the sequence to the class as well as to the instructor's own perspective. An instructor can also vary the emphasis in each chapter. For example, an introductory course might place the most emphasis on Chapters 2 through 13 (the basic design process). An advanced course might place more emphasis on Chapters 10–16 (evaluation, design of technology-based instruction, project management, role of the designer, and implementation). Another approach is to start with the chapters on evaluation and assessment (11 to 13) or project management (16), then teach the basic design process (2 to 9), and end with the new chapter on designing for technology-based instruction. Other instructors might decide to start with a theoretical foundation (Chapter 14) and then teach the basic design process (2 to 13).

### What's New

In this edition, we have made significant updates to all the chapters to include recent trends and research, added one new chapter, and changed the organization and content of the final chapters. The new chapter, Chapter 10, focuses on design considerations for technology-based instruction. In this chapter we examine design considerations for computer-based, web-based, and distance instruction. We have also reorganized the planning and implementation chapter and the project management chapters at the end of the text. Chapter 15 has a new section that describes the decision stages involved in adopting an innovation as well as a brief discussion of the supervisor's role in supporting employee training. Chapter 16 now includes a complete example of a project agreement and a new section on design process shortcuts.

### Pedagogical Features

We have created a design for this textbook that includes various features to stimulate thinking and to provide additional explanations in the book.

**Getting Started.**    Each chapter begins with the "Getting Started" section that provides a real-world scenario of an aspect of the chapter. Instructors can use these scenarios as stimulus for discussion during class time or as part of a discussion conducted via a mailing list or online forum discussion.

**Expert's Edge.** What happens when an instructional designer tries to design a project in the real world? The "Expert's Edge" pieces were contributed by practicing instructional designers and scholars who share their knowledge, successes, failures, and perspectives from the real world. The Expert's Edge pieces reflect an international perspective as well as different contexts in which instructional design is conducted.

**The ID Process.** Instructional design texts, as most scholarly texts, tend to take a sterile approach to writing. The "ID Process" sections allow us to present a "here's how it is really done" discussion of each element of the model.

**Applications and Answers.** At the end of each chapter, we present one or two exercises for the readers to test their skills and knowledge. Many of the chapters present the reader with realistic problems where they can apply and expand their knowledge.

**Quality Management.** This section will help the designer conduct a quick quality check of the design project. Key questions and issues are presented to help the designer keep the project aligned with solving the instructional problem. If you require your students to develop a project as part of this course, they can use this feature to do a quality check during the design and development process.

**Instructional Design: Decisions and Choices.** This section tracks an instructional design project through the ID process. Our approach is to provide a realistic example of the instructional design process along with commentary from the designer on the decisions and choices made at each step of the process.


## ACKNOWLEDGMENTS

Since the first edition of this text in 1994, we have received feedback, ideas, and encouragement from colleagues far and near. Although the list is too long to name each individual, we would like to thank each of you for your ideas and suggestions and encourage you to continue to provide us with your feedback. Last, we would like to thank the numerous students in our classes and those of our colleagues who have provided us with valuable insights into ways of improving the book.

# ABOUT THE AUTHORS

**Gary R. Morrison** Received his doctorate in instructional systems technology from Indiana University in 1977. Since then, he has worked as an instructional designer at the University of Mid-America, Solar Turbines International, General Electric Company's Corporate Consulting Group, and Tenneco Oil Company; and as a professor at the University of Memphis and Wayne State University. He is currently a professor at Old Dominion University, where he teaches courses in instructional design. His credits include print projects, multimedia projects, and over 30 hours of instructional video programs, including a five-part series that was aired nationally on PBS-affiliated stations. He has worked on projects involving pest management for farmers, small business management, gas turbine troubleshooting, systems engineering for electrical engineers, beam-pumping performance analysis, vessel design, microcomputer sales, and microcomputer repair.

Gary has written more than 100 papers on topics related to instructional design and computer-based instruction, as well as contributing to several book chapters and instructional software packages. He is co-author of *Integrating Computer Technology into the Classroom*. He is the editor of the *Journal of Computing in Higher Education*, editorial board member of two journals, and a past president of the Association for Educational Communication and Technology's (AECT) Research and Theory, Design and Development, and Distance Learning Divisions.

**Steven M. Ross** Received his doctorate in educational psychology from Pennsylvania State University. He is currently a senior research scientist and professor at the Center for Research and Reform in Education at Johns Hopkins University. Dr. Ross is the author of six textbooks and over 120 journal articles in the areas of educational technology and instructional design, at-risk learners, educational reform, computer-based instruction, and research and evaluation. He is a noted lecturer on school programs and educational evaluation, the editor of the research section of the *Educational Technology Research and Development* journal, and a member of the editorial board for two other professional journals. In 1993, he was the first faculty recipient of The University of Memphis Eminent Faculty Award for teaching, research and service, and recently held the Lillian and Morrie Moss Chair of Excellence in Urban Education and a Faudree Professorship at The University of Memphis. He has testified on school restructuring research before the U.S. House of Representatives Subcommittee on Early Childhood, Youth, and Families, and is a technical advisor and researcher on current federal and state initiatives regarding the evaluation of technology usage, supplemental educational services, State Systems of Support (SSOS), and No Child Left Behind.

**Howard K. Kalman** Received his doctorate in instructional systems technology from Indiana University in 2001. He joined the faculty at Ithaca College in 2002, is currently an associate professor in strategic communication, and also serves as the graduate program chair. He teaches courses in strategic communication management, learning, and performance improvement. Earlier in his career, he worked as a district audiovisual specialist for the Aurora City School District (Ohio) and as an instructional designer for Chevron Information Technology Company. He has consulted on projects involving needs assessments, program evaluation, and strategic planning for Fortune 500 firms as well as instructional projects involving custom computer applications, hazardous materials handling, new supervisor orientation, network operations, and data communications. He has authored or co-authored publications on strategic planning, knowledge management, process improvement, and instructional strategies and contributed to the *Handbook of Human Performance Technology* (2nd ed.).

**Jerrold E. Kemp** Received his doctorate in audiovisual education from Indiana University in 1956. For 30 years, he served as professor of instructional technology and coordinator of instructional development services at San Jose State University, California. Jerry first wrote *Instructional Design: A Plan for Unit and Course Development* in 1971 (Fearon), from which the present book, as the fourth version, emerged. In addition, he has authored or coauthored three other books dealing with training and technology. Jerry has been an instructional design consultant and conducts training workshops for many computer and electronics companies in Silicon Valley, California, and elsewhere.

# CONTENTS

# CHAPTER FOUR
## Task Analysis                                                   76

# CHAPTER FIVE
## Instructional Objectives                                       106

**CHAPTER SIX**
## Designing the Instruction: Sequencing                              134

**CHAPTER NINE**
## Developing Instructional Materials

## CHAPTER FOURTEEN

## CHAPTER FIFTEEN

## CHAPTER SIXTEEN
## Instructional Design Project Management                    424

# CHAPTER 1

# Introduction to the Instructional Design Process

## GETTING STARTED

At last, you have finished your degree and are now ready to start practicing instructional design at your new job at a Fortune 25 company. Your first day on the job, however, holds a few surprises. Of most concern is that the manager you thought you were going to work for has transferred to a different division. Your new manager does not have a background in instructional design, but rather has worked as a chemical engineer and project manager for this corporation for the past 15 years. Needless to say, you are a little apprehensive about your predicament, considering that you are the *first* instructional designer hired by this corporation. Shortly after the morning coffee break, your manager invites her staff in for an introductory meeting. The staff includes three trainers who have more than 35 years' combined experience in teaching courses for the corporation, an administrative assistant who schedules and makes arrangements for courses, two engineers who write new curricula (each of whom has worked in the department for 4 years), and you. The meeting starts with each individual describing his or her background and role in the department. The other staff members can easily impress the new manager with their mastery of company lingo and the number of hours of training they produce each quarter.

## QUESTIONS TO CONSIDER

"Why examine the teaching/learning process?"

"What are the components of a comprehensive instructional design plan?"

"What premises underlie the instructional design process?"

"What benefits can result from applying the instructional design process?"

"What is the value of instructional design to teachers?"

"What is the relationship between instructional design and human-performance technology?"

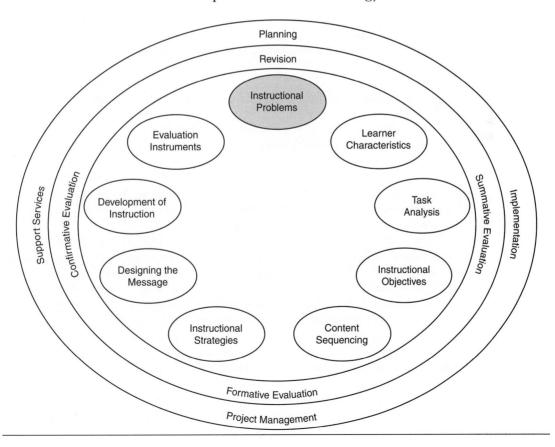

Turning slowly, the manager sizes you up and asks you to describe your background and your role in *her* new department. The manager and other staff members are not impressed by your degree in instructional design or the fact that you received it from a leading program in the area—probably because they have never heard of instructional design (although one of the engineers was familiar with your university's field hockey team). After a brief pause and a few frowns, one of the senior trainers asks you to explain exactly what it is that you do—it's as if they all think you are an *interior* designer, there to spruce up their offices and classrooms.

The next few minutes are critical. You can either win over this manager and staff to a new way of viewing training, or you can overwhelm them with your knowledge so they decide you are one of those intellectual types. What will you say to this group that will help ensure your longevity with the company?

The Questions to Consider listed earlier represent the important concepts treated in this introductory chapter. Understanding them is the basis for systematic instructional design.

## WHY INSTRUCTIONAL DESIGN?

The goal of instructional design is to make learning more efficient and effective and less difficult. Often, well-designed instruction saves time and money. A classic example of the value of instructional design is a case study conducted at AT&T in the 1960s and 1970s. AT&T offered a course for Long Lines craftsmen (Mager, 1977) that was 45 days in length, that is, nine weeks of classroom time, away from the job. To the dismay of local managers, that meant individuals taking this training were unavailable to repair telephone lines for over two months.

In an effort to improve the training, an instructional design team conducted a task analysis to determine the essential content for the course. The results of this analysis revealed that 25 days of the course focused on irrelevant content. Additional instructional design techniques were applied to reduce the course duration from nine weeks to nine days, an 80% reduction in training time. The cost of developing this new course in the 1960s was $350,000 but resulted in savings of $37 million over a five-year period between 1968 and 1973.

Why instructional design? We do not mean to imply that each instructional design project will yield the same return as described by AT&T's example. Of more relevance is the fundamental difference between the initial course and the revised course. The instructional designers focused on improving human performance to solve an instructional problem. By narrowing the content to the information and skills needed to perform the tasks or job, they were able to reduce the instructional time from 45 days to just 9 days. Sometimes, as we have found in our work, there is not a cost savings but rather a significant improvement in course quality as a result of the improved focus as described in the AT&T example.

A subject-matter expert or instructor often approaches the design of a course from a content perspective, that is, what to cover. In contrast, an instructional designer approaches the task by first defining the problem and then determining what knowledge and skills are needed to solve the instructional problem. This difference between a subject-matter expert's approach of determining what to cover and the instructional designer's approach of first defining the problem and identifying an instructional need offers insight into the course revision and subsequent cost savings in the AT&T example. The instructional design process focuses on what the learner "needs to know" and avoids including nonessential content that is "nice to know." There are times when the problem is not one that is best solved through an instructional intervention. A competent instructional designer can identify a variety of problems and then determine the most effective solution even when it means other individuals are needed for the solution.

## Why Do Instructional Design?

Training is expensive, yet it is essential to the healthy functioning of any organization. In 2004, the American Society for Training and Development (ASTD, 2004) estimated that employees averaged between 28 and 38 hours of training per year and that the average percentage of payroll invested in learning ranged from 1.99 to 4.16, depending on the size of the organization and the nature of the work. Of importance to us as instructional designers is the cost per learning hour, which ranged from $596 per hour to $1430 per hour. If we consider the training investment of a single company, the costs in time and expense are overwhelming. For example, IBM estimated they would spend approximately $700 million on training their workforce in 2005, with employees spending more than 15 million hours engaged in training (Davenport, 2005). The costs for employee training in business in the United States grew from approximately $63 billion in 1999 to over $134 billion in 2007 (Paradise, 2007). This increasing cost of training signals the importance of designing efficient and effective training.

Given that the cost of training includes not only development costs but also the time participants are away from their jobs, it is important that the training is effective, efficient, and on target. Thus, the goal for the instructional designer is to design and develop instruction that will improve performance in a most effective and efficient manner. Instructional designers want to avoid developing a course similar to the original AT&T linesman course, one that had irrelevant content and required workers to spend extra hours (actually weeks) away from the job. Given the more than 30 years since the publication of the AT&T case study, it is surprising that we continue to hear about and observe similar mistakes being made today.

## What Are the Benefits of Instructional Design?

Given that the investment needed to develop training is quite substantial, what are the benefits of using an instructional design approach to develop the training?

First, let's consider the financial benefit of instructional design. The AT&T case study reported a savings of $37,800,000 over a period of five years based on an initial investment of $350,000, or a savings of $108 for each development dollar spent (Mager, 1977). In another example, Motorola reported a return of $33 for every dollar spent on training (Wiggenhorn, 1990). This calculated return rate also included the wages of the participants who attended the training.

Second, let's consider how you as an instructional designer can improve the return on the investment in training whether it is for a Fortune 500 company or your classroom of third-grade students. Instructional design is a process for solving skills and knowledge deficiencies, whether it be troubleshooting an aircraft engine or learning the 50 states and their capitals. The process starts by identifying the performance problem of the worker or student and then determines whether instruction is the appropriate solution. If instruction is required, the designer then uses a systematic process to design the instruction. The process described in this book is similar in many ways to the one used in the AT&T course, which can be contrasted to the "What content should we include?" approach used for the original linesman course. In contrast, a systematic instructional design process asks, "What information and skills are needed to perform the task?"

## Applying the Process to Both Academic Education and Training Programs

Specific job training has precise, immediate requirements with identifiable and often measurable outcomes. The instructional program must stress the teaching of knowledge and skills for the performance of assigned tasks. Formal education, on the other hand, often has broad purposes and more generalized objectives. Application of the knowledge and skills taught may not become important until sometime in the future.

Whether one is studying history or carpentry, the identical principles of learning apply to structuring experiences for individuals. Although the emphasis, terminology, and details differ, both situations involve similar elements of the instructional design plan. Thus, the process presented in this book can be effective for either an academic or a training situation. Where particulars differ, special explanations and examples are included in either the academic instruction or the planning for training.

**Benefits of Instructional Design in Business.**   The benefits of the application of instructional design in business can take many forms. Results can vary from simply reducing the amount of time it takes to complete a course to solving a performance problem by designing effective instruction that increases worker productivity. The role of instructional design and training varies from company to company, as do its benefits. For example, Speedy Muffler King, which experienced high revenues and profits for 1994, made extensive use of training. During 1994, the company provided more than 100,000 hours of employee training to improve customer satisfaction and loyalty (Canada NewsWire, 1995). Appropriate training can produce a return on investment for both tangible (e.g., increased output) and less tangible (e.g., worker loyalty) measures.

**Benefits of Instructional Design in PK-12 Education.**   Do PK–12 teachers have to be instructional designers in addition to their traditional roles of classroom manager, presenter-lecturer, and mentor? Our definitive answers are "to some degree'' and ''it all depends.'' By saying ''to some degree,'' we mean that textbooks, workbooks, basal readers, and other standard instructional resources rarely, if ever, are sufficient to satisfy benchmarks and standards while keeping students engaged and interested. There are numerous occasions (many teachers might say ''every day'') in which the need for teacher-developed materials—drill-and-practice exercises, remedial lessons, problem-based lessons, or even full-fledged instructional units—arises. Knowing the basic principles of instructional design can help to ensure that what is produced serves a necessary purpose, meets the needs of students, is attractive and well organized, is delivered in an appropriate mode, and is continually evaluated and improved. Unlike professional instructional designers, however, the typical teacher is not likely to need formal expertise in the various instructional design processes. However, basic familiarity with major principles and procedures (e.g., how to present text, design and deliver a lecture, and prepare a test) can be extremely helpful, both for the teacher's own work and for evaluating commercial educational products.

How teachers use the instructional design process also depends a great deal on situational factors. Teachers working in today's restructured schools may find themselves increasingly involved in design activities. Specifically, in recent years, national initiatives for educational reform have generated support for both teacher-centered instruction and activity-oriented, student-centered methods of teaching that stress meaningful learning applied to real-world problems (see Desimone, 2009; Rowan, Camburn, & Barnes, 2004). The choice between these approaches often depends on school preference, instructional needs, the nature of instructional objectives, the instructional time available (student-centered learning approaches take longer to implement), and available resources. Recently, ''stimulus funds'' and grant monies were being offered to states and school districts for developing innovative curricula and programs for increasing student achievement. For example, a recent federal grant program offered by the Institute for Educational Sciences concentrates on bringing designers, researchers, and practitioners together to devise solutions to barriers faced by ''chronically low-performing schools'' to raising test scores. Given the importance of designing contemporary educational programs to address technology literacy and twenty-first-century learning skills, Morrison and Lowther (2010) provide a inquiry-based instructional design model for teachers to use in integrating computer technology into classroom instruction.

Implementing these approaches obviously requires well-designed instructional activities and projects. Where do they come from? For the most part, the responsibility of design falls on individual teachers. Not surprisingly, however, many teachers find themselves unprepared for the task, and the implementations of the new strategies suffer as a result (Desimone, 2009; Mishra & Koehler, 2006; Niess, 2005). By learning more about instructional design, teachers should become better equipped either to create high-quality, student-centered lessons or to adapt commercial materials to fit their course needs.

In the remainder of this chapter, we will introduce the instructional design process by examining the context in which it is used and the premises underlying the process and introduce you to the model described in this book.

## WHAT IS INSTRUCTIONAL DESIGN?

Using a systematic design process is termed *instructional design* (often abbreviated *ID*). It is based on what we know about learning theories, information technology, systematic analysis, educational research, and management methods. Dewey (1900) saw a need in the early part of the twentieth century for a science that could translate what was learned through research into practical applications for instruction. This science would make decisions about instructional practices based on sound research rather than intuition. Snellbecker (1974) and others have proposed that instructional design is the linking science described by Dewey. We agree with Snellbecker and see instructional design as the process for designing instruction based on sound practices.

Instructional design starts by first identifying the performance problem and never assumes that instruction is the answer to *all* problems. *If* instruction is the most appropriate solution, *then* the design process can begin. The instructional design approach considers instruction from the perspective of the learner rather than from the perspective of the content. The traditional approach simply asks, "What information should I include in this course?" In some courses, the chapters in the textbook determine the content. In contrast, the ID approach focuses on many factors that influence learning outcomes, including the following:

- What level of readiness do individual students need for accomplishing the objectives?
- What instructional strategies are most appropriate in terms of objectives and learner characteristics?
- What technology or other resources are most suitable?
- What support is needed for successful learning?
- How is achievement of the objectives measured?
- What revisions are necessary if a tryout of the program does not match expectations?

Other issues inherent in the instructional design process also influence student learning. This process is applicable for designing instruction in public education, higher education, and the workplace. The information, concepts, and procedures presented here can aid teachers and instructors, instructional designers, and planning teams—anyone who wants to develop effective, appealing instruction.

How would you answer this question: "If you were about to start planning a new unit in a course or training program, what issue would first receive your attention?" Various individuals might answer as follows:

**Primary-grade teacher:** "I think first about the state and district benchmarks and how this content aligns with those benchmarks. Then, I would ask, *How well prepared are my students to learn it (physically, emotionally, intellectually)?*"

**High school teacher:** "First, I would start by identifying the relevant state standards, then I'd start writing down what I want to accomplish in teaching the unit to meet these standards. These statements become the goals around which I'll plan the instruction."

**College professor:** "My approach is to list the content that needs to be covered relative to the selected topic. This list would include the terms, definitions, concepts, and principles that I feel need to be communicated to my students."

**Instructional designer in industry:** "I would start by determining whether the problem the training is to address is an instructional problem. If instruction will help solve the problem, then it's important to start by listing the skills and knowledge the trainees are to develop as a result of this instruction. These would be the outcomes or objectives to be accomplished."

The foregoing replies represent a sampling of approaches that might be taken as different individuals initiate their instructional planning. There could be other replies to the question. For example, one community college instructor always starts by writing the final examination for a new unit. He believes that passing the final exam is the students' greatest concern. Therefore, he writes questions that indicate what should receive emphasis in his teaching. His reasoning seems plausible.

As you read the replies to the question and formulate your own answer, two conclusions become apparent. First, a number of different considerations appeal to educators and instructional designers as each starts planning. Second, each of us selects an order or sequence of our own to treat these elements.

*Instructional development* is often interpreted in different ways, and the term is sometimes used interchangeably with *instructional design*. Frequently, instructional development is defined as the production process, that is, the translation of the instructional design plan into the instructional materials such as print, video, multimedia, or Web-based materials. Another definition describes instructional development as the management function in systematic instructional planning. This term includes assigning and supervising personnel, handling allocated budgets, arranging for necessary support services, and checking time schedules for compliance.

## Education versus Training

We might also want to consider the distinction between education and training. Both education and training are concerned with learning; however, each has a different perspective and purpose. One of the goals of formal education is to prepare an individual to be a contributing member of the society. The focus of an education is quite broad and can range from history to English to chemistry to physical fitness to political science to music. Formal education also occurs during a fixed time frame. For example, classes for students in grades 1 to 6 typically start in late August and continue to early June. University courses follow a similar schedule: Classes typically start by the first week of September and end in early December with a second semester starting in January and ending in May. The content of a course is typically defined by its time frame and the number of chapters in the textbook used. However, with the recent emphasis on student performance, the content of many elementary and secondary education programs is more likely to be defined by benchmarks or standards than by a textbook.

In contrast, training in an organizational setting is defined by the information needed to perform a specific task or related tasks. For example, a course in using a fire extinguisher would not include information on how the pump on a fire truck works or a lecture on the history and use of fire. The course would focus on selecting the correct fire extinguisher and then how to use the fire extinguisher. The length of the course would be determined by the content rather than a specific time frame. The purpose of training is more narrowly focused than is education in that training centers on very specific information—only the information needed to perform the task.

## Instructional Design and Human Performance Technology

An area of interest to the instructional designer is the applied field of human performance technology, or human performance improvement. This field focuses on "maximizing the valued achievements of people within work settings" (Stolovitch & Keeps, 1999, p. 4). Human performance technology places a strong emphasis on front-end analysis to identify the performance problem and the cause. Similarly, a performance technologist takes a broader perspective on performance problems than does a trainer by considering nontraining interventions as a solution to a problem. The performance technologist might involve an organizational development specialist, a compensation specialist, an information technologist, an ergonomics specialist, or an industrial engineer to provide a nontraining intervention. Performance improvement interventions might include restructuring job compensation, redesigning a workstation, or designing a simple job aid—in addition to or in place of training.

Although scholars and practitioners are still debating whether human performance technology is part of instructional design or instructional design is part of human performance technology, we prefer to think of the two as overlapping. A good human performance technologist is knowledgeable about instructional design, and a good instructional designer is knowledgeable about human performance technology. This text focuses on instructional design and provides the instructional designer or performance technologist with essential skills for developing training interventions as well as some nontraining interventions such as job aids and electronic performance support systems (EPSS). More important, instructional designers will learn how to identify performance problems and then decide whether instruction is the best solution or part of the solution for addressing the problem.

## Contexts for Instructional Design

We can apply instructional design in any context in which people are performing a task. Let's examine some of the contexts in which instructional designers work.

**Business and Government.**  Training in business and industry is *big* business, as indicated by IBM's projected expense of $700 million for employee training in 2005. A recent report indicates that companies spent over $134 billion in 2007 on training (Paradise, 2008). Training represents a major investment by corporations and companies. Similarly, local, state, and the federal governments also make a sizeable investment in training. Training in business and governmental agencies can be grouped into four broad areas: *Technical training* can include developing materials that focus on repairing a piece of equipment, performing an accounting audit, or learning to use computer software. *Soft-skill training* includes interpersonal communication skills such as building teams or working at help desks to solve customer or employee problems. *Management and supervisory training* is another focus area of instructional designers. Supervisory training often involves learning how to assess employee performance and correct behavioral problems. The last group is *sales training*, and it includes not only sales techniques but also product knowledge training.

**Medical.**  Hospitals, medical schools, and other medical-related agencies hire instructional designers to design training and employ other techniques for improving performance. Professionals from doctors to nurses to technicians participate in continuing education to update skills knowledge and to maintain certification. Instructional designers working in a medical school typically focus on developing instructional materials as well as collaborating with teams to develop innovative instructional tools to allow students to practice and learn critical techniques in a simulated environment. Instructional designers also create patient education materials such as nutritional programs on diabetes, stress reduction, and wellness.

**Military.**  The various branches of the U.S. military are constantly training people. This activity can range from basic training to performing maintenance and repair on atomic submarines. The military employs instructional designers and also contracts with corporations to develop the needed courses. Unlike most other organizations, the military utilizes a very strict process that all designers must follow for the development of instructional materials.

**Education.**  Although limited, there are some positions for instructional designers in PK–12 schools, usually in very large school districts. The requirements for certification vary between states, and some states do not recognize the instructional design specialist. More commonly, teachers select instructional design as a major for their master's degree and then find employment as a technology specialist in their school or district.

There are many opportunities for instructional designers in higher education. Many community colleges, colleges, and universities hire instructional designers to work with faculty to improve teaching skills and assist with course development. Today, a growing number of instructional designers are employed to work on the design and development of distance education courses.

One can see that there are a variety of employment opportunities for instructional designers. The basic process we describe in this book is applicable in all these various contexts in which instructional designers are employed. Before we overview the instructional design process and our instructional design model, let's examine the premises underlying the instructional design process.

## Premises Underlying the Instructional Design Process

We have identified seven basic premises to help you understand the ID process and apply it successfully. These premises can influence both your thinking and your treatment of the instructional design plan.

> **Premise 1: The instructional design process requires attention to both a systematic procedure and specificity for treating details within the plan.**

The term *systematic* refers to an orderly, logical method of identifying, developing, and evaluating a set of strategies aimed at attaining a particular instructional goal. This task is accomplished using the nine interrelated elements of the instructional design plan.

Treating each element requires exacting mental effort. Each element of the plan (if it is relevant to your project) must be applied with attention to precise details. This means being specific. For example, an instructional objective is a statement that includes a verb. We can use this verb and other information in the objective to determine whether we are designing content that will address the performance problem we have identified. Consider this objective: The learner will list in order the steps for restocking the soft-drink machine. The objective has all the necessary information and specificity of performance. However, if the problem is one of personnel incorrectly restocking the machine, then our objective does not address the problem. The learners can write down the steps, but there is no guarantee they can actually do the task. The content and verb in the objective also guide the development of an instructional strategy and indicate how achievement will be evaluated. The details of the instructional strategy are used to develop the instruction that will support objective. Similarly, the details included in the specification of the objective are used to determine how to assess the learner's mastery of the objective. These are examples of factors that indicate the specific treatment required when implementing the instructional design process. Each part of the process depends on one or more earlier tasks to design appropriate instruction.

Attention to detail is critical for the success of any instructional design work. By applying systematic procedures and being attentive to specific details, you can design effective instruction.

> **Premise 2: The instructional design process starts by identifying an instructional problem.**

Instructional designers first determine if there is a performance problem. Once a problem is identified, the designer must determine whether it can be solved efficiently by instruction *before* he or she starts designing the instruction. In contrast, organizations often bring in guest speakers or provide workshops on general topics such as time management or business writing without first clearly identifying a need. To answer the question of what to include, the instructional designer begins by identifying the performance problem and then uses a variety of tools to determine what knowledge and skills are needed to solve the problem.

**Premise 3: An instructional design plan is developed primarily for use by the instructional designer and planning team**.

Some people believe that all details developed as part of the design process (e.g., needs analysis, instructional objectives, content sequencing, etc.) should be given to learners, often in the form of a study guide. This assumption is not true. The learners will use many of the items written as elements in the plan, but not always in the form or order in which they are being developed. We distinguish between the instructional design documents (e.g., needs analysis, instructional strategies, task analysis, etc.) and the instructional materials the learners will actually see and use. The design team prepares a design document to manage the development of the instructional units. Once the instructional materials are in final form, the design documents lose their value and usually are filed.

Also, the order in which elements are treated during planning may differ substantially from the order in which they are eventually presented to learners. For example, a pretest might be developed after the final examination is devised, even though students will complete it prior to the start of instruction.

**Premise 4: While planning, every effort should be made to provide for a level of satisfactory achievement rather than minimal achievement for all learners**.

A classic study by Bloom (1976) concluded that up to 95% of all public school students can accomplish what is required of them if each individual has suitable academic background, appropriate instruction, and sufficient time for learning. Other research has shown that, if a student is prepared to learn and puts forth the effort to study but is unsuccessful in learning, a more careful design of the instructional plan can help overcome this shortcoming. This conclusion applies to training as well as to education. It justifies the need to test a plan before its implementation, as illustrated in the revision oval in Figure 1-1.

**Premise 5: The success of the instructional product is dependent on the accuracy of the information flowing into the instructional design process**.

To solve a performance problem, the designer must identify the performance problem or need through the use of needs analysis, goal analysis, and/or performance analysis. Creating instruction for a task that is not a performance problem is not likely to lead to an improvement in performance. Similarly, the designer must accurately identify the target audience to design materials that are appropriate for the audience's reading and skill levels. The information obtained from the subject matter expert must be accurate and complete. Selecting an appropriate instructional strategy for the content and objectives is essential for both efficient and effective instruction. And last, accurate information is needed from the formative evaluation of the materials to make appropriate modifications. Failure to obtain accurate information and to make the correct decisions can result in ineffective instruction.

**Premise 6: The instructional design process focuses on the individual rather than the content**.

**FIGURE 1-1**
Components of the instructional design plan

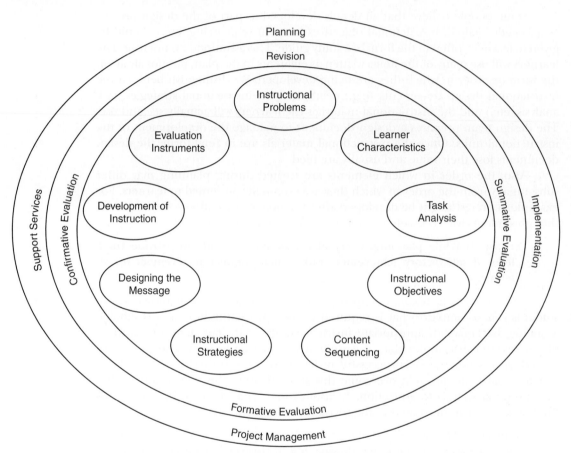

Instructional design focuses on the individual and how to improve individual performance rather than on what content to cover. During the learner analysis, the process focuses on audience characteristics. As we design the instruction, we consider these characteristics in the selection of the instructional strategies and delivery methods that are adapted to the individual members of the target audience. Throughout the design process, the designer focuses on the individual learner and what the learner must master to alleviate a problem rather than focusing on what content to cover.

**Premise 7: There is no single best way to design instruction.**

Applying the instructional design process can reduce reliance on intuition or trial and error in planning. Yet the instructional design process has not reached a level of scientific exactness. Many paths can reach the same goals and objectives. Instructors and designers are unique individuals, just as learners are unique. Each designer formulates activities and applies elements of the instructional design plan in individual ways. The proof of an instructional plan's success is whether a satisfactory level of learning is achieved in an acceptable period of time.

## Expert's Edge

### Is ADDIE a Blond, Brunette, or Bald?

One of the terms you hear most frequently in the field of instructional design (ID) is "the ADDIE model." Critics might say, for example, that the ID model presented in this book is "a variation of the basic ADDIE model." But what is the ADDIE model? As it turns out, there is no such thing as *the* ADDIE model or even *an* ADDIE model.

If you search the dictionaries and encyclopedias of instructional technology, education, and training, ADDIE does not appear in any of them. Nor in the histories of instructional technology and ID. Nor in the textbooks on ID. Most notably, ADDIE does not appear in any of the books that survey and critique the various ID models. And yet everyone talks about it as if it actually existed.

After an extensive survey of the literature and numerous interviews with the "seasoned citizens" of ID, I have concluded that the term *the ADDIE model* is merely a colloquial label for a systematic approach to instructional development, virtually synonymous with *instructional systems development* (ISD). It is an acronym referring to the major stages in the generic ISD process: Analysis, Design, Development, Implementation, and Evaluation. The label seems not to have a single author but rather to have evolved informally through oral tradition around the 1980s. There is no original, fully elaborated model, only a label that refers to a family of models that share common basic elements.

Although the origin of the *label* itself is obscure, the underlying concepts of ISD can be traced to the model developed for the United States armed forces in the mid-1970s. As Branson (1978) recounted, the Center for Educational Technology at Florida State University developed detailed procedures that evolved into the Interservice Procedures for Instructional Systems Development (IPISD), intended for the Army, Navy, Air Force, and Marine Corps. The Center's graphic depiction of the IPISD model (Branson, 1978, p. 13) shows five top-level headings: Analyze, Design, Develop, Implement, and Control. This model is referenced in subsequent historical reviews of ID, but notably, users do not refer to it by the *ADDIC* acronym, only IPISD.

The underlying concepts of the IPISD model can be found in an earlier handbook by Leslie Briggs (1970). Briggs's model incorporates ideas similar to the IPISD model but without the ADDIC headings.

Some ID authors are now trying to retroactively create an ADDIE model because the label is so popular. They take the five-stage outline and then go on to spell out procedural steps for each stage and to give narrative descriptions of those procedures. However, it should be recognized that authors who do this are essentially creating and disseminating *their own* models, as there does not appear to be an original, authoritative version of the ADDIE model to be revealed and interpreted. Anyone is free to impute whatever attributes they want to this label . . . and they do.

## References

Branson, R. K. (1978, March). The interservice procedures for instructional systems development. *Educational Technology*, pp. 11–14.
Briggs, L. J. (1970). *Handbook of procedures for the design of instruction.* Pittsburgh: American Institutes for Research.

A longer version of this story, complete with references, appears in Molenda, M. (2003). In search of the elusive ADDIE model. *Performance improvement 42*(5), 34–36.

Michael Molenda is an associate professor emeritus. He recently retired from the Instructional Systems Technology program at Indiana University. He continues to do research and writing related to the history and conceptual foundations of instructional technology.

## OVERVIEW OF OUR DESIGN MODEL

Think back to how the primary-grade teacher, high school teacher, college professor, and instructional designer answered the question of how they would design a course (see pages 6–7). Of the planning elements identified by the four individuals, four are fundamental in instructional design. You will find them addressed in almost every ID model. They can be represented by these questions:

1. For whom is the program developed? (i.e., characteristics of learners or trainees)
2. What do you want the learners or trainees to learn or demonstrate? (i.e., objectives)
3. How is the subject content or skill best learned? (i.e., instructional strategies)
4. How do you determine the extent to which learning is achieved? (i.e., evaluation procedures)

These four fundamental components—learners, objectives, methods, and evaluation—form the framework for systematic instructional planning (Figure 1-2).

These components are interrelated and could conceivably make up an entire instructional design plan. In actuality, additional components should require attention (i.e., the context in which the learner learns and works) and, when integrated with the basic four, form a complete instructional design model. The following paragraphs describe the elements of our instructional design model.

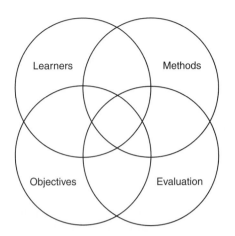

**FIGURE 1-2**
The fundamental components of instructional design

## Instructional Problems

The first step of the process is to identify the need of the client or the performance problem the client wishes to solve. If the need identified is best addressed by instruction, then the designer proceeds with the project. If the need identified requires a noninstructional solution, the designer may implement a noninstructional intervention, refer the problem to other specialists, or work with a team of specialists to implement the most appropriate solution. For example, the designer might work with other specialists to redesign a workstation to make it ergonomically correct. The performance problem is associated with the target audience, and the client is often a manager or supervisor of the audience.

## Learner and Context

One aspect of the analysis is defining the characteristics of the target audience, or those individuals who are not performing as expected. You might collect information about the learner's reading level, general background knowledge, assumptions, or work experience. The information you collect will depend on the problem and the audience. For example, a fifth-grade teacher might find value in the students' scores on the previous year's benchmark or achievement tests. A designer for an accounting firm might find knowing the number of years the learners have worked in accounting more useful for planning instruction than information about their general background or reading level.

## Task Analysis

Task analysis is one of the most, if not the most, important component of the process. You will use this process to determine what knowledge and procedures you need to include in the instruction to help the learner master the objectives. You will also find that there are different techniques you will need to use for analyzing different types of content.

## Instructional Objectives

The instructional objectives specify exactly what the learner must master. The objectives provide a map for designing the instruction and for developing the means to assess learner performance. We use the objectives as one of our first quality checks to make sure that the instruction (including the learning activities) we develop is focused on solving the performance problem. As we begin to design the instruction, the objectives establish a focal point to make sure our strategies and assessments are appropriate.

## Content Sequencing

The order in which the information is presented plays an important role in helping the learner understand and learn the information. At first glance, one might expect to present the information in the same sequence as defined by the task analysis. However, ordering the information in a logical sequence may help the learner grasp the ideas in a more efficient and effective manner.

## Instructional Strategies

Many designers consider this part of the process the creative step. It involves designing creative and sometimes innovative ways of presenting the information that help the learner integrate the new information with ideas they already understand. The process involves numerous approaches ranging from a simple analogy to a complex simulation.

## Designing the Message

The message is the pattern of words and pictures we create to communicate with our learners. The design of the message is the specific and deliberate process we use to arrange the words and pictures (Fleming & Levie, 1978). Once you have designed the instructional strategies, you can turn your focus to designing the message. This process uses techniques ranging from the way you structure a sentence using signal words such as ''Recall in the last step . . . '' to the use of typographical elements such as bold or italics to direct the learner's attention. Selecting appropriate graphics, text, and typographical design can further enhance the readability and the learner's understanding of the instruction.

## Development of the Instruction

Once you have completed the analysis and design, you are ready to develop the instruction. This part of the process involves putting all the parts together to produce instructional materials such as video recordings, Web pages, print materials, or audiotapes.

## Evaluation Instruments

The evaluation instruments are used to assess the learner's mastery of the objectives. Some objectives are easily assessed by familiar methods such as multiple-choice test items, whereas other objectives require more complex approaches such as a portfolio that is a collection of exemplary work products over a period of time.

These nine elements just described are the basic components of the design process presented in Figure 1-1. They overlap and are presented in an oval shape (see Figure 1-1) to indicate that *there is no one specific sequence or order to completing the steps*. It would seem logical to start with the instructional problem and then proceed clockwise. However, it is also logical to complete the design of the evaluation instruments immediately after defining the objectives. Similarly, if your job requires you to design instruction for the same group of learners (e.g., a fifth-grade class or field service engineers), you will probably not need to complete the learner analysis in great detail after the first or second project, because those characteristics remain stable.

## Ongoing Processes

In the two outer ovals of Figure 1-1 are presented eight processes that are ongoing throughout the life of an instructional design project. The following paragraphs describe these processes.

**Planning and Project Management.**   Instructional design projects vary in degree of complexity and the amount of planning and management that they require. These two processes are essential for developing and managing the schedule and budget for a project. The effort required for project management is determined by the scope of the project.

**Support Services.**   The size and scope of the project will determine the resources that are essential for its success. For smaller projects and those with a short time frame, the instructional designer might provide, in addition to the instructional design processes, all the services required, from typographer to evaluator to graphic artist. For large-scale projects, support services might include a number of specialists such as graphic artists, scriptwriters, video producers, or programmers to support the development and production of the instructional materials.

**Formative Evaluation and Revision.**   Your design and development work on a project is evaluated at multiple places during the process. Such "formative evaluation" processes (see Chapter 13) can start with the problem identification step to ensure that you have correctly identified the problem. Similarly, you may conduct reviews of the task analysis and objectives to verify that you are correctly addressing the problem. Once you have designed the strategies and created a draft or prototype of the instruction, you can conduct additional reviews to test their effectiveness. Using the information that you or the evaluator gather, you can make revisions to improve the quality of the instruction.

**Implementation.**   As you design the instruction, you must also plan for the implementation. Careful planning and involvement of key individuals during the design of the instruction can improve the implementation and use of the instruction. Implementation, like formative evaluation, starts early in the instructional design process. Planning for the implementation early can help ensure a smooth rollout of the instructional program.

**Summative Evaluation.**   Once the instruction is implemented, you or your evaluator can conduct a summative evaluation. This evaluation is used to evaluate the effectiveness of the final materials when they are used as planned (see Chapter 13).

**Confirmative Evaluation.**   In business, training courses are often institutionalized and offered to employees long after the problem they addressed is gone. Confirmative evaluation (see Chapter 13) is a process instructional designers use to determine whether a course or instruction remains appropriate over time.

## WHO'S WHO IN THE INSTRUCTIONAL DESIGN PROCESS

As you prepare to study the instructional design process, you will want to view it from your own perspective. What role or roles will you assume in an instructional project? What specific responsibilities might you have? What relationship do you have with other individuals in your organization who are involved in aspects of designing or delivering instruction? These are all matters to keep in mind as you study the elements of instructional design. Let's examine three essential roles in the instructional planning process. You may be expected to fill one or more of these roles.

### Instructional Designer

This person is responsible for carrying out and coordinating the planning work and is competent in managing all aspects of the instructional design process. The instructional designer has the primary responsibility for designing the instruction.

### Subject-Matter Expert (SME)

The subject-matter expert is qualified to provide information about content and resources relating to all aspects of the topics for which instruction is to be designed. This individual is responsible for checking accuracy of content treatment in activities, materials, and examinations. The teacher or instructor may serve also as an SME.

### Evaluator

This person is qualified to assist the staff in developing instruments for pretesting and for evaluating student learning (i.e., posttesting) and is responsible both for gathering and interpreting data during program tryouts and for determining the effectiveness and efficiency of the program after it's been fully implemented.

During various stages of the process, you may involve other individuals such as media production personnel, instructors, and facility planners and managers.

---

### Expert's Edge

## Does He Know That I Know That He Knows That I Know?

**Why should I care about philosophy?**   Our philosophies shape what we think and do. Few of us, however, take the time (or have the time these days) to examine our beliefs or to contemplate life. I barely have enough time to figure out what to wear each day, let alone the meaning of life. Yet, understanding our beliefs can go a long way toward removing the roadblocks we face each day in life—and in instructional design.

Whether it's life in general or an applied field of study in particular, some things are black or white and others are gray. Yet, when we take the time to understand the beliefs that guide and direct us, we become better prepared to solve problems and manage difficult situations. Our philosophies are the beliefs, values, and attitudes that filter how we interpret situations and make decisions.

In addition, those of us who work in the field of instructional technology will most likely encounter those core values that underlie our profession, including these:

1. The systems approach is the field's foundation.
2. Learning is a change in knowledge or behavior.
3. Achievement is the desired outcome of the instructional design process.

Our philosophies influence how we make sense of these core values. Sometimes we become so wrapped up in living our lives that we forget to consider our values and beliefs. Our philosophy sheds light on what we do, how we do it, and why we do it, because philosophy is all about thinking. Long ago, when Socrates claimed that "the unexamined life is not worth living," philosophy was a way of life intended for ordinary people. It provided practical advice for living. So, let's take a look now at how all this might apply to instructional design.

**Is it a line or an oval?**   The systems approach means different things to different people. Some interpret the systems approach as *systematic*, a concept best illustrated by the vast array of procedural models that describe instructional design as a linear, step-by-step process. Others believe that the systems approach is a systemic orientation that is more recursive and organic than linear. Of course, gray areas between these two extremes integrate bits and pieces of both explanations.

What do you think? Is the systems approach a line, an oval, or something else? Does it ever make sense to follow a rigid plan, or should you always plan to follow a flexible process?

**Is learning internal or external?**    Speaking of gray areas, the field has yet to discover a single theoretical perspective that completely explains the complex phenomenon of learning. Generally, the black-and-white opinions on this subject describe learning either as something that occurs in the mind or as a behavior that must be observed. Added to this issue are various beliefs about how learning occurs. Some believe knowledge is what the learner acquires through instruction. Others suggest that learning is an active process of constructing rather than acquiring knowledge. Clarifying views about the nature of learning helps you make sense of the perspectives and expectations about instructional design that stakeholders hold. As an instructional designer, you will be constantly challenged to understand multiple viewpoints and interpret theories of learning into appropriate strategies.

**Stuff, experiences, or environments?**

> **Student:** Is the focus of instructional design on instruction or learning?
> **Professor:** Yes!

The instructional design process yields achievements that align with various orientations to the field. An orientation often focuses on development of instructional materials. A product orientation reflects a focus on structuring meaningful learning experiences, whereas a focus on the environment is oriented toward creating an atmosphere that fosters learning. But there are no absolutes, and more times than not, instructional design integrates all these views. From a philosophical perspective, however, these various orientations often lead to learning outcomes that include anything from knowledge to skills to attitudes. If you're clear about whether your focus is materials, experiences, or environments, you'll be more likely to deliver the results you desire.

**Is unexamined instruction worth designing?**    When was the last time you came face-to-face with your philosophies about learning and instruction? Philosophy can help instructional designers find solutions that are compatible with those beliefs surrounding the instructional design process. Some believe that instructional design needs to address more than practical issues; it should provide for the human spirit as well. The ultimate benefit of this approach is insight into the impact of our actions on the learner . . . and it may help a few people figure out what to wear tomorrow!

David L. Solomon has more than 13 years' experience designing, developing, and implementing training and performance improvement solutions for multinational and privately held businesses. David teaches part-time at the secondary and postsecondary level, and his research interests include explicating the role of philosophical inquiry in our field.

## ANSWERING THE CRITICS

Isn't the instructional design process actually a mechanistic rather than a humanistic method of instructional planning? Doesn't this procedure discourage creativity in teaching? Isn't teaching more of an art than a science? These and similar questions are frequently raised and must be answered realistically. After studying this book, you should make up your own mind about how to answer them. Following are our responses to such questions:

**Question: Isn't the instructional design process actually a mechanistic rather than a humanistic method of instructional planning?**

Some ID models exhibit rigidity, following only a single, linear path for planning, represented by a chain of boxes and arrows, without exception. Figure 1-3 illustrates this approach. The sequences should be flexible, with elements addressed in a logical order for each project. The instructional designer's style of working, the nature of the subject, environmental constraints, and the learner's needs can all influence how the components are addressed in planning. The ID process would only be mechanistic if elements were treated in a fragmented manner rather than in an integrated approach. That is, the elements must work together rather than be treated as isolated steps.

A humanistic approach to instruction recognizes the individual learner (i.e., student or trainee) in terms of his or her own capabilities, individual differences, present ability levels, and personal development. It should be apparent that these matters do receive attention in the instructional design process. Elements of the process include examination of learner characteristics and identification of readiness levels for learning. Furthermore, systematic planning is applied to designing various forms of individualized or self-paced instruction to address an individual learner's needs.

Philosophically, as the planning starts, the instructional designer or instructor might have the following perspective: "I am designing a program of learning

**FIGURE 1-3**
A typical instructional design model

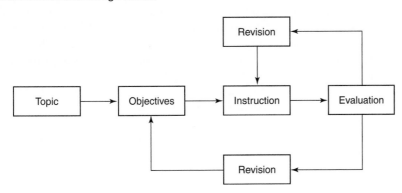

experiences for learners so that together we will be successful in accomplishing the stated goals and objectives. Although it is important for each person to learn, it is equally important to me that the learner become proficient." A successful instructional program is one in which as many students as possible have succeeded, reaching a mastery level for accomplishing the specified outcomes. Grading on a bell-shaped normal curve and assigning letter grades would have no place in such instruction designed to improve performance.

**Question: Doesn't the ID procedure discourage creativity in teaching?**

When a fine work of art is created, the artist has used creatively a number of widely accepted design elements (unity, emphasis, balance, space, shape, color, etc.). This same principle applies to instructional design. The effective instructional designer considers all the elements of the process to design a creative instructional approach. A good design goes beyond just effectiveness. It is efficient, engaging, and interesting.

Design requires creatively applying learning principles while taking into account characteristics of individual components and necessary relationships among elements that may constrain the design. These nine design elements, discussed earlier, can be developed and manipulated in imaginative and creative ways. Although the nine elements are the basis for good instruction, innovative and creative approaches result from how you, the instructional designer, apply the process.

Two individuals teaching the same subject or topic and targeting the same outcome goals might very well design different plans. Both can result in equally satisfactory student learning. The process demands dynamic interactions between students and instructor and between student and content, and different activities may be developed to satisfy those demands. This process encourages creativity, even to the extent of providing for open-ended or unanticipated learning experiences.

**Question: Isn't the main attention in ID given to low-level, immediate learning outcomes rather than to higher-order, long-term outcomes?**

Low-level, immediate outcomes are typical of instructional designs that implemented a strict behavioral approach using such strategies as mathemagenic behaviors (Rothkopf, 1970). Designers and researchers tend to implement strategies, such as inserted questions, proposed by Rothkopf, with a focus on very narrow, specific bits of information. Learners quickly discover they can search for a specific answer (intentional information) by skimming and ignoring all other supporting information (incidental information). As a result, learning is primarily rote; the *task* requires only the recall of specific information. In contrast, instructional design models based on cognitive strategies can provide a means to facilitate the development of higher-level learning involving analysis, synthesis, and problem solving.

In many academic subject areas, learners achieve major learning outcomes only after they have completed a class and then enrolled in an advanced course or begun working on the job. Instructional design includes procedures for directly and indirectly evaluating postcourse behavior and content application outcomes.

**Question: Doesn't instructional design take too long?**

Instructional design is often criticized for taking too long. But time is relative, and time requirements are dictated by number of circumstances. For example, you might take your car to the local garage or full-service filling station to have a flat tire fixed. Given the interruptions of customers wanting gas and those only asking for directions, it might take an hour or more to have your tire changed or repaired. In contrast, crews at the Indianapolis 500-Mile Race routinely change *all* four tires in under 10 seconds. Your local mechanic will probably receive around $20 regardless of how long it takes to do the job, where thousands of dollars are riding on the efficiency of the pit crew on race day.

Does that mean that all design tasks should be done with the speed of a pit crew working the Indy 500? No, not all the time. However, you will need to make some critical decisions. For example, consider an organization that is changing to a different telephone system and in a two-hour training session must train 600 employees in how to use the system. Given that this process is a one-shot training program, a designer would need to consider what value the design process could add. A simple task analysis presented as a lecture outline for the trainer might suffice in place of a lengthy development project. In contrast, a troubleshooting course for field service staff is more complex and has a longer life. In this example, the company's field service staff is growing at a high rate, and there is a high turnover due to promotions. An investment in design of the course would prove worthwhile even though it might take six months to complete. Recall the AT&T example from earlier in this chapter. An instructional design approach was not used for the first version of the course, which was lengthy and not focused on the performance requirements of the job.

To answer the critics, instructional design does take an investment of time and resources. However, the alternative is even more costly, as illustrated by the AT&T example. There are also times when instruction is not the answer (see Chapter 2) or when the problem does not warrant the investment of resources. A missed application of the instructional design process is a costly investment.

These answers to the critics may seem unconventional. Many teachers and trainers, based on their beliefs and experiences, might not accept them. Often people must become dissatisfied with present practices or results before they recognize the need for change and improvement (e.g., getting beyond passive learning, beyond accepting recall as an acceptable goal, when improved performance on a task or application of knowledge is a more appropriate outcome). Then, they are probably ready to explore a fresh approach to creating effective instruction. Providing explanations and offering opportunities, as described in this introductory chapter, can help counter criticism of the instructional design process.

## QUESTIONS . . . QUESTIONS . . . QUESTIONS

As you read and study the following chapters, you will frequently see questions raised or referred to in relation to the topic under consideration. Such questions may appear at the beginning of a chapter to indicate the important matters that follow. Then, as the discussion proceeds, other questions help direct thinking toward decisions that must be made.

An instructional designer continually probes for clarification, explanations, and details. You must help the persons with whom you carry out instructional planning to communicate effectively with you. This can best be done by using questions. Therefore, pay particular attention to the questions raised throughout the book. Then, let questioning become a common part of your behavior as you explore and eventually practice the instructional-designer role.

## SUMMARY

1. The use of instructional design to design and develop training can shorten training time and focus the training on the specific performance issue that can result in significant cost savings.
2. The instructional design process is applicable to a broad range of contexts that focus on improving human performance. These contexts can include but are not limited to education, business, health care, and the military.
3. A complete ID plan consists of nine elements arranged in a flexible configuration and formative, summative, and confirmative evaluations for potential revisions and judgments of success.
4. A number of expressions are synonymous with the term *instructional design* in the literature and in practice.
5. The ID process has the following qualities: It follows a systematic procedure with specific details, it usually starts at the course development level, and the process is applied in different ways by different designers but produces equally effective learning interventions.
6. The ID process can benefit program managers, administrators, instructional designers, instructors, and learners.
7. Roles in the ID process include instructional designer, instructor, subject-matter expert, and evaluator.
8. Criticisms of the ID process include the opinions that it is a mechanistic rather than humanistic planning method, it discourages teacher creativity, and its main attention is given to low-level, immediate outcomes. The ID process emphasized in this textbook is counter to these criticisms.
9. Asking questions during all phases of the ID process can help direct thinking toward decisions.

## THE ID PROCESS

As you read through this book, you will use the instructional design process to create a unit of instruction similar to the one in Appendix B. In this section, we provide guidance for applying the concepts, skills, and processes described in the chapter. This section also provides you with additional heuristics on the design process.

To start, we recommend that you reflect on your own definitions and philosophies. First, what is your definition of instructional design? Second, which learning theory or theories do you subscribe to for designing instruction? Third, what is your view of the learner?

## APPLICATION

In the "Getting Started" section at the beginning of this chapter, we described an unfortunate scenario of an instructional designer's first day on the job. How would you respond to the group's questions?

Write a job description for your ideal job. Next, refer to the nine elements in Figure 1-1 and see how many of them are described in your job description. Which elements did you include in your description?

## ANSWERS

How would you respond to the "Getting Started" scenario? It seems the key issue, if you are to do your job, is not to overwhelm your new colleagues with instructional design terminology while clearly selling them on the concept of design. A friendly approach might be to discuss what you can do in concrete terms that they can understand. This job is going to take some gradual selling and building of both rapport with and support from the manager and staff. We suggest proceeding cautiously, but do everything you can to be helpful. As part of a sales job, you might work with the group to identify a performance problem and then work with them to design an appropriate solution. Again, keep in mind your audience of coworkers, and approach the task in a way that will help them adapt your instructional design approach.

Which design elements would you include in your job description? Asking us to pick one or two is like asking parents to select their favorite child! Each of us enjoys doing certain tasks more than others but we recognize that all the different elements are essential and important in the design, development, and implementation of an effective and efficient product. We hope that you have a real interest in two or three of the elements but that you also develop your skills in all aspects of the design process.

## REFERENCES

*ASTD 2004 State of the Industry Report.* (2004). Retrieved from http://www.astd.org/astd/research/research-reports

Bloom, B. (1976). *Human characteristics and school learning.* New York: McGraw-Hill.

Canada NewsWire. (1995, August). Speedy Muffler King announces second quarter results. Retrieved from http://www.newswire.ca/releases/August1995/03/c2085.html

Davenport, R. (2005). A new shade of big blue: IBM reinvents its workforce. *Training and Development, 59*(5), 34–41.

Desimone, L. (2009). Improving impact studies of teachers' professional development: Toward better conceptualizations and measures. *Educational Researcher*, 38, 181–199.

Dewey, J. (1900). Psychology and social practice. *Psychological Review*, 7, 105–124.

Fleming, M., & Levie, W. H. (1978). *Instructional message design: Principles from the behavioral sciences.* Englewood Cliffs, NJ: Educational Technology Publications.

Mager, R. F. (1977). The "winds of change." *Training and Development Journal, 31*(10), 12–20.

Mishra, P., & Koehler, M. J. (2006). Technological pedagogical content knowledge: A framework for teacher knowledge. *Teachers College Record, 108*(6), 1017–1054.

Morrison, G. R., & Lowther, D. L. (2010). *Integrating computer technology into the classroom* (4th ed.). Columbus, OH: Merrill.

Niess, M. L. (2005). Preparing teachers to teach science and mathematics with technology: Developing a technology pedagogical content knowledge. *Teaching and Teacher Education, 21*, 509–523.

Paradise, A. (2008). State of the industry report. Alexandria, VA: ASTD Press.

Rowan, B., Camburn, E., & Barnes, C. (2004). Benefiting for comprehensive school reform: A review of research on CSR implementation. In C. T. Cross (Ed.), *Putting the pieces together: Lessons from comprehensive school reform research* (pp. 1–52). Washington, DC: The National Clearinghouse for Comprehensive School Reform.

Rothkopf, E. Z. (1970). The concept of mathemagenic activities. *Review of Educational Research, 40*, 325–336.

Snellbecker, G. (1974). *Learning theory, instructional theory, and psychoeducational design.* New York: McGraw-Hill.

Stolovitch, H. D., & Keeps, E. J. (1999). What is human performance technology? In H. D. Stolovitch & E. J. Keeps (Eds.), *Handbook of performance technology: Improving individual and organizational performance worldwide* (pp. 3–23). San Francisco: Jossey-Bass/Pfeiffer.

Wiggenhorn, W. (1990, July/August). Motorola U: When training becomes an education. *Harvard Business Review*, pp. 71–81.

# CHAPTER ( 2 )

# Identifying the Need for Instruction

## GETTING STARTED

You have just transferred to the U.S. division of the Electric Green Wind Company. This company installs and maintains wind turbines that generate electricity. When you arrive, your manager is very agitated because he has a problem. There have been two deaths due to trucking accidents in the first eight months of the year, plus the company is averaging 5.3 more accidents per miles driven than the national average for trucking companies. The chief executive officer has told the division manager that he wants to see a perfect driving record in three months.

Your manager is convinced that the accidents are caused by drivers not obeying the speed limit, and he wants to initiate a program that will impose a company fine for every speeding ticket a driver receives. However, he is not sure how effective this approach will be, because he does not always receive information on speeding tickets. He knows that the drivers are not performing at their best. Thus, he is giving you this problem to solve.

There are eight areas in the division (Texas, Florida, Oklahoma, Colorado, North Carolina, North Dakota, and two in California). He quickly explains that each area has a dispatcher who assigns jobs to the drivers, two to five supervisors who manage 12 to 15 drivers each, and a safety manager. All training is done at the Florida training facility. You have permission to travel to each area, in which a manager will provide you with access to all personnel. Your manager would like to discuss your plan of action for addressing this problem tomorrow morning. What is your plan?

## QUESTIONS TO CONSIDER

"What is the problem we are asked to solve?"

"Will instruction solve the problem, or is there another approach?"

"What is the purpose of the planned instruction?"

"Is an instructional intervention the best solution?"

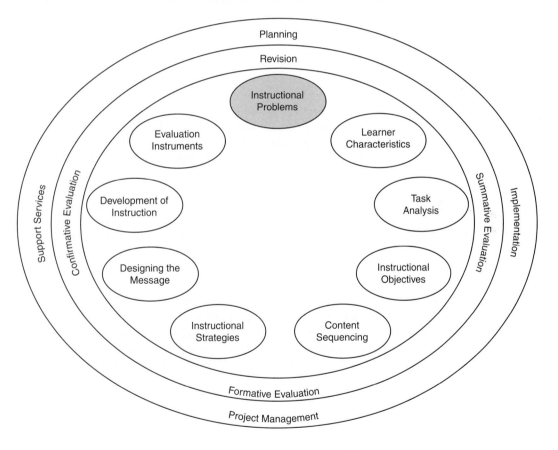

Before starting an instructional design project you should ask, ''Why is instruction (i.e., training) needed? Under what conditions is it advisable to undertake a task that is often both costly and time-consuming?'' Let's examine some situations that *might* require an instructional intervention.

First, suppose performance is not meeting expectations. For example, emergency personnel who answer 911 phone calls are not providing accurate, complete information to the police and fire departments responding to emergency situations; or the mean score for a fifth-grade class on the fractions section of the state's benchmark test is below the state and district means. In these two situations the operators and students are not performing to expectations.

Second, the work environment can change as a result of modifications in procedure or the installation of new equipment. When one corporation purchases another corporation, there probably will be procedural changes for minor operations such as requesting travel or completing travel expense forms. More complex procedures can also change—for example, how to prepare packages for exportation. In an elementary school the principal may decide to adopt a problem-based learning approach, requiring staff development and changes in teaching methods. Or a school might receive money to purchase five programmable calculators for every math classroom. Teachers would then need training not only on how to operate the calculators but on how to integrate this technology into their curricula.

Third, a company or industry can expand so rapidly that qualified personnel are in short supply. In the 1970s, the petroleum industry grew faster than the industry could prepare its engineers for higher-level positions and faster than universities could provide qualified graduates. The solid-state electronics industry experienced similar growth in the late 1970s and early 1980s, which created problems. A similarly rapid industry growth occurred for information technology specialists in the 1990s. Inexperienced professionals were often hired, promoted to higher-level positions, and advised to learn through experience on the job. In the near future, we might see similar rapid growth in the need for health care professionals as the baby boomers retire and create additional needs.

In situations like the three just described, training interventions might help improve productivity or achievement. More specifically, instructional design would provide a means for developing appropriate training or increasing the cost-effectiveness of existing training. Let's examine one more example of when instruction might be the answer. Consider a corporation that has hired an outside consulting group to teach a course on time management. Could a similar course be designed in-house to reduce costs and more directly reflect the corporation's work environment? The vendor-offered course might require that employees attend for five full days. Perhaps a mixture of self-paced instruction and classroom instruction would reduce time away from the job.

## IS INSTRUCTION THE ANSWER?

At first glance, it seems that the 911 operators mentioned earlier need training in how to record correct information, and the fifth-grade students need to study one or more units on fractions. But do we know that more instruction will solve these problems? Could something in the environment account for the inaccuracies of the 911 operators? A careful analysis of the situation might reveal that the earpieces on the headsets may not fit the operators properly or that transmissions have an unacceptable level of static. Training for the operators would not solve any of these problems. The fifth-graders' low test scores might be the result of the students' taking the annual achievement test *before* they have completed the planned unit on fractions.

The purpose for identifying the problem is to determine whether instruction should be part of the solution. A team who develops new training for the 911 operators or requires them to repeat existing training would be squandering company resources if the cause of poor performance is poor audio quality. Similarly, simply rescheduling the teaching of fractions or the achievement test might easily solve the fifth-graders' performance problem. Consider our Electric Green Wind Company problem. What are the potential solutions to this problem? One option might be training or improved training. Another option to consider is the scheduling of the jobs. Further analysis might indicate that the time frame for each job allows little flexibility, resulting in the need for drivers to drive above the speed limit and take risks. A problem of this nature would require a change in policy and procedure as well as in the work environment. Data from the National Highway Traffic Safety Administration (http://www-nrd.nhtsa.dot.gov/Pubs/TSF2006FE.PDF) provides statistics that suggest that there are more accidents in some months than others. Thus, an analysis of the timing of the accidents might provide additional insight as to the cause. An analysis of the driving conditions might indicate that the roads driven are hazardous (e.g., narrow, two-lane roads as opposed to freeways), requiring additional training for drivers.

The instructional design process begins with the identification of a problem or need. Why is performance below expectations? Once we know the root cause of the problem, we can determine whether an instructional intervention will solve the problem. Instructional designers can use three different approaches to identify instructional problems: needs assessment, goal analysis, and performance assessment. Once the problem is identified, the instructional designer must determine the most appropriate intervention. Problems that on the surface seem to require an instructional intervention can often be solved with a change in policy, coaching, or the environment. Our focus in this book is on designing instructional interventions *when* instruction is an appropriate solution to the problem.

When does an instructional designer conduct an assessment to determine whether there is a problem to address? Rossett (1999) identifies four opportunities for identifying performance problems. First is the introduction or rollout of a new product. When an automobile company introduces a new vehicle such as an electric or hybrid car, this change represents an opportunity to provide some type of support—either training or other—to improve the mechanics' ability to troubleshoot and repair the vehicle. Second is responding to an existing performance problem. If a computer mail-order company notices an increase in returned power supplies that were incorrectly installed, then an analysis is probably warranted to determine the cause of the problem. Third, a company recognizes a need to develop its people so they can continue to contribute to the growth of the company. For example, in the early 1980s, with the growth of micro-computer chips, many appliance-manufacturing companies found that the knowledge of their design engineers was suddenly out of date due to the introduction of microprocessors into home appliances. Companies were faced with either replacing their current staff with new college graduates or developing their existing staff. An analysis was used to identify an appropriate solution—retraining the existing staff. Fourth is strategy development, in which an analysis provides useful information for making decisions for strategic planning.

Individual and organization needs are ever changing. The needs or performance problems you identify today are likely to change in a month or six months. Similarly, training or change in the workplace implemented to address the problem affects existing needs and may change priorities. Problem identification often has a limited life span and requires continual updating to identify critical performance problems. The remainder of this chapter will focus on three tools instructional designers can use to identify performance problems: needs assessment, goal analysis, and performance assessment.

## NEEDS ASSESSMENT

The terms *needs assessment* and *needs analysis* are often used interchangeably. A needs assessment is used to identify gaps in performance and then determine whether the gaps are worth addressing through an intervention. If a gap is worth addressing, then recommendations are made to improve performance through some type of intervention. In contrast, a needs analysis involves examining the gap and identifying potential causes of the gap (also called cause analysis). The causes of the gap are used to determine an appropriate intervention.

Needs assessment is a tool designers use to identify performance problems in many different areas. For example, Sampson (2007) summarizes a needs assessment conducted to determine the needs of individuals who must read Department of Defense briefs. The assessment revealed that those writing the briefs failed to consider their audience's needs. A needs analysis conducted at General Motors focused on identifying performance problems of skilled workers in a metal fabrication plant (Finson & Szedlak, 1997). In contrast, a case study of a needs assessment in a bank resulted in a change from a management-driven training program to one focused on the trainee. The needs assessment recommended changes in objectives and design of the training, as well as in the organization (Lucier, 2008). The use of needs assessment to identify performance problems is not limited to business and industry. For example, Meeker and Byers (2003) describe how a needs assessment was used to redesign a master's degree program in nursing. Hilbert, Renkl, Schworm, Kessler, and Reiss (2007) describe the use of needs assessment to analyze instructional math materials. Consequently, computer-based instruction using worked examples was designed (Sweller & Cooper, 1985).

Needs assessment is described as a tool for identifying the problem and then selecting an appropriate intervention (Kaufman & English, 1979; Kaufman, Rojas,

& Mayer, 1993). If the designer fails to identify the problem properly, then the intervention may address only the symptoms, with no resultant change in the target audience's performance. For an instructional designer, the needs assessment process serves four functions:

1. It identifies the needs relevant to a particular job or task, that is, what problems are affecting performance.
2. It identifies critical needs. Critical needs include those that have a significant financial impact, affect safety, or disrupt the work or educational environment.
3. It sets priorities for selecting an intervention.
4. It provides baseline data to assess the effectiveness of the instruction.

Gathering baseline data is not always possible or cost-effective. For example, a designer may determine that one cause of meter damage is due to water-meter inspectors using the wrong technique for turning off meters. Is it feasible or cost-effective to observe a number of individuals in order to document the incorrect procedure, when no records exist that indicate the cause of the damage? Or could the designer simply record the total number of meters replaced before and after the training was implemented?

We define a need as a gap between what is expected and the existing conditions. Instructional designers are primarily interested in gaps when actual performance does not equal or exceed *expected* performance. The next section describes how to plan and conduct a needs assessment.

## Types of Needs and Data Sources

Six identifiable categories of needs are used for planning and conducting a needs assessment (Burton & Merrill, 1991). These six categories provide a framework for designers to determine the type of information to gather and a means to classify needs.

**Normative Needs.** A normative need is identified by comparing the target audience against a national standard. Normative needs in education include national achievement test norms such as those of the California Achievement Test (CAT), the Scholastic Aptitude Test (SAT), or the Graduate Record Exam (GRE). Normative data for identifying training needs in industry often do not exist because of a lack of record keeping at the national level. Some normative data exist for safety records (e.g., plant safety and transportation), service (e.g., an airline's on-time rating), and sales (e.g., projected sales of a product or service for a metropolitan area). A normative need exists when the target population's performance is below the established norm. Thus, a fifth-grade class that scores 15 points below the norm on the math section of the CAT has a defined normative need. A trucking company that averages six more accidents than the industry norm per million miles driven has an identified normative need.

The first step in defining a normative need is to obtain the normative data. The test administrator's handbook or test publisher typically provides test norms. Norms related to specific industries (e.g., insurance, transportation) may be available from professional societies, trade groups, and government agencies (e.g., the Department of Transportation). Once the norm is defined, the instructional designer must collect data from the target audience for comparison with the norm. Again, summarized test data are often available in schools. Sales, manufacturing, and safety data are often included in company reports, databases, internal newsletters, and annual reports.

**Comparative Needs.**   Comparative needs are similar to normative needs in that both are defined by comparing the status of the target audience to an external measure or status. A comparative need, however, is identified by comparing the target group to a peer group, that is, to another company or school as opposed to a norm. In education, a comparative need is identified by comparing one class to another, equivalent class (e.g., two sixth-grade classes) or comparing two equivalent schools to identify differences such as available equipment or test scores. However, federal and school district regulations involving privacy protection, as well as human-subject review committees, in the case of university-based studies, have made such data collection more difficult in recent years. Still, the data gathering may be even more challenging in a business environment. For example, public schools in many states administer an achievement test developed by the state each spring. School districts can prepare profiles for all of their schools for the different subtests. Administrators, teachers, and parents can then compare their school to similar schools to identify comparative needs. Many universities and colleges maintain a list of institutions they use for comparisons of faculty salaries, class size, and budgets. Businesses often study competitors to define training needs, facilities, compensation, and incentives. A comparative need exists when there is a gap between the groups. This difference, however, may not reflect a true need that can be addressed through training but rather an attitude of "keeping up with the Joneses."

To identify comparative needs, the designer must first determine areas for comparison (e.g., math scores, manufacturing waste, management development). Data are then collected on the target audience to determine the current status. Next, data are collected from the comparative audience. In education, this process may be as simple as calling the other school and requesting the information. Data gathering is usually not as simple in the business environment because of the proprietary nature of information and because of government antitrust regulations, which often prohibit such discussions between different companies. A designer may need to revert to interviewing employees who have a knowledge of other organizations and to reading journals (e.g., *Performance and Instruction, Training and Development*) to obtain the comparative data. When identifying comparative needs, the designer must make sure that the need is a viable training need as opposed to a status need. For example, is the rationale valid that because a competitor has an elaborate training facility your company is justified in constructing a similar or even bigger facility?

**Felt Needs.**   A felt need is a desire or want that an individual has to improve either his or her performance or that of the target audience. Felt needs express a gap between current performance or skill level and desired performance or skill level. When searching for felt needs, designers must identify needs related to improving performance and individual wants that are motivated by a desire other than performance improvement. For example, one company offered a training course that involved travel to several locations in the United States and the Bahamas to study and observe various geological formations. The training manager had to determine who had a need for the course to improve job performance and who had a "need" to travel to interesting places. Another example is a college professor who decided to revise a course. She "felt" the need to add new information to the course to make the course current, which would result in an improvement for the learners.

Felt needs are best identified through interviews and questionnaires. Face-to-face interviews are often more effective, because the designer can alleviate anxieties and probe for additional details. Questionnaires are effective only when individuals are willing to express their needs on paper. Typical questions to elicit felt needs are, "What could be done to improve your work performance?" or "What could be done to improve the performance of (target audience)?" Such questions may open a Pandora's box of problems; the designer would need to separate needs into those that are addressable by training (e.g., "a better understanding of the accounting system") and those that require other interventions (e.g., "reduce the amount of paperwork, add more lights to the work area").

**Expressed Needs.**   An expressed need is a felt need turned into action (Bradshaw, 1972). People are often willing to pay to satisfy expressed needs (Burton & Merrill, 1991). An individual who chooses one of two or more options—for example, enrolling in a specific course or workshop—is also demonstrating an expressed need. Again, instructional designers are primarily interested in expressed needs that improve the performance of the target audience or person. An example of an expressed need is the list of employees who are placed on a waiting list for a training course. As a student you may have been confronted by an expressed need when more students than anticipated *expressed* a need for a course and you found the course closed when trying to register. The employees on the waiting list have expressed a desire to enroll in the course and willingness to wait for an opening. The expressed need is the waiting list, which indicates a need for another section, a larger room, or a change in course formats to allow more students to take the course. In industry, professionals are often encouraged to attend one or more training courses a year as part of their professional development. Expressing an interest in attending such a course or having a manager recommend that an employee attend a specific course are means of identifying expressed needs. Similarly, an individual can express a need by indicating a need to update skills such as with a new version of a software package or an interest in developing management skills.

Data on expressed needs come from a variety of sources. A need for more sections of a course is expressed in the enrollment data. Individual personnel files and performance reviews often include goals in the form of either expressed or felt needs. Although the right to privacy may restrict an individual designer from reviewing files, a designer could ask the appropriate supervisor or manager to review the files and report any needs. Finally, expressed needs are often identified in suggestion boxes and in-house publications with a question-and-answer or suggestions column.

**Anticipated or Future Needs.**   The instructional design process often focuses on identifying needs related to existing performance problems. Anticipated needs are a means of identifying changes that will occur in the future. Identifying such needs should be part of any planned change so that any needed training can be designed prior to implementation of the change. For example, a school principal and supervisors might decide to implement a new instructional technique (e.g., argumentation skills) next year. An anticipated need is the knowledge teachers need to use problem-based learning effectively in a classroom. By anticipating the need, a principal can arrange for the appropriate training before the teachers start the year and difficulties develop with the method. Similarly, the introduction of new software in a customer service center at a major corporation would probably require training for customer service representatives. Anticipating this need as the software is developed will allow the designers an opportunity to design the training so that it is ready prior to the transition to the new software. The customer service representatives are then knowledgeable about the new software and better able to do their job when they start using it.

Anticipated needs are often identified through interviews and questionnaires similar to those used with felt needs, but with additional questions about what future changes the employee anticipates will affect the way the job is done. A second approach to identifying anticipated needs is to identify potential problem areas. For example, assume that a manually controlled drill press will be converted to a computer-controlled machine next year. An analysis of this change might find that the maintenance staff will need training on repairing and replacing the digital controllers on the drill presses.

**Critical Incident Needs.**   Critical incident needs are failures that are rare but have significant consequences—for instance, chemical spills, nuclear accidents, medical treatment errors, and natural disasters such as earthquakes, hurricanes, and tornadoes (Mager, 1984b). A typical reaction to a critical incident need was the planning and education that occurred in Memphis, Tennessee, in 1990 in the wake of the 1989 San Francisco earthquake. An earthquake was predicted to occur in Memphis in December 1990. In anticipation of the disaster, several government agencies, schools, and corporations developed earthquake awareness programs by analyzing the events associated with the 1989 San Francisco earthquake.

Critical incident needs are identified by analyzing potential problems. For example, chemical plants, manufacturing facilities, and petroleum refineries often develop employee training programs for handling emergencies such as fires, explosions, or spills. Other critical incident needs are identified by asking ''what if'' questions: for example, "What would happen if the main computer or phone system failed?"

## Conducting a Needs Assessment

Four phases constitute a needs assessment: planning, collecting data, analyzing data, and preparing the final report. Figure 2-1 identifies the individual steps in each of these four phases.

**Phase I: Planning.** An effective needs assessment focuses on one job classification or target audience. Once the audience is defined, a strategy is developed for collecting the needs data. The designer first determines whether data are required for each type of need. For example, normative needs might not be essential when

**FIGURE 2-1**

Needs assessment process

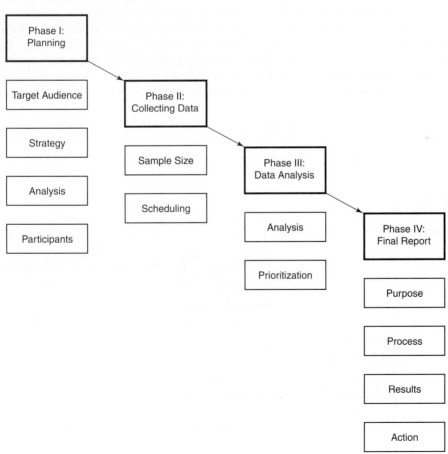

identifying anticipated needs due to a change in software or database system an organization uses. Careful consideration should be given to what type or types of needs are most relevant to the analysis. If you are examining the need for future training, then you might focus only on anticipated needs. A designer who is new to an organization or client might gather data on several types of needs to gain a more robust picture and data.

The next step of the planning phase is to determine who will participate in the study. In industry, the participants (i.e., individuals to interview) might include a sampling of the target audience, supervisors and managers of the target audience, and experienced individuals who once were members of the target audience but have received promotions to higher levels. Figure 2-2 illustrates a sample organizational chart for a telephone company and identifies target participants (i.e., installers). Members of this target audience and the managers are asked to share their perceptions of the current needs. The line workers and repair people are also interviewed because they once worked as installers (i.e., the target audience) and can provide a different perspective. Experienced individuals provide another perspective based on their experiences and their interactions with the target audience.

Similar decisions are also required for school-based needs assessments. Major participants in those assessments are parents, students, and administrators. For example, we conducted a technology assessment for a school to identify teacher training needs and hardware and software needs. Our focus was primarily on felt and anticipated needs. We collected data by interviewing teachers and asking teachers, parents, and students to complete surveys.

The last step of the planning phase is to determine how to collect the data. Common data collection techniques include questionnaires, rating scales, interviews, small-group meetings, and reviews of paper trails. Consider the population

**FIGURE 2-2**
Needs assessment participants (shaded boxes indicate individuals participating in needs assessment).

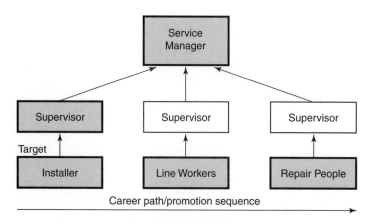

who will participate in your assessment and determine the best means for collecting the data. For example, sending a questionnaire via e-mail to an audience that is not composed of frequent e-mail users could result in a low return rate. Similarly, paper questionnaires mailed to a group of executives may also yield a small return rate. Find one or two data collection methods that will produce the best results. Needs assessment results are often reported as frequencies (e.g., 60% of the employees indicated they did not know how to complete an expense advance request). Identification of the analysis methodology early in the process aids in designing the instruments and ensures that appropriate data are collected. The planning step is complete when you have designed the data collection instruments.

**Phase II: Collecting the Data.**   Careful consideration of the sample size and distribution is required when collecting data. It may not be logistically or economically feasible to interview every participant at each company site, plant, or division. Thus, the sample must include individuals from representative sites and regions. For example, manufacturing companies produce a variety of products at a number of different locations. Interviewing employees in only one area could provide a false picture of the training needs for a companywide target audience. Data collection also includes scheduling appointments, making travel arrangements, and distributing and collecting questionnaires. Individual experience will determine the optimum number of interviews to plan per day and the return rate for questionnaires. Note that a 100% return rate often is unrealistic. Although a 75% to 85% return rate is desirable, the acceptable level depends on the context. Also, unlike experimental or basic research, large samples may be less important than samples that are representative relative to the target population of employees or students.

**Phase III: Analyzing the Data.**   Once the data are collected, you are ready to analyze the data. The output of the analysis is a prioritization of needs. Needs can be prioritized on the basis of economic value (e.g., the cost value to the company), impact (i.e., the number of people affected), a ranking scale, frequency of identification, or timeliness. One method for prioritizing needs, the Delphi method, is an iterative process: The designer might mail a list of goals to a group of managers and ask them to rank the goals. In a second mailing, the designer might send the same group a list of the top 40 goals and ask them to rank them again, and then send the top 20 in a third mailing. This process is repeated until it establishes a focus. The advantage to the Delphi approach is its systematic and thorough data-gathering process; its disadvantage is its relatively high effort and time demands. Another method for prioritizing is to use the identified needs as an input to a goal analysis (see the "Goal Analysis" section later in this chapter), which is then used to set the goals for training intervention.

**Phase IV: Compiling a Final Report.**   The last phase of needs assessment is to prepare a final report. A needs assessment report should include four sections:

1. Summary of the study's purpose
2. Summary of the process (how it was done and who was involved)

3. Summary of the results in one or more tables and a brief narrative
4. Necessary recommendations based on the data

The recommendation should be appropriate to the problem. If the needed intervention focuses on restructuring wages or on an organizational development intervention, then either a new team or additional team members may be needed to implement the solution. If instruction is an appropriate intervention, the designer can proceed with the design and development process.

## Example Needs Assessment Plan

The Electronic Phone Company (EPC) offers business customers discounted day-time phone rates for domestic and overseas calls. EPC has customer service and operator information centers in New York, Atlanta, St. Louis, and San Francisco. The caller information department consists of information operators (entry level), operator supervisors, and chief operators. Information operators are promoted to operator supervisors. Operator supervisors monitor operator activity, provide coaching to entry-level operators, and handle problem situations for 10 to 15 operators. Chief operators monitor the activities of 5 to 10 operator supervisors and have the final authority and responsibility for all actions. EPC has decided that training is needed to improve the skills of the operator supervisors.

**Phase I.**   A decision was made to collect data on five types of needs: comparative, felt, expressed, anticipated, and critical incident. The decision was made in part because of an international conflict that began at the beginning of the needs assessment. Operator supervisors are the target audience (approximately 70 in the four locations). Face-to-face interviewing was selected as the primary method for data collection. Two operators at each of three levels were interviewed individually. A structured interview form was developed to guide the interviews.

**Phase II.**   A decision was made to interview employees at all four locations because the New York and San Francisco locations had a greater percentage of overseas calls, and the St. Louis and Atlanta locations handled primarily domestic calls. The designers scheduled two days in each location to conduct 6 interviews (two operators at each of three levels), for a total of 24 interviews at the four locations. Table 2-1 includes the interview questions that were used.

**Phase III.**   A frequency count was made for each need identified in the interviews. The needs were categorized as either customer oriented or employee oriented. Customer-oriented needs were ranked by estimated loss of income (e.g., inability to find a phone number, misdirection of customer complaints). A group of operator supervisors and chief operators participated in a ranking process using the Delphi method to rank the employee-oriented needs.

**Phase IV.**   The final report identified three training problems. First, operator supervisors needed training in the use of advanced searching techniques to identify

**TABLE 2-1**
Interview questions

How long have you served as an operator?
What resources do you use to help to answer caller questions?
How well do the resources work for you?
Does anything get in your way while doing your job?
What changes do you want to see?
Are there any things/issues that impact employee efficiency and effectiveness?
If you could change one thing about your job, what would it be?
How do you learn about new products that affect your job?
What changes might affect your job?

phone numbers. Second, they needed training in handling difficult customers. Third, they needed training in coaching entry-level operators in communication techniques.

Needs assessment is a useful tool for identifying training needs. It is particularly effective when very little is known about an organization. Gathering data from a number of individuals provides a broad perspective for correctly identifying the problem or needs.

## GOAL ANALYSIS

Sometimes, conducting a needs assessment is neither practical nor feasible. An alternative approach is to use a goal analysis to define the problem. Goal analysis is a method for "defining the undefinable" (Mager, 1984b). Some designers consider goal analysis to be an integral part of the needs assessment process. Unlike needs assessment, which seeks to identify problems, a goal analysis begins with input suggesting a problem. For example, a manager might determine that supervising operators are having a problem coaching the information operators. Goal analysis is then applied to this "need" to develop the goals for the training intervention. Applying goal analysis to a need suggested by one individual assumes that the need exists and that a training intervention is required to address the need. For example, a manager might contact you indicating that HVAC service personnel *really* need a course in troubleshooting. Similarly, a principal might ask you to conduct an in-service workshop on webpage development for the teachers in her school. While you might first propose a needs assessment for each of these two situations, time and financial constraints will not allow you to conduct a needs assessment. An alternative then is to meet with supervisors or senior personnel and conduct a goal analysis.

A goal analysis could also use the data from a needs assessment to set priorities. Take, for example, a needs assessment that identifies the need to train managers in how to conduct hiring interviews. A goal analysis would use this need assessment data to determine goals for the instruction.

$\overline{\text{Expert's Edge}}$

## "Getting Blood out of a Turnip": An Instructional Design Approach

In an ideal world, focus groups would consist of 8 to 10 participants—experts in the field—who take turns addressing issues, allow the facilitator to control the conversation, and have unlimited time to participate. What happens, however, when you have 15 to 20 participants who are experts at their jobs, many of whom refuse to share information because supervisors are present, and who have only one hour to spend? Clearly, such a situation calls for some changes to the traditionally run focus group. Here's what our training team did.

Prior to the focus group, we circulated a list of 10 questions we would ask and requested that participants review them. At the beginning of the session, we handed out the list again, this time with room for the participants to write down potential answers. They were told that we would collect these notes at the end of the session, and we requested that they not write their names on the notes unless they wanted to be contacted directly for their answers.

The facilitator read each question, clarifying, if necessary, and allowed a couple of minutes for the participants to make the notes. Discussion followed with note takers recording answers. (We were not allowed to tape these sessions.)

As with any focus group this large, there were a few who did not participate. With 10 minutes to go, we stopped the process and gave each person an opportunity to make one last statement about anything he or she felt strongly would affect training. These ideas were also captured.

In the debriefing session that followed, we reviewed the participants' notes and were surprised to find that many mentioned topics that we didn't have time to discuss. We also received some strong comments that may not have been politically correct to express in a focus group setting. Finally, we had substantial reinforcement for all the comments that were made, making it easier for us to determine consensus of opinion. In one hour we had collected more data than we normally gained in much longer sessions.

Bailey F. Hanes, Ed.D, is an independent consultant and educational psychologist specializing in performance management and employee training. He has over 30 years' experience in working with major corporations all over the United States.

Carol Diroff is an instructional technologist at Ford Motor Company's Power-Train Core Competency, in which she has done extensive work in technical training. She is currently working on training for complex problem solving.

## Six Steps of Goal Analysis

Klein, Hoepfner, Bradley, Wooley, Dyer, and Strickland (1971) and Mager (1984b) have suggested similar steps for conducting a goal analysis. Our six steps for a goal analysis are a synthesis of theirs. A goal analysis is generally done with a small group of individuals (4 to 12) who are familiar with the problem. The makeup of the group can include individuals from different levels in the organization, as with a needs assessment, or it can include more homogenous group. We tend to prefer a mixed group so that we can collect different perspectives.

**Identify an Aim.**   Have the group determine one or more aims related to the need. An aim is a general intent that gives direction. For example, the aim could be to conduct an effective interview for a real estate sales position.

**Set Goals.**   Have the group generate a number of goals for each aim. These goals should identify behaviors that describe learner performance. Here are some goals a group might generate that are related to the example aim:

> Prepare an agenda for the interview.
> Prepare a series of questions to ask during the interview.
> Prepare a structured interview form.
> Identify people to take the interviewee to lunch.
> Identify individuals to provide transportation for the interviewee.
> Identify a real estate agent to work with the interviewee.
> Obtain benefits information.
> Identify the steps for conducting an interview.
> Determine the type of questions to ask.

**Refine Goals.**   The group then sorts through the goals and deletes duplicates, combines similar goals, and refines those that are vague. This step is primarily a refinement stage to clarify the goal statements. The example goals could be refined as follows:

> Prepare a series of questions to ask during the interview.
> Prepare an agenda and transportation for the interview.
> Identify a real estate agent for the interviewee.
> Obtain benefits information.
> Identify the steps for conducting an interview.
> Determine appropriate business clothing for the interview
> Determine the type of questions to ask.

**Rank Goals.**   Next, the group ranks and selects the most salient goals. Ranking can be by order of importance, items most likely to cause problems if ignored, or other relevant criteria. Some goals may be eliminated and others identified as critical to job performance.

1. Prepare an agenda for and transportation to and from the interview.
2. Obtain benefits information.
3. Prepare a series of questions to ask during the interview.
4. Determine the type of questions to ask.

    5.  Identify the steps for conducting an interview.
    6.  Identify a real estate agent for the interviewee.
    7.  Determine appropriate business clothing for the interview

**Refine Goals Again.**   The group then identifies discrepancies between the goals and existing performance. This step verifies that the need exists and that the goals are related to the job task(s). For example, after examining the goal, you might find that your target audience does not perform the task as with Goal 2 described below.

> Goal 2 was dropped because the personnel office handles benefits information. Goal 6 was dropped because it was not considered part of the interview process. Goal 7 was dropped as company policy requires business dress when in the office and all employees abide by the policy.

> The remaining goals represent existing performance problems.

**Make a Final Ranking.**   Last, the group develops a final ranking of the goals. They start by determining how critical or important each goal is to performing the tasks. Second, consider the overall effect of the goal. Relevant factors may be the cost of not doing the training, the probability the need will disappear if ignored (e.g., because of an impending change in the system), and the number of people affected by the training intervention. The final ranking is then used to design the training. The following are the final, ranked goals for the example:

    1.  Determine the type of questions to ask.
    2.  Prepare a series of questions to ask during the interview.
    3.  Identify the steps for conducting an interview.
    4.  Prepare an agenda for and transportation to and from the interview.

## Comparing Goal Analysis and Needs Assessment

Goal analysis takes less time than a needs assessment, and its focus is typically much narrower. The goal analysis starts with a problem someone has identified, and then it focuses on a solution to the given problem. A goal analysis is typically conducted with a few individuals who are knowledgeable about the problem and target audience. The designer is relying on this small group of individuals to provide accurate input rather than gathering a variety of data from a number of sources as with a needs assessment. Deciding which method to select depends on a number of factors, including cost, time, scope of the project, and validity of the information the designer obtains from the participants. Typically, a needs assessment is reserved for projects that can justify the time and cost involved. A goal analysis is used when a problem is identified and the designer has confidence that the problem is valid. For example, a university implements a new online record system so that faculty and advisors can access student and class information. Because this system is new, training of some sort is probably needed. In contrast, a manager indicating that a group of employees needs a course on troubleshooting may need verification before the designer starts the task of designing the course. A goal analysis with appropriate individuals could be used to further define the training.

## PERFORMANCE ASSESSMENT

Instructional designers often receive requests to design a training program to address a perceived problem. A manager, chairperson, principal, or vice president may offer additional funding or rewards as an incentive to complete the project. Although it is often tempting to "take the money and run" with the project, the first step prior to initiating design is to determine whether training intervention will actually solve the problem. Some problems, for example, may result from a failure to follow procedures rather than from the improper execution of a task. An overnight shipping company saved thousands of dollars on training by recognizing such a problem. One facility had a consistently large number of package-sorting errors. The company's initial reaction was to design a training program to improve the sorters' skills. After careful observation of the process, however, the manager found that the crew loading the packages on the conveyor was starting the sort earlier than scheduled and before the full complement of sorters arrived. The few sorters who arrived early were overwhelmed by the packages and made errors trying to keep up with the packages loaded by the crew. Simply enforcing the procedure that the sort would not start until the designated time solved the sorting problem. The appropriate solution to this problem was one of following procedures rather than one of providing retraining for the employees.

Similarly, a petroleum company requested that a designer develop a course to help petroleum engineers plan an acid treatment on an oil well to increase oil production. An analysis of the problem indicated that treatments were adequately planned, but they were done on wells that were already producing as much oil as possible given the pipe diameter and well pressure. Any increase in oil production would not be physically possible nor economically feasible compared with the cost of the treatment. The training emphasis shifted from planning the treatment to determining when a treatment was needed. The performance assessment, in this case, identified a different problem that was addressed with training.

For training to be effective, it must address the appropriate problem, not simply its symptoms. Mager (1984a) describes a performance analysis as an aid to identifying performance problems. Rossett (1999) describes this process as finding the source of the problem. If we know the source of the problem, then we can determine the appropriate solution! Developing training for the package sorting problem just described would be a waste of company resources and would fail to solve the problem. Often, there is a simpler solution (such as reaffirming the starting time) than developing and implementing a training program. Rossett (1999) and Kalman (1987) suggest a number of causes of performance problems. We have combined these two approaches in Table 2-2. If you discover a problem during a needs assessment or goal analysis, or someone "identifies" a performance problem,

**TABLE 2-2**

Causes of performance problems

| Cause | Example | Intervention |
|---|---|---|
| Lack of knowledge or skills | Production personnel do not know how to set the computer controller for the drill press.<br><br>New-hire insurance sales personnel do not know the difference between whole life and term life insurance. | Training. |
| Lack of motivation or incentive | Employees are not returning unused parts to the correct bins.<br><br>Students are not completing homework assignments due on Mondays. | Improve motivation and/or offer incentives for performance. |
| Environmental factors | Professional staff are experiencing an increase in carpal tunnel syndrome after receiving PCs.<br><br>Lighting in the shop is not adequate to perform tasks. | Modify environment or change workstation to facilitate task. |
| Management factors | Manager fails to provide adequate direction for staff concerning scope and time frame for jobs.<br><br>Manager's style is confrontational. | Change management practices or train/coach manager. |
| Interpersonal relations | Dispersed workgroup flounders on collaborative projects.<br><br>Rivalry between staff members disrupts job/task. | Change work environment; provide coaching, conflict resolution; change management practices or policy. |

you can use Table 2-2 to help guide your assessment of the problem. By identifying the real cause of the problem, you can determine the appropriate intervention strategy. Your analysis may require additional interviews, observations, surveys, and focus groups (Rosset).

Another technique, job analysis, is a listing of all the tasks an individual performs in a job. Such an approach is useful for developing a curriculum for training rather than identifying performance gaps or problem areas. Although this method is very time-consuming, it does yield a complete task listing for a job. The use of job analysis to define a program assumes that training is needed on the tasks. Such an approach is appropriate for certain environments, such as a trade school course or military training that involves entry-level learners who have little knowledge or skill in the area. The outcome is typically a series of courses based on a body of knowledge the learner must master.

## SUMMARY

1. Like a good problem-solving model, instructional design begins with identification of the training problem. Needs assessment, goal analysis, or performance assessment can help identify the problem. In practice, problem identification often involves a combination of these techniques rather than just one.

**FIGURE 2-3**
Identifying instructional problems

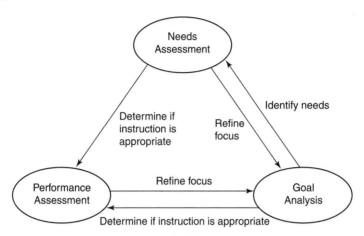

2. Needs assessment is an effective tool for identifying a range of problems in an organization, particularly if the designer is unfamiliar with the organization.
3. A needs assessment can identify six types of needs: normative, comparative, felt, expressed, anticipated, and critical incident.
4. A goal analysis can use either a needs assessment or a request for instruction as a starting point to establish priorities. The goal analysis process first identifies aims, then establishes, refines, and prioritizes the goals.
5. Performance assessment helps determine whether the goals of the training program actually address a training problem or another intervention would be more appropriate.
6. The problem-identification process may require multiple techniques to refine the problem (see Figure 2-3). For example, you might start with a needs assessment or performance assessment, and then use a goal analysis to refine the problem.

## THE ID PROCESS

This element of the ID process provides the first contribution to instructional design documentation. During this phase, you meet with your manager to identify your client and maybe the target audience. In most cases, one of your clients will have an idea or focus area for the performance problem. That is, someone will have identified a gap between performance and expectations. Or, in some instances, you might be asked to identify where a performance problem might develop because of upcoming changes in the job or work environment. There are also times when you might identify a performance problem during your analysis of an unrelated problem.

Now is the time to delve into your toolbox and determine the best tool or tools to use to define the problem. You must find an approach that is both effective and efficient. If instructional design is a new concept in your company, you may need to sell your management on the concept of defining the correct performance problem.

The output of this phase is a definition of a performance problem. If it is a problem that you can solve with training, then you further refine the problem statement with a goal analysis that will guide the next phase: task analysis. If the performance problem is easily solved with a job aid, then you can begin the process of developing the job aid. If the problem is one that is not best addressed by an instructional intervention, then you must determine who can more appropriately provide a solution. Depending on your own skills, you might provide the solution, or you could find another resource in the company to provide the appropriate solution.

## APPLICATIONS

Consider the next two problems you might face as an instructional designer. What actions would you take?

**Problem 1**. It is your first day on the job at Global Plastics and you are meeting with your manager in her office. Looking around, you notice that it is professionally decorated and has various symbols indicating her success in the company (and probably access to the corporate interior designer). Obviously, she is someone who is viewed favorably by upper management and has the necessary political connections. As you talk with her, she is fumbling with a malfunctioning mechanical pencil. From her actions, you might infer that she lacks any mechanical ability and wonder what effect it might have on her ability to understand technical training problems. Noticing that you are not paying full attention to what she is saying, she places the pencil in her desk drawer and closes it with extra effort for emphasis. She explains that she wants video instruction developed on how to change the oil in all the diesel engines in the 10 manufacturing plants; the video will be posted on the company's website for easy viewing and testing. She is unsure how many engines there are in all, but there are four in this plant. Furthermore, she explains that the in-plant technical training program must start with the basics. As you walk out the door, she mentions that her neck is on the line for the $2.5 million video studio she installed last year, and there are still no training materials on the training department's website. She needs to show management that video instruction can affect the company's bottom line. She urges you to collect data to support this point. "Now," she charges, "determine where you want to begin shooting, and I will make the arrangements for you to begin tomorrow afternoon."

**Problem 2**. After your two-day meeting with the regional field service managers, you have a list they generated of 56 "training" courses. A quick analysis of the topics suggests that they are potential performance problems caused by either a lack of knowledge or skill, or they are tasks that are not performed frequently. These managers are quite adamant that their field service staff definitely needs this type of training if they are to continue offering a quality product to clients.

After some investigation, you grow weary of the list. It seems some of your sources question the need for certain topics and some topics are deemed too simple to need training. Your task is to improve the performance of the field service engineers, who have acquired the reputation of replacing part after part until the equipment is fixed rather than troubleshooting the problem.

What is your plan of action? One of your clients is the group of managers, who fully believe they have identified the training needed to solve the problem. On the other hand, these training topics do not appear to support troubleshooting but rather the removing and replacing of parts. Considering you are new to the company, what will you do?

## ANSWERS

What is the real problem with changing the oil in the diesel engines? There are two issues. First, your manager needs to justify the expensive purchase of the video equipment that you will use for producing video-based training. Second, there may be a need for in-house technical training. You are new on the job, and you do not have a lot of credibility or support yet. This situation may be an instance in which it is best to "bite the bullet" and spend an afternoon producing a simple tape on how to change the oil. You will gain the support of your manager, who can then show upper management the nice product you have produced. Then, she might more readily listen to your plan for addressing the larger issue. Presenting her with reasons why the company does not need the video training might fall on deaf ears.

In every situation, there are typically two or more clients. Your manager is one of your clients. The field service managers are also clients, as are the field service engineers—probably the most important ones because you are trying to improve their productivity. Although it might be politically expedient to develop the 56 courses identified by the managers, the burden of not solving the performance problem would probably ultimately fall on you. Given the results of your initial research, it appears that the problem is not defined. We would recommend that you sell your manager and the field service managers on trying to identify the "real" problem: lack of troubleshooting skills.

To accomplish this task, you might do a needs assessment and an analysis of the type of work completed during the past two years on the job. Obvious trends might emerge, such as the fact that the engineers replace the heat transfer element whenever a problem occurs. A check with your engineering department might indicate that the number of failures reported by this service department far exceeds those expected or performed by other service groups. The combination of the needs assessment data and repair data might convince the managers to take a different approach to solving the problem. This problem illustrates that there is a political side (not only in business, but also in education) of instruction. The successful designer must often balance the political and instructional needs of the organization and individuals. Designers must consider the political issues to ensure that all stakeholders buy in, that is, understand and support the plan. Similarly, the designer must report the needs to the stakeholders and help them make the most appropriate decision for addressing the problem.

## QUALITY MANAGEMENT

There are two questions to ask at this stage of the instructional design process. First, is the problem correctly identified? A needs assessment should provide adequate data to support your problem identification. However, if you use only a goal analysis or performance assessment, there often will be a lack of such data. Before proceeding, you should verify that you have correctly identified the problem by either reviewing your data or posing some additional follow-up questions to those familiar with the target audience and/or problem. Second, is this problem one that is best addressed by an instructional intervention? If instruction is the answer, then you should proceed with the instructional design process. If you have determined that another intervention is more appropriate, such as by using the performance assessment process, you must determine the most appropriate action. You might add new members to your team or suggest another specialist form a team to address the problem.

## INSTRUCTIONAL DESIGN: DECISIONS AND CHOICES

This morning you have received a phone call from the corporate security director. The corporate security director tells you, "We need you to put on a safety training course for employees. When can you have it ready?"

Although you are excited about the opportunity to design a course that could promote a safer workplace, you immediately recognize that the security director has proposed a solution (i.e., instruction) without describing the underlying problem. You want to know more about the current situation to ensure that instruction is an appropriate solution, so you arrange to meet with the security director.

At the meeting, you ask the security director to tell you more about the situation. "Last week a trash can caught fire in the mail room and the mail room clerk didn't know what to do. By the time he figured out how to use the fire extinguisher, the fire was almost out of control. Worse, he didn't follow emergency procedures. He should have sounded the fire alarm before attempting to put out the fire! We should require that all employees be trained on using fire extinguishers as part of their new employee orientation put on by the human resources department."

As an experienced designer, you hypothesize that the mail room clerk has either forgotten what to do (because he was trained several years ago) or he never really learned the procedure correctly when he was trained. Further investigation reveals that the "training" the mail room clerk received consisted of being given an information sheet that described emergency procedures when he was first hired eight years ago. Because the mail room clerk never actually practiced using a fire extinguisher, you are confident that a knowledge/skills gap exists and that training is an appropriate solution.

You prepare a needs assessment document that describes what you learned from your interviews and explains your rationale for recommending that training is needed. Here's an excerpt from your report:

Training on fire emergency procedures is needed for all administrative support personnel, maintenance staff, and security officers to ensure employee safety, prevent damage to company property, and reduce potential workman's compensation costs in the event of a fire. Although administrative support employees may have some familiarity with emergency procedures, they have limited confidence carrying out emergency procedures because they have had no hands-on practice using a fire extinguisher. Second, although hands-on training on the proper use of fire extinguishers is mandated by state law for security officers, making this training available to all employees who voluntarily wish to attend may result in preventing lawsuits and may reduce annual liability insurance costs. Making this course available to all employees will enhance safety awareness and may also contribute to enhanced employee morale. The cost of relocating employees as a result of smoke and water damage and lost productivity will more than offset the cost of providing this training program.

The final ranking of the goals is as follows:

- Differentiate types of fires (paper, grease, chemical)
- Differentiate types of fire extinguishers
- Recognize when a fire is too large to attempt to extinguish
- List, in sequence, fire evacuation procedures
- Aim the spray nozzle of a fire extinguisher
- Recognize how to hold a fire extinguisher (carbon dioxide type)
- Describe the historical development of the fire department
- Describe the organizational structure of the company's emergency personnel

## REFERENCES

Bradshaw, J. (1972). The concept of social need. *New Society, 19*(4), 640–643.

Burton, J. K., & Merrill, P. F. (1991). Needs assessment: Goals, needs, and priorities. In L. J. Briggs, K. L. Gustafson, & M. H. Tillman (Eds.), *Instructional design: Principles and applications* (2nd ed., pp. 17–43). Englewood Cliffs, NJ: Educational Technology Publications.

Finson, K., & Szedlak, F. (1997). General Motors does a needs analysis. *Training and Development, 51*(5), 103–104.

Hilbert, T. S., Renkl, A., Schworm, S., Kessler, S., & Reiss, K. (2007). Learning to teach with worked-out examples: A computer-based learning environment for teachers. *Journal of Computer Assisted Learning, 24*, 316–332.

Kalman, H. K. (1987, March). *Is it a training problem?* Paper presented at the National Society of Performance and Instruction, Washington, DC

Kaufman, R., & English, F. W. (1979). *Needs assessment: Concept and application.* Englewood Cliffs, NJ: Educational Technology Publications.

Kaufman, R., Rojas, A. M., & Mayer, H. (1993). *Needs assessment: A user's guide.* Englewood Cliffs, NJ: Educational Technology Publications.

Klein, S. P., Hoepfner, R., Bradley, P. A., Wooley, D., Dyer, J. S., & Strickland, G. P. (1971). *Procedures for needs-assessment evaluation: A symposium.* (Report No. 67). Los Angeles: University of California, Center for the Study of Evaluation.

Lucier, K. H. (2008). A consultative training program: Collateral effect of a needs assessment. *Communication Education, 57*(4), 482–489.

Mager, R. F. (1984a). *Goal analysis* (2nd ed.). Belmont, CA: Lake.

Mager, R. F. (1984b). *Analyzing performance problems* (2nd ed.). Atlanta, GA: The Center for Effective Performance.

Meeker, P. G., & Byers, J. F. (2003). Data-driven graduate curriculum redesign: A case study. *Journal of Nursing Education, 42*(4), 186–188.

Rossett, A. (1999). Analysis for human performance technology. In H. D. Stolovitch, & E. J. Keeps (Eds.), *Handbook of performance technology: Improving individual and organizational performance worldwide* (pp. 139–162). San Francisco, CA: Jossey-Bass/Pfeiffer.

Sampson, J. F. (2007). A systematic approach to writing in the Department of Defense. *Performance Improvement, 46*(3), 31–35.

Sweller, J., & Cooper G. A. (1985). The use of worked examples as a substitute for problem solving in learning algebra. *Cognition and Instruction, 2*, 59–89.

# Learner and Contextual Analysis

## GETTING STARTED

Your manager has asked you to design a training program to improve the collaborative skills of cell phone designers who are using a new online collaborative design tool. Each group of cell phone designers includes, for example, engineers, programmers, human interface specialists, or artists that must bargain with the other designers or groups. For example, the group working on the battery might ask all the teams for a few more ounces of weight in exchange for a longer talk time. It is November, and the training design document is due in late January. Time is therefore short, and as you soon discover, the target employees are very busy and not highly accessible for providing information. First, what do you need to know about your target audience that might influence the design of the materials? Second, how will you collect the information?

Suppose you had never heard about the instructional design process. You start giving a lecture at the first class meeting of your course on the success of school reform. You have put a lot of work into developing this new introductory unit to impress students with the value of the subject. The lecture contains detailed statistical content from recent research and complex explanations. As you proceed, you sense reactions: A few students are listening intently and rapidly taking notes; others look puzzled; some appear completely indifferent. This is a one-time opportunity for all of them to get this important information! What is wrong? Perhaps, in your preparation, you have given little consideration to the nature of the student group, the students' preparation levels, degree of motivation, or other traits that contribute to their interest and success in learning. One of the key elements of the instructional design process mentioned in Chapter 1 is the need to consider the learners for whom a program is being developed. Obviously, the measure of success of an instructional plan will depend principally on the learning level of the learners involved. Learner populations, from elementary levels through high school and college and in training areas (whether industrial, business, health,

## QUESTIONS TO CONSIDER

"Why is it important to give attention to learner characteristics when planning instruction?"

"Which characteristics are most useful, and how is information about them obtained?"

"What limitations might these characteristics place on your design?"

"What factors in the environment will affect the instruction?"

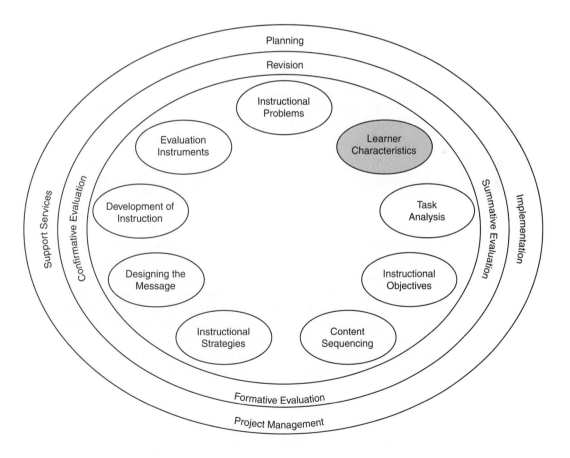

government, or military), are composed of varied types of people. As designers, we need to understand the relevant characteristics of our learners and how those characteristics provide either opportunities or constraints on our designs.

Just as people differ in many respects, so do ways in which they learn. Some of these differences are evident in the kinds of experiences each person requires to learn and, if competence in a skill is to be acquired, in the amount of time and practice each person needs to acquire it. It is essential, therefore, early in the planning process, to give attention to the characteristics, abilities, and experiences of the learners—both as a group and as individuals. To serve either a training group or an academic classroom, the instructional designer must obtain information about the capabilities, needs, and interests of the learners. This information should affect certain elements in planning, such as the entry point, selection of topics (and the level at which topics are introduced), the choice and sequencing of objectives, the depth of topic treatment, and the variety of learning activities. Related to learner analysis is environmental analysis: that is, what variables in the learning environment can or will affect the design and delivery of the instruction.

When designing an instructional plan, decide early in the initial design stages which characteristics of your learners or trainees to identify to help with the design decisions. Then, decide how to acquire the necessary information. As you complete the design process, you may find that you need additional information about your learners or the learning environment.

Let's consider an example from a learner analysis that two of the authors (Ross and Morrison) conducted for a project involving the design of computer-based support tools. What follows is the summary section of our final report (fictitious labels are substituted):

- The employees to be trained are generally motivated to improve their skills and efficiency.
- New employees often start the job without adequate training.
- More employees with experience work in section GM than in section EO.
- Most employees are very knowledgeable about their jobs.
- Employees are generally positive about their jobs, but feel that they are inhibited by limitations of the existing computer system.
- Other employee frustrations stem from a perceived lack of understanding by other groups as to what their group needs. This frustration is particularly strong among section EO employees, who feel that section A's staff needs to better understand section EO's needs for orders and other tasks.
- Most users characterize themselves primarily as problem solvers.
- Employees are generally well educated and have good reading and cognitive skills.
- Employees feel great time pressure to complete their job requirements.

Based on the preceding characterizations and more detailed, job-specific information, we were able to make much more informed decisions about different aspects of the instructional design plan. For example, we determined that computer-support tools requiring any substantive off-task time (e.g., receiving a Web-based tutorial lesson on a particular job procedure) would rarely be used by the target audience. To derive this information, however, we needed to orient our learner analysis around characteristics most likely to affect the learning task. Let's now examine strategies and schemes for identifying these key learner differences.

## TYPES OF LEARNER CHARACTERISTICS

Countless traits differentiate learners. In initiating a learner analysis, the important task for the designer is to identify those characteristics most critical to the achievement of the specific training objectives. Also, in most applied contexts, the accessibility of learner information is a major factor in deciding which characteristics to consider. For example, where general intellectual ability is considered an important variable relating to success in the training program, administering individual IQ tests at several hundred dollars per student may be viewed as extravagant, or certainly impractical, relative to using some existing ability or aptitude score. On the other hand, a variable such as gender or prior employment may be highly accessible but have little relevance to the particular instructional design decisions.

Heinich, Molenda, Russell, and Smaldino (1999) suggested that designers initially consider three categories of learner characteristics: general characteristics, specific entry characteristics (prerequisite skills for the instruction), and learning styles. In addition to these three categories, we will also describe five additional categories that include academic information, personal and social characteristics, culturally diverse learners, learners with disabilities, and adult learners. Let's briefly examine each category; remembering that on an actual design project (e.g., training accountants to use a new tax preparation application) the importance of specific traits within each category depends on both the relevance of the trait to the task and the accessibility of learner information.

### General Characteristics

General characteristics are broad identifying variables such as gender, age, work experience, education, and ethnicity. We examine several of these variables in more detail later, but for now consider an example of training employees to use a new tax-preparation application. Recognizing that you may not have yet conducted a needs assessment (see Chapter 2) or task analysis (see Chapter 4), try to form preliminary impressions of some training approaches you might use. Would you rely primarily on a workshop, lecture, or printed manual or on Web-based instruction? on-the-job coaching? job aids or guide sheets? some combination? At this point, it's probably pure speculation, but would your "best guess" first idea change if you were told that the employees are all novice workers in their early 20s? What if all were disadvantaged teenagers hired for the summer on a school-to-work program? What if they were senior accountants with extensive experience in numerous accounting applications? And, finally, the designer's frequent challenge: What if the employees comprise a mixture of experts, novices, and paraprofessionals with diverse job and software experiences? Given these variables, the importance of both a prior needs assessment (or goal analysis) and present understanding of how general learner characteristics may affect addressing those needs in the training design should be evident.

## Specific Entry Characteristics

Specific entry competencies are prerequisite skills and attitudes that learners must possess to benefit from the training. Based on our experiences, we have found the analysis of such competencies is important at two stages in the design process. One stage precedes the design of the instruction and determines the entry characteristics of typical target students or trainees. In the example of the accounting project, it would certainly help to know, for example, that the majority of employees to be trained have had limited experience in using computers in their work, or that most are highly educated with strong reading skills, or that most are extremely negative about using the new application and are likely to resist the training. Knowing the learners' skills, attitudes, or aptitudes is obviously important in determining the appropriate difficulty level of instruction. We recommend making the difficulty level slightly higher than that considered optimum for the average learner. Consequently, the instruction will be challenging but not overly demanding for most learners, and it is usually easier to provide supplementary support for learners experiencing difficulty than it is to make too-easy content interesting and challenging for the majority.

The preceding sentence suggests the second stage of design during which the assessment of specific entry competencies comes directly into play. Once the instruction is designed, it is highly useful and often essential to include entry tests that determine the learners' readiness. For example, if one of the accounting trainees were completely unfamiliar with the computer used in the training (e.g., switching from a Macintosh to a PC), a prerequisite training session to provide the needed background could prevent a situation in which that individual becomes lost and frustrated during the instruction. At the opposite extreme, an entry assessment might identify several trainees who have already mastered the instructional objectives and, therefore, do not need the training. Heinich et al. (1999) suggested clearly stating prerequisite competencies as part of the instructional program: "The accounting trainee must be able to boot the computer and connect to the network for saving files." We might expect to revise our specific entry competencies after completing the task analysis or after completing the strategy design.

## Learning Styles

Learning styles are traits that refer to how individuals approach learning tasks and process information. Simply put, some learners find certain methods of learning more *appealing* than others. For a long time it has been known that, rather than attending lectures and reading textual material, some individuals are more *comfortable* learning from a visual approach to studying and others learn from physical activities and the manipulation of objects. Attempting to identify a person's unique learning style preference might aid planning for small-group or individualized instruction.

Despite the extensive literature on learning styles, questions remain regarding the degree to which such styles can be matched to teaching methods with any benefits for learning (Knight, Halpin & Halpin, 1992; Park & Lee, 2004; Snow, 1992). This concern has been raised in general with the research that attempts to systematically adapt instructional methodologies to individual learner characteristics (see the review by Jonassen & Grabowski, 1993). For the designer, then, the potential value of knowing students' learning styles must be weighed against the effort required to obtain that information (e.g., administer and score a learning styles inventory) and the likelihood that useful and practical adaptations of instructional strategies can be achieved. Jonassen and Grabowski concluded that there are very limited applications of learning style information. In our view, the primary context in which you may want to consider learning styles is one-to-one instruction, for which materials and strategies can be easily adapted to accommodate individual needs.

Again, you as the instructional designer must weigh, on the basis of practical considerations and instructional needs, the degree to which assessing learning styles is useful to the design project. The limited support for adapting instruction to specific learning styles suggests that designers focus their attention on other types of data to make design decisions (Jonassen & Grabowski, 1993). Academic information, our next focus, is more often a key variable for instructional planning and delivery.

## Academic Information

Probably the most easily obtainable and often used category of information about individual learners is the academic record. This record would include the following:

- School grade or training level completed and major subject areas studied
- Grade-point average or letter grades for academic studies
- Scores on standardized achievement tests of intelligence and in such basic skills as reading, writing, and mathematics
- Special or advanced courses completed relating to the academic major or area of training

Data from prior-year achievement tests can provide useful information to a designer and teacher. For example, if the majority of your seventh-grade students failed to master the section on converting basic measurement units in grade 6, you can plan accordingly when teaching the conversion of metric units.

Much of this information is available from student records on file in a school's administrative office or from an individual's personnel or training records. Some of it is available from employment applications, in personnel files, or in the individual's training history. Confidentiality and ethical considerations must be kept in mind when referring to student or personnel records. If a specific type of information about learners is not available, specialized tests can be obtained and administered through a testing or personnel office.

Closely associated with the academic information about learners is the knowledge and skills that learners may already possess directly relating to the subject content or skills to be learned. Obtaining knowledge and skills information is one of the purposes for the pretesting element of the instructional design process (see Chapter 12). Thus, there is a close relationship between the information gathered about learner characteristics and the data to be acquired from pretests.

## Personal and Social Characteristics

You should also consider personal and social characteristics of the learners for whom the program is intended when those characteristics might affect the design and delivery of the course. Typically, information about the following types of variables is helpful to the designer:

- Age and maturity level
- Motivation and attitude toward the subject
- Expectations and vocational aspirations (if appropriate)
- Previous or current employment and work experience (if any)
- Special talents
- Mechanical dexterity
- Ability to work under various environmental conditions, such as noise, inclement weather (for those working outdoors), or high elevations

Looking at this list and thinking of your recent experiences, which variables do you feel are most important for instruction or training? Much depends on the nature and conditions of the learning activities. For many instructors learner motivation is actually considered to be the most important determinant of success (Driscoll, 2005; Keller, 2007; Pintrich, Roeser, & De Groot, 1994). Learners who "just don't care" or, worse, are actively resistant to the instruction are not likely to respond in the same way to the learning activities as would highly motivated students. Design strategies that create interest and keep attention would be appropriate for the former group.

Learner attitude is different from motivation. For example, a learner may be interested in taking a basic electronics course, but he may feel doubtful that he can pass it based on his poor abilities. This type of self-fulfilling prophecy breeds failure by anticipating failure (Slavin, 2006). If the designer finds that such negative attitudes are common for the target learner groups, she might employ strategies specifically intended to build confidence in the learners' abilities as the lesson proceeds (Jonassen & Grabowski, 1993). One possibility is to start the instruction with very easy content and gradually increase difficulty over time. B. F. Skinner (1954), in fact, employed a similar orientation, called "successive approximations," or "shaping," in designing programmed instruction. More recently, researchers have examined having learners complete some of the steps in worked examples, which is similar to Skinner's shaping and fading methods (Atkinson & Renkl, 2007).

Manual dexterity and other special motor skills of the learner may be of major importance in certain training programs. As is discussed in Chapter 5, the classification of motor skills has had fewer acceptances and less practical impact than has that of the cognitive and affective domains. Yet, several potential useful taxonomies exist, such as those by Heinich et al. (1999) and Kibler (1981).

Learner analysis may also reveal physical characteristics of potential students, such as health, physical fitness, weight, or disabilities that are relevant to training decisions. For example, a training program offered to a school district included, as a team-building exercise for administrators and teachers, an outdoor expedition requiring hiking and climbing. For several participants, these activities proved highly strenuous and produced negative feelings about the training (not to mention soreness and muscle aches the next day as a continuing reminder!).

Useful data about personal and social characteristics may be obtained by observation, interviews, and informational questionnaires, as well as from attitudinal surveys completed by learners. (See Chapters 12 and 13 for further discussion about these information-gathering methods.) If special groups constitute a significant percentage of the student population, social characteristics peculiar to each group should be given due consideration.

Although it is important during planning to gather and use the usual kinds of information—academic, personal, and social—about all learners, attention also should be given to additional characteristics of the target audience. This section examines the characteristics of culturally diverse learners, learners with disabilities, and adult learners.

## Culturally Diverse Learners

Learner groups may include members of ethnic cultures with backgrounds and behaviors that differ markedly from those of the majority of learners or trainees. Also, both the instructional designer and instructors who deliver the instruction may differ in ethnic background from members of the student group. The growth of global corporations and outsourcing also bring together learners from different cultures. For these reasons, characteristics of culturally diverse learners need special attention during planning.

One obvious problem may be deficiency in the English language and the implications for communication and reading comprehension (see Slavin & Cheung, 2004). In some situations, remedial training in English (or the language in which the instruction will be conducted) must be provided as needed (Ovando, 1989). Cultural and social differences should be recognized because they can affect such things as the ability to take responsibility for individualized work or to engage in creative activities. In some cultures, an accepted, strong authority figure such as, for example, the father in a family, influences the freedom and decision-making abilities of others, in this case, his children. If background experiences are limited, a resulting naivete and lack of sophistication may affect a learner's readiness for and participation in a program. In planning instruction for culturally diverse learners, take care to select bias-free materials and providing alternative resources and activities to support instructional objectives.

Five "standards" for effectively teaching culturally diverse learners have been proposed by researchers (see Bradford, 1999; Tharp, 1998). The standards include the following:

- Joint productive activity, in which the teacher (i.e., expert) and students (i.e., novices) work closely together to accomplish joint projects
- Developing language and literacy across the curriculum, where language development is continually emphasized and assisted through modeling, eliciting, probing, restating, clarifying, questioning, and praising
- Making meaning, where learning is highly situated within and connected to the real-world contexts of students' lives
- Teaching complex thinking, where students are involved in complex tasks and instruction shifts from basic skills to complex manipulation of problem solving in content domains
- Teaching through conversation, where students are engaged in learning through the use of language and dialogue, especially in relation to real-world tasks

Information about the abilities of learners in ethnic groups can be obtained through the usual testing, interview, and questionnaire procedures, as well as from the literature (e.g., Garcia, 1991). In addition, another source of information is counselors in an organization or the community who have had direct experience working with such individuals. However, at the same time, it is extremely important for designers to avoid stereotyping different ethnic or cultural groups and thus creating adaptations that aren't needed or, worse, unequal opportunities to learn (Pollock, 2001). We advise carefully checking the appropriateness of such design variations using formative evaluation and expert review (see Chapter 13).

## Learners with Disabilities

The category of learners who are disabled includes individuals with physical disabilities and others with learning disabilities such as hearing and vision loss, speech impairment, and mild mental retardation. Each type of disabled learner has unique limitations and requires special consideration. Although some persons with physical disabilities can participate in regular classes, others cannot (Friend & Bursuck, 2002). A careful analysis of individual abilities should include observation, interviews, and testing.

Many learners with disabilities require special training and individual attention. Therefore, an instructional program may require extensive modification to serve such learners appropriately. Specialists who are capable of working with individuals with disabilities should be a part of any instructional-planning team.

## Adult Learners

An important factor reducing the homogeneity of learner populations is the increasing number of adults who have become learners in these settings: those returning to colleges and universities, enrolling in distance education programs, engaging in community adult education programs, and participating in job training or retraining for new skills in business, industry, health fields, government service, and the military.

The field of adult education, known as andragogy, has been studied at length. Those who work in this field recognize a number of generalizations (Knowles, Holton, & Swanson, 2005) regarding adults and their accommodations in the educational process:

- Adults often enter an education or training program with a high level of motivation to learn. They appreciate a program that is structured systematically with requirements (i.e., objectives) clearly specified.
- Adults want to know how the course's content will benefit them. They expect the material to be relevant, and they quickly grasp the practical use of the content.
- To adults, time is an important consideration. They expect the class to start and finish on schedule, and they do not like to waste time.
- Adults respect an instructor who is fully knowledgeable about the subject and who presents it effectively. Students quickly detect an unprepared instructor.
- Adults bring to class extensive experience from their personal and working lives. These experiences should be used as major resources for helping students relate to the subject being studied.
- Most mature adults are self-directed and independent. Although some adults lack confidence and need reassurance, they would prefer that the instructor serve as facilitator to guide and assist rather than as an authoritarian leader.
- Adults want to participate in decision making. They want to cooperate with the instructor in mutual assessment of needs and goals, the choice of activities, and decisions on how to evaluate learning.
- Adults may be less flexible than younger students. Their habits and methods of operation have become routine. They do not like to be placed in embarrassing situations. Before they accept a different way of doing something, they want to understand the advantages of doing so.
- Some adults may prefer to cooperate in groups and socialize together. Small-group activities and an atmosphere for interaction during breaks are important.

For adults, as well as for other learners, the same principles of human learning and behavior must form the basis of an instructional program. (These principles receive attention in Chapter 7.) The degree and specificity for applying the principles among certain groups differ during planning, when media are designed, and when instructional activities are carried out. By being sensitive and alert to the characteristics of special groups of learners, a designer can plan programs especially effective for them.

Expert's Edge

## Old Technology Is Still Good Technology . . . for Some

A major industrial corporation had its top executive-level suites completely remodeled. The work was to be completed after the New Year's holiday break and included remodeling all the executive conference rooms. In addition to a more comfortable and plush headquarters, the design team for the remodeling also wanted to include the latest technology wherever possible. In their zeal to impress the executives, they equipped every conference room with new electronic whiteboards—boards that could download scribed information directly to a computer for saving. "They'll love this!" was the general thinking.

Within the first week of activity after the holidays, I began receiving the usual requests to scan, digitize, and transcribe the executives' flip-chart musings from the old paper easels. After a week or two of business as usual, I asked one of the vice presidents why they weren't using the nifty computerized whiteboards. It seems the executives, while technically aware, were not very technically knowledgeable. In addition, the use of paper easel flip charts with colored felt-tipped pens was ingrained in the corporate culture for use at any meeting or brainstorming session involving scribing. They would scribble and write like crazy on these pages, then tear them off and hang them around the room so they could refer to them during the meeting. None of them had a clue what the whiteboard with the computer even did, much less how to use it.

Nobody took the time to analyze how the executives used conference rooms. The executives generally were 40-plus years old and well paid to make major decisions and conduct strategic planning. Each executive had one or two assistants who dealt with any technology such as faxing, preparing presentations, and using voice mail, and various computer applications. A few interested assistants eventually found the time to study the instruction manual and experiment with the boards to discover, on their own, what they could do. I later learned that some of them tried to encourage their bosses to be innovative and use the boards; only two were successful after a year. They reported results of slowed meetings, too much focus and wasted time on learning what they were doing, and nearly instantaneous grumbling to "get those easels back in here!" The effort failed. Currently, the boards mostly just sit there, unused. A small monument to wasted effort and cost, and a reminder to take the time to understand the learners and the environment!

Paul Burry works in customer service, providing projection room and conference support for the executive staff of a Fortune 500 company. He has been responsible for digital still reproduction, multimedia applications, video conferencing, and projection systems management for several years.

## CONTEXTUAL ANALYSIS

Cognitive science research has found that embedding the instruction in a familiar context enhances both student achievement and student attitudes (Boyd & Jackson, 2004; Ku & Sullivan, 2000; Papadopoulos, Demetriadis, & Stamelos, 2009; PT3 Group at Vanderbilt, 2003). Context, for example, plays a key role in the design and development of problem-based learning (Barrows & Kelson; 1996; Morrison & Lowther, 2002; Spronken-Smith, 2005) and anchored instruction (Bransford, Brown, & Cocking, 1999). For example, consider a course for legal professionals on searching electronic databases. A very simple approach to teaching how to use a database such as Westlaw would be to display the search screen and point to where to enter data and which button to click to search. This same presentation could be enhanced by embedding the teaching of the search strategy within a context. For example, the instruction could create a scenario in which the student is searching for information on disputed property lines to keep Big Al's Super Food Market from encroaching on a client's backyard. Providing a context for teaching the search strategy makes the content concrete and realistic and helps the student understand not only the search strategy but also how it can be applied on the job.

Analysis of the instructional context provides rich data for designing real-world examples and scenarios (Tessmer & Richey, 1997). Why should a designer be concerned with this larger environment? First, instruction and learning do not take place in a vacuum. The context influences every aspect of the learning experience. Second, context is a collection of factors that can inhibit or facilitate instruction and learning. For example, a classroom across the hall from the break room will probably have noise and other distractions from other students that can disrupt the instruction. However, a classroom that is well equipped with a video projector and computers for each student, for example, can facilitate instruction in creating database queries. Third, a single class can require multiple contexts. For example, a fifth-grade classroom using a problem-based learning approach might survey historical buildings in the neighborhood, do research at the historic society, use a computer lab, and conduct small-group meetings in the hallway. Learners in a popular geology course offered by an oil company might visit various geological sites in Texas and the Grand Canyon and end with a snorkeling trip in the Caribbean, all to observe different geological structures. Each of these contexts provides a unique learning environment for the course. A thorough context analysis ensures the planned instruction fits the instructional environment (Hannafin, 2005; Tessmer & Harris, 1992).

## Types of Context

There are three types of context an instructional designer should analyze when designing instruction (Tessmer & Richey, 1997). First is the orienting context, which focuses primarily on the learner. Second is the instructional context, which provides information about the physical environment and scheduling of training. Third is the transfer context, which considers the opportunities for transferring the knowledge and skills to new situations. The following is a description of each of these context types.

**Orienting Context.**   The first part of this chapter focuses on learner characteristics, that is, the knowledge, skills, and attitudes the learner brings to the instruction. A designer might want to consider three other variables. First, what goals do the learners have for taking or attending this course or instruction? Some individuals in business approach a course simply as another week of paid vacation! As a new student or trainee, what were your goals for your first course? Were you simply concerned with getting an A or obtaining a certificate, or were you more concerned with learning new knowledge and skills? With knowledge of the learners' goals or lack thereof, you can consider how to design the preinstructional strategy (see Chapter 8) as well as the instruction.

Second, what is the learners' perceived utility of the instruction? Do the learners see the course as providing them with useful information? For example, a university installed new Touch-Tone phones in faculty members' offices many years after they had Touch-Tone phones at home. The communications department prepared a four-hour training program on the new phones. Faculty and staff perceived little utility in the training because the only features the phones had were for receiving incoming calls and making calls. Voice mail, call forwarding, and conferencing would not be available for a year or more. As a result of the low perception of utility, only a few people attended the training.

The third factor to consider is the learners' perceptions of accountability. Are the learners accountable for mastering the content presented in the course? For example, many faculty members have discovered that students will not participate in an online discussion or create personal Webpages if these do not count toward their grades. Similarly, adults attending training that does not lead to certification or some other form of accountability (e.g., pay increase or promotion) may have a low perception of accountability and may demonstrate less transfer of the knowledge or investment in the course. A designer who understands the learners' goals, utility, and accountability can use this information in the design of the instruction.

**Instructional Context.**   Simple strategies such as planning to use a PowerPoint presentation on Thursday can turn to disaster when you discover the hotel does not have a video projector (they thought you wanted an overhead projector)! Several years ago, it was common practice to have both a PowerPoint presentation and overhead transparencies. Few follow this precautionary practice due to the ready access, in most places, to video projection equipment.

Some of the common environmental factors to consider in instruction are described in Table 3-1. Many corporations employ meeting coordinators who help instructors address some of these issues. Each of these factors requires careful consideration. For example, you might plan a course on using Excel to calculate the return on investment (ROI) of a project or improvement. Such a course assumes that students have access to computers; thus, you need a computer lab with the

**TABLE 3-1**
Analysis of the instructional environment

| Factor | Considerations |
|---|---|
| Lighting | Can you control the lights for presentations by turning off the lights above the screen and dimming the other lights? Are the controls easily accessible and usable? Are there shades or blinds on the windows? |
| Noise | Are there sources of noise such as mechanical devices (e.g., elevators, motors), office areas, hallways, or break rooms that will distract the learners? Is there any way to control these noises? |
| Temperature | Can you or someone else easily adjust the temperature in the room? |
| Seating | Are the tables the correct size and shape for activities? Can you move the chairs for small-group exercises? Does everyone have a clear view of the screen and presenters? |
| Accommodations | Are there hotel or housing accommodations in close proximity? Can learners eat lunch on-site to avoid disruptions? Are facilities or entertainment available after course hours? |
| Equipment | Is equipment such as projectors, computer labs, tools, shops, and other equipment available or available for renting? |
| Transportation | Do students and instructors have easy access to the meeting area and accommodations? Do you need to arrange for transportation? |

software installed or each student will need to bring a laptop to class with the software installed. If you are planning to offer the course at a hotel, is it feasible to set up a computer lab? Your only option might be to create a self-paced course using printed materials, a CD-ROM, or the Web so that learners can complete the training at their computer workstations. Careful consideration of the instructional environment early in the design process is essential.

Another environmental factor to consider is the scheduling of the course. For example, what are the problems with offering a course in January in Minneapolis or another city in the snowbelt versus Houston or Atlanta? Similarly, offering a two-week course the second week of December may not generate a large enrollment because of the holidays. If you are planning a workshop for teachers, what are the date and time limitations during the school year? Another factor to consider is the length of a course and its meeting times. It is not unusual to find one-week or even six-week courses offered in business. But how do you accommodate a course you planned as a weeklong course (e.g., 5 days for 8 hours a day) when management dictates that the course must be offered one or two days a week for only two hours and that it must start one hour before the regular workday begins? What modifications will you need to make? Some companies also require courses be offered on weekends. For example, one Fortune 500 company's introductory management course is always held on Saturdays. Management's philosophy is that only those employees who are really interested in moving into the management track will be willing to give up a few Saturdays to make the transition.

**Transfer Context.**    A goal of any instruction should be the continual application of the knowledge and skills learned. This last type of context analysis focuses on creating an environment that promotes the application of the newly learned knowledge and skills to a diverse range of situations. Learners are more likely to transfer the knowledge if they perceive that it can help them do their jobs. Similarly, a learner needs access to the tools and resources required to apply the skills. For example, work assignments that require the use of spreadsheets to perform calculations will need access to a computer with Excel installed if students are to use the information learned in the course. Thus, sending an engineer to a course on using an Excel template to calculate ROI requires that the engineer have access to a computer in the work environment if she is to transfer the new knowledge to the job.

Two other factors that can inhibit the transfer of knowledge and skills are opportunities and support. If learners do not have frequent opportunities or need to calculate expected ROI, then they are unlikely to transfer the skill to new situations. If the learners' manager does not support the use of Excel or even punish learners for using it, then they are less likely to transfer the knowledge to new situations.

## Conducting a Contextual Analysis

The common tools for conducting a contextual analysis include surveys, observations, and interviews. Start by identifying factors that might affect your instructional design plan by providing either opportunities or constraints. Then, determine how to collect the necessary data. You may need to refine your contextual analysis after you start designing the instruction (see Chapter 7) and when you refine your delivery strategy and instructional strategies.

**Collecting Data.**    Rich data are needed to provide the designer with an accurate picture of the instructional environment. Surveys using both forced-choice (e.g., rating scales and multiple-choice items) and open-ended questions can provide a quick picture of the environment (see Chapters 12 and 13). For example, a designer might send a survey to several sites to gather information about the training room facilities or the types of computers and software available in the labs. Surveys can also be used to assess learner perceptions and the organizational support for the instruction. A designer might send such an instrument to both the target audience and the supervisors and/or managers of the audience.

Consider an instructional designer planning a multimedia unit on how to operate cash registers in a national chain of grocery stores. You might start first with a survey to determine the availability and the type of computer(s) each store has for training. Second, you might want to know what type of cash register each store is using. By collecting these two pieces of data, you can determine the lowest common denominator for the computers used to deliver the instruction. If over 35% of the stores have computers that are 6 years old, you can make some initial assumptions about the capabilities of the machines and take this limitation into consideration when designing animations. If the results of the survey indicate that more than one type of cash register is used, the instruction will need to include instructions for each type. To make the instruction more efficient, the instruction will need to have a means of selecting or preselecting the appropriate cash register for the training.

Observations provide the instructional designer with a firsthand picture of the environment. Designers can observe the layout of facilities to determine their applicability for various instructional strategies. A room with fixed seating might not be appropriate for a course that relies heavily on small-group work or role plays. The senior author once presented in a room that was touted as a well-equipped, state-of-the-art presentation room. Yes, it had a large screen and video projector. Unfortunately, there was no way to connect the laptop to the video projector, the windows faced east and let the morning sunlight shine on the screen and in the presenter's face, and the two entrances to the room were on either side of the screen and behind the presenter. Although the author could use the facility's desktop computer and deal with those arriving late, he could not control the air-conditioning vents placed directly behind the projection screen, which caused it to wave continuously! Although a survey might suggest the rooms are appropriate, a direct observation can reveal any problems or enhancements.

Interviews can provide a picture of potential learners in their work environments. Interviewing members of the target audience and their supervisors can provide a rich source of contextual information. Tessmer and Richey (1997) suggested using open-ended questions that allow for a wide range of potential answers. Interviews conducted in the workplace can also provide insights into the factors that can support or inhibit the transfer of learning.

**Analyzing Data.** The collected data are analyzed to identify environmental factors that will influence the design and delivery of instruction. This analysis should identify factors that place limitations on the design and delivery of the instruction, that facilitate the design and delivery, and that are missing from the analysis.

## S U M M A R Y

1. By considering the results of task or goal analysis and the likely conditions of training (i.e., practical constraints, setting, duration), the designer must identify the learner characteristics most likely to have an impact on instructional outcomes.
2. Three categories of learner traits are general characteristics (gender, age, ethnicity), specific entry characteristics (prerequisite skills for the instruction), and learning styles (preferred ways of learning).
3. Knowing about students' *preferences* for learning provides a potentially valuable basis for designing instruction, but valid learner classifications and beneficial instructional adaptations may be difficult to achieve in practice.

4. Academic records can reveal the extent and quality of schooling or training that learners have already received.

5. Through observation, interviews, and questionnaires, indications of learners' personal and social characteristics can be obtained.

6. The target audience can include culturally diverse learners, adult learners, and learners with disabilities. Special characteristics of such individuals should be recognized and considered during planning.

7. Contextual analysis provides information about environmental factors that will affect the design and delivery of the instruction.

## THE ID PROCESS

Learner analysis and contextual analysis are easily viewed as identifying constraints to the design or delivery of the instruction. Learners who do not have the prerequisites expected, who cannot be away from work for extended periods to attend a course, or who have a short attention span may require the designer to make necessary changes in the design plan. On the other hand, a learner analysis might reveal a highly motivated group of learners, and the contextual analysis might reveal not only a supportive environment from management but a state-of-the-art training facility! If you approach learner and contextual analysis as a means of identifying both limitations and opportunities, then you are likely to generate a more positive attitude and product.

When initiating a learner analysis, consider the performance problem you have identified. Then, reflect on practical considerations involving your time schedule and the accessibility of information about the prospective trainees. General characteristics of interest might include age, work experience, work level, education, and ethnicity as relevant, easily obtainable information. A good source of specific characteristics is the subject-matter expert who helps you with the task analysis. This individual can help you identify specific characteristics related to the task or content that are needed to solve the problem. Your initial contextual analysis may be very broad at this stage of the design process. You can refine it and the learner analysis as the design plan gathers more information in the task analysis and strategy-design steps.

Based on your data collection and analysis of findings, you will begin the next phase of the design process—task analysis (see Chapter 4)—with an initial conceptualization of the target audience and the instructional environment. This information facilitates your decisions throughout the remainder of the design process.

## APPLICATION

Your design consulting group has just accepted a contract to revise a conflict resolution course for managers for one of the largest accounting companies in the country. This course met for three full days and had a one-day follow-up meeting six weeks after the course. According to the training manager, the majority of the managers have already completed the course. The focus now is on managers who need to take it again and on the 10 to 20 new managers promoted or hired each month. Currently, the course is taught by six different instructors, who use a combination of excellent video recordings, lecturettes, and role plays. The training manager wants the course revised so that it can be offered at a variety of company locations rather than at the corporate training center. He also wants the course to be offered in two- to four-hour blocks over a period of four weeks.

What type of information would you want to collect in a contextual analysis before beginning your design?

## ANSWERS

The following is our initial list of data we would want to collect to determine the factors to consider when revising this course:

1. The best times and days to offer the training
2. The type of video equipment that is available
3. The expected number of new managers in each location each quarter
4. The layout of the training rooms
5. The closeness of the training room to the place of work (i.e., how much travel time is needed between work and the class)
6. The amount of time learners might have for studying outside of class
7. Any distractions the place of work might present during the training
8. Perceived benefits of training

## QUALITY MANAGEMENT

Updating and verifying your learner analysis is an ongoing process as you design the instruction. Initially, you need to confirm that you have identified the correct target audience—the individuals who will receive the instruction. Next, you need to consider how the audience characteristics and environmental characteristics can provide opportunities or limitations to the design of the course. For example, discovering that your course cannot run for five continuous days but can be offered only for two hours a day creates opportunities to build in self-reflection time after each class meeting. If you find that many of the students taking a computer course have physical limitations, you can collect additional information on their fine motor skills and then determine whether adaptive technologies (e.g., large keypads, large buttons, or voice-activated software) can be used to enhance the functionality of the computers.

## INSTRUCTIONAL DESIGN: DECISIONS AND CHOICES

During your initial client meeting, while collecting data about the need for instruction, you also asked questions about the audience. As a result, you divided your audience into a primary and a secondary audience based on whether using a fire extinguisher could reasonably be expected to be part of performing one's job.

Later, you talked with a member of the human resources department and learned some additional information: "20 lbs. is our standard for anyone who works in a position where some lifting is required such as in the mailroom or maintenance department. We are also aware that about 2% of our employees have some difficulty reading. Everyone in our U.S. as well as worldwide operations speaks English."

Here is your initial draft of your learner analysis:

**Primary Audience** *(training will be mandatory for these employees):*

- Physical plant and maintenance department personnel
- Mailroom staff
- Security officers
- Food-service workers

**Secondary Audience** *(training will be voluntary for these employees):*

- Administrative assistants
- Professional salaried employees
- Summer interns

**General Learner Characteristics**

- Age: 18–65
- Gender: 48% men, 52% women (primary audience: 60% men, 40% women)
- Education: High school diploma–graduate degree (all read at the eighth-grade level or above)
- Work experience: 1 week to 25+ years
- Physical strength: all are capable of lifting 20 lbs. (except for those with a physical disability)

**Entry Characteristics**

Prerequisite skill and knowledge:

- Most are familiar with the concepts "grease," "fat," and "combustible materials."
- Most understand that water and electricity create a life-threatening situation.

Attitudinal and motivational characteristics:

- All recognize the consequences of fire (damage to property, smoke inhalation)
- Previously trained personnel may believe they will learn nothing new taking this course
- Some learners may be motivated to take the training because it is applicable for personal use as a home owner

Prior experience:

Although many learners may have general knowledge about how to use a fire extinguisher, few have actually practiced operating one.

Common errors made by novice learners:

- Aiming the fire extinguisher at the body of the fire rather than sweeping at the base of the fire
- Failing to ensure a safe evacuation route prior to attempting to use a fire extinguisher
- Failing to recognize when a fire is too large to fight
- Using the wrong type of fire extinguisher

[The instructional designer has discovered these common errors while thinking about the learner analysis and as a result of talking with the security director. These errors would also surface from talking with a subject-matter expert, such as the local fire marshal. The designer will later move these common errors to the section on task analysis. The point is that the design process is iterative. Other critical learner characteristics may surface during other phases of the design process, such as the fact that in this organization English is not the primary spoken language for 80% of the custodial staff. As a result, the designer must consider whether the program should be offered in multiple languages.]

## Potential Audience Misconceptions:

– Any type of fire extinguisher will be effective to put out any type of fire.
– Some learners may believe no fire can start because the sprinkler system would activate.

## Learning Styles:

Individual learning styles will not be considered for this project. However, some learners may be apprehensive or nervous about making mistakes (or being embarrassed in front of others) while practicing using a fire extinguisher.

[The designer will later decide that the instruction will be delivered to groups of 12 to 18 learners in a classroom laboratory and that providing one-on-one training is cost prohibitive. The designer rationalizes that an experienced and well-prepared instructor can verbally reassure an apprehensive learner. The instructional designer also makes a note concerning whether work teams should take the training together and whether a separate training session should be held for office personnel and professionals. (Providing separate training for these two groups raises professional ethical issues.) Notice here how the designer is constantly engaged in making decisions concerning the design of the instruction as well as how the learner analysis affects content decisions, the potential need to produce materials in multiple languages, and delivery issues as well as ethical concerns. Notice too that gathering data from appropriate individuals is critical, affects the quality of the analysis, and has implications for the effectiveness of the instruction.]

## REFERENCES

Atkinson, R. K., & Renkl, A. (2007). Interactive example-based learning environments: Using interactive elements to encourage effective processing of worked examples. *Educational Psychology Review, 19,* 375–386.

Barrows, H. S., & Kelson, A. M. (1996). Problem-based learning: A total approach to education. Unpublished monograph, Southern Illinois School of Medicine, Springfield.

Boyd, A. M, & Jackson, M. L. (2004). An effective model for rapid skills acquisition through a simulation-based integrated learning environment. *Journal of Educational Computing Research, 30*(1–2), 1–21.

Bradford, D. J. (1999). Exemplary urban middle schoolteachers' use of five standards of effective teaching. *Teaching and Change, 7,* 53–78.

Bransford, J., Brown, A., & Cocking, R. (Eds.). (1999). *How people learn: Brain, mind, experience, and school.* Washington, DC: National Academy Press.

Driscoll, M. P. (2005). *Psychology of learning from instruction* (3rd ed.). Needham Heights, MA: Allyn & Bacon.

Friend, M., & Bursuck, W. (2002). *Including students with special needs* (3rd ed.). Boston, MA: Allyn & Bacon.

Garcia, R. L. (1991). Teaching in a pluralistic society: Concepts, models, and strategies. New York: HarperCollins.

Hannafin, M. (2005). Functional contextualism in learning and instruction: Pragmatic science or objectivism revisited? *Educational Technology Research and Development, 54*(1), 36–40.

Heinich, R., Molenda, M., Russell, J., & Smaldino, S. (1999). *Instructional media and technologies for learning* (6th ed.). Englewood Cliffs, NJ: Prentice Hall.

Jonassen, D. H., & Grabowski, B. L. (1993). Handbook of individual differences, learning, and instruction. Hillsdale, NJ: Erlbaum.

Keller, J. M. (2007). Motivation and performance. In R. A. Reiser & J. V. Dempsey (Eds.), *Trends and issues in instructional design and technology* (2nd ed., pp. 82–92). Columbus: Merrill/Prentice Hall.

Kibler, R. J. (1981). *Objectives for instruction and evaluation.* Boston: Allyn & Bacon.

Knight, C. B., Halpin, G., & Halpin, G. (1992, April). *The effects of learning environment accommodations on the achievement of second graders.* Paper presented at the annual meeting of the American Educational Research Association, San Francisco, CA.

Knowles, M., Holton, E. F., & Swanson, R. A. (2005). *The adult learner: The definitive classic in adult education and human resource development,* 6th ed. Burlington, MA: Elsevier.

Kolb, D. (1984). *Experiential learning: Experience as the source of learning and development.* Englewood Cliffs, NJ: Prentice Hall.

Ku, H. -Y., & Sullivan, H. (2000). Learner control over full and lean computer-based instruction under personalization of mathematics word problems in Taiwan. *Educational Technology Research and Development, 48*(3), 49–60.

Morrison, G. R., & Lowther, D. L. (2002). *Integrating computer technology into the classroom* (2nd ed.). Columbus: Merrill/Prentice Hall.

Ovando, C. J. (1989). Language diversity and education. In J. Banks & C. McGee Banks (Eds.), *Multicultural education: Issues and perspectives* (pp. 208–228). Boston: Allyn & Bacon.

Park, O., & Lee, J. (2004). Adaptive instructional systems. In D. H. Jonassen (Ed.), *Handbook of research on educational communications and technology* (2nd ed., pp. 651–684). Mahwah, NJ: Erlbaum.

Papadopoulos, P. M., Demetriadis, S. N., & Stamelos, I. G. (2009). *Prompting students' context-generating cognitive activity in ill-structured domains: Does the prompting mode affect learning? Educational Technology Research and Development, 57,* 193–210.

Pintrich, P. R., Roeser, R. W., & De Groot, E. A. M. (1994). Classroom and individual differences in early adolescents' motivation and self-regulated learning. *Journal of Early Adolescence, 14,* 139–161.

Pollock, M. (2001). How the question we ask most about race in education is the very question we most suppress. *Educational Researcher, 30*(9), 2–12.

PT3 Group at Vanderbilt. (2003). Three AMIGOs: Using "Anchored Modular Inquiry" to help prepare future teachers. *Educational Technology Research and Development, 51*(1), 105–23.

Skinner, B. F. (1954). The science of learning and art of teaching. *Harvard Educational Review, 24*(1), 86–97.

Slavin, R. E. (2006). *Educational psychology: Theory and practice* (6th ed.). Needham Heights, MA: Allyn & Bacon.

Slavin, R. E., & Cheung, A. (2004). How do English language learners learn to read? *Educational Leadership, 61*(6), 52–57.

Snow, R. E. (1992). Aptitude theory: Yesterday, today, and tomorrow. *Educational Psychologist, 27*, 5–32.

Spronken-Smith, R. (2005). Implementing a problem-based learning approach for teaching research methods in geography. *Journal of Geography in Higher Education, 29*(2), 203–221.

Tessmer, M., & Harris, D. (1992). *Analysing the instructional setting*. London: Kogan Page.

Tessmer, M., & Richey, R. C. (1997). The role of context in learning and instructional design. *Educational Technology, Research, and Development, 45*, 85–111.

Tharp, R. (1998). *Theory into practice*. Santa Cruz, CA: National Center for Research on Cultural Diversity and Second Language Learning.

# CHAPTER ④

# Task Analysis

## GETTING STARTED

At last, you have the opportunity to work on a really neat project. The project focuses on teaching new hires how to design the interior of an automobile. This project will really test your skills as an instructional designer because it goes beyond the "simple" assembly tasks you designed in the past. In fact, your two subject-matter experts are legends within the company. Ms. Makeena is credited with the recent designs for women drivers that pushed your company's sales to new highs. Dr. Royce is the chief interior designer and has worked on over 30 different designs. If you can capture their knowledge and talent, you can develop a training program that will ensure your status in the training department as well as the company.

Your initial meeting is going quite well. Ms. Makeena and Dr. Royce both explain the process and the many factors they consider. You have had a tour of their design lab and the usability-testing studio. Now that lunch is over, it is time to start defining the content to address the problem. Your first few questions are answered in detail, and it looks like this will be an easy task analysis. Then, Dr. Royce pauses and stares into the distance, much as you might expect him to do as he ponders the placement of the off-on switch for the cruise control. He states that he has two concerns. First, you are not an automobile designer, so how can you expect to "write" a course on this topic? Second, this process of designing the interior of a car is an art and not something like teaching someone how to assemble a radiator. How could you possibly expect to teach someone this art?

It is apparent that Ms. Makeena supports Dr. Royce's concerns. How will you reply to obtain their confidence?

## QUESTIONS TO CONSIDER

"What skills and information are necessary to address the identified needs?"

"What knowledge does the expert have that is essential for the task?"

"What related subject content should be taught?"

"How can the subject content items be organized?"

"How is a task analyzed to identify its components and then to sequence the actions required?"

"To what other elements of the instructional design process is task analysis most closely related?"

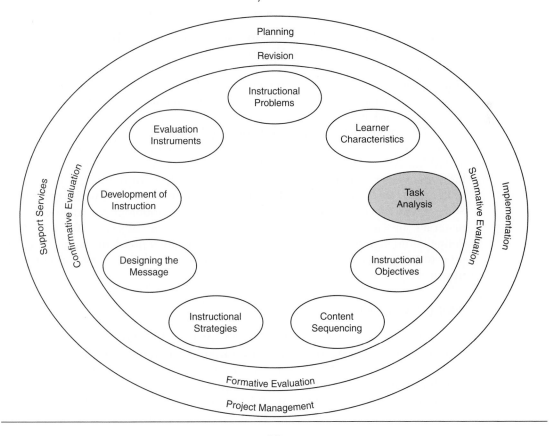

Task analysis is probably the most critical step in the instructional design process. If a designer has not defined the content to include in the instruction, there is little value in or need for designing an instructional strategy, producing appropriate media, or conducting an evaluation. A survey of designers by Loughner and Moller (1998) found that over 78% of the designers agreed that it was not possible to design good instruction without first conducting a task analysis. Unfortunately, only 38% of the designers felt their clients understood the purpose of a task analysis. The instructional design process depends on the concise definition of the content that is the object of the instructional materials. Task analysis is considered the most critical part of the instructional design process (Jonassen, Hannum, & Tessmer, 1999). The analysis solves three problems for the designer:

1. It defines the content required to solve the performance problem or alleviate a performance need. This step is crucial because most designers are working with unfamiliar content.
2. Because the process forces the subject-matter expert to work through each individual step, subtle steps are more easily identified.
3. During this process, the designer has the opportunity to view the content from the learner's perspective. Using this perspective, the designer can often gain insight into appropriate teaching strategies.

Jonassen and his colleagues (Jonassen, Hannum, & Tessmer, 1989) have identified 27 different task-analysis procedures that instructional designers can use to define the content for an instructional package. Selecting the best or most appropriate technique depends on a number of factors, including the purpose for conducting the task analysis, the nature of the task or content, and the environment in which the task is performed.

The terminology associated with topic and task analysis is often confusing. The instructional design literature frequently refers to the process of analyzing content as task analysis. Specific analysis procedures also go by a host of names. Some individuals refer to task analysis as a specific procedure for defining psychomotor skills, which leads to further confusion. The term *content analysis* is also confusing. Some researchers use this term to describe a methodology for analyzing text materials. Instructional designers use content, topic, or subject-matter analysis to define knowledge or content related to the instructional problem. In this book, we refer to *task analysis* as the collection of procedures for defining the content of an instructional unit.

## TASK ANALYSIS

An analysis of the content required for instruction does not begin in a vacuum. It begins with the needs or goals derived from the definition of the instructional problem (see Chapter 2). These needs or goals provide an initial definition of the breadth of the project and provide the designer a focus. For example, if you were designing a unit of instruction on cardiac care for medical doctors, would you start with emergency-room care, bypass surgery, or rehabilitation of a patient who had suffered a heart attack? If you have properly defined the instructional problem, the problem statement and needs or goals will provide the initial direction and breadth of your analysis. Thus, a unit on cardiac care might focus only on rehabilitation as a result of the problem identification. A second input is from the learner analysis (see Chapter 3). An understanding of the learner's knowledge and background related to the topic helps the designer determine the beginning point for the analysis as well as the depth and breadth of analysis. The output of the analysis is documentation of the content to include in the instructional materials. This output then serves as an input for developing instructional objectives (see Chapter 5).

## Preparing to Conduct a Task Analysis

A task analysis can take many different forms. The methods and individuals involved vary depending on the circumstances. Designers most often work with a subject-matter expert (SME), an individual who is an expert in the content area. The SME is our link to the content; we rely on this individual (or individuals) to provide accurate, detailed information for use in developing the instructional unit. Our task as designers is to help the SME elaborate on the content and tasks in a meaningful, logical manner. The designer is responsible for obtaining a complete analysis, whereas the SME is responsible for providing accurate information and suggesting where gaps may exist in the original goals.

In educational settings, the instructor often serves as both the SME and instructional designer, a difficult but often necessary combination of responsibilities. The teacher/SME/designer is responsible for providing a global view ("Are all the steps and information defined?") as well as a microscopic view ("What result or condition is required before doing the next step?").

In this chapter, we describe three specific techniques for analyzing knowledge and tasks. First, you will learn how to conduct a topic analysis that is well suited for defining cognitive knowledge. Second, you will learn how to conduct a procedural analysis for use with psychomotor tasks, job tasks, or cognitive sequences involving a series of steps. Third, you will learn about the critical incident method, which is useful for analyzing interpersonal skills.

## TOPIC ANALYSIS

Assume you are a student attending a lecture. As the instructor delivers the lecture, what are you doing? Probably taking notes so you can capture the essence of the content. You may take notes in detailed sentences or in an outline form, such as the following:

*Topic: The Circulatory System*

    I. Types of vessels in closed circulatory system
        A. Arteries—carry blood away from heart
        B. Veins—carry blood toward heart
        C. Capillaries—final division of arteries that unite to form first small veins
   II. Circulation
        A. Systemic—supplies most of body (aorta)

    B. Pulmonary—supplies lungs
    C. Coronary—within heart

We are all familiar with this procedure of outlining information as it is presented in a lecture. Now, reverse the procedure. You are the individual who will deliver the lecture. What is your preparation? You might either write out the lecture in a narrative form you can read as written, or with experience, you might prepare an outline consisting of the main headings, supporting details, and examples. This outline becomes a framework to refer to as a guide to your presentation.

Change the situation yet again, and imagine you are a designer working for Big Box Home Store, who must prepare a manual for customers on how to select an appropriate wood fastener. Your manager has assigned an SME to work with you on the project. You would follow a similar process to define the content; the outline becomes a reference for designing the instruction.

The topic analysis is used to define the facts, concepts, principles, and rules that will make up the final instruction. Such an analysis is typically done in layers much like what an archaeologist finds when excavating a site. First, the top layer of soil is scraped away. Then layers of earth are removed, and each artifact's identity and location are recorded. Similarly, a designer working with the SME carefully reveals the first layer of information while looking for indicators of content structure (i.e., facts, concept, and principles). Once the structure is revealed, additional detail is gathered for each structure, and new information appears as the designer digs deeper into the content.

A topic analysis thus provides two types of information. First, it identifies the content that is the focus of the intended instruction. Second, it identifies the structure of the components (Bruner, 1963). Let's first examine these content or knowledge structures and then describe the process for conducting a topic analysis.

## Content Structures

Most instructional design models provide a scheme for classifying information into discrete categories (Reigeluth, 1983). These classifications are then used to identify the appropriate instructional strategy (see Chapter 7). Six structures are often associated with a task analysis: facts, concepts, principles and rules, procedures, interpersonal skills, and attitudes.

**Facts.**    A fact is an arbitrary association between two things. For example, ''The chemical symbol for potassium is K'' is a fact that describes a relationship between potassium and *K*. Learning a fact requires only the memorization and recall of the fact. Examples of facts are listed here:

    Names, symbols, labels, places, dates
    Definitions
    Descriptions of objects or events
    Topic Analysis

Most topics include many facts because they are the building blocks or tools of any subject—the "vocabulary" the learner must master for understanding. Verbal information or facts are preparation for more complex ways of organizing content. Unless the facts are arranged in structured patterns, they will be of limited use to a learner and are often quickly forgotten. Facts are easy to identify but often confused with the second category, concepts. Consider our example, "The chemical symbol for potassium is *K*": There is one "potassium" and one symbol—*K*. The fact refers to this one element.

**Concepts.** Concepts are categories used for grouping similar or related ideas, events, or objects. For example, we might use the concept "soft drinks" to categorize the aisle in the grocery store that contains colas, orange drink, root beer, and so forth. The concept of fruit would include apples, oranges, bananas, and dates, but not potatoes. We use concepts to simplify information by grouping similar ideas or objects together and assigning the grouping a name (e.g., fruit). Some concepts such as fruit are considered concrete concepts because we can easily show an example. Concepts such as safety, liberty, peace, and justice are abstract concepts because they are difficult to represent or illustrate. As instructional designers, we have to be careful to not confuse facts with concepts. There is a concept related to our fact about potassium: Potassium is an example (i.e., member) of the concept "elements." There are many members of this category including carbon, magnesium, and vanadium. Chemistry books are filled with facts about each of these elements.

**Principles and Rules.** Principles and rules describe a relationship between two concepts. In microeconomics, we can derive several principles from a supply-and-demand curve. For example, "as price increases, the supply increases" is a principle that describes a direct relationship between two concepts (i.e., price and supply) that increase and decrease together. "As price decreases, the demand increases" describes a different relationship between price and demand that causes one to increase as the other decreases. "Stop at a red light" and "release the pressure before opening a pressure cooker" are also examples of principles.

**Procedures.** A procedure is an ordered sequence of steps a learner must execute to complete a task. For example, the back of many bank statements lists a series of steps for balancing a checkbook. This series of steps is a procedure. Similarly, a recipe for making a cake or casserole is a procedure. A procedure could be a series of psychomotor steps needed to plant a rosebush, or it could be a complex series of cognitive processes required to debug a computer program.

**Interpersonal Skills.** Verbal and nonverbal (e.g., body language) skills for interacting with other people are grouped in this category. This broad category includes behaviors and objectives related to interpersonal communication. An objective for a manager-training program requiring the development of interviewing skills is an example of this category. Content related to solving group conflict, leading a group, and demonstrating how to sit (e.g., appropriate body language) when being interviewed on television are also examples of behaviors in this category.

**Attitudes.**   Attitudes are predispositions to behavior. Although often overlooked, attitudes are a part of many instructional programs. For example, a training program might emphasize the safety precautions for replacing a seal on a gas valve or courteous driving habits in corporate vehicles. Corporate employees who have access to confidential financial information must complete a course that explains the misuse of this information (e.g., insider trading). Such programs contain information on the laws governing the use of this information (i.e., concepts and rules) as well as a component to develop appropriate attitudes toward corporate responsibility and proper behavior.

## Analyzing a Topic

Let's examine a topic analysis on wood fasteners and define each of the content structures with an example. To begin, we first asked our SME to describe the different types of wood fasteners. Our question prompts the following outline:

  I. Nails
  II. Screws
  III. Bolts

Our SME considered these three major categories adequate to describe the various types of fasteners.

Next, we asked the SME to further define each of these categories. He expanded our outline as follows:

  I. Nails
    A. Generally made from wire
    B. Range in size from 2-penny to 60-penny
      1. Length of nails 10-penny or less is determined by dividing size by 4 and adding 0.5 inch
        a. Example: 7-penny nail is 2.25 inches long
    C. Typically driven into one or more pieces of wood with a hammer
  II. Screws
    A. Made from steel
    B. Size determined by the gauge (thickness) and length
      1. Length varies from 0.25 to 6 inches
    C. Usually twisted into a hole with screwdriver
    D. Screws provide a more secure joint than nails
  III. Bolts
    A. Made from steel
    B. Measured by length and diameter
      1. Available in fine or coarse threads
    C. Bolt is placed through a hole and then a nut is tightened from opposite side

Let's examine the content structure identified in the outline. Some of the facts identified in the outline are as follows:

Generally made from wire
Made of steel
Measured by length and diameter
Available in fine or coarse threads

The concepts identified in the topic analysis are these:

Nail
Screw
Bolt

One procedure was identified in the task analysis:

Length of nails 10-penny or less is determined by dividing size by 4 and adding 0.5 inch.

Our SME helped us identify one principle in the content:

Screws provide a more secure joint than nails.

Next, our SME decided to provide detailed information on each fastener category, starting with nails. Once we finished the analysis, we organized the content. This organization process included the following steps:

1. Review the analysis, and identify the different content structures (facts, concepts, principles, interpersonal skills, and attitudes).
2. Group related facts, concepts, principles, interpersonal skills, and attitudes. For example, in our full outline of wood fasteners, we would group all the information about nails, then the information about screws, and so forth.
3. Arrange the various components into a logical, sequential order.
4. Prepare the final outline to represent your task analysis.

The completed topic analysis on nails was as follows:

I. Nails
  A. Generally made from wire
  B. Range in size from 2-penny to 60-penny
    1. Length of nails 10-penny or less is determined by dividing size by 4 and adding 0.5 inch
      a. Example: 7-penny nail is 2.25 inches long
    2. Size is written as 2d for "2 penny"
  C. Typically driven into one or more pieces of wood with a hammer
  D. Types of nails
    1. Common nails
      a. Most commonly used nail
      b. Available in sizes from 2d to 60d
        (1) 8d size is most common
      c. Identified by flat head
      d. Used for general purposes

    2. Box nails
       a. Smaller in diameter than common nails
       b. Available in sizes ranging from 2d to 40d
       c. Also identified by its flat head
       d. Used in lumber that may split easily
       e. Often used for nailing siding
    3. Finishing nails
       a. Have a very small head that will not show
          (1) Head can be sunk into wood and hole filled
       b. Available in sizes 2d to 20d
       c. Used primarily for finishing work and cabinetry
    4. Common brads
       a. Similar to finishing nails but much smaller
       b. Available in various lengths
          (1) Length expressed in inches or parts of an inch
       c. Used for finishing work
    5. Roofing nails
       a. Similar to common nails but with a larger head
       b. Available in lengths from 0.75 inch to 2 inches
          (1) Available in various diameters
       c. Used for roofing[1]

How detailed should a topic analysis be? A designer needs to break down the content to a level appropriate for the learner. Two sources are used for determining the needed level of detail. First, the learner analysis describes the learner's knowledge of the content area; it is used as a general guide for the amount of information needed. A course on home repair for apprentice carpenters, for example, will require a different amount of detail than a course for home owners. Second, the SME is often a source of information concerning the learners' entry-level knowledge. A combination of these two sources provides a basis for determining the level of detail needed in this initial analysis. During the development and formative evaluation stages, you might find a need for additional information.

## PROCEDURAL ANALYSIS

Procedural analysis is used to analyze tasks by identifying the steps required to complete them. The process breaks tasks into the steps needed for learning. Some designers distinguish between procedural analysis and information-processing analysis (Jonassen et al., 1989). The major distinction is that procedural analysis focuses on observable tasks (e.g., changing a tire), whereas information-processing analysis focuses on cognitive or unobservable tasks, such as deciding which stock to add to a portfolio for diversification. In recent years, the distinction between the two methods has decreased due to the influence of cognitive psychology that has

---

[1] Information from this task analysis is based on a chapter by Phipps (1977).

shown the importance of cognitive steps in observable processes. We use *procedural analysis* to refer to the analysis of both observable and unobservable behaviors.

Conducting a procedural analysis is a matter of walking through the steps with an SME, preferably in the environment in which the task is performed. For example, if you are conducting a procedural analysis for replacing an electric meter, the SME should have an electric meter and the necessary tools. Similarly, if you are analyzing how to calculate your home's electric bill, you will need an electric meter (or at least a picture of the dial) and the electricity rates. Sometimes it may not be possible to use the actual equipment for your procedural analysis. For example, you might analyze how to change the fuel filter on a gas turbine generator. Given the size, cost, and availability of the equipment, it may not be possible to actually conduct the analysis on the engine. However, you may be able to obtain a smaller component that you can use for your task analysis. Each step of analysis includes three questions:

1. What does the learner do?
   - Identify the action in each step that the learner must perform.
   - These actions are either physical (e.g., loosening a bolt) or mental (e.g., adding two numbers).
2. What does the learner need to know to do this step?
   - What knowledge (e.g., temperature, pressure, orientation) is necessary?
   - What does the learner need to know about the location or orientation of the components that are a part of this step (e.g., how to position a wrench to remove a hidden nut)?
3. What cues (tactile, smell, visual, etc.) inform the learner that there is a problem, the step is done, or a different step is needed (e.g., a blinking light indicates you can release the starter switch)?

In the following procedural analysis, a designer visited a cabinetmaker and asked him how to prepare a piece of woodwork for the final finish. During the analysis, the designer asked him variations of the three questions described in the previous paragraphs to identify the steps, knowledge, and cues. As part of the analysis, the cabinet maker informed him that someone who finishes furniture would already know the basics of sanding and using a paint sprayer. The designer's analysis produced the following steps:

1. Inspect all surfaces for defects.
   Tactile cue: Feel for dents, scratches, and other surface defects.
   Visual cue: Splits or cracks are normally visible.
2. Repair defects in surface.
   a. Sand, glue, or fill minor defects.
   b. Reject pieces that you cannot repair for rework.
3. Spray two coats of lacquer sanding sealer on all surfaces.
   Visual cue: Dry, misty appearance indicates too-light application.
   Visual cue: Runs or sags indicate too-heavy application.
4. Prepare for final finish.
   a. Allow a 20-minute minimum drying time for sealer coat.
   b. After drying, rub out all parts with #400 grit silicon carbide abrasive paper.

      c. Remove dust from all surfaces with air gun, then wipe with clean, lint-free cloth.

5. Complete the final finish.
    a. Spray two coats of finishing lacquer on all parts.
      Visual cue: Dry, misty finish indicates too-light application.
      Visual cue: Runs or sags indicate too-heavy application.
    b. Allow a minimum of four hours for second coat to dry.

6. Inspect final finish.
    Tactile cue: Feel for grit or runs that may not be visible.
    a. Rub out all surfaces with #000 steel wool.
    b. Remove dust from all finished surfaces with air gun and lint-free cloth.
    c. Apply a thin coat of wax to all finished surfaces.
    d. Buff all surfaces to high gloss.
    Visual cue: Wax becomes dull prior to buffing.

In addition to an outline, designers often use tables (see Table 4-1) and flowcharts (see Figure 4-1). The table format provides a visual prompt for the designer to ask questions to obtain information about the cues associated with each step. A flowchart is useful for identifying a specific sequence of steps the learner must follow as well as the key decision steps. Flowcharts are also useful for helping SMEs identify missing components and for identifying alternative procedures that may have been missed in the initial analysis. A rectangle indicates an action or knowledge in the flowchart. Diamonds indicate a question or decision point with branches off each tip to another question or action. The arrows indicate the path through the flowchart.

After you have collected the data for a procedural analysis, you need to organize the information in a logical fashion. Because most procedures are sequential, they are often organized in a linear manner by the order of the steps.

You could also use a procedural analysis for a task involving primarily cognitive operations, such as calculating the amount of paint needed to paint a room. Again, you need to identify the steps, the knowledge associated with each step, and any cues associated with each step:

1. Measure and record the length of each wall.
2. Add the lengths of the walls to obtain a sum.

**TABLE 4-1**
Procedural analysis table

| Step | Cue |
| --- | --- |
| 1. Inspect all surfaces for defects. | Feel for dents, scratches, and other surface defects. Splits or cracks are normally visible. |
| 2. Repair defects.<br>  a. Sand, glue, or fill minor defects.<br>  b. Reject pieces that are not repairable for rework. | |
| 3. Spray two coats of lacquer sanding sealer on all surfaces. | Dry, misty appearance indicates too-light application. Runs or sags indicate too-heavy application. |

**FIGURE 4-1**
Flowchart of a procedure

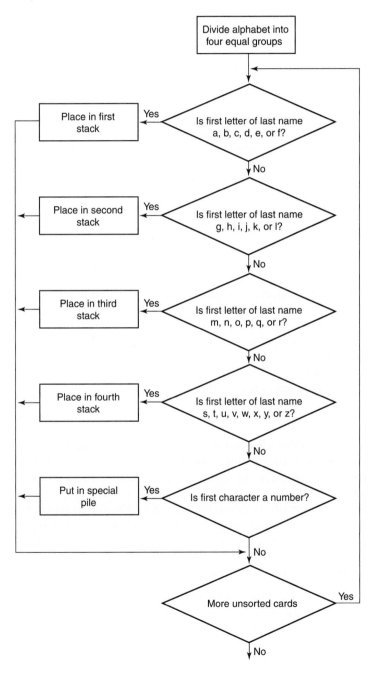

3. Measure the height of the wall (baseboard to ceiling).
4. Multiply the sum of the walls' length by the height to obtain the square footage of the walls.
5. Measure the height and width of each door and window.
6. Calculate the number of square feet for each door and window.
   a. If the windows are the same size, measure one and multiply the square footage by the window count.
7. Add the square footage of doors and windows to obtain a total of the area not to paint.
8. Subtract the square footage of the doors and windows (Step 7) from the square footage of the walls (Step 4) to obtain the area to paint.
9. Determine the number of square feet a gallon of paint will cover by reading the paint can or manufacturer's data.
10. Divide area to paint (Step 8) by the coverage per gallon to determine the number of gallons needed.
11. If two coats of paint are needed, double the number of gallons in Step 10.
12. For fractional amounts, determine value of purchasing an additional gallon or smaller sizes.

Following is a checklist for conducting a procedural analysis:

- Are the relevant cues and feedback identified for each step of the procedure?
- Does the analysis identify the generally acceptable procedure rather than the personal preferences of the SME? Tips that make a step easier are usually acceptable as long as they do not violate a safety rule.
- Are the decision steps identified (e.g., "If the blue light is on, then turn to the right; if not, turn to the left.")?
- Are all steps accurately described?
- Are critical steps that could result in personal injury, equipment damage, or other loss identified?

Procedural analyses also reveal a content structure much as a topic analysis does. For the cognitive information, you need to identify the related facts, concepts, and principles to complete the related topic analysis. Procedures or steps are grouped in several ways. One method is to classify the steps by frequency of execution (e.g., frequently, occasionally, seldom). A second method is by difficulty level (e.g., easy, moderately difficult, difficult). Psychomotor tasks may be grouped according to gross- or fine-motor skills or level of proficiency (see Chapter 5).

## Going Beyond Procedural Analysis

The limitations of a behavioral task analysis, which focuses exclusively on observable tasks of the subject-matter expert, became clear a few years ago with the development of cognitive psychology research (Anderson, 2007). Its limitations became obvious while designers were analyzing the tasks an air traffic controller performs (Chipman, Schraagen, & Shalin, 2000). The traditional analysis approach focused on the observable psychomotor skills of using the equipment but failed to consider the

**FIGURE 4-2**
Task diagram

various cognitive operations the controller performed. As a result, a combination of researchers and designers developed a new approach to task analysis, cognitive task analysis, to analyze tasks that involve a cognitive component. Cognitive task analysis is typically used with more traditional task analysis and provides additional information that is not obvious when watching an expert perform a task. The goal of cognitive task analysis is to identify those covert cognitive operations associated with the overt behaviors we can easily observe.

There are many approaches to conducting a cognitive task analysis. For example, GOMS (which stands for "goals, operators, methods, and selection rules") (Card, Moran, & Newell, 1983) focuses on the goals of the expert in doing the task, the operations or small tasks the expert performs, the methods (i.e., approaches or means) available to achieve the goals, and the selection of the most appropriate method. GOMS has been used extensively to design human–computer interfaces (Williams, 2000). Militello and Hutton (1998) described the applied cognitive task analysis (ACTA) process, which is very flexible and applicable to a wide variety of tasks. This method involves four steps (Figure 4-2 and Tables 4-2 through 4-4 are excerpts from a cognitive task analysis of an insurance-underwriting submission-review task conducted by Jennifer Maddrell). First, the designer asks a subject-matter expert to identify three to six broad steps that are performed as part of this task (see Figure 4-2). The purpose of this step is to identify broad steps rather than a sequence like a procedural analysis. The second step is a knowledge audit

**TABLE 4-2**
Excerpt from knowledge and audit table

| Aspect of expertise | Cues and Strategies | Why Difficult? |
|---|---|---|
| ***Past and future***<br>Example: Call from broker about account where incumbent carrier messed up on claim and insured's legal department insisting the account must move. | • High-level nature of incumbent mess-up<br>• Level of people involved in decision (low-level versus high-level) | • Novice may not recognize significance of messed up claim handling<br>• Novice may not link level of insured to severity of problem<br>• Novice may not link severity of problem to increased chance of writing account. |

**TABLE 4-3**
Excerpt from simulation interview

| Events | Actions | Assessment | Critical Cues | Potential Errors |
|---|---|---|---|---|
| Discussion about prospect with broker | • Ask probing questions about opportunity<br>• Sensing tone from broker of urgency and desire to have your quote | • Answers to question make sense or not with what is in the submission<br>• Broker wants to work with you or just wants a quote for comparison purposes | • Can you meet the insured<br>• There is disaffection with incumbent<br>• Openness of the broker<br>• Willingness to provide additional information | • Being overly optimistic about *any* opportunity<br>• Not probing deeply for hidden facts about situation<br>• Not reading the verbal and nonverbal cues the broker is giving you |

that is used to generate examples of the task (see Table 4-2). For the knowledge audit the designer uses probes, asking what is important about the big picture, describing a situation in which the expert immediately knew the problem after studying it for just a few minutes, or asking whether the expert has ever noticed things others did not. The knowledge audit is conducted for each of the broad steps identified in the first step. The third step is to conduct a simulation interview in which the expert describes how he or she would solve a realistic problem (see Table 4-3). As part of this interview, the expert is asked to first identify the major events. Next, the expert is asked a series of questions about each event, including what actions to take, what is going on, and what errors a novice might make. The last step of the process is to create a cognitive demands table that synthesizes the information from the first three steps (see Table 4-4). A designer should focus on those steps that require complex cognitive processing when performing a cognitive task analysis. The cognitive demands table is used along with the traditional task analysis to design the training.

**TABLE 4-4**
Excerpt from cognitive demands table

| Difficult Cognitive Elements | Why Difficult? | Common Errors | Cues and Strategies Used |
|---|---|---|---|
| Assessing whether broker's answers make sense or not with what is in the submission | • Novice underwriters tend to focus on basic facts in the submission versus what the broker is telling them<br>• Brokers reluctant to voluntarily air dirty laundry about account | • Don't recognize or probe for hidden "red flags"<br>• Focus exclusively on information in submission | • Consider whether you really know the story behind the story<br>• Get and keep the broker talking to elicit information beyond the submission |

Teaching the process of cognitive task analysis is beyond the scope of this book. A CD-ROM training program on ACTA is available from www.decisionmaking.com/approach/ACTA_CD.html. The Militello and Hutton (1998) article also provides an excellent description of the ACTA process. There are, however, some ideas you can borrow from cognitive task analysis to enhance a procedural analysis.

First, you can use a talk-aloud protocol when conducting a procedural analysis. When working with a subject-matter expert, you can ask him or her to verbally describe each action and step as it is performed. You may need to use continual prompting of the subject-matter expert to talk aloud (e.g., "Could you tell me what you are [doing, seeing, thinking, hearing, smelling, feeling]?"). Second, you can use the talk-aloud protocol to identify important cues. These cues are used by the experts to complete the task and make decisions. It is important to collect with the cues any information identifying errors a novice might make. Table 4-5 provides examples of different types of cues an instructional designer might identify in a task analysis and the types of errors a novice might make.

## THE CRITICAL INCIDENT METHOD

The two methods we have described—topic and procedural analyses—work well with concrete content and highly structured tasks that are easily analyzed. Analyzing a process, such as how to conduct an interview, resolve an interpersonal conflict, or close a sales opportunity, is more difficult because processes vary from instance to instance. Although the instances share certain elements, typically the breadth of skills and techniques account for one's success. Procedural analysis works quite well for analyzing how to apply the final finish to a wooden table, for example, because the basic process is repeated time after time, with variations due to size and type of wood. Closing a sale, however, depends on several conditions (e.g., personality of the buyer, financial status of the buyer) that change with each sale. To define the content for this type of training adequately, we need a method that provides different points of view. For example, we might interview a salesperson who uses a very calm approach and another individual who uses high-pressure tactics.

A *critical incident analysis*, then, can identify the commonalities of various approaches. Interviewing several individuals for the critical incident analysis provides a rich context for analyzing interpersonal skills. In some situations, you may need to combine the results with a procedural analysis to define content for designing the instruction.

The critical incident method was developed by Flanagan (1954) during World War II to determine why Army Air Force pilots were not learning to fly correctly. Pilots were interviewed to determine which conditions led to a successful mission and which conditions led to an unsuccessful one. A critical incident interview is based on three types of information:

1. What were the conditions before, during, and after the incident?
   - Where did the incident occur?
   - When did it occur?

**TABLE 4-5**
Cues for enhancing a procedural analysis

| Input | Example | Questions to Extract Cues from SME | Errors a Novice Might Make |
|---|---|---|---|
| Decisions | Determining when a board is sanded smooth | What do I do next? Is the procedure finished? | Might not know alternative steps to take when a problem arises |
| | Determining when a wood joint is a good fit | Do the two pieces fit properly? | Might misinterpret a snug fit for a secure fit |
| Visual | The closed lock at the bottom of browser window indicating a secure Website | How do we know the Website is secure? | Sending a credit card number to a nonsecure Website |
| | A good recording is distortion free | What is the correct recording level on the meter? | Setting the recording level too high, which results in unintelligible recording |
| | Swelling in the lower leg | What are the symptoms of a blood clot? | Diagnosing a blood clot as a sprained ankle |
| | Patterns in a data set or display | What does the initial inspection of the data set indicate? | Might miss an incorrect piece of data that is out of range, which creates problems with the analysis |
| Tactile | A physical exam | How do you identify a lump in the breast? | Failing to identify a lump could result in cancer |
| | Stiffness of dough as it is kneaded | How long do you knead the dough? | Not kneading the dough enough will result in bread not rising |
| | The resistance of a nut as it is tightened or loosened | How do you know when a bolt is tightened enough? | Overtightening the nut can result in weakening or breaking the bolt |
| Aural | The pitch of the sound produced by a turbine engine or generator | What do variations in the pitch or sound indicate? | A change in pitch can indicate a different speed or part failure |
| | Sounds of a fire crackling or metal stressing | What sounds does a burning building make? | Failing to recognize the crackling of a fire or sound of metal stressing could cause injury or death due to building collapse |
| | Car engine making a knocking sound | What types of unusual noises might one hear from an engine? | Failure to identify engine knock can result in costly damage to internal engine parts |
| Smell | The smell of gasoline at a fire | What can you tell about a fire from the odor of the smoke? | Smell of gasoline changes as it heats up and might be missed |
| | The aromas of a wine | What can you detect from the aroma of a wine? | May miss subtle fruit aromas |
| Taste | The "message" sent by a food | What taste sensations are aroused by the food? | Failing to discriminate between sour and bitter |
| | Patient complaints of frequent metallic taste | What can a metallic taste indicate? | A patient taking certain oral medicines could experience a metallic taste, which might be mistaken for a symptom of kidney disease |

- Who was involved?
- What equipment was used, and what was its condition?
2. What did you do?
   - What did you do physically (e.g., grabbed the rudder)?
   - What did you say and to whom?
   - What were you thinking?
3. How did this incident help you reach or prevent you from reaching your goal?

Primhoff (1973) suggested two questions to ask as part of a critical incident analysis: First, ask the SME to identify three instances when he or she was successful in doing the task. Second, ask the SME to identify three instances when he or she was not successful in doing the task. An analysis of the interviews will identify knowledge and techniques the SME used to accomplish the task. Once this information is identified, performing a topic and/or procedural analysis can further define the content.

The critical incident method is well suited for analyzing interpersonal skills and attitudes. If you were designing a course on classroom management for prospective teachers, you might use a critical incident analysis to determine how teachers handle disruptive students. Similarly, you might use this method to determine the content and skills needed to teach a workshop on conducting job interviews or employee performance reviews. It is also useful for initially defining complex tasks that an SME might consider an "art." For example, a designer might use this method for initial analysis when determining where to drill an oil well, predicting successful stocks or mutual funds to purchase, or determining which type of psychotherapy to use on a patient.

## Expert's Edge

### Hitting an Invisible but Moving Target

Our experience with task analysis over the years has led to tailoring the procedures to meet characteristics of the organization and tasks themselves. No one situation should be expected to be the same as others.

For example, in large organizations with many job incumbents who are geographically and organizationally disbursed, there may be variations in how tasks are performed and under what conditions. Even trying to sample these differences through a few SMEs is often not satisfactory. To ensure that differences and commonalities of task performance are identified, a stepwise approach is used. First, we define a task list with representative SMEs and then administer a task questionnaire to a large sample of the jobholders. The questionnaire asks for criticality, difficulty, and frequency judgments under various conditions of the task. The results are then analyzed to determine priorities for training as well as any differences among organizational elements.

Another organizational factor is the maturity of the job. In some cases, the job does not yet exist or is evolving. For example, a job might evolve because a new concept of operations is anticipated due to a major equipment change. In such situations it is necessary to both lean on existing SME experience and to analyze details of the differences as the changes emerge. It is often the case for emerging jobs that the task analysis and resulting training will lead to the actual job development and standards for the job.

Primary among the task factors is determining the type of learning, including the category of knowledge. There is an increasing awareness among analysts that higher-level cognitive tasks need more attention than straightforward procedural or skill tasks. For example, many cognitive tasks require looking at the task structure conditions. A task can be ill or well structured. An ill-structured task is one that may have more than one solution, more than one path to a solution, or unknown task constraints and one for which not all of the information needed is available. These tasks require deeper interviews with SMEs, and not all SMEs can verbalize the task well. This process may require some SMEs to develop examples to help other SMEs explain what they do under such situations and various conditions. The analysis then becomes a cognitive task analysis. There are many types of content domains this applies to, such as medical diagnosis, troubleshooting complex equipment, any decision making under uncertainty, and engineering design problems.

Higher levels of cognitive tasks, such as designing, planning, strategic, and tactical decision making and problem solving, often require a deeper interview even when the task is well structured. An overlooked aspect of task analysis is the executive processing or metacognitive-type task elements involved. Many job incumbents have developed, through experience, cognitive techniques for processing the knowledge of the task. This is what makes them experts. It is part of the information needed if future experts are to be trained. Contrasting interviews with experts and those with novices sometimes help identify the differences.

The job of the task analyst is to structure the analysis, including interviews, questionnaires, and other instruments, to account for these aspects of the organization and the task characteristics. Each situation should be approached with a view that there may be something different needed from the last analysis.

Dewey Kribs, past president of Instructional Science and Development, has over 30 years of experience in the development of interactive training systems and computer-based courseware.

## CONDUCTING A TASK ANALYSIS

Your SME and the environment will influence how you conduct a topic, procedural, or critical incident analysis. If you are an instructional designer working in a hospital, university, government agency, or business, a knowledgeable SME will most likely be assigned to work with you on the project. If you are a classroom teacher or a part-time instructor, such as a nursing supervisor responsible for training your staff, you will most likely be your own SME. The environment may vary from your office to a retail store, an operating room, or an offshore oil-drilling rig. Each environment offers advantages and disadvantages.

## Serving as Your Own SME

Serving as your own SME has two major advantages. First is the ease of access and of scheduling of meetings—you need only motivate yourself! Second, you are already familiar with the learners and the problems they have with the task. The major disadvantage is your familiarity with the content, which may cause you to skip steps and fail to identify important cues. Four techniques can counter this disadvantage. First, find another SME and assume the role of the designer. In the latter role, you need to ''forget'' everything you know about the task and approach it from a naive point of view. Second, if you are conducting a procedural analysis, once you have the initial version done, ask someone else to perform the task. As the other person does the task, ask him or her to verbally describe the task. You can then check this description with your own. Third, have another expert review or actually work through your analysis to identify any missing steps, cues, or topics. Fourth, talk both a novice and an expert through the task using your task analysis. Their feedback can help you revise your analysis.

## Techniques for Gathering Data

Each designer develops a repertoire of techniques for analyzing content. The first rule is to be prepared when working with SMEs. Typically, they are on loan from their regular jobs for an hour or a few days. These individuals are usually experts who perform a valuable service for the organization. Adequate preparation on your part is not only courteous but also shows that you respect their expertise and time. Adequate preparation includes that of your materials as well as adequate knowledge of the goals and problems you are trying to reach and solve. This information was defined when you identified the instructional problem (see Chapter 2). Review those materials and, if necessary, contact some of the individuals who helped you define the problem to obtain additional clarification and understanding. The following paragraphs describe three techniques for conducting content and procedural analyses. You might use only one or a combination of all three.

**Literature Research.**    Reading technical manuals and other materials is the least preferred method for conducting an analysis. It is an inefficient way to master the content in a relatively short time. However, if the materials can give you an expert's understanding, they may be adequate for use as training materials. Reading materials to prepare for a meeting with an SME may be beneficial, but reading the materials to become an expert is often counterproductive.

**Interviewing an SME.**    This technique is the most preferred method of defining information for all three analyses. The individual interview was the task analysis methodology designers reported using most often (Loughner & Moller, 1998). Meeting in the SME's office for an analysis that involves primarily a cognitive task has the benefit of providing easy access to the SME's resources. These resources include books as well as data to use for examples and case studies in your instruction. For example, the first author was developing a course on how to prepare engineering proposals. During the analysis, the SME was able to retrieve several good and bad examples from the office files. Analyzing these proposals helped in developing a procedure and checklist for proposal development as well as examples for instruction.

When conducting a procedural analysis that depends primarily on psychomotor skills, it is beneficial to schedule the SME meeting in a location where the SME can demonstrate the skills. These meeting locations can range from an operating room to a manufacturing plant. Sometimes a location is not available or travel or access is prohibited. For instance, one of the authors needed to analyze the tasks involved in setting the vanes on gas turbine engines that the client company manufactured but was unable to visit an operating site. After several phone calls, the SME found that each new turbine engine was run through a series of operational tests in a test cell at the plant. The SME was able to obtain the use of an engine for an afternoon while the analysis was conducted. For other analyses, a part was often obtained from the parts warehouse, and then a meeting was scheduled with the SME in a shop to analyze the repair and maintenance of that specific part. A network of key individuals, built and maintained by the designer, is a necessary resource.

**Developer Modeling.**   This method is typically used after the initial analysis with the SME to confirm the accuracy of your analysis. You can model the analysis by explaining the content in the topic analysis or demonstrating the steps in the procedural analysis. If an instructional designer is conducting a topic analysis, the information is explained to the SME. This technique helps the designer check his or her understanding and interpretation of the content. Explaining the information to the SME also identifies topics that were not adequately explained and prompts the SME to provide additional details and examples. In a procedural analysis, the task should be demonstrated or simulated. A designer can identify additional cues and steps that were missed in the initial analysis by walking through the steps and doing the motions. For some tasks (e.g., those that are hazardous or require a great deal of skill), the designer may need to resort to simulated actions or observe the SME performing the task.

## Recording Methods

Another aspect of task analysis is recording the information for use in developing the instruction. Notepads and index cards are helpful for recording the topics and steps. If the task analysis is outdoors, a notepad is often preferable because it will not scatter if dropped. Index cards provide flexibility in adding new topics or steps; it is very easy to label an index card as 10A and place it in the stack between cards 10 and 11. Another tool for recording information is a laptop computer, netbook, or smart phone, but the user should make sure it has adequate battery life or an extension cord and power source. A laptop computer, netbook, or a smart phone with an outliner provides a very flexible method for conducting an analysis. Simply clicking at the appropriate point allows you to easily insert a new step or rearrange other steps and information. Tape recorders are also useful for taping the analysis; however, they are difficult to reference later unless transcribed.

A digital camera is very helpful when conducting a procedural analysis. Taking pictures of the equipment, tools, and various steps is useful for refreshing the designer's memory. Some of the photographs can be printed in the manuals to illustrate a procedure. Designers should check first, however, to make sure they are allowed to take photographs—some locations have security regulations or may prohibit the use of flash lighting. A portable video camera is also useful for documenting a procedural analysis, with the SME describing each step as it is performed. One author's project involved the development of a training program for maintaining a portable computer. The procedural analysis involved the only prototype available, and it was in a location different from the author's office. When the notes were inadequate, the video recording was cued and played to review the specific steps. Still, the SME had to be telephoned several times for clarification (e.g., "Do you need to rock it as you remove the board or pull it straight up?").

## SUMMARY

One of the key steps of the design process is defining the content needed to address the instructional need or problem. This content is then used to identify the objectives, design the instructional strategies, develop test items, and create the instruction.

Topic, procedural, and critical incidence analyses are three methods for defining the content. A topic analysis is used to identify the facts, concepts, and principles needed for the instruction. Procedural analysis is applied to a task to identify the individual steps, cues, and sequence for performing steps. Critical incidence analysis is used to identify the content related to interpersonal interactions and attitudes. Cognitive task analysis provides a method for determining the "mental" steps the professional uses when performing a task. This method goes beyond what is observable.

Our experience has shown that almost every project uses at least two of these methods. The designer may switch between a topic and procedural analysis several times during an interview with the SME. When conducting a task analysis, the designer must keep accurate records of the transactions. Notepads and index cards can be supplemented with photographs or video recordings.

## THE ID PROCESS

You are now ready to analyze the content and tasks needed for the instruction. The first step is to identify an SME who can provide you with the needed information. We always start by contacting individuals with whom we have worked in the past and soliciting their recommendations for an SME. Once you have identified the expert or experts, contact them and discuss the problem. They can help you determine whether you need to meet in an office or at a location that has the appropriate equipment or conditions. Also, during this initial contact, inquire about whether any special equipment or training is needed. For example, you might need to complete a course in first aid, winter survival, or hydrogen sulfide training, or you might need special equipment such as a hard hat and safety shoes. Arriving unprepared can result in a lack of access.

Next, you need to set a time and place for your meeting. You might also mention to your SME what type of examples (e.g., written reports, diagrams, pictures) you might need for the final unit. Finally, you need to prepare for the analysis. We always like to take one or two notepads, note cards, and a camera. If the conditions are favorable, we like to take a computer or smart phone for note taking, but we always have our notepad and note cards as a backup.

Remember to respect the expert's time during your meeting. Simply preparing a brief summary of the problem or goals and the target audience can set the stage for the analysis. While you are conducting the analysis, ask plenty of questions and seek clarification; don't wait until you return to your office. Once you finish the analysis, you will develop the objectives for the instruction.

## APPLICATION

What are the steps for creating a peanut butter and jelly sandwich? Assume that the learner is given a knife, two pieces of bread, peanut butter, jelly, and a paper plate. Now, perform a task analysis.

## ANSWER

The following is our task analysis for making a peanut butter and jelly sandwich. (Rather than using "dominant" and "nondominant hand," we have used "right" and "left hand.")

I. Place paper plate with top side facing up directly in front of you.
II. Place two pieces of bread side by side on plate with top edge of each facing same direction.
Visual cue: Top edge of bread is usually round.
III. Remove lid from jelly jar.
   A. Grasp jelly jar with left hand and hold between thumb and fingers.
      1. Move jar 3 inches above and over slice of bread on right side of plate.
      2. Position so mouth of jar is one-third of way between top and bottom of bread and approximately 6 inches above bread.
      3. Tilt mouth of jelly jar approximately 45 degrees toward center of bread.
IV. Grasp knife handle in right hand so that top (dull, smooth, flat side) of blade is facing up.

A. Place index finger on top edge of knife blade for control.

Visual cue: One edge of knife may be rounded as opposed to straight. This edge is pointing down.

B. Insert knife approximately 1 inch into jelly with index finger on edge of blade closest to ceiling.

  1. Gently pull knife through jelly to accumulate approximately 1 tablespoon of jelly on tip.
  2. Slowly twist knife clockwise so that flat part of blade with jelly is facing ceiling.
  3. Gently remove knife from jar while keeping jelly on blade.
  4. Set jar down out of the way with mouth up.
  5. Place bread in palm of left hand.

C. Carefully maneuver knife to center of bread on right side without dropping jelly.

  1. Turn knife blade over and gently brush jelly onto bread.
  2. Working from center out, use knife blade to spread jelly over the bread, leaving an eighth-inch border at each edge.
     a. Hold knife blade barely off of bread and at a 25-degree angle to bread to spread jelly.
  3. Spread jelly evenly over piece of bread.
     a. Add additional jelly as needed to meet personal preferences.
  4. Place bread back on plate in original position with jelly up.

D. Move knife to second piece of bread.

  1. Hold blade flat against piece of bread and gently wipe both sides of blade clean.
  2. Set knife down on clean surface.

V. Replace lid on jelly jar and tighten.

A. Place jelly jar out of immediate workspace.

VI. Remove lid from peanut butter jar.

A. Grasp peanut butter jar in left hand between thumb and fingers.

B. Position mouth of peanut butter jar approximately one-third of distance from top to bottom of second piece of bread, approximately 6 inches above bread.

C. Tilt mouth of peanut butter jar approximately 45 degrees toward center of bread.

VII. Grasp knife handle in right hand so that top, dull, or smooth side of blade is facing up.

A. Place index finger on top edge of knife blade.

Visual cue: One edge of knife may be rounded as opposed to straight. This edge is pointing down.

B. Insert knife approximately 1 inch into peanut butter with index finger on edge toward ceiling.

  1. Gently pull knife through peanut butter to accumulate approximately 1 tablespoon of peanut butter on tip.

2. Slowly twist knife clockwise so that flat part of blade is facing ceiling.
3. Gently remove knife from jar while keeping peanut butter on blade.
4. Set jar down with mouth up and out of way.
5. Place "clean" bread in palm of left hand.

C. Carefully maneuver knife to center of bread without dropping peanut butter.
  1. Turn knife blade over and gently brush peanut butter onto bread.
  2. Working from center out, use knife blade to spread peanut butter gently on bread, leaving an eighth-inch border at each edge.
    a. Hold knife blade off of bread and at a 25-degree angle to bread to spread peanut butter.
  3. Spread peanut butter evenly over piece of bread.
    a. Add additional peanut butter as needed to meet personal preferences.
    b. Gently scrape each side of knife blade on edge of bread to remove excess peanut butter from knife blade.
    c. Place bread on plate in original position.
  4. Place knife in a clean spot.

D. Gently grasp crust at top edge of bread of peanut-buttered piece with fingers of left hand and crust of bottom edge of same piece with right hand.
  1. Grasp only edge to avoid getting peanut butter on fingers.

E. Lift bread approximately 1.5 times width of bread above plate.

F. Move piece of bread directly over piece of bread with jelly.

G. Carefully rotate piece of bread with peanut butter so that peanut-buttered side is facing down.
  Visual cue: Clean side of bread is facing up.

H. Align two pieces of bread so that tops and right edges are aligned.

I. Slowly lower bread with peanut butter toward piece that's jellied so that all four corners align.

J. When two pieces of bread are barely touching, make any final adjustment in alignment.

K. Release hold on bread.

L. Gently pat top piece of bread to ensure adhesion of peanut butter and jelly.

VIII. Place lid on peanut butter jar and tighten.
  A. Move jelly and peanut butter jars out of way.

IX. Determine how sandwich should be cut.
  A. To cut at angle from edge to edge
    1. Turn left corner of edge toward you at a 45-degree angle.
    2. Hold bread in position with gentle pressure from left hand on left corner.
    3. Grasp knife with right hand as before.

      4. Cut bread from top right corner to bottom left corner to create two right-angle triangles.
  B. To cut sandwich in half creating two equal rectangles
      1. Turn bread so that the longest side is parallel to your body.
      2. Gently hold bread into position with left hand by grasping top or bottom edge.
      3. Grasp knife in right hand as before.
      4. Select position halfway on longest edge on farthest side.
      5. Cut bread by drawing knife toward you.
  C. Arrange two pieces into pleasing presentation.
  D. Place knife in sink or dishwasher.

There several potential ways of completing this task analysis. For example, one designer might start with a trip to the grocery store to gather the materials. Another might start with the gathering of all the materials in the kitchen. Similarly, another SME might suggest putting the top of the bread closest to the learner, whereas another might start with applying the peanut butter. The task analysis simply defines the content; it does not specify the sequence. As the process progresses, you may need and want to make changes in the task analysis.

## QUALITY MANAGEMENT

There are two tasks to help ensure quality. First, you need to verify that your task analysis is thorough and accurate. For procedures, you can have another SME or naive person walk through the steps as you read them. An SME can help you identify inaccurate information and missing steps, whereas the naive person can help you identify missing steps and missing cues. For a topic analysis, you can conduct a review with one or more SMEs. We recommend giving them your verbal explanation rather than having them review your task analysis, because they may not know how to accurately read the task analysis. The second task is to determine whether your task analysis is in alignment with your needs assessment and goal analysis. That is, will the content and skills you have identified alleviate the instructional problem? If not, you can take two actions. First, you can revise your task analysis to correct the error. Second, you can revise your goals to more accurately reflect the task analysis. This second solution may be the result of new or additional information that has resulted in a refinement of the problem. Such a decision should not be made haphazardly but should include information from multiple sources.

## INSTRUCTIONAL DESIGN: DECISIONS AND CHOICES

Now that you've completed your draft of the learner analysis, you are ready to concentrate on the task analysis. Actually, you began the task analysis during the initial meeting with the client. As you gathered information about the instructional need and the audience, the client also talked about the content in broad general terms. While listening to the client describe the mistakes made by the mailroom clerk, you began to list the learning goals and categorize the types of learning tasks (e.g., conceptual tasks, procedural tasks, and affective behaviors).

Next, you prepare to meet with a subject-matter expert to conduct the task analysis in depth. However, before meeting with the SME (because his/her time is extremely limited), you conduct a Web search to learn all you can about fire extinguishers. You learn about the types of fire extinguishers, the procedures for using a fire extinguisher, how a fire extinguisher works, the history of fire extinguishers, types of combustible materials, policy planning for fire safety, fire extinguisher laws, and so on. You don't want to attempt to become an expert, but you do want to become knowledgeable before you meet with the SME.

## Instructional Goals

With the SME, you prepare an initial task analysis. You facilitate the SME's identifying the content by brainstorming. The initial analysis follows. [As you examine the task analysis note (1) how the identified goals are broken down into greater detail, (2) how the analysis includes both conceptual and procedural learning tasks, and (3) that the initial analysis includes a mix of "nice-to-know" content and critical content. Consider which instructional goals should be eliminated or reordered.]

1.0 How fires start
2.0 Importance of fire in the development of civilization
3.0 History of the development of fire extinguishers
4.0 Historical development of municipal fire departments
5.0 Types of fire extinguishers
6.0 Nuts and bolts about the inner parts of how a fire extinguisher works
7.0 How to use a fire extinguisher
8.0 Types of fires
9.0 Fire emergency procedures

Your meeting with the SME has included a spirited discussion concerning many of these instructional goals. [On larger projects, several SMEs and other stakeholders often meet together to conduct the task analysis. It's important to clearly establish how your role as the designer is different from that of the SME from the start of your interaction. The SME's role is to ensure that all essential content is included and that the content is accurate. As an instructional designer, your role is to organize and sequence the content efficiently by applying learning and instructional theories.]

Here's the revised task analysis. Nice-to-know content (e.g., the history of fire extinguishers) has been eliminated. Although nice-to-know content is interesting, it overburdens the learner's cognitive capacity, dilutes attention from important information, and gets in the way of learning that is essential. Notice in the following task analysis how sequencing is critical (e.g., the classes of fires must be presented before instruction on the types of fire extinguishers).

1.0 How fires start
    1.1 The fire triangle principle

      1.1.1 Oxygen, heat, and a fuel source create a chemical reaction (fire)

    1.2 Fire extinguishers remove one or more of these components to put out a fire

2.0 Types of fires

    2.1 Class A: Wood, paper, cloth, trash

    2.2 Class B: Flammable liquids (gasoline, oil, grease, acetone)

    2.3 Class C: Electrical

    2.4 Class D: Metals (potassium, sodium, aluminum, magnesium)

3.0 Types of fire extinguishers

    3.1 Using the wrong type of fire extinguisher can make the situation worse

      3.1.1 Example: Using water-based fire extinguisher on an electrical fire

      3.1.2 Example: Using water on a grease fire will make the fire spread out

    3.2 Water Type

      3.2.1 Physical characteristics: large metal can filled with water

      3.2.2 Use only on Class A fires

      3.2.3 Will spread out rather than extinguish flammable liquids (Class B fires)

      3.2.4 Places user at electrocution risk if used on an electrical fire (Class C fires)

      3.2.5 Often found in college dormitories

    3.3 Carbon Dioxide

      3.3.1 Physical characteristics: cone-shaped nozzle; has no pressure gauge

      3.3.2 Use on Class B and C fires

      3.3.3 May be ineffective on Class A fires

      3.3.4 Often found in kitchens, laboratories, and mechanical rooms

    3.4 Dry Chemical

      3.4.1 Physical characteristics: has a pressure gauge

      3.4.2 "DC" means dry chemical

      3.4.3 Come in two versions: ABC and BC

      3.4.4 Powder used interrupts chemical reaction

      3.4.5 BC versions usually found in commercial kitchens

[Notice that each of the four types of fire extinguishers is a concept. The designer has intentionally used a parallel structure to analyze each type of extinguisher to make salient the similarities and differences among the types for the learner. First the physical characteristics of each extinguisher are described. Second, the classes of fires the extinguisher is used for are discussed, and third, places the extinguisher is commonly found are identified.]

4.0 Emergency Procedures

    4.1 Evacuate people and call for help

      4.1.1 Assist anyone in immediate danger

      4.1.2 Pull the building fire alarm

          4.1.2.1 The alarm will automatically notify the fire department

4.1.2.2 The alarm will automatically shut down the HVAC to prevent the spread of smoke
4.1.3 Call 911 if the alarm does not activate
4.2 Determine whether you can safely attempt to use a fire extinguisher
4.2.1 Determine what is burning
4.2.1.1 If you aren't sure what is burning, do not attempt to fight the fire
4.2.2 If the fire is spreading rapidly, do not attempt to fight the fire
4.2.2.1 Close doors behind you as you leave
4.2.3 If there is a large amount of smoke, do not attempt to fight the fire
4.2.3.1 Beside carbon monoxide, synthetic materials (e.g., carpets) that catch fire produce toxic gasses
4.3 Ensure that you can escape quickly before attempting to use the fire extinguisher
4.3.1 Ensure that you will not become trapped by the fire
5.0 How to use a fire extinguisher
5.1 Acronym: PASS
5.2 Pull the pin
5.3 Aim at the base of the fire (not at the flames)
5.4 Squeeze the handle or lever
5.5 Sweep (at the base of the fire) from side to side

[Notice that tasks in 4.0 and 5.0 are procedures. Tasks in 4.0 include both mental and physical procedures whereas tasks in 5.0 are physical procedures. Notice too that the learner will make judgments and decisions as part of the mental and physical procedures.]

## REFERENCES

Anderson, J. R. (2007). *How can the human mind occur in the physical universe?* New York: Oxford University Press.
Bruner, J. S. (1963). *The process of education.* New York: Vintage Books.
Card, S. T., Moran, T. P., & Newell, A. (1983). *The psychology of human-computer interaction.* Hillsdale, NJ: Erlbaum.
Chipman, S. F., Schraagen, J. M., & Shalin, V. L. (2000). An introduction to cognitive task analysis. In J. M. Schraagen, S. F. Chipman, & V. L. Shalin (Eds.), *Cognitive task analysis* (pp. 3–23). Mahwah, NJ: Erlbaum.
Flanagan, J. C. (1954). The critical incident method. *Psychological Bulletin, 51,* 327–358.
Jonassen, D., Hannum, W., & Tessmer, M. (1989). *Handbook of task analysis procedures.* New York: Praeger.
Jonassen, D., Hannum, W., & Tessmer, M. (1999). *Task analysis methods for instructional design.* Mahwah, NJ: Erlbaum.
Loughner, P., & Moller, L. (1998). The use of task analysis procedures by instructional designers. *Performance Improvement Quarterly, 11,* 79–101.

Militello, L. G., & Hutton, R. J. B. (1998). Applied cognitive task analysis: A practitioner's toolkit for understanding cognitive task demands. *Ergonomics, 41,* 1618–1641.

Phipps, C. J. (1977). *Mechanics in agriculture.* Danville, IL: Interstate.

Primhoff, E. (1973). *How to prepare and conduct job element examinations.* Washington, DC: U.S. Civil Service Commission.

Reigeluth, C. M. (1983). Current trends in task analysis: The integration of task analysis and instructional design. *Journal of Instructional Development, 6,* 24–30, 35.

Williams, K. E. (2000). An automated aid for modeling human-computer interaction. In J. M. Schraagen, S. F. Chipman, & V. L. Shalin (Eds.), *Cognitive task analysis* (pp. 165–180). Mahwah, NJ: Erlbaum.

# 5

# Instructional Objectives

## GETTING STARTED

For the past six years, you have worked for a petroleum company and are responsible for the training of civil, electrical, and chemical engineers at the various company refineries. When you visited one of the refineries recently while working on an instructional program for new engineers, you met an engineer, Ms. Calle, who had developed a program to determine the maximum output for the refinery based on the type of crude oil being refined. Ms. Calle demonstrated the program and pointed out that many engineers were requesting what she thought was unnecessary maintenance work. She had determined that the refinery was working at its maximum for the quality of crude oil input and the output it was producing. The problem, she said, was that the engineers were spending money for maintenance and repairs that simply were not needed. As a follow-up, you did your own analysis and verified the problem. Seeing the opportunity for fame and immediate recognition, you rushed to complete the task analysis and develop the objectives for a training program to teach engineers how to use the software to solve problems.

## QUESTIONS TO CONSIDER

"What is the purpose of this instruction?"

"How can learners demonstrate their understanding of the material?"

"How can you assess whether the learners have mastered the content?"

"If you have good test items, do you really need objectives?"

"Don't instructors know what needs to be taught in a course?"

"What types of content and performance are specified in the objectives?"

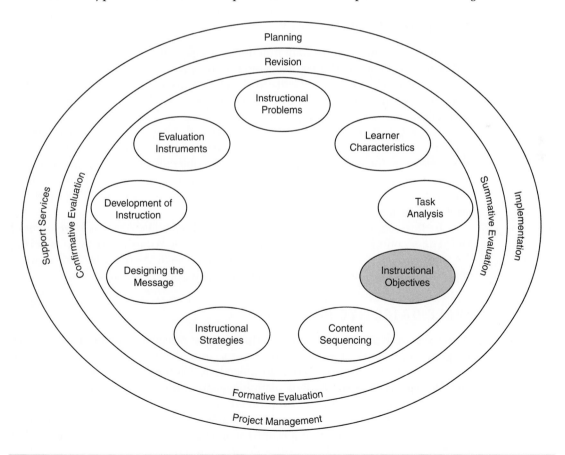

After returning to your office, you showed your plan to the chief engineer, who thought it was a good idea—except, that is, for your objectives. He stated that his engineers knew how to solve problems and that there was no need for any problem-solving objectives. The unit should focus on how to enter the data and run the software. You pled your case with your data, which clearly showed money was wasted on needless maintenance. Again, the chief engineer directed you to remove the problem-solving emphasis from the proposed training. What would you do in this situation?

Why do instructional designers need instructional objectives? Unless the requirements are specifically defined, the instructional designer will not know what to include in the instruction. Also, without a clear statement of intent, the designer will have difficulty measuring the specific learning achieved. The benefits of the instruction are indicated in terms of what the learner is to accomplish—hence the expression *instructional objectives*. Clearly defined objectives are also essential for selecting the optimum instructional strategies to facilitate the learner's achievement of the objectives.

## FUNCTION OF OBJECTIVES

Objectives perform two important functions for instructional designers, instructors, and teachers. First, they offer a means for the instructional designer to design appropriate instruction, specifically to select and organize instructional activities and resources that facilitate effective learning. The result is a highly focused unit of instruction.

Second, instructional objectives provide a framework for devising ways to evaluate student learning. Because written tests and performance activities are the major means of measuring student achievement, objectives should guide the design of relevant testing items and procedures. Thus, the writing and use of instructional objectives can have a worthwhile impact on improving both teaching and the resultant learning.

In this chapter, we focus on the first function, objectives as a development tool. The second function is addressed in Chapter 11. We will start by considering the three domains or classifications of objectives. Next, we describe how to write objectives and then how to classify them for making instructional decisions.

## THREE OBJECTIVE DOMAINS

Objectives are typically grouped into three major categories (or domains, as they are generally called): cognitive, psychomotor, and affective. These areas are often discussed in the literature related to objectives. Understanding the levels within each domain is important when planning instruction. For example, if you were designing a course that focuses on problem solving, you would not expect to have the majority of your objectives written at the knowledge level of the cognitive domain. You may also find that it is difficult to classify your objectives at one level of a domain. Designers, teachers, and evaluators often disagree as to the classification of objectives as they may feel they fit at different levels in a domain. Often agreement is reached when we consider both the verb and the content, or the whole objective.

## Cognitive Domain

The domain receiving the most attention in instructional programs is the cognitive domain, which includes objectives related to information or knowledge, naming, solving, predicting, and other intellectual aspects of learning. Bloom, Englehart, Furst, Hill, and Krathwohl (1956) developed a widely used taxonomy for the cognitive domain. (A taxonomy is a method of sequential classification on different levels.) The taxonomy is organized within two major groups: (a) simple recall of information and (b) intellectual activities. Bloom labeled the lowest level knowledge, and the higher mental abilities are classified into the five increasingly more intellectual levels of comprehension, application, analysis, synthesis, and evaluation.

Table 5-1 illustrates several examples of instructional objectives in each of the six levels in the cognitive domain.

Too often, major attention is given in a course to memorizing or recalling information—the lowest cognitive level. One reason for the abundance of recall

**TABLE 5-1**
Taxonomy of cognitive objectives

| Level of Bloom's Taxonomy | Course: Chemistry Topic: Gas Laws | Course: Fundamentals of Electricity Topic: Connecting a Three-Way Switch |
|---|---|---|
| **Knowledge**: Recall of specific information | Define pressure. | List the tools required to wire a three-way switch. |
| **Comprehension**: Lowest level of understanding | Describe the relationship between pressure and volume. | Explain the purpose for each of the three wires used in connecting a switch. |
| **Application**: Application of a rule or principle | If you have a fully inflated basketball and you add more air, what is the effect on pressure inside the ball? | Sketch a diagram for connecting a three-way switch to an existing circuit. |
| **Analysis**: Breaking an idea into component parts and describing the relationships | Explain why an automobile's tire will not appear underinflated after being driven several miles at a high speed. | Determine the gauge and length of wiring needed to connect a three-way switch to a junction box. |
| **Synthesis**: Putting the parts together to form a new whole | If you double the absolute temperature of a gas and double the pressure of the gas, what is the effect on volume? | Develop a plan for converting the single switch on a dining room chandelier to a three-way switch. |
| **Evaluation**: Making judgments | Before you is a container of water vapor with a temperature of 150°C and a container of oxygen at 150°C. Which gas is more likely to behave in accordance with the gas laws? | Given a diagram of an existing two-way switch for a dining room light, determine whether it can be converted to a three-way switch. |

objectives may be the ease of writing them. One of the challenges in an instructional design, however, is to devise instructional objectives and then design related activities that can direct students to accomplishments on the five higher intellectual levels. If the task for which you are designing instruction requires application, problem solving, or evaluation, then objectives will not help the learner master the task. Although Bloom's taxonomy is used to design instructional strategies, others such as Merrill (1983) have developed specific strategies for classifying objectives and then prescribing appropriate instructional strategies. We describe these methods in Chapter 7.

## Psychomotor Domain

The second category for grouping instructional objectives is the psychomotor domain, which encompasses the skills requiring the use and coordination of skeletal muscles, as in the physical activities of performing, manipulating, and constructing. Although no taxonomy is universally accepted for this domain, Heinich, Molenda, and Russell (1993) presented a taxonomy based on the degree of coordination that is applicable to many design projects (Table 5-2). Most muscular movements required for performing a task, whether it's doing a somersault or using a screwdriver, can be derived from this taxonomy.

Another grouping of psychomotor skills, proposed by Kibler (1981; see Table 5-3), is not a sequential taxonomy (in other words, the different levels are not sequentially organized). The value of Kibler's grouping is the recognition of separate gross- and fine-movement skills in the first two psychomotor behavior categories. Because each one requires the use of different sets of muscles, teaching such skills can be better organized by giving attention first to gross movements and then to fine movements.

**TABLE 5-2**

Domain of psychomotor objectives

| Level | Description | Example |
|---|---|---|
| Imitation | Demonstrates an observed action | After watching the video recording on drilling countersink holes, you will drill a countersink hole for a wood screw. |
| Manipulation | Performs an action | After practicing on scrap wood, you will drill a hole for connecting two pieces of wood, scoring 8 of 10 points on the performance checklist. |
| Precision | Performs an action with accuracy | You will catch 75 percent of the ground balls hit to your position. |
| Articulation | Performs a coordinated activity in an efficient and coordinated manner | During a tennis game, you will properly execute a backhand swing as required by the volley. |

**TABLE 5-3**
Kibler's psychomotor skill grouping

| Level | Examples |
|---|---|
| Gross bodily movements of arms, shoulders, feet, and legs | Throwing a ball for a distance, picking up a heavy object so as not to strain the body, performing a backward dive |
| Finely coordinated movements of hands and fingers, of hand and eye, of hand and ear, and of hand, eye, and foot | Knitting a scarf, guiding wood through a table saw, using a laptop, driving a car, sight-reading music while playing an instrument |
| Nonverbal communication through facial expression, gestures, bodily movements | Showing emotions through facial expressions, employing gestures to communicate directions, pantomiming a message |
| Speech behavior in producing and projecting sound, coordinating sound and gestures | Giving instructions in a foreign language or presenting a literary reading with gestures for emphasis |

## Affective Domain

The third category of instructional objectives is the affective domain, which involves objectives concerning attitudes, appreciations, values, and emotions such as enjoying, conserving, and respecting. This area is typically believed to be very important in education and training, but it is the one area in which we have been able to do the least, particularly in writing useful instructional objectives.

Krathwohl, Bloom, and Masia (1964) organized the affective domain into five levels (see Table 5-4). The levels of the affective domain, like those of the cognitive domain, form a continuum for attitudinal behavior, from simple awareness and acceptance to internalization, as attitudes become part of an individual's practicing value system.

## Interrelation of Domains

As you plan your instruction, keep in mind all three domains and attempt to treat the higher levels as they affect your topics and general purposes. Remember, too, that even though we are examining the three domains separately, they are closely related in two ways. First, a single major objective can involve learning in two or even all three domains. For example, when a technician learns to mix chemicals, he or she must first acquire knowledge about the different chemicals and their relationships as well as the psychomotor skills of performing the mixing operation. To this knowledge we might add the affective behavior of neatness and the practice of safety during the mixing procedure.

Second, attitudinal development may even precede successful learning in the other domains. Learners often need to be motivated to learn subject matter before instruction is successful. This step may be particularly true in a self-paced learning or distance education program because these students must take responsibility

**TABLE 5-4**
Affective domain

| Level | Description | Example |
|---|---|---|
| Receiving | Willing to give attention to an event or activity. | Listen to, aware of, perceive, alert to, sensitive to, show tolerance of |
| Responding | Willing to react to an event through some form of participation. | Reply, answer, follow along, approve, obey, find pleasure in |
| Valuing | Willing to accept or reject an event through the expression of a positive or negative attitude. | Accept, attain, assume, support, participate, continue, grow in, be devoted to |
| Organizing | When encountering situations to which more than one value applies, willing to organize the values, determine relationships among values, and accept some values as dominant over others (by the importance to the individual learner). | Organize, select, judge, decide, identify with, develop a plan for, weigh alternatives |
| Characterizing by a value complex | Learner consistently acts in accordance with accepted values and incorporates this behavior as a part of his or her personality. | Believe, practice, continue to, carry out, become part of his or her code of behavior |

for their own learning, and both receptiveness and cooperation can, in some measure, determine their level of achievement. Once motivation is established, a well-organized program in which the learners participate successfully usually encourages them to have a positive attitude toward the subject and instructor.

## DEVELOPING INSTRUCTIONAL OBJECTIVES

Some instructional designers insist that instructional objectives be defined immediately after formulating the goal or statement of general purposes for a topic. Sequentially, this approach may sound correct, but in actual practice it is not always feasible. Although some subject-matter experts (SMEs) can verbalize the direction the instruction should take, others are not able to provide detailed information this early in the design process. To an instructional designer, the content may be unfamiliar, and additional information may be needed to formulate meaningful objectives. Thus, the task analysis element is placed in the instructional design plan preceding the element of instructional objectives.

Writing instructional objectives is a design activity that requires changes and additions as the instruction is developed. Sometimes it is not until the instructional strategies are selected or evaluation methods stated that the ''real'' objectives for a topic are evident. Thus, your project may start with broadly defined objectives that you refine as design progresses. Our experiences have shown that designers often refine and modify the objectives as the SMEs provide additional details during the design process.

## The Basis for Objectives

Objectives are based on the results of the task analysis and provide a refinement and implementation of the needs of and/or goals for a project. If you use only a needs assessment to define your problem, the objectives will relate directly to those needs. If you use a goal analysis, the objectives will reflect a refinement of the goals. There are two cases, however, in which a discrepancy may exist between the goals or needs and the objectives. First, the SME who helps with the task analysis may have a better understanding of the problem and provide different content and focus. Second, the SME simply may take a different approach to solving the problem. In either case, when this discrepancy exists, you should verify the accuracy and validity of the objectives with the group that helped you with the goal analysis or identification of needs.

Instructional objectives identify information necessary to solve the performance problem. Deriving the objectives is a four-step process to be completed after the task analysis. These steps are as follows:

1. Review the task analysis and identify the essential knowledge, tasks (i.e., procedures), and attitudes the learner must master to solve the performance problem.
2. Group the task analysis in clusters with the goals or needs you have identified.
3. Write an objective for each of the goal statements or needs.
4. Write objectives for any additional information that is essential and that is not addressed by an objective.

## Approaches to Objectives

Historically, instructional designers have insisted on the use of precise objectives (often referred to as Mager-style objectives), which evolved from the design and research on programmed instruction. This approach is based on behavioral psychology principles that require the learner to demonstrate an overt response indicating mastery of the content. The Mager (1984c) approach was applied to writing objectives for all three domains of learning: cognitive, psychomotor, and affective. Recent trends in cognitive psychology, however, have prompted a reconsideration of the specification of objectives for each of the learning domains.

In the following sections, we describe how to write different styles of objectives. We begin with the behavioral and cognitive approaches to writing objectives in the cognitive domain, then we describe how to write objectives for the psychomotor and affective domains.

## WRITING OBJECTIVES IN THE COGNITIVE DOMAIN

There are two generally recognized approaches to writing objectives: behavioral and cognitive. The behavioral orientation is typically applied to writing objectives in all the domains, whereas the cognitive approach is best suited for the cognitive domain. The following sections focus on their application in the cognitive domain.

## Behavioral Objectives

A behavioral objective is a precise statement that answers the question, "What behavior can the learner demonstrate to indicate that he or she has mastered the knowledge or skills specified in the instruction?" Ask yourself this question each time you start to formulate an objective; your answer will guide your efforts. To answer this question satisfactorily, you need to recognize that behavioral objectives consist of at least two essential parts and two optional parts.

**Essential Parts.**   Start with an action verb that describes the learning required by the learner or trainee:

> To name
> To operate
> To arrange
> To compare

Follow the action verb with the subject-content reference (e.g., the name of a piece of machinery or the focus of the action) that describes the content addressed by the objective:

> To name *the parts of speech used in a sentence*
> To operate *a video recorder*
> To arrange *parts in order for assembly*
> To compare *points of view expressed on political issues*

Taken together, the action verb (e.g., to name) and the subject-content reference indicate what the student is to achieve.

Undoubtedly, you or the SME can easily choose the content for an objective. Selecting the appropriate action verb to describe the learner's performance is the difficult part of writing objectives. For instructional objectives developed in the cognitive domain, a "shopping list" of verbs that express behaviors on each of the six levels in Bloom's taxonomy can be helpful (see Table 5-5). These verbs can help you identify (and give attention to) the higher intellectual levels in your planning.

## Optional Parts

You may feel that stating the action verb and the content reference completely expresses an instructional objective. Although these two components are adequate in many situations, sometimes it is desirable or necessary to include other parameters as part of the learning requirement. This additional information is particularly important when the instruction has specific or minimum outcome requirements for proficiency. Objectives for such a competency-based program require two additional parts.

**Level of Achievement.**   The performance standard, or criterion, indicates the minimum acceptable performance. It answers questions such as, How well? How

**TABLE 5-5**
Observable verbs for the cognitive domain

| 1. Knowledge | | 2. Comprehension | | 3. Application | |
|---|---|---|---|---|---|
| Recall information | | Interpret information in one's own words | | Use knowledge or general-ization in a new situation | |
| arrange | name | classify | report | apply | operate |
| define | order | describe | restate | choose | practice |
| duplicate | recall | discuss | review | demonstrate | prepare |
| label | relate | explain | select | dramatize | schedule |
| list | repeat | express | sort | employ | sketch |
| match | reproduce | identify | tell | illustrate | solve |
| memorize | | indicate | translate | interpret | use |
| | | locate | | | |

| 4. Analysis | | 5. Synthesis | | 6. Evaluation | |
|---|---|---|---|---|---|
| Break down knowledge into parts and show rel-ationships among parts | | Bring together parts of knowledge to form a whole and build relationships for new situations | | Make judgments on basis of given criteria | |
| analyze | differentiate | arrange | manage | appraise | evaluate |
| appraise | discriminate | assemble | organize | argue | judge |
| calculate | distinguish | collect | plan | assess | predict |
| categorize | examine | compose | prepare | attack | rate |
| compare | experiment | construct | propose | choose | score |
| contrast | inventory | create | set up | compare | select |
| criticize | question | design | synthesize | defend | support |
| diagram | test | formulate | write | estimate | value |

Note: Depending on the meaning for use, some verbs may apply to more than one level.

much? How accurate? How complete? and In what time period? Here are ways in which the performance standard is stated:

> In proper order
> At least 8 out of 10 correct (or 80 percent correct)
> With an accuracy of 2 centimeters
> Within 3 minutes
> Meeting the criteria stated in the manual

The following examples illustrate objectives with an action verb, content, and performance standard:

> To arrange the six steps of water purification *in proper order*
> To troubleshoot circuit problems with *a correct solution rate of 90 percent*
> To measure a client's blood pressure *within 5 mm Hg accuracy as determined by the instructor*
> To design a display that received a rating *of at least 4 relative to the criteria discussed in class*

**Conditions of Performance.**   Conditions result from answers to questions such as, "Is specific equipment required?" "Is access to a certain book, chart, or other reference allowed?" "Are time limitations imposed?" and "Are other specific factors set as conditions for testing?" Conditions are resources necessary for establishing evaluation requirements. They specify the conditions under which the evaluation takes place.

The following statements exemplify instructional objectives, each of which includes a condition:

> Using the hospital's floor map as a guide, locate all fire extinguishers and emergency exits on the floor with 100% accuracy.
>
> Based on assigned readings, compare the cultures of two past civilizations, enumerating at least five characteristics of each.
>
> Given the chart showing the normal growth rate of a redwood tree, predict within 15% accuracy the size of a tree over a five-year period.
>
> Within a three-minute period, set up, zero in, and operate a multimeter tester.

Mager-style instructional objectives follow the form of the objectives illustrated in these examples. When appropriate, include either or both of the optional parts. When no performance standard is included, the assumption is that only a 100% correct response or performance is acceptable. Keep your statements simple and brief. Avoid including so much detail that the effort of writing the objectives becomes discouraging and the requirements seem overwhelming to learners and instructors.

An alternative approach for specifying behavioral objectives is the use of terminal and enabling objectives. A major objective for a topic or task is called a terminal objective. It describes, in behavioral terms, the overall learning outcomes expressed originally as the general purpose for a topic. More than a single terminal objective may be necessary for accomplishing a general purpose. Here are examples of terminal instructional objectives:

> **Topic:** Fetal circulation
> **General purpose:** To acquire knowledge and understanding of the anatomy and physiology of fetal circulation
> **Terminal objective:** To describe the normal circulation pattern within a fetus

> **Topic:** Renaissance and Reformation
> **General purpose:** To understand the changes that took place in European civilization during the late Middle Ages
> **Terminal objective:** To interpret the significant developments taking place as Europeans broke the Continental bonds and established a world hegemony

> **Topic:** The automobile distributor
> **General purpose:** To clean and adjust the distributor for a smooth-running engine
> **Terminal objective:** To service a distributor

The subobjectives that lead to accomplishing the terminal objective are referred to as enabling, or supporting, objectives. Enabling objectives describe the specific behaviors (i.e., single activities or steps) that must be learned or performed, often sequentially, to achieve the terminal objective. For the terminal objectives cited previously, the following enabling objectives are required:

**Terminal objective:** To describe the normal circulation pattern within a fetus
**Enabling objectives:**
1. To name the two types of blood vessels found in the umbilical cord
2. To locate the two shunts that are normal in fetal circulation
3. To label a diagram of fetal circulation, indicating differences in systolic pressure between the left and right sides of the heart

**Terminal objective:** To interpret the significant developments taking place as Europeans broke the Continental bonds and established a world hegemony
**Enabling objectives:**
1. To identify economic developments that emerged in medieval Europe
2. To analyze the political, religious, social, and psychological forces that helped create the Reformation
3. To relate the intellectual and architectural accomplishments of the twelfth century to the foundations for the Renaissance

**Terminal objective:** To service a distributor
**Enabling objectives:**
1. To identify the four main parts of a distributor
2. To remove and clean the distributor cap
3. To remove and clean the rotor
4. To clean and install breaker points
5. To set breaker points

**A Caution.** When instructional designers first start to write objectives, they sometimes tend to write descriptions of what is to occur during the instruction and then consider these statements to be instructional objectives (e.g., "To view a videotape on ecological safeguards," "To teach the student how...," or "To read pages 45 through 70 in the text"). These statements are activities or processes; they do not indicate learning outcomes. An instructional objective should focus on outcomes or products rather than on process. If you are not sure whether what you are stating is an objective, ask yourself, "Is this outcome what I want the learner to know or demonstrate after completing the topic or unit?" If the answer is no, you need to revise your objective. Similarly, designers often confuse the terminal and enabling objectives, resulting in an overly complex objective. We prefer the Mager style rather than the terminal-enabling format for instructional design projects because they are precise and easier to use for designing instructional strategy.

## Cognitive Objectives

Gronlund (1985, 1995, 2004) suggested an alternative approach to Mager's for writing instructional objectives in the cognitive domain. Both behavioral objectives and cognitive objectives specify learning as outcomes. Cognitive objectives, however, are stated in two parts. First is a statement of the general instructional objective. General objectives are stated in broad terms to encompass a domain of learning (e.g., comprehend, understand, apply, use, interpret, evaluate):

Selects information using ERIC
Understands the meaning of the terms used in the gas laws
Interprets a graph
Comprehends the meaning of a poem

These general statements indicate the overall outcome of the instruction. Like a behavioral objective, they focus on the products or outcomes of the instruction, not the process. Statements that include words such as *gains, views*, or *acquires* are indicators that the designer is focusing on the learning process instead of the outcomes. Thus, an objective written as "The learner will gain ..." is focusing on the process and should be rewritten as "The learner interprets ..." to focus on the outcome.

The second part of a cognitive objective is one or more samples of the specific types of performance that indicate mastery of the objective. Following are examples:

Selects information using ERIC
1. Finds an article on a given topic
2. Compiles a bibliography of related literature
3. Identifies narrower and broader terms for a search
Interprets a graph
1. Determines the group that sold the most
2. Determines the groups that were below average
3. Determines the year with the greatest number of sales
Conducts effective meetings
1. Prepares an agenda prior to the meeting
2. Arranges the room for effective communication
3. States the intended outcomes at the beginning of the meeting

Why use cognitive objectives instead of behavioral objectives? If we compare cognitive objectives to Mager-type behavioral objectives, we find they both specify a student performance in specific, measurable terms. However, behavioral objectives become the end rather than the means for instruction. Cognitive-style objectives overcome this problem by first stating a general objective (similar in structure to the terminal objective) to communicate the intent (e.g., "To interpret the graph"). A behavioral objective might oversimplify the intent by stating the outcome as "Identify the tallest bar on the chart." The resulting instruction from the behavioral objective, then, focuses on measuring the elements of the graph rather than interpreting it. The sample performances of the cognitive objective simply indicate behaviors that help the teacher or instructor to determine when the learner has achieved the higher-level intent.

$$\boxed{\text{Expert's Edge}}$$

## Legal Outcomes

One of my first projects as an instructional designer for the University of British Columbia's Department of Distance Education and Technology was the development of a new (not repurposed) Web-based course on Online Mediation, for the Dispute Resolution Program, Faculty of Law. The faculty member selected to teach it was an experienced classroom instructor but new to Web-based instruction. Nevertheless, she was open to new approaches and particularly wanted to look at problem-based learning (PBL) as a major learning strategy.

The main target audience for the course was second-year law students from the University of British Columbia and the University of Victoria. At the time when I began to work with her, the faculty member had only a rough idea of what the course structure might entail, but had a relatively solid understanding of the content and skills she wanted the students to learn. The content was to include such concepts as types of online dispute resolution available, online dispute resolution terminology, and issues in online dispute resolution, with a strong emphasis on such "practical" online dispute resolution skills as advocacy, rapport building, and client–counsel communication.

At this stage, I decided the best course of action was to work with the faculty member to look carefully at her course learning outcomes. In my experience, most university faculty are well practiced in writing instructional objectives and, while they may not always be cognizant of the range of possibilities, they either come to a project with a preference or are bound by a faculty approach or existing curriculum document. In this case, the faculty member was open to suggestion, although opposed to the perceived narrowness and detail of performance objectives. Clearly, this was a situation that indicated the use of some sort of cognitive learning outcomes, but which of the many approaches and taxonomies would suit her needs?

This faculty member, like many educators, was most familiar with the general categories of Bloom et al.'s (1956) taxonomy and had developed an initial list using the six groupings: knowledge, comprehension, application, analysis, synthesis, and evaluation. Not surprisingly, the largest category was knowledge. This emphasis presented a problem since the whole point of the course was to teach the students to analyze a dispute and then decide on (or even design) an appropriate method of mediation that they would then carry out (apply). There seemed to be insufficient focus on the "higher-order" learning outcomes she wanted the students to achieve.

What I decided to do was to continue to work with Bloom's taxonomy (in a slightly modified format as per the following), since she was comfortable with that approach. We examined and discussed the wording in her initial list and made modifications to it, including rewording some outcomes and switching them to "higher-level" categories. To complement this process, since she was open to rethinking her learning outcomes, we also looked over a couple of other taxonomies (e.g., the Iowa Department of Education's Integrated Thinking Model) that place designing, problem solving, and decision making—all-important skills for this course—at the top of the pecking order and that, it can be argued, subsume Bloom's process categories of analyzing and evaluating. While we didn't switch to a new taxonomy, we were able to use aspects of the other approaches to revise some of the initial outcome wordings to take into account these processes. As a result, I believe we were able to improve the range and breadth of what she wanted the students to learn from the course. We also used the new learning outcomes to guide us in developing instructional strategies appropriate to help them achieve these outcomes. Here is a sampling of what we came up with:

Remember
Recall the basic terminology for online dispute resolution (DR)
Recall the options available for online dispute resolution (synchronous/ asynchronous mediation, arbitration, blind bidding, etc.)

Understand
Explain the process of online mediation
Interpret the issues raised by an Agreement to Mediate

Apply
Practice the skills required of an advocate in an online environment (reframing, paraphrasing, context building through documentary exchange, etc.)
Apply client interview skills through conduct of live client interview and follow-up e-mail interviews

Analyze
Analyze a transcript of online mediation to identify strengths and weaknesses of advocates' approaches
Compare and contrast effectiveness of a variety of online DR processes in resolution of single dispute

Create
Recommend the choice of DR process for a client in specific circumstances based on integration of knowledge regarding process choice, client profile, legal and nonlegal factors raised by facts
Utilize existing information to develop a range of available options for other party

Evaluate
During online mediation, argue for client's preferred resolution
Assess arguments and offers of opposing counsel

### Reference

Bloom, B. S., Englehart, M. D., Furst, E. J., Hill, W. H., & Krathwohl, D. R. (1956). *A taxonomy of educational objectives: Handbook I. The cognitive domain*. New York: McKay.

Richard F. Kenny is an instructional designer with the Department of Distance Education and Technology and an adjunct professor with the faculty of education at the University of British Columbia, Canada. Rick works with members of such faculties as agriculture, education, forestry, law, and nursing to design and develop Web-based instruction. He also edits the *Canadian Journal of Learning and Technology*. Rick's research agenda focuses on the design and development of emerging technologies to foster higher-order thinking.

Behavioral objectives are particularly well suited for mastery learning instruction for which the learner must demonstrate specific behaviors to advance to the next level. For example, a course that stresses how to produce a specific report, such as sales by departments for a given month, might best be defined with behavioral objectives. These objectives will accurately describe the outcome, in this case, "The learner will print a report indicating sales revenue by department," which involves a repetitive task of entering the month and department name.

Cognitive objectives are well suited for describing higher levels of learning. For example, in a course that emphasizes labor negotiation skills, the designer might develop a cognitive objective to describe the outcome related to evaluating a contract offer: "The learner will comprehend the implications of an offer." The examples of behaviors related to this outcome could focus on specifics such as "calculating the cost of the contract to the company," "identifying possible counteroffers," and "determining long-range implications." Cognitive objectives can be written for all three domains of learning.

## WRITING OBJECTIVES FOR THE PSYCHOMOTOR DOMAIN

Psychomotor skills are the most easily observed of the three domains. Objectives in this domain rely on the same four objective parts; however, the emphasis is often different. For example, the verb *demonstrate* is frequently used to describe the behavior. Explicitly stated conditions are often required for psychomotor objectives. For example, is the learner to use an electric drill or a manually powered drill? Are the ground balls thrown or hit by a batter? Similarly, psychomotor objectives are more likely to require specific criteria because 100% accuracy (e.g., all 10 shots in the bull's-eye) often is not expected of a novice. Thus, we might have a number of objectives ranging from hitting a large target by the end of the first practice to eventually scoring a specific number of points. Following are examples of behavioral objectives in the psychomotor domain:

> Given five rounds of ammunition, the learner will shoot each round from 50 feet so that each hits within a 7-inch circle.
> Given five rounds of ammunition, the learner will score a total of 30 points while firing from a distance of 50 feet.

> Given two 15-inch straight needles and yarn, the learner will cast on 50 stitches of equal size and correct tension.

Time is often used with psychomotor objectives, but it may be difficult to determine whether time is a condition or a criterion in behavioral objectives.

Let's examine two additional psychomotor objectives:

> Students will run a quarter-mile around a track in under 2 minutes.
>
> Given a malfunctioning light switch, the student will correctly replace the switch in 30 minutes.

In the first objective, time (2 minutes) is a criterion because it is conceivable that some students are not capable of running a quarter-mile in less than 2 minutes. Thus, the time is a standard for measurement. The 30-minute time limit in the second objective is a condition, because almost any physically able student will be capable of completing the task in less than 30 minutes.

To summarize, if the time factor is used to measure the performance, then it is a criterion for the objective. If the time factor is used to set a maximum time limit and there is another criterion (e.g., "correctly replace"), then time is a condition.

## WRITING OBJECTIVES FOR THE AFFECTIVE DOMAIN

The affective domain encompasses more abstract behaviors (e.g., attitudes, feelings, and appreciations) that are relatively difficult to observe and measure. One method of developing objectives in this domain is for the designer to specify behaviors indirectly by inferring from what he or she can observe. What a learner does or says is assumed as evidence of behavior relating to an affective objective.

Some behaviors in this area are difficult to identify, let alone to name and measure. How, for instance, do you measure an attitude of appreciating the importance of good nutrition or developing a positive relationship with company clients? Such attitudes are inferred only indirectly from secondary clues. When developing an affective objective, it is often useful to divide the objective into two parts. First, identify the cognitive component, or "thought," that describes the attitude. Second, identify a behavior that when observed would represent the attitude. This behavior is then used to write the affective objective.

To measure an attitude about an activity, we must generalize from learner behaviors that indicate the student is developing or has developed the attitude. The following examples illustrate behaviors indicating a positive attitude:

> The learner says he or she likes the activity.
>
> The learner selects the activity in place of other possible activities.
>
> The learner participates in the activity with much enthusiasm.
>
> The learner shares his or her interest in the activity by discussing it with others or by encouraging others to participate.

If the instructional objective is "to appreciate the importance of good nutrition," accomplishment is demonstrated by the following behaviors:

> Is observed eating only foods of high nutritional value (no junk foods or refined products)

Readily advises other people about the value of nutritious foods
Voluntarily reads books and articles describing good nutrition practices
Attends lectures and workshops presented by nutrition authorities

If the instructional objective is "to develop a positive relationship with company clients," evidence of accomplishment can be shown if the employee does the following:

Is prompt for appointments with clients
Calls each client by name, is courteous, and speaks in a friendly tone
Shows an interest in the client as a person by talking about matters other than
    business that are mutually interesting
Spends extra time with a client, as necessary
Provides requested information promptly

Admittedly, the evidence in these examples indicates only the possible fulfill-ment of an attitudinal objective and does not measure it directly. Mager (1984a) called these behaviors tendencies toward exhibiting a positive attitude to a subject or a situation. The learner's attitude is considered negative if he or she shows avoid-ance tendencies. Notice, however, that Mager's approach to affective objectives is very similar to Gronlund's (1985, 1995) cognitive approach. They both begin with a general behavior and then proceed to specific example behaviors that the instructor uses to infer the presence of the attitude.

In the book *Goal Analysis*, Mager (1984b) suggested that, if employees are to exhibit safety consciousness, they are expected to practice the following behaviors: "Report safety hazards; wear safety equipment; follow safety rules; practice good housekeeping by keeping the work area free of dirt and loose tools; encourage safe practice in others by reminding them to wear safety equipment; and so forth" (pp. 46–47). This example is similar to a cognitive objective in that it states a general purpose—safety consciousness—and then provides specific examples of behaviors indicating the practice of safety.

Gronlund's and Mager's approaches can help you refine ways of indicating attitudinal objectives and then setting a degree of measurement for them. (For additional help in identifying and writing affective domain objectives, refer to the work of Lee and Merrill, 1972.) Table 5-6 is a list of verbs you may find useful as you state instructional objectives in this domain.

**TABLE 5-6**
Affective verbs

| | | |
|---|---|---|
| acclaims | cooperates | joins |
| agrees | defends | offers |
| argues | disagrees | participates in |
| assumes | disputes | praises |
| attempts | engages in | resists |
| avoids | helps | shares |
| challenges | is attentive to | volunteers |

Realistically, we must recognize that there are many important objectives that cannot result in measurable outcomes. Eisner (1969) uses the term *expressive objectives* to describe those for which specific outcomes are not readily stated. These objectives identify situations for the learner. An expressive objective may allow for self-discovery, originality, and inventiveness, with a result that surprises both the learner and the instructor. For example, "To develop a feeling of personal adequacy in athletic performance" is an expressive objective. By stating such nonmeasurable objectives during planning, you can at least identify aspects of instructional goals that have personal or social importance and thus can make a start on deciding how to achieve them.

## CLASSIFYING OBJECTIVES

The cognitive and affective domains comprise sequential hierarchies starting from low levels of learning or behavior and progressing through more intellectual or sophisticated levels. The psychomotor domain does not exhibit as consistent a sequencing pattern as do the other two domains.

These three domains are useful for determining the level of learning for each objective and for checking that the objectives are distributed across several levels rather than clumped as rote memory objectives. The next element of the design process is to use the objectives as a basis for developing the instructional strategies. We accomplish this task by classifying the objectives into a matrix that is then used to prescribe the instructional strategy. The three taxonomies just discussed are not well suited for developing instructional strategies for two reasons: First, an objective can often be classified into more than one level because the levels are not mutually exclusive. Second, the taxonomies do not provide prescriptive instructional strategies for each level. The following pages describe two different models for classifying objectives and then prescribing instructional strategies. The Mager and Beach (1967) model is particularly suited for classroom instruction, whereas the performance-content matrix provides a structured instructional design approach.

### Mager and Beach's Model

Mager and Beach (1967) described a performance classification approach in their book *Developing Vocational Instruction*. Objectives are classified into one of five categories, or performance types, and then ranked by difficulty (see Table 5-7).

Objectives that require the learner to speak in a specific manner are classified as speech performance objectives. This category is limited to speaking; written verbal responses are not classified in this performance category. *Manipulation* is the execution of a psychomotor skill, which can range from a simple skill such as dialing a phone number to a complex machine operation. Objectives requiring the rote memorization of information (e.g., listing two types of screwdrivers) are classified in the recall category. The discrimination category requires the learner to distinguish between two objects (e.g., a Phillips-head and a flat-head screwdriver) or two events (e.g., a strike and a ball). Objectives that require the student to

**TABLE 5-7**

Mager and Beach's performance types

| Objective | Performance | Learning Difficulty |
|---|---|---|
| When answering the phone, the salesperson will correctly identify the company and self. | Speech | Easy |
| Salesperson will correctly enter the customer's ID number into the computer. | Manipulation | Easy |
| The student will demonstrate how to properly sharpen a serrated knife. | Manipulation | Difficult |
| Salesperson will identify to whom he or she transfers a customer with a problem. | Recall | Easy |
| Salesperson will determine shipping time based on zip code and package size. | Discrimination | Moderately difficult |
| When an article is out of stock, the salesperson will suggest an alternative item. | Problem solving | Difficult |

determine what to do are classified as problem-solving performances. Finally, each objective is classified as easy, moderately difficult, difficult, or very difficult to perform based on both the instructional designer's observations during the task analysis and input from the SME.

## Expanded Performance-Content Matrix Model

In his component display theory, Merrill (1983) proposed another useful tool for classifying objectives. Although Merrill's performance-content matrix is not hierarchical like Bloom's taxonomy, it does provide a means of determining which type of instructional strategy to use to master the objective. The expanded model (see Table 5-8) builds on Merrill's model to account for psychomotor, affective, and interpersonal tasks that are not included in Merrill's component display theory. Unlike Bloom's taxonomy, this model classifies types of content and performance as opposed to levels of learning. In addition, Bloom's model is descriptive in that it describes different levels of learning. Instructional design models must prescribe optimum instructional strategies for achieving an objective. Thus, like Merrill's model, the present model uses content categories that are then used to prescribe instructional strategies (see Chapter 7).

The content aspect of the matrix provides six categories for classifying objectives. Each objective is classified into one category. If the objective fits into two categories, it needs to be refined and stated as two separate objectives. The following paragraphs briefly review each of the content categories.

**Fact.**  A fact is a statement that associates one item with another. The statement "Columbus was an explorer" associates the words *Columbus* and *explorer*. Learning

**TABLE 5-8**
Expanded performance-content matrix

| Content | Performance | |
|---|---|---|
| | **Recall** | **Application** |
| Fact | | |
| Concept | | |
| Principles and rules | | |
| Procedure | | |
| Interpersonal | | |
| Attitude | | |

that the symbol *H* represents hydrogen in a chemical equation is also a fact that associates *H* with hydrogen. Facts are memorized for later recall.

**Concept.**    Concepts are categories we use for simplifying the world. It is much easier to refer to two-wheeled, self-propelled vehicles as bicycles than to remember the brand name of every bike. Examples of concepts are *circle, car, box, woman, mirror*, and *tree*. We can identify several different models of automobiles, but we classify each as a car, just as we group maple, oak, and pine trees in the category of *tree*.

**Principles and Rules.**    Principles and rules express relationships between concepts. For example, "Metal expands when its temperature is increased" expresses a causal relationship between the concepts of metal and temperature. Similarly, "Providing reinforcement increases the chances the behavior will be repeated" expresses a relationship between learning (repeating a behavior) and reinforcement.

**Procedure.**    A procedure is a sequence of steps one follows to achieve a goal. Procedures can describe primarily cognitive operations such as solving a quadratic equation, operations that involves both cognitive and psychomotor operations such as taking a voltmeter reading, and primarily psychomotor operations such as driving a nail. Procedures can also vary in difficulty from repetitive tasks (e.g., driving a nail) to problem-solving tasks (e.g., debugging a computer program).

**Interpersonal Skills.**    This category describes spoken and nonverbal (i.e., body language) interaction between two or more people. For example, an objective that describes the phone skills of a help-desk professional or the skills in making an effective presentation would be classified as interpersonal skills. Similarly, a course designed to improve the skills of managers interviewed on television by improving their posture and sitting habits to project confidence would be grouped in this category.

**Attitude.**    Objectives that seek to change or modify the learner's attitude are classified in this category. Affective objectives can vary from simply developing an awareness of different options to changes in attitudes that result in action, such as stopping theft of company materials.

The second part of the model is the performance specified in the objective. The behavior or performance specified in the objective is considered and then classified as either recall or application.

**Recall.**   Objectives that specify that the learner simply memorize information for later recall (e.g., "Name an explorer," "Define reinforcement") are classified as recall performance. Recall performance encompasses those behaviors at the lower levels of Bloom's taxonomy. Verbs such as *list, define,* and *name* are often cues of recall performance.

**Application.**   When the performance requires the learner to use or apply the information, the objective is classified as application. For example, an objective that requires the learner to demonstrate the use of reinforcement in a microteaching lesson would be classified as application. Verbs such as *demonstrate, discriminate,* and *solve* are cues that the performance requires an application of the content. Note that facts are always classified as recall because they cannot be applied.

Later chapters use this expanded performance-content matrix to prescribe instructional strategies to help the learner achieve the objective.

## DIFFICULTIES IN WRITING OBJECTIVES

One reason many people shy away from stating precise objectives is that formulating them demands much thought and effort. Each objective should be unambiguous. It must communicate exactly the same thing to all learners and to other instructors and designers. Many instructors are not accustomed to such exactness in instructional planning. For too long we educators have based our teaching on broad generalizations, often leaving it up to the learner to interpret what we actually mean.

Not until the importance of objectives for an instructional program becomes apparent are instructors or designers willing to put sincere effort into preparing them. Then the difficulties and frustrations are taken in stride, and they gradually develop a habit and pattern for expressing as many of the desired outcomes of effective learning as possible in specific, meaningful terms.

## PROS AND CONS OF WRITING OBJECTIVES

As you studied the content of this chapter, you no doubt considered your own feelings and attitudes relative to the importance of writing instructional objectives. Some designers and instructors readily accept the position taken in this book: that it is important to write observable and measurable objectives whenever possible. Others have strong views against such specificity, believing that objectives are often unnecessary or that the important outcomes of a program do not lend themselves to objective statements. These latter individuals may feel that the more important long-term outcomes of an instructional program are hard to define and often are unmeasurable.

This position should not be an either/or situation. Admittedly, most objectives relate to short-term goals, attainable during a course or training program. Some, however, may contribute to long-term goals, such as the development of analytical skills or decision-making abilities. These high-level objectives may not be *fully* measurable until sometime in the future. Therefore, it is reasonable at times to assume that certain objectives cannot be completely satisfied during the planned instructional program. For example, if we design a course to teach a manager how to make an effective presentation, then it is unlikely that a manager will fully develop this skill in a couple of days. Rather, the managers would develop a basic level of competence during the course, and then we would expect their presentation skills to improve over time as they ''practice'' making presentations. Instructors and designers can do a follow-up evaluation after a course to determine learner competencies relative to such important long-term objectives.

If you would like to read a rationale that examines all aspects of this topic of objectives, Davies (1976) may be most helpful. He puts objectives in perspective, based on his review of literature and research in the field of curriculum design.

## SUMMARY

1. The specification of instructional objectives plays a key role in the procedure for systematically planning instruction.
2. The objectives indicate what a learner is expected to do after completing a unit of instruction, and they are expressed in precise, unambiguous terms. We have provided both a strict behavioral approach and a more flexible cognitive approach to specifying instructional objectives.
3. Objectives are important for instructional designers and instructors. They guide them in planning instruction and devising tests.
4. Objectives are grouped into cognitive, psychomotor, and affective domains within which increasingly higher levels of intellectual aptitude, skill ability, and emotional behavior are recognized. The domains are closely related because a single major objective can require learning in more than one area.
5. Behavioral objectives consist of an action verb and subject-content reference; they may also include a performance standard and/or conditions. Cognitive objectives consist of a general objective and then samples of student performance.
6. Objectives for higher intellectual levels are more difficult, yet more important, to specify. Objectives in the affective domain are identified indirectly by inferring learner acceptance of an attitude from observable behavior.
7. Objectives are organized and sequenced by various methods to ensure that the more advanced objectives receive suitable attention. After the objectives are specified, they are classified into categories using one of the schemes presented. These classifications are then used to prescribe an appropriate instructional strategy.

8. The subject matter relating to instructional objectives as treated in this chapter provides the essential information to guide you in developing your own objectives and in assisting a subject-matter expert to write instructional objectives.

## THE ID PROCESS

A list of instructional objectives and their classification in the expanded performance-content matrix is the output for this step of the instructional design process. The objectives are derived from the task analysis and represent the major tasks, knowledge, and attitudes defined by the analysis. These objectives are the starting point for the design of the instructional strategies. However, as you design the strategies and develop the instruction you will often find the need for more details in your task analysis. This additional analysis and even the strategy design process can lead to a refinement of your objectives.

Once you have written your objectives, you can collect feedback from your SME and other instructional designers (see Chapter 13 for specific formative evaluation strategies). Your SME and other content experts can help you determine whether the objectives will support a solution for the performance problem. Other instructional designers can help you ensure that your objectives are appropriate for the task analysis and for solving the performance problem.

## APPLICATION

1. Change the verb in each of the following phrases to one that is observable.
   a. The learner will understand . . .
   b. The learner will recognize . . .
   c. The learner will feel . . .
2. Write a cognitive objective for the following task: *The customer service representative will calm an upset customer*.
3. Classify each of the following objectives into the expanded performance-content matrix.
   _____ a. On a posttest following the completion of this instructional unit, the learner will state the inherent rate of the sinus node, atrioventricular node, and His-Purkinje system with 100% accuracy.
   _____ b. The system operator will remove the pH sensor.
   _____ c. Given a control panel, the system operator will identify the location of the override switch.
   _____ d. Given five black-and-white photographs of insects, the learner will correctly identify the three insects detrimental to corn.
   _____ e. Given a list of three insecticides and a list of five insects, the learner will correctly match the insect to the insecticide that kills or controls it.
   _____ f. The learner will list the four steps to reconcile a discrepancy in the piece count.

_____ g. Given the hearing evaluation form and a patient, the learner will correctly administer a hearing test.

_____ h. Given a choice of various musical CDs, the student will listen to those from the Baroque period.

## ANSWERS

1. Change the verb in the following phrases to one that is observable:
   a. The learner will understand (classify, discuss, identify, select, analyze, distinguish) . . .
   b. The learner will recognize (identify, select, categorize, indicate, locate) . . .
   c. The learner will feel (express, attempt, defend, share, participate in, choose) . . .
   (Note the problems of dealing with ambiguous verbs and attempting to find agreement on their meaning!)
2. Write a cognitive objective for the following task: *The customer service representative calms an upset customer.*
   • Listens to customer's complaint without interrupting
   • Asks appropriate questions to define customer's problem/concern
   • Assures customer complaint will be addressed
   • Demonstrates desire to help customer
   • Takes responsibility for helping customer
   • Maintains a balance between customer's request and company's interests
   • Keeps a log of the call
   • Uses questions to gather information before taking action
3. Classify each of the following objectives into the expanded performance-content matrix.
   a. Fact/Recall
   b. Procedure/Application
   c. Fact/Recall
   d. Concept/Application
   e. Fact/Recall
   f. Procedure/Recall
   g. Procedure/Application
   h. Attitude/Application

## QUALITY MANAGEMENT

The quality check for objectives consists of two steps. First, you need to check each objective to determine that it is complete and adequately describes the intended outcome. The objectives should be concise to avoid misinterpretation. Behavioral objectives should include a verb and related content, conditions, and criteria. Cognitive objectives should have a general objective and adequate descriptions of learner performance. Second, determine whether the objectives are in alignment with your task analysis and goals. The objectives should represent the knowledge and skills identified in your task analysis. To avoid having a large number of objectives, you may need to write your objectives at a higher level of learning. Next, check your objectives against the goals and/or needs identified for the problem. The objectives should support the achievement of the goals and alleviation of the needs. If there is a discrepancy between the objectives and the problem, then there are two courses of action. First, you can revise your problem and goals to more accurately reflect the problem. Second, revise the task analysis and/or objectives to focus more on the problem and goals.

## INSTRUCTIONAL DESIGN: DECISIONS AND CHOICES

### Writing Objectives

You began to think about what the learner needs to *know* and *do* during your initial client meeting, and then you considered the goals in-depth as you conducted the task analysis. With the task analysis as your guide, you are ready to formulate the instructional objectives.

To begin, you write the phrase, "The learner will . . ." as a prompt to start the objective:

*The learner will **use** a fire extinguisher.*

[The action verb has been set boldface to help ensure that the action or performance is clear to anyone who reads the objective.]

On rereading the objective, however, you realize that the action (i.e., using a fire extinguisher) does not reflect the final performance (i.e., putting out a fire). Using a fire extinguisher is the *means* or *process*, whereas putting out the fire is the *end* (i.e., product), or the accomplishment. Some designers would take the position that "putting out" the fire is not the intent of the objective because the learner could use the fire extinguisher yet fail to put out the fire. The desired performance is the "attempt to use" and "skill in using" the fire extinguisher and the "decision" that the learner makes that fighting the fire does not place him or her at risk. Either action (using a fire extinguisher or putting out the fire) can be employed for the objective—but judging the correctness of the performance changes based on the verb. Your next step is to make the objective more specific by adding conditions (i.e., givens):

*Given a dry-chemical, multiclass fire extinguisher and a trash container full of burning paper, the learner will **put out** the fire.*

The conditions make clear the size of fire (as opposed to an entire house engulfed in flames) as well as a common context. The criterion is implied in the action verb—if the fire is extinguished, then the learner has successfully mastered the objective. You consider adding a criterion: *Given a dry-chemical, multiclass fire extinguisher and a trash container full of burning paper, the learner will **put out** the fire within three minutes.* However, as you think more deeply about the performance and recall your interview with the client concerning the errors made by the mailroom clerk, you realize that if the learner does not pull the fire alarm and evacuate employees from the building, then the learner will have failed to follow emergency procedures and act safely. Here's your final version of the objective:

*Given a dry-chemical, multiclass fire extinguisher and a fire burning in a trash container full of paper in an office setting, the learner will **extinguish** the fire by correctly using the fire extinguisher.*

[You have revised the objective several times to improve precision and clarity. The criteria for this objective were derived from reviewing the task analysis. You have included the phrase "by correctly using the fire extinguisher" as the criterion; otherwise, the learner could conceivably use a 2-liter bottle of soda to attempt to extinguish the fire.]

## Refining the Objectives

Let's examine another objective from the instructional program that needs revision: *The instructor will **describe** types of fire extinguishers.*

[Although the action verb is clear, this is not an objective. An objective focuses on what the learner must know or do, not what the instructor will do to help the learner.]

Here's a rewrite of the objective: *The learner will **use** PowerPoint to learn types of fire extinguishers.*

[This is a poor objective. The objective focuses on the learning process (i.e., using PowerPoint), rather than on the knowledge or skill that the learner must acquire. As written, the objective says that the learner needs to learn how to use PowerPoint.]

Here's the third rewrite: *Given one of several types of combustible materials, **select** an appropriate type of fire extinguisher.*

[The phrase "the learner will" or "the learner will be able to" does not have to be included in an objective. It is understood that an instructional objective specifies what the learner must know or do. The conditions are adequate yet could be made more specific (e.g., related to class A, B, and C combustible materials). The criterion for mastery is implied as "100% accuracy." Stating the level of mastery required would improve precision.]

## Putting It All Together

Here's the final set of objectives for the project:

> *Given a dry chemical multiclass fire extinguisher and a fire burning in a trash container full of paper in an office setting, the learner will **extinguish** the fire by correctly using the fire extinguisher.*
>
> *After completing this unit, the learner will correctly state the three components necessary to start a fire.*
>
> *Given an example of a fire, the learner will correctly classify the class of fire.*
>
> *Given a variety of fire extinguishers, the learner will correctly identify each type of fire extinguisher.*
>
> *Given a description of the combustible material in a fire, the learner will select the correct fire extinguisher to extinguish the fire.*

*The learner will demonstrate the appropriate response to a fire in an office setting.*
  a. *Demonstrates how to activate the fire alarm*
  b. *Describes how to assist with evacuation of employees*
  c. *Describes when to and when not to attempt to fight the fire*
  d. *Ensures that there is an evacuation route before attempting to fight the fire*
  e. *Selects the appropriate type of fire extinguisher*

[Notice how each objective relates back to the task analysis. All the content in the task analysis is incorporated into these objectives. Second, note how a cognitive objective was used for the final objective. The focus is on a broad task (i.e., response to a fire), and then specific types of performance are provided to evaluate the learner's response. Third, note how some objectives involve the *recall* of concepts and procedures (e.g., list, describe, identify), whereas other objectives involve *application* (e.g., select, extinguish). Fourth, the instructional designer determines the level of detail and the inclusion of conditions and criteria based on the project context, the preferences of the client, and the audience for the instruction. A client might prefer the full-blown Magerian-style performance objective or view this objective as excessive. The key deciding factor is, does the objective clearly communicate what the learner must know or do?]

## REFERENCES

Bloom, B. S., Englehart, M. D., Furst, E. J., Hill, W. H., & Krathwohl, D. R. (1956). *A taxonomy of educational objectives: Handbook I. The cognitive domain.* New York: McKay.

Davies, I. K. (1976). *Objectives in curriculum design.* New York: McGraw-Hill.

Eisner, E. W. (1969). Instructional and expressive objectives: Their formulation and use in curriculum. In W. J. Popham (Ed.), *Instructional objectives: An analysis of emerging issues* (pp. 13–18). Chicago: Rand McNally.

Gronlund, N. E. (1985). *Stating behavioral objectives for classroom instruction.* New York: Macmillan.

Gronlund, N. E. (1995). *How to write and use instructional objectives* (5th ed.). Englewood Cliffs, NJ: Prentice Hall.

Gronlund, N. E. (2004). *Writing instructional objectives for teaching and assessment* (7th ed.). Upper Saddle River, NJ: Prentice Hall.

Heinich, R., Molenda, M., & Russell, J. D. (1993). *Instructional media and the new technologies of instruction* (4th ed.). New York: Macmillan.

Kibler, R. J. (1981). *Objectives for instruction and evaluation.* Boston: Allyn & Bacon.

Krathwohl, D. R., Bloom, B. S., & Masia, B. B. (1964). *A taxonomy of educational objectives: Handbook II. The affective domain.* New York: McKay.

Lee, B. N., & Merrill, D. M. (1972). *Writing complete affective objectives: A short course.* Belmont, CA: Wadsworth.

Mager, R. F. (1984a). *Developing attitude toward learning* (2nd ed.). Belmont, CA: Pitman.

Mager, R. F. (1984b). *Goal analysis* (2nd ed.). Belmont, CA: Lake.

Mager, R. F. (1984c). *Preparing instructional objectives* (2nd ed.). Belmont, CA: Pitman.

Mager, R. F., & Beach, K. M. (1967). *Developing vocational instruction.* Belmont, CA: Pitman.

Merrill, M. D. (1983). Component display theory. In C. M. Reigeluth (Ed.), *Instructional-design theories and models: An overview of their current status* (pp. 282–333). Hillsdale, NJ: Erlbaum.

CHAPTER ( **6** )

# Designing the Instruction: Sequencing

## GETTING STARTED

You work for a national telecommunication corporation that employs 2,000 people in 30 call centers around the country. These individuals sell the company's services, which range from simple telephone service to voice mail, 800 numbers, and Internet access. This group experiences a high turnover rate of approximately 30% a year. In 12 months, the company will install a new computer system that integrates all the services into one system (as opposed to the 14 individual computer systems needed now for the various products). You are responsible for developing the training to teach this group of salespeople the products the company offers and the process for determining the pricing of each product based on past or projected usage. There are several options for sequencing the content. For example, you could organize the sequencing of the products based on their appeal to the learner (i.e., interest), their sales rate, or the number of inquiries they elicit from customers (e.g., residential long-distance service before voice mail). Or you could sequence them based on prerequisites such as 800 numbers, for example, before discussing the total small business package, which includes voice mail and 800 numbers. How would you sequence the information for both the naive and the experienced learners?

# QUESTIONS TO CONSIDER

"Can sequencing the content improve the learner's understanding?"

"What strategies are available to help me sequence a unit?"

"When do I determine the sequencing of the content?"

"What are the benefits of using a sequencing scheme?"

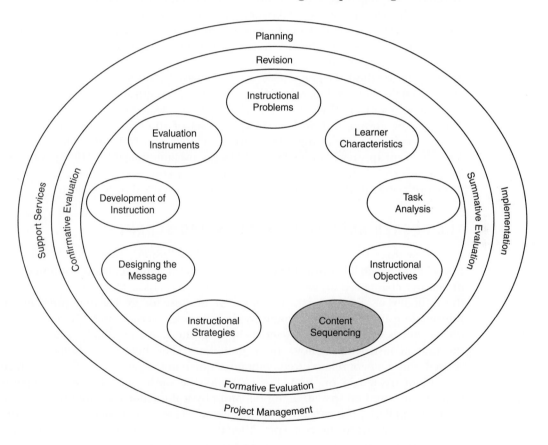

Once you have developed the objectives, you are ready to determine the optimum sequence for the instruction. As you completed the task analysis, you may have made mental notes as to how you might present the content. Instructional designers recognize that the sequence the subject-matter expert (SME) presented during the task analysis may not be the most appropriate sequence for learning the content. This chapter focuses on how to determine the most appropriate sequence for presenting the content related to each objective.

Sequencing is the efficient ordering of content in such a way as to help the learner achieve the objectives. For some objectives, the sequence is suggested by the procedure. For example, when teaching someone how to change a tire, it would seem more appropriate to teach where the tools are located before teaching how to remove the lug nuts. Other topics, however, have a less obvious sequence. A course on how to write a research paper has several possible sequences, all of which are equally effective. For example, one instructor might start with how to read a research paper, whereas another might first teach how to use the library. There are several general methods of sequencing content. One well-known method is the prerequisite method (Gagné, 1985), which is based on a learning hierarchy that identifies skills that are dependent on other skills. Prerequisite skills are taught first (e.g., how to sort checks before marking them as cleared). A second approach, described by Posner and Strike (1976), is a set of strategies for sequencing the instruction based on learning-related, world-related, and concept-related content. A more recent approach is one described by English and Reigeluth (1996) as part of Reigeluth's elaboration theory. This chapter focuses on two sequencing strategies: those prescribed by Posner and Strike and those prescribed by Reigeluth.

## THE POSNER AND STRIKE SEQUENCING SCHEMES

We review three sequencing schemes proposed by Posner and Strike (1976). The first scheme, which is learning related, suggests ways of sequencing the content based on learner characteristics identified in the learner analysis. This scheme considers the difficulty of the material, its appeal or interest to the learner, prerequisite information, and the learner's cognitive development. Because this scheme is based on the needs of the learner, it seems appropriate that the initial sequencing of the unit of instruction follows these guidelines. The next two schemes, world-related and concept-related, recommend sequencing schemes based on the type of content treated in the unit. For example, the world-related scheme suggests sequencing based on spatial, temporal, and physical relationships identified in the content. Similarly, the concept-related scheme suggests sequencing based on the relationships between the concepts. After the initial sequencing based on learner characteristics, you must select a best-fit scheme for the content from either the world-related or concept-related schemes. Thus, if you are trying to sequence a series of related concepts (e.g., herbivores, carnivores, omnivores, and examples of each), the concept-related guidelines would be most appropriate for determining which concept to present first, second, third, and so forth. The following sections describe each of the sequencing schemes.

## Learning-Related Sequencing

This strategy for sequencing content is based on five student-learning concepts (see Table 6-1). First, there are identifiable prerequisites a learner must master before demonstrating a more complex task. For example, one needs to learn the alphabet before using a dictionary or encyclopedia or before arranging data alphabetically. The prerequisite skills and knowledge are identified in the task analysis. Second is teaching about the familiar or known before teaching about the unknown. When teaching a math unit on measurement in the United States, for example, you might begin with inch-, foot-, and yard-measurement problems before teaching problems involving calculations with centimeters and meters. A third learning-related scheme is difficulty. Posner and Strike (1976) stated that difficulty is determined by the fineness of the discrimination the learner must make, how quickly the procedure is executed, and the amount of cognitive processing required. Guidelines prescribe teaching the easier tasks first, such as spelling short words before longer words and replacing a button before sewing a seam. Similarly, a French horn tutor would first teach a student about intervals and then move to complex chords. Fourth is the sequencing of content based on interest. An introductory course on programming a robot might start with how to make the robot move (i.e., high-interest content) before introducing structured programming techniques (i.e., content of less interest). Fifth, the content is sequenced according to a development theory, such as that of Bruner, Piaget, or Kohlberg. For example, following Bruner's (1964, 1966) theory, words (i.e., symbols) would be introduced only after the learner had learned the appropriate visual images (i.e., icons) related to the words. Suppose a professor asks for help in redesigning a course in photography. The objectives might cover learning the basic operation of the camera, the concepts of exposure control and depth of field, and how to produce prints. We might first sequence the content using learner interest by allowing the learners to shoot several pictures using the camera's automatic exposure. Learners can enjoy immediate satisfaction with the hands-on experience.

When we organize the content related to controlling a camera's exposure, we would first teach the learner how to set the digital camera so that it automatically selects either the aperture or the shutter. Next, we would teach when to use aperture settings to control the image. Sequencing for the information on controlling exposure begins with the easiest step of simply setting a selected exposure and proceeds to a more difficult step of selecting the shutter speed and f-stop to stop action or to obtain different depths of field. Finally, we would teach how to print a picture before teaching how to improve the quality of a picture through software manipulations. This sequencing is based on the identifiable prerequisite of printing a simple picture before manipulating it. More recent research suggests that a sequential approach is most effective with novices. For example, if you are teaching math concepts and spreadsheet use, then the most effective approach is to first teach the procedure for using the spreadsheet followed by the math operations; teaching both concurrently is ineffective (Clarke, Ayres, & Sweller, 2005; Kester, Kirschner, & Merriënboer, 2004).

**TABLE 6-1**
Learning-related sequencing

| Phenomenon | Example/Prescription |
| --- | --- |
| Identifiable prerequisite | Teach a skill required to perform another skill first<br>e.g., Teach addition of whole numbers before teaching addition of fractions |
| Familiarity | Begin with the most familiar information and then progress to the most remote<br>e.g., Teach about mammals in the surrounding area before teaching about mammals of another country |
| Difficulty | Teach the less difficult before the more difficult<br>e.g.,Teach how to complete a simple income tax form before teaching how to complete a form with itemized deductions |
| Interest | Begin with the topics or tasks that will create the most learner interest<br>e.g., Teach a recruit how to fire a rifle before teaching how to clean it |
| Development | Ensure that the learner has reached the appropriate developmental level before teaching a task or topic<br>e.g., Teach students to recognize the color green before teaching them how to read the word *green* |

A procedural analysis typically reveals a temporal sequence, whereas a topic analysis usually reveals a logical sequence. Although the sequence identified by the procedural analysis is usable in a unit of instruction, a more effective unit might result from a different sequence or combination of sequences. A detailed analysis of basic photography techniques might proceed from composing a picture, manipulating lighting, and using a histogram to adjusting exposure and so forth. A teaching strategy might start with how to take a picture and proceed to how to manipulate the image using an application such as PhotoShop to increase the student's interest and motivation. Thus, basing the sequence first on interest rather than a logical sequence might heighten the learner's motivation for learning.

## World-Related Sequencing

Suppose you are developing a unit of instruction for automobile salespeople on the features of a new car model. Do you start at the front of the car or the back in your presentation? Or do you begin by describing what the drivers see when they approach the car, then describe what happens when they enter the door, start the car, and so on? Or do you describe the different systems in the car, such as all the safety features, the electrical system, and the power system? Obviously, there are several different ways to organize and describe the features of the car for a sales training program. Sequencing the content by walking around the car and viewing it from a driver's perspective might be appropriate for salespeople learning the features so that they can point them out to prospective customers. Describing what the driver sees in sequence is probably most appropriate for the new owner. The third approach of describing the related systems is probably more appropriate for mechanics, who require and use a different conceptualization of a car. The

**TABLE 6-2**
World-related sequencing

| Phenomenon | Example/Principle |
|---|---|
| Spatial | Left to right, top to bottom, north to south |
| | e.g., Describe a plant starting with the flower and moving toward the roots in sequence |
| Temporal | Historical first, second, third, etc.; fast to slow |
| | e.g., When describing the mailing options at the post office, begin with the fastest and proceed to the slowest |
| | When describing how to give an insulin injection, describe the steps in sequence |
| Physical | Roundness, hardness, large to small, color, smoothness |
| | e.g., When teaching the different types of wines, group them by color (e.g., white, red, blush) |

sequencing strategy you select, then, depends largely on the characteristics and needs of the target audience.

Content that represents objects, people, and events is presented in a sequence that is consistent with the real world. Thus, as designers we want a one-to-one correspondence between the sequence of the instruction and the sequence of the objects and events in the real world. Sequencing is typically done according to spatial relations, temporal relations, or physical attributes that occur in the real world (see Table 6-2). A unit for salespeople on the introduction of a new electric car might group the new features in sequence as they are found while walking around the car. Basing the organization on the physical layout of the car is referred to as *spatial organization*. A mechanic might be more interested in the individual components of each system (electrical, power, etc.). This grouping by related features is referred to as grouping by physical phenomena, which is the presentation of similar items together. Finally, a unit organized on an orderly sequence of steps, such as what the driver sees when approaching the car, entering the car, and then starting it, is based on a temporal sequence. Temporal sequences use a timeline to sequence the content.

Once a sequence is selected, the content is presented in an orderly fashion according to the scheme. For example, if we were using a temporal organization for talking to new car owners, we would not begin with explaining how to adjust the radio. Rather, we would start with what the driver sees when approaching the car and continue to present the content in the sequence it would occur in the real world (e.g., opening the door, sitting in the seat, putting on a seat belt). Adjusting the radio would come sometime after the key is inserted in the ignition. A spatial organization might begin with the front bumper, then the engine or electric motor, the tires, the front disk brakes, the door latches, and finally the trunk. The presentation sequence follows an orderly plan from left to right, top to bottom, and so forth. Table 6-2 describes the three sequences for world-related phenomena and a sample sequence using each.

Consider the sequencing in the classic computer simulation, Oregon Trail (2001), of a wagon train trip. If we organized the simulation in alphabetical order

**TABLE 6-3**
Concept-related sequencing

| Phenomenon | Example/Principle |
|---|---|
| Class relations | Teach characteristics of a class before teaching members of the class<br>e.g., Teach concept of central tendency before teaching about mean, mode, and median |
| Propositional relations | Provide examples first, then the proposition<br>e.g., Show students examples of metal expansion (cookie sheet, bridge on a hot day, etc.), and then explain that metal expands when heated |
| Sophistication | Begin with concrete or simple and then proceed to abstract or complex concepts<br>e.g., Teach the concepts of mean, mode, and median before teaching analysis of variance |
| Logical prerequisite | Teach the logical prerequisite concepts first<br>e.g., Teach the concept of the mean before teaching the concept of standard deviation |

(i.e., temporal order), then the students would be searching for food at *Chimney Rock* before they loaded their wagons for departure on the trail in *St. Louis, Missouri*! A spatial sequencing based on the east-to-west travel along the trail makes much more sense for the computer simulation. A unit on types of rocks might organize the rocks according to their hardness or softness (i.e., physical order). The unit, then, might start with the softest rocks and progress to the hardest rocks. Such a sequencing scheme is based on naturally occurring physical attributes. Following a world-related scheme for sequencing provides a concrete organization that reflects the sequence of the content as it exists in nature.

## Concept-Related Sequencing

Content can also be sequenced in a manner consistent with how we organize the world conceptually or logically. Posner and Strike (1976) present four schemes for sequencing conceptual content (see Table 6-3). The first is class relations, grouping things or events (i.e., concepts) that are similar. The recommended sequence is to teach the concept of the "class" first (i.e., personal computers) and then the concepts of the individual "class" members. For example, a unit on computers might start with a description of the general concept of a computer (e.g., input, output, central processor) before moving on to specific types of computers (e.g., desktop, laptop, netbook). In a course on database programming, an instructor would begin by teaching the concept "database" before discussing specific types of databases, such as hierarchical, relational, and multidimensional databases.

A second concept-sequencing scheme, propositional relations, prescribes teaching the relationship between propositions before teaching the proposition. An application of this principle is the sequence for teaching the relationship among volume, temperature, and pressure of an ideal gas (i.e., Boyle's law). A prescribed sequence might be to present a variety of different volume, temperature, and pressure conditions to illustrate relationships between the three variables before teaching Boyle's law.

---

### Expert's Edge

## What Do Procedures, Chains, and Learners Have in Common?

Let's assume you are an instructional designer working on a particular instructional design project. You have completed many of the design tasks discussed in the chapters of this book, including needs assessment, learner analysis, task analysis, and objective development. The primary goal that you identified for the students describes a procedural task. At some point in the design process you will have to decide how the instruction you design will be sequenced. Will the instructional sequence "start at the beginning" or "go from simple to complex"? Will the learners structure their own instructional sequence, or will the instruction be sequenced using some other approach?

A classic approach to sequencing was described by Gilbert (1962) in his discussion of *mathetics*. Mathetics as a technology of instruction was a pioneering effort to systematically apply reinforcement theory in order to help students master instructional content and develop skills. A well-known aspect of mathetical procedures related to sequencing is that of "backward" chaining.

But first, what is a chain? A *chain* is a procedure that requires the performance of a sequence of tasks including the condition that the performance of each task depends on the outcome of the previous task (Mechner, 1971). Classic examples of chains include learning how to tie your shoes, solving mathematical problems such as long division, or writing a computer program. Let's consider the task of students learning to successfully use a word-processing system. In particular, the goal is to create and print a word-processing document. The "basic" tasks involved include loading the word-processing software, creating and naming a file, entering text and numeric information, editing the entered information, and printing the word-processing document. A typical instructional sequence for the word-processing task would be to order the tasks in the order listed. However, we could sequence differently using Gilbert's idea of "starting the students at the terminal acts of mastery." In the word-processing example, the first step in the instructional sequence would be printing the document. The next step would be editing the entered information and then printing the document. The next step in the instructional sequence is entering text and numeric information, editing entered information, printing the information, and so on. The general idea is to start with the final goal and always make each new subtask lead directly to the goal. This mathetical procedure is referred to as *backward chaining* (Markle, 1969). It should be noted that the learner always goes forward through the performance sequence to the goal. *Backward chaining* only refers to the method used in the design process for sequencing the instruction. One argument for sequencing the instruction using backward chaining is that the learner always masters the terminal act in each step of the instructional sequence, and this type of sequencing helps learners maintain their motivation.

## References

Gilbert, T. F. (1962). Mathetics: The technology of education. *Journal of Mathetics, 1,* 7−73.

Markle, S. M. (1969). *Good frames and bad: A grammar of frame writing.* New York: Wiley.

Mechner, F. (1971). Complex cognitive behavior: The teaching of concepts and chains. In M. D. Merrill (Ed.), *Instructional design readings* (pp. 264−284). Englewood Cliffs, NJ: Prentice Hall.

Gary J. Anglin is associate professor and program coordinator of the instructional systems design program at the University of Kentucky. He teaches courses in instructional design and technology and consults with private-sector organizations. His current research interests are in the areas of visual learning and the design and delivery of distance-learning programs.

The third concept-sequencing scheme is to organize the content by sophistication. Examples of concept sophistication are the continuums of concrete to abstract and simple to complex. The prescription is to start with concrete, simple, or precise concepts and then proceed to abstract, complex, and imprecise concepts. For example, a chemistry instructor might start a unit with an explanation of a simple compound such as salt before discussing ionic bonding (concrete to abstract). The fourth concept-sequencing scheme is the logical prerequisite, which prescribes that concepts necessary to understand another concept be taught first. In chemistry, an instructor would need to teach the concept of a chemical reaction before introducing the concept of an enzyme that hastens a chemical reaction.

Suppose you are developing a unit on pests for a firm that specializes in pest management for the agricultural business. One of the objectives requires the learners to identify the different types of agricultural pests, including insects, plants, fungi, nematodes, and viruses. The unit might begin with a definition of *pest* (class relations) and then provide examples of the different types of pests (class members). The remainder of the unit might be organized by beginning with the simplest, most concrete pests (e.g., weeds) and proceeding to the more complex and abstract types of pests (e.g., viruses, nematodes, bacteria, and drought) based on the sophistication of the concepts. In the section on insects, an objective might require the learner to explain the relationship between the weather (temperature) and the developmental stages of insects. Before the learners read the section on this relationship, you would present information on the life cycle (e.g., egg, larva, pupa, and adult) of insects (logical prerequisite). Examples would then be organized showing the different life cycles of the insects in relation to the temperature. Finally, the learners would receive information about the relationship between temperature and insect development (propositional relations).

The sequence of a unit of instruction may use strategies from each of the three sequencing schemes—learning related, world related, and concept related—identified by Posner and Strike (1976). The actual decision is based first on the characteristics of the learner and then on the nature of the content.

## ELABORATION THEORY SEQUENCING

To determine the sequence of the instruction, elaboration theory makes distinctions between the types of expertise the learner will develop (English & Reigeluth, 1996). Content expertise describes instruction that will help the learner master a body of knowledge such as chemistry or management. Task expertise describes a unit that will help the learner become an expert at a task such as using a bow and arrow, completing a tax form, or solving a mathematical story problem. Let's examine the sequencing schemes for each type of expertise.

### Content Expertise Sequencing

A conceptual or theoretical elaboration sequence is used for developing content expertise. The conceptual sequence arranges concepts according to their superordinate, coordinate, and subordinate relationships. For example, in a statistics course, a superordinate concept would be measures of central tendency. The coordinate concepts would be mean, mode, and median. Subordinate concepts would include scores and sum.

A theoretical elaboration sequence organizes the content in much the same way a researcher might have followed to discover an idea. For example, when teaching Boyle's law, we might start with several observations of gases expanding when heated. Then, we might introduce learners to a computer-based animation that allows them to observe the pressure in a vessel as they increase and decrease the temperature. This sequence follows the recommendation by Reigeluth (1987) for starting with the readily observable and then proceeding to the more detailed and complex aspects of the theory or discovery.

### Task Expertise Sequencing

The elaboration theory sequence for teaching tasks uses the simplifying conditions method. Sequencing for a task should start with the simplest task and proceed to the more complex task. For example, when training bank tellers, we might start with a simple task such as how to accept a deposit of cash into a savings account. Next, we might show the tellers how to check the balance of a checking account. After they know how to check the balance of an account, we could show them how to check the balance and then cash a check if there are adequate funds. Teaching these naive learners how to assess a loan application or how to react in a robbery are more complex tasks and would come near the end of the training.

## FROM OBJECTIVES TO SEQUENCING

Your task analysis will provide a general outline, whereas the classification of your objectives in the expanded performance-content matrix (see Chapter 5) will identify the types of content in your task analysis. Based on your content and performance, you can select a sequencing strategy for each objective. If your unit is primarily concerned with teaching a procedure (e.g., how to tie knots for fly fishing), you might use the same sequencing strategy for the total unit, such as arranging the notes from simple to most difficult and then presenting the steps in a temporal sequence.

## SUMMARY

1. Once you have completed your task analysis and written the objectives, you are ready to begin designing the instruction by determining the most appropriate sequence for presenting the information.
2. Posner and Strike (1976) suggested three sequencing strategies based on how objects or events occur in the real world, concepts and their relationships to other concepts, and the interests and needs of the learner. Organizing the content according to one of these schemes provides a systematic method for presenting the content that is likely to match the learner's expectations.
3. The elaboration theory suggests sequencing content based on whether the learner is developing task expertise or concept expertise. Concept expertise sequencing presents the logical relationships between the concepts or presents the content in a sequence similar to what one might have used to discover the idea. Task expertise sequencing proceeds from the simplest to the more complex tasks.

## THE ID PROCESS

The output of this step of the instructional design process is a sequencing of your objectives. If your unit is of sufficient complexity, you might use multiple sequencing strategies (i.e., different strategies for different objectives). For example, you might start with the basic concepts sequenced by order of interest, then use a temporal approach for a procedure, introduce some additional concepts sequenced according to class relations, and finally end with a series of rules presented according to difficulty.

You will use your sequencing strategy to design the instructional strategies and finally as input for developing the instructional materials. The sequencing strategy creates a high-level outline that corresponds to the roman numerals I, II, III, IV, and so on of your task analysis.

## APPLICATION

Assume that you have contracted with a paint store franchise to develop a training program for new employees on how to mix (i.e., tint) paints. Your task analysis has produced the following objectives:

1. After completing this unit of instruction, the learner will correctly distinguish between a paint tint and a paint base.
2. Given a painting problem, the learner will correctly select the type of paint base for a task.

3. Given a stock color, the learner will demonstrate how to select the appropriate amount of tint.
4. Given a tinted base, the learner will correctly demonstrate how to mix the paint.

Develop a sequencing strategy for these four objectives.

## ANSWERS

There are several options for sequencing these objectives. We chose to sequence the fourth objective first (using interest as a guide), as it seems we are all fascinated by the mechanical shaker in a paint store! The remaining three objectives were sequenced according to a temporal plan, that is, the sequence performed or used.

1. Given a tinted base, the learner will correctly demonstrate how to mix the paint.
2. After completing this unit of instruction, the learner will correctly distinguish between a paint tint and a paint base.
3. Given a painting problem, the learner will select the correct type of paint base for a task.
4. Given a stock color, the learner will demonstrate how to select the appropriate amount of tint.

## QUALITY MANAGEMENT

Our quality check at this stage of the design process focuses on the objectives and task analysis. First, as you sequence the objectives, you need to check each objective for clarity. Does it communicate the intended outcomes? Does the objective include the needed parts (i.e., verb and content, conditions, and criteria for behavioral objectives)? Is the objective measureable? Second, as you sequence the objectives, you can review the task analysis to ensure that it is adequate. That is, does the analysis include the required information for the sequencing strategy? For example, if you are using an identifiable prerequisite strategy, are those prerequisites identified in the task analysis?

## INSTRUCTIONAL DESIGN: DECISIONS AND CHOICES

With the objectives completed, you are ready to sequence the instruction. You believe that motivating the learner is essential, so you will begin the instruction by presenting how to use the extinguisher and then immediately engage the learner in practice. After the learner has learned to aim and discharge the extinguisher, he or she will recognize the need to learn about the different types of extinguishers and emergency procedures. Here's the sequence that you propose:

| Sequence | Description | Objective |
|---|---|---|
| 1 | Demonstrate how to extinguish a fire using a fire extinguisher | 6 |
| 2 | Differentiate the types of fire extinguishers | 3 |
| 3 | Describe the types of fire classes | 2 |
| 4 | Select the correct fire extinguisher | 4 |
| 5 | Describe the emergency procedures | 5 |
| 6 | Describe how a fire gets started | 1 |

[The sequence of the instruction does not have to follow the sequence of the task analysis. In this example, the hands-on practice enhances the desire to learn about the different types of fire extinguishers and the emergency procedures. The disadvantage of this sequence is that once the learner has practiced using the fire extinguishers, he or she may not attend to the rest of the instruction—or worse, leave early.]

The SME and another designer have additional concerns about the sequence you propose. The hands-on practice must take place outside. Thus, valuable time will be wasted moving between the classroom, the outdoor location, and then back to the classroom. Using an extinguisher before the learner understands which type of extinguisher to use (which is based on understanding the fire classes) and the emergency procedures could lead to unnecessary learner errors.

Here's an alternative sequence proposed:

| Sequence | Description | Objective |
|---|---|---|
| 1 | Describe how a fire gets started | 1 |
| 2 | Describe the types of fire classes | 2 |
| 3 | Differentiate the types of fire extinguishers | 3 |
| 4 | Select the correct fire extinguisher | 4 |
| 5 | Describe the emergency procedures | 5 |
| 6 | Demonstrate how to extinguish a fire using a fire extinguisher | 6 |

[This sequence builds on concepts in a logical order. However, the learner could remain passive until the end of the instruction or may not understand how the conceptual content contributes to learning the procedure. The use of generative strategies (see Chapter 7) will be critical.]

Here's one more possible sequence:

| Sequence | Description | Objective |
|---|---|---|
| 1 | Describe how a fire gets started | 1 |
| 2 | Describe the types of fire classes | 2 |
| 3 | Differentiate the types of fire extinguishers | 3 |
| 4 | Demonstrate how to extinguish a fire using a fire extinguisher | 6 |
| 5 | Select the correct fire extinguisher | 4 |
| 6 | Describe the emergency procedures | 5 |

[This sequence places the demonstration component in the middle of the instruction. It aims to minimize the initial time spent on conceptual content. The advantage is the potential increase in learner motivation. Although any of these sequences is viable, the designer must trade off logistics, learner motivation, and logical order.]

## REFERENCES

Bruner, J. S. (1964). The course of cognitive growth. *American Psychologist, 19*, 1–15.

Bruner, J. S. (1966). *Toward a theory of instruction.* Cambridge,: The Belknap Press.

Clarke, T., Ayres, P., & Sweller, J. (2005). The impact of sequencing and prior knowledge on learning mathematics through spreadsheet applications. *Educational Technology Research & Development, 53*, 15–24.

English, R. E., & Reigeluth, C. M. (1996). Formative evaluation research on sequencing instruction with elaboration theory. *Educational Technology and Research Journal, 44*, 23–41.

Gagné, R. M. (1985). *Conditions of learning and theory of instruction* (4th ed.). New York: Holt, Rinehart and Winston.

Kester, L., Kirschner, P. A., & van Merriënboer, J. J. G. (2004). Timing of information presentation in learning statistics. *Instructional Science, 32*, 233–252.

Oregon Trail. (2001). [Computer software]. Novato, CA: Broderbund.

Posner, G. J., & Strike, K. A. (1976). A categorization scheme for principles of sequencing content. *Review of Educational Research, 46*, 665–690.

Reigeluth, C. M. (1987). Lesson blueprints based on the elaboration theory of instruction. In C. M. Reigeluth (Ed.), *Instructional theories in action: Lessons illustrating selected theories and models.* Hillsdale, NJ: Erlbaum.

# CHAPTER 7

# Designing the Instruction: Strategies

## GETTING STARTED

You are developing an introductory course on management information systems (MIS) for a company. Your task analysis has identified three different types of databases (i.e., concepts) and information on how to determine which database is appropriate for the user's data (i.e., rules). The next step is to design the strategies for teaching the concepts and rules.

The concepts include relational, hierarchical, and multidimensional databases. You have also identified a total of seven rules that will help a user determine which database is most appropriate for the task. In your task analysis, you have identified one excellent example of an existing database for each of the three that you will include in the unit. You also have two or more examples of each rule. How would you design the instructional strategy to help the learner master this content? Remember, you want the learner not only to pass the test at the end of the instruction but to apply this new knowledge while on the job to make appropriate decisions.

# QUESTIONS TO CONSIDER

"What is the best way to teach a fact, a concept, a rule, a procedure, an interpersonal skill, or an attitude?"

"How can I make the instruction meaningful?"

"How can I teach an objective that focuses on interpersonal skills?"

"What is the best way to present the content so that each learner will master the objectives?"

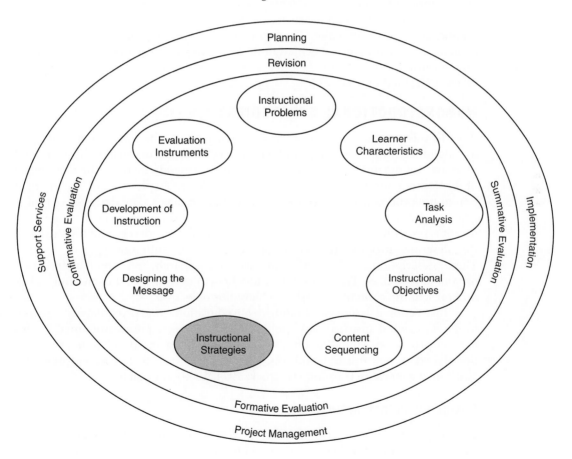

Decisions on the design of the instruction are made at two levels. The first decision is the delivery strategy, which describes the general learning environment. General learning environments can range from a typical lecture presentation to a highly interactive multimedia or Web-based lesson. These strategies are often classified according to their degree of individualization. Individualized instruction presents the content (or objectives) to each student at an appropriate rate for the individual. Thus, one student might be working on unit 1 while another student is on unit 5. A more sophisticated approach to individualization adapts the instruction for each individual. For example, when teaching students how to solve a story problem, you might create unique problems for each student that include mention of his or her birthday, favorite friends, pets, and favorite candy (Ross & Anand, 1987). A group-paced approach is that of the typical classroom-lecture course with scheduled examinations that all students take at designated times.

The second decision is the instructional strategy, which prescribes sequences and methods of instruction to achieve an objective. These prescriptions provide guidance on how to design instructional sequences, and they are generalizable to a number of delivery strategies. These prescriptions are determined by the types of content and performance specified in the objectives (see Chapter 5). This chapter presents instructional strategies for each cell of the expanded performance-content matrix presented in Chapter 5.

## WHY INSTRUCTIONAL STRATEGIES?

Prior to this stage of the instructional design process, the instructional designer has identified an instructional problem, the content to correct the problem, and objectives for the instruction. The design of the instruction includes the sequencing of the content and the preinstructional strategy (see Chapters 6 and 8). The next step in the process is to design the instructional strategies. The designer's primary goal is to design effective and efficient instruction that produces reliable results each time it is presented to the learner. We achieve this goal by developing prescriptions that describe an optimum method of instruction for different types of content. These prescriptions, or heuristics, are based on research; you modify them based on your experiences. This chapter provides heuristics to answer the question, ''How do I present the content needed to achieve this objective?''

Instructional design uses findings from educational and psychological research to develop sound instructional applications. The prescriptions presented in this chapter provide a foundation on which you should add and develop new prescriptions based on new research and your experience with each. The prescriptions are based on a generative-learning (Wittrock, 1974, 1989) approach.

### Designing an Instructional Strategy

Learning is an active process in which the learner constructs meaningful relationships between the new knowledge presented in the instruction and the learner's existing knowledge. A well-designed instructional strategy prompts or motivates the learner to actively make these connections between what the learner already knows and the new information. Wittrock (1974, 1989), and others (Grabowski, 1996; Jonassen, 1985) describe this learning process as generative learning. The advantages of generative learning are the learner's deeper understanding and longer retention of what is learned.

## Foundations for the Prescriptions

Craik and Lockhart (1972) suggest that a learner can process new information on a continuum that ranges from phonemic to semantic processing. For example, in one study a researcher might ask one group to read through a passage and put an $X$ through every $e$ on the page. She might tell a second group that they will have a test on the passage when they finish. The first group, the one marking the $e$'s, would process the material at a phonemic level; that is, they are looking for $e$'s and not reading for meaning. The second group will most likely read the material for a greater depth of meaning to achieve a higher test score (especially if they are offered a reward for the performance). They will try to relate the new material to what they already know. This second group is said to process the material at a semantic, or deeper, level of processing. This type of processing produces meaningful learning. Processing the new information at a deeper level allows the learner to relate the information to several existing ideas and generate more meaningful relationships. Thus, stronger memory traces that make the information more resistant to forgetting are created.

One of the goals of an instructional strategy, then, is to design the instruction so that the learner is motivated to generate or construct these meaningful relationships. The design should activate the existing knowledge structures (i.e., recall of prior knowledge) and then help the learner to alter and encode the new structures. The current literature refers to this process also as *explanations* (Wittwer & Renkl, 2008). Instructional strategies are central to helping the learner develop an understanding when learning new materials (Leinhardt & Steele, 2005; Treagust & Harrison, 2000). If you are to develop an effective instructional strategy or instructional explanation for use in your instructional materials, then you must take into account the prior knowledge your learners possess (Leinhardt & Steele, 2005; Wittwer & Renkl, 2008). A strategy that ignores the learner's prior knowledge and is too difficult can result in misconceptions and a lack of understanding. Similarly, an explanation that is too easy can cause problems in comprehension. Thus, an effective instructional strategy must consider the learner's prior knowledge and offer the appropriate level of challenge (Wittwer & Renkl, 2008).

This cognitive approach to instructional design is different from the often used strategy of mathemagenics, which attempts to control the learner by manipulating the instructional materials. The mathemagenic approach was first suggested by Rothkopf (1960, 1996). Its most common implementation has been the insertion of adjunct questions, either before or after a paragraph, designed to guide the learner's processing of the content. The results of a mathemagenic approach typically have been rote learning or very shallow levels of processing (Andre, 1979; Jonassen, 1985; Rickards, 1979).

As an alternative to earlier emphases on rote (i.e., memorization) learning, Jonassen (1988) identified four different information-processing strategies a learner can use to promote deeper processing. Designers can embed these strategies into the instruction to motivate the learner to process the new information in a meaningful way. The following section describes the four strategies.

## Generative Strategies

The four generative categories identified by Jonassen (1988) are recall, integration, organizational, and elaboration.

- The first strategy, recall, is helpful for learning facts and lists for verbatim recall. Specific instructional strategies that facilitate recall include repetition, rehearsal (e.g., mental practice), review, and mnemonics.
- The second type, integration strategies, is useful for transforming information into a more easily remembered form. Strategies that help the learner transform new content include paraphrasing, which requires learners to describe the new material in their own words, and generating questions or examples from the new information.
- The third type of strategy, organizational, helps the learner identify how new ideas relate to existing ideas. Sample strategies include analyzing key ideas, which requires the learner to identify the key ideas and then interrelate them; outlining; and categorizing. West, Farmer, and Wolff (1991) suggest the use of tables for categorizing and integrating new information. An example of a strategy requiring the learner to integrate information is illustrated in Table 7-1, in which the learner completes the table by describing the type of cut each blade makes.
- The fourth strategy type is elaboration, which requires learners to add their ideas (i.e., elaborations) to the new information. Strategies that facilitate elaboration include the generating mental images, creating physical diagrams, and relating existing knowledge to the new information

**TABLE 7-1**
Categorization table

| Saw Blade | Type of Cut |
|---|---|
| Cross cut | |
| Rip | |
| Hollow ground planer | |
| Combination | |

## PRESCRIPTIONS FOR INSTRUCTIONAL STRATEGIES

The following prescriptions are useful basic guides for developing instructional strategies to achieve each of the content-performance types in Table 7-2.

This expanded content-performance matrix was first described in Chapter 5. Each instructional objective (and the general objective for cognitive objectives) for a unit is classified into one of the cells based on the type of content the objective treats (i.e., fact, concept, principle, procedure, interpersonal skill, or attitude) and

**TABLE 7-2**
Expanded performance-content matrix

| Content | Performance | |
|---|---|---|
| | Recall | Application |
| Fact | | |
| Concept | | |
| Principles and rules | | |
| Procedure | | |
| Interpersonal | | |
| Attitude | | |

the type of performance the learner must demonstrate (i.e., recall or application). Prescriptions are provided for each cell to use in developing the strategies.

Recall performance relies on rote memorization of the content. For example, the learner would recall a fact, state the definition of a concept, state a rule, list the steps of a procedure, describe a type of interpersonal behavior (e.g., how to deal with a domineering individual), and state a previously described example of a behavior indicating an attitude. Application performance requires the learner to apply the content (e.g., concept) to a new situation or problem. For example, an application for a concept (e.g., herbivore) would be to identify new examples as either belonging to the class (as, e.g., a cow) or *not* belonging to the class (as, e.g., a lion). Application objectives for rules and procedures would require the learner to apply the rule or procedure to solve a problem, explain an instance, or complete a task. For example, the instructor could ask the learner to list the steps for creating a formula for determining the average of a column of numbers in a spreadsheet (i.e., recall) or to demonstrate how to enter a formula to determine the average of a column of numbers (i.e., application).

---

( **Expert's Edge** )

### How to Fit 25 Days of Training into Three

The training team at Perfect Software Corporation (not its real name) had a problem: It was December and the rollout of PSC's new software system for collaborative work groups was scheduled for February 1. On that date, all PSC field engineers would assemble at headquarters for their annual three-day Field Service Convention. The training team's mandate was to get all 175 field engineers trained in how to troubleshoot the new system.

Using the classic methods of job task analysis, the team had identified well over 200 troubleshooting procedures. Details of each procedure varied based on the way the software system was installed on a client's network of mainframes. The team could see the disaster coming: At the convention, they would have time to teach perhaps two dozen procedures, at most. Months of agonizing service problems would result, and the hotline would be overwhelmed with calls from field service technicians. Not a pretty picture!

I was called in to see if PLATO could help automate the training. But it soon became clear that a computer-based training solution for teaching over 200 procedures would be overwhelmingly large and expensive and would take months too long to develop. There had to be a better way.

After a little dialogue, a few additional facts emerged:

- The new system consisted of 10 major modules. Clients would install them on their mainframe networks in different ways. Almost all of the procedures involved failures or conflicts of communication between the modules.
- The field technicians were already certified network engineers, with experience in troubleshooting network problems.

The principles of problem solving, grounded in cognitive psychology, look like they might apply here, I thought. One of these principles is that expert problem solving is the ability to manipulate a mental model of the system to predict what kinds of faults could cause the observed symptoms.

I reasoned that our instructional strategy should focus on the mental model, not the individual procedures. The strategy had three basic steps:

1. Teach the technicians the functions of each kind of system module and how the modules communicate when performing various tasks.
2. Point out that, in a client's installation, any module could reside on any mainframe in a network, and more than one instance of a module was allowed in order to assure fast performance. In short, we would teach how the system worked normally.
3. Finally, we would give the technicians practice in manipulating their mental models of the system to predict probable causes of symptoms. In other words, the technicians would be asked to predict and explain how and why the system behaves as it does when it doesn't work. We would be careful to select a range of symptoms that would involve every kind of communication and every kind of communication fault possible for each communication. A few of the symptoms would be used as case studies to illustrate, and the rest would be used in practice and tests.

The team estimated that this training could easily be completed by the end of the second day of the conference. That would leave the third day for proficiency testing, certification on the new system, and remedial tutoring as needed. Not only did this instructional strategy save training time, but also it solved another problem: The product was expected to evolve right up to product release, so the details of the more than 200 troubleshooting procedures were not stable. Visions of being overwhelmed by last-minute revisions to the training concerned the team. By emphasizing the basic structure of the system, however, last-minute training updates could be expected to be minimal. Since technicians could practice with a stand-alone real installation that could be "broken" as needed for training, training materials didn't need to include these details. Furthermore, it was likely that, in the future, technicians could easily master product upgrades with no further procedure training; only a brief orientation to new features would be needed.

Rob Foshay is director of research for the Education Technology Group of Texas Instruments. His 30 years of experience in educational technology has included technology management, instructional design, and human performance technology at the secondary and postsecondary levels and in industry, with particular interest in teaching and assessment of expertise and high-level problem solving. He served as chief instructional architect of the PLATO Learning system for 15 years.

The remainder of this chapter presents a series of heuristics based on the research literature. Heuristics present a problem-solving strategy, rather than a set of rules, that allows for a flexible approach that you can refine and modify with each new experience.

Thus, we encourage you to develop your own set of heuristics to expand and modify based on experience and your interpretation of the research literature. These prescriptions represent a number of heuristics based on behavioral and cognitive research for each of the content-performance matrix cells in Table 7-2. A prescription is designed for each of your objectives based on the type of performance (i.e., recall or application) and content, and is included as part of the instructional design plan. Each prescription has a minimum of two parts: (1) a description of how the information is initially presented to the learner and (2) the generative strategy to increase the depth of processing. The initial presentation is a means of structuring the information in your task analysis for the learner in a form that facilitates learning. Design of the initial presentation must consider what information is needed (e.g., definitions, examples, cues, steps) to achieve the objective and how best to present it (e.g., model, pictures, narrative). The generative strategy incorporates one of the four groups of strategies identified by Jonassen (1985) to help the learner make the necessary connections between existing knowledge and the new knowledge.

## Prescriptions for Teaching Facts

A fact is a statement of association between two things (e.g., "The earth is 92.96 million miles from the sun."). Facts can only be recalled—they have no specific application (see Table 7-2). The prescriptions in Table 7-3 describe how to present a fact to the learner for optimum learning when the objective is classified as factual content and the performance is recall.

Concrete facts are those that you can sense, such as "fire trucks are red." For concrete facts, the initial presentation should provide the student with experience with the objects of the fact (see Table 7-3). For example, to teach the fact that tomato sauce is red, you might open a can of tomato sauce and

**TABLE 7-3**
Example fact strategies

| Factual Content | Example | Initial Presentation and Generative Strategy |
| --- | --- | --- |
| Concrete facts | McIntosh apples are red. | Show a McIntosh apple and ask for the color. Allow for practice/rehearsal by showing the color and asking which apple is that color, or by naming the apple and asking for its color. |
| Abstract facts | The airport code for Memphis is *MEM*. | Show luggage tag with MEM and explain that it indicates "Memphis." Allow for practice/rehearsal by showing tag or the word *Memphis* and asking for the city or code. |
| Abstract facts | It's best to wear safety goggles when hammering. | Show students a picture or model of someone hammering and wearing safety goggles. Have student explain why this safety rule is important. |
| Lists | The lines of the musical staff are EGBDF. | Show a musical staff with each line labeled. Provide students with the mnemonic to practice, "Every Good Boy Does Fine." |

let each learner see the color. In contrast, abstract facts cannot be observed or experienced. When teaching abstract facts, the designer should first attempt to find a concrete representation of the fact (e.g., a picture or other artifact) for the initial presentation. To teach the learner that the capital of Indiana is Indianapolis, you might present a map of Indiana with only Indianapolis identified. The map forms a concrete representation of the fact.

Applicable generative strategies for learning facts are rehearsal/practice, elaboration, and the development of mnemonics (see Table 7-3). A rehearsal/practice strategy might involve covertly rehearsing by simply repeating the fact mentally, overtly practicing by writing the fact, or answering questions related to the fact. Elaboration can include answering questions as to why a fact is true or explaining relevant information such as importance or context of the fact. Mnemonics are devices that help recall facts. For example, photography students must often learn the primary colors and their complements (red–cyan, blue–yellow, and green–magenta). A simple mnemonic (*red cars by General Motors*) will assist the learner in recalling the colors later. The instruction can prompt the learner to generate a mnemonic (e.g., "Can you think of a picture that will help you remember that cotton is the main export of Egypt?"), or the instruction can introduce and provide directions on how to use a mnemonic ("You can use the word, 'FANBOYS' to remember the seven conjunctions—for, and, nor, but, or, yet, and so—to help"). For example, when students were provided with a mnemonic, they recalled more information than students who studied without guidance (Rummel, Levin, & Woodward, 2003). Another useful approach is elaborative interrogation (McCrudden & Schraw, 2007; Ozgungor, & Guthrie, 2004; Woloshyn, Paivio, & Pressley, 1994), in which the learner is asked to explain why a fact is true. For example, if you are teaching students that they must wear safety goggles in the work area, you might ask them to explain why it is important for them to wear the goggles. Answering this question requires them to relate this new fact to knowledge they already know, which is a generative activity.

Back to the example of wood fasteners introduced in Chapter 4, assume you are designing a unit of instruction for employees of a newly opened hardware store. One of the objectives is to teach the fact that most screws are made of steel. To teach this fact, your strategy might start with a picture of a steel screw and text stating that screws are made from steel. Your instructional strategy, then, gives the fact (screws are made from steel) and a concrete representation of the fact (the steel screw). Note that this strategy does not teach the concept of a screw; rather, you are teaching a fact of its composition. Your generative strategy might involve having the learner write this fact 10 times on a sheet of paper (i.e., practice) or explaining why screws are often made from steel (i.e., elaborative interrogation).

## Prescriptions for Teaching Concepts

A concept is a category used to group similar ideas or things (e.g., jewelry) to organize knowledge. Concepts are representations that reflect the structure of the real world (Goodman, Tannebaum, Feldman, & Griffiths, 2008). Performance for a concept can be either recall (e.g., state the definition of) or application, such as identifying new examples of the concept (see Table 7-2). Recommended recall strategies for a concept are the same as those used for a fact: repetition, rehearsal, review, and mnemonics. The instructional strategies for application-type performance, summarized in Table 7-4, are described next. The initial presentation of the concept includes the concept name, definition, and best example (Tennyson & Cocchiarella, 1986) that illustrates the category, such as a diamond ring for the concept jewelry. Additional examples of the concept are then presented to refine the category further (e.g., necklaces, bracelets, earrings, etc.), as are nonexamples of the concept (e.g., silverware, figurines). For abstract concepts such as in chemistry, models are often used to illustrate the different types of chemical bonds. Similarly, a number of Ping-Pong balls can be glued together to illustrate the concept of hole in a chemical structure.

**TABLE 7-4**

Example concept strategies

| Concept Example | Strategy | Initial Presentation and Generative Strategy |
|---|---|---|
| Open-end wrench | Integration | Present the student with the concept name, definition, and best example of the concept. |
| | | Provide the student with a catalog of tools, and ask the student to identify examples of open-end wrenches. |
| Box wrench | Organizational | Present the student with the concept name, definition, and best example of the concept. |
| | | Ask the student to list the characteristics of a box wrench and compare the box wrench to other wrenches and pliers. |

If the purpose of the objective is simply to remember the concept (e.g., "define herbivore"), then the same generative strategies recommended for a fact are applicable to the recall of a concept. Students could use a rehearsal/practice strategy or develop a mnemonic to help them recall the definition of the concept. Both integration and organization strategies are useful for facilitating generative learning of concepts for application. An integrative strategy might have the learners generate new examples and nonexamples of the concept by making two columns on a piece of paper and writing examples in one column and nonexamples in the other. Another integration strategy is practice in determining whether new instances are examples or nonexamples of the concept. For example, provide students with a tool catalog and have them circle examples of all the wrenches. Students would need to discriminate between wrenches and pliers, both of which are used to grip nuts and bolts. Organizational strategies include analysis of key ideas, categorization, and cognitive mapping. A strategy to induce the learners to analyze key ideas might ask them to identify the features (i.e., critical attributes) that define the concept. The instruction could direct the learner to use a categorization strategy by presenting the learners with a list of examples and nonexamples. Similarly, Hamilton (2004) found that asking students to describe the similarities and differences between concepts was beneficial. The learners would identify those items that are examples. More recent research suggests that having students engage in argumentation, that is answering questions others pose about a concept or about members of "class" (e.g., elaboration) supports the learning of the concept (Asterhan & Schwarz, 2008). This research found that the use of argumentation was most effective when it was done with a peer rather than individually. Finally, the instruction could encourage the learners to develop a cognitive map to determine how this new concept relates to concepts they have already learned. One advantage of both argumentation and concept maps is that they place the concepts within a framework that shows their relationships to one another rather than presenting them as isolated entities (Jonassen, 2006). Table 7-4 provides examples of how a designer might use an integration and organizational strategy to design the instruction to teach two concepts.

Consider another objective from the example training unit on wood fasteners. The objective is to have the learners identify various types of screws. For your initial presentation you would select the one best example (e.g., a flat-head wood screw) and present it as an example of a wood screw. The presentation would then include various types (e.g., oval-head, round-head, and Phillips-head) and sizes of wood screws. Nonexamples could include bolts and sheet-metal screws.

If the intent of this objective was to have learners identify a screw for a customer who needs a replacement for a stripped one or additional screws of the same or different size, you might choose an organizational strategy (see Table 7-4). Organizational strategies help the learner transform the new information into a more easily remembered form by having the learner classify new examples. This approach matches your objective of having the student identify examples of screws. Your instructional strategy, then, is to send the learners through the store and have them select 25 different packages of screws, which will require the students to actively process the content and classify each package as either screws or a nonscrews.

## Prescriptions for Teaching Principles and Rules

A principle or rule is a statement that expresses a relationship between concepts, such as "The sum of the angles in a triangle is 180 degrees." The type of performance for learning a principle or rule can be either recall or application (Table 7-2). Principle application includes both explanation of the effect of the rule and prediction of consequences based on the rule.

There are two general approaches to principle and rule learning (Markle, 1969). The first, RULEG, includes a statement of a rule followed by several examples. Using the RULEG approach, the instruction begins with a statement of the rule or principle (e.g., "The sum of the angles in a triangle is 180 degrees") and then provides several triangles with the angle measurements listed and summed. A second, more active, learning approach is EGRUL, which provides the learner with several examples (e.g., the triangles with their angles summed) and asks the learner to generate the rule (see Table 7-5).

**TABLE 7-5**
Example principle and rule strategies

| Rule Example | Strategy | Initial Presentation and Generative Strategy |
|---|---|---|
| Brush painting requires 1/3 more labor than spray painting. | RULEG and integration | State the rule and then show examples. |
| | | Have the learner complete a table illustrating the required time for each painting method. |
| A higher gear-ratio is harder to pedal. | EGRUL and integration | Have the student try pedaling three different gear ratios. Ask the student the relationship between the three gears. |
| | | Have the learner complete a table indicating the relative effort needed to pedal each gear ratio. |
| Fusion welding is used when the base metal and weld metal colors must match. | EGRUL and organizational | Show examples of fusion welding and bronze welding. Ask the student to generate the rule. |
| | | Ask the student to identify the visual differences between the two. |
| | | Have the student develop a decision tree for selecting the welding process. |
| Metal expands when heated. | EGRUL and elaboration | Show an example of a cookie sheet warping in an oven. Ask the student to explain what has happened. |
| | | Have the student explain why a bridge has expansion joints. |
| | | Have the student predict the effect of temperature on the expansion joints. |

If the purpose of the objective is simply to recall the principle or rule, the initial presentation strategy would be either an example or demonstration of the rule for the learner. The generative strategies are the same as those recommended for a fact. For example, the learner might employ a covert rehearsal strategy of repeating the rule or an elaboration strategy of explaining why the rule is true. Integrative, organizational, and elaboration strategies can facilitate generative learning of principles and rules. Using an integrative strategy, the learners can paraphrase the principle using their own words or generate examples, of different types of triangles, for instance, to illustrate the principle. An organizational strategy might include having the learners identify key components of the principle and then compare the principle to similar principles (e.g., the number of degrees in a square). An elaborative strategy might ask the student to develop a diagram that explains the principle. Another approach is to require the students to develop an argument (e.g., explain why something happened; Jonassen, 2006; Wiley & Voss, 1999). Returning to the example unit on wood fasteners, the next objective is to learn the rule that a nail should be driven through the thinner piece of wood into the thicker piece. The student will use this rule to explain to customers how to select the size of the nail. Table 7-5 illustrates the use of the RULEG and EGRUL initial presentation strategies and the use of integration and elaboration generative strategies.

The fourth suggestion, EGRUL and elaboration, would be selected because this strategy is most similar to the job performance condition of explaining this principle to the customer. An elaboration strategy encourages the learner to add more information to the content, such as explaining why the rule works in a specific instance, which makes the content meaningful (Wiley & Voss, 1999).

The initial presentation of the rule could show several mocked-up pieces of wood nailed together. The learners then would be asked to identify which piece of wood to drive the nail into first (i.e., EGRUL). An alternative would be to have the learners nail several thin and thick pieces of wood together to observe the results. The generative strategy (i.e., elaboration) would ask the learners to draw a diagram for a customer to explain how to nail a $1'' \times 6'' \times 6'$ fence piece to a $2'' \times 4''$ fence rail.

## Prescriptions for Teaching Procedures

A procedure is a sequence of steps the learner performs to accomplish a task such as threading a needle or solving a calculus problem. Like concepts and principles, the performance for a procedure can take the form of recall or application (see Table 7-2). Recall performance requires the learner to list or describe the steps of the procedure, whereas application requires the learner to demonstrate the procedure. The generative strategy involves two steps, which include the development of a mental model and then practice. The prescriptions for procedures are summarized in Table 7-6. The following sections describe the strategy design for cognitive procedures and psychomotor procedures.

**Cognitive Procedures.**    The initial instruction is the demonstration, or modeling, of the procedure. Because cognitive procedures are not directly observable, the

**TABLE 7-6**
Example procedure strategies

| Procedure Example | Strategy | Initial Presentation and Generative Strategy |
|---|---|---|
| Removing and installing piston rings | Demonstration, organization, elaboration, practice | While watching a video recording of the process, students are encouraged to take notes on each step. |
| | | After viewing the video, students are encouraged to develop a mental image of the positioning of the piston ring expander for removing and installing the rings. Then they are encouraged to practice the procedure on an engine. |
| Calculating the amount of paint needed to paint a house | Demonstration, organization, elaboration, practice | Students are presented with a worked example that illustrates how to calculate the amount needed using the square footage of the house and coverage of the paint. |
| | | Learners are then encouraged to paraphrase the steps for doing the calculation. Last, they are given three examples and asked to calculate the amount of paint needed. When they complete an example, they compare their work against a worked example of the problem. |

instructional designer must find a means of representing the procedure for the learner. The initial presentation is particularly important when learning cognitive procedures because well-developed conceptual knowledge is essential for effective learning of the procedure (Rittle-Johnson, Siegler, & Alibali, 2001). Worked examples (see Table 7-7) are one method used to teach cognitive procedures such as solving a math problem (Sweller & Cooper, 1985; Van Gerven, Paas, van Merriënboer, & Schmidt, 2002; van Merriënboer, 1997). The worked example shows each step of the problem-solving process. A learner studies the problem by working through each step of the example.

If the purpose of the objective is simply to recall the procedure, the initial strategy would be an example. The generative strategies (e.g., recall, rehearsal of step names, mnemonics) would be the same as those recommended for a fact. For example, you might suggest a verbal mnemonic to help the learner remember either the steps or possibly a rule associated with a step.

The generative strategy for an application performance involves two steps. First, the learner must either paraphrase the procedure or use an elaboration strategy to embellish the processes. Another approach is to prompt learners by asking them, "Can you create a list of steps in your mind that you will follow to complete this task?" Or, the instruction could direct the learner to describe the model's behavior or the process (Bandura, Grusec, & Menlove, 1966) Second, the instruction must provide the learner with practice in applying the procedure (Hazeltine, Aparicio, & Weinstein, 2007). One approach is the presentation of similar example problems for practice. More recent research suggests that the worked examples are more effective if the prompts are faded (Atkinson & Renkl,

**TABLE 7-7**
Worked example

**Problem:** In baking a cake, the baker must combine 4 parts flour with 1 part milk. This particular cake will use 16 cups of flour. How much milk needs to be added?

**Solution:** Let's make 4 the number of cups of milk that are needed. It is the unknown quantity. Now let's summarize the problem information in a table.

|  | Recipe | Baker's Cake |
|---|---|---|
| Flour | 4 parts | 16 cups |
| Milk | 1 part | $y$ cups |

Note that to solve the problem you need equal ratios of milk to flour. Thus,
$1/4 = y/16$
$16 = 4y$
$4 = y*$
The baker needs 4 cups of milk.

*If the designer were to use fading, this last step would be omitted, and the learner would need to provide the answer from the final step. This process could be repeated several times until the learner could solve the problem.

2007; Gerjets, Scheiter, & Schuh, 2008; Renkl, Atkinson, & Grobe, 2004). For example, for the first problem, the last step is removed, and the learner must complete the final step of the problem. For each additional example, one or two additional steps are removed from the worked example, which the learner must complete. In a classroom, the instructor can provide feedback, and model answers or checklists for feedback are provided in a self-paced environment.

**Psychomotor Procedures.** The initial strategy for psychomotor procedures also involves modeling, or demonstrating the task. For tasks involving psychomotor skills, the demonstration may need to have motion (e.g., a live demonstration or a video recording), or a series of still pictures may be adequate. Motion is often required for teaching complex psychomotor tasks or when teaching psychomotor tasks to naive learners. A skilled individual such as an experienced car mechanic may find a series of still pictures (see Figure 8-4) adequate to learn a familiar procedure (e.g., replacing the brake pads on an automobile). A naive learner who is unfamiliar with the basic skills may find a more realistic demonstration, such as a video recording or streaming video, more beneficial because it helps develop a model for executing the task. The initial learning for a psychomotor procedure is enhanced by encouraging the learner to develop mental images of the procedure and by adding verbal labels to the steps (Anshel & Singer, 1980; Bandura & Jeffery, 1973).

One procedure consists of a series of *if-then* statements (Eley & Norton, 2004). Eley and Norton suggest using the sequence of the cue (IF) followed by the action (THEN) for the initial presentation when teaching a procedure. For example, if you were training a new group of heating and air-conditioning installers you might need to teach when to use a box-end wrench, which is used when the nut is hard to reach. Thus, you might include the following in our initial presentation: ''IF the

**TABLE 7-8**
Wood fastener worked example

---

**Problem:** Determine the length in inches of a 9d (penny) nail.

**Solution:** Divide the penny size by 4 and add 0.5 inch.

$$9d \div 4 = 2.25 \text{ inches}$$
$$2.25 + 0.5 = 2.75 \text{ inches}$$

---

nut is hard to reach, THEN use a box-end wrench.'' This statement is more effective than ''Use a box end wrench when the nut is hard to reach.'' The first example uses the if-then format (IF hard to reach, THEN use . . . ) where the second example uses a *then-if* sequence ([THEN] use IF it is . . . ).

Again, the generative strategy involves two steps. First, the learner is encouraged to develop a mental image of the procedure, paraphrase the procedure, or elaborate on the steps of the procedure (e.g., connecting cues or decisions to each step). Second, the learner is encouraged to practice the procedure either using a simulator or the materials and equipment in a real or realistic setting. Feedback can be provided by an instructor, samples for comparison, or a checklist. If the objective is recall performance, then the generative strategies are the same as those recommended for a fact (e.g., recall, rehearsal of step names, mnemonics).

The sample wood fastener unit has an objective of converting the length of a nail given in pennies to inches. The initial presentation is a worked example that illustrates the steps (see Table 7-8). The generative strategy involves two steps: (1) ask the learners to paraphrase the procedure, and then (2) provide the learner with five problems to solve. The learners will then compare their answers with a worked example of each problem for feedback.

## Prescriptions for Teaching Interpersonal Skills

Interpersonal skills deal with the development of communication skills. Performance for interpersonal skills is either recall or application, with a primary emphasis on application (see Table 7-2). The strategy for designing instruction for interpersonal objectives, based on Bandura's (1977) social learning theory, involves four steps. The first step is the initial instruction that presents the model to the learner. Models of the interpersonal behavior (e.g., how to coach an employee who has difficulty working with other team members) are usually presented as live demonstrations, role plays, videos, or printed scenarios. As part of the observation process, the learner's attention may need to be directed to identify key steps of the behavior as a generative activity (see Table 7-9).

The second step is to help each learner to develop verbal and imaginal models of the behavior. A verbal model is derived from the key steps—the process (e.g., modeling) can be paraphrased, or a cognitive map can be developed showing the relationship between the steps. The imaginal model is developed either by offering the learner an image (e.g., ''Remember how the manager focused the employee's

**TABLE 7-9**

Example interpersonal skills strategies

| Interpersonal Skill Example | Strategy | Implementation |
|---|---|---|
| Facilitate a group problem-solving meeting | Model | Show students a video of a facilitator demonstrating the appropriate behaviors for a group. |
| | Verbal and imaginal models (organization) | Have students identify the key behaviors and when they are used. |
| | Mental rehearsal (elaboration) | Provide students with several instances that require the application of a facilitative behavior, and ask them to imagine how they would react to these. |
| | Overt practice | Provide opportunities for each student to facilitate a group as part of a role play. |

attention on the primary issue?'') or by directing the student to develop an image of the behavior. Third is providing for mental rehearsal (i.e., covert practice) of executing the skill. Strategies for mental rehearsal can include examples or case studies presented in print or on video that prompt the learners to determine how they would respond. Fourth is setting up overt practice, which can include role plays involving two or more learners. Some environments might allow the development of interactive programs that present a situation, allow the learners to select a response, and then show the effects of the response.

If the purpose of the objective is simply to recall the interpersonal skill, the initial strategy would be a video or role play. The generative strategies are the same as those recommended for a fact (e.g., rehearsal of the step names, practice in reciting the names, mnemonics).

The sample unit on wood fasteners includes a unit on sales techniques. One of the unit's objectives is for the student to demonstrate how to greet a customer correctly. The first step of the strategy is for the learner to view a video in which an expert demonstrates how to greet a customer. During a second viewing of the video, words describing each of the steps for greeting a customer (e.g., making eye contact, smiling, verbal greeting) are superimposed on the video image to cue the student. The second step is for the learner to develop the verbal and imaginal models. After viewing the video, students are asked to paraphrase the process (i.e., create a verbal model). Next, learners are directed to imagine themselves working in the wood fastener department when a customer approaches them. They are then told to visualize the scenario of greeting the customer in their minds (i.e., create an imaginal model).

Mental rehearsal, the third step, is accomplished by presenting the learners with three scenarios with different situations (e.g., you are stocking new screws, you are busy with another customer) and asking them to imagine how they would greet the customer. For the fourth step, the learners are divided into pairs and directed to role-play the different roles of the customer and sales associate as overt practice.

**TABLE 7-10**
Example attitude strategies

| Attitude Example | Strategy | Implementation |
|---|---|---|
| Discussion of work projects with others may be giving away proprietary information. | Model | Have two students role-play a casual conversation between two individuals from two different companies in which each describes a problem he or she is having with a work project. |
| | Develop verbal and imaginal models (organization) | Have students identify the type of information exchanged. |
| | Mental rehearsal | Provide students with several instances in which (elaboration) they might inadvertently give information away, and ask them to imagine how they would react. |
| | Overt practice | Provide opportunities for each student to practice the appropriate behaviors. |

## Prescriptions for Teaching Attitudes

An attitude consists of a belief and associated behavior or response. The strategy for teaching (i.e., changing) attitudes is similar to the strategy for interpersonal objectives. Both are based on Bandura's (1977) social learning theory (see Chapter 14). The prescription for attitudes is to model the behavior, develop the verbal and imaginal models, use mental rehearsal, and provide for both covert and overt rehearsal (see Table 7-10). The last objective for the example sales associates' training concerns an attitude that all nails need to be weighed accurately. If the purchase weighs more than marked, then the store loses money; if the package weighs less than measured, then the customer loses. (Students learned how to weigh the nails in an earlier unit.) The instructional strategy employs the same four steps used for interpersonal skills.

In the first step, the instructor models how the exact weight of the nails is recorded on the sales slip. Second, the learner identifies the consequences of over- and undercharging the customer (i.e., creates a verbal model) and imagines the consequences of each action (i.e., creates an imaginal model). Third, the learner practices the imaginal model. Fourth, the learner practices the behavior of weighing the nails with an emphasis on marking the sales slip accurately.

## SUMMARY

To design effective instruction, the designer must concentrate on how to present each individual objective in a manner that will help the learner achieve the objective. We consider the design the instructional strategies to be the most crucial step in the process and the one that can contribute the most to making the instruction successful. Unfortunately, however, the design of the instructional strategies is often the most neglected step of the instructional design process.

Instructional strategies begin with determining the content and performance type of each objective using the expanded content-performance matrix. This classification of the objectives helps the designer identify how the learner is to perform the behavior specified in the objective and the type of content the learner must master. Specific strategies are then prescribed for each cell of the content-performance matrix.

There are six categories of content. Facts are associations that learners recall. Concepts are categories learners use to classify similar things or events, such as circles or strikes in baseball. Principles and rules are relationships between two concepts, such as "metal expands when heated." Procedures are sequences of steps a learner must follow to accomplish a task. Interpersonal skills describe spoken and nonverbal communications. Attitudes are predispositions a learner has toward an object, such as about wearing safety goggles when using power equipment.

Each prescription involves two components. The first component is the initial presentation of the content for the learner. Our preferred form is direct, purposeful (i.e., concrete) experience with the content. Typically, the prescriptions recommend either hands-on learning experiences or the use of visuals or representations for abstract ideas.

The second component of the prescription is a generative strategy to make the content meaningful and to encourage active processing by the student. The generative strategies include recall, integration, organization, and elaboration. These strategies are then embedded—that is, made a part of the instructional unit—to encourage the student to respond actively.

The prescriptions presented in this chapter form the basis of a set of heuristics for designing instruction. Each designer should attempt to modify and expand these heuristics based on experience.

The following steps describe how to design your instructional strategies:

a. Review each objective and determine in which cell it best fits in the performance-content matrix.
b. Refer to the appropriate table of prescriptions in this chapter and select an initial and generative strategy.
c. Develop the instruction, which consists of the initial presentation and the generative strategy.

## THE ID PROCESS

The instructional design product from this step of the process is the strategy design for treating each objective. The instructional strategies provide a guide for developing the instructional materials presented in the sequence you specified in Chapter 6. You use the initial presentation component to direct the development of the basic information for the objective. The generative strategy component provides the active learning aspect of the instruction. Consider the instructional strategy as a blueprint for developing the unit. It should allow you flexibility for creatively presenting the information interestingly, motivationally, and effectively. Designing the instructional strategy requires that you integrate your creative skills with the science of instructional design to create an approach that will help the learner understand and learn the content and skills. Interesting strategies that have the flavor of a real-world application not only motivate the learner but also make the instruction exciting.

## APPLICATIONS

As part of your job, you have been asked to review the design document for a course on decision making. Your review of the objectives for the course indicates that the learners will demonstrate how to use data to make decisions. Several of the objectives focus on different types of decisions (e.g., regarding costs, sales, forecasting) the learners will need to make using available data. As you review the instructional materials, you realize that all the strategies are focused on memorizing either the steps for decision making or the types of data that are available for managers. What would you recommend to improve the effectiveness of the instructional strategies in this course?

Your technology company has recently hired a number of young professionals "to pave the way of the future" in information technology. The wise old CEO (she is 31 years old) is genuinely interested in all her employees. Because everyone is paid an excellent salary, she feels that the young staff should be educated in proper investment strategies so they can have a comfortable life. She has personally asked you to design an investment-training program and has hired a personal financial consultant as your subject-matter expert.

One of your tasks is to teach about bonds, mutual funds, and stocks. What type of strategy would you design to teach this information?

## ANSWERS

There is an obvious discrepancy between the performance described by the objectives—decision making—and the instructional materials, which are using strategies to help the learner memorize the decision-making steps and other information. Assuming that the client has already agreed with the problem-solving focus of the objectives, a different set of instructional strategies that will support the development of the decision-making skills is needed. A closer analysis of the objectives probably would indicate that they could be classified as concept, rule, or procedure with application-level performance. Once you have correctly classified the objectives, you can select the appropriate instructional strategies that will develop application performance rather than recall performance.

Bonds, mutual funds, and stocks are concepts. A concept-application strategy will enable the employees to identify each type of investment. Your initial presentation would include the name of the concept (e.g., bonds), the definition provided by the SME, and a best example of the concept. You could use an integrative strategy that asks the learner to identify new examples of each concept from various investment websites. This instruction would address the current instructional goal: understanding the facets of investment options. Subsequent units, if required by additional training goals, might then address applications, such as choosing between investment options and buying and selling stocks.

## QUALITY MANAGEMENT

The first question to ask is whether the instructional strategies really support the development of the skills and knowledge specified in the objectives. The first application problem (i.e., the decision-making course) illustrates instructional strategies that do not support the development of the objectives. Your quality check should compare the strategies against the objectives to determine whether your instruction will develop the appropriate knowledge and skills. Consider, for example, a series of objectives that focus on teaching troubleshooting skills at the application level. The instructional strategies, however, focus on memorizing faults and steps for troubleshooting. This mismatch between the objectives will not help the learners achieve the objectives. If your objectives accurately reflect what is needed to address the problem, then the instructional strategies must be revised. It is more time- and cost-efficient to correct these mistakes before you have developed the materials.

The second question to ask is whether the objectives, content, and instructional strategies address the instructional problem you have identified. We are always amazed at how different individuals attempt to influence our design process and begin to move us away from our original purpose. When this deviation occurs, it is often because we have accepted personal viewpoints on what should be included rather than remaining focused on the problem and the instruction needed to solve the problem. This final check of the alignment of your task analysis, objectives, and instructional strategies is needed before you begin development of the instructional materials. Changes at this stage are relatively inexpensive compared to major revisions of developed materials. Last, review your instructional strategies and sequencing. Is the logic of the sequencing still appropriate now that you have designed the instructional strategies? If not, make the needed changes in the sequencing before beginning the development work.

## INSTRUCTIONAL DESIGN: DECISIONS AND CHOICES

### Instructional Strategies

Now that the task analysis and objectives are complete, you're ready to engage in designing the instructional strategies. For each objective, you think about how to actively engage the learner with the material (i.e., identify one or more generative strategies). Here's your strategy design document:

### Objective 1

After completing this unit, the learner will correctly state the three components necessary to start a fire. *(Principle/Recall)*

**Initial Presentation.**    Present three components of combustion as a graphic showing three sides of a triangle. Second, present common examples that the learner could encounter in the workplace (e.g., paper as a fuel source, oxygen, and cigarette as a heat source). Third, describe how fire extinguishers remove one of the three components of combustion (e.g., a dry chemical extinguisher removes oxygen).

**Generative Strategy.**    Have the learners develop a mnemonic to help them remember the three components needed for a fire.

## Objective 2

Given an example of a fire, the learner will correctly classify the class of fire. *(Concept/Application)*

**Motivational Strategy.**    Ask the learner to speculate what would happen if a water extinguisher were used to fight an electrical fire. [This scenario demonstrates why understanding the fire classes is important and thus places the instruction in context.]

**Initial Presentation.**    Present a definition of each class, the title for the class, and an example of a fire in the class (Class A, paper, wood, and cloth; Class B, gasoline, oil, and grease; Class C, electrical equipment; Class D, metals: magnesium, aluminum).

**Generative Strategy.**    Ask the learner to classify new examples of materials into the appropriate fire class (e.g., acetone, magazine, alcohol, clock radio).

## Objective 3

Given a variety of fire extinguishers, the learner will correctly identify each type of fire extinguisher. *(Concept/Application)*

**Initial Presentation.**    Present the name and a description of each type of fire extinguisher followed by an example of each. Highlight features that are unique to each type of extinguisher (e.g., a water-filled extinguisher looks like a metal can and has no pressure gauge; a dry chemical extinguisher always has a pressure gauge; a carbon dioxide extinguisher has a cone-shaped nozzle).

**Generative Strategy.**    Show pictures of extinguishers in various workplace settings (e.g., hallway, kitchen, mailroom, garage, etc.) and ask the learner to identify the extinguisher type. [This generative activity also enables the learner to recognize places where various types of extinguishers are commonly found.]

## Objective 4

Given a description of the combustible material in a fire, the learner will select the correct fire extinguisher to extinguish the fire. *(Principle/Application)*

**Initial Presentation.**    Restate the importance of matching extinguisher type to fire type. Identify types of fires each type of extinguisher is designed to extinguish (e.g., water-type extinguishers fight Class A fires; carbon dioxide extinguishers fight Class BC fires; dry chemical extinguishers fight Class ABC fires). [This objective synthesizes content knowledge from objectives 2 and 3.]

**Generative Strategy.**    Give the learner several fire scenarios and ask the learner to select an appropriate type of fire extinguisher (e.g., "Given a grease fire on an electric stove, what type of extinguisher would you use?").

## Objective 5

The learner will describe the appropriate response to fire in an office setting. *(Procedure/Recall)*

**Initial Presentation.**    Describe step-by-step emergency procedures. Explain why following the procedure is critical. Describe the criteria for evaluating the risk of attempting to fight the fire using a fire extinguisher. Use illustrative example cases describing errors made by well-intentioned people that resulted in personal harm.

**Generative Strategy.**    Show brief video vignettes of fire situations. Ask the learner how he or she would respond. In the initial vignettes, the video segment will show individuals incorrectly responding to fires. Ask the learner to identify the procedural errors. In more advanced video vignettes, no responder will be shown, and the learner will describe actions as well as how he or she evaluated the risk of fighting the fire. [Ideally, the learner would demonstrate the procedure, but the designer has determined that this is not feasible in a classroom setting and given the time constraints. This is why the verb for the objective "list" rather than "demonstrate" is used. The video vignettes will enable the learner to walk through the procedure.]

## Objective 6

Given a dry chemical multiclass fire extinguisher and a fire burning in a trash container full of paper in an office setting, the learner will extinguish the fire by correctly using the fire extinguisher. (*Procedure/Application*)

**Initial Presentation.**    Demonstrate holding, aiming, and discharging a generic multiclass extinguisher using streaming video. Emphasize aiming the extinguisher at the base of the fire and using a sweeping motion. Demonstrate how far to stand away from the fire. Then show variations in holding and using a carbon dioxide and water-type extinguisher.

**Generative Strategy.**    First, the learner visualizes how he or she would hold and use each type of fire extinguisher. Second, in a carefully controlled outdoor environment, each learner practices holding, aiming, and discharging a multiclass extinguisher. Next, the learner practices using a carbon dioxide and water-type extinguisher. [Some designers think about instructional strategies as consisting of (1) presentation, (2) practice, and (3) feedback. Experienced designers also think about learner motivation and the real-world context to ensure that the instruction links directly to the workplace performance requirements. In addition, it is also important to consider how the learner will receive feedback after completing each generative strategy. Last, in this example, the designer saves design time by determining the instructional sequence and the instructional strategies simultaneously.]

## REFERENCES

Andre, T. (1979). Does answering higher-level questions while reading facilitate productive learning? *Review of Educational Research, 49*(2), 280–318.

Anshel, M. H., & Singer, R. N. (1980). Effect of learner strategies with modular versus traditional instruction on motor skill learning and retention. *Research Quarterly for Exercise and Sport, 51,* 451–462.

Asterhan, C. S. C., & Schwarz, B. B. (2008). The effects of monological and dialogical argumentation on concept learning in evolutionary theory. *Journal of Educational Psychology 99*(3), 626–639.

Atkinson, R. K., & Renkl, A. (2007). Interactive example-based learning environments: Using interactive elements to encourage effective processing of worked examples. *Educational Psychology Review, 19,* 375–386.

Bandura, A. (1977). *Social learning theory.* Englewood Cliffs, NJ: Prentice Hall.

Bandura, A., & Jeffery, R. W. (1973). Role of symbolic coding and rehearsal processes in observational learning. *Journal of Personality and Social Psychology, 26,* 122–130.

Bandura, A., Grusec, J., & Menlove, F. (1966). Observational learning as a function of symbolization and incentive set. *Child Development,* 37, 499–507.

Craik, F. I. M., & Lockhart, R. S. (1972). Levels of processing: A framework for memory research. *Journal of Verbal Learning and Verbal Behavior, 11,* 671–684.

Gerjets, P., Scheiter, K., & Schuh, J. (2008). Information comparisons in example-based hypermedia environments: Supporting learners with processing prompts and an interactive comparison tool. *Educational Technology Research and Development, 56,* 73–92.

Goodman, N. D., Tannebaum, J. B., Feldman, J., & Griffiths, T. L. (2008). A rational analysis of rule-based concept learning. *Cognitive Science, 32,* 108–154.

Grabowski, B. L. (1996). Generative learning: Past, present, and future. In D. Jonassen (Ed.), *Handbook of research for educational communication and technology* (pp. 897–918). New York: Macmillan Library Reference USA.

Hamilton, R. J. (2004). Material appropriate processing and elaboration: The impact of balanced and complementary types of processing on learning concepts from text. *British Journal of Educational Psychology, 74,* 221–237.

Hazeltine, E., Aparicio, P., & Weinstein, A. (2007). Configural response learning: The acquisition of a nonpredictive motor skill. *Journal of Experimental Psychology: Human Perception and Performance, 33,* 1451–1467.

Jonassen, D. H. (1985). Generative learning vs. mathemagenic control of text processing. In D. H. Jonassen (Ed.), *Technology of text: Vol. 2. Principles for structuring, designing, and displaying text* (pp. 9–45). Englewood Cliffs, NJ: Educational Technology Publications.

Jonassen, D. H. (1988). Integrating learning strategies into courseware to facilitate deeper processing. In D. H. Jonassen (Ed.), *Instructional designs for microcomputer courseware* (pp. 151–182). Hillsdale, NJ: Erlbaum.

Jonassen, D. H. (2006). On the role of concepts in learning and instructional design. *Educational Technology Research & Development, 54*(2), 177–196.

Leinhardt, G., & Steele, M. D. (2005). Seeing the complexity of standing to the side: Instructional dialogues. *Cognition and Instruction, 23*(1), 87–163.

Markle, S. (1969). Good frames and bad: A grammar of frame writing. New York: Wiley.

McCrudden, M. T., & Schraw, G. (2007). Relevance and goal-focusing in text processing. *Educational Psychology Review, 19*(2), 113–139.

Ozgungor, S., & Guthrie, J. T. (2004). Interactions among elaborative interrogation, knowledge, and interest in the process of constructing knowledge from text. *Journal of Educational Psychology, 96*(3), 437–443.

Renkl, A., Atkinson, R. K., & Grobe, C. S. (2004). How fading worked solution steps works—A cognitive load perspective. *Instructional Science, 32*, 59–82.

Rickards, J. P. (1979). Adjunct postquestions in text: A critical review of methods and processes. *Review of Educational Research, 49*(2), 181–196.

Rittle-Johnson, B., Siegler R. S., & Alibali, M. W. (2001). Developing conceptual understanding and procedural skill in mathematics: An iterative process. *Journal of Educational Psychology,* 93(2), 346–362.

Ross, S. M., & Anand, P. G. (1987). A computer-based strategy for personalizing verbal problems in teaching mathematics. *Educational Communications and Technology Journal, 35*, 151–162.

Rothkopf, E. Z. (1960). The concept of mathemagenic activities. *Review of Educational Research,* 40, 325–336.

Rothkopf, E. Z. (1996). Control of mathemagenic activities. Generative learning: Past, present, and future. In D. Jonassen (Ed.), *Handbook of research for educational communication and technology* (pp. 879–896). New York: Macmillan Library Reference USA.

Rummel, N., Levin, J., & Woodward, M. M. (2003). Do pictorial mnemonic text-learning aids give students something worth writing about? *Journal of Educational Psychology, 95*(2), 327–334.

Sweller, J., & Cooper, G. (1985). The use of worked examples as a substitute for problem solving in learning algebra. *Cognition and Instruction, 2*, 59–89.

Tennyson, R. D., & Cocchiarella, M. J. (1986). An empirically based instructional design theory for teaching concepts. *Review of Educational Research, 56*, 40–71.

Treagust, D., & Harrison, A. (2000). In search of explanatory frameworks: An analysis of Richard Feynman's lecture "Atoms in Motion." *International Journal of Science Education, 22*, 1157–1170.

Van Gerven, P. W. M., Paas, F. G. W. C., van Merriënboer, J. J. G., & Schmidt, H. G. (2002). Cognitive load theory and aging: Effects of worked examples on training efficiency. *Learning and Instruction, 12*, 87–105.

van Merriënboer, J. J. G. (1997). *Training complex cognitive skills.* Englewood Cliffs, NJ: Educational Technology Publications.

West, C. K., Farmer, J. A., & Wolff, P. M. (1991). *Instructional design: Implications from cognitive science.* Englewood Cliffs, NJ: Prentice Hall.

Wiley, J., & Voss, J. F. (1999). Constructing arguments from multiple sources: Tasks that promote understanding and not just memory for text. *Journal of Educational Psychology, 91*, 301–311.

Wittrock, M. C. (1974). A generative model of mathematics learning. *Journal of Research in Mathematics Education, 5,* 181–197.

Wittrock, M. C. (1989). Generative processes of comprehension. *Educational Psychologist, 24,* 345–376.

Wittwer, J., & Renkl, A. (2008). Why instructional explanations often do not work: A framework for understanding the effectiveness of instructional explanations. *Educational Psychologist, 43*(1), 49–64.

Woloshyn, V. E., Paivio, A., & Pressley, M. (1994). Use of elaborative interrogation to help students acquire information consistent with prior knowledge and information inconsistent with prior knowledge. *Journal of Educational Psychology, 86,* 79–89.

# Designing the Instructional Message

## GETTING STARTED

You have worked diligently on an instructional project, including creating the design of the graphics and printed page. At the last minute, your manager decides that your project is just the thing to showcase the training department. He makes arrangements for you to meet with a production house that will transform your document into something to rival a *National Geographic* publication, at least in looks. During your first meeting with the graphic designers, you explain your design scheme with the headings, indentations, and your use of bold and italic text, stressing their importance for communicating the structure of the text. You also stress the importance of keeping the graphics very simple so as not to confuse the learner with too much detail. The graphic designers agree and promise to follow your suggestions. Two weeks later you receive the page proofs from the production house. After a cursory examination, you can find absolutely no trace of the original structure that you conveyed to the graphic designers. In addition, the artists have turned your carefully crafted drawings into balloon-style cartoons, which detract from the potential dangers of working with high-voltage electrical equipment. In fact, the unit looks more like a comic book than a copy of *National Geographic*. Having seen the invoice included with the work, you wonder if you should mention the problems to your manager. Assuming that you have your anger and surprise under control, how would you approach this problem and correct it?

## QUESTIONS TO CONSIDER

"What is the best way to introduce the content to a learner?"

"What is the best way to implement your instructional strategies?"

"How can you cue the learner to the most important information?"

"Should you use pictures with your instruction?"

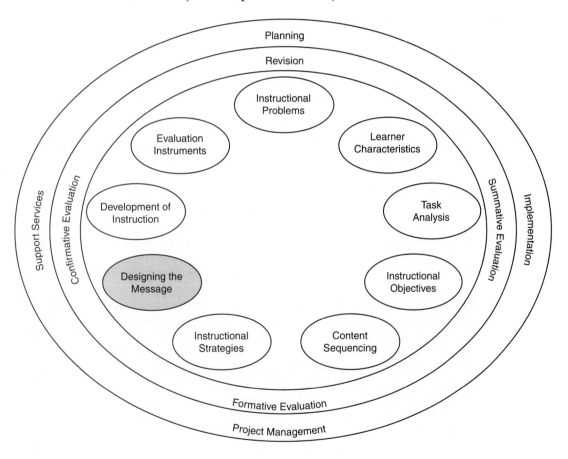

Thus far, we have focused on defining the problem and content, defining the characteristics of our audience, specifying the objectives, and designing the instructional strategies. The next step is to prepare the instructional materials by translating the instructional design plan into a unit of instruction. Translating the plan into an effective instructional unit requires more than simply "writing" the instruction. Effective instruction is developed by carefully structuring and presenting the materials that both engage the learner and signal the important points. Now that we have determined the content and strategies for the instruction, we must shift our focus to the design of the message (Fleming, 1993). In this chapter, we divide this message design process into three sections. First is the preinstructional strategy, which is a technique for preparing the learner for the instruction. Second are strategies for signaling the structure of the text through words and typography. Third is discussion of the use of pictures and graphics in your instructional materials.

## PREINSTRUCTIONAL STRATEGIES

Once the sequence for the instruction is established, the designer can begin to focus on how to present the information. Each unit of instruction begins with some form of an introduction that prepares the learner for learning the task. Hartley and Davies (1976) identified four different methods of preinstructional strategies for introducing an instructional unit: the traditional written-paragraph introduction (i.e., overview) plus three alternative approaches. Each of the four preinstructional strategies has specific applications for use in creating a better introduction for the unit. The first preinstructional strategy is a pretest, which is a set of questions directly relevant to the instruction. The second type of preinstructional strategy is a set of objectives, often simply a restatement the objectives the designer has developed or goal statements describing the behavior the student must master. A third technique is the overview, which is similar to a summary. Unlike pretests and objectives, an overview is written as a paragraph(s) of prose rather than a list of items. The fourth preinstructional strategy is the advance organizer, which is similar to an overview but written at a higher level of abstraction. A variation of an advance organizer is the graphic organizer, which uses a graphic to illustrate the content. Table 8-1 summarizes the applications and prescriptions derived from Hartley and Davies (1976) for each of these strategies. The "Function" column describes the instructional purpose of the preinstructional strategy. "Content Structure" describes the nature or length of the content. Some topics are labeled as loosely structured (e.g., "How to sell a vacuum cleaner") because there is not one set method for each of them. A highly structured topic (e.g., "How to balance a checking account") has a set of well-defined steps that are easily identified and recognized by experts. A subject area that is primarily rule based, such as math, is described as having a dominant structure, as opposed to a topic such as visual literacy, which is more loosely structured. The "Learner" column describes the characteristics of the target audience in terms of maturity or intelligence. The last column, "Task Attributes," identifies the learning conditions best suited for this preinstructional strategy. The following sections provide guidelines for developing each type of preinstructional strategy.

**TABLE 8-1**

Preinstructional strategies

| Strategy | Function | Content Structure | Learner | Task Attributes |
|---|---|---|---|---|
| Pretests | Alert student to what is expected | Length of the instruction is relatively short and loosely structured | Above-average IQ, older, or more mature learners | Learners should have some familiarity with the content if the questions are to be meaningful |
| Behavioral objectives | *Precisely* inform the student of what is expected | Used to preface a passage of fewer than 2,500 words[a] | Middle-ability students | Works best with traditional methods such as lectures |
| Overviews | Prepare the learners for the learning task | Little or no structure | Lower-ability students | Facts |
|  |  |  | Higher-ability students | Concepts |
| Advance organizer | Conceptual framework needed to clarify content for learner | Should have a dominant structure | Above-average ability, maturity, and sophistication | Factual information |

[a]Klauer (1984).

## Pretests

A pretest used as a preinstructional strategy differs from a pretest used to assess the learner's prior knowledge (see Chapter 11). When used as a preinstructional strategy, a pretest is designed to heighten the student's awareness of the content by giving cues to the key points. These cues will help the learner identify and focus on the main ideas in the unit of instruction. Pretests work best when the instructional time is relatively short, allowing the learner to remain focused on the questions. Answers to the pretest questions are typically not provided because the answers are derived from the instructional materials. (Additional guidelines for developing pretest questions are provided in Chapter 11.)

The following pretest might be used with a chapter on measures of central tendency:

> Think about the following questions as you read this unit.
> What are three measures of central tendency?
> When is it appropriate to use each of the measures?
> What are the steps to follow when calculating the mean?

Each question is open ended and serves to make the learner aware of three main points in the chapter. The designer does not expect the learners to answer the questions (if they can, they may not need to complete the unit). Instead, the questions should direct the learner to the key areas in the instruction identified by the questions.

**Pretest Guidelines.**

1. A preinstructional pretest should be relatively short so as not to delay the start of the instruction.
2. Typically, the questions are open ended and answered mentally to stimulate the student to think about the answer as he or she reads the content.
3. If there are several objectives for the unit, the pretest items can address a sampling of the objectives rather than every one.

## Objectives

The use of behavioral objectives has been the subject of much research for many years (Jegede, 1995; Klauer, 1984; Klein & Cavalier, 1999; McNeil & Alibali, 2000; Zumbach & Reimann, 2002). Davies (1976) has suggested that objectives may even be superfluous with highly designed materials such as computer-assisted instruction and other instructional design products. Another issue is whether students actually know how to use objectives for learning. Klauer's (1984) analysis found that learning directions and questions were more effective than specific (e.g., Mager-style) objectives. One possible explanation was that the learners were better able to interpret and understand the implications of the learning directions and questions because they were presented in simpler sentences. Although the general trend continues to be the use of objectives as a preinstructional strategy, the research results suggest they are not as effective for promoting student learning as once thought. However, research and practice strongly support the use of objectives by instructional designers and teachers when designing instruction. And, if learners see over time that test items are directly linked to objectives (see Chapter 12), the orienting influences of the objectives should greatly increase.

Here is an example of the use of objectives as a preinstructional strategy for a unit on job aids:

At the end of this unit, you will

- describe the difference between a job aid and a unit of instruction,
- determine when a job aid might be more appropriate than training, and
- design a job aid.

**Objective Guidelines**

1. Use a statement that clearly indicates the behavior the student needs to master rather than including the condition and criteria (cf. Klauer, 1984).
2. If there are several objectives for the unit, create more general statements to keep the list shorter than seven items long. Too many objectives will place too many requirements on working memory, resulting in confusion rather than mastery of the material.
3. Write the objectives in a style the learner can understand (e.g., ''At the end of this unit you will...'' as opposed to ''At the termination of the instructional presentation, the learner will be able to...'').
4. Objectives are less effective with units of instruction that are longer than 2,500 words (Klauer, 1984). Researchers theorize that it is too difficult for learners to remember the objectives and the content for lengthy passages.

As a result, the effectiveness of the objectives as a preinstructional strategy is decreased.

## Overviews

Overviews and advance organizers are often referred to synonymously; however, they are quite different. Overviews are written at the same level of abstraction as the unit of instruction and simply serve to introduce the student to the central themes. Overviews are most often identified as introductions because they are written as prose. The following is an example of an overview for a unit on job aids: A job aid is a step-by-step guide for performing a task on the job. Job aids are often used for complex tasks or infrequently performed tasks. An example of a task is the instructions on a pay telephone for making different types of long-distance calls. Although most individuals making such calls have received instruction on the task, the task is performed so infrequently that a job aid is used to prompt the user in performing the steps.

The "Getting Started" section of each chapter in this textbook is an overview for the chapter.

### Overview Guidelines

1. There are four general approaches to designing an overview. The first and most common approach is simply to provide a summary of the content. Most "introductions" that serve as an overview present a summary. The second is to pose a problem that the unit will help the learner solve (e.g., finding a discrepancy in your bank account). Presenting a problem can enhance motivation and increase learners' interest in the materials as they recognize the direct applications. The third approach is to describe how the content will help the learner. For example, as part of the overview we might state "this unit will help you develop job aids" to show how the learners can use the materials in their job. A fourth approach, suggested by McCrudden, Schraw, and Hartley (2006), uses prereading instructions to show learners how the instructional materials are relevant to their goals. For example, an overview would include instructions that are germane to the learner, such as adopting a perspective or reading for a specific purpose. The learner must then evaluate the relevance of each text segment based on the pre-reading instructions.
2. An overview should be relatively short (i.e., less than one page). A longer overview places an extra burden on the learner's short-term memory, which can interfere with the actual learning task.

## Advance Organizers

An advance organizer is written at a higher level of abstraction and serves to provide a conceptual framework to increase the meaningfulness of the content. This conceptual framework is hypothesized to make it easier for the learner to grasp the new material (see Mayer, 1984, for a review of studies). There are two forms of advance organizers. If the learner is familiar with the content, then a comparative organizer, which compares the new content with what the learner already knows, is used. If the learner is unfamiliar with the content, then an expository organizer, which incorporates relevant information the learner already knows, is used. The following comparative organizer is from a study by Glover, Bullock, and Dietzer (1990). Notice how the authors compare the idea of model testing to the development of a car using a model car.

> Many scientific advances are the result of testing models that describe natural phenomena. Scientific models are similar in some ways to the models with which we are all familiar. For example, a model car represents a real car but is easier to manipulate and study than the real car. Consider how a car easily can be put into a small wind tunnel to test the means by which the car's form allows it to slip through the air. By testing the model car, engineers can quickly and inexpensively test many possible forms of new cars before settling on one. On the next several pages you will read more about how astronomy uses models. (p. 296)

**Advance Organizer Guidelines**

1. State in general terms ideas that learners can understand and remember.
2. Ideas presented should be inclusive of the content covered.
3. If the learner is unfamiliar with the content, use an expository advance organizer. Expository organizers include relevant information the learner already possesses and compares this known information to the new information in the instruction.
4. If the learner is somewhat familiar with the content, use a comparative organizer to compare the new idea to known ideas.

The selection of a preinstructional strategy should be based on the factors in Table 8-1. The process is one of finding the best fit among the function, content structure, target audience, and task attributes.

## MESSAGE DESIGN FOR TEXT

An instructional unit—whether a textbook, printed manual, computer-based instruction, multimedia instruction, or video recording—is an artifact of the design process that will endure (Simon, 1981). This artifact represents the interface or interaction between the learner and the instructional materials. In Simon's terms, the artifact will serve its purpose if it is appropriate for the learner. Thus, our task as designers is to create an appropriate interface between the instructional materials and the learner. One part of this process is to design the message so that it is communicated effectively. In this section, we consider how we can design the message by manipulating the text (e.g., structure of the writing) and the typography.

After analyzing science textbooks, Chambliss and Calfee (1989) concluded that there are three critical design elements essential to good printed instruction. First is a set of distinctive elements such as words or typography that signal the structure of the text to the learner. For example, in this book the words at the beginning of each chapter signal the structure of the text through an overview and a series of questions. The headings signal the structure of the chapter. You might also choose to use italic type to signal key words or phrases. Second is the coherence of the text structure, which aids the organization and recall of information. We can affect this structure by using redundancy and familiar words and phrases. Third, there must be a match between the content and the learner's background if the learner is to comprehend the text. Other research also supports the notion that we can affect learners' cognitive processes by designing the message (Britton & Gülgöz, 1991; Jonassen, 1982; Mannes, 1994; Schraw, Wade, & Kardash, 1993). Similarly, Wiley and Voss (1999) suggested that the amount of information learners retain from the instruction is dependent on the "considerateness" of the text. Let's examine how we can manipulate or structure the text to communicate the schema or topic structure to the learner.

## Signaling the Text's Schema

When learners are presented with a signal that identifies the text's structure, they can use this information to form a model of expectations that will aid their comprehension (Mannes, 1994). Signals can be global or local in nature (Lemarié, Lorch, Eyrolle, & Virbel, 2008). Global signals work together and are part of the overall design, such as the heading on each page of a textbook that, typically, states the chapter name or section name and page number. The heading and page numbers appear on each page, thus they are global in nature. Similarly, some computer and technical books may use icons for warnings, cautions, or tips that may not appear on every page but are used throughout the materials. These icons work together to signal the structure of the text and share common properties as global signals. Global signals can be thought of as a system; they are consistent and used throughout the material, whether it is print, a web page, or a computer-based instruction unit. An individual heading, such as "Signaling the Text's Schema," above, is local in nature and provides a signal to the text that follows. As the learner encounters new information, this information is placed within the existing model. The preinstructional strategies described in the first part of this chapter are one means of signaling the overall structure of the text, through headings and typographical layout. Another approach is to alert the learner to specific information within a paragraph or section of the material. For example, how can you alert the reader that six different tools are needed to complete a task, or that a particular paragraph will compare RAM memory to ROM memory? Armbruster (1986) identified five common text structures that a designer can use to signal important text for the learner:

- **Lists of items or ideas,** which are in no significant order. Examples of lists in instructional materials could include the clothing you would need to take on a raft trip or the instruments needed to extract a tooth.
- **Comparisons or contrasts** of ideas or objects. In a science unit we might contrast the features of a planet and a moon. Similarly, a course on corporate finance might compare two methods of cost accounting.

- **Temporal sequences** connected by time or specific sequences. The steps for testing and replacing an automobile battery or for solving a quadratic equation are examples of temporal sequences of events.
- **Cause-and-effect structures or explanations.** These structures describe the relationship between two ideas or events. That is, one idea or event is explained as a result of the second. For example, an economics text explains the relationship between consumer demand and price. An instructional unit on crude oil production explains the relationship between well-pipe diameter and maximum flow rate through the pipe.
- **Definition and example structures.** These are used to teach concepts by defining the concept and then offering examples of it. An example concept in a biology textbook is a capillary. Similarly, a concept in a database management training manual is a relational database.

Once the designer has identified the different topic structures in the instruction, the task is one of signaling these structures to the learner. These signals do not add new content to the text; rather, they provide emphasis to the structure or message the designer wishes to convey (Meyer, 1985). There are two methods for signaling these structures. *First* is through explicit statements that alert the learner to the structure. For example, we have signaled this list of two items by first mentioning that there are two methods, and then by starting the sentences with first and second. *Second* is through typographical conventions that signal the structure through change. Examples of typographic signals are the use of boldface or italic type and spacing (e.g., indenting and vertical space).

## Explicit Signals

Probably the most common method of explicit signaling is through the use of what Meyer (1985) calls "pointer words." These words, such as "There are two methods...," alert the learner to what to expect in the following sentence, paragraph, or chapter. By combining Meyer's pointer words with Armbruster's (1986) content structures, we can create a table of explicit signals used as part of the message design process (i.e., Table 8-2).

Table 8-2 provides a general guide for manipulating your textual information to signal important points for the learner. It is important that you use signals wisely and not overload the learner. Using too many signals on a page, whether in printed or electronic text, can result in too much distraction, with the learner failing to identify what is important. A second method for signaling the structure of the text is through the use of typography.

## Typographical Signals

With the increased availability and ease of use of desktop publishing, the instructional designer now has greater control over the use of typographical signaling. We can use typography to signal the structure of the text by identifying changes

**TABLE 8-2**
Explicit signals

| Text Structure | Example | Signaling Words[a] |
|---|---|---|
| Lists | *The following* items are essential for a weeklong raft trip . . .<br><br>Humans have five senses. *First is* . . . | *First, second, third, etc.; subsequent; another* |
| Comparisons or contrasts | A sole proprietorship is a business that is owned by one individual and typically managed by the owner. *In contrast*, a corporation is owned by a few to several thousand individuals and is incorporated under the laws of one of the fifty states.<br><br>A prime number is divisible by itself and 1, *whereas* a composite number is divisible by at least one other whole number in addition to itself and 1. | *But, in comparison, however, while, to differentiate, a distinguishing* |
| Temporal sequence | Hold down the Command key *while* pressing S to save the document.<br><br>*Finally*, switch the main breaker to on and close the fuse box door. | *Beginning with, after, next, then, first, second, etc.* |
| Cause and effect | *If* the application works properly with the start up files off, *then* there is probably a conflict with a start up file.<br><br>*One result* of increased recycling is the development of new industries to convert these items into new products. | *Consequently, as a result, if/then, the reason, one explanation* |
| Definition and example | Assets are items or resources of value that are owned by an individual or business. *Examples* of assets include cars, buildings, homes, furniture, and computers.<br><br>Hibernation is a period of inactivity in cold-blooded animals. Animals that hibernate *include* snakes, rodents, and bees. | *For example, include, another* |

[a]See Meyer (1985) for a detailed list.

in topic, and we can signal important words, phrases, and ideas by making them look different from the surrounding text. Let's examine how we can use headings, layout, and typographical variations to signal the learner.

**Headings.**   Authors use headings to signal a change of topic and to provide the learner with a picture of how the materials are organized. The use of headings to signal changes of topic is prominent even in electronic documents. The tags used to create Web pages for the Internet provide six different levels of headings for a Web document (see examples of two of these heading levels in Figure 8-1).

Headings are key words or short phrases that identify the content of the sections of text information. We have found that most instructional materials need two or three levels of headings. A heading level corresponds to the different levels

**FIGURE 8-1**
Using headings as signals

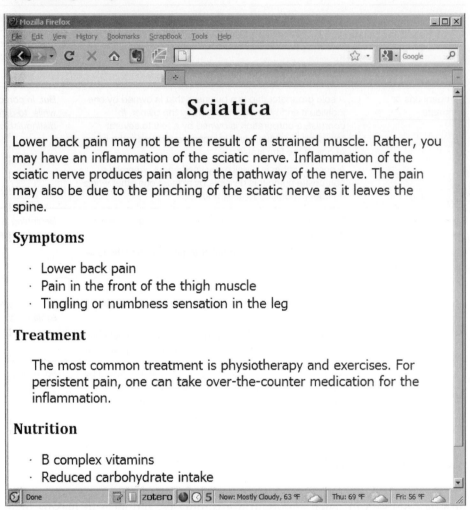

in an outline you might use for writing a paper. For example, first-level headings would correspond to the points listed as Roman numerals I, II, III, and so forth.

Second-level headings would correspond to the A, B, and C points under each of the Roman numeral headings. The third level of headings would correspond to the points under the 1, 2, and 3 points under the A, B, and C headings.

Each level of heading has a different typographical design. For example, in an early draft of this book's manuscript, the first-level headings were in 18-point boldface type and centered on the line. The second-level headings were left justified (i.e., flush against the left margin) and in 14-point boldface type. Finally, the third-level headings were the first few words of a paragraph and were printed in boldface.

This style is similar to the one specified by American Psychological Association's (APA) Publication Manual (2010) for writing articles and works well for manuscripts or documents that are desktop published.

To design headings for instructional materials, we suggest that you start with the objectives for the unit. Often, the objectives can function as the first-level headings. The second-level headings will signal the major ideas or steps needed to achieve the objectives. For complex content, you may want to also add a third level of heading that identifies specific ideas, tasks, or concepts in the unit. Next, you will need to select a typographical style that signals the heading. If you look through a number of books, magazines, and instructional materials, you will find a variety of styles used to identify the various levels. Your style should be easily recognizable by the learner. For example, using left-justified headings and only subtle changes in type size (e.g., 14-, 12-, and 11-point) might be a unique typographical design, but it may be confusing to the learner. The design specified in the APA Publication Manual is a good starting point with minor variations used to make it unique. A unique approach that does not signal the changing level of headings for the learner is likely to result in ineffective communication of the structure of the information.

If a graphic designer designs your materials, you may want to meet with this individual before you start developing your materials and seek his or her input on the design. In some instances, you may not have any decision-making authority on the typographical design of the final document. For example, a textbook author seldom has any input in the actual typographical design of the book. Yet, an instructional designer working in industry may have total control. Similarly, many graphic designers and editors are requesting that authors (including instructional designers) use a style template that assigns a specific style to text and graphics in a document. The graphic designer can then take the disk copy of the manuscript and easily create a layout on a personal computer by assigning different typographical styles (e.g., boldface, italics, type size, and spacing) to the document. This process can greatly streamline the production process and reduce the cost of materials.

**Layout.**   A designer can also use the layout of the page to signal the structure of the information. For example, you can divide the page into vertical spacing and horizontal spacing, which graphic designers refer to as "white space." By increasing the number of lines or points between a heading and the previous and next paragraphs, you can emphasize the heading. Similarly, you can indent a list of items from the left margin to signify that the items are grouped together.

**Typographical Variations.**   Another means of signaling the structure of the information is by varying the type—adding boldface, italics, or a change in type size—which creates a variation in the pattern of the page. Out of curiosity, the human eye is drawn to this difference. Thus, type variations are used to signal important words and new information. There are three factors to consider when using typographical variations. First, using too many variations on a page can overwhelm the reader, making it difficult to determine what is important. Second, the use of a single variation must be consistent throughout your materials. For example, you should not use boldface to identify new terms in one chapter of a book and then switch to italics for this same function in another chapter. Decide on how you will use variations, if any, before you start writing, and then be consistent. Third, the mixing of different typefaces or fonts on a page requires an understanding of concord and contrast in typography. Designers who lack experience in typography should avoid mixing typefaces and should rely primarily on the use of boldface, italics, and size variations of one type font to signal the structure of the text.

---

### Expert's Edge

#### The 10% Solution (for Learning)

One of the most widely disseminated nostrums in education and training is the "retention chart" that typically is phrased, "People generally remember 10% of what they read, 20% of what they hear, 30% of what they see, 50% of what they hear and see, 70% of what they say or write, 90% of what they say as they do a thing."

Where does this nostrum come from? You will see it attributed to Edgar Dale, Jerome Bruner, William Glasser, the NTL, and many other sources. All these attributions are entirely bogus.

The most likely author is Paul John Phillips, who prepared training materials for the petroleum industry at University of Texas in the summer of 1939 and 1940. Phillips then spent the World War II years as a lieutenant colonel in charge of the Training Methods branch of the Ordnance School, Aberdeen Proving Ground. After the war he returned to the University of Texas. Records at the University of Texas show that Phillips developed a mimeographed handout, "Some Training Principles" (TIM-151) in 1947, and this handout contains the now infamous retention chart.

One of the earliest published mentions of the retention chart is by Treichler (1967), who refers to it as a well-known finding but gives no source. Treichler was affiliated with the oil company that was known as Socony-Vacuum Oil Co. prior to 1955 and Mobil Oil Corp. after 1966, hence there are some early references to Socony-Vacuum or Mobil Oil Corp. as the sources of the percentages. Since P. J. Phillips (who died in 1950) had prepared training materials for oil industry workers, it is quite likely that Treichler encountered the percentages in the University of Texas handout.

The remaining issues are whether the percentages were based on controlled experiments and whether the percentages are a literal report of the research or a rounded estimate. There are no detailed records at Aberdeen Proving Grounds documenting a systematic program of research, but it is likely that they conducted research on training methods and retention at the Ordnance School, as this would have been consistent with the work done in other training branches of the U.S. military during World War II.

However, if there was research, the retention table could only be a very roughly rounded summary, for several reasons. First, it is implausible that any field research results would yield such even numbers. Second, any statistical findings would be pertinent only to some specific content, presented to a specific audience; they would not be pertinent to the retention of all knowledge in general. Third, not only is different content retained by different people at different rates, the retention rates would differ when measured by different sorts of tests. We know enough about visual and verbal learning to know that there are no simple generalizations.

The retention chart is often used to encourage teachers and instructional designers to select more "active" instructional strategies. That's not a bad idea, but it is a bad idea to attempt to support that practice by reference to ghost sources and oversimplified data.

### References

Treichler, D. G. (1967). Are you missing the boat in training aids? *Film and Audio-Visual Communications, 1,* 14–16.

[A longer version of this story, complete with references, appears in Molenda, M. (2004, January/February). Reader comments: On the origins of the "retention chart." *Educational Technology*, p. 64.]

Michael Molenda is an associate professor emeritus. He recently retired from the Instructional Systems Technology program at Indiana University. He continues to do research and writing related to the history and conceptual foundations of instructional technology.

## PICTURES AND GRAPHICS IN INSTRUCTION

The final consideration is the use of pictures and graphics in instruction. Considerable research (e.g., Anglin, Vaez, & Cunningham, 2004) and books (e.g., Willows & Houghton, 1987) are devoted to the study and use of pictures in instruction as well as their ability to increase motivation (Ainsworth, 1999; Peeck, 1993). In this section, we describe the effectiveness of pictures in instructional materials, the functions pictures can serve, and some general design considerations for using pictures for instruction.

### Effectiveness

There is a general consensus that illustrated text is conducive to learning the related text information. Pictures help readers learn the text information that was illustrated (Levie & Lentz, 1982; Mayer, Hegarty, Mayer, & Campbell, 2005). The pictures neither helped nor hindered the learning of textual information that was not duplicated in the illustrations. Pictures are particularly helpful when used to show spatial relationships described in the text (Peeck, 1987). For example, in a text describing the relationship between the position of the moon relative to the earth and sun during a lunar eclipse, a picture of these spatial relations would benefit the reader. Pictorial representations are also beneficial when used to illustrate abstract material and the main ideas in the text. However, no one type of information benefits more from illustrations than another.

Extensive research on the effectiveness of different types of illustrations was the subject of much of Dwyer's (e.g., 1970, 1972) work. A series of his studies focused on the use of photographs, realistic drawings, and simple line drawings in instruction. He concluded that, if the learner has limited time for viewing the illustration, as in an externally paced presentation like a video recording or lecture, then a simple line drawing tends to be most effective. If the learning environment is self-paced, then the learner is more likely to take advantage of the details in a more realistic picture such as a photograph. However, there is always the possibility that the learner may focus on inappropriate parts of an illustration with too much detail.

Simply placing an illustration in the instruction, however, does not guarantee that the learner will examine the illustration and gain any benefits. Directing the learner's attention to the illustration through prompts such as ''Examine the difference . . . '' is not always effective (Peeck, 1987). Researchers, however, have had more success when the learner interacts with or studies the illustration (Dean & Kulhavy, 1981; Winn & Holliday, 1982). For example, the designer might require the learner to label parts of a diagram or picture, answer questions about the picture, or trace and study a picture. A balance is needed between the picture and the activity, as overprompting the learner is also detrimental to learning from a picture (Winn & Holliday, 1982). Similarly, Mayer et al. (2005) found that static pictures were more effective than animations when teaching the operation of a system, and suggest that learners may need assistance in learning how to process animations to make them effective. According to Mayer et al., the static pictures reduced extraneous processing, which resulted in additional memory resources (i.e., germane load) for developing appropriate schema.

## The Function of Pictures

One can examine almost any textbook with pictures and see a variety of styles (e.g., simple to complex, black and white or color, line drawings or color drawings). On a more careful examination of the pictures and prose, one can identify pictures that serve different functions in a textbook. Levin (1981) has identified five different learning functions that pictures can perform in text. He also suggested that these functions are not equal in their effects on learning. Following is a summary of his categories with examples of how you might use each in designing instructional materials.

**Decoration.**    Pictures at the beginning of a chapter often serve no other purpose than to decorate and to signal that a new chapter is about to start (see Figure 8-2). From a publisher's standpoint, the inclusion of these pictures increases sales by making the text appealing. An instructional designer might view the pictures as motivational for the student. Graphic designers also use decorative pictures in the

**FIGURE 8-2**
Decorative picture

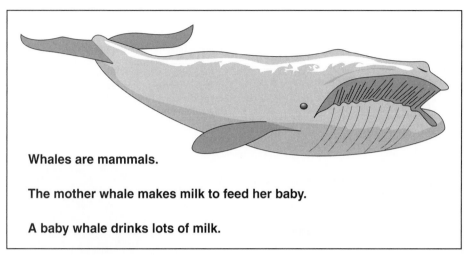

Whales are mammals.

The mother whale makes milk to feed her baby.

A baby whale drinks lots of milk.

From a unit by Reneé Weiss, used by permission.

text to "break up" the page so that it is appealing to the reader. The general idea is that a full page of text is threatening to the reader. Decorative pictures have no direct connection to the text information.

**Representation.**   When a picture is used to represent people, tools, things, or events in the text or other media, it may be classified as representational. Such pictures illustrate a major portion of the important textual information (Figure 8-3). For example, a designer might use two pictures in a science unit to illustrate the difference between rotation and revolution of a planet. Representational pictures provide a concrete reference for verbal information, which makes the information easier to grasp and more meaningful to the learner. These pictures are often used in children's books to illustrate poems, fairy tales, and stories. They are also used in technical training materials to illustrate new ideas.

**Organization.**   If you have ever purchased a car repair manual or tried to use your DVD player's instructions, you have probably seen a series of pictures that performed an organizational function. Designers can use pictures, such as step-by-step how-to pictures, to provide a framework for the text (Figure 8-4). The pictures in a manual on how to program an answering machine or a cell phone provide a map or path for completing the process. In many cases, the pictures provide more information than the few words associated with each picture. Pictures that perform an organizational function are not limited to procedural tasks. They are often used to describe the various attributes or features of an object (e.g., a new car) or a concept (e.g., a tornado).

**Interpretation.**   Pictures that help the learner understand difficult or abstract information are classified as performing an interpretation function (Figure 8-5).

**FIGURE 8-3**
Representational picture

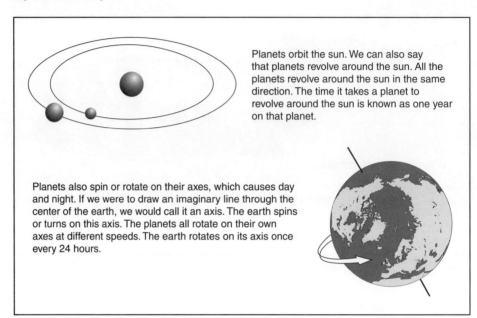

Planets orbit the sun. We can also say that planets revolve around the sun. All the planets revolve around the sun in the same direction. The time it takes a planet to revolve around the sun is known as one year on that planet.

Planets also spin or rotate on their axes, which causes day and night. If we were to draw an imaginary line through the center of the earth, we would call it an axis. The earth spins or turns on this axis. The planets all rotate on their own axes at different speeds. The earth rotates on its axis once every 24 hours.

Carefully selected pictures can add comprehensibility to a passage by providing visual interpretation of the content. For example, a science book that uses pictures to explain Ohm's law by comparing it to the flow of water or that compares the heart to a water pump is using interpretative pictures. According to Levin, Anglin, and Carney (1987), the distinction between the representation, organization, and interpretation functions is one of their underlying mechanisms (i.e., how the picture is used). Representational pictures add concrete representations to familiar information. Organizational pictures add coherence to easy-to-process material. Interpretative pictures, on the other hand, provide added comprehensibility to difficult or abstract materials.

**Transformation.**    Pictures that provide the learner with a mnemonic learning aid perform a transformation function (Figure 8-6). Transformational pictures are useful in passages that require the memorization of facts by providing the learner with a visual anchor for recalling the fact. A transformation picture often combines concrete images to help the student recall an abstract idea.

## Using Pictures in Instruction

The decision to use pictures in instruction is influenced by three factors. The first and most influential is whether it enhances learning. Second is the availability of the picture or illustration. Third is the cost of reproducing the materials with the

**FIGURE 8-4**
Organizational picture

## The Surgeon's Knot

The surgeon's knot is used to tie different diameter lines. Although it is not a very neat knot, it is very strong and easy to tie. It can be used to add tippet to the end of your line. This is especially useful when modifying your line to imitate dry flies, and when you want to do it quick, use the surgeon's knot.

Lay the new line parallel to the end of the leader, so that the lines overlap about four inches.

Make an overhand knot by forming a loop, bringing the tippet and leader around and through the loop. Keep the strands together.

Bring the same double strand around and through the loop once more, forming a double overhand.

Wet the knot, and then tighten by pulling all four ends to set the knot. Apply equal tension to both sides as you pull. Trim the tag ends as close as possible.

From a unit by Elizabeth Mathis, used by permission.

**FIGURE 8-5**
Interpretative picture

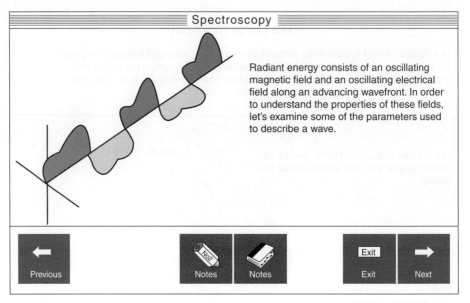

added pictures. We have examined the first factor in the previous sections, and now address the last two factors.

**Availability.**    With the advent of desktop publishing, computer-based instruction, and multimedia productions came the introduction of new technologies and processes for incorporating pictures and illustrations in instructional materials. For our purposes, we will classify pictures into three categories: original art, clip art, and photographs.

Original art is typically drawn by the instructional designer, an artist, or a graphic artist. The work can be a simple pen-and-ink line drawing, a watercolor, or a computer drawing. Original art requires someone with the artistic ability to render the picture.

Computer drawing and drafting programs make it relatively simple for an individual with limited artistic ability to produce an illustration. More complex illustrations require more expertise. Thus, the use of original art can substantially increase the cost of your materials.

Clip art is widely available on CD-ROMs and the Internet, where a designer can find a wide variety of photographs and line art (e.g., line drawings). Some of the materials are available for little or no royalty costs, and any royalty paid is often less than the cost of creating an original drawing. One problem with clip art is that it is generic and may not fit a designer's needs without some alteration. Also, the art may be outdated—depicting, for example, computers that are several years old or different from those used in the designer's organization. However, for those with

**FIGURE 8-6**
Transformation picture

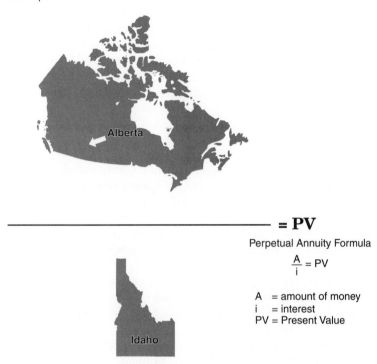

limited artistic ability and limited access to a graphic artist, clip art provides a viable alternative.

Designers have the option of hiring a photographer to take specific photographs, purchasing stock photographs, or selecting photographs from a CD-ROM. Again, CD-ROM photographs are often generic in nature and may not fit the specific need. Digital cameras have made it relatively easy for a designer to take a picture and incorporate it into the instructional materials whether they are distributed on paper or electronically via CD-ROM or the Internet. The quality of the photograph depends on the skill of the individual taking the picture.

**Cost of Reproducing.**    The cost of reproducing the instructional materials is the final factor that influences the use of pictures in instructional materials. The cost of reproducing pictures is seldom a factor when the materials are distributed electronically as in computer-based instruction, in Web publishing, or on CD-ROM. Typically, cost is a factor only when the large number of pictures necessitates additional disks. Cost, however, is often a factor when preparing print materials that use either color and/or photographs.

Accurate reproduction of photographic images in paper materials typically requires the use of a printing process (e.g., offset printing) as opposed to photocopying. Before a photographic print can be reproduced, it must be converted to a screened image, which adds an additional cost. Each photograph must be individually screened and prepared for printing. Digital photographs do not require this process when making electronic copies and may produce an acceptable photocopy. Black-and-white line drawings add no additional cost to the duplication of materials. These drawings can be scanned into a computer and included with text or simply pasted in electronically if they are clip art or computer drawings. Documents composed of only text and line drawings can be reproduced by photocopying or offset printing. The addition of color either for text or drawings will add cost for any method of reproduction.

## SUMMARY

1. Once you have completed the design of your instructional strategies, you are ready to concentrate on how to present the information. In this chapter, we have described how to create a preinstructional strategy to focus the learner's attention on the instruction, how to signal different aspects of the instruction through words and typography, and finally, how to use pictures to enhance learner understanding. This message design process provides a means for effectively communicating your instructional strategies.
2. There are four types of preinstructional strategies—pretests, objectives, overviews, and advance organizers—you can use to introduce the learner to the content. Each strategy performs different functions and works with different content structures (see Table 8-1).
3. You can enhance the communication of your instructional message by signaling the text's structure to the learner. Signaling can take the form of explicit pointer words, such as ''There are two methods...,'' or typographical signals, such as boldface or italics.
4. Pictures can provide concrete references for abstract terms presented in the text. Pictures can provide a decoration, representation, organization, interpretation, or transformation function in the text.

## THE ID PROCESS

The outcomes for this chapter include two different products: the preinstructional strategy and the message design plan. The preinstructional strategy product includes two parts. First is the rationale for the selection that is based on Table 8-1. Your rationale should describe the best fit considering the function, content structure, learner, and task attributes. As you develop this rationale, you will need to consider the results of your learner analysis, task analysis, and goal analysis. As you make your decision, you will need to consider which of the variables (e.g., function, content structure, learner, or task analysis) has the most weight for the project. Second is the design of the preinstructional strategy. This activity will result in the first page or part of your instructional unit. You need to design this strategy so that it accurately reflects the function of the preinstructional strategy you have selected. As you design and write the strategy, keep your audience in mind so that you write it at the appropriate level to appeal to the learner.

The message design product is a plan and a template for the unit. A good place to start is by examining your task analysis and identifying the text structures shown in Table 8-2. After identifying these structures, you can make notes as to the signal words and typographical signals you can use to alert the reader. This stage is also a good time to identify any pictures you will need and make arrangements for clip art, an illustrator, or a photographer. The second part of the message design is a word-processing template that defines the various styles for headings, text, lists, and so forth. Templates are an excellent method for providing consistency across multiple units of instruction or when more than one designer is working on a project.

## APPLICATIONS

Assume you are working for an energy company that has assigned you the job of developing the training for an in situ uranium-mining operation. You are responsible for developing training as prescribed by the federal government. Failure to design and offer the training can result in legal action against the company. One of the first training tasks you are directed to design is how to dispose of contaminated water that is spilled from one of the injection wells that pumps the water into the uranium veins. The mining engineers as well as the field operators have traditionally ignored such spillage and simply let the water seep back into the ground. The unit you are developing requires proper disposal activities that run counter to field practices. Failure to dispose of the contaminated water and contaminated soil in a proper manner can result in substantial fines to the company.

Given this information, which preinstructional strategy would you select for your instruction? Explain your rationale.

The sales personnel and company representatives for your plastics manufacturing company have requested that they have wireless access to the sales server so they can retrieve data from the field or from home. Management has refused the request for several years, but has finally agreed to provide access through a national Internet provider. As senior instructional designer, you are assigned the task of preparing a three-hour, lab-based course on how to access the server using wireless communication as well as how to log on to the server. Which preinstructional strategy would you select for your instruction? Explain your rationale.

## ANSWERS

One primary factor in designing the uranium-mining unit and the preinstructional strategy is the audience. The prospective trainees are using an unacceptable practice and may see this unit as a "waste of time." Thus, we can make a strong argument that the function of this strategy should precisely inform the learner of what is expected. Behavioral objectives would perform this function. Similarly, we might consider an overview that prepares the learner for the task. Our overview might take the form of a case study that describes the legal problems of a company that ignored the proper disposal methods.

The learners in the second example are familiar with the task (task attribute) of using the server, and the process is highly structured. Learners will range from those of low to high ability as well as low to high maturity. The function of the task will probably guide your decision for selecting either an objective or overview as your preinstructional strategy.

The new unit provides you with an opportunity to develop instruction for a highly motivated audience. Access to the sales information could lead to increased sales, which could result in increased income for the audience. The learners in the audience have used the data on the company server, so they are familiar with part of the task. They are not familiar with wireless access procedures.

The procedure is highly structured, and the audience is of middle to high ability. The task is straightforward and will be short in duration. Given the workshop/lecture format of the instruction, the length of the instruction, and the motivation of the learners, objectives would be a good choice for the preinstructional strategy. An advance organizer is also a viable choice given the dominant structure and the need to memorize the individual steps.

## QUALITY MANAGEMENT

The first quality check is to determine whether the preinstructional strategy you have selected represents the best fit between your learners and instruction. You can use Table 8-1 to determine whether you have the best match. As you develop your preinstructional strategy, keep your focus on the learners and consider what will help them prepare for the instruction.

The second quality check focuses on the message design of the unit. First, make sure that you have selected illustrations that properly illustrate the instruction. Are the illustrations accurate? Are they legible when reproduced? Have you obtained copyright clearance or paid the royalty if required? Second, as you edit your materials, try to identify the different text structures listed in Table 8-2 and then use the appropriate signal words to alert the learners. Third, check your headings. Do they convey the structure of the text? Can the reader easily identify the different headings? Are the headings distinct from one another and from the text?

## INSTRUCTIONAL DESIGN: DECISIONS AND CHOICES

You've probably been itching to get to the creative component of instructional design for quite some time. But you've remained patient and disciplined, aware that designers who shortchange or skip the analysis typically create ineffective instruction and waste time having to do a lot of rework.

You begin by building an overall design plan (see the following matrix). The plan provides an outline for the instruction and is useful for planning classroom as well as self-paced instructional materials. You decide to use an overview for the preinstructional strategy by presenting a problem based on a fire in the mail room that caused extensive damage because no one tried to extinguish a small fire that then spread after all employees exited the building. The fire disaster story heightens learner motivation and makes clear the importance of the instruction.

Notice that the "Instructional Strategy" column identifies the media (if any) that will be used for the initial presentation as well as a brief reference to the generative strategies.

| Design Sequence | Description | Objective | Time | Instructional Strategy |
|---|---|---|---|---|
| Preinstructional Strategy | Overview Fire disaster story | — | 3 min | |
| Instruction (Background concepts) | How a fire starts Types of fires Types of extinguishers Selecting a fire extinguisher | 1, 2, 3, 4 | 10 min. | Initial presentations with slides Generative presentation Learner practice activities |
| Instruction (Procedures) | Emergency procedures | 5 | 10 min. | Slide presentation Learner practice activities (video vignettes) Discussion |
| Instruction (Procedures) | How to use an extinguisher | 6 | 25 min. | Hands-on practice (outdoors in open field) |
| Posttest | Written test | — | 10 min. | |

Now you are ready to begin designing the instructional materials. Figures 8-7 and 8-8 are some example graphics that you have sketched:

**FIGURE 8-7**
Example graphic

## Fire Classifications

### Class A
Solid Materials (paper, wood, cloth, trash, plastics)

### Class B
Flammable Liquids (cooking oil, gasoline)

### Class C
Electrical Equipment

### Class D
Metals (magnesium, aluminum)

[The layout and use of typographical elements facilitates rapid comprehension of the content. Notice how the bolding, font size, and indentation affect how you read this slide. By including all four fire classifications on a single slide, the learner can compare how fire class relate to each other. The use of images would make this slide harder to read. Last, notice how the examples have been subordinated within parentheses.]

**FIGURE 8-8**
Example Graphic

Water Extinguisher      Dry Chemical      Carbon Dioxide ($CO_2$)

[This visual highlights key features to help the learner differentiate among the three types of fire extinguishers. Notice that the size of each extinguisher is shown in relative proportion to each other. Size of the extinguisher, the presence of a pressure gauge, and the shape of the nozzle are the key characteristics. Notice how the illustration eliminates all other nonrelevant cues. Notice that the label on each extinguisher reinforces the instruction. However, the inconsistency of the label on the $CO_2$ extinguisher impedes ease of learning. The water-type and dry chemical make clear the fire classes that apply, but the $CO_2$ extinguisher does not show its fire classes (B and C).]

## R E F E R E N C E S

Ainsworth, S. (1999). The functions of multiple representations. *Computers and Education, 33*, 131–152.

American Psychological Association. (2010). *Publication manual of the American Psychological Association* (6th ed.). Washington, DC: Author.

Anglin, G. J., Vaez, H., & Cunningham, K. L. (2004). Visual representations and learning: The role of static and animated graphics. In D. Jonassen (Ed.), *Handbook of research for educational communication and technology* (2nd ed., pp. 755–794). New York: Macmillan Library Reference USA.

Armbruster, B. B. (1986). Schema theory and the design of content-area textbooks. *Educational Psychology, 21,* 253–267.

Britton, B. K., & Gülgöz, S. (1991). Using Kintsch's computational model to improve instructional text: Effects of repairing inference calls on recall and cognitive structures. *Journal of Educational Psychology, 83,* 329–345.

Chambliss, M. J., & Calfee, R. C. (1989). Designing science textbooks to enhance student understanding. *Educational Psychologist, 24,* 307–322.

Davies, I. K. (1976). *Objectives in curriculum design.* New York: McGraw-Hill.

Dean, R. S., & Kulhavy, R. W. (1981). The influence of spatial organization in prose learning. *Journal of Educational Psychology, 73,* 57–64.

Dwyer, F. M. (1970). Exploratory studies in the effectiveness of visual illustrations. *AV Communication Review, 18,* 11–15.

Dwyer, F. M. (1972). *A guide to improving visualized instruction.* State College: Pennsylvania State University, Learning Services Division.

Fleming, M. (1993). Introduction. In M. Fleming & W. H. Levie (Eds.), *Instructional message design: Principles from the behavioral and cognitive sciences* (pp. ix–xi). Englewood Cliffs, NJ: Educational Technology Publications.

Glover, J. A., Bullock, R. G., & Dietzer, M. L. (1990). Advance organizers: Delay hypothesis. *Journal of Educational Psychology, 82,* 291–297.

Hartley, J., & Davies, I. K. (1976). Preinstructional strategies: The role of pretests, behavioral objectives, overviews, and advanced organizers. *Review of Educational Research, 46,* 239–265.

Jegede, O. J. (1995). An investigation of student's disposition to the use of objectives in distance learning materials. *Educational Research, 37,* 293–304.

Jonassen, D. (1982). *The technology of text.* Englewood Cliffs, NJ: Educational Technology Publications.

Klauer, K. J. (1984). Intentional and incidental learning with instructional texts: A meta-analysis for 1970–1980. *American Educational Research Journal, 21,* 323–339.

Klein, J. D., & Cavalier, J. C. (1999, February 10–14). *Using cooperative learning and objectives with computer-based instruction.* Proceedings of selected research papers presented at the National Convention of the Association for Educational Communications and Technology, Houston, TX.

Lemarié, J., Lorch, R. F., Jr., Eyrolle, H., & Virbel, J. (2008). SARA: A text-based and reader-based theory of signaling. *Educational Psychologist, 43*(1), 27–48.

Levie, W. H., & Lentz, R. (1982). Effects of text illustrations: A review of research. *Educational Communications and Technology Journal, 30,* 195–232.

Levin, J. R. (1981). On the functions of pictures in prose. In F. J. Pirozzolo & M. C. Wittrock (Eds.), *Neuropsychological and cognitive processes in reading* (pp. 203–228). New York: Academic Press.

Levin, J. R., Anglin, G. J., & Carney, R. N. (1987). On empirically validating functions of pictures in prose. In D. M. Willows & H. A. Houghton (Eds.), *The psychology of illustration: Volume 1. Basic research* (pp. 51–85). New York: Springer-Verlag.

Mannes, S. (1994). Strategic processing of text. *Journal of Educational Psychology, 86,* 577–588.

Mayer, R. E. (1984). Twenty-five years of research on advance organizers. *Instructional Science, 8,* 133–169.

Mayer, R. E, Hegarty, M., Mayer, S., & Campbell, J. (2005). When static media promote active learning: Annotated illustrations versus narrated animations in multimedia instruction. *Journal of Educational Pscyhology, 11,* 256–265.

McCrudden, M. T., Schraw, G., & Hartley, K. (2006). The effect of general relevance instructions on shallow and deeper learning and reading time. *The Journal of Experimental Education, 74*(4), 293–310.

McNeil, N. M., & Alibali, M. W. (2000). Learning mathematics from procedural instruction: Externally imposed goals influence what is learned. *Journal of Educational Psychology, 92,* 734–744.

Meyer, B. J. F. (1985). Signaling the structure of text. In D. J. Jonassen (Ed.), *The technology of text* (Vol. 2, pp. 64–89). Englewood Cliffs, NJ: Educational Technology Publications.

Peeck, J. (1987). The role of illustrations in processing and remembering illustrated texts. In D. M. Willows & H. A. Houghton (Eds.), *The psychology of illustration: Volume 1. Basic research* (pp. 114–151). New York: Springer-Verlag.

Peeck, J. (1993). Increasing picture effects in learning from illustrated texts. *Learning & Instruction, 3,* 227–238.

Schraw, G., Wade, S. E., & Kardash, C. A. (1993). Interactive effects of text-based and task based importance on learning from text. *Journal of Educational Psychology, 85,* 652–661.

Simon, H. A. (1981). Sciences of the artificial (2nd ed.). Cambridge, MA: MIT Press.

Wiley, J., & Voss, J. F. (1999). Constructing arguments from multiple sources: Tasks that promote understanding and not just memory for text. *Journal of Educational Psychology, 91,* 301–311.

Willows, D. M., & Houghton, H. A. (Eds.). (1987). *The psychology of illustration: Volume 1. Basic research.* New York: Springer-Verlag.

Winn, W. D., & Holliday, W. G. (1982). Design principles for diagrams and charts. In D. Jonassen (Ed.), *The technology of text* (Vol. 1, pp. 277–299). Englewood Cliffs, NJ: Educational Technology Publications.

Zumbach, J., & Reimann, P. (2002). Enhancing learning from hypertext by inducing a goal orientation: Comparing different approaches. *Instructional Science, 30*(4), 243–267.

# CHAPTER  9

# Developing Instructional Materials

## GETTING STARTED

You have spent almost nine months working on a business economics course for your international consulting company. The vice president of your division believes that this course will provide a significant revenue stream for your company. Your manager said that your design plan is a model for future projects: "The task analysis was very thorough, you have a good grasp of the learners, and your instructional strategies were creative." You now have to prepare the instructor's manual and the student's manual. The instructor's manual will include fairly detailed lecture notes and exercises. The student's manual consists of an outline for the lectures, readings, and problems that are done either before or after the lectures. You are responsible for writing every word in the manual. Where will you start?

## QUESTIONS TO CONSIDER

"How do I use the design plan to develop the instruction?"

"What guidelines can I follow when 'writing' the instruction?"

"What makes good instruction from the learner's perspective?"

"Shall I do role playing somewhere in this unit because my students are likely to benefit from such an activity?"

"Are there alternatives to having an instructor lecture?"

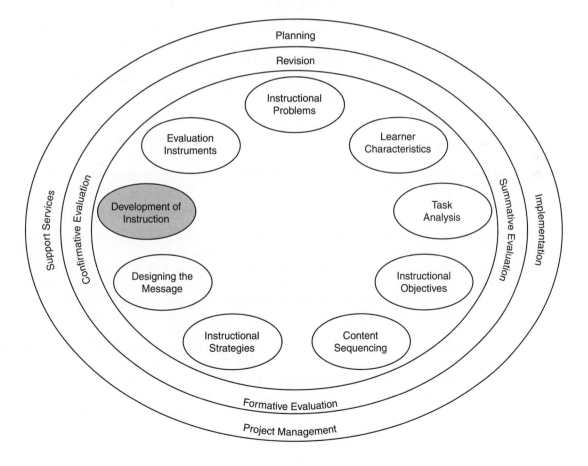

Once the instructional strategies are designed (see Chapter 7), the instructional designer is ready to start developing the instruction. This task is the process of translating the design plan into instruction. An instructional designer can choose from a wide variety of formats for the instruction, ranging from a simple printed manual to a DVD to a multimedia unit that includes video, coaching, and immediate feedback. The common feature of almost all instruction is text. Each medium offers a different challenge and opportunity for the designer. However, many principles apply to the development of the instruction regardless of the medium used to deliver it to the learner. This chapter has two main sections. In the first section, we discuss heuristics for developing the instruction with an emphasis on print-based materials. The second section of the chapter focuses on three different instructional delivery methods: group presentations (e.g., lectures), self-paced instruction, and small-group activities. Chapter 10 will address specifics for computer-based and web-based delivery systems.

## STARTING THE DEVELOPMENT OF THE INSTRUCTION

How do we craft effective, exciting, and motivating instruction using your instructional design plan? Instruction does not need to be dry and pedantic like that of a technical manual. Although we would not expect the instruction to be as captivating as a mystery novel, we would expect it to be more exciting and interesting than instructions on how to assemble a gas grill. Let's examine how to get started in developing the instruction.

### Staying Focused

As you develop the instruction, it is important to stay focused on solving the performance problem.

**Objectives.**   Make sure the objectives support the resolution of the instructional problem. Each objective should address either content or skill that will help the learner improve performance related to the problem. Similarly, the instructional strategies you have designed should support the mastery of the objectives. Now is an excellent time to review the strategies and make sure each strategy supports the content and performance specified for the objective in the expanded content-performance matrix. If you designed the strategy correctly, the performance—recall or application—specified in the objective will be reflected by the strategy you designed to support the intended performance. One common error is to have an objective classified as an application-level performance and then design a strategy that focuses on recall. For example, the objective might state that the learner will demonstrate how to correctly balance the cargo load in an aircraft, but the designed strategy simply focuses on helping the learner recall the steps. Thus, a quick review of your objectives classifications and the strategies you designed will help you maintain a focus on the problem.

**Learner Analysis.**   Next, you should review the learner analysis. First, the learner analysis should help you determine the appropriate reading level for your audience. If you make the text too difficult to understand, then the learners may fail to complete the instruction. If it is too simple, they may become bored and tend to ignore it or feel that the information is unimportant. It is unlikely you will know the exact average reading level of your audience; however, you should be able to determine a typical range of abilities. Once you start developing the materials, you can use the readability index included with some word processors to judge and modify the level of your materials (see Figure 9-1).

Second, you can use the learner analysis to determine the learners' familiarity with the content and technical terms. If you were designing the introductory unit in a computer repair course, could you use the terms ROM, RAM, USB port, and network without first defining them? If you had recruited your learners from a high school that also offers a network administrators' certificate and has extensive computer resources, then your learners might be familiar with the terms. However, if you recruited your learners from a group of students at a high school with very limited computer resources, then your learners might not be familiar with the terminology. Assuming that your learners know too much can result in instruction

**FIGURE 9-1**
Readability Index

| Readability Statistics | ? X |
| --- | --- |
| **Counts** | |
| Words | 2582 |
| Characters | 14743 |
| Paragraphs | 35 |
| Sentences | 135 |
| **Averages** | |
| Sentences per Paragraph | 5.1 |
| Words per Sentence | 18.8 |
| Characters per Word | 5.5 |
| **Readability** | |
| Passive Sentences | 20% |
| Flesch Reading Ease | 25.6 |
| Flesch-Kincaid Grade Level | 12.0 |
| | OK |

that is too difficult. Third, understanding the audience's background can help you select an appropriate context for illustrations used in the instruction. For example, when describing Ethernet ports to computer-naive students, you might use the analogy of the phone jack. Similarly, our designer in the "Getting Started" scenario might need to use a variety of examples for different industries or parts of the country. Using an auto-manufacturing company as an example for teaching the students how to calculate return on investment might work for learners in Michigan. For learners in Texas, a more appropriate context might be an oil industry example.

## HEURISTICS FOR DEVELOPING INSTRUCTION

Each time we develop instructional materials, we learn something new. This approach is the heuristic process described in Chapter 1. We modify existing heuristics, and add new heuristics, as we learn what works and what does not work. These heuristics are general rules we can apply to the design process. The following discussion provides several heuristics that will help you develop a unit of instruction.

### Make It Concrete

The positive benefits of learning from concrete materials have been well established by Paivio 1971, 1986. Unfortunately, because text materials are often abstract, learners may have difficulty understanding the ideas the author wants to convey. We might initially think that the best way to make instruction concrete is to add a picture. Carter (1985) suggested that carefully crafted words have their benefits: "If a picture is worth a thousand words, a good concrete example is worth at least several hundred words of further definition and explanation" (p. 151). As designers who may slip into the mode of an author while developing materials, we may easily be seduced by the idea that abstract presentations are better for our learners and a necessary part of learning. Research, however, suggests that a mix of abstract and concrete information increases both the learner's interest and recall of the information (Sadoski, Goetz, & Fritz, 1993). Research suggests that presenting material in a personalized style can also aid learner comprehension and transfer, possibly because it increases interest and thus the learner is more likely to engage in cognitive processing (Mayer, Fennel, Farmer, & Campbell, 2004). However, Mayer et al. raise concerns about extensive personalizations because they can be distracting. They recommend subtle changes like using "you" and "your."

**What Is Concrete?**   Concrete words are those that readily create a mental image for the learner. For example, the word *truth* is considered abstract because it does not bring to mind an image. The word *house*, though, is concrete because our minds easily conjure an image of a house. Similarly, sentences can be abstract or concrete. Sadoski et al. (1993) gave the example, "The traditional customs fascinated the tourists" (p. 292) as abstract because the subject, *traditional customs*, is abstract (i.e., not something represented by a single picture or image). In contrast, the subject of the sentence "The tribal marriage customs fascinated the tourists" (p. 292) is concrete and is more likely to be remembered by the reader.

**Making Text Concrete.**     There are three ways to make instructional text concrete and thus more comprehensible. First is the use of illustrations (see Chapter 8). Drawings, graphics, graphs, and photographs provide a referent, or an image, for words. By providing this image for the learner, we can make the text more concrete. Simply adding a picture to the text, however, is typically not adequate. You will need to direct the learner's attention to the picture with words such as, "Note the roundedness of the upper edge . . . " or through some interaction such as, "Label the three points subject to stress on the chassis in the figure below."

Second, we can create concrete text through the use of concrete words, shorter words, and active sentences. Simple words tend to increase the readability of the text, making it easier to comprehend. Active sentences are easier to understand than passive sentences. For example, "The pointer should be aimed at the 2 o'clock position" is more difficult to comprehend than "Move the pointer to the 2 o'clock position." Given the passive text, your learner might stand before the control panel for hours waiting for the pointer to move to the 2 o'clock position!

The third method is to use ample examples to illustrate the ideas (Carter, 1985). Interspersing examples of the abstract ideas can add concreteness to the text. For example, consider the previous subsection of this book, the paragraph with the heading "What Is Concrete?" Notice how we used examples of abstract and concrete words and sentences to explain concrete text. The research does not advocate removing all abstract ideas from instructional materials. Rather, these abstract ideas need elaborations in the form of pictures, concrete text, and examples to improve learners' comprehension.

Generally, creating a concrete context for learning is supported by the research literature when the desired outcome is a basic understanding of the ideas. If the outcome is the transfer of the knowledge to other areas, then providing limited contextual or concrete examples can reduce the transfer (Son & Goldstone, 2009). When your objective is the transfer of skills and knowledge, then learners need to be presented with multiple contexts or concrete examples to support the transfer.

## Control the Step Size

If you have read a research article, especially in an unfamiliar area, you may have found it difficult to follow the literature review. The reason is that the authors are typically writing for individuals who are familiar with background information, and they make large jumps between ideas. These jumps or transitions are referred to as step size. Researchers assume that readers of their articles have the background knowledge and can follow the logic leading to the new idea. As a result, the naive reader may find it quite difficult to read the article because of a lack of prior, supporting knowledge.

As designers, we can control the step size of instruction. There are two strategies for reducing step size. First, use consistent terminology throughout the instruction. For example, do not refer to the *mesh screen* in step 1 and then refer to it as the *filter* in step 4. Select one term and use it consistently throughout the instruction. Second, make explicit references back to what the learner has previously learned. You can use the references when transitioning from one unit to the next and from one idea to the next idea. Simple statements such as, "Remember examining the mesh screen of the filter in step 1? If it was dirty, you can now remove it and clean it." Or, "Yesterday we examined how to use a predefined formula in Excel." Using consistent terminology and providing references to prior learning provide contextual cues to the learner. These cues make the new information easier to comprehend by providing a context or frame of reference. Step size can vary for different audiences. A small step for one group might be a large step for another group (Fleming & Levie, 1978). Having conducted an appropriate learner analysis can help you determine the appropriate step size for your target audience.

## Use Appropriate Pacing

When we think of pacing, we often think of how fast the lecturer speaks. Pacing, however, also refers to text materials. Pacing is a function of the number of examples, problems, interactions, or exercises presented with an idea. Designers can control the pacing of the instruction by varying the number of examples and/or problems in the instruction. If we were to create a map of a unit of instruction, a fast-paced unit would look like the map at the top of Figure 9-2. A unit that has several examples (bottom of Figure 9-2) would have a slower pacing. The fast-paced unit might define the first concept and then immediately define a second concept. To slow the pacing of this unit, the designer might add one or more examples of the first concept.

For example, a unit begins by introducing the concept "rectangle" by defining it. Then, the concept "square" is introduced. To slow the pacing of this unit, we might add several examples of rectangles after we define the concept (rectangle). Then, we could introduce the concept of square and provide examples of squares. After these examples, we could further change the pacing by presenting the student a mixture of five rectangles and five squares. The student is directed to place an X in each square. Increasing the "distance" (see Figure 9-2) between two ideas slows the pacing. Selecting an appropriate pacing requires familiarity with the learner's prior knowledge, general ability, and the difficulty of the material. For novel and/or difficult material, slower pacing can provide the learner with adequate time and support to develop an understanding. For reviews or less difficult material, a faster pace may be necessary to maintain the learner's interest.

**FIGURE 9-2**
Illustration of pacing

## Maintain Consistency

Using consistent terms throughout a unit can aid learner understanding. An editor will often direct you to create a style guide before you start writing. One part of this guide is a list of terms/words you will use. For example, will you spell email as "E-mail," "email," or "e-mail"? Consider a unit in which the spelling "E-mail" is used at the beginning to describe how to communicate with people within the company, and then the spelling "e-mail" is used during discussion of communication to and from a mailing list. Your learner might incorrectly assume that "E-mail" is a term describing internal company messages and "e-mail" is a different form of communication that is used with mailing lists. Consistent terminology is important when preparing instructional materials for technical areas. Naive learners are easily confused by similar terms. Referring to a covering as a "port cover" in one paragraph and the same object later as the "lower access" can lead to confusion. Although it is not always possible to use familiar terms, instructional designers should strive to use consistent terms to reduce the cognitive load on and confusion of the learner.

## Use Cues

Our last heuristic focuses on the use of cues in the instruction. As you completed your task analysis, you may have identified different cues that either make the process easier or are essential. For example, when explaining how to splice two electrical wires, the SME would probably indicate that, before cutting the wires, you first need to make sure the power is turned off. A learner might need to "turn the indicator until the arrow is at the 12 o'clock position." Developing the instruction includes identifying the cues and then accurately communicating them to the learner. We might cue the learner to "First turn off the electricity and check for voltage." In Chapter 8 we described several methods for cueing the learner using words (e.g., *first, second*) and using typographical conventions such as boldface and italics. Combining signaling with the cues will help the learner both identify the cue and increase the probability that it will be recalled (Lorch & Lorch, 1996; Lorch, Lorch, & Inman, 1993; Naumann, Richter, Flender, & Christman, 2007).

## PUTTING PEN TO PAPER OR FINGERS TO KEYBOARD

Tweaking the instructional design plan, identifying another cue, or coming up with just one more example must end sometime, and the writing must start. There will come a time when each refinement to the design plan becomes less and less productive. As a designer, you need to identify this stage of diminishing returns long before the returns are minuscule and recognize the signal to start developing the materials. In this section, we provide some final guidelines for translating your design plan into instruction.

## Preinstructional Strategy

If you have followed the model presented in this text, you have already designed and developed your preinstructional strategy. Once you have completed the title page for a manual, the opening logo for the video program, the index page for the Web instruction, or the splash (i.e., opening) screen for the multimedia program, you are ready for the preinstructional strategy. The preinstructional strategy is the learner's first contact with your unit of instruction.

Start your unit by copying the preinstructional strategy (e.g., just the overview, pretest, objectives, or advance organizer) from your design documentation and pasting it into your unit. Your next step is to address each of the objectives according to your sequencing plan. You will present the initial presentation and then the generative strategy for the first objective, then the initial presentation and generative strategy for the second objective, and so on until you have completed the unit of instruction.

## Initial Presentation

The initial presentation for an objective provides the learner with the information needed to achieve the objective. Each initial presentation in your design plan includes a brief plan for how to present the information. For example, the initial presentation of a concept will include the concept name, definition, and best example. Your task analysis will include this information. During the development of the initial presentations, you may identify a need to vary the step size or pacing. You can include summaries or refer to specific ideas presented earlier to reduce step size. To increase step size, you can reduce or remove redundancy and transitions. Similarly, you can vary the pacing by adding or removing examples and elaborations.

The initial presentation will include the cues to signal the learner to critical information. Signals in the initial presentation include those that indicate critical information such as cues or lists of items, the use of headings to identify the content structure (e.g., Tools Needed, Safety Precautions, Steps, Definition, Example), and headings that signal the structure of the unit (e.g., Introduction, Practice, Application). Signaling the intent will influence not only how much is remembered but also the type of knowledge that is learned (Anderson & Armbruster, 1985). The initial presentation for an objective is followed immediately by that objective's generative strategy.

## Generative Strategy

The generative strategy creates an active learning opportunity for the learner. Implementing the strategy from the design plan provides the learner with the guidance and chance to relate the new information to existing information by generating new linkages. Thus, it is essential that the initial presentation provide the learner with the appropriate information to accomplish this task. Once the learners have completed the generative strategy, how will you provide them with feedback? One effective approach used with the audiotutorial method (Postlethwait, Novak, & Murray, 1972) is to present the learner with the instructor's response after the learner completes one of the embedded exercises. Other research has also demonstrated that providing the learners with an expert's paraphrase is an effective strategy (Johnsey, Morrison, & Ross, 1992). Generative strategies differ from the more traditional strategies, such as mathemagenic activities (Rothkopf, 1996) that typically were designed to have a single, narrowly focused answer. Responses to generative strategies, such as asking the learner to paraphrase or generate questions, do not have clear-cut right and wrong answers. Thus, any feedback should include directing the learners to compare their responses to those of the expert to identify differences.

## Transitions

As you finish the development of one objective and start the next, you may want to include a transition. Transitions can help reduce the step size, or jump from one idea to the next, for the learner. Similarly, you can use a transition to alert the learner that the instruction is moving to a new idea. Transitions can consist of a single sentence at the end of the previous section or one at the beginning of the next section. For example, note the last sentence in the section on "Initial Presentation," which provides a transition to the generative strategy. You can also create short paragraphs that help the learner transition from one idea or objective to the next. The following is an example of a transition. "Now that you have completed the installation of the Ethernet card and installed the software, we are ready to modify the operating system so that we can share a folder and a printer connected to the computer." This transition refers back to the section the learner has just completed (i.e., installation) and shows how the completed steps are related to the next section (i.e., modifying the operating system). When you prepare a transition, avoid the trap of providing extensive summaries that overwhelm the learner.

Developing the instruction may seem like a daunting task both to novice and to experienced instructional designers. We can simplify this task if we consider our design plan as a blueprint for the unit of instruction. By following the instructional design plan and addressing each objective, the development process becomes a manageable task. Developing the materials is a combination of following the instructional design plan and using a good dose of creativity.

## Cognitive Load

Many introductory psychology courses introduce students to the "magic number 7 plus or minus 2" (see Miller, 1956). The basic conclusion from this rule is that learners can remember between five and nine items at one time. As instructional designers, we concluded that when giving the learner a list of items to memorize, such as airport codes, we should design our strategy to present only five to nine codes at a time rather than a list of two or three hundred codes at one time. Although this heuristic is an important guideline, Sweller (1999) and his associates, who have researched the cognitive load placed on the learner during instructional tasks, have suggested other factors to consider. In this section, we examine the application of cognitive load theory to the design of instructional materials. First, we examine the learning process. Second, we define two types of cognitive load. Third, we examine how we can manage cognitive load as we develop our materials.

**FIGURE 9-3**
A simple memory model

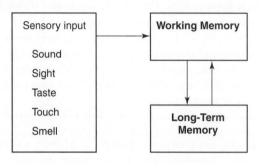

**The Learning Process.**   For you to read or watch television, three important processes take place. First, you must attend to or be aware of the information coming from your senses. Second, you process the information, or transform it into another form, so you can easily encode it in a manner that you will remember it for future recall (see Figure 9-3). These processes occur in working, or short-term, memory. Information held in working memory will remain there only for a few seconds unless it is refreshed by rehearsal.

For example, you might use the phone book to look up the phone number for the pharmacy. As you walk across the room to the phone, you keep repeating the phone number in your memory to keep it from fading from working memory. Most often we are trying to remember a seven-digit number such as 555–1212. But what if we needed to call another country and the number was 5475-4329? The additional number and unusual pattern would require us to expend extra effort to remember the phone number as we walked across the room. We have developed a schema that helps us recognize 555–1456 as a telephone number; more precisely, it is probably a local telephone number because it does not have an area code preceding the seven digits. When we use our schema to organize or recognize a seven-digit number, we can easily remember it for a few short seconds. The foreign number, 5475-4329, does not match our schema for phone numbers and requires extra effort to remember. This extra effort is the mental effort, or cognitive load, we must expend to remember, or process, the number. As instructional designers, we need to be concerned with the cognitive load we place on learners as they work with the materials we have designed. How can we control the effort the learner must expend to process the information?

**Two Types of Cognitive Load.**   Most of us have found that some subjects are easy whereas others are difficult. Some topics, such as the symbols for the chemical elements, are easy to memorize. We can create a list and start memorizing *O* for oxygen, *S* for sulfur, *C* for carbon, and so forth. Each element is learned by itself, and the learning task has little dependence on learning the other elements.

Sweller (1999) referred to this content as having low element interactivity. Other tasks require us to grasp several factors and consider the relationships between them before we can understand the content. For example, in microeconomics we must first understand fixed costs and variable costs to understand the concepts of total costs and marginal costs. Memorizing the definitions of each term would not contribute to our understanding of total or marginal costs. Similarly, we must go beyond memorizing the variables for calculating acceleration (acceleration = [Final rate − Initial rate]/time) and understand the meaning of each element to understand the concept of acceleration. These two examples identify content that has a high degree of element interactivity; that is, we must understand the different parts and their relationships to gain an understanding of the total concept.

The first type of cognitive load, intrinsic load, is determined by the interactivity of the elements of the content. As designers, we have no control over the interactivity. If there is a high degree of interactivity between the elements, then there will be a high intrinsic cognitive load. If there is low interactivity, as between the chemical element symbols, then the intrinsic cognitive load will be low. One approach to managing high intrinsic load is to break the ideas into smaller components rather than using a whole, or molar, view (Gerjets, Scheiter, & Catrambone, 2004; van Merriënboer & Sweller, 2005).

In contrast is the second type, extraneous cognitive load, which is introduced in the design or layout of the instructional materials. We can control the extraneous cognitive load imposed on the learner by careful use of instructional design and message design elements. For example, consider the task of teaching a student how to calculate the area of a trapezoid. To calculate the area, you must add the two bases, then divide by 2, and multiply by the height. We can simplify the process further by providing a formula: area = $([b + b_2]/2)h$.

Because the intrinsic cognitive load for calculating acceleration and the area of a trapezoid is high, we want to avoid introducing or increasing the extraneous cognitive load. We can significantly reduce the cognitive load required to understand this calculation by providing a diagram (see Figure 9-4). The diagram provides the

**FIGURE 9-4**
Using illustrations to reduce cognitive load

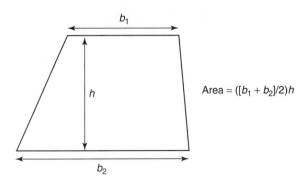

Area = $([b_1 + b_2]/2)h$

learner with a concrete reference for the terms in the formula, thus reducing the need for the student to use working memory to make those transformations. Instead, the student can focus on the calculation process.

As designers, our task is twofold. First, we must recognize content that has a high intrinsic cognitive load. Second, we must use appropriate instructional design and message design strategies to reduce the extraneous cognitive load imposed on the learner by our designs. The following paragraphs describe four ways of controlling cognitive load.

**Goal-Free Effect.**   When faced with a novel problem, learners often use a means-ends analysis to solve the problem. That is, they determine what is known, then try to find the shortest path to the solution of the problem. This approach is often highly efficient and effective for solving problems; however, Sweller (1999) suggested that it is not the best approach for learning how to solve problems. When learning how to solve a problem, the learner needs to develop a schema, such as one we have for determining the area of a rectangle so that we can apply it, for example, to determining the area of our yard in order to purchase the correct size bag of fertilizer. As we learn how to make this calculation, we learn to recognize elements such as length and width so that we can determine the area. The means-ends analysis does not help us understand the relationship between the elements (i.e., length and width), nor does it help us automate the calculation process.

This approach also increases the intrinsic cognitive load for the learner. Sweller (1999) suggests that we incorporate goal-free problems to reduce the cognitive load. For example, when presented with the problem in Figure 9-5, the learner would focus on finding the value of $C$, and finding the value of $B$ will become a subgoal. However, if we add the statement, "Determine the value of as many variables as you can," the learner will take a different approach, which also reduces the cognitive load. That is, the learner will first see that she can substitute 3 for the value of $A$ and then determine the value of $B$. Then, the learner will see that the value of $B$ can be substituted in the next equation to determine the value of $C$. According to Sweller, this goal-free approach reduces the cognitive load and allows the learner to develop a problem-solving strategy.

**Worked-Example Effect.**   If you developed a math anxiety in your early years, you probably felt the return of the same anxiety when you first opened a statistics textbook. You were ready for the instructor to introduce a math-related topic, provide an example, and then expect you to solve a similar problem. Again, you were faced with trying to determine what steps were required to arrive at the correct answer. In recent years, we have seen considerable research on the use of worked examples (e.g., Atkinson & Renkl, 2007; Kalyuga, Chandler, & Sweller,

$$A = 3$$
$$B = A + 4$$
$$C = B + 5$$

**FIGURE 9-5**
Means-ends analysis problem

2000, 2001; Paas & van Merriënboer, 1994; Sweller, 1999; Tuovinen & Sweller, 1999; van Merriënboer, Schuurman, de Croock, & Paas, 2002). The worked-example illustrates how to solve the problem by presenting each individual step rather than just the problem and final solution step. A sample worked-example is presented in Table 7-7. The worked examples direct the learners' attention to the steps of the process and reduce the cognitive load needed to transform the steps in the more traditional presentation of a math example. Recent studies (Atkinson & Renkl, 2007; Renkl, Atkinson, & Grobe, 2004) have suggested additional benefits for fading the steps in a worked example. That is, the last one or two steps are not completed for the learner, which requires the learner to engage in working the example to complete it. When the interactions (completion steps) are directly relevant to the learning task, then they can enhance learning.

**Split-Attention Effect.**   If you have ever tried to follow instructions for replacing spark plugs, installing a graphics card in a computer, or installing a zipper, then you have probably experienced a split-attention effect (Chandler & Sweller, 1992). "How-to" guides and textbooks often unintentionally create layout that increases the learners' cognitive load when trying to learn tasks. This effect is created when an illustration is introduced into the text. Typically, the learner must divide his attention between the text and the graphic to comprehend the material. Figure 9-6 illustrates a passage that has introduced a split-attention affect and then how we corrected the problem to reduce the cognitive load imposed on the learner. In the first example, the learner must split her attention between the text that has the explanations and the labels (i.e., A, B, and C) on the drawing. Thus, the learner is not only learning the parts A, B, and C but must keep track of her location in the text and on the picture as she switches between the two presentations. Thus, more cognitive effort is required for the first example than the second example, in which the text explanation and the graphic are integrated. The second example results in a reduction of cognitive effort required for understanding the text. We can prevent extraneous cognitive load by integrating their text and graphics rather than keeping them separated, as in the first example.

**Redundancy.**   While correcting a problem that creates a split-attention effect, you might decide that, if text integrated with an illustration is good, then keeping the similar information in the text should further enhance the instructional quality of the materials. Sweller (1999), however, has found that repeating the same information in both the illustration and text creates a redundancy effect that actually increases the cognitive effort to process the information. The learner must pay attention to both the text and the graphic source, resulting in less working memory available to process the information (Bodemer, Ploetzner, Feuerlein, & Spada, 2004). Figure 9-7 illustrates the redundancy effect. The information should be presented either in the graphic or in the text rather than in both.

During the design and development phase, the instructional designer needs to identify strategies for reducing the cognitive load of the instructional materials. The

**FIGURE 9-6**
Split-attention effect

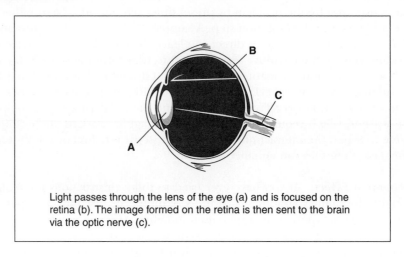

Light passes through the lens of the eye (a) and is focused on the retina (b). The image formed on the retina is then sent to the brain via the optic nerve (c).

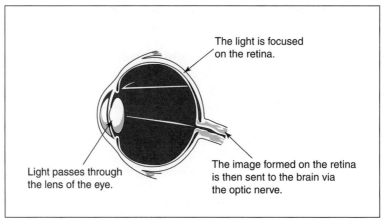

The light is focused on the retina.

Light passes through the lens of the eye.

The image formed on the retina is then sent to the brain via the optic nerve.

four effects—goal-free, worked-example, split-attention, and redundancy—provide examples of ways cognitive load can be increased as well as strategies for decreasing it. The effort might require working closely with a graphic artist, because the integration of text and graphics is not the traditional method used in the layout and design of materials.

The next section of this chapter focuses on three different instructional delivery methods: group presentations (lectures), self-paced instruction, and small-group activities. Examples of each method are described, followed by a discussion of the method's strengths and limitations.

**FIGURE 9-7**
Redundancy effect

The light is focused on the retina.

Light passes through the lens of the eye.

The image formed on the retina is then sent to the brain via the optic nerve.

Light passes through the lens of the eye and is focused on the retina. The image formed on the retina is then sent to the brain via the optic nerve.

Expert's Edge

## Taking a Load off the Learner's Mind

**Helping the learner comprehend.**  Some time ago, we noticed that our students were often overwhelmed by the abundance of irrelevant hits that were generated by their scientific literature search activities and were amazed by the results of an expert searching for literature using different databases and Boolean operators. As a result of this observation, we realized that searching for scientific literature is a complex task for which we might have a training problem. A quick analysis of the task and a closer look at the current training practice revealed that the task consisted of many interactive elements. The training focused on isolated elements and almost immediately began with authentic search assignments. From our experience as "cognitive" instructional designers, we knew that high element-interactivity material is highly cognitively demanding and difficult to understand. Although the elements can be learned individually, meaning full learning or deep understanding can only commence if the learner is able to attend to the important aspects of the presented material, mentally organize it into a coherent cognitive schema, and integrate it with relevant existing knowledge.

To tackle this training problem, we used the four-component instructional design (4C/ID) approach (Van Merriënboer, 1997). With its heavy reliance on cognitive load theory (CLT) (Sweller, Van Merriënboer, & Paas, 1998), the methodology is especially suitable to developing training for these complex cognitive tasks, which, without the appropriate instruction, may easily impose a high burden on the cognitive system of the learner. CLT is concerned with the development of innovative instructional methods that efficiently use people's limited cognitive-processing capacity in order to stimulate meaningful learning. Although 4C/ID considers authentic learning tasks as the driving force for learning, it acknowledges that the intrinsic load of these tasks in combination with the load caused by the manner in which the information is presented may hamper learning. When the load is necessary and enhances learning, it is referred to as germane load. After a thorough task analysis, use the following techniques to manage the cognitive load.

**Organization of learning tasks in a simple-to-complex sequence to task classes.** To prevent the excessive cognitive load that is typically associated with authentic tasks, learners will typically start working on learning tasks that represent relatively simple versions of the whole task. They progress toward tasks that represent more complex versions of the whole tasks as their expertise increases. Cognitive load is optimized because at any time in the training program learners receive tasks that are challenging to them but never too demanding on their cognitive capacities. The intrinsic aspects of cognitive load can be reduced by this simple-to-complex sequencing.

Task classes are used to define these simple-to-complex categories of learning tasks. The basic idea is to use a whole-task approach in which the first task class refers to the simplest version of whole tasks that experts encounter in the real world. For increasingly more complex task classes, the assumptions that simplify task performance are relaxed. The final task class represents all tasks, including the most complex ones that professionals encounter in the real world.

For example, some of the task factors that determine how complex it is to perform the scientific literature search skill are (1) the clearness of the concept definitions within the domain, (2) the number of articles written about the topic of interest, and (3) the number of search terms and Boolean operators needed to identify the topic of interest. Using these factors, we can define the simplest task as a category of learning tasks in which the concepts are clearly defined, with only few search terms, and which yields a limited amount of relevant articles. In contrast, the most complex task class is defined as a category of learning tasks for which concept definitions within the domain are unclear and searches require many terms and Boolean operators in order to limit relevant articles. Additional task classes of an intermediate complexity level can be added in between by varying one or more of the task factors.

**Timing of supportive and prerequisite information.** From a cognitive load perspective, the distribution of essential information over a training program and the timing and the format of presentation to students is critical. In many contemporary training programs, all information is provided before practice starts and is presented in a manner that unnecessarily increases extraneous cognitive load. The 4C/ID model takes this problem into account by making a distinction between supportive and prerequisite information and by prescribing how, when, and where in the program it should be presented. Supportive information is helpful to the learning and performance of the variable aspects of learning tasks. It can be information that describes how a learning domain is organized and therefore allows for reasoning in that domain. It can also be information that describes the way problems in a domain may be effectively approached and therefore guides problem solving. To keep the load resulting from the presentation of supportive information within manageable proportions, the supportive information within a 4C/ID training program is connected to task classes and evenly distributed across the whole training program.

Prerequisite information is conditional to the learning and performance of the consistent aspects of learning tasks. It consists of step-by-step knowledge that exactly describes how consistent skills need to be performed. This information is always applied in the same manner. Once a learner has mastered a consistent skill, the declarative information of how the skill is performed (e.g., procedures for selecting and filling in search fields) is no longer necessary. We can decrease the extraneous load imposed by organizing the consistent skills (i.e., how to fill in search fields) in small units or information displays and presenting it precisely when learners need it (just in time) during their work on the learning tasks.

**Part-task practice to automate consistent skills.**   Learning tasks are designed in such a way that they primarily promote knowledge construction for the performance of the variable aspects of the to-be-learned complex skill. However, in some cases the use of repeated practice in order to automate the consistent aspects of the skill is needed. For example, in complex literature searches a learner has to formulate search queries in which many search terms are combined with Boolean operators (e.g., learning and psychomotor) to decrease the otherwise large amount of hits. The cognitive load resulting from performing this consistent skill might be so high that learners have no cognitive resources available to organize the different literature search problems. As a result, the learning of the whole skill is disrupted. Repeated short isolated practice sessions are used to automate the performance of the consistent skill and to free up cognitive resources to cope with the variable aspects of the learning task.

**High variability of practice within task classes.**   The learning tasks within the same task class are sequenced in a randomized order so that each next learning task differs from the previous one. High variability is known to promote meaningful learning by stimulating learners to compare the solutions to the different learning tasks and to abstract more general knowledge for solving a wide range of problems. So, high variability of learning tasks is used as a technique to increase germane cognitive load.

**Learner support.** To compensate for the increased germane load that is created by the high variability of learning tasks, a task class will typically start with learning tasks having a large amount of learner support. As learners acquire more expertise in working on the learning tasks, learner support is gradually decreased until learners are practicing with no support at all. One popular way to realize the reduction in extraneous load is by providing the substantial scaffolding of worked examples initially, followed by completion problems and then full problems. Each of these problem forms may provide product and/or process support. Product support is provided by giving more or less of the solution to the problem that the learner has to solve in the learning task. Process support is also directed to the problem-solving process itself. Full process support can be provided as a modeling example in which the learner is confronted with an expert who is performing a literature search and simultaneously explains why the task is performed as it is.

### References

Sweller, J., van Merriënboer, J. J. G., & Paas, F. (1998). Cognitive architecture and instructional design. *Educational Psychology Review*, 10, 251−296.
Van Merriënboer, J. J. G. (1997). *Training complex cognitive skills: A four-component instructional design model for technical training*. Englewood Cliffs, NJ: Educational Technology Publications.

Fred Paas is senior educational technologist at the Educational Technology Expertise Center of the Open University of the Netherlands. His interests include research and development with a main focus on the instructional control of cognitive load in the training of complex cognitive tasks.

Marcel de Croock is an assistant professor of educational technology at the Educational Technology Expertise Center of the Open University of the Netherlands. He is currently involved in the development of computer-based tools for the design of personalized training for complex skills. His research interests include transfer of training, cognitive load and learning, training of troubleshooting skills, and adaptive computer-based learning environments for complex skills.

## GROUP PRESENTATIONS

In the group presentation, or lecture, method, the instructor tells, shows, demonstrates, dramatizes, or otherwise disseminates subject content to a group of learners. This pattern can be utilized in a classroom, an auditorium, or a variety of locations through the use of radio, amplified telephone, closed-circuit television transmission, interactive distance television, the Internet, or satellite communication (teleconferencing). While lecturing, the instructor may include media materials, such as PowerPoint slides, sound recordings, slides, video recordings, or multimedia presentations, either singly or in multi-image combination. These activities illustrate the one-way transmission of information from instructor to learners, often for a set period of time (generally a 40- to 50-minute class period). In small classes there may be some degree of two-way communication between teacher and learners, but most frequently learners are passively listening and watching.

## Strengths

The benefits of choosing a group presentation method to accomplish certain learning objectives include the following:

- A lecture format is familiar and conventionally acceptable to both instructor and learners. This method is the most common form of instructional delivery.
- Lectures can often be fairly quickly designed because the instructor is familiar with the material and will make the actual presentation. The designer often works with the subject-matter expert to provide the instructor with a list of objectives and a topic outline with the unwritten agreement that the instructor will follow the outline. The assumption is that the instructor can make the necessary strategy decisions. This strength is a particular advantage when instruction is needed to address a critical, short-term need.
- A lecture places the instructor in direct control of the class and in a visible authority position. For some instructors and in many teaching contexts, these factors are advantageous for achieving the objectives.
- Large numbers of learners can be served at one time with a lecture. The group is limited only by the size of the room; thus, lectures can be highly economical.
- As instructional needs change, a presentation can be easily modified by deleting content or adding new content just before or even during the delivery. Also, the presentation can be easily adapted for a specific group of learners (e.g., made longer or shorter, more or less difficult).
- Lectures are a feasible method of communicating when the information requires frequent changes and updates or when the information is relevant for only a short time period, such as the implementation of a new travel policy.
- A good lecture can be motivating and interesting for the students.

## Limitations

The group presentation method of instruction suffers from the following limitations:

- Learning is typically very passive, involving listening, watching, and taking notes, with little or no opportunity for exchanging ideas with the instructor.
- To maintain learners' attention during a presentation, the lecturer needs to be interesting, enthusiastic, and challenging.

- When an instructor lectures, demonstrates, shows a video, or otherwise presents subject content to a class of learners, the assumption is made that all learners are acquiring the same understanding, with the same level of comprehension, at the same time. They are forced to learn at a pace set by the teacher. Thus, lectures are not adaptive to individual differences.
- If questioning is permitted, instruction stops and all learners must wait until the question is answered before the presentation can proceed.
- In a large lecture class, it is difficult for the instructor to receive individual feedback from learners pertaining to misunderstandings and difficulties encountered during the presentation. Thus, some learners may leave the class with incorrect learning.
- A presentation may be inappropriate for teaching psychomotor and affective objectives, as these objectives typically require some form of practice or active learning environment.
- A large-group presentation may vary from presentation to presentation. Thus, the consistency of information and topics covered may not be the same for any two groups. This problem is particularly relevant when the training needs to be consistent, such as when teaching policies or procedures.
- Students who have difficulty with auditory learning will be at a disadvantage throughout the presentation.

## Applications

There are specific situations and times at which a presentation to a group of learners is most valuable:

- As an introduction, overview, or orientation to a new topic
- To create interest for a subject or topic
- To present basic or essential information as common background before learners engage in small-group or individual activities
- To introduce recent developments in a field, especially when preparation time is limited
- To provide such resources as a one-time guest speaker, a video, or other visual presentation that can most conveniently and efficiently be shown to the whole group at one time
- To provide opportunities for learners to make their own presentations as reports to the class
- As a review or summary when the study of the topic or unit is concluded
- To teach a large group of learners in a highly economical manner

## Guidelines for Effective Lecturing

Keep in mind that learning is enhanced when learners are actively involved. Therefore, it is important to develop a plan for including learner participation activities when lecturing. Also, to facilitate learners' understanding of the material, lectures should be clear and well organized. We recommend the following components:

- *Active interaction with the instructor.* Prepare questions to use at various points during the verbal presentation; encourage or direct learners to answer and enter into discussion with the instructor. Decide on places to stop a presentation (often at the conclusion of a section or the end of information presented on a concept), and ask questions to measure understanding and encourage discussion.

- *Note taking.* Encourage note taking by learners so that they will actively work with the material. Notes taken in the students' own words are useful in producing meaningful learning rather than rote memorization. If a PowerPoint presentation is used as part of the lecture, handouts with the slides can be provided so students do not need to copy each word from the slide but can focus on the lecture and take relevant notes.

- *Handouts.* Consider preparing structured notes on topics requiring the learner to (1) fill in an outline of content (e.g., structured notes), (2) complete diagrams that accompany visuals used in the presentation, (3) write replies to questions, (4) solve problems, and (5) make applications of content and concepts as the presentation proceeds. Learners can also complete self-check exercises or quizzes of the content presented. The key is to stimulate active processing of the information. For this reason, detailed notes are generally not recommended because they eliminate the need for the students to generate their own. Other forms of handouts include slides from a multimedia presentation such as PowerPoint that allows you to print three slides per page with room for notes.

- *Other mental activity.* Encourage thinking by helping learners verbalize answers mentally to rhetorical or direct questions that you or another learner pose. You can also ask learners to formulate their own questions relating to the materials for use in follow-up small-group sessions.

- *Terminology.* Use clear terminology and meaningful examples to illustrate concepts.

- *Organization.* Organize the lecture by constructing an outline. Bring the outline (or note cards) to the presentation and talk "from" it rather than reading it verbatim (a guaranteed painful experience for listeners). Unless you are very accomplished as a lecturer and highly familiar with the presentation, do not try to speak extemporaneously; a frequent result is a disorganized and rambling presentation.

- *Enthusiasm.* Show enthusiasm and interest in your subject.

- *Format.* A standard model (adapted from Slavin, 1995) is as follows:

  1. Orient the students to the topics (an outline, story, or overview).
  2. Review prerequisites.
  3. Present the material in a clear, organized way.
  4. Ask questions.
  5. Provide independent practice.
  6. Review and preview.

## Distance Education

With the rising cost of gathering individuals in business for an on-site class and the increased competition for students in higher education, distance education is gaining in popularity as a cost-effective delivery system. As Simonson (1995) pointed out, although few students prefer to learn at a distance relative to being in the same room with the instructor, there are times when the convenience of distance education outweighs other factors. Keegan (1996) identified two categories of distance education. According to his first category of distance education, the learner and the instructor are separated in time and space for the majority of the course. Examples include correspondence courses, broadcast television courses, and Web-based courses. The second category is those with delivery systems, such as interactive distance television, that separate the learner and instructor in space but not time. That is, all the students must meet at the same time, but in different locations. He labeled this category "virtual education" rather than seeing it as a form of distance education. In the typical virtual education setting, there is a host classroom or studio in which the instructor actually presents the instruction. Remote sites contain one or more video monitors, TV cameras, or microphones, along with other, optional equipment (e.g., a fax machine), permitting the two-way transmission of voice, video images, written communications, and computer animations and simulations. Also, it is becoming increasing common for students to connect to the classroom from their home or office computer.

In essence, the students at the remote site can hear, see, and interact with the instructor as he or she presents material in real time. Naturally, differing degrees of instructor-to-student interaction are possible depending on the number of remote sites to which the instruction is transmitted. Another type of distance education is one using the Internet to deliver the instruction. Instruction offered via the Internet can take many forms, ranging from Web pages to mailing lists to course management systems such as Blackboard to virtual classrooms created with software such as Adobe Connect®. Students can interact in real time or asynchronously by posting to bulletin boards or forums. Various Web sites also provide software and hosting services for instructors who want to create either Web-based resources for their classes or a Web-based course (e.g., www.blackboard.com). Another form of Internet-based instruction is asynchronous courses that have many features common to the personalized system of instruction (discussed later in the chapter). Today, it is not unusual for a distance education course to include a mix or blend of media or delivery systems. Campus courses often make use of Web-based instruction through applications such as Blackboard, allowing a blend of traditional and distance education delivery systems.

**Strengths.**    Distance and virtual education have additional strengths beyond the traditional classroom lecture and self-paced instruction for both training and education environments as follows:

- Students can "attend" a class without going to campus.
- Very large audiences situated miles apart can be served.

- Quality communications equipment at the host site can transmit professional-level, multimedia presentations.
- Unlike with conventional video presentations, students can experience instruction as it happens, thus permitting updates, announcements, and the spontaneity of live events.
- Unlike conventional instructional television, students can interact with the instructor by asking questions or making comments.
- Students can study and complete course activities anytime, anywhere.

**Weaknesses.**    There are also weaknesses associated with distance education that one would not encounter in a traditional classroom. These weaknesses are as follows:

- Depending on the sophistication of the telecommunications system and other resources, the quality of the video and/or audio transmission may be inferior to a seeing and hearing a presentation given in the same room (e.g., video images that are not well synchronized with the sound may be distracting to learners; the layout of the room may limit viewing of monitors).
- Despite the two-way communication capabilities, interactions between individuals at the host and remote sites are more constrained and less fluid than those taking place in the same room. Because such interactions interrupt the main presentation or are difficult to follow aurally and visually, students may lose interest in the instruction.
- The hardware requirements for some distance education delivery systems may prove too expensive for some organizations.
- Students working independently in a distance course lack a pacing mechanism, such as a weekly lecture, and may fall behind.
- Students in distance education courses tend to have a higher dropout rate than students attending campus courses.

**Guidelines for Effective Learning.**    The following heuristics can help you plan an effective distance education lesson.

- Consider the cost of delivering the instruction, and use distance education selectively where it fits special instructional conditions and needs (e.g., enables you to reach learners who are geographically dispersed).
- At the remote site, use multiple monitors rather than a single monitor where appropriate to achieve greater closeness between students and the presentation (Gopalakrishnan Jayasinghe, Morrison, & Ross, 1997).
- At the host site, favor an eye-level rather than high-angle camera position to increase eye contact by the presenter (Gopalakrishnan Jayasinghe et al., 1997).
- Carefully balance the amount of two-way communication permitted so that appropriate opportunities for interactivity are provided without compromising the pace or continuity of the lesson.
- Where appropriate, integrate multiple media (e.g., professional-quality videos or software presentations) to increase variety and impact, so that

the distance instruction is more interesting than watching an essentially TV-type lecture.

- Provide a means for students to contact the instructor, and then provide a response in a reasonable time frame.
- Provide detailed feedback on assignments.
- Materials must be designed in a way that creates a guided-didactic conversation (Holmberg, 1983). In distance education, the teaching (i.e., design of the instruction) and the learning (i.e., when the student studies the materials) are often separated by weeks or even months. Keegan (1996) suggested that we need to reintegrate the teaching and learning acts, which were separated due the design of the materials prior to their delivery to the students. That is, design the instruction to engage the learner with the content so that it is actively processed rather than passively read.
- Asynchronous components need to be designed and developed prior to the start of the course (and hopefully, tested).

## SELF-PACED LEARNING

Self-paced learning has received the most attention in instructional design. As the principles of learning indicate, much evidence supports the belief that optimum learning takes place when a student works at his or her own pace, is actively involved in performing specific learning tasks, and experiences success in learning. Self-paced learning methods are also called *individualized learning* or *self-instruction*.

Although these terms may have different meanings, the important features for the learner are responsibility, pacing, and successful learning based on specific learning objectives and a variety of activities with accompanying resources. Most frequently, the instructor selects the learning objectives and sets the requirements learners must follow. A "true" individualized learning, or learner-controlled, program would require the design of separate objectives and learning activities for each learner according to that individual's own characteristics, preparation, needs, and interests. Implementation of such a system usually requires a computer-managed instructional system to track the progress of each student and to select the appropriate objectives. Self-paced instruction, however, can occur at several different levels. Classic models from the literature are mastery learning (Block, 1971) at the precollege level and the Personalized System of Instruction (PSI) at the college level (Keller & Sherman, 1982). In school contexts, comparable approaches are sometimes referred to as continuous-progress grading, in which students' evaluations depend on the number of units they complete in a given time period (Slavin, 1994).

Drawing from these models, a quality self-paced learning program includes the following specific features:

- Learning activities are carefully designed to address specific objectives. A typical self-paced unit is organized into comparatively small, discrete steps, each one treating a single concept or segment of content. The size of the steps can vary, but it is essential that they are carefully sequenced.

- Activities and resources are carefully selected in terms of the required instructional objectives.
- The learner's mastery of each step is checked before he or she proceeds to the next step. Therefore, it is necessary to require the learner to demonstrate mastery of the content.
- The learner then must receive immediate confirmation of mastery of the objectives. With each success, the learner confidently advances to the next step.
- When the learner has difficulty understanding the material or fails to master the objectives for a unit, further study may be necessary, or the learner may ask the instructor for help. Thus, the learner is continually engaged in active learning and receives immediate feedback.

Most objectives in all three domains can be treated through some form of self-paced learning activity. In some learning environments, the instructor and students may feel more secure using a mixture of self-paced and group-paced instruction (i.e., lecture). The instructor and designer must determine the most appropriate delivery method for each of the objectives. In some situations, background and factual information might be assigned to a self-paced mode to ensure that all learners have mastered the basic information. Then, the group presentation (i.e., lecture) can build on this foundation. In another situation, the lecture might provide the background material, and some form of individualized instruction treatment would help the learners achieve the higher-level objectives. The instructor can then work with individual students who have difficulty mastering the material, and the faster learners can proceed to the next unit. Today, the greater emphasis being placed by educators on cognitive theory and self-constructed knowledge has altered the assumption that self-paced units must be highly rigid in content and linked to highly specific mastery criteria. That is, units that are project based and discovery oriented would certainly represent desirable types of self-paced instruction (e.g., using the Internet as an information source for creating a classroom exhibition on world-renowned natural history museums).

## Strengths

Evidence suggests that, in many situations, learners participating in self-paced learning programs work harder, learn more, and retain more of what is learned than do learners in conventional classes. Self-paced learning offers a number of unique advantages as an instructional method:

- Both slow and advanced learners can complete the instruction according to their own abilities and under appropriate learning conditions.
- The self-reliance and personal responsibility required of learners by a self-paced learning program may carry over as habits to other educational activities, job responsibilities, and personal behavior.
- Increased attention can be given to the individual learner by the instructor.
- The activities and responsibilities of an instructor involved in a self-paced learning program change because less time is spent in making presentations

and more time is devoted to addressing learners in group sessions, consulting with individuals, and managing the learning environment.

- Although major approaches to self-paced learning are not always immediately cost effective, as the lessons and resources are employed over time with additional classes, the cost of a program can be reduced appreciably. (For a consideration of program costs and measuring program efficiency, see Chapter 13.)
- The information presented to each learner remains consistent (i.e., each learner receives the same basic ideas) over time, which reduces variations caused by lectures presented on different days.

## Limitations

There are also some limitations to self-paced learning that make it less suitable for some environments:

- There may be a lack of interaction between instructor and learners or among learners if a self-paced program is the sole method of instruction in a course. Therefore, it is important to plan for periodic instructor–learner and small-group activities as appropriate.
- If a single-path, lockstep method is followed, learning can become monotonous and uninteresting. On the other hand, open-ended (discovery-type) projects may allow for too much divergence in what learners experience and accomplish.
- Lack of self-discipline combined with procrastination can result in delaying the completion of required study by some learners. Many learners must develop new habits and patterns of behavior before they are successful in self-paced learning. Setting deadlines (weekly or monthly) within which learners can adjust to their own study pace is often required and beneficial for some learners.
- The self-paced method often requires cooperation and detailed team planning among the faculty involved in the course. Also, coordination with other support services of the organization (e.g., facilities, media, reproduction, etc.) may become necessary or even critical. Such an effort is in contrast to the usual single-person operation characteristic of conventional teaching.
- More preparation and expense is typically involved in developing self-paced units compared with lecture presentations.

## Guidelines for Effective Learning

A self-paced unit typically includes a great deal of active learning. If existing materials (e.g., textbook, films, video recordings) are adapted, then the designer needs to develop materials to encourage active learning. These materials can include study guides, worksheets, and exercises. The Keller Plan or Personalized System of Instruction (PSI) is a good example of how an instructor can adapt existing materials for use in an individualized program. Because individuals learn at different rates, there should be time to study when it is convenient for them and also time in which to pace themselves. Individuals may want to linger over some material and speed through that which they understand quickly. A preferable way to plan for individualized learning is to start with a variety of materials serving the objectives and then plan more than one instructional sequence to provide for differences among individual learners. Depending on preparation and need, some learners may take the fast track, even skipping ahead and using few materials before concluding their study. Other learners may require a slower track that contains a greater number of concrete illustrations or examples, more review exercises, or even smaller segments of subject content with a repetition of explanations in different contexts. A designer needs to include a management system in the course design to accommodate these learners. The Keller Plan is easily adapted to asynchronous and hybrid courses and can make use of the learning management system such as Blackboard or Moodle.

Individuals also differ in how they prefer to learn (see Chapter 3). Some learners prefer visual materials, whereas others prefer to work with printed resources or hands-on experiences. Therefore, it may be advisable to collect or prepare a variety of materials to treat a set of instructional objectives and then allow each learner to select a preferred way to study. For example, if an objective requires the operation of a piece of laboratory equipment, the program for mastering this objective may include printed instructions, a set of still photographs, a video sequence, and the equipment. One learner may choose to begin with the video demonstration and then go on immediately to practice with the equipment; another learner might prefer to read the instruction sheet and then examine the still pictures before attempting to practice; a third might go immediately to the equipment and learn in a trial-and-error fashion.

By recognizing that active participation is a key element for learning, instructional designers can design a variety of experiences for learners. These can range from a carefully structured program that allows learners to proceed at their own pace to one that gives individuals virtually complete freedom and responsibility for choosing their own activities and materials according to their own learning styles or preferences.

## Design Checklist

If you are developing a self-paced program, the following checklist of questions for evaluating your planning may prove useful.

1. Is the program adaptable to the characteristics of learners who have different cultural and ethnic backgrounds?
2. Are learners who need remedial help identified before they start on a unit or module?
3. Are learners allowed to skip ahead if they already show competencies in part of the topic being treated?
4. Are low-level cognitive knowledge and psychomotor skills mastered before requiring higher-level learning experiences and practical applications of subject content?

5.  Is adequate attention given to affective objectives? That is, are learners developing positive attitudes toward the subject or its applications?
6.  Are options provided so that a learner may select learning experiences and resources?
7.  Are learners permitted or encouraged to progress at their own rates?
8.  Do learners have opportunities for checking their progress as they proceed through a program?
9.  Do learners have opportunities to share their learning or otherwise interact among themselves and with the instructor?
10. Do instructors consult with or assist individual learners and small groups?
11. How will self-pacing for the particular unit impact other activities in the course?

## Changing Roles

Finally, as a the team designs a self-paced learning program, the instructors involved should recognize that, not only are they changing their methods of instruction, but they also must change their own roles in working with learners. These changes can become both stimulating and more demanding. Some of the changes that can be anticipated are the following.

- Freedom from routine teaching of basic facts and skills
- More time spent with individual learners in diagnosing their difficulties, giving help, and monitoring their progress
- More opportunities to interact with learners on higher intellectual levels concerning their problems, interests, and uses of the subject content
- More time required for preparing, gathering, and organizing materials for use by learners
- More time required to orient and supervise aides, tutors, proctors, and other assistants

## SMALL-GROUP FORMATS

In the small-group teaching/learning format, instructors and learners, or learners themselves, work together in groups of 2 to 10 or so individuals to discuss, question, pursue problems cooperatively, and report. This approach provides students an opportunity to synthesize the content and improve their communication skills.

## Strengths

Small-group formats have the following strengths.

- A small-group format can engender synthesis of content by allowing individuals to discuss materials, share ideas, and problem solve with others.
- Learners acquire experiences in listening and oral expression through reacting to others' ideas and presenting their own. The more able learners can strengthen their own learning by explaining points or principles to other learners (also known as ''peer teaching'').

- By listening to students' discussion in a small-group session, an instructor can gain an increased awareness of the successes or shortcomings of various phases of an instructional program as well as obtain suggestions from learners for revisions.
- Small-group sessions promote active learning.
- Learners develop social skills by working with others.

## Limitations

Small-group learning may have the following drawbacks:

- Students need to complete the assigned readings before the small-group activities so they will be ready to participate.
- Instructors who are not prepared or who are inexperienced with small-group activities may fall back on lecturing for their own security or may provide too much input at the expense of the discussion.
- Careful planning of group composition and management is required to create an atmosphere that encourages all group members to participate.
- Individual groups require feedback on their progress and prompting to keep them on task.
- Students are not trained instructors; thus, the group activities should be used to supplement rather than replace other forms of instruction (i.e., lecture or individualized).
- Logistics of providing space for small groups and the expense associated with using additional rooms may prohibit the use of this approach.

## Formats

A number of different techniques are available to encourage and provide for interaction within small groups. These eight techniques are useful in both large-group and self-paced formats.

**Discussion.**    Discussion is the most common form of face-to-face teaching in which facts, ideas, and opinions can be exchanged. As learners think about a subject under discussion and present their views, learning can take place on higher intellectual levels (specifically analysis, synthesis, and evaluation) than is possible with a focus solely on the recall of information.

Discussions can take three forms:

1. Instructor-directed discussion is characterized by questions posed by the instructor and answered by individual learners. Such a format provides for a limited exchange of ideas within the group.
2. Group-centered discussion allows for a free-flowing exchange of ideas without the controlling influence of the instructor. Cooperation between participants provides their own direction and control of the pace. This method is open ended, as the discussion can go in any number of directions depending on learner interactions and reactions.

3. Collaborative discussions often focus on solving a specific problem. The instructor has neither a dominant nor a passive role but serves as a resource person and also as a contributor. All participants share decision-making responsibilities and are obliged to accept and integrate the ideas presented and to critically evaluate alternative solutions. This method is the most difficult form of discussion to implement; it is best used after a group has experience with the other two forms of discussion.

**Panel Discussion.**    In the panel discussion, three to six qualified persons (from the community or a professional group) present information or their views on an assigned topic in front of the class. The individuals may represent different viewpoints, various interest groups, or special experiences. Learners may research topics and serve on the panels themselves to present their findings. Following the presentations, learners in the class are encouraged to ask questions of the panel members.

**Guided Design.**    The guided-design method, developed by Charles E. Wales (Wales, Nardi, & Stager, 1987), focuses on developing the learners' decision-making skills as well as on teaching specific concepts and principles. Learners work in small groups to solve open-ended problems that require them to gather information (outside class), think logically, communicate ideas, and apply steps in a decision-making process. Learners are required to look closely at each step in the decision-making operation, apply the subject matter they have learned, exchange ideas, and reflect on solutions developed by others. The instructor acts as a consultant to the class.

**Case Study.**    In a case study, learners are provided with detailed information about a real-life situation. All related circumstances, issues, and actions of persons involved are carefully described. Learners must study and analyze the situation as presented. They decide what was done correctly and what mistakes might have been made in terms of principles and accepted practices in their field of specialization. During discussion, each person must explain, justify, and defend his or her own analysis of the case situation. This method is widely used in the business management field.

**Role Playing.**    Role playing involves the spontaneous dramatization by two or more persons of a situation relating to a problem. The incident might have to do with interpersonal relations or an operational problem within an organization (see Chapter 7 for specific strategies for interpersonal skills). Each person acts out a role as he or she feels it would be played in real life. Other learners or trainees observe the performance and then, when the performance ends, discuss the feelings expressed and actions observed. This process promotes an understanding of other persons' positions and attitudes as well as the procedures that might be used for diagnosing and solving problems.

**Simulation.**    Simulation is an abstract representation of a real-life situation that requires a learner or a team to solve a complex problem. The instructor creates aspects of the situation that are close to reality, and the learner must perform manipulations, make responses, and take actions to correct deficiencies or maintain a proper status. Many simulations are computer controlled, such as a mock-up simulator of an airplane cockpit used for pilot training. The simulator allows the instructor to set up appropriate conditions that require specific responses by the trainee. The participants become deeply involved, undergoing the same stress and pressures they would experience in reality. The instructor discusses and evaluates the results of the activity with the learners.

**Games.**   Games are formalized simulation activities. Two or more participants or teams compete in attempting to meet a set of objectives relating to a training topic. The game takes place under a set of rules and procedures, with information being provided that requires decision making and follow-up actions. The subjects of most instructional games are typical real-life situations related to a training topic. Periodically, the results are evaluated by the instructor, other learners, or a group of judges. A wide variety of prepared games is available for use in many areas of instruction. A recent innovation is the use of serious games for instruction. Serious games combine the realistic features of a simulation with goals of a game to create an instructional method that engages the learner in a new type of learning strategy.

**Cooperative Learning.**   Cooperative learning is a specific type of group activity that attempts to promote both learning and social skills by incorporating three concepts into the instruction: (1) group rewards, (2) individual accountability, and (3) equal opportunity for success (Slavin, 1995). Consideration of these components suggests that cooperative learning must be carefully planned and systematically implemented. It is much more than assigning learners to groups and telling them to ''tutor each other'' or complete a project. Two major forms of cooperative learning involve having students work in groups to (1) help one another master material and (2) complete a project, such as a written report, presentation, experiment, or artwork. In both situations it is desirable to follow these guidelines:

- Limit group size to three to five students.
- Compose groups so that they are heterogeneous in ability level, gender, and ethnicity.
- Carefully plan the activities with regard to room arrangement, task materials, and time frame.
- Establish some reward (either recognition or something tangible, depending on the age level of the learners) to motivate the groups.
- Ensure that everyone in the group has a specific task with which he or she can succeed with appropriate effort. Otherwise, shy or lower-ability students may defer to others and not benefit from the activity.
- Teach the lesson using an instructor presentation or appropriate individualized approach; use cooperative learning as a supplement for review, practice, remediation, or enrichment.
- Monitor and assist the groups as needed.
- Base grades as much as possible on individual group members' personal contributions or achievement; use the group reward as the means of recognizing the group's success.

Cooperative learning has proven very successful in research studies. Several models, such as Student-Teams Achievement Divisions, Co-op Co-op, Cooperative Controversy, and Jig Saw, have become quite popular in recent years. Also consider that the way cooperative learning is designed may depend on the conditions of instruction. In a computer-based learning context, for example, the lack of sufficient computers for all students may necessitate employing some form of cooperative groupings. However, the availability of space around the computers may further dictate how many students can work together at the same time.

As Sherman and Klein (1995) demonstrated in a study, strategies for making cooperative learning more effective may be integrated with the main instruction. Specifically, they designed a computer-based unit to cue students working in groups to perform various interactive cooperative activities (e.g., ''Yulanda, explain to Gerry why the first statement below is an example of an observation, but the second statement is not.''). Their findings indicated that both learning interactivity and achievement increased relative to a noncued condition. For more ideas on cooperative learning, the books by Slavin (1995) and Johnson and Johnson (1986) should be valuable in suggesting alternative approaches and outlining implementation procedures.

## SUMMARY

1. The development of the instruction materials is the implementation of the instructional design plan. Designers must consider how to accurately convey the information to the learner in a manner he or she can comprehend. During the development process, the designer should keep a focus on the problem and objectives to ensure the instruction supports the resolution of the problem.

2. There are two types of cognitive load. Intrinsic cognitive load is a function of the content and is highest when there is a high degree of interactivity between the elements. Extraneous cognitive load can be increased or decreased through the design and layout of the instructional materials.

3. The three patterns we have examined in this chapter—presentation to class, self-paced learning, and small-group interaction activities—provide the framework for delivering a variety of instructional formats. As you consider the selection of methods, the following important questions should be asked:

   a. Is there subject content or other material that can best be uniformly presented to all learners at one time?

   b. Is there subject content that learners can better study on their own, at their individual paces?

   c. Are there experiences that would best be served by discussion or other group activity, with or without the instructor being present?

   d. Is there need for individual learner–instructor discussion or consultation in private?

In considering these questions, the planning team should consider some degree of balance among the three delivery patterns.

1. Although the large-group presentation format is still the most widely accepted method in schools, it keeps learners in a generally passive mode and may not be cost effective in training contexts in which learners are geographically dispersed or highly varied in experiences and training needs. Distance learning is gaining popularity as a mode for reaching many learners located at remote sites as a means to reduce costs and increase enrollments.
2. In business, many companies are switching to a self-paced delivery format to reduce travel costs and time away from the job and to increase the efficiency of the instruction. Greater access to computers by businesses and schools is making self-paced instruction more practical and potentially more powerful.
3. In many situations, there are no clear-cut divisions among the three patterns. A presentation to a regular-sized class can incorporate questions and discussion. A self-paced learning period may be supplemented periodically with tutorial interaction as one learner helps another or as the instructor replies to a trainee's question. Combining orientations to fit instructional conditions and individual needs is a sensible approach that can potentially yield benefits much greater than could be attained by using any one method alone.

## THE ID PROCESS

Developing the instructional materials gives the instructional designer an opportunity to test the design plan. The "testing" process, formative evaluation, is explained in Chapters 11 and 13. You can use these procedures to test some of your materials as you develop them and then make modifications to improve their effectiveness. Developing instructional materials is very similar to writing an article or a book; however, we designers have one advantage. It seems that many of our high school English teachers always tried to convince us to create a complete outline before beginning to write an essay. The design plan is a very detailed outline of the content and structure of the instructional materials. By following this outline, we are more likely to produce an effective unit of instruction.

## APPLICATION

The city police department requests the development of a training unit to teach officers a new protocol for testing drivers for possible intoxication. The officers work three different shifts a day, have rotating days off, and must appear in court on short notice. Thus, you cannot select one day that everyone or even every officer on a specific shift will attend the training. The department also hires approximately 20 new officers a year. Your contextual analysis reveals that the department does not have computers for delivering computer-based instruction. What type of approach would you suggest for the instruction?

## ANSWER

The officers' schedule makes it difficult to offer a group-paced course. Another factor against a group-paced course is the need to train 20 new officers each year. Given these constraints, a self-paced approach appears to be most viable. A computer-based or Web-based unit that simulates the testing process and the equipment would make an excellent choice; however, the department does not have computer resources. One option is to offer the instruction individually with printed materials, and then use pairs or small groups for simulations with the actual equipment.

## QUALITY MANAGEMENT

Managing the cognitive load imposed by the instructional materials consists of two activities. First, the designer must make sure that any unnecessary cognitive load is not created through poor designs that create a split-attention effect or redundancy. Second, the designer can use goal-free problems, worked examples, and integrated text and graphics to reduce the cognitive load imposed by the materials. During the development process, the designer needs to regularly check to make sure the materials are supportive of the objectives. It is easy to fall into a mode of writing instruction rather than following the design plan when the designer is overly familiar with the content. As the material is developed, the designer should check to make sure it is presented in a concrete manner and add examples and illustrations as needed. Once the first draft is prepared, you can check the flow of the instruction while paying particular attention to step size and pacing. Last, check to make sure the initial presentation and generative strategy are implemented for each objective.

## INSTRUCTIONAL DESIGN: DECISIONS AND CHOICES

As you formulated the instructional strategies, media selection criteria also began to emerge. You realized early on, during your initial client interview, that the instruction would probably include a conceptual component and a hands-on component. Now, you ask yourself, "How best to deliver each component of the instruction?"

You know that the cognitive component (i.e., classes of fires, types of fire extinguishers, and the description of the emergency procedures) can be delivered as a classroom lecture, as a printed self-instructional manual, as a Web site, as a video recording, or as a combination of these. You also know from media research studies that any of these delivery approaches will be equally effective. For the hands-on component, however, you have decided that practice using a fire extinguisher will be essential. However, the hands-on component is time consuming and will require outdoor space and special equipment to create a controlled fire. (During your discussion with the SME, you learned that the local fire department has access to this special equipment and might be able to assist you.)

You've decided to create a classroom program that will include the conceptual component and the hands-on component. In addition, you will make the conceptual component available on the organization's Web site. The Web site will enable new hires and those who want or need "refresher training" to have easy, on-demand access to the instruction anytime—and from anywhere in the world. The Web site will also serve as a stop-gap measure until the employee can attend the classroom program. The Web site will consist of the same PowerPoint slides that will be used in the classroom and include online activities based on the generative strategies. Last, both the classroom and online versions will include a posttest. The posttest will be used to document successful completion of the training.

[Your decision making regarding media selection has considered a number of constraints and requirements, including:

- Ease of access (anytime, anywhere, any place)
- Scheduling and physical logistics (the desire for on-demand, just-in-time learning)
- Recognition that the organization has local, national, and global office locations
- Ease of updating the instructional materials
- Availability of resources (availability of classroom instructors and special equipment)
- Cost of delivery
- Ability to deliver consistent, replicable instruction

The use of the posttest may also reduce the potential for employee lawsuits and help reduce the cost of insurance liability for the organization.]

## REFERENCES

Anderson, T. H., & Armbruster, B. B. (1985). Studying strategies and their implications for textbook design. In T. M. Duffy & R. Waller (Eds.), *Designing useable texts* (pp. 159–177). Orlando: Academic Press.

Atkinson, R. K., & Renkl, A. (2007). Interactive example-based learning environments: Using interactive elements to encourage effective processing of worked examples. *Educational Psychology Review*, 19, 375–386.

Block, J. H. (Ed.). (1971). *Mastery learning: Theory and practice.* Englewood Cliffs, NJ: Prentice Hall.

Bodemer, D., Ploetzner, R., Feuerlein, I., & Spada, H. (2004). The active integration of information during learning with dynamic and interactive visualizations. *Learning and Instruction, 14,* 325–341.

Carter, J. F. (1985). Lessons in text design from an instructional design perspective. In T. M. Duffy & R. Waller (Eds.), *Designing useable texts* (pp. 145–156). Orlando: Academic Press.

Chandler, P., & Sweller, J. (1992). The split-attention effect as a factor in the design of instruction. *British Journal of Educational Psychology, 62,* 233–246.

Fleming, M., & Levie, W. H. (1978). *Instructional message design: Principles from the behavioral sciences.* Englewood Cliffs, NJ: Educational Technology Publications.

Gerjets, P., Scheiter, K., & Catrambone, R. (2004). Designing instructional examples to reduce intrinsic cognitive load: Molar versus modular presentation of solution procedures. *Instructional Science, 32,* 33–58.

Gopalakrishnan Jayasinghe, M., Morrison, G. R., & Ross, S. M. (1997). The effect of distance learning classroom design on student perceptions. *Educational Technology Research and Development, 45*, 5–19.

Holmberg, B. (1983). Guided didactic conversation in distance education. In D. Stewart, D. Keegan, & B. Holmberg (Eds.), *Distance education: International perspectives* (pp. 114–122). London: Routledge.

Johnsey, A., Morrison, G. R., & Ross, S. M. (1992). Promoting generative learning in computer-based instruction through the use of elaboration strategies training. *Contemporary Educational Psychology, 17*, 125–135.

Johnson, D. W., & Johnson, R. T. (1986). Learning together and alone. Englewood Cliffs, NJ: Prentice Hall.

Kalyuga, S., Chandler, P., & Sweller, J. (2000). Incorporating learner experience into the design of multimedia experience. *Journal of Educational Psychology, 92*, 126–136.

Kalyuga, S., Chandler, P., & Sweller, J. (2001). Learner experience and efficiency of instructional guidance. *Educational Psychology, 21*, 5–23.

Keegan, D. (1996). *Foundations of distance education* (3rd ed.). New York: Routledge.

Keller, F. S., & Sherman, J. G. (1982). *The PSI handbook: Essays on personalized instruction.* Lawrence, KS: International Society for Individualized Instruction.

Lorch, R. F., & Lorch, E. P. (1996). Effects of organizational signals on free recall of expository text. *Journal of Educational Psychology, 88*, 38–48.

Lorch, R. F., Lorch, E. P., & Inman, W. E. (1993). Effects of signaling topic structure on text recall. *Journal of Educational Psychology, 85*, 281–290.

Mayer, R. E., Fennell, M. S., Farmer, L., & Campbell, J. (2004). A personalization effect in multimedia learning: Students learn better when words are in conversational style rather than formal style. *Journal of Educational Psychology, 96*, 389–395.

Miller, G. A. (1956). The magical number seven, plus or minus two: Some limits on our capacity for processing information. *Psychological Review, 63*, 81–97.

Naumann, J., Richter, T., Flender, J., & Christman, U. (2007). Signaling in expository hypertexts compensates for deficits in reading skill. *Journal of Educational Psychology, 99*, 791–807.

Paas, F. G., & van Merriënboer, J. J. G. (1994). Variability of worked examples and transfer of geometrical problem-solving skills: A cognitive-load approach. *Journal of Educational Psychology, 86*, 122–133.

Paivio, A. (1971). *Imagery and verbal processes.* New York: Holt, Rinehart and Winston.

Paivio, A. (1986). *Mental representations: A dual coding approach.* New York: Oxford University Press.

Postlethwait, S. N., Novak, J., & Murray, H. (1972). *The audio-tutorial approach to learning.* Minneapolis, MN: Burgess.

Renkl, A., Atkinson, R. K., & Grobe, C. S. (2004). How fading worked solution steps works—A cognitive load perspective. *Instructional Science, 32*, 59–82.

Rothkopf, E. Z. (1996). Control of mathemagenic activities. In D. Jonassen (Ed.), *Handbook of research for educational communication and technology* (pp. 879–897). New York: Macmillan Library Reference USA.

Sadoski, M., Goetz, E. T., & Fritz, J. B. (1993). Impact of concreteness on comprehensibility, interest, and memory for text: Implications for dual coding theory and text design. *Journal of Educational Psychology, 85*, 291–304.

Sherman, G. P., & Klein, J. D. (1995). The effects of cued interaction and ability grouping during cooperative computer-based science instruction. *Educational Technology Research and Development, 43*, 5–24.

Simonson, M. (1995). Does anyone really want to learn at a distance? *Tech Trends, 40,* 12.

Slavin, R. E. (1994). *Educational psychology* (4th ed.). Needham Heights, MA: Allyn & Bacon.

Slavin, R. E. (1995). *Cooperative learning: Theory, research, and practice.* Englewood Cliffs, NJ: Prentice Hall.

Sweller, J. (1999). *Instructional design in technical areas.* Camberwell, Victoria: ACER Press.

Son, J. Y., & Goldstone, R. L. (2009). Contextualization in perspective. *Cognition and Instruction, 27*(1), 51–89.

Tuovinen, J. E., & Sweller, J. (1999). A comparison of cognitive load associated with discovery learning and worked examples. *Journal of Educational Psychology, 2,* 334–341.

van Merriënboer, J. J. G., Schuurman, J. G., de Croock, M. B. M., & Paas, F. G. W. C. (2002). Redirecting learners' attention during training: Effects on cognitive load, transfer test performance and training efficiency. *Learning and Instruction, 12*(1), 11–37.

van Merriënboer, J. J. G., & Sweller, J. (2005). Cognitive load theory and complex learning: Recent developments and future directions. *Educational Psychology Review, 17*(2), 147–177.

Wales, C. E., Nardi, A. H., & Stager, R. A. (1987). *Thinking skills: Making a choice.* Morgantown, WV: Center for Guided Design.

# Design Considerations for Technology-Based Instruction

### GETTING STARTED[1]

Wind and Solar Power Incorporated has hired you to improve their sales training. Although the company is only seven years old, they have a rich history of training their sales personnel in how their wind and solar electricity-generating equipment functions so that they can explain it to potential customers. As the company has grown beyond expectations, the need for training new sales and support personnel has also grown. To meet this need, the company has produced online training materials that consist simply of the PowerPoint® presentations used in the classroom. Employees read the slides but do not have the narrative that the instructor provides in the classroom. Thus, they are missing much of the content. Your goal is to improve their online training. Can you fix what they have, or must you start from scratch? What approach will you use in either case?

---

[1] We would like to thank Ginger Watson for her ideas in the development of this chapter.

## QUESTIONS TO CONSIDER

"Where do you begin?"

"What design skills will you need when designing technology-based instruction?"

"Who are the other team members?"

"Will the techniques you have learned thus far work with technology-based instruction?"

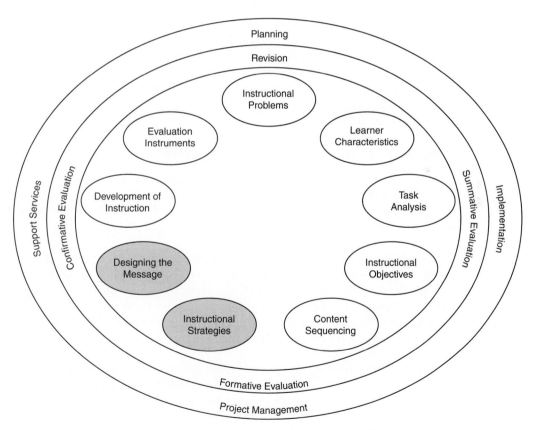

In Chapter 7 we described two levels of decisions on the design of the instruction. The first level was the delivery strategy, which describes the general learning environment, which can range from a lecture format to Web-based instruction. The second decision concerned designing the instructional strategy for helping the learner achieve a specific objective. In this chapter, we will focus again on the types of decisions involved in applying specific instructional strategies, when used within the delivery strategy of technology-based instruction. To answer the last question in the Questions to Consider, the approaches you have learned thus far will work with designing technology-based instruction.

Before we begin to examine the design issues, let's define technology-based instruction. Technology-based instruction is the use of computers and other electronic devices to communicate the instruction to the student and to allow students and instructors to communicate with one another. Although we agree that printed materials are a form of technology, we will limit our definition to instruction delivered via electronic devices. The more common forms of technology-based instruction include distance education, in which the student and instructor are separated in both time and geographic location (asynchronous), and virtual classrooms (synchronous), in which case the instructor and student are separated by geographic location but meet at the same time (Keegan, 1996). Another example is Web-based and other computer-based instruction, which often incorporate individualized instruction, as opposed to the group-paced instruction in virtual and traditional classrooms.

## Affordances of Technology-Based Instruction

Just as an electric starter in our automobile offers affordances (e.g., turning a key as opposed to turning a crank or pushing the vehicle), technology-based instruction offers additional affordances over traditional teacher-led instruction. For example, we can use a distance education delivery strategy to reach additional members of our target audience and we can save time and money by making the instruction available at multiple locations rather than at one central location. Similarly, we could teach foreign vocabulary words to a learner using a drill-and-practice program that can manage the sequence and content of the material as well as provide immediate feedback. Unlike a teacher, the program can perform these tasks endlessly without tiring or becoming bored with the process. Teachers have used flashcards in both large and small classes for years; however, the technology makes the instructional delivery more efficient.

Although technology can provide more *efficient* instruction, it does not necessarily provide more *effective* instruction. While the issue of the effect of technology on learning has been debated since the earliest days of our field, the research fails to support any advantage for technology over other delivery modes using comparable instructional strategies (Clark, 1983, 1994, 2001; Clark & Salomon, 1986; Cobb, 1997; Knowlton, 1964; Levie & Dickie, 1973). For example, a researcher might argue that a multimedia presentation with inserted questions is more effective than a lecture. Such a study would be comparing apples and oranges as the multimedia presentation is presented to each individual learner with feedback but the lecture is given to a group without feedback. It is unlikely the content or strategy (e.g., questions) would be the same in both treatments. If the content and strategy are both held constant and only the technology is varied, as in a multimedia unit with questions versus a video recording with the same questions, why would we expect a difference? The references cited earlier in this paragraph (i.e., Clark, 1983, etc.) will provide you with a starting point to explore this argument, as will two issues of *Educational Technology Research and Development* (issues 2 and 3) published in 1994.

The remainder of this chapter will focus on instructional design considerations for both individualized instruction and group-paced distance education instruction. The next section will focus on individualized instruction delivered in either a computer-based or Web-based delivery system. The following section will focus on design considerations for group-based distance education.

## INDIVIDUALIZED COMPUTER- AND WEB-BASED INSTRUCTION

An image of a young student sitting in front of a computer answering questions presented flash-card style is often evoked when someone mentions computer-based instruction (CBI). Although electronic flash cards, or drill-and-practice, is a form of CBI, there are other strategies we can use. In this section, we will focus on five types of individualized instruction. All five CBI strategies can be delivered via (a) an individual computer by installing the software; (b) a computer connected to a server, CD-ROM drive, or DVD player; and (c) a computer connected to the Internet, where the application is delivered via a Web browser or Web interface. We refer to this type of delivery as individualized due to the characteristics. First, an individual student usually works on the instruction alone, although an instructor could assign two to four students to work together. Second, the instruction is self-paced; that is, the user clicks a button to move forward or backward or is advanced after inputting or selecting a response. Third, the instruction can adapt to the individual by providing different responses to a variety of answers. For example, if Mark mistakenly identifies an example of an adjective as an adverb, the instruction would branch to a remedial section to help him understand the difference between the two concepts. In contrast, Michelle might select the correct answer, and the instruction would present her with either a new example or the next step of the instruction. Fourth, the instruction can allow the learner to select the sequence, context, or the number of examples to study so that each learner has a unique path through the instruction. Individualized instruction, whether CBI or Web based, is not limited to an isolated student sitting alone or apart from others. Instructors can incorporate individualized instruction into their traditional classroom. We will use the term *CBI* to encompass both computer-based and Web-based individualized strategies. The following paragraphs describe five types of CBI or Web-based instruction.

### Drill-and-Practice

One of the earliest forms of CBI was drill-and-practice. This strategy is useful for practicing the memorization of information (''rote learning'') such as vocabulary words, names of presidents, chemical element symbols, and multiplication tables.

At home and in the classroom, drill-and-practice strategies are often used as flash cards. CBI offers a more efficient approach than traditional flash cards. Manual flash cards require two individuals—one to present and one to respond, whereas the CBI version requires only the learner. A CBI drill-and-practice application can easily manage the number of "cards" presented at a time, and can then track which were answered correctly and which incorrectly so that more time is given to those the learner has not yet mastered. For example, on one trial the application might ask when Lincoln served as a president. On another trial, the instruction might present the dates "1861—1865" and asked who was president during this period. Last, a CBI application has continual patience and availability.

A drill-and-practice strategy is used to provide practice rather than initial learning. That is, the learner has prior exposure to the information such as having read a chapter or viewed a video recording. The drill-and-practice application is used to strengthen the association between the stimulus and response or question and answer.

## Tutorials

While drill-and-practice applications are used to strengthen associations between a stimulus and response, tutorials are used to present new material for initial learning. An instructor in a biology class might use a tutorial that explains how the lungs and heart work to deliver oxygen to cells in the body, or a company might use a tutorial to teach basic procedures for keeping files secure. A tutorial is similar to a textbook chapter or training manual in that each helps the learner develop an understanding of specific content. Unfortunately, too many CBI tutorials are nothing more than "electronic page turners" that simply present text on a computer as a textbook does. There are several affordances that give computer and Web-based tutorials potential advantages. When compared to printed tutorials, CBI tutorials are easier to update and can be distributed more quickly throughout the organization. However, they do require a computer and possibly Internet access for the learner. CBI tutorials can include interactive components that make use of generative strategies with feedback to promote active learning. Both interactive and static graphics as well as animations and video are easily incorporated into a CBI tutorial. Last, tutorials can provide alternative explanations and remediation based on the learner's answers and progress.

## Simulations

Simulations model real-world phenomena by presenting a realistic representation. Learners can engage in full-scale physical simulators, such as aircraft simulators, driving simulators, and nuclear power plant control room simulators, that have a high fidelity—that is, they closely reflect the actual equipment and/or setting. In contrast to a full-scale flight simulator is a computer-based flight simulator or game that is much lower in fidelity. For example, the larger flight simulator closely resembles the cockpit of an airplane including instruments and controls. The computer-based simulator might use a joy stick or keyboard for the controls and screen images that resemble the instruments, which results in lower fidelity than would a full-scale simulator. The amount of fidelity required for instruction varies depending on the level of the learner. For example, a novice might be overwhelmed by a full-scale simulator while a knowledgeable learner could benefit from the higher fidelity (Allessi & Trollip, 2001). Simulations are based on a mathematical model of a phenomenon. Although some animations, movies, and games superficially appear to be simulations, they lack the underlying model that controls the events (Allessi & Trollip, 2001). Simulations offer a cost-effective strategy for learning. For example, it is extremely costly to practice landing an airplane or navigating a large ship. There are also instances where practice is impractical, as in learning to take an electrical generator plant off the grid. Simulations provide a means to create learning and practice experiences in a cost effective and efficient manner.

## Games

Instructional games are a means of adding a motivational factor to drill-and-practice programs, tutorials, and simulations. A game may have a simple story line such as blasting space aliens, or it may be a more involved scenario such as rescuing a hostage or saving a life. The nature of the story line and reward of winning can increase learner motivation to engage in the game. Games can be designed for the single user or multiple players, as in multiple-player online games. Dickey (2007) identified five types of computer games: strategy, adventure, role-playing, action, and massively multiple online role-playing games. Although instructional designers and educators have shown an interest in computer games for the past two decades, there is a lack of empirical evidence that games influence student achievement (Fe, 2008).

## Hypermedia

If you have used a search engine such as Google and then clicked on one of the results, you have used hypermedia, or hypertext. The World Wide Web is based on the concept of hypertext, which allows the user to click on a link to obtain additional information. A common use of hypermedia is to connect to reference information such as an encyclopedia (e.g., a wiki). Other uses include locating archived material including documents and visuals or browsing the contents of a museum. Advocates of hypermedia suggests that it is useful for accessing large amounts of nonlinear information, such as a Web search on learning theories, allowing learners to explore new ideas, capturing attention, and representing how the human mind works (Dillon & Gabbard, 1998). The effectiveness of hypermedia for learning, however, has not yet been established (Dillon & Gabbard, 1998). Azevedo and Jacobson (2008) caution designers to approach this technology with caution because allowing learners to "access, manipulate, or restructure" (p. 93) information without the necessary scaffolding is challenging for learners of all ages. Such designs require careful consideration that will help the learners develop the needed understanding. Hypermedia is best used when learners must search through multiple sources and then compare or manipulate the information. Outside of this limited application, the use of hypermedia for instruction appears to be limited (Dillon & Gabbard, 1998).

## DESIGN CONSIDERATIONS FOR INDIVIDUALIZED COMPUTER AND WEB-BASED INSTRUCTION

A common concern that designers express is that a new instructional design model is required for each new technology; however, if you recall Clark's (1983, 1994, 2001) argument, it is the strategy or method that makes the difference, not the technology. The strategies such as mnemonics, paraphrasing, and categorization tables presented in Chapter 7 are also applicable to CBI. In addition, we can take advantage of the affordances offered by the technology to make the instruction more efficient and accessible. Given the ability to input or select answers, judge answers, and then provide feedback, a designer might feel that the use of inserted questions (see Chapter 7) is an appropriate strategy. However, there is little evidence to suggest that such a strategy would be any more effective in a technology-based environment than in a printed-text environment. Thus, the model presented in this book is applicable for designing instruction for delivery in a variety of different technologies including CBI.

The following sections address six design considerations for individualized CBI that you should consider and incorporate into your designs. However, a designer should not use a "feature" just because it is there. For example, in the early days of CBI on personal computers, programmers discovered that they could create a variety of sounds. Using this newfound "discovery," the sounds were used for feedback. Learners would often select the wrong answer on purpose because the negative feedback sounds were more exciting than the sounds for correct feedback.

### Interface Design

If you have ever suffered through a major upgrade of your favorite software such as a word processing or graphics program, you are aware of how the interface affects your work. For example, when Microsoft changed their interface from drop-down menus to ribbons, many users spent extra time trying to find that one command that seemed to be placed in the most illogical ribbon. Interface design is not limited to technology-based products. Instructional materials such as books also have an interface. Parts of this interface include page numbers, running heads, different levels of headings, and typographical features. The instructional materials that we design represent the interface between the learner and the instruction (Simon, 1969). What features create a good interface? Creating an interface can be a difficult task because there is not a general standard for computer interface design (Cheon & Grant, 2009). However, even in the absence of a standard, there are some general principles that can guide your design. An interface should be simple and easy to use. Tognazzini (2003) provides a clear perspective on interface design: "Effective interfaces are visually apparent and forgiving, instilling in their users a sense of control. Users quickly see the breadth of their options, grasp how to achieve their goals, and do their work'' (p. 1).

Interfaces should be intuitive such that a learner is able to open a web page or tutorial and immediately start learning without having to guess what to do next. Adams et al. (2008) found three levels of intuitiveness in their evaluation of physics simulations: Learners found nonintuitive interfaces difficult to use even when instruction was provided. Semi-intuitive interfaces were easy to use once the learner saw an example or was given instructions. Intuitive interfaces were easily used without instruction. What are the characteristics of an intuitive interface? Consistency is a primary attribute. For example, navigation buttons are always in the same position and the layout of the screen is constant not only within a lesson but also among different lessons. Objects with which the learner interacts should respond as expected. Consider for example, a lesson teaching college freshmen how to sort their clothes to do laundry. One CBI task is to drag the ''whites'' to one basket and the dark clothes to another. When the user clicks on a T-shirt icon and drags it, he expects it to follow a natural path as if it were tossed and landed in the basket rather than taking off like a paper airplane and doing a couple of loops before gliding from the ceiling to the basket.

Once you have designed the interface, you need to test it. What may seem perfect to you might be nonintuitive to your learners. You can use the formative evaluation methods in Chapter 13 to test the usability of your design.

## Learner Control

Allowing learners to take control of the instruction is one of the earliest computer-based instruction concepts (Merrill, 1975). When using CBI, learners would have the ability to select tactics at any moment to support their learning. One of the earliest implementations of learner control allowed learners to select different presentations (i.e., initial presentation) consisting of expository and inquisitory examples, practice, help, hard or easy examples, and forward and backward navigation (Merrill, 1988). This initial conception of learner control has generated numerous empirical studies comparing learner control with program control (i.e., the designer making the decisions) resulting in mixed findings (Corbalan, Kester, & van Merriënboer, 2006; Kopcha & Sullivan, 2008; Morrison, Ross, & Baldwin, 1992; Swaak & de Jong, 2001; van Gog, Ericsson, Rikers, & Paas, 2005; van Merriënboer, Schuurman, de Croock, & Paas, 2002; Yang & Chin, 1996).

There are three general types of decisions learners can make when using learning control. The first type is navigation, which allows the learner to move forward or backward in a unit of instruction or to stop, start, and replay an audio or animation sequence. Using this type of control, learners can adjust the pacing of the material. By comparison, ''program control'' determines *for the learner* how quickly to present the content, much like watching a video recording as opposed to reading a book. There may be instances, however, when the designer wants to limit navigation, such as not allowing the learner to review during a test.

The second type of learner control decision allows the learner to choose the context of the lesson materials and examples (Morrison et al. 1992; Ross, Morrison, & O'Dell, 1989). Students learning the metric system, for example, could select the context of sports, animals, clothing, or no theme for the instruction and examples (see Figure 10-1).

The third type is controlling the content by determining how much material to study or how many examples (see Figure 10-2) to try (Hannafin & Sullivan, 1996; Morrison et al., 1992; Ross et al., 1989). For example, in the Morrison and Ross studies, learners made a decision to try another example or to move to the next section. Hannafin and Sullivan allowed the learner to determine the number of examples, reviews, and problems they studied. The first two types of learner control, navigation and context selection, do not allow the learner to skip some of the instruction. In the third type of learner control, learners can determine how much instruction and practice they receive. Kopcha and Sullivan (2008) suggested that learners who elect to bypass some of the instruction can be expected to perform less well than learners who do not have that option (e.g., due to program control). Similarly, learners who have the option to add additional instruction (and choose to do so) would be expected to perform better than those receiving minimal instruction. When making a decision on how to use learner control, careful consideration needs to be given. Learners with a prior knowledge of the content tend to make better decisions with learner control than learners with little prior knowledge (Kopcha & Sullivan, 2008).

**FIGURE 10-1**
Learner control of context

In the next lesson you will be able to choose the topic area for the examples you would like to study. Note that the first choice is called "no topic" because it uses only numbers for the examples.

What type of examples would you like for the next lesson?
  A.  No topic (just numbers)
  B.  Sports
  C.  Pets
  D.  Clothing
  Enter your choice_____

**FIGURE 10-2**
Learner control of content

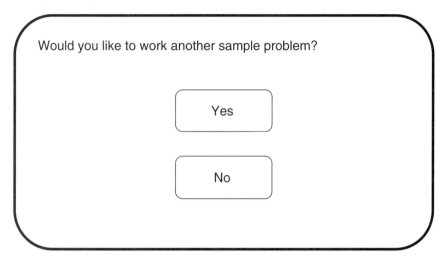

## Feedback

Feedback has been a topic of interest for researchers since the early 1900s (Kulik & Kulik, 1988; Thorndike, 1927). One of the affordances of CBI is the use of feedback, which is related to answer judging. As designers, we have several options for judging answers, providing feedback, and then making decisions on what content the learner will engage in next. Although the research concludes that feedback is clearly more effective for learning than is no feedback, the evidence comparing different types of feedback is less conclusive (Narciss, 2008). There are five basic types of feedback. The first and simplest form of feedback is simply providing the learner with *knowledge-of-result*, or *KR*. Knowledge-of-result feedback would simply inform the learner whether the response was correct or incorrect. Second, *knowledge-of-correct-response* (KCR) feedback provides the learner with the correct response. A variation requires the learner to enter the correct response before proceeding (see Figure 10-3). The third type of feedback is *answer-until-correct* (AUC), which requires the learner to keep responding until the correct answer is selected. Answer-until-correct feedback is often paired with knowledge-of-result feedback to inform the learner of the correctness of the response (Morrison, Ross, Gopalakrishnan, & Casey, 1995). The fourth type of feedback is *elaborated* feedback, which provides additional information beyond the correctness of an answer or correct answer itself (Narciss, 2008). Common functions of elaborated feedback are directing the learner to relevant sections of the text, providing suggestions for the use of metacognitive strategies, and providing additional information that goes beyond the original instruction. The fifth type of feedback is *response-sensitive*, or error-contingent, feedback. Response-sensitive feedback is unique to each answer to help

**FIGURE 10-3**
Knowledge of correct response

How is time used in the following objective?
". . . will complete the test in 30 minutes."

A. Behavior
B. Condition
C. Norm
D. Criterion
E. Modifier

Your answer is incorrect. The correct answer is B.
Enter the correct answer to continue:_____

Based on stimulus materials used in Morrison, G. R., Ross, S. M., Gopalakrishnan, M., & Casey, J. (1995). The effects of feedback and incentives on achievement in computer-based instruction. *Contemporary Educational Psychology, 20,* 32–50.

the learner understand why the answer is incorrect (see Figure 10-4) or correct, and can even provide information to help the learner correct a particular type of error.

A second factor to consider after selecting the type of feedback is the timing of feedback. Feedback can be given immediately after a response, or it can be delayed until the end of the instruction or test. For example, Morrison et al. (1995) embedded 24 multiple-response questions in the instructional unit. Two of the treatments provided immediate feedback while a third treatment provided judgment of the response (i.e., correct or incorrect) immediately but did not give the correct answer until the unit was completed. The rationale for using delayed feedback is that the immediate information about one's performance may be interfering or distracting at a time when learning the material is more important than one's score (Mory, 2004). Delayed feedback provides more opportunity for the material to be assimilated and the learner to be less preoccupied with his or her performance. Again, the research on feedback timing is inconclusive. Kulik and Kulik (1988) concluded that instructional designers should use immediate feedback. The research suggests immediate feedback is more effective for the less experienced learner learning a motor task, and delayed is more effective for the experienced learner (Smits, Boon, Sluijsmans & van Gog, 2008). Our suggestion is for designers to consider the nature of the particular task and the learners' characteristics when making decisions about the best timing of feedback. For example, if a task is difficult

**FIGURE 10-4**
Response sensitive feedback

> 12
> +6
> ———
> Answer: 6
>
> Your answer is incorrect. You have subtracted 6 rather than added 6. Note the + sign before the 6 indicating you are to add the two numbers. The correct answer is 18.

and making errors early in a lesson can result in cumulative misunderstandings, it certainly would make sense to favor immediate feedback.

The final factor to consider when using feedback is the mode of presentation. Designers generally have the option of presenting the feedback as text, audio, or as an image. Bruner (1966) suggests that feedback must be in a mode the learner can understand. For example, if the learner cannot read, then the feedback should be provided as a picture or audio.

## Remediation

Directly related to feedback is remediation. If a learner answers one or more questions incorrectly, what actions do you plan as a designer to remediate or correct the incorrect responses? Since Crowder (1959) introduced the concept of intrinsic programming, or branching, in programmed instruction, instructional designers have considered how to provide remediation to correct learner responses. One common technique is simply to have the learner reread the material a second time. Although there is considerable research on rereading (Dunlosky & Rawson, 2005; Haenggi & Perfetti, 1992; Rawson & Kintsch, 2005), these studies examined rereading prior to taking the test. The research is unclear on the effects of rereading as a remediation strategy after taking a test. One adaptive approach is to advise or coach learners on the level of instructional support (e.g., number of examples) they should select for the next section based on their performance (Ross & Morrison, 1993). Similarly, a response-sensitive feedback approach can provide highly specific feedback based on the learner's answer. Park and Tennyson (1980) sequenced and selected the instruction based on the learner's response when teaching concepts. For example, when the learner was presented with an example of Concept A and she incorrectly labeled the example as Concept C, then the next example presented was Concept C. This response-sensitive feedback provided more appropriate remediation than reading the same material a second or third time. More recently, Moreno (2004) found that elaborative feedback, which explained why the answer was incorrect, lead to greater learning gains than just corrective feedback. Computer-based instruction, therefore, provides an efficient means for providing response-sensitive feedback as well as remediation that is adapted to the individual learner's responses.

## Designing Interactions

Computer-based instruction affords a variety of interactions ranging from entering individual words or a letter as a response to clicking on a button or object. Although, intuitively, it would seem that interactions are important, care must be taken when designing the interaction. Interactions should engage the learner and require cognitive processing on the part of the learner. For example, a learner could interact with a program by simply clicking the next button. Such interaction takes little effort or thought, yet it is interactive. It is primarily a behavioral interaction (i.e., clicking). An interaction has two components: a behavioral activity and a cognitive activity (Mayer, 2004, 2009). When designing CBI, we need interactions that actively promote cognitive processing rather than simply pressing buttons. Let's examine five types of computer input that we can use to engender meaningful interactions *once* we have designed our instructional strategy (see Table 10-1).

The first form of CBI input is using the keyboard. A learner could enter a short answer to a question, a letter for a true-false item or multiple-choice item, a numeric

**TABLE 10-1**

Types of user input

| Input Type | Example |
| --- | --- |
| Keyboard | Arrows keys for navigation<br>Providing a single letter to a paragraph answer or input<br>Manipulation of object on screen with arrow keys or I, J, K, L keys |
| Mouse or touch screen | Selecting an answer or object by clicking<br>Highlighting a phrase or screen area |
| Clicking a button | Clicking buttons for an answer<br>Clicking and moving sliders for control such as increase or decreasing speed or temperature, or rotating an object |
| Mouse or touch screen to drag and drop | Click and drag to sort or rearrange objects |
| Speech | Control of applications or objects<br>Record voice for an answer |

answer to a math problem, or a paragraph as part of a paraphrase. The second type of interaction is using a mouse or touch screen to click an answer. Answers can take the form of words or phrases, objects such as an example of a concept, or multiple-choice or true-false items. Clicking on buttons to control an event is the third type of interaction. For example, in working with a chemistry program, the learner might click on different buttons to raise or lower the temperature and observe the effect (see Figure 10-5). A fourth type of interaction also uses a mouse to drag and drop objects. Consider for example an interactive program for college freshmen on how to do laundry. The first task might be sort the white clothing from colored clothing by dragging individual items into one of two baskets. A specialized mouse such as one that vibrates can also provide tactile feedback. The fifth type of interaction is speech. A common use of speech interaction is teaching a foreign language where the learner's input is recorded and then played back with the instructor's answer so that the student can compare pronunciation. There are also other specialized input devices for individuals with physical limitations. Interactions are carefully planned instructional strategies that require the learner to cognitively process the content rather than only engaging the learner behaviorally at a low level.

**FIGURE 10-5**
Interacting with buttons

Expert's Edge

## Designing Effective Instructional Animations

Much instructional content deals with situations that change over time. Common examples include climate change, engine operation, volcanic eruption, equipment assembly, military tactics, chemical reactions, and population growth. Although traditional print-based instruction struggles to do justice to such dynamic information, computer-based instruction is much better suited due to its capacity to animate content.

Computer animation seems ideal for presenting dynamic subject matter because it can depict changes directly and explicitly. Further, easy-to-use software tools are now available that make the authoring of animations far more straightforward than ever before (Custom Animations in PowerPoint® being a prime example). However, the mere inclusion of animations in a resource does not necessarily improve its educational effectiveness. Indeed, animations can actually be detrimental to learning if they distract the learner from central aspects of the content. For animations to be effective, careful thought must be given to both the reason for using this type of presentation and the specific design features each animation contains.

Current learning resources use animations in two main ways. In many cases, animation is used primarily for *affective* purposes—as an "add-on" intended to serve functions such as attracting initial interest, providing extrinsic motivation, or sustaining engagement. Because animations engage visual perception so powerfully, their inclusion can divert the learners' attention away from the aspects they are meant to be studying. For this reason, affective animations within an instructional resource should be positioned so they do not compete with the content for learner attention. All the added motivation in the world will not overcome the flaws in a poorly designed content presentation that fails to build learner understanding.

This brings us to the other main way instructional designers use animations: for cognitive purposes. If affective animations are directed toward the learner's "heart," then cognitively oriented animations are directed to the learner's "head." They are designed with the express intention of making key content more accessible, more understandable, and/or more memorable. Although they may well also be (and should be) attractive in terms of their graphic design, affective impact is not their prime function. The most obvious use for cognitive animations is to provide a dynamic depiction of the changes in position and form that occur in the subject matter over time.

Unfortunately, this process is not quite so simple. Animations can present their own interpretative challenges to learners unless they are instructionally well designed. The nature of the depiction is an important aspect of animation design. A prevailing myth about instructional animations is that their effectiveness depends largely on how faithfully they depict the dynamic subject matter. A high degree of realism is equated with a high degree of instructional effectiveness. This mistaken belief is influential even when the animation presents its subject matter in a diagrammatic style. Despite its lack of realism in terms of *appearance*, it will be animated so it *behaves* in a realistic manner. Several challenges for learners can arise as a result. One problem is that a behaviorally realistic animation may make it difficult for the learner to identify some of the changes that are occurring. For example, crucial events may occur too quickly to resolve perceptually or be so short-lived that they are missed. This problem can be exacerbated if other events occurring in the animation at the same time compete for the learner's attention.

Instructional designers have long accepted that highly modified and simplified static pictures such as diagrams are beneficial for learners. Diagrams work so well because they strip away the unnecessary from a complex reality and present just the essence of the content. A similar approach needs to be taken for instructional animations. If behavioral realism causes learners to miss high-relevance information in an animation, then the presentation should be modified and simplified so that crucial events are readily accessible to learners. One way to help learners cope with the demands of animation is to give them control over how it presents its information. Rather than having the animation play in a fixed, system-controlled way, control buttons and sliders can be provided that allow the learner to vary the playing regime. Not only can the animation then be repeatedly viewed (a vital feature if the presented content is complex), it can also be interrogated at different speeds, in different directions, as a whole or in segments, and continuously or discontinuously. These varied viewing options improve learners' opportunities for being able to extract information that is most relevant to the nominated learning task.

Although providing learner control can be helpful with simple animations depicting familiar content, it may be less effective for complex, unfamiliar content. Animations are often used for this latter type of subject matter on the assumption that their explicit portrayal will make the content intrinsically accessible for learners. However, learners tend not to be very effective in interrogating animations of complex, unfamiliar content. They have problems in knowing which of the depicted items have greatest relevance, which events in the animated sequence are most important, and how the depicted items and events are related to one another. As a result, their interaction with the user-control facilities can be ineffective—they look in the wrong places, at the wrong things, and at the wrong times. Their attention is drawn to aspects that are readily noticeable rather than those that are most important to their learning.

For animations to fulfill their instructional potential, a balance should be struck between freedom for the learner to explore the available material and guidance to make that exploration effective. Learner control is likely to be more beneficial if the learner receives direction about where to look, what to look at, and when to look at those things. Instructional designers can provide such direction by approaches that include presegmenting the animation to identify crucial events, nominating useful interrogation approaches (e.g., "Play this segment at half speed and take particular note of . . . "), cueing high-relevance items, and signaling key relationships. These forms of support are important for all but the simplest animations portraying the most familiar types of content.

Richard Low is a professor of learning technologies at Curtin University in Perth, Australia. In addition to his research, he continues to work as a practicing instructional designer for industry and government organizations that rely on complex and dynamic graphic information displays for their operations.

## Using Multimedia

Multimedia instruction is the incorporation of both pictures and words or narration in the instruction (Mayer, 2009). Often this mix results in a narrated animation. Although Clark and Feldon (2005) show the lack of evidence that multimedia instruction produces superior results over live or other forms of mediated instruction, multimedia can offer an efficient and cost-effective delivery strategy. Before we discuss the design of multimedia instruction, let's define the term. Mayer (2009) defines multimedia instruction "as the presentation of material using both words and pictures, with the intention of promoting words" (p. 5). Words include both written text and narration. Pictures include both static pictures such as drawings and photographs and dynamic graphics such as animations. Mayer also makes a critical distinction for instructional designers concerning the design of multimedia instruction. The first approach he describes is one that focuses on the technology. A technology approach is a solution searching for a problem. That is, the designer asks how the features of the technology can be used to design instruction. The result is often a presentation-rich program that has all the bells and whistles but ignores good instructional design. Unfortunately, this is a common approach that we have witnessed with the introduction of new technologies. For example, we once saw a program designed by a student that displayed the cumulative time the learner spent on each individual "frame" of the instruction. When asked why it was included, the student simply replied "because the feature was *available*." The display of time spent was not part of the instructional design; rather, it was a technology-based approach of using an available feature. A second, much more desirable, approach described by Mayer is the learner-centered approach, which asks how we can use the technology to enhance learning. This approach considers the learner, the content, and environment to produce effective and efficient instruction. According to Mayer, an approach that uses technology in a manner that is consistent with how the human mind works is a more effective approach for fostering learning.

As a designer, you might ask if the design of multimedia instruction is different from CBI or printed instruction. The answer is yes and no. The principles you have learned thus far are applicable to all forms of instruction. That is, you can use mnemonic devices to enhance recall of information in both printed text and in multimedia. Similarly, you can use paraphrasing in printed instruction, CBI, and multimedia instruction. In fact, you could use it with a video-recording or a streaming-video presentation. So, the first answer to our question is no—it is essentially the same. But, there are also differences. CBI and multimedia instruction offer opportunities or features not available or easily implementable in print or in a teacher-led environment. For example, a teacher could show an animation using a projector or larger monitor. However, the individual students cannot pause, rewind, and move forward at their own individual pacing as they can with multimedia instruction. So, the answer is also yes—multimedia and print instruction are different. As a designer, you will need to consider how to incorporate the special features of multimedia into your design of the instruction. Given all the features available, explaining each is beyond the capacity of this text. The following is a summary of ten principles described by Mayer (2008) that are applicable to the design of multimedia instruction.

**Principles for reducing extraneous overload.**   Mayer (2008) presents four principles based on research to reduce cognitive load on working memory (see Chapter 9) to facilitate schema formation. First is the *coherence* principle, which recommends the exclusion of extra information in animations or narrations. The instruction should be focused on the needed content rather than including peripheral information that can be distracting. For example, we might ask an artist to prepare a *simple* background for an animation that depicts pollution from a power plant. When we see the artwork, the artist has taken the liberty to go beyond our design by including other items around the power plant such as a lake, flowers, wildlife, and trash. All these extra features distract from the main point—the power plant and its smoke stack. The second principle is *signaling*, which suggests that learning is enhanced when we include cues that draw attention to text, animation, or narration (see Chapter 8).

*Redundancy*, the third principle, is based on Sweller's (1999) work and is often a result of a technology-based approach. Consider a design team that has produced an excellent animation with narration. At the last minute, the team learns that they can scroll the narration across the bottom part of the animation and decides to incorporate this feature. The unfortunate result, however, is an overload on working memory because of redundant information. That is, the learner must process the spoken narration and the written narration, and then compare the two to determine whether they are the same or different. The fourth principle is *spatial contiguity*, which recommends that relevant text (e.g., labels) and graphics or animations be placed in close proximity of each other rather than be separated on the screen. In the top part of Figure 10-6, the information on the angle of the razor blade is separated from the illustration and placed in the text. In the bottom part of Figure 10-6 the drawing illustrates the principle of *spatial contiguity* by placing the text (45°) on the drawing with arrows indicating the angle. Including the text with the illustration also reduces split attention (see Chapter 9). *Temporal contiguity*, the fifth principle, recommends that the animation and narration be presented

**FIGURE 10-6**
Spatial contiguity

simultaneously rather than one before the other. Consider, for example, a study by Mayer and Anderson (1992) in which they were teaching how a bicycle pump works. In one treatment, the participants first heard the narration and then saw the animation of the pump. A second treatment viewed the animation first, and then heard the narration. The third treatment viewed the animation and heard the narration simultaneously (temporal contiguity). The simultaneous-presentation group performed better.

**Principles for managing essential overload.**    The next three principles from Mayer (2008) describe how to manage cognitive load so as not to overwhelm the learner's working memory. The sixth principle, *segmenting*, recommends presenting narrated animations in learner-paced segments rather than as a continuous presentation. Although this option provides the learners with the ability to control the animation, the research suggests that learners do not always take advantage of this feature (Lowe, 2008). Mayer recommends that an animation should be presented in small, individual animations the learner can review rather than in one longer segment. The smaller, meaningful segments allow the learner time to process the information before clicking a button to proceed to the next idea. Thus, we might have two individual animations to teach two concepts. After viewing each of the concept animations, the learner would view the animation that relates the two concepts in a principle. The three animations are controlled by the learner so that the learner moves to the next only when he or she understands the content. The seventh principle is the *pre-training* principle. According to this principle, the learner should understand the basic information before viewing the animation. If we were designing a unit on the operation of the gas engine, we might first start with the parts of the engine, then cover the injection of air and gas, next would be combustion, and finally the exhaust function. After the learner understands the basic components, we could show an animation of the gas combustion engine working.

The eighth principle, *modality*, states that animation and narration are more effective than animation and on-screen text. Let's consider an animation we might create demonstrating how to cut a piece of cardstock with a razor blade, as illustrated in Figure 10-6. In the first example we will use the bottom half of the picture and animate the razor blade as it moves across the cardstock to cut it. Several cuts are made to cut through the cardstock. Rather than narrating the animation, we decide to add the narration as text below the animation, as in Figure 10-6. As our learners view the animation, they must read the text. Thus, their eyes (and attention) must move between our written narrative and the animation, causing an increased load on their working memory. Now, consider the effect if we remove the text and record it in sync with the animation. The learner's eye can follow the animation *while* the learner listens to the narration, resulting in a lower load on their limited working memory (see Chapter 9).

This process is explained using Baddeley's (1992) model of working memory (see Figure 10-7). Working memory consists of three parts. First is the visual component, which processes pictures and written text. Second is the auditory component, which processes audio information and language. Third is the manager that moves information between the three components of working memory and into long-term memory. When we see a picture, it is processed by the visual working memory. When we hear narration, it is processed by the auditory component. But, when we read text, it is *first* processed by visual working memory and then *transferred* to the auditory and language working memory. Thus, when we view the animation and read the text, we are unnecessarily increasing the load on working memory.

**Principles for fostering generative processing.**    The last two principles suggested by Mayer (2008) relate to the narration and generative processing. The ninth principle, *personalization*, recommends that the narration be written in a conversational style rather than a formal style such as one might use for printed materials. The tenth, the *voice* principle, suggests the narration be spoken in standard-accented human voice rather than a machine- or computer-synthesized voice. These ten principles from Mayer are summarized in Table 10-2.

**FIGURE 10-7**
Baddeley's model of working memory

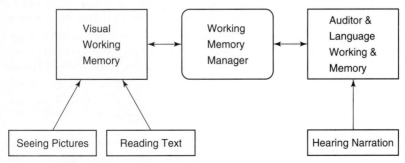

Based on Baddeley, A. (1992). Working memory. *Science, 255,* 556–559.

**TABLE 10-2**
Mayer's principles for multimedia design

| Principle | Application |
| --- | --- |
| 1. Coherence Principle | Remove extraneous information from animations to reduce distractions. |
| 2. Signaling Principle | Include cues such as arrows to focus learner's attention on important information. |
| 3. Redundancy Principle | Avoid presenting information in multiple formats (e.g., text narrative and text on graphics or spoken and written narration). |
| 4. Spatial Contiguity Principle | Present illustration and labels together rather than the labels in the text narrative. |
| 5. Temporal Contiguity Principle | Present narration and animation at the same time rather than narration before or after the animation. |
| 6. Segmenting Principle | Present shorter meaningful animations controlled by the learner rather than one longer animation. |
| 7. Pre-Training Principle | Present the basic information such as components and individual processes before showing an animation that incorporates these ideas into a single animation. |
| 8. Modality Principle | Animations with narration are more effective than animations with text. |
| 9. Personalization Principle | Use a conversational style with a text and narration. |
| 10. Voice Principle | Use a human voice for narration rather than a computer-generated voice. |

Based on Mayer, R. E. (2008). Research-based principles for learning with animation. In R. Lowe & W. Schnotz (Eds.), *Learning with animations: Research and implications for design*. (pp. 30–48). New York: Cambridge University Press.

## DESIGN CONSIDERATIONS FOR GROUP-BASED DISTANCE INSTRUCTION

The growth of distance education in higher education and in business is a significant factor in offering instruction and training. During the 2006–2007 academic year, over 65% of two- and four-year postsecondary institutions reported offering courses via distance, and 65% of those institutions offered courses for college credit (Parsad & Lewis, 2008). Distance education is also growing in businesses and the military, with a combined projected expenditure of $52.6 billion by 2010 (Kopf, 2007). Rapid growth, however, does not necessarily translate into examples of well-designed instruction. In this section, we will describe two general approaches to group-based distance instruction. We define group-based instruction as a class or cohort working at the same pace to complete a course even though the students may be physically separated.

### An Individualized Approach to Distance Instruction

The first approach addresses instruction of a group as individual learners separated by time and location. Although this approach can include CBI or multimedia instruction, it often takes the format of written text. Unfortunately, many instructors have simply dumped their PowerPoint presentations, lecture notes, and recorded lectures into a course management system or onto the Web and labeled the materials as an online course. Such courses have been referred to as "shovelware" (Morrison & Anglin, 2006) or "shrink wrapped" materials (Stevens-Long & Crowell, 2010). An alternative approach to shovelware is Holmberg's (1996) guided didactic conversation in which he suggests designing the materials to emulate a conversation with the learner. This approach reflects his belief that learning is an individual activity and is facilitated by materials that facilitate an interaction between the new content and what the learner already knows. A similar approach, reintegration of the teaching acts, was proposed by Keegan (1993). This reintegration process must occur in order to learn, because the instructional materials are designed in one time frame and the learner engages with the materials in another time frame. The materials must be designed in a manner that engages the learner in the second half of the learning conversation to learn the material.

## A Group Approach to Distance Instruction

The second approach is labeled by Keegan (1966) as the "virtual classroom." Newer definitions of distance education do not require the learner and instructor to be separated in both time and location as Keegan describes, but rather define distance education as taking place at the same time in different locations and mediated by electronic technologies such as two-way audio and video (Simonson, Smaldino, Albright, & Zvacek, 2006). One method used in the virtual classroom is the Community of Inquiry (CoI) framework (Garrison, Anderson, & Archer, 2000). The CoI framework posits that learners are able to construct meaning through communication. There are three elements considered essential to this process. First is cognitive presence, which is believed to be essential for critical thinking. Second is social presence, which is the ability of individuals to be perceived as a "real" person by others in the class. Third is teaching presence, which includes the design of educational experience (e.g., organization and selection of content, activities, discussion topics, and assessment) and the facilitation of the communication. Garrison et al. (2000) consider these three elements essential for creating the instruction in a distance environment. CoI is based on a constructivist philosophy for designing an online instructional environment that encourages the development of understanding through interactions with other students and the instructor. Recently, researchers have questioned the effectiveness of CoI for fostering critical thinking and deeper levels of learning (Rourke & Kanuka, 2009) due to a lack of assessment of learning in the research of CoI. They concluded that designing a course using the CoI framework does not facilitate the development of critical thinking or meaningful learning. Rather, student reports suggest that most learning from CoI has been factual knowledge.

## Avoiding the Shovelware Trap

In recent years, we have seen a surge in the number of Web-based, or e-learning, courses in businesses and military with the expectation of increasing effectiveness (Cone & Robinson, 2001) and reducing costs (Strother, 2002). To achieve these

**FIGURE 10-8**
Disassembled content example

You have two choices: Pay in full or finance over time. If you finance, the total cost of the car increases. That's because you're also paying for the cost of credit, which includes interest and other loan costs. You'll also have to consider how much you can put down, your monthly payment, the length of the loan, and the annual percentage rate (APR). Keep in mind that annual percentage rates usually are higher and loan periods generally are shorter on used cars than on new ones.

    I. Two choices for financing total cost of car
      a. Pay in full
      b. Finance
          i. Total cost increases [Fact]
            1. Paying interest [Fact]
            2. Paying other loan costs [Fact]
         ii. How much to put down [Rule]
            1. Affects
               a. Monthly payment [concept]
               b. Length of loan [concept]
               c. Annual percentage rate (APR) [concept]
            2. APR is
               a. Higher on used cars [Fact]
               b. Payment period is shorter [Fact]

From Federal Trade Commission. (2002). *Buying a Used Car*. Washington, DC: Government Printing Office. Retrieved from http://permanent.access.gpo.gov/lps39791/usedcar.pdf

goals, existing course materials such as PowerPoint presentations, video-recorded lectures, and handouts have been digitized and uploaded to create Web-based courses (Stevens-Long & Crowell, 2010). Although experience and logic suggest that one cannot simply place existing course materials online and create an effective course, a designer may be able to use the existing classroom materials to design an effective course. Morrison and Anglin (2006) proposed a strategy to evaluate existing materials to determine what additional instruction is needed to provide effective Web-based instruction.

The first part of the process is the disassembly of the existing materials (Morrison & Anglin, 2006) through a reverse engineering process. Existing materials are broken down into individual ideas much like an initial task analysis (see Figure 10-8). The result is a detailed outline of the existing content. Next, the content structures are identified using the expanded-content performance matrix (see Chapter 7). The third step is to determine the adequacy of the instructional strategies used to teach the identified content by comparing the strategies used with the prescriptions for each type of content presented in Chapter 7. If any deficiencies are identified, the designer can devise a revision plan to improve the strategies. If the design team does not have ownership or access to the original materials, supplemental materials may be developed.

## SUMMARY

1. Distance education is defined by Keegan (1996) as the separation of the teacher and learners in time and location. A synchronous classroom, in which the teacher and students are in different locations but meet at the same time, is labeled a "virtual classroom."
2. There are five types of computer-based or Web-based instruction: drill-and-practice, tutorials, simulations, games, and hypermedia.
3. Designing CBI requires the instructional designer to address the interface design, learner control, implementation of feedback, remediation, format of interactions, and use of multimedia.
4. Distance education can be offered in either an individualized or group-based format. An individualized approach is used with asynchronous courses and often uses guided didactic conversation (Holmberg, 1996) or Keegan's (1996) reintegration of the teaching acts. Although it has received recent criticism, one popular group-based approach is the Communities of Inquiry method.
5. When designing distance instruction, designers should avoid creating "shovelware" (i.e., repackaging existing materials) and put careful and thoughtful effort into designing good instruction.

## THE ID PROCESS

The instructional design product for this step of the process is the strategy for the specific delivery technology you have selected. Strategy design for technology-based instruction is a combination of the strategies described in Chapter 7 and the affordances of the technology that allow you to design efficient and effective instruction. As described in Chapter 7, designing the strategy requires that you to integrate your creative skills with the science of instructional design. When designing the strategies for instruction that will be delivered with technology, you have additional options to incorporate into your design. However, you should not include an option simply because it is available.

## APPLICATION

As part of your job, you have been tasked to modify two classroom courses so they can be offered on the Web on demand for individual learners. You have access to professional-quality videos that were developed for the class, the instructor's guide, and the student guide in both hard copy and electronic formats. One course focuses on interviewing job applicants, and the second focuses on recognizing sexual harassment in the work place.

## ANSWER

This task appears to be a typical shovelware assignment. The materials already exist, and management may believe that it is simply a matter of uploading the materials and opening the course for enrollment. What is missing is the instructor. The instructor's guide is simply that, a guide. Good instructors personalize the instructor's guide and add additional information to help the learners understand the content and to make the course interesting. We would start by analyzing the content, disassembling the existing instruction (Morrison & Anglin, 2006). Based on the results of our analysis, we would determine what additional content and instructional strategies are needed to create an online course with the existing materials.

The ideal situation would allow you to revise the materials and create any additional instruction required from your analysis. If time and resources do not allow this option, an alternative is to use your analysis to create a study guide that directs the learner through the material and provides additional information that you found to be missing from the classroom course. Although this option is not the optimal solution, it can provide a better approach than creating a shovelware course.

## QUALITY MANAGEMENT

The first question to ask when designing for technology-based instruction is, How can I use the technology to create efficient instruction? One example is the cost savings resulting from using technology to rapidly change content for, and frequently update the training of, a large number of employees. We recall one trainer telling us that, by the time he finished updating his presentation materials and the student handouts, the content (computer screen shots) had changed again. Selecting a technology-based delivery system for such a situation could reduce the cost of the training materials and make them readily available to all employees. Similarly, deciding to deliver training via Web-based instruction, using either a synchronous or asynchronous format, can significantly reduce travel costs and time away from the job while still providing opportunities for employees to network. Deciding to use CBI allows the designer to take advantage of affordances such as response-sensitive feedback and answer judging to create more efficient instruction that is available anytime anywhere.

The second question to ask when converting existing materials to a Web-based delivery system, is the time and resources for making needed changes. The quality of the materials can be evaluated using the instructional disassemble. Based on these results, the designer can then prepare a design plan to create an effective online course within the time and resource constraints.

## INSTRUCTIONAL DESIGN: DECISIONS AND CHOICES

Earlier, you had decided to make the conceptual component available on the organization's website. But now you have been asked to offer the entire fire extinguisher training course as computer-based instruction—including a simulation of the hands-on component. You will build off the presentation and generative strategies that you have already designed (see Chapter 7). You recognize that CBI will require the use of a tutorial, practice, and simulation. Now you need to make decisions about the interface design, learner control, use of feedback, remediation, and use of multimedia. You also recognize that you will need the assistance of a computer programming specialist to help develop your design. You and the computer programmer will develop a screen template to ensure that the user interface for navigating the course is consistent. Last, you know that careful consideration must be given to how to use the affordances of a CBI system most effectively. Here's a look at the design decisions for each objective.

## Objective 1

After completing this unit, the learner will correctly state the three components necessary to start a fire. *(Principle/Recall)*

For the initial presentation, the learner will view a simple animation of the combustion graphic showing the effect on the fire when one of the sides is removed. The animation will be narrated to reduce cognitive load. The tutorial will suggest a mnemonic and direct the learner to rehearse the mnemonic. [Rather than allow the learner to remove parts of the fire triangle, the animation will play through the removal of each side; learners do not always interact with all the options.]

## Objective 2

Given an example of a fire, the learner will correctly classify the class of fire. *(Concept/Application)*

Using a tutorial, we will present each concept by giving the name (e.g., Class A), a definition, and best example. For the generative strategy, we will use a drill-and-practice routine using knowledge of correct response feedback, in which we present examples of different types of combustible materials and ask the learner to identify the class of fire. The drill-and-practice will continue until the learner answers 75% of the items correctly.

## Objective 3

Given a variety of fire extinguishers, the learner will correctly identify each type of fire extinguisher. *(Concept/Application)*

Using a tutorial, we will present each concept by giving the name (e.g., Class A fire extinguisher), a definition, and a best example, and highlighting the differences between the concepts. For the generative strategy, we will use a drill-and-practice routine using knowledge of correct response feedback, in which we present examples of different extinguishers and ask the learner to indicate the proper classification. The drill-and-practice will continue until the learner answers 75% of the items correctly.

## Objective 4

Given a description of the combustible material in a fire, the learner will select the correct fire extinguisher to extinguish the fire. *(Principle/Application)*

A tutorial will present the rules followed by examples of the application of the first extinguisher. For the generative strategy, the learner will be presented with a scenario and then select the appropriate fire extinguisher. [You think about how many scenarios should be provided. You also consider the feedback that will be needed if the learner selects the incorrect fire extinguisher. To help guide these decisions, you plan to construct an early prototype and test the scenarios using formative evaluation procedures.]

## Objective 5

The learner will describe the appropriate response to fire in an office setting. *(Procedure/Recall)*

A tutorial will be used to explain and illustrate the proper emergency procedures. The generative strategy will include video segments of fire situations that require the learner to identify procedural errors.

## Objective 6

Given a dry chemical multiclass fire extinguisher and a fire burning in a trash container full of paper in an office setting, the learner will extinguish the fire by correctly using the fire extinguisher. (*Procedure/Application*)

A video tutorial using avatars with narration will present an actor demonstrating the dry chemical multiclass fire extinguisher. After viewing the demonstration, the learner will paraphrase the proper procedure. Then, the learner will practice in a controlled environment using a mouse or touchpad to simulate pressing the fire extinguisher lever, aiming the nozzle at the base of the fire, and demonstrating a sweeping motion. The computer-based system will provide corrective feedback to differentiate whether the learner points the extinguisher at the body or base of the fire and whether a sweeping motion is used. [You decide to use animated avatars to simplify the images, focus the learner's attention to highlight the critical cues, and to avoid distracting detail that could create cognitive overload. You also consider whether a game controller could be used to simulate the psychomotor task of using the extinguisher.]

## REFERENCES

Adams, W. K., Reid. S., Lemaster, R., Mckagan, S. B., Perkins, K. K., Dubson, M., & Wieman, C. E. (2008). A study of educational simulations: Part II. Interface design. *Journal of Interactive Learning Research, 19*(4), 551–577.

Allessi, S. M., & Trollip, S. R. (2001). *Multimedia for learning: Methods and development*. Needham Heights, MA: Allyn & Bacon.

Azevedo, R., & Jacobson, M. J. (2008). Advances in scaffolding learning with hypertext and hypermedia: A summary and critical analysis. *Educational Technology Research and Development, 56*, 93–100.

Baddeley, A. (1992). Working memory. *Science, 255*, 556–559.

Bruner, J. (1966). *Toward a theory of instruction*. Cambridge, MA: Harvard University Press.

Cheon, J., & Grant, M. M. (2009). Are pretty interfaces worth the time? The effects of user interface types on web-based instruction. *Journal of Interactive Learning Research, 20*(1), 5–33.

Clark, R. E. (1983). Reconsidering the research on learning from media. *Review of Educational Research, 53*(4), 445–459.

Clark, R. E. (1994). Media will never influence learning. *Educational Technology Research and Development, 42,* 21–29.

Clark, R. E. (2001). *Learning from media.* Greenwich CT: Information Age.

Clark, R. E., & Feldon, D. F. (2005). Five common but questionable principles of multi-media learning. In R. E. Mayer (Ed.), *The Cambridge handbook of multimedia learning* (pp. 97–115). New York: Cambridge University Press.

Clark, R. E., & Salomon, G. (1986). Media in teaching. In M. C. Wittrock (Ed.), *Handbook of research on teaching* (2nd ed., pp. 464–478). New York: Macmillan.

Cobb, T. (1997). Cognitive efficiency: Toward a revised theory of media. *Educational Technology Research and Development, 45,* 21–35.

Cone, J. W., & Robinson, D. G. (2001). The power of e-performance. *Training and Development, 55*(8), 32–41.

Corbalan, G., Kester, L., & van Merriënboer, J. J. G. (2006). Towards a personalized task selection model with shared instructional control. *Instructional Science, 34,* 399–422.

Crowder, N. A. (1959). Automatic tutoring by means of intrinsic programming. In E. Galanter (Ed.), *Automatic teaching: The state of the art* (pp. 109–116). New York: Wiley.

Dickey, M. D. (2007). Game design and learning: A conjectural analysis of how massively multiple online role-playing games (MMORPGs) foster intrinsic motivation. *Educational Technology Research and Development, 55,* 253–273.

Dillon, A., & Gabbard, R. (1998). Hypermedia as an educational technology: A review of the quantitative research literature on learner comprehension, control, and style. *Review of Educational Research, 68*(3), 322–349.

Dunlosky, J., & Rawson, K. A. (2005). Why does rereading improve metacomprehension accuracy? Evaluating the levels-of-disruption hypothesis for the rereading effect. *Discourse Processes, 40*(1), 37–55.

Fe, K. (2008). Computer games application within alternative classroom goal structures: Cognitive, metacognitive, and affective evaluation. *Educational Technology Research and Development, 56,* 539–556.

Garrison, D. R., Anderson, T., & Archer, W. (2000). Critical inquiry in a text-based environment: Computer conferencing in higher education. *The Internet and Higher Education, 2*(2-3), 87–105.

Hannafin, R. D., & Sullivan, H. J. (1996). Learner preferences and learner control over amount of instruction. *Journal of Educational Psychology, 88,* 162–173.

Haenggi, D., & Perfetti, C. A. (1992). Individual differences in reprocessing of text. *Journal of Educational Psychology, 84,* 182–192.

Holmberg, B. (1996). *Theory and practice of distance education* (2nd ed.). New York: Routledge.

Keegan, D. (1996). *Foundations of distance education.* New York: Routledge.

Knowlton, J. Q. (1964). A conceptual scheme for the audiovisual field. *Bulletin of the School of Education Indiana University, 40*(3), 1–44.

Kopf, D. (2007). E-learning market to hit 52.6B by 2010. Retrieved from http://thejournal .com/articles/2007/07/30/elearning-market-to-hit-526b-by-2010.aspx?sc_lang=en

Kopcha, T. J., & Sullivan, H. (2008). Learner preferences and prior knowledge in learner-controlled computer-based instruction. *Education Technology Research Development, 56,* 265–286.

Kulik, J. A., & Kulik, C. C. (1988). Timing of feedback and verbal learning. *Review of Educational Research, 58*, 79–97.

Levie, H. W., & Dickie, K. E. (1973). The analysis and application of media. In R. M. W. Travers (Ed.), *Second handbook of research of teaching* (pp. 858–882). Chicago: Rand McNally.

Lowe, R. (2008). Learning from animation. In R. Lowe & W. Schnotz (Eds.), *Learning with animations: Research and implications for design* (pp. 49–68). New York: Cambridge University Press.

Mayer, R. E. (2004). Should there be a three-strikes rule against pure discovery learning? The case for guided methods of instruction. *American Psychologist, 59*(1), 4–19.

Mayer, R. E. (2008). Research-based principles for learning with animation. In R. Lowe & W. Schnotz (Eds.), *Learning with animations: Research and implications for design* (pp. 30–48). New York: Cambridge University Press.

Mayer, R. E. (2009). *Multimedia learning* (2nd ed.). New York: Cambridge University Press.

Mayer, R. E., & Anderson, R. B. (1992). The instructive animation: Helping students build connections between words and pictures in multimedia learning. *Journal of Educational Psychology, 84*, 444–452.

Merrill, M. D. (1975). Learner control: Beyond aptitude–treatment interactions. *AV Communications Review, 23*, 217–226.

Merrill, M. D. (1988). Applying component display theory to the design of courseware. In D. J. Jonassen (Ed.), *Instructional designs for microcomputer courseware* (pp. 61–96). Hillsdale, NJ: Erlbaum.

Moreno, R. (2004). Decreasing cognitive load for novice students: Effects of explanatory versus corrective feedback in discovery-based multimedia. *Instructional Science, 32*, 99–113.

Morrison, G. R., & Anglin, G. J. (2006). An instructional design approach for effective shovelware: Modifying materials for distance education. *Quarterly Review of Distance Education, 7*(1), 63–74.

Morrison, G. R., Ross, S. M., & Baldwin, W. (1992). Learner control of context and instructional support in learning elementary school mathematics. *Educational Technology Research & Development, 40*, 5–13.

Morrison, G. R., Ross, S. M., Gopalakrishnan, M., & Casey, J. (1995). The effects of feedback and incentives on achievement in computer-based instruction. *Contemporary Educational Psychology, 20*, 32–50.

Mory, E. H. (2004). Feedback research revisited. In D. H. Jonassen (Ed.), *Handbook of research on educational communications and technology* (2nd ed., pp. 745–783). Mahwah, NJ: Erlbaum.

Narciss, S. (2008). Feedback strategies for interactive learning tasks. In J. M. Spector, M. D. Merrill, J. van Merriënboer, & M. P. Driscoll (Eds.), *Handbook of research on educational communications and technology* (3rd ed., pp. 125–143). New York: Taylor Francis.

Park, O., & Tennyson, R. D. (1980). Adaptive design strategies for selecting number and presentation order of examples in coordinate concept acquisition. *Journal of Educational Psychology, 72*, 362–370.

Parsad, B., & Lewis, L. (2008). *Distance education at degree-granting postsecondary institutions: 2006–07* (NCES 2009–044). Washington, DC: National Center for Education Statistics, Institute of Education Sciences, U.S. Department of Education.

Rawson, K. A., & Kintsch, W. (2005). Rereading effects depend on time of test. *Journal of Educational Psychology, 97*, 70–80.

Ross, S. M., & Morrison, G. R. (1993). Personalization of feedback in computer-based instruction. In G. Sales & J. Dempsey (Eds.), *Feedback and interactive instruction* (pp. 177–195). Englewood Cliffs, NJ: Educational Technology Publications.

Ross, S. M., Morrison, G. R., & O'Dell, J. K. (1989). Uses and effects of learner control of context and instructional support in computer-based instruction. *Educational Technology, Research, and Development, 37*, 29–39.

Rourke, L., & Kanuka, H. (2009). Learning in communities of inquiry: A review of the literature. *Journal of Distance Education, 23*(1), 19–48.

Simon, H. A. (1969). *The sciences of the artificial.* Cambridge, MA: MIT Press.

Simonson, M., Smaldino, S., Albright, M, & Zvacek, S. (2006). *Teaching and learning at a distance: Foundations of distance education.* Upper Saddle River, NJ: Pearson/Merrill/Prentice Hall.

Smits, M. H. S. B., Boon, J., Sluijsmans, D. M. A., & van Gog, T. (2008). Content and timing of feedback in a web-based learning environment: Effects on learning as a function of prior knowledge. *Interactive Learning Environments, 16*, 183–193.

Stevens-Long, J., & Crowell, C. (2010). Revisiting the design and delivery of an interactive online graduate program. In K. Rudestam & J. Schoenhotz-Read (Eds.), *Handbook of online learning* (2nd ed., pp. 252–266). Thousand Oaks, CA: Sage.

Strother, J. (2002). An assessment of the effectiveness of e-learning in corporate training programs. *International Review of Research in Open and Distance Learning.* Retrieved from http://www.irrodl.org/index.php/irrodl/article/view/83/161

Swaak, J., & de Jong, T. (2001). Learner vs. system control in using online support for simulation-based discovery learning. *Learning Environments Research, 4*, 217–241.

Sweller, J. (1999). *Instructional design in technical areas.* Camberwell, Victoria: ACER Press.

Thorndike, E. L. (1927). The law of effect. *American Journal of Psychology, 39*, 212–222.

Tognazzini, B. (2003). First principles of interaction design. Retrieved from http://www.asktog.com/basics/firstPrinciples.html

van Gog, T., Ericsson, K. A., Rikers, R. M. J. P., & Paas, F. (2005). Instructional design for advanced learners: Establishing connections between the theoretical frameworks of cognitive load and deliberate practice. *Educational Technology Research and Design, 53*, 73–81.

van Merriënboer, J. J. G., Schuurman, J. G., de Croock, M. B. M., & Paas, F. G. W. C. (2002). Redirecting learners' attention during training: Effects on cognitive load, transfer test performance and training efficiency. *Learning and Instruction, 12*, 11–37.

Yang, Y.-C., & Chin, W.-K. (1996). Motivational analyses on the effects of type of instructional control on learning from computer-based instruction. *Journal of Educational Technology Systems, 25*(1), 25–35.

# The Many Faces of Evaluation

## GETTING STARTED

You are asked by a school system to evaluate a new health sciences program that it has purchased to teach "healthy habits" to elementary school children. Before you design the evaluation, you first determine what questions the school system is trying to answer. Because the program is "complete" as purchased and implemented (i.e., it cannot be easily modified), summative rather than formative evaluation is desired. But the program hasn't been used enough to justify conducting a confirmative evaluation. The teachers and administrators involved with the program indicate that, aside from issues concerning cost and training requirements, their main interest is in the effects of the program in increasing positive attitudes and knowledge about healthy practices.

To increase the validity of your findings, you decide to use multiple data collection instruments, including a teacher survey and interview, student interview, parent interview, student attitude survey, and a test of student learning of health principles. For the last two measures (attitudes and learning), you also arrange to assess control students who attend schools similar to those of the program students. In constructing the test of learning, you create some criterion-referenced sections to determine the percentage of students who have mastered particular program objectives. One performance-based section asks students to demonstrate treatment for minor cuts using actual first-aid materials. You also create some norm-referenced sections especially designed to compare program and control students on knowledge and application of key health principles. Your synthesis of results from these multiple data sources will form the basis for your conclusions about the effectiveness of the program for achieving the district's objectives in the health education area. A member of the school board, however, asks why the evaluation contains "so many things." What would you say to defend the use of multiple measures? What would you concede to be disadvantages?

## QUESTIONS TO CONSIDER

"How can I determine whether this course is teaching what it is supposed to?"

"What are some ways to measure the accomplishment of performance skills besides observing a person at work on a job?"

"When is it appropriate to use a performance test instead of an objective test?"

"The questions on this test don't relate to the objectives the teacher gave us at the beginning of the unit. Shouldn't they?"

"Should I pretest my students? If so, how can that information be used to improve instruction?"

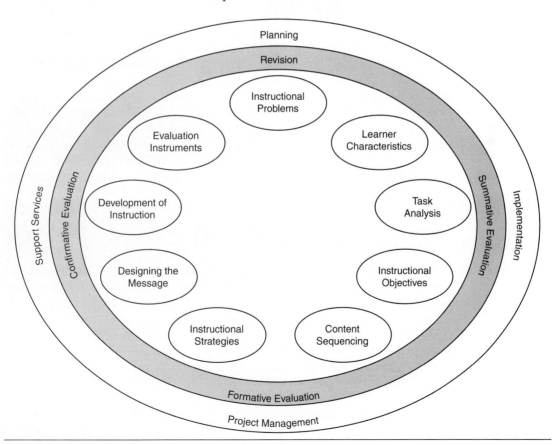

As reflected by these questions, evaluating learning is essential in the instructional design process. After examining learner characteristics, you identified instructional objectives and selected instructional strategies to accomplish them. Now, finally, you must develop the testing instruments and materials to measure the degree to which learners have acquired the knowledge, can perform the skills, and exhibit changes in attitudes as required by the objectives. In this chapter we examine the purposes and major forms of evaluation and important concepts concerning the role of evaluation in the instructional design process. In Chapter 12, we focus on specific procedures for constructing different types of tests and instruments to evaluate student learning. Before we begin, however, here is a quick overview of terminology. In these chapters, the term *evaluating* refers to the process of using measurement or assessment to make judgments about something. Is the training unit achieving its goals? Has the trainee attained the criteria required, for instance, for licensing as a day care van driver? The terms *measuring* and *assessing* are used interchangeably to denote the systematic collection of data about programs or people.

## PURPOSES OF EVALUATION

As just stated, evaluation is used for the purposes of making judgments about the worth or success of people or things (e.g., lessons, programs, projects). Before initiating an evaluation, you must determine its goals. The overall goal in training and educational settings is to determine student success in learning. But will the evaluation results be used primarily for improving how the course is taught or for identifying the effectiveness of the course? Will the results be used to judge a course that is being developed, has just been completed, or has been offered for some time? These varied interests clearly go hand in hand, but the nature of the evaluation approach employed is likely to differ depending on which is assigned greater importance. Specifically, depending on the stage of the instructional design process, one of three types of evaluation will become most useful: the formative, summative, or confirmative approach.

### Formative Evaluation

Even the most talented and conscientious designer is not likely to develop the "perfect" lesson or course the first time through. What seems excellent as a concept or idea may not work as well as planned when actually put to use in the classroom. Formative evaluation thus becomes an important part of the instructional design process. Its function is to inform the instructor or planning team how well the instructional program is serving the objectives as it progresses. Formative evaluation is most valuable when conducted during development and tryouts. It should be performed early in the process, before valuable time and resources are wasted on things that aren't working. If the instructional plan contains weaknesses, they can be identified and eliminated before full-scale implementation.

Expert's Edge

## But Did They Get Their Money's Worth?

Several years ago, Kmart Corporation needed to take numerous initiatives to improve its competitiveness in the retail field. Among the initiatives was the use of new learning technologies for training. The training management team determined that the "buddy system" used to train new hires in register skills could no longer meet the demand and that they were going to use technology to accelerate a change in training methods. But what were the benefits of this change?

A four-year plan for conversion of existing register-skills training to computer-based training (CBT) format was adopted with an embedded evaluation plan to determine effectiveness and return on investment (ROI). The computer-based training approach was adopted with the following projected benefits:

- Increased flexibility across and within stores
- Reduced delivery costs
- Consistency of application and administration
- Reduced employee training time
- Greater skill development

A comprehensive evaluation plan was devised that included measures before, during, and following implementation. Key measures for data collection included training time savings, learning gains, register productivity improvements (e.g., minutes per customer, transaction voids, number of overrides), team member turnover reduction, store usage figures, and increases in the customer satisfaction measurement index. A set of general guidelines was developed to ensure that various levels of management reviewing the progress of implementation accepted the resulting evaluation data. These guidelines included the following:

- Verifying measures with field and operations staff
- Defining measures and data sources up front
- Using conservative figures (when such options existed)
- Focusing on change management interventions
- Allowing an eight-month to one-year lag for initial reporting

ROI calculations typically provide a snapshot in time that may not provide an accurate picture during the implementation. We decided to use a "rolling ROI" that was calculated at different time periods to provide a truer picture of the impacts. In general, ROI can be applied to projects for which the following conditions are in place: (1) the projects are of longer duration (more than one year); (2) training is tied to organizational objectives or change; and (3) there exists significant management support and interest. On the other hand, ROI data analysis might be questioned when senior management is skeptical of the value of training, training is required to break the "not invented here" syndrome, the "bean counters" (financial staff) demand hard evidence, or the CEO asks for the data (it is probably too late!).

During the first six months of the rollout, 37 stores participated in an in-depth pilot study to determine bugs in the implementation process, including training materials, technical computer support, job aids, and ease of computer usage by trainees. The second six months involved the participation of a total of 197 stores throughout the United States. The third phase, during the next 18 months, was implementation in all of Kmart Super K stores (the large superstores) and about one-third of the Big K stores (regular Kmarts) for a total of about 650 stores. The fourth phase, over the final 18 months, included all 2,161 stores in the United States and Puerto Rico.

Because stores participating in the four phases were included at various stages of implementation, CBT stores could be compared with non-CBT stores for any given time period. Variables such as differences in region, economic environment, and size were controlled during the implementation. In addition, baseline quantitative data could be collected on all key measures for any given time through the use of an enterprise-wide data collection system. A comprehensive data collection system with key and control variables was available for analysis. Initial results for the first year of implementation showed that approximately 40,000 training hours were saved, CBT trainees had 6% higher productivity, and there was less turnover during the first 90 days of employment. The ROI calculation for this first year was a very conservative 126%. During the second year, it was determined that the turnover data was maintained in the CBT stores, there were 10% fewer overrides, and checkouts were 13% faster. These data together with the reduction in training hours resulted in an ROI calculation of about 400%.

Overall conclusions drawn by training management and reported to senior operations management showed that register trainee performance demonstrated significant improvements in that trainees were both faster and better (fewer errors). The impact on turnover was significant—much more than what was originally projected. The only downside was the failure to show any demonstrated impact on the customer service index. It was suggested that this measure was too "global" in nature and was beyond the control of direct impact of register operators.

Dale C. Brandenburg is research professor and director of workplace education and training at Wayne State University. He has over 30 years of experience in needs assessment, training evaluation, technical training strategy, and the impacts of technology deployment on workforce issues, with an emphasis on manufacturing and advanced technology organizations.

Test results, reactions from learners, observations of learners at work, reviews by subject-matter experts, and suggestions from colleagues may indicate where there are deficiencies in the learning sequence, procedures, or materials.

Formative evaluation is the quality control of the development process. Starting in Chapter 2, we have included a section titled Quality Management—a formative evaluation step during the design of the instruction. This section in each chapter includes suggestions on how to evaluate your progress as you design a project. The suggestions provide guidelines for determining whether you are focused on the original problem and whether the instruction you are developing would solve the problem you identified.

Formative testing and revision (and retesting and further revision, if necessary) are important for the success of an instructional design plan. They should relate not only to the suitability of objectives, subject content, instructional strategies, and materials but also to the roles of personnel, the use of facilities and equipment, the schedules, and other factors that together affect optimum performance in achieving objectives. Remember, the planning process is highly interactive—each element affects other elements.

Keep in mind that both instructional designers and instructors need to use formative evaluation. For designers, the usual focus is the effectiveness of materials. Thus, if students perform poorly, the conclusion will be that the materials, not the students, are at fault (Hellebrandt & Russell, 1993, p. 22). For instructors, the focus will be placed on the students. If students don't perform up to expectations and the effectiveness of instruction has been previously demonstrated, the conclusion will be that the students, not the materials, are at fault.

The following questions might be used by designers to gather data during formative evaluation:

1. Given the objectives for the unit or lesson, is the level of learning acceptable? What weaknesses are apparent?
2. Are learners able to use the knowledge or perform the skills at an acceptable level? Are any weaknesses indicated?
3. How much time did the instruction and learning require? Is this acceptable?
4. Did the activities seem appropriate and manageable to the instructor and learners?
5. Were the materials convenient and easy to locate, use, and file?
6. What were the learners' reactions to the method of study, activities, materials, and evaluation methods?
7. Do the unit tests and other outcome measures satisfactorily assess the instructional objectives?
8. What revisions in the program seem necessary (content, format, etc.)?
9. Is the instructional context appropriate?

We more closely examine the procedures for conducting formative evaluations in Chapter 13. For now, consider the purposes of the formative approach in comparison to those of an alternative orientation—summative evaluation.

## Summative Evaluation

Summative evaluation is directed toward measuring the degree to which the major outcomes are attained by the end of the course. Key information sources are therefore likely to be the results of both the unit posttests and the final examination for the course. In addition to measuring the effectiveness of student or trainee learning, summative evaluations frequently also measure the following:

- Efficiency of learning (material mastered/time)
- Cost of program development
- Continuing expenses
- Reactions toward the course or program
- Long-term benefits of the program

Long-term benefits may be determined by following up on learners who complete the program to discover whether and when they are using the knowledge, skills, and attitudes learned. Depending on the length of the time frame, this process may be labeled "confirmative evaluation" (see the next section), which represents an extended type of summative evaluation. (Summative and confirmative evaluations receive full attention in Chapter 13.) As for formative evaluation, instructional designers focus summative evaluations on the effectiveness of materials, whereas instructors focus them on the effectiveness of students.

## Confirmative Evaluation

Suppose you've developed a training unit to teach the accounting staff of a company how to use a new billing system. The unit was subjected to continuous formative evaluation, and appropriate revisions were made at each stage of the design process. Summative evaluation further confirmed that the training unit was effective in preparing employees to use the system accurately and efficiently. Everyone seems happy in the accounting department until it is realized over time that employees are making numerous mistakes and reacting negatively toward the software system. You investigate by conducting a follow-up evaluation. Your findings reveal that increasing numbers of customers are paying for purchases through automatic bank withdrawals, a type of transaction that was not sufficiently addressed in the initial training. The evaluation also yields a number of useful suggestions by the accounting staff for how other aspects of the training could be strengthened to provide better preparation for actual job tasks.

The type of evaluation performed in the preceding example is called confirmative evaluation. It was originally introduced by Misanchuk (1978) based on the rationale that evaluation of instruction needs to be continuous and, therefore, extend beyond summative evaluation. Similar to formative and summative evaluations, confirmative evaluations rely on multiple data-gathering instruments, such as questionnaires, interviews, performance assessments, self-reports, and knowledge tests (Moseley & Solomon, 1997). Of special interest to the confirmative evaluator are questions such as these:

Do learners continue to perform successfully over time?
Do materials still meet their original objectives?
How can clients' needs be best met over time?
If improvements are needed in the training or materials, how can they be made most effectively?

If the instruction isn't working as well as it did originally, what are the reasons?
Should the instruction be continued as is?
Should it be revised?
Should it be terminated?

## RELATIONSHIP AMONG FORMATIVE, SUMMATIVE, AND CONFIRMATIVE EVALUATIONS

At this stage, you probably have noted some similarities as well as differences among formative, summative, and confirmative evaluations. Let's now take a closer look at similarities and differences between these components in addressing different evaluation needs.

### The Role of Instructional Objectives

For all three evaluation approaches, what is evaluated is determined directly by instructional objectives. If one objective, for example, is to teach trainees how to file an accident report correctly, then assessing how well they do this task becomes an essential part of an evaluation, regardless of whether the primary interest is to improve the instruction (formative) or judge its effectiveness after completion (summative) or over time (confirmative). If improving student attitudes toward the accident-reporting process is not an instructional goal, there will be little rationale for including an attitude measure (however, as you will see, attitude assessments can be valuable in interpreting why particular objectives are or are not achieved successfully). Instructional objectives, however, provide only part of the basis for determining evaluation objectives. Broader educational or training goals may suggest looking at "summative" effects of instruction on personnel, administration, resource allocation, and cost-effectiveness (see Chapter 13). As will be discussed later, analyzing processes of instruction (e.g., instructional strategies, teaching methods, student behaviors, or student feelings) becomes especially important when conducting formative evaluations to describe how well particular course features are operating. Confirmative evaluation, like summative evaluation, examines all training effects, but it takes place some time after the completion of instruction and usually in the actual performance environment (i.e., at the workplace). Key idea: All three types of evaluation are driven by instructional objectives and goals.

### Multiple Data Sources Equal Increased Information

Because most units of instruction have multiple objectives with different focuses, all three evaluation approaches require varied sources of outcome data. Examples include measures of knowledge, skills, behaviors, attitudes, and completion time, as well as information about the instructional delivery, learning activities, resources, teacher characteristics, and so on. The more the designer knows about the instruction and its outcomes, the more confidently he or she can make conclusions and recommendations. Generally speaking, there is a greater need for multiple data sources in formative evaluations because the interest is not only the effectiveness of particular elements but also how to improve those that are not working as planned. Similarly, if trainees or materials are not maintaining expected standards over time, the confirmative evaluator will want to determine the causes of the problem and possible remedies. Key idea: All three types of evaluation (but especially formative) typically require multiple data sources.

## Processes and Products

Formative evaluation asks, "How are we doing?" Summative evaluation asks, "How did we do?" Confirmative evaluation asks, "How are we still doing?" To answer these questions, different types of measurement orientations are needed. Specifically, formative evaluation emphasizes the measurement of outcomes *as instruction evolves* (or "forms"). Interest is as much with process as with product. Summative evaluation stresses measurement of criterion outcomes that occur *at the end* of instruction. Here interest is more with products than with processes. Confirmative evaluation stresses the measurement of criterion outcomes that occur after the instruction *has been completed for some time*. Its interest is, therefore, the long-term maintenance of products. Key idea: Formative evaluation gives equal attention to processes and products. Summative and especially confirmative evaluations give greater weight to products.

## Time of Testing

For formative evaluations, testing is important at all phases of instruction— pretesting (before), embedded testing (during), and posttesting (after). Although all three types of testing may be used in both summative and confirmative evaluation, posttesting is clearly the most critical and the main basis for forming conclusions about the instruction. (In the final section of this chapter, we examine uses of pretesting in more detail.) Confirmative evaluation, however, should generally include repeated posttesting to monitor performance over time. Key idea: Formative evaluation gives equal attention to pretesting, embedded testing, and posttesting. Summative and confirmative evaluation give greater weight to posttesting.

## When to Evaluate

Formative evaluations are most valuable before instruction is fully developed, when it is inexpensive to make changes. They are also most valuable when used in a continuous manner, at different phases of the design process. As is discussed more fully in Chapter 13, some common modes of formative evaluation are connoisseur-based (i.e., expert-based) review, one-to-one trials, small-group testing, and field testing. All these are used to refine instruction at different developmental stages. Summative and confirmative evaluations, in contrast, are designed to examine the effectiveness of completed versions of instruction. Summative comes after the instruction is first used, but before sustained implementation, whereas confirmative is used after implementation has occurred and the design has been used for a reasonable time (usually at least six months to a year).

## RELATIONSHIP BETWEEN EVALUATION AND INSTRUCTIONAL OBJECTIVES

The broad purpose of evaluation is to determine to what extent the objectives of the instruction are being attained. The assessments used to inform the evaluation should therefore have a direct relationship with the objectives. In the case of knowledge testing, some authorities even suggest that, as soon as a subject content list and the details of a task analysis are first completed, you should immediately write examination questions relating to the content. In turn, the questions can be reworded as instructional objectives. This procedure may seem to be a backward way of planning, but it points to the importance of relating evaluation directly to instructional objectives. Usually, once you are satisfied with the extent and completeness of the instructional objectives, you are ready to develop ways for evaluating them. For accomplishing this, two key ideas are crucial. First, obtain a good match between types of assessment instruments and types of objectives. Second, consider using several data sources to gain as complete a picture as possible about to what degree the learner has attained each objective and the processes involved. Remember, not all instructional objectives lend themselves to direct, precise measurement or to a simple "success/fail" answer.

### Matching Measures to Objectives

In Chapter 5 we discussed the fact that various forms of objectives are useful for describing different types of learning outcomes—for instance, cognitive objectives for knowledge, psychomotor objectives for skills, and affective objectives for attitudes. To complete the cycle, those objectives, coupled with the evaluation goals, in turn suggest certain types of measures. Finding the measures that best fit each objective is an important evaluation task. Note the following real-life examples, for each of which the measure–objective fit could be seriously questioned:

- A corporate training course on group leadership skills included objectives that were nearly all performance or skill based: for example, "The student will distribute an agenda for the meeting." Yet, the sole assessment measure employed was a 25-item multiple-choice knowledge test administered as a pre- and postassessment! Not surprisingly, students "significantly" improved their scores across the two testings (after all, they were taught new material). Should the course be viewed as successful in meeting its objectives?
- A college professor assessed achievement on the midterm and final exams of a history course by asking students to list the "major developments" that led to the Vietnam War. Scoring was based on how closely the students' listings matched the one given in class. These assessments accounted for about 85% of the final course grade. Does this evaluation approach appear

valid given instructional objectives that emphasize analysis and synthesis of historic events?

- A department chairman wanted to evaluate the effectiveness of teaching in a certain core course. Toward the end of the year, he scheduled sessions in which he would visit a class, dismiss the instructor for 20 minutes, and ask class members to react in a group discussion to the teaching methods and teacher qualities. Was he likely to obtain an accurate picture of teaching effectiveness in that course?

The answer to the questions in all three illustrations is a definite no. Inappropriate instruments were employed in each situation. For the corporate training evaluation, improvement on the knowledge test says little about trainees' abilities to perform the desired skills. Similarly, verbatim recall of historical facts from a listing appears to be a trivial, lower-level measure of learning in the history course. Finally, although the department chairman was on the right track by employing student attitudes as a data source, the specific measure used (i.e., a group discussion) probably would generate invalid results because students may feel pressured and self-conscious about speaking openly in front of a group to the department chairman.

## Suggested Measures for Alternative Outcomes

Suggested instrument selections for assessing different types of instructional outcomes are provided in Figure 11-1. For now, we will simply identify the instruments and save discussion of the procedures for developing them for Chapter 12. Keep in mind that the ultimate choice of evaluation measures depends on a variety of factors other than what is considered in an ideal sense to be most desirable and valid. These factors include costs, time, skill required for test administration, instrument availability, and accepted practices in the educational or training context concerned.

## VALIDITY AND RELIABILITY OF TESTS

Once you have determined the types of measures for assessing objectives, selecting or developing the instruments becomes the next major task. Whichever route is taken, it is important to ensure that those instruments possess two necessary qualities: validity and reliability.

## Validity

Attention was previously given to the validity of testing when the necessity for a direct relationship between instructional objectives and assessment items was indicated. A test is considered valid when it specifically measures what was learned, as specified by the instructional objectives for the unit or topic.

In Chapter 5 we described the benefits of developing a performance-content matrix that relates objectives to learning levels. One way of ensuring a high degree of test validity is to devise a second table of specifications that relates test items

**FIGURE 11-1**

Various evaluation instruments for different outcomes

---

**A. Knowledge**

Data Sources:    **Objective Tests**

Objective test questions have one correct answer and thus can be easily ("objectively") graded.

1. Multiple choice

Example:    *Which state is the farthest west in longitude?*
*a. Hawaii*
*b. California*
*c. Alaska*
*d. Washington*

2. True-False

Example:    *In the sentence "The boys enjoyed the movie," the subject is "movie."(T/F)*

3. Matching

Example:    *Match the choice in column B that described the term in column A.*

| A | B |
|---|---|
| Mean | Midpoint |
| Mode | Most frequent score |
| Median | Variability |
| | Average |

Data Sources:    **Constructed-Response Tests**

Constructed-response tests require the learner to generate ("construct") responses to questions. Thus, alternative answers and/or solution strategies are usually possible.

1. Completion (fill-in-the-blank)

Example:    *Instructional objectives that describe the use and coordination of physical activities fall into the _____ domain.*

2. Short essay

Example:    *Define formative and summative evaluation and describe two ways in which they might differ procedurally.*

3. Long essay

Example:    *Discuss the purposes of instructional evaluation. Using an example lesson or course, describe the considerations or steps that would be involved in such evaluations with regard to (a) planning, (b) implementation, and (c) interpretation and dissemination of results.*

4. Problem-solving

Example:    *Complete the following math problem, showing the correct formula, your work, and the solution.*

*Four electricians install 1,327 outlets in 70 apartments. What is the average number of outlets in each apartment?*

**B. Skills and Behavior**

Data Sources:    1. Direct testing of performance outcomes

Example    *A test of tying different types of knots used in sailing*

2. Analysis of naturally occurring results

Example:    *Number of accidents, attendance, sales increases, etc.*

*(continued)*

**FIGURE 11-1**
(*continued*)

---

3. Ratings of behaviors based on direct observation
Example:    *Rate teacher clarity on a five-point scale.*

4. Checklists of behavior based on direct observation
Example:    *Check each safety precaution exhibited by trainees while wiring circuits.*

5. Ratings or checklists of behavior based on indirect measures
Example:    *Peer evaluation of the student's communication skills while dealing with clients*

6. Authentic tests
Example:    *Portfolios or exhibitions that display students' work in meaningful contexts.*

**C. Attitudes**

Data Sources:

1. Observation of instruction
Examples:    *What percentage of the students is attentive? How frequently does the typical student participate in class discussion? Do students appear to enjoy the lesson?*

2. Observation/assessment of behavior
Examples:    *How many plays do students attend following an arts appreciation course? What percentage of students enroll in Algebra II following completion of Algebra I?*

3. Attitude surveys
Examples:    *Ratings of instructor preparedness, lesson difficulty, clarity, and organization, open-ended evaluation by hospital patients of the bedside manner of the nurses who cared for them*

4. Interviews
Examples:    *What appear to be the strengths of the instruction? Why? What appear to be the weaknesses? Why?*

---

to objectives. Such a table can serve two purposes. First, it helps verify that outcomes at the higher learning levels (e.g., application, analysis, synthesis, and evaluation) receive adequate attention. Second, it shows the number of questions needed for measuring individual instructional objectives or groups of related objectives. These frequency values reflect the relative importance of each objective, or the proportion of emphasis it is given during instruction.

Table 11-1 indicates the nature and number of test questions for instructional objectives in a knowledge-based unit. Table 11-2 relates the number of test items to the instructional objectives on a task involving different cognitive levels and psychomotor performances. By designing such tables, you can be reasonably certain you will test for all instructional objectives and give each the proper amount of attention. Although validity is typically associated with knowledge tests, it has the same importance for all types of assessment measures. The key idea is that the test assesses what it is supposed to measure. Thus, course attitude surveys need to measure reactions to the course (and not primarily instructor popularity or some

**TABLE 11-1**
Specifications relating number of test items to learning objectives on cognitive levels
Topic: Community Services for the Elderly

| Objective | Knowledge | Comprehension | Application | Analysis | Synthesis | Evaluation |
|---|---|---|---|---|---|---|
| 1. Recognize misconceptions and superstitions about the elderly. | 3 | | | | | |
| 2. Differentiate between facts and opinions about physical and social behaviors of the elderly. | | 2 | | | | |
| 3. Describe attitudes toward the elderly as practiced by various ethnic groups. | | 2 | | | | |
| 4. Locate information relative to community programs for the elderly. | | 4 | | | | |
| 5. Classify community organizations according to types of services offered for the elderly. | | | | 2 | | |
| 6. Develop a plan for judging the value of individual community programs for the elderly. | | | | | 3 | |
| 7. Assess the merits of a community program for the elderly. | | | | | | 2 |
| 8. Given a hypothetical or real situation, analyze the needs of a senior citizen and recommend one or more community programs. | | | 4 | | | |

**TABLE 11-2**
Specifications relating number of test items to learning objectives on cognitive levels
for psychomotor performance
Task: Measuring Electrical Values in Series Circuits

| Objective | Knowledge | Comprehension | Application | Psychomotor |
|---|---|---|---|---|
| 1. List symbols used to identify components in an electrical circuit. | 2 | | | |
| 2. Recognize the makeup of a complete series circuit. | | 3 | | |
| 3. Identify a series circuit in a schematic diagram. | | 1 | 2 | |
| 4. Assemble a series circuit on a board using component parts. | | | | 2 |
| 5. Set up and adjust a multimeter for measuring. | | | | 1 |
| 6. Measure and calculate voltage, current flow, and resistance in a series circuit. | | | 3 | 3 |

other incidental variable); performance tests need to assess processes and outcomes relating to the skills or competencies of concern; and observations of instruction need to describe events and impressions that accurately capture what occurred when the instruction was delivered.

Validity is not always easy to measure or quantify. Several different types exist and are discussed in most measurement texts (e.g., face, content, predictive, concurrent, and construct validity). The two most important types for the instructional designer are face validity and content validity, which both involve judgmental processes. Face validity is supported by the judgment (often by an expert panel) that the measure appears (''on the face of it'') to assess the measure of interest. Content validity is similar to face validity but typically involves a more specific examination of individual items or questions to ensure that each ''content domain'' is appropriately addressed. For example, a final achievement exam that draws 90% of its items from only one out of four primary course units would have questionable content validity. Tables of specification (see Tables 11-1 and 11-2) are especially useful in making content validity judgments.

## Reliability

Reliability refers to a test's ability to produce consistent results whenever used. If the same learners, without changes in their preparation, were to take the same test or an equal form of the test, there should be little variation in the scores. Certain procedures can affect the reliability of a test:

- The more questions used relating to each instructional objective, the more reliable the test will be. If only one question is asked about a major objective or an extensive content area, it can be difficult to ascertain whether a learner has acquired the knowledge or guessed the correct answer. (See the previous procedure for developing a specification table relating the number of test questions to the objectives.)

- The test should be administered in a standardized way. If more than one person directs testing, similar instructions must be given to each group of individuals who take the test over a period of time.
- Everyone should be tested under the same conditions so that distractions do not contribute to discrepancies in the scores.
- Testing time should be the same length for all learners.
- Possibly the most important factor that can affect test reliability is the scoring method, especially when marking an essay test or judging performance on a rating scale. Despite attempts to standardize how different persons score tests, criteria can be viewed in various ways, and variations are unavoidable. The less subjective the scoring, the more reliable the test results will be. As is discussed in Chapter 12, ensuring adequate reliability has been the main challenge for instructors using performance assessments (e.g., evaluating students on the quality of their oral reports) and authentic measures (e.g., reviewing portfolios showing the students' work in mathematics over the past six weeks). There are a number of different methods for assessing reliability.
- The test–retest method correlates students' scores on two different administrations of the same measure.
- The parallel forms method correlates scores on similar (i.e., "parallel" or matched) tests taken at different times.
- The split–half method correlates students' scores on half of the test with those on the other half. (The split should be every other item, rather than the first versus the second half, to ensure items of similar content and difficulty are compared.)
- Internal-consistency reliability is comparable to performing all unique split–half correlations. High internal consistency means that different test items are measuring the same abilities or traits. Popularly used formulas such as KR-20 and coefficient alpha are described in basic educational measurement texts and can be easily run by most computer-based statistical packages.

## Relationship Between Validity and Reliability

A final question to consider is the relationship between validity and reliability. Does validity require reliability? Does reliability require validity? The answers to these two questions are yes and no, respectively. For an assessment to be valid, it must be reliable. Think about it: How could a test measure what it is supposed to if the scores vary from testing to testing (without any change in testing conditions or learner states)? On the other hand, you could have reliability without validity.

For example, an instructor might attempt to assess students' ability to design lessons by giving them a 50-item true/false test on learning theories. The scores might remain consistent from one testing to the next, but they would hardly reflect instructional design skills, the outcome of major interest.

## STANDARDS OF ACHIEVEMENT

Suppose you have completed planning your evaluation. Not only have you identified the types of measures needed, but you also have outlined the domains to be assessed and the amount of weight to be given to each one to establish high content validity. Before you develop the actual tests, there is another decision to be made: how to judge achievement. Two standards of achievement can be applied when interpreting test scores and assigning grades: relative and absolute. Understanding each standard, as well as its particular implications within the instructional design process, is an important part of evaluation.

### Relative Standards

In most conventional educational programs, the performance of one learner is compared with those of other learners in the class. A test based on relative standards indicates that one learner has learned more or less than other learners have, which results in a relative rating of each learner within the group. The rating does not necessarily signify the level of proficiency of any learner in the group with respect to a specific standard of accomplishment. For example, assume that scores on an 85-point test range from 44 to 73. The instructor would assign grades, starting with the 73 score as the highest A. He might then decide, for example, to have about 7.5% of the learners receive a grade of A, 17.5% a B, 50% a C, 17.5% a D, and 7.5% an F (see Figure 11-2). This approach is called a normal distribution, or "grading on the normal curve." Grades are assigned in a relative or normative fashion. Note the characteristics of the normal distribution: It is symmetric (you can fold it in half); the mean (average), mode (most frequent score), and median (halfway

**FIGURE 11-2**
Grading on a normal curve

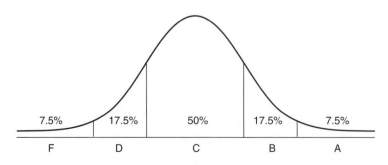

point or fiftieth percentile) are identical and positioned in the exact middle of the distribution; and the frequency of scores decreases as you move from the middle to the extremes of the distribution in either direction. Many human characteristics (e.g., height, weight, and intelligence) tend to be normally distributed. Note, however, that normal distributions facilitate the use of (but are not required for) norm-referenced grading.

Regardless of the distribution, the critical element is that people are being compared with one another rather than against a standard. Norm-referenced scoring, grading, and reporting conventions are therefore designed to convey these comparisons. But, under norm-referenced systems, it cannot be assumed, for example, that a learner who received an A this year in Biology 101 is comparable in achievement to another learner who received an A in the same course last semester. The high grades convey that both students did well relative to their classmates, but they do not indicate which specific competencies or skills the students have mastered. Standardized scores, such as those for the American College Testing (ACT), Scholastic Achievement Test (SAT), and Graduate Record Examination (GRE) exams, also illustrate norm-referenced scores. Perhaps the type of relative score with which you are most familiar is percentile scores. If you know that Micah scored at the 89th percentile on the geometry final, what have you learned? Essentially, you know that Micah performed well, surpassing close to 9 out of 10 of his classmates. What you do not know from that information alone is what his actual score was (i.e., the number or percentage he answered correctly) or types of learning he demonstrated.

Norm-referenced testing procedures are important for comparing the overall accomplishments of individuals or a class with established local, state, or national norms. They are also useful when the purpose of evaluation is to select individuals who stand out from the group (at the high or low extremes) for special programs. For example, there seems to be a good reason to want one's heart or brain surgeon to be someone who not only passed all the competencies but also excelled relative to other medical students in the knowledge and skills required. Because of this property, norm-referenced testing may not fit well with plans to make instruction and resulting learning effective for the great majority of learners in a class or training program.

## Absolute Standards

In many instances, the primary goal of the instructional design is to have as many learners as possible reach a satisfactory level of achievement. Therefore, learning outcomes must be measured against a specific standard rather than a relative standard.

The specific standard is the criterion specified by the instructional objectives. Criterion-referenced testing includes the measurement of how well each learner attains the required level of comprehension and competence specified for each objective. This degree of achievement is independent of the performance of other students. The terms *competency-based instruction, performance-based instruction,* and *mastery-based instruction* are used interchangeably with criterion-referenced instruction. These methods identify a program that provides experiences intended to bring most learners to a satisfactory level of proficiency in learning or performing a task that will be measured by testing. When criteria are set and learners successfully meet them, the concept of mastery learning is realized. This goal partly justifies giving increased attention to self-paced learning methods and providing more than one opportunity for a learner to restudy, self-test, and then be retested until the mastery level is attained. There is concern about the emphasis on mastery learning in some programs. Although it is successful when identifiable competencies are required (e.g., in the training of dental technicians or airline pilots), some people fear that use of conventional letter grading (A-B-C-D-F) will lead to "grade inflation" and lower academic standards. In a well-designed and properly executed instructional program, each learner could attain mastery of each topic and receive an A. Students are especially likely to obtain high grades when the learning situation satisfies a combination of the following conditions:

- The learner group has been carefully selected on the basis of ability.
- Each learner is highly motivated to learn.
- Learners have received excellent prerequisite training.
- Instruction has been carefully prepared, pretested, and proven to be effective.

On the other hand, mastery can be accepted as attainment of minimum or essential knowledge and skills at a reasonable competency level (e.g., an 80% performance standard), which may guarantee a B or C grade (or possibly a *P* for "pass," or credit). Then, to reach a higher level, or an A grade, additional accomplishments may be required, such as answering 95% to 100% of the posttest questions correctly or achieving optional objectives and engaging in additional activities. If a number of performance levels above the acceptable minimum are set, each learner could be permitted to choose a goal on the basis of his or her capabilities, background, and motivation. This procedure is similar to the contract concept used in some educational programs.

## Measurement Issues

In comparing norm-referenced and criterion-referenced testing and grading methods, a final matter should be emphasized. First, in the norm-referenced approach, tests are constructed so that expected learner attainment levels are purposefully spread out to achieve high, average, and low scores. In measurement terms, the key concern is that items discriminate, or differentiate, between learners. Given this goal, what item-difficulty level (i.e., proportion of learners answering correctly) would provide maximum discrimination? The answer is 0.50—an item that is answered correctly by half the examinees and missed by half. Note, by comparison, that an item that is answered correctly or missed by 100% of the examinees provides zero discrimination.

In most normative instances, we would not want a test to consist exclusively of items having 0.50 difficulty (nor would our students or trainees be very happy about such a test). Some easier items should be included to increase motivation and morale. In the criterion-referenced method, test items are included as relevant to the required standards. The results clearly indicate what a learner has learned and can do. Assuming that training has been effective, you would expect and probably want most students to demonstrate mastery. Items with difficulty levels of 0.80 or higher would therefore be desirable in the criterion-referenced situation. In summary, guiding and assessing learners to help them accomplish their objectives is a normal procedure in criterion-referenced measurement and mastery learning. This orientation fosters cooperation among learners. The norm-referenced approach, on the other hand, emphasizes competition, resulting in differentiation among learners based on achievement levels.

## Standards Versus Conventional Measurement

In K–12 contexts, controversy has been generated in recent years regarding the use of norm-referenced tests (NRTs) versus criterion-referenced tests (CRTs). Perhaps you remember taking NRTs, such as the Iowa Test of Basic Skills (ITBS), the Scholastic Achievement Test (SAT), or the California Achievement Test (CAT), when you were in school. These tests involved answering multiple-choice questions in language arts, mathematics, and other core subjects under strictly controlled conditions. In many school districts, school means on the standardized tests are published in the local newspaper and interpreted by the public and often by district and state administrators as indicators of the success of the individual schools.

Starting in 2001, the No Child Left Behind Act (2002) holds schools and districts responsible for demonstrating adequate yearly progress (AYP) on state-mandated tests by all targeted subgroups of students (e.g., disadvantaged, African American, special education). Needless to say, these conditions typically create a high-stakes testing environment in which teaching to the test, coaching, and sometimes even cheating may occur in the quest to raise scores (Kim & Sunderman, 2005; Linn, 2003).

In an effort to link testing directly to performance and content standards, states have been replacing formerly used norm-referenced tests (such as ITBS) with curriculum-linked CRTs, such as the Illinois Standardized Achievement Test (ISAT) and the Tennessee Comprehensive Assessment Program (TCAP). Schools are evaluated on the basis of the percentages of students performing at or above "benchmark," defined as surpassing cutoff scores for "proficient" or "advanced" status in reading and mathematics. Under No Child Left Behind, schools that fail to demonstrate such AYP face sanctions of increasing severity for each successive year of failure. However, what constitutes proficiency in a subject area (i.e., the specific cutoff levels for benchmark) is arbitrary and differs from state to state. Would you be surprised to learn that, given the sanctions faced by schools and districts for not achieving AYP, the cutoff scores in many states are quite low and decreasing over time? For example, one of us recently worked with test data from a state in which from 35% to 40% correct on most grade-level reading and math CRTs constitutes proficiency. And, to make matters worse, the assessment is a four-item multiple-choice test (see Chapter 12) (i.e., students have a 25% chance of guessing each answer correctly). We hope to never fly with a pilot or be operated on by a surgeon who mastered only 40% of the content on his or her proficiency test!

The advantage of standardized objective tests is their high reliability of measurement. On the other hand, a growing number of educators have questioned the validity of the scores for reflecting students' ability to apply the knowledge and skills they have learned (Baker, 2007). These concerns have given rise to national efforts to develop standards of achievement (as alternatives to or to supplement conventional NRTs or CRTs) that focus on students' demonstrating higher-level learning (e.g., by writing essays, solving problems, participating in debates, completing and presenting a project) rather than simply recalling knowledge. You may remember from Chapter 5 that a traditional behavioral-type instructional objective might read something like, "Given a familiar topic and 30 minutes' time, the student will write a 500-word essay on that topic containing no grammatical errors and fewer than five errors of spelling or punctuation." A language arts content standard in the same area, however, might read, "The student will write a persuasive essay that shows a clear sense of purpose and audience and that uses language forms accurately, clearly, and appropriately." Associated benchmarks for that standard would then specify what students should know and be able to do at developmentally appropriate levels (e.g., for a ninth-grader: "introduces and clearly states a position," "supports main points by relevant and accurate information," and "clearly conveys the main points of the opposing argument").

The standards approach shares some similarities with Gronlund's (1985, 1995) cognitive objectives (see Chapter 5) in that this approach operationally defines a generally stated outcome (i.e., the standard) in terms of more specific competencies (i.e., the benchmark). The main difference is that objectives tend to be more narrow and unit specific, whereas standards delineate an entire curriculum, quite possibly for all subjects and all grades in the school system. Associated with content standards are performance standards, which specify the criteria for assessing student achievement at different skill levels (e.g., for exiting primary grades, intermediate grades, middle school, or high school). These assessments are criterion referenced in nature and employ tasks requiring relatively realistic or "authentic" demonstrations of skill and knowledge. An example would be requiring students to test a hypothesis in science by performing a simple experiment.

This approach contrasts with reading about an experiment and answering multiple-choice questions about it, as on a norm-referenced achievement test. What is the advantage of the performance assessment? Clearly, it is increasing external validity (i.e., realism) and orienting instruction toward meaningful learning. The disadvantage, however, is the difficulty of scoring such performances reliably for both everyday feedback and formal grading, such as by report cards. (We return to the reliability issue in Chapter 12.) What does the standards movement mean for instructional designers? Designers working with schools using standards-based curricula will need to link instructional material directly to those standards and benchmarks (as they would with conventional objectives). Although lower-level learning (e.g., memorizing facts and dates) will still be required, greater emphasis than in the past will be placed on teaching such knowledge as a natural part of performing more complex, real-world tasks (e.g., learning history facts by completing a project on the Civil War or learning punctuation through reading and writing). Assessments will also need to be integrated with learning activities; students will demonstrate what they know and can do through portfolios, exhibitions, and projects (see Chapter 12 for more discussion).

For classroom teachers, instructional design skills (formal or otherwise) will likewise become increasingly valuable as they attempt to address standards by creating meaningful performance-based tasks to replace traditional seatwork and drill exercises.

## STUDENT SELF-EVALUATION

Successful learning is enhanced when individuals receive feedback on how well they are learning as instruction takes place. This can be accomplished by allowing learners to grade their own short tests at the end of a unit or set of learning activities. The results indicate to them whether the material has been learned satisfactorily or whether further study is needed. By completing such self-check tests, learners can individually evaluate progress, recognize difficulties or confusion in understanding, and review material prior to taking the instructor's test covering the same objectives. This procedure can better ensure learner preparation for and success with the unit posttest.

### Pretesting

Up to this point, we have discussed different approaches to evaluation, assessment, and measurement instrument selection. Our final focus will be on the question of when and how to use pretests as part of the evaluation design. Suppose you want to begin a strenuous swimming, cycling, or running program. What should you do before starting? Having a physical examination seems necessary to ensure that your body is prepared for rigorous exercise. A similar practice is important in the instructional process. Specifically, pretesting is used to assess learners' entry skills for a course or a particular unit of study. Pretesting serves two important roles in the instructional design process. One role has two functions: (1) to assess the learner's preparation to study the course or topic, and (2) to determine which competencies for the course or topic the learner may have already mastered. The second major role is to measure the degree of improvement after instruction is completed.

### Testing for Prerequisites

A prerequisite test determines whether students are prepared for starting a course or studying a topic. For example,

- Can junior high school students perform basic arithmetic at a level that qualifies them to start learning algebra?

- Is an apprentice entering a furniture-manufacturing training program competent in using such machines as a table saw, a belt sander, and a router?

Refer to the list of subject content for the topic or the analysis of the task to be taught (see Chapter 4) as well as your learner analysis (see Chapter 3). Enumerate the required competencies that a learner should have before starting this phase of the program. From the list, develop appropriate methods, such as those in the following list, to gather information about necessary prerequisite knowledge and abilities:

- Paper-and-pencil tests (sometimes standardized tests in fundamental areas such as reading, writing, mathematics, chemistry, or physics)
- Observations of performance and rating of competencies exhibited by learner
- A questionnaire to determine learner background, training, and experiences
- Review of learner's previous or related work
- Talks with supervisors or other persons with whom the learner has worked

The results of this prerequisite testing will indicate which learners are fully prepared to start studying the topic, which need some remedial work, and which are not ready and should therefore start at a lower level. Do not assume that grades in previous or related courses necessarily indicate the degree of readiness for a learner to be successful in a program. The objectives of courses taken elsewhere may be quite different from what you interpret them to be by reading the titles or descriptions of those courses. Do your own prerequisite evaluation of each learner's preparation. To determine learners' previous experience with a topic, you might use a pre-topic questionnaire or even an informal, oral questioning of the class (e.g., "How many of you have ever used an ohmmeter?") instead of a formal test. Have learners reply with a show of hands. For mature learners, a questionnaire, in which each learner indicates his or her level of skill or knowledge for all items to be studied, will go further than the few questions of a pretest.

## Testing for Improvement in Performance

A second reason for pretesting is to determine the degree to which learners improve in critical competencies as a result of the instruction. Because the accomplishment of instructional objectives is measured by the evaluation test for each objective, some authorities recommend using the actual evaluation test (or a modified form of it) for both pretesting and final evaluation (i.e., the posttest). In this case, the amount of learning is determined from the gain in score from the pretest to the posttest. An illustration of this is shown in Figure 11-3. Note that large gains are indicated for objectives 1, 5, and 7, whereas only small improvements occurred for objectives 3 and 8. If the final examination is too detailed for use as a pretest, select only the most important or representative test items. Do not test only the easiest objectives (often knowledge-level) or the most difficult (i.e., higher cognitive levels). Maintain a fair balance.

**FIGURE 11-3**
Using pretests and posttests to determine improvements in performance

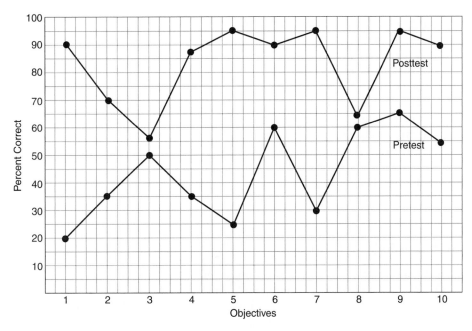

## Benefits of Pretesting

For the more traditional group instruction situation, in which learners move together through all teacher-controlled activities, pretesting may have limited value for adapting instruction to individuals. The instructor may discover a range of preparation within the group. Not much can be done to provide for the differences among learners other than to recommend some remedial work while the instruction moves ahead as planned. If some learners show on the pretest that they already are competent with some of the content to be treated in the class, they most often still have to sit through the regular instruction. Only infrequently does a concerned instructor adjust assignments to accommodate these learners. In recent years, however, the need for adaptive instruction in K-12 districts has become increasingly pressing as schools and districts strive to achieve the adequate yearly progress required by the No Child Left Behind Act of 2001 (2002). The effective delivery of individualized or small-group instruction, particularly in expanded learning (i.e., after-school) contexts (Stonehill, Little, Ross, Neergaard, Harrison, et al., 2009), depends strongly on assessing the learner's prior knowledge and skills by administering pretests. Accordingly, if you plan to individualize or provide for self-paced learning, then pretesting will be important for the following reasons:

- It determines learners' readiness for the program by alerting each of them to what they do and do not know about the topic.

- It indicates to both learners and the instructor the point at which to begin the program or what remedial (or lower-level) course work to complete before starting the program.
- It may motivate learners to study the topic by arousing their curiosity and interest as they read pretest questions or otherwise experience what they will be learning (a preinstructional strategy; see Chapter 8).
- It informs learners of what will be treated during study of the topic so that they realize what will be required of them (see Chapter 8).
- It indicates the testing methods the instructor will use in the final examination, because there is a close relationship between pretest and posttest.
- It provides baseline data for determining learner growth in learning by comparing scores on pretest and posttest.
- It provides formative evaluation information that will help the instructor modify parts of the course or program (adding or eliminating objectives and/or activities) so that the program can start at the point of learner readiness.

## Whether or Not to Pretest

Given the advantages of pretesting, you may believe that pretests are always desirable. This is not the case. Disadvantages of pretests are that they take time away from instruction, involve extra work in creating the tests, may cue the learner to concentrate on certain things while neglecting others, and may produce negative feelings. The last point seems the most critical. When learners have little background in the topics to be taught and therefore are likely to perform at a very low level (e.g., by making random guesses) on the pretest, there is little point in administering a pretest. Without useful performance information, anxiety or frustration can easily result when the pretest is too difficult. In light of these concerns, when you do pretest, be sure that learners have sufficient readiness and understand the purpose. Explain clearly why the pretest is being given and that it in no way counts toward grades.

### S U M M A R Y

1. Evaluation is used to provide information about the success of a course or unit of instruction.
2. One general category of evaluation is the formative evaluation, which focuses on instructional processes and outcomes during development, tryout, and the progression of the course.
3. Summative evaluation assesses the degree to which instructional objectives have been achieved at the end of the course.
4. Confirmative evaluation assesses the degree to which instructional objectives are being achieved over an extended period of time after the course.
5. Whatever evaluation approach is used, there must be a direct relationship between instructional objectives and assessment measures. Multiple data sources are particularly valuable in providing a more accurate and comprehensive picture of a particular outcome than any single measure could provide.

6. For assessing knowledge, both objective tests (e.g., completion, multiple-choice, true/false, and matching) and constructed-response tests (e.g., short essay, long essay, and problem solving) may be used.

7. For assessing skills and behavior, recommended measures are direct testing of performance, analysis of naturally occurring events, ratings and checklists of behavior, and performance testing.

8. Attitudes are commonly assessed by observing instruction, observing behavior, using rating scales, surveying, and interviewing.

9. A test has a high degree of validity if it measures the behavior or trait specified by the instructional objectives. Test scores have a high degree of reliability if they remain consistent from one testing to the next. To be valid, a test must be reliable.

10. Relative standards of evaluating achievement are reflected in norm-referenced (NRT) grading, in which people are compared with one another, often for selection purposes.

11. Absolute standards are reflected in criterion-referenced (CRT) grading, in which performance is judged relative to established criteria regardless of how other learners score.

12. An alternative form of criterion-referenced testing in K–12 schools is standards-based assessment. These tests ask students to demonstrate the application of knowledge and skills by performing authentic, real-world tasks.

13. Student self-testing allows learners to check their own learning level as they progress through a program.

14. Pretesting is used to determine how well prepared a learner is to start an instructional program or a specific unit. Pretests are also useful in providing a baseline performance from which to judge the degree of improvement resulting from the instruction.

## THE ID PROCESS

Evaluation is an essential component of instructional design. Contrary to the beliefs of some inexperienced designers, evaluation is not something that occurs only at the "back end" of a project, after the unit of instruction has been completed. Nor is it conducted only one time. Rather, evaluation is a continuous process that should occur early in a design process and then be repeated at different phases. Determine your evaluation approach early in the process of planning the overall instructional design (see Chapter 1). You will want to include formative evaluation as the instruction is developed, summative evaluation after it is completed, and perhaps confirmative evaluation as it is being implemented over time. Whether you have the opportunity to conduct confirmative evaluations may depend on your involvement with the course or instructional unit after it has been delivered to your clients. In negotiating with clients about instructional design projects, it is important to educate them about the need for continuous evaluation for supporting quality development of the instruction and quality control over its implementation.

Sufficient funds must be allocated to support the immediate and long-term evaluation functions. Early in the planning process, you need to decide who will conduct the evaluation. Depending on budget and the complexity of the design project, you or members of the design team may be able (or need) to conduct the evaluation, or outside experts may be judged more suitable. External evaluators may add cost to the project, but they bring expertise in instrument design and validation, data analysis, and reporting. They also add credibility and objectivity because they are not personally involved in the project's success. Internal evaluators (design team members), however, are experts in the project and can directly benefit by collecting evaluation data firsthand. In our work, we have often used a combination of internal and external people to collaborate on the evaluations, especially for formative purposes.

Part of the evaluation planning should also include deciding how often evaluations need to be conducted and at what critical times. Several formative evaluations will probably be needed. Although summative evaluation is formally conceived as a one-time process—to make a judgment about a project's success—in reality, the distinctions among formative, summative, and confirmative evaluations often become blurred. That is, if you conduct a summative evaluation and the instruction is judged "unsuccessful," do you just scrap it? Suppose it could be easily fixed following simple suggestions from some trainees whom you interviewed in your "summative" evaluation? If the revisions are then made, does that make the previous evaluation summative or formative?

Based on the preceding discussion, here are some key points to consider for including evaluations in the ID process:

- Educate stakeholders about the need to support and use continuous, long-term evaluation.
- Devise your evaluation plan early in the planning process.
- Begin evaluations early in the design process.
- Determine where internal evaluators (i.e., design team members) versus external evaluators might be used, given the type of evaluation, budget, and complexity of the project.
- Consider designing all evaluations (summative, too) so that they yield data for improving the instruction, not only for judging it.

## APPLICATIONS

A design group has developed a training course for basketball referees who work youth games for the park commission in a large city. The course meets five nights for three hours and includes, as main components, a manual on basketball rules, a software program on refereeing hand signals, classroom lectures on rules and techniques, and simulated practice sessions. The main objectives of the course address the preparation of trainees in three areas: (1) the rules, (2) working games, and (3) interactions with players, coaches, and spectators. You have been hired to evaluate the completed program. What basic approach and data-gathering methods would you use in a summative evaluation?

A N S W E R S

A summative evaluation is intended to examine instruction after its completion. The primary focus is whether instructional objectives are being achieved. Thus, outcomes resulting from the course rather than learners' reactions to the course are the main concern. Given the objectives of the refereeing training course, three outcomes need to be assessed. We suggest the following possible strategies, although you may have proposed reasonable alternatives. You be the judge (i.e., a self-evaluator). One objective deals with knowledge of rules. This outcome might be addressed by administering, at the end of the course, a comprehensive written posttest that includes both simple knowledge items (e.g., "How many fouls is each player allowed?") and higher-order thinking items (e.g., "A player with the ball calls time-out while in the air before landing out of bounds. What is the call?"). Test items should be carefully developed and validated. A second objective deals with performance in working games. For this objective, a random sample of 25 trainees who successfully completed the course could be evaluated by experts while refereeing a game. The experts would be given checklists of specific behaviors to observe (e.g., use of correct hand signals, calling of defensive fouls and offensive fouls, etc.) as well as rubrics (see Chapter 12) for making a global categorizations of overall performance ("highly skilled," "skilled," "acceptable," "weak," etc.). A third objective deals with the trainees' interactions with coaches, players, and spectators. This objective can also be evaluated as part of the observation of the trainees' working game. Also, 10 randomly selected trainees might be interviewed and asked to react to scenarios in which they are refereeing and someone from one of the three target groups reacts to them in a certain way (e.g., a parent continually yells during the game that the referee is blind and unfit to be refereeing).

As a summative evaluator, you also have to interpret the data to support a conclusion about each objective. It is likely that on each measure some trainees will perform at a high level whereas some will perform poorly. Making an overall judgment requires synthesizing the multiple data sources and comparing this picture to what is viewed as an acceptable standard in each outcome area (i.e., what is an "acceptable" knowledge score or performance score?).

I N S T R U C T I O N A L   D E S I G N :   D E C I S I O N S
A N D   C H O I C E S

As you complete the task analysis and determine objectives, you ask yourself, "How can I be sure that I haven't missed something? How can I be sure that I'm on target with the instruction?" Uncovering "blind spots"—missing content, content accuracy errors, extraneous content, sequence problems, or examples that the learner cannot relate to—is important—that is, if you want to avoid rework, save time, and contain costs. You realize that evaluation should be "ongoing" throughout the project.

You begin to devise an evaluation plan that will include (1) ongoing review (i.e., formative evaluation) as design of the instruction progresses, (2) formative evaluation of the prototype instructional materials, and (3) design of a posttest for the instructional program.

Formative evaluation during the design of the instruction will include several "checkpoints" to ensure quality and catch errors early. For the first checkpoint, to ensure that the instruction is focused on the "right" learning problem, you will ask the client to review the analysis phase of the project. The client will review the needs assessment, learner analysis, and objectives. To ensure that no essential content has been omitted and to eliminate any extraneous content, you plan to ask the subject-matter expert to review the task analysis and objectives. [An evaluation of the needs assessment phase of the project might have revealed that using existing "off-the-shelf" materials had not been considered. Purchasing ready-made materials (and modifying them) might have eliminated the need to design custom materials and reduce costs to the organization.]

For the second checkpoint, you will ask the subject-matter expert to review a draft of the instructional materials to verify technical accuracy. You will also ask the client and other key stakeholders (e.g., the security director) to review the design phase of the project including the prototype materials and test items, primarily to obtain their support and to reinforce buy-in. [On a large-scale project, one or more external evaluators might be asked to review the task analysis and instructional content. Evaluation activities also promote open communication throughout the project and help create stakeholder buy-in.]

You also begin devising a plan to formatively evaluate the prototype (more on this in Chapter 13). In addition, you anticipate that documenting each learner's successful completion of the program will be necessary to ensure compliance with federal or state regulations (e.g., OSHA standards). Determining what the minimum standards for successful completion will be is a critical task. You make a note to contact the human resources department and the legal department to check on compliance requirements. Lastly, you begin to think about how you will demonstrate to senior management the value of investing in the instructional program.

Here's a chart representing the project's overall evaluation plan:

| Phase/Time (Checkpoint) | Questions to Consider | Individuals Involved |
|---|---|---|
| After initial client meeting and completion of initial needs assessment | Is the project worth doing? <br> Is the project a priority for organization? <br> Do any off-the-shelf materials already exist? | Project manager <br> Immediate supervisor <br> Client |
| Completion of task analysis and objectives | Is the instructional program on target? | Project manager <br> Subject-matter expert <br> Client <br> External reviewer |

*(continued)*

| Phase/Time (Checkpoint) | Questions to Consider | Individuals Involved |
|---|---|---|
| Completion of prototype instructional materials (draft of Website) and posttest | Is the instructional content accurate? | Subject-matter expert<br>Client |
| | Are the test items reliable and valid? | Designer or evaluator |
| Formative evaluation | Are the instructional strategies effective? | Test subjects<br>Designer or evaluator |
| | Does the instruction motivate the learner?<br>Is the instruction effective? | Subject-matter expert |
| Confirmative evaluation | Do advances in technology require modifying the instruction? | Instructor<br>Training department project owner |

## REFERENCES

Baker, E. (2007). The end(s) of testing. *Educational Researcher, 36*(6), 309–317.

Gronlund, N. E. (1985). *Stating behavioral objectives for classroom instruction*. New York: Macmillan.

Gronlund, N. E. (1995). *How to write and use instructional objectives* (5th ed.). Upper Saddle River, NJ: Prentice Hall.

Hellebrandt, J., & Russell, J. D. (1993). Confirmative evaluation of instructional materials and learners. *Performance and Instruction, 32*, 22–27.

Kim, J. S., & Sunderman, G. L. (2005). Measuring academic proficiency under the No Child Left Behind Act: Implications for educational equity. *Educational Researcher, 34*(8), 3–13.

Linn, R. L. (2003). Accountability responsibility and reasonable expectancies. *Educational Researcher, 32*(7), 3–13.

Misanchuk, E. R. (1978). Beyond the formative-summative distinction. *Journal of Instructional Development, 2*, 15–19.

Moseley, J. L., & Solomon, D. L. (1997). Confirmative evaluation: A new paradigm for continuous improvement. *Performance Improvement, 36*, 12–15.

No Child Left Behind Act of 2001, Pub. L. No. 107-110, 115 Stat. 1425 (2002, January 8).

Shepard, L. A. (2000). The role of assessment in a learning culture. *Educational Researcher, 29*(7), 4–14.

Stonehill, R. M., Little, P. M., Ross, S. M., Neergaard, L., Harrison, L., Ford, J., Deich, S., Morgan, E., & Donner, J. (2009). *Enhancing school reform through expanded learning*. Naperville, IL: Learning Point Associates.

# 12

# Developing Evaluation Instruments

## GETTING STARTED

You have just finished designing a training unit for computer repair technicians working for a large aviation company. At this point, you want to add an evaluation component both to assess trainee skills and to evaluate the effectiveness of the instruction. Because a main emphasis of the unit is learning the specific components and terminology for the computer systems employed, you first create an objective test featuring 125 multiple-choice questions and 25 short-answer questions (e.g., "List the main hardware components of the employee workstations."). However, correctly applying rules and using proper protocol are also critical outcomes. For this area, you simulate five scenarios (e.g., "computer freezes," "slow response time," "no access to Internet," "cannot save to disk," and "doesn't allow password access") to which trainees will be asked to react via open-ended responses (e.g., "What would you do here?"). Next, you develop a ratings instrument, using rubrics defining four categories of skill level, to evaluate each trainee during an actual problem situation. Finally, you create a brief open-ended survey to collect feedback from the trainees regarding the effectiveness of the training unit. Would portfolios possibly be useful here as well? What is your reaction to the overall evaluation strategy? Is it likely to provide useful data? Why or why not?

## QUESTIONS TO CONSIDER

"How do instructional objectives dictate the selection of evaluation methods?"

"What type of test should I use to measure comprehension rather than simple memorization?"

"How can I assess what students like and don't like about the instruction?"

"If it is not practical to assess skills in real-life situations, are there any alternative ways of assessing performance?"

"How should portfolios be evaluated?"

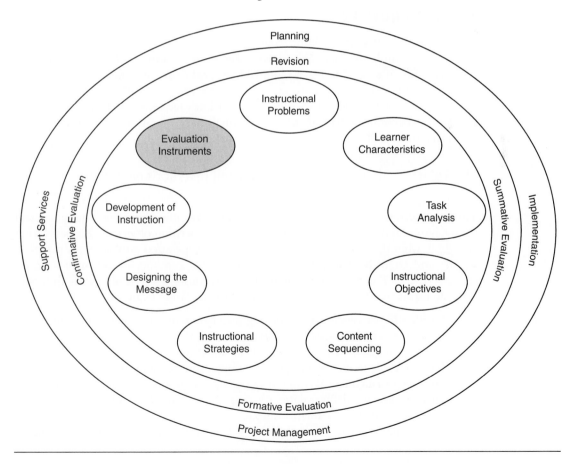

In Chapter 11 we discuss the purposes of evaluation in training and education and major principles relating to designing and conducting evaluations. As the opening questions suggest, we now turn to the more specific topic of constructing instruments to address each evaluation interest. Begin the process by asking questions such as these:

- What measures are likely to provide the most valid assessment of learning outcomes?
- Is using a particular measure complicated or precluded by practical constraints (e.g., cost, time, accepted practices)?
- What are appropriate procedures for constructing the selected measures and analyzing results?

Reexamine the first question concerning the types of measures needed. To answer it, classify the learning outcomes according to whether they deal primarily with knowledge, skills and behavior, or attitudes. We work with this scheme, as we do in Chapter 11, to identify and discuss alternative measures relating to each category.

## TESTING KNOWLEDGE

The acquisition of relevant knowledge is central to most instructional programs. Pilots, for example, need to know principles of aeronautics before attempting to fly planes, doctors need to learn medical facts and concepts, and teachers require procedures for classroom management and grading (as well as expertise in the subjects they teach). Given the importance of knowledge in the learning process, assessing it becomes a critical part of instructional evaluations. This area mainly concerns the cognitive domain of instructional objectives.

### The Relationship between Evaluation and Instructional Objectives

A direct relationship between instructional objectives and test items must exist. Thus, it is customary to derive test items directly from the objectives. You may recall from Chapter 5 that two recognized approaches to writing objectives are behavioral (in which what the learner must do to master the specified knowledge is precisely stated) and cognitive (in which general outcomes and specific behavior samples are described). The verb component of both of these types of objectives indicates possible forms that test items should take. Here are some examples:

**To identify or recognize:** Choosing an answer in an objective-type test item (see types in following discussion)

**To list or label:** Writing a word or brief statement

**To state or describe:** Writing or speaking a short or lengthy answer

**To solve or calculate:** Writing or choosing a solution or numerical answer

**To compare or differentiate:** Writing about a relationship or choosing an answer that shows a relationship

**To operate or construct:** Rating the quality of performance or product against criteria

**To formulate or organize:** Writing a plan or choosing an order of items relative to a plan

**To predict or judge:** Writing a description of what is expected to happen or choosing from alternative decisions

Although some variation in interpreting the verb's meaning is inevitable, these examples illustrate the close relationship that is necessary between an instructional objective and a test item. A student should anticipate being tested on the same type of learning or behavior indicated by the objective, and the verb in an objective alerts the student to the content that is particularly important to study. Most cognitive-domain objectives are evaluated by various types of paper-and-pencil tests grouped into two categories: objective and constructed response. Some instructional objectives might preferably be measured by one type of test rather than another. You should therefore become familiar with the considerations that can influence your choice. Let's look at the features of each of the commonly used test types. (For further help with formulating properly stated test questions, see the references at the end of this chapter.)

## Objective Tests

Individuals scoring objective test items in the cognitive domain can easily agree on the correct answer; hence, the term *objective test* is used. This category includes questions for which the student must recognize and select an answer from two or more alternatives or respond to prepared statements. Typically, no writing, other than marking an answer, is required. Objective tests are of three major types: multiple choice, true/false, and matching.

**Multiple Choice.**   Multiple choice is the most useful and versatile type of objective testing. It consists of a stem, which is a question or an incomplete statement, plus the alternatives, which consist of a correct answer and several incorrect answers, called distractors. Typically, it is best to use from three to five alternatives. More than five may stretch the test developer's creativity for devising reasonable options while increasing the reading demands on the student. Multiple-choice items can be written at all levels of Bloom's taxonomy. Thus, compared with true/false and matching items, they can more easily test higher-order learning, including conceptual reasoning. You will probably find them to be somewhat limited, however, especially compared with essay questions, for testing synthesis and evaluation, the two highest levels in the taxonomy. Here are examples of multiple-choice questions on the first four levels of the Bloom taxonomy:

1. Knowledge
   How does cardiovascular death rank as a killer in the United States?
   a. First
   b. Second
   c. Fifth
   d. Tenth

2. Comprehension
   When the temperature of a moving air mass is lower than that of the surface over which it is passing, heat transfer takes place vertically. This principle results in which designation for the air mass?
   a. k
   b. w
   c. A
   d. P
3. Application
   An operator can be expected to drill six holes a minute with a drill press. What is the amount of time required to drill 750 holes?
   a. 3 hours, 14 minutes
   b. 2 hours, 30 minutes
   c. 2 hours, 5 minutes
   d. 1 hour, 46 minutes
4. Analysis
   Examine the sample photographic print. What should you do to correct the condition shown?
   a. Use a different grade of paper.
   b. Expose the paper for a longer time.
   c. Develop the paper for a longer time.
   d. Use dodging to lighten shadows.

Multiple-choice tests have two advantages: (1) that of measuring a variety of learning levels and (2) that of being easy to grade. They have the disadvantages, however, of testing *recognition* (i.e., choosing an answer) rather than *recall* (i.e., constructing an answer), allowing for guessing, and being fairly difficult to construct. Some novice developers think that the best multiple-choice item is one that is "tricky" or complex. Actually, the key to writing valid items is to make them as clear and straightforward as possible. The purpose is to test learning, not reading skill, mind reading, or puzzle solving. Here are some guidelines for writing multiple-choice items, with examples of both poor and good questions (an asterisk denotes the correct answer):

1. Make the content meaningful relative to the instructional objectives. Do not test trivial or unimportant facts.
   **Poor:** Skinner developed programmed instruction in _____
   a. 1953.
   *b. 1954.
   c. 1955.
   d. 1956.
   **Better:** Skinner developed programmed instruction in the _____
   a. 1930s.
   b. 1940s.
   *c. 1950s.
   d. 1970s.

Note that even though the "better" version would be much preferred, the test developer should question the importance of students knowing particular isolated facts, names, and dates in the first place. Some are *essential* (imagine your doctor saying, "Your problem is with that pinkish organ next to your 'wacha-ma-call-it'"), but other factual information may matter little for furthering specific course or life learning. A growing trend in standardized testing, such as in the Scholastic Achievement Test (SAT) and entrance or certification exams for specific professions (e.g., medicine, law, nursing, accounting) is emphasizing problem solving and higher-order learning (e.g., application, synthesis, evaluation) in objective testing. On a medical exam, for example, a "set" of four or five items may start with a scenario in which a patient comes to a doctor's office with a medical complaint and various symptoms. The various items then present different application or synthesis questions about what might be done in diagnosing the problem or treating the patient. Each item, though, should be independent of all other items in the set. That is, how the student answers Item 1 should have no direct influence on how she should logically answer any of the remaining items. Otherwise, the negative impact of an early error would be unfairly multiplied across the item set.

2. Reduce the length of the alternatives by moving as many words as possible to the stem. The rationale is that additional words in the alternatives have to be read four or five times, in the stem only once.

   **Poor:** The mean is _____
   *a. a measure of the average.
   b. a measure of the midpoint.
   c. a measure of the most popular score.
   d. a measure of the dispersion of scores.

   **Better:** The mean is a measure of the _____
   *a. average.
   b. midpoint.
   c. most popular score.
   d. dispersion of scores.

3. Construct the stem so that it conveys a complete thought.

   **Poor:** Objectives are _____
   *a. used for planning instruction.
   b. written in behavioral form only.
   c. the last step in the instructional design process.
   d. used in the cognitive but not the affective domain.

   **Better:** The main function of instructional objectives is _____
   *a. planning instruction.
   b. comparing teachers.
   c. selecting students with exceptional abilities.
   d. assigning students to academic programs.

4. Do not make the correct answer stand out as a result of its phrasing or length.

**Poor:** A narrow strip of land bordered on both sides by water is called an _____

*a. isthmus.

b. peninsula.

c. bayou.

d. continent.

(Note: Do you see why *a* would be the best guess, given the phrasing of the question?)

**Better:** A narrow strip of land bordered on both sides by water is called a(n) _____ (The same choices as in the preceding question would then follow.)

**Poor:** In Bloom's cognitive taxonomy, analysis involves _____

a. memorizing.

b. valuing.

c. understanding.

*d. breaking down knowledge into parts and showing the relationships between the parts.

**Better:** In Bloom's taxonomy, analysis involves _____

a. memorizing information verbatim.

b. learning to value something.

c. understanding the meaning of material.

*d. breaking a whole into parts.

5. Avoid overusing always and never in the distractors. Students who are good test takers quickly learn to avoid those choices.

6. Avoid overusing "all of the above" and "none of the above." When "all of the above" is used, students can eliminate it simply by knowing that one answer is false. Or they will know to select it if any two answers are true. When "none of the above" is the correct answer, the student moves on from the question having recognized what is not true but still may not know the correct answer. For example,

The capital of Tennessee is _____

a. Birmingham.

b. Atlanta.

c. Albany.

*d. None of the above

Some designers routinely add "all of the above" or "none of the above" when they run out of ideas for good distractors. A better strategy might be to include fewer choices rather than to use these two options indiscriminately.

7. Questions phrased in a positive direction are generally preferred over those phrased negatively. Negative stem: Which of the following is false? Positive stem: Which of the following is true? Negative stems may be good choices in some instances, but use them selectively. One disadvantage of such items is that the correct answer is a noninstance rather than the actual response to be learned (see number 6). Also, students may have more difficulty when interpreting negative phrasing. Underline, capitalize, or italicize the *not* to make sure the student notices it.

8. Randomly select the position of the correct answer. This guideline is probably the easiest to follow, but many instructors seem to rely instead on making these selections subjectively. The problem is that they may have unintentional biases in favor of certain response positions. Consequently, students may learn, for example, that alternative *a* is a better guess than alternative *d* in Mr. Tessmer's class.

**True/False Items.**   True/false test questions are presented as statements that the learner judges to be correct or incorrect. Only content material that lends itself to either/or answers should be written in this format. Consequently, the range of content that can be tested is fairly narrow, often limited to factual information. True/false tests have the advantage of being fairly easy to write and very easy to grade. Their disadvantages are that they test recognition rather than recall, allow for a high probability (i.e., 50%) of guessing the correct answer, and limit assessments to lower levels of learning (e.g., knowledge and comprehension). Some guidelines for true/false testing are as follows:

1. Be certain that the statement is entirely true or entirely false.
   **Poor:** A good instructional objective will identify a performance standard. (True/False) (Note: The correct answer here is technically *false*. However, the statement is ambiguous. Although a performance standard is a feature of some "good" objectives, it is not necessary to make an objective good.)
   **Better:** A performance standard of an objective should be stated in measurable terms. (True/False) (Note: The answer here is clearly *true*.)
2. Convey only one thought or idea in a true/false statement.
   **Poor:** Bloom's cognitive taxonomy of objectives includes six levels of objectives, the lowest being knowledge. (True/False)
   **Better:** Bloom's cognitive taxonomy includes six levels of objectives. (True/False)
   Knowledge is the lowest-level objective in Bloom's cognitive taxonomy. (True/False)
3. Unless there are special circumstances, use true/false questions sparingly.

The 50% probability of guessing correctly is a major disadvantage of this type of item. This factor, along with the limited levels of learning that can be assessed, make true/false, in general, less desirable than other testing forms. Strategies for reducing these weaknesses are (1) requiring learners to write a short explanation of why false answers are incorrect and (2) incorporating third or fourth choices such as "opinion" (as opposed to fact), "sometimes, but not always true," "cannot be resolved," and the like (see McBeath, 1992, for additional discussion and examples). Note that in the first case we are converting the standard true/false question into a type of short-answer item; in the second case, it is being converted to a three- or four-alternative multiple-choice item. We might therefore consider whether we would have been better off using an alternative to the true/false format in the first place.

**Matching Items.**   Matching items is a specific form of multiple-choice testing. It requires the learner to identify the relationship between a list of entries in one column and a list of responses in a second column. A matching test is highly appropriate when each listing forms a category of related items (e.g., state capitals, chemistry elements, levels of Bloom's taxonomy). It is most suitable for testing ability to discriminate between the following:

- Definitions and terms
- Events and dates
- Achievements and people
- Descriptions or applications and principles
- Functions and parts

The main advantage of a matching test is that a large amount of material can be condensed to fit in less space on a page than would be required for multiple-choice testing of the same content. By your careful selection of terms, students have substantially fewer chances for guessing correct associations than on multiple-choice and true/false tests. A disadvantage of matching tests is that they assess recognition rather than recall and test lower levels of learning (i.e., of knowledge).

Here are examples of matching tests:

A. In column I are descriptions of geographic characteristics of wind belts. For each statement, find the appropriate wind belt in column II. Answers may be used more than once.

*Column I*

1. Region of high pressure, calm, and light, baffling winds
2. The belt of calm air nearest the equator
3. A wind belt in the Northern Hemisphere
4. The belt in which most of the United States is found

*Column II*

a. Doldrums
b. Horse latitudes
c. Polar easterlies
d. Prevailing easterlies
e. Prevailing westerlies

B. Select a lettering device in column II to carry out the task in column I. Answers may be used only once.

*Column I*

1. Making a thermal transparency quickly
2. Preparing a transparency directly on clear acetate
3. Quick lettering for a paste-up sheet
4. Producing colored lettering for a poster
5. Preparing titles, without equipment, to be photographed as slides

*Column II*

a. Soft-lead pencil
b. Broad-tipped felt pen
c. Fine-tipped felt pen
d. Mechanical pen
e. Dry pen
f. Photocopying
g. Word-processing software

Following are some guidelines for constructing matching tests:

1. Limit the number of items to a maximum of six or seven. It becomes very confusing for learners to try to match a greater amount.
2. Limit the length of the items to a word, phrase, or brief sentence. In general, make the items as short as possible.
3. Provide one or two extra items (i.e., distractors) in the second column. Their inclusion reduces the probability of correct guessing. This also eliminates the situation that may occur in equal-sized lists, in which, if one match is incorrect, a second match must also be incorrect. Note from Example A that this "double-jeopardy" limitation can also be removed by allowing answers to be used more than one time.

## Constructed-Response Tests

The major limitation of objective-type tests is that learners are not required to plan answers and express them in their own words. These shortcomings are overcome by using constructed-response tests. The requirements of such tests may range from a one-word response to an essay of several pages. An important advantage of constructed-response tests is that high-level cognitive objectives can be more appropriately evaluated. The main disadvantage, as will be seen, is obtaining reliable scores.

**Short-Answer Items.**   Short-answer items require a learner to supply a single word, a few words, or a brief sentence in response to an incomplete statement or a question. The terms *fill-in-the-blank* and *completion* are also used in referring to this type of constructed-response question. As a category of test, these items fall between objective types and essay questions. Because the expected answers are specific, scoring can be fairly objective. Another advantage, and a similarity of short-answer to multiple-choice tests, is that they can test a large amount of content within a given time period. A third advantage is that these items test recall rather than simply recognition. On the other hand, short-answer items are limited to testing lower-level cognitive objectives, such as the recall of facts (i.e., knowledge level), comprehension, or the application of specific information. Also, scoring may not be as straightforward and objective as anticipated. Here are examples of short-answer test questions:

1. The type of evaluation designed to assess a program as it develops or progresses is called _____ evaluation.
2. Guessing is considered the greatest problem for which type of objective item?
3. List the four types of reliability defined in your text.
4. Define criterion-referenced testing.

The most important guideline for writing short-answer items is to word them so that only one answer is correct. Otherwise, scoring will become more subjective, and when grades are at issue, arguments with students will become more frequent.

**Poor:** The first president of the United States was _____ (two words)
(Note: The desired answer is George Washington, but students may write "from Virginia," "a general," "very smart," and other creative expressions.)
**Better:** Give the first and last name of the first president of the United States:
_____

**Essay Questions.**  Essay questions are most useful for testing higher levels of cognitive learning. In particular, instructional objectives emphasizing analysis, synthesis, and evaluation can be measured effectively when learners are required to organize and express their thoughts in writing. A "short" essay, which may be restricted to a few paragraphs or a single page, typically requires a highly focused response. A "long" essay allows the learner more opportunity to express and defend a point of view. The trade-off, of course, is that, the more expansion or divergence that is allowed, the more difficult the grading. (We return to the grading issue shortly in discussing advantages and limitations of essay tests.) Among the advantages of essay questions are these:

- They are relatively easy to construct, taking less time than does the design of a comparable objective-type test.
- They require learners to express themselves in writing, a language skill that is highly important for students at all levels to develop.
- They are superior to objective tests for assessing higher-order learning, such as application, analysis, synthesis, and evaluation.
- They provide instructors with considerable information about learners' understanding of the content taught.

Disadvantages of essay tests include these:

- Because students will have time to write only a few essays, a limited number of concepts or principles relating to a topic can be tested.
- If the questions asked are not focused, students may stray off the topic or misinterpret the type of response desired. Scoring becomes more difficult and unreliable as a result.
- Because of the subjective nature of grading essay tests, an instructor paying attention to "style over substance" may award a learner with good writing skills higher grades than his or her knowledge of the subject warrants. Similarly, a student who is a poor writer will be at a disadvantage.
- Time required for different learners to complete an essay test will vary greatly.
- Much time and care must be taken when grading to be as objective as possible and avoid making personal judgments about individual learners.

Here are examples of essay questions:

1. Prepare a hypothetical route weather forecast from your station to a location 500 miles away. Assume that a winter cold front exists at the beginning of the forecast period halfway between the two locations, with squall lines and

icing conditions below 12,000 feet MSL. Make reference to the general situation, sky conditions and cloud base, visibility, precipitation, freezing level, winds aloft, and other factors you deem important. (20 points)

2. In your judgment, what will be the most difficult change to which human society will have to adapt in the twenty-first century? Support your position with reference to at least three utopian objectives and their significance for the future. (15 minutes maximum; two-page limit; 20 points)

Guidelines for constructing essay tests are as follows:

1. Make the questions as specific and focused as possible.
   **Poor:** Describe the role of instructional objectives in education.
   Discuss Bloom's contribution to the evaluation of instruction.
   **Better:** Describe and differentiate between behavioral (Mager) and cognitive (Gronlund) objectives with regard to their (1) format and (2) relative advantages and disadvantages for specifying instructional intentions.
2. Inform students of the grading criteria and conditions. Will spelling count? How important is organization? Are all parts of the essay worth the same number of points? Can a dictionary be used? Do dates of historic events need to be indicated? Unless you specify the criteria, students may perform poorly simply because they do not know what type of response you expect. Also, keep in mind that certain criteria may be less relevant to evaluation needs; it may be desirable to derive separate scores for various criteria.
3. Write or outline a model answer. Essays are difficult to grade reliably. Incidental qualities such as length, handwriting, vocabulary, and writing style can all influence the overall impression and divert attention from the content. Writing a model answer makes it easier to focus on content, assign points to key concepts included, and grade more objectively and reliably.
4. Do not give students a choice of essays; have all respond to the same questions. All essay questions are not created equal. If one student selects a biology question on, say, cell division, whereas another selects a question on oxidation, they will be taking essentially two different tests. Also, when students are given a choice, they can adapt the test to their strengths in the process.
5. Grade essays "in the blind," that is, without knowing the writers' identities. As noted already, the subjectivity involved in evaluating essays can reduce reliability. When you grade an essay knowing the identity of the writer, you may be swayed by an individual's prior performance and attitude. To reduce this effect, have students write the last four digits of their social security number (or some other code) instead of their names on their answer sheets. True, you may identify some individuals by handwriting or other telltale signs (purple ink, smudges, etc.), but you'll have enough doubt about most papers to make blind scoring worthwhile.
6. When multiple essay questions are required, evaluate a given question for all students before scoring the next essay. It is challenging enough

to obtain reliable scores while concentrating on one question at a time;
jumping around from question to question will complicate the scoring task
immensely.

**Problem-Solving Questions.**    Like essays, problem-solving questions are well suited
to evaluating higher-level cognitive outcomes such as application, analysis, and
synthesis. Another advantage is that such questions are generally easy to construct.
The main disadvantage, as you probably have anticipated, is scoring. In some
instances, the problem will have a single correct answer that can be derived in only
one way. Scoring those answers is easy. The other extreme is a situation in which
there are alternative solution approaches and possible answers. An example would
be statistically describing and interpreting a set of test scores. A top performance
(based on the class mean) in the eye of one analyst may appear mediocre to another
(who focuses on the median or some other property of the results).

An increasingly popular form of problem-solving assessments is associated
with a form of instruction called *problem-based learning*, or PBL. Initiated in the 1960s
for use in medical education, PBL is now employed in a variety of subject areas to
give students exposure to real-life problems and events, often linked to professional
practice (Himelo-Silver, Duncan, & Chinn, 2007; Schmidt, Loyens, van Gog, &
Pass, 2007). In a PBL setting, students usually work in groups to solve a complex
problem, such as diagnosing a medical patient's symptoms or developing a classroom
management strategy to help a teacher control student behavior problems. Because
the answers will be detailed and open ended, evaluation of performance will focus
on higher-level cognitive applications such as analysis, synthesis, and evaluation.

### Expert's Edge

### Three Blind-Grading Principles . . . See How They Run

In the next few paragraphs, I would like to describe three principles that constitute
a "blind-grading" procedure that I employ in one of the classes I teach. For many
years, I have employed these principles when I grade student responses to a series
of essay questions that are part of two take-home open-book exams I administer.
Moreover, I have recently started to use the blind-grading technique to grade
student responses to some open-ended questions I ask them to do for homework.
Indeed, I feel that this method could be effectively employed in grading student
responses to a wide variety of questions or assignments for which there is no one
"correct" answer. The principles I describe here certainly were not developed by
me. I am sure that they have been described in many textbooks on measurement
and testing. Nonetheless, I hope that this account of how an instructor (me!) has
actually employed such principles may encourage you, and/or the instructors you
will be working with, to employ these methods.

The first basic principle is that, when I assign papers to my students, I ask them to not put their names on their papers. Instead, I ask them to simply list their student identification number on the back of the last page of their responses. Because students do not list their names, I am usually unaware of who wrote a particular paper. Not knowing this information allows me to be much more objective when grading papers. By not knowing who wrote a particular paper, my grading is not influenced by factors that might otherwise affect my grading-factors such as how often the student participates in class and the quality of his or her in-class comments. Personality factors, such as how much I like a student or how likely it is that the student will complain about the grade he or she receives, also cease to be issues. As easy as it may be for us to think that the aforementioned factors do not affect how we score an exam, I would bet that in many cases these factors do have some influence. Indeed, I would wager that in many cases instructors are influenced by these factors but are unaware of this fact. By scoring papers without knowing who wrote them, the chances of being influenced by such factors are greatly diminished, although not totally so (there may be a tendency to guess who wrote a particular paper, a tendency I am usually able to beat into submission).

The second principle I adhere to is that I grade each student's response to one question before I grade any student's response to the next question. By doing so, I am able to keep the same criteria clearly in mind as I review each student's answer to that particular question. Moreover, although in most cases I judge student responses in light of some specific criteria I have in mind (or have specified in writing), I am better able to judge how good (or bad) an answer to a question may be by comparing it with another answer to the same question. I know to many individuals this practice might appear to be antithetical to the principles of criterion-referenced testing, but I don't agree. I believe that in most of the cases when we are grading open-ended responses for which there is no one right answer, a certain degree of subjectivity comes into play; in other words, our criteria are rarely so well defined as to rule out all subjectivity. In such instances, I believe we may be better able to judge the quality of a response to a question after having read several other responses to the same question, or after having reread a model response from a previous semester. Another advantage of reading everyone's response to one question before reading anyone's response to the next question is that it lessens the likelihood of a halo effect. That is, it lessens the likelihood that how you judge a student's response to one question will be influenced by how you judged his or her response to a previous question.

I further ensure that the halo effect will not occur by requiring my students to start their responses to each essay question on a new page. When I finish grading a student's response to one question, I record the student's grade on the last page of his or her response to that question, then turn to the first page of the next response and place the student's paper aside with the others I have already graded. When I have graded all the students' answers to the first question and begin to grade their answers to the next one, all their papers have now been turned to a page that gives me little, if any, clue as to how well any of the students responded to the first question. Thus, I greatly reduce the likelihood of my grading being influenced by a how well or poorly a student responded to the previous question.

The third principle I adhere to is closely related to the second one. When I complete grading students' answers to one question and begin grading their answers to the next question, I change the order in which I grade the papers. I usually do this by randomly shuffling the papers, or reversing the order in which I reviewed the papers when I graded student answers to the previous question. By changing the order in which I grade papers, I lessen the likelihood that a student will benefit from, or be hurt by, some idiosyncrasy in the way I score papers as I move from grading the first to last response to a given question. For example, it may be that as I review a series of responses to a question, I get more critical as I proceed through that set. If so, then the student whose paper is graded last will be at a disadvantage. Again, one may think that if the criteria for judging responses have been clearly identified, then the order in which a series of responses is reviewed should have no influence on how an individual paper is judged. However, after many years of experience, I have found that no matter how carefully I identify the criteria I will use, my judgment of an individual response is often influenced, at least to some small degree, by the other responses I have read. I believe this circumstance is likely to be more common than many adherents of criterion-referenced testing are inclined to admit. If my opinion is correct, then by changing the order in which you grade students' responses, you are likely to lessen the impact of this phenomenon.

In summary, when I administer essay exams, the three principles I adhere to when grading those exams are the following:

1. Grade each exam without knowing who wrote it.
2. Grade all of the answers to one question before grading any of the answers to the next question.
3. When moving from question to question, change the order in which papers are graded.

I have employed these principles for many years and have found that they really enable me to grade students' responses much more objectively. Moreover, many of my students have indicated how much they appreciate my use of these methods. In conclusion, these techniques have worked very well for me and my students, and I believe they will work just as well for you and those you work with. I hope you will give these techniques a try.

Dr. Robert Reiser is a professor in the instructional systems program in the Department of Educational Psychology and Learning Systems at Florida State University. Dr. Reiser has written four books and more than 40 journal articles in the field of instructional design and technology. His most recent book, which was published in 2002, is *Trends and Issues in Instructional Design and Technology* (edited with John V. Dempsey).

Following are some examples of problem-solving questions:

1. One worker can build 5 benches in 1 day. For a particular job, 20 benches are needed in 1 day's time. How many workers need to be assigned to this job? Show all work, and circle your final answer.
2. You are given a beaker that contains one of the five chemical solutions used in previous laboratory exercises. Describe a procedure that you would use to positively identify the particular solution and rule out the other alternatives. (Be sure to list each major step in your procedure.)

Here are some guidelines for constructing problem-solving items:

1. Specify the criteria for evaluation. For example, indicate whether students should show their work in addition to the final answer.
2. Award partial credit or give a separate score for using correct procedures when the final answer is incorrect. On many problems, a careless error may result in a wrong answer, even though the work shown conveys full understanding of the problem.
3. Construct a model answer for each problem that indicates the amount of credit to be awarded for work at different stages.

Remember that regardless of which type of test you employ (multiple-choice, essay, problem-solving, etc.), the key concern is that it provides a valid measure of performance. In the case of objective tests, validity will mostly depend on the appropriateness of the content tested and the clarity of the items. For constructed response tests, an additional element becomes the reliability of scoring. The guidelines provided here for the different constructed response modes should be helpful toward that end.

## TESTING SKILLS AND BEHAVIOR

In evaluating skills and behavior, we examine overt actions that can be directly observed. Frequently, the target behavior is some type of performance reflecting how well a trainee or student can carry out a particular task or a group of related tasks. Some examples are as follows:

- Using a power saw to cut boards of different thickness
- Doing a dance step for 10 repetitions without error
- Debugging a computer program so that it runs effectively
- Giving a speech that incorporates the ''10 speaking skills'' taught in a course
- Leading a group to resolve a conflict successfully

The standards of performance are judged according to the requirements of the instructional objectives and should be the same as those covered during instruction. Accordingly, each of the preceding general goals would need to be broken down into more precise descriptions of expected performance. Prior to testing, the learner should have had sufficient opportunities to practice and apply the skills to be able to demonstrate the learning. If so, he or she should be prepared to complete the test successfully.

---

$\qquad$ Expert's Edge $\qquad$

## The Proof Is in the Pudding, or Is It in How You Make the Pudding?

A large company we shall call Info Avenue is in an interesting and highly profitable business. It acquires sensitive, unpublished information from and about other companies—for which it pays nothing—and subsequently sells the information to customers. Obviously, this business relies heavily on the skills of Info Avenue employees who acquire this information; without their success, there is no product to sell. However, extracting this information is difficult; strong interpersonal, interviewing, and selling skills are required.

Because this job is so critical and difficult, Info Avenue had invested in extensive instruction to train new hires in how to perform this role. The instruction included weeks of self-study and coordinated follow-up with supervisors who were to perform important coaching and feedback functions for these employees. The investment in the training was so substantial and concern for verifying competence among these employees was so high that Info Avenue also wanted a good performance assessment tool. The instrument was to be used to screen new hires for competence before they were released to go into the field and begin interacting with organizations and collecting information. Performance assessment was planned to occur during a large, national meeting convened for this purpose.

When we were called by Info Avenue to assist with the development and validation of this performance-assessment instrument, we knew this would be a challenging project. However, we assumed that the challenges would be largely technical in nature. After all, this appeared to be among the "softest" of "soft skills." It was apparent that these competencies could not be assessed using multiple-choice test questions: A performance test was essential.

Performance tests actually have two components: the observation support tool, usually a rating scale or checklist, and the observer or rater. For performance tests to work and to be legally defensible, the rating scale must reflect job-related competencies (a validity issue), and the raters must be consistent in their use of the scale (a reliability issue). Both aspects require serious attention from the test developer.

The rating scale development began with a job analysis drawing on the expertise of those within the company who were knowledgeable about how the information-gathering position is best performed. We drafted the tool, and then an iterative process of review and revision began. The tool was piloted with a sample of raters, and its content validity (job relatedness) was documented by subject-matter experts. So far, so good.

The next technical hurdle was training the Info Avenue raters to use the observation tool. Even the best rating instruments or checklists can seldom be used consistently by untrained raters. Unfortunately, this part of performance testing is often overlooked. The good news is that training raters to score performances reliably—even soft skills performances—is easier than most people think. Interestingly, the process follows the same general pattern as a concept lesson. In other words, competent performance becomes a concept that the raters must master at the comprehension level: They must become consistent with one another in classifying previously unseen instances of the performance as examples or nonexamples of competent performance.

The process for training the raters generally looks like this:

- Create sample cases of performance that reflect competent and typically incompetent performance.
- Bring the raters together.
- Review the rating scale or checklist.
- Present the model-case competent performance for rating.
- Compare ratings and discuss any discrepancies.
- Present a "far-out" nonexample.
- Compare ratings and discuss discrepancies.
- Present nonexamples including "near-in" nonexamples, compare ratings, and discuss until discrepancies disappear.
- Present final trials to calculate interrater reliability for documentation.

Following this process, we were able to bring the Info Avenue raters to acceptable levels of interrater reliability in one morning session. Info Avenue was delighted with the assessment. It proceeded to implement the training for new hires and scheduled the nationwide testing session at the culmination of the training period. The day of the testing session turned out to hold a major insight regarding the implementation of sound and rigorous testing in an organization. The assessment process worked beautifully, and the vast majority of new-hire candidates passed the test. However, *all* those who did not pass were from one region in the southeastern United States. The candidates from that region were obviously less well prepared than they should have been, and all of them were under the supervision of the same regional training manager. It quickly became apparent that the problem was with this regional manager. In the process, the test—designed to assess new-hire competence—had shed unflattering light on management. Higher management, fearing embarrassment within middle management, suddenly announced that Info Avenue had "only winners" within its ranks and that the testing session would henceforth be regarded as a "coaching opportunity" rather than a performance evaluation. And so it is with well-constructed, valid performance assessments. They often turn up performance problems elsewhere besides among the test takers. We now consider learning outcomes assessment more than simply a step in the instructional design process: It is truly *organizational* change. And the better the test, the more profound the change is likely to be, because comfort is sometimes found in error and uncertainty. Be ready.

Sharon Shrock is professor of instructional development and evaluation at Southern Illinois University, where she is the coordinator of graduate programs in instructional design and technology. She has consulted with a number of global corporations in developing criterion-referenced assessment systems. She is first author of the award-winning book *Criterion-Referenced Test Development: Technical and Legal Guidelines for Corporate Training and Certification.*

Bill Coscarelli is professor of instructional technology at Southern Illinois University and coauthor of *Criterion-Referenced Test Development: Technical and Legal Guidelines for Corporate Training and Certification.* Dr. Coscarelli has been an active testing consultant. He is a former editor and a past president of the International Society for Performance and Improvement.

## Preliminary Considerations

When preparing to evaluate performance, look for answers to the following questions:

1. Will process, product, or both be evaluated? When a learner performs a task, the confidence, care, and accuracy with which he or she carries out the procedures usually are important. This is a measurement of the process portion of the task, which may include elements such as these:
   - Following a proper sequence of actions or steps
   - Performing detailed manipulations
   - Using tools or instruments properly
   - Working within a specified time period

Product evaluation focuses primarily on the end result or outcome of the effort. Attention is on the quality and possibly quantity of a product or on the final action that results from applying the process. The evaluation of most tasks includes both process and product components.

2. What constraints or limitations should be recognized when planning a performance evaluation? The conditions under which a task is normally performed should be considered before developing the test. Such elements as the following can help you decide whether to use a realistic or a simulated testing situation:
   - Size and complexity of the task
   - Cost for materials or services required
   - Human safety factors
   - Time needed for testing

Other matters that need attention when deciding on the method of testing include the following:

   - The required place for testing
   - Necessary or specialized equipment
   - Instruments, tools, and supplies needed
   - The required involvement of other persons

3. Will the testing conditions be simulated or realistic? By considering the various factors indicated in the answer to the previous question, you can

be prepared to decide whether the test can be conducted under realistic conditions or, if this is impractical, whether it can be handled in some abbreviated or simulated fashion. The simulation should be as joblike as possible to serve as a valid measure of performance.

Today many of those involved in K–12 education are placing increasing emphasis on assessing student performance in addition to students' recall or recognition of content. Performance assessments are frequently confused with authentic assessments, even though they do not mean the same thing. Authentic assessment involves the student's demonstrating the performance in a real-life context (Meyer, 1993). In your opinion, would going on a field trip, returning to class, and then writing an essay in a one-hour class period be an authentic assessment of writing? Probably not, because the conditions for the writing performance are contrived. A more authentic context would be one in which, similar to journalists given an assignment and a deadline, the students have a day or two in which they can use a variety of resources (e.g., school or community library, Internet, textbooks) to generate the written report.

The instructional designer should also keep in mind that assessment is not useful only for measuring the outcomes of instruction. Another valuable contribution is enhancing the process of learning. As Lorie Shepard (2001) suggested, building meaningful "formative" assessment into instructional units can be extremely helpful to the learner. Shepard favors authentic performance measures that build learner motivation, require student self-assessment, and promote the transfer of knowledge in contrast to, say, merely inserting a few multiple-choice items in different sections of a lesson.

Whether the testing takes place under realistic or simulated conditions, an evaluator should give consideration to recording the performance on video. With this procedure, evaluation of a performance can take place at a later time and may involve the learner in the review. Depending on the evaluation needs and conditions, one or more of the alternative measures described next may be used.

## Types of Skill/Behavior Assessments

**Direct Testing.**    For certain types of performances, it may be feasible to test the student or trainee directly to determine skill level. The primary focus is on products (i.e., final outcomes), but examining processes (i.e., the actions that lead to the products) will also be of interest in most situations.

### *Examples*

Keyboarding speed and accuracy
Operating equipment
Marksmanship
Assembling parts
Using a hammer
Drawing geometric shapes

**Procedure.**    The first step in developing the test is to review the instructional objectives and details of the task to be evaluated. Then use the following procedure:

1. Review the task analysis (see Chapter 4), and identify the steps or specific procedures of the task that constitute the criteria to be judged. Establish the proficiency level that will be accepted (as indicated by the performance standard component of the objective).
2. Plan how the performance will take place, including its location and the application of the procedure.
3. List the equipment, tools, materials, and printed resources to be made available.
4. Consider any special matters like safety and other persons needed.
5. Write the instructions that direct the actions of the learners during the test.

For example, for evaluating nursing trainees' skills at taking blood pressure, a designer might establish the standard of achieving an accuracy level averaging a 95% proximity to experts' readings on 15 patients. Trainees perform in a simulated examining room where they are scheduled at 30-minute intervals; given instructions, the necessary equipment, and volunteer patients; and tested under controlled conditions (e.g., with proper safety precautions and sanitary conditions). Because the scores obtained will be reflective of each individual, it is highly important to establish appropriate conditions of testing to ensure that the scores are valid. For example, it would hardly seem appropriate to assess taking blood pressure in a noisy room with insufficient lighting.

**Analysis of Naturally Occurring Results.**    Certain skills or behaviors may be evaluated as products of activities naturally performed in realistic contexts. By assessing these products, the evaluator obtains a direct measure of the objective in question, without having to develop instruments or collect new data.

*Examples*

Number of absences from school
Number of traffic citations received this year
Sales volume during the second quarter
Verbal score obtained on the Graduate Record Exam
Courses selected for the spring semester

As with direct testing, the score by itself reflects the target performance (or behavior), which thus makes the validity of that score the key concern. For example, if the measure of interest were sales volume in a given month, an evaluator would want to be sure that nothing unusual happened during that period to change outcomes that would normally occur. Weather, student illness, or special conditions in the business could have unanticipated effects in this regard. Similarly, following their completion of a driver's safety course, students may receive very few traffic citations, but the main reasons for their increased "driving success" may be local sales on radar detectors and the city's cutback on traffic officers. The evaluator, therefore, must make sure that the available data are valid indicators of performance associated with the instruction.

Analysis of naturally occurring events is especially useful for confirmative evaluations. Recall from Chapter 11 that the purpose of confirmative evaluations is to examine the effectiveness of instruction over an extended time. Available data, such as quantity of sales, number of patient complaints, and percentage of trainees passing the certification examination, provide a practical and cost-effective basis for judging the stability of instructional outcomes over time. Depending on needs and resources, supplementary measures may also be desired.

### Procedure

1. Based on the instructional objectives for the instruction, identify any relevant results (i.e., behaviors or products) that naturally occur as the individual performs his or her job or normal activities.
2. Arrange to obtain the results. (Permission from the student and/or other individuals, such as supervisors or administrators, often will be required.)
3. Ensure that the results reflect representative performance/behavior. If conditions seem unusual (e.g., a bad month for sales), increase the time frame to include additional data collection periods.

**Ratings of Performance.**   In many situations, especially when the process component of performance is to be evaluated, it becomes necessary for the instructor or other qualified judge to observe learner actions and rate them in terms of the necessary criteria.

### Examples

Speaking ability
Applying colors in a painting
Technical skill in a gymnastics routine
Interpersonal skills
Carpentry ability in building a deck

The ratings are commonly made using one of the following instruments.

**Checklists.**   A checklist can be used to determine whether sequential steps in a procedure or other actions are successfully performed. The evaluator indicates "yes" or "no," "done" or "not done," for each element. A checklist, however, does not allow assessments to be made of quality of performance. An example of a checklist is shown in Figure 12-1.

**Rating Scales.**   With a rating scale, special values can be assigned to each element of a performance. Only behaviors that can be observed and rated reliably should be included in a rating scale. A numerical scale is commonly used. It consists of standards from low to high, such as these:

| 0 | 1 | 2 |
|---|---|---|
| Unacceptable | Acceptable with corrections | Acceptable |

| 1 | 2 | 3 | 4 |
|---|---|---|---|
| Poor | Fair | Good | Excellent |

**FIGURE 12-1**
Checklist for packaging medical specimens (nonhazardous)

| Skills | Performed (Yes/No) |
|---|---|
| 1. Primary container in watertight. | _____ |
| 2. Primary container contains no more than 500 mL or grams. | _____ |
| 3. Primary container can withstand at least 95 kpa internal pressure. | _____ |
| 4. Absorbent material is place inside secondary packaging. | _____ |
| 5. Enough absorbent material is added to absorb all the contents of the primary container. | _____ |
| 6. Primary container is placed so the absorbent material isolates primary container from secondary container. | _____ |
| 7. Selected outer packaging that can withstand a drop from 6 feet. | _____ |
| 8. Secondary container is placed inside outer packaging. | _____ |
| 9. Item list is placed between secondary container and outer packaging. | _____ |
| 10. Voids between secondary container and outside packaging are filled with soft material to prevent movement. | _____ |
| 11. Outside package is sealed with shipping tape. | _____ |
| 12. Sender and receiver information is clearly legible on outside of package. | _____ |

Using descriptive terms is recommended to differentiate and clarify the meaning of the individual rating categories. It would make little sense, for example, to ask an observer to rate a manager's "leadership skills" given only a rating scale of 1 to 10. What would a 10 indicate? How would a 4 differ from a 5? Without clearer definitions, the ratings will be completely arbitrary and unreliable. Depending on the situation and the descriptors used, rating scales may be either norm referenced, such that learners are judged in comparison to each other, or criterion referenced, so they are judged relative to the acceptable standards for performance. Here is an example of a norm-referenced descriptive rating scale:

| 1 | 2 | 3 | 4 | 5 |
|---|---|---|---|---|
| Unsatisfactory | Below average | Average | Above average | Superior |

An important limitation of rating scales can be any personal bias an evaluator may have in preferring one learner over another for any number of reasons. Also, careful attention is required to discriminate each level of performance from the others on a scale; thus, limiting rating scales to three to five levels is usually advisable. Training of evaluators to standardize their measurements is also strongly encouraged. In addition to evaluating the process component of a skill, the designer should use a rating form to judge the quality (and quantity) of a resulting product. Such factors as these may be included:

- General appearance of product
- Accuracy of product details (e.g., shape, dimensions, finish)
- Relationships between components or parts (e.g., size, fit, finish, color)
- Quantity of products produced during a time period

**FIGURE 12-2**
Rating scale for using direct instruction

| Procedure | Rating | | | |
|---|---|---|---|---|
| | Poor | | | Excellent |
| 1.  Introduces objectives | 0 | 1 | 2 | 3 |
| 2.  Gives overview | 0 | 1 | 2 | 3 |
| 3.  Reviews prerequisites | 0 | 1 | 2 | 3 |
| 4.  Shows enthusiasm | 0 | 1 | 2 | 3 |
| 5.  Uses clear examples/explanations | 0 | 1 | 2 | 3 |
| 6.  Asks appropriate questions | 0 | 1 | 2 | 3 |
| 7.  Keeps students on task | 0 | 1 | 2 | 3 |
| 8.  Provides sufficient independent practice | 0 | 1 | 2 | 3 |
| 9.  Provides review | 0 | 1 | 2 | 3 |
| 10. Closes lesson effectively | 0 | 1 | 2 | 3 |
| 11. Summary rating | 0 | 1 | 2 | 3 |

Figure 12-2 illustrates a rating scale that includes both process and product evaluations.

Before the rating instrument is used, it should be tried out with a sample of two or three persons from the potential learner group or equivalent. This trial allows checking for (1) the learner's clear understanding of the testing procedure, (2) the effectiveness of each part of the instrument, and (3) the length of the testing period required for each learner. Also, if more than one evaluator will use the scale, the procedure must be standardized so that evaluators will grade similar performances equally. That is, interrater reliability (i.e., consistency) must be established.

**Rubrics.**   A newer evaluation approach involves the use of rubrics to judge the quality of performance. In contrast to a conventional rating scale, a rubric is intended to give a more descriptive, holistic characterization of the quality of students' work. Specifically, where multiple rating items might be used to evaluate isolated skills in a complex task (see Figure 12-2), the rubric represents a general assessment of the overall product. In designing and using a rubric, the designer's concern is less with assigning a number to indicate quality than with selecting a verbal description that clearly communicates, based on the performance or product exhibited, what the student knows and is able to do. Thus, rubrics can be highly informative and useful for feedback purposes. On the other hand, the need to develop distinct categories and meaningful verbal descriptions makes them challenging to develop and to score reliably. Figures 12-3 and 12-4 illustrate rubrics used in evaluating writing in grades K–1 and at the secondary-school level, respectively. Note that these types of assessments are much more informative about students' skill levels than a simple letter grade or numerical score. To the extent that standards-based education remains prevalent, you can expect to see rubrics used frequently as an evaluation and feedback tool for evaluating student and school performance.

**FIGURE 12-3**

Rubric used in evaluating writing in grades K and 1

| Holistic Evaluation Scale (K and 1) |
|---|
| 5  Focused to starter sentence; story structure is recognizable; contains successful attempts in sentence construction (i.e., capitalization, punctuation, etc.) |
| 4  Focused to starter sentence; story structure is recognizable but contains little evidence of sentence mechanics |
| 3  Some words are recognizable; may or may not have mechanics; has connection with starter sentence, but little story development |
| 2  Some words are recognizable; no connection with starter sentence; no mechanics and little story content |
| 1  No recognizable words, mechanics, or story content |

Created by Michele Woodward. Used with permission.

**Anecdotal Records.**    An anecdotal record is an open-ended instrument for evaluating performance in a narrative fashion. An outline-type form containing behaviors to be observed is prepared. In addition to a description of performance, interpretations of what was done along with recommendations for improvement may be included in such a record. The written record should be made while observing the performance, or brief notes should be taken and then expanded on the record form immediately after the evaluation session.

*Examples*

Observing a student teacher

Attending a presentation given by a student who has completed a public speaking course

Spending a day in an office to evaluate how a manager interacts with her employees

*Procedure*

1. Develop a general set of guidelines to focus your observations according to the objectives of the evaluation. (The guidelines may be modified over time as considered appropriate.)
2. Determine whether the observation will be prearranged or unannounced. The advantage of the prearranged visit is ensuring that the observation can be done at a particular time and that your appearance will be accepted. The advantage of the unannounced visit is observing events as they naturally take place, without special preparation (to impress an observer). Regardless of the orientation used, permission to observe from school or company officials will most likely be required.
3. If you want to use a tape recorder or video camera, be sure to obtain approval from the individual(s) being observed as well as from school or company authorities. (Note: Approval might be needed even if you are simply observing, so check this out.)

**FIGURE 12-4**

Rubric used for evaluating writing at the high school level

| Score | Content | Organization | Expression | Mechanics |
|---|---|---|---|---|
| 4 | Focus is clear and on a limited topic; ideas are developed and supported with concrete details; evidence of consideration of possibilities and complexities of the issue | Strong introduction; transitions between paragraphs help tie information together; strong conclusion | Varied sentence structure; use of vivid language; tone is consistent with text; audience and purpose clearly defined; individual voice present | Use of standard grammar and punctuation; correct spelling |
| 3 | Focus may be clear but ideas developed minimally; no consideration for complexity of an issue | An introduction but may not be strong; transitions made between paragraphs; conclusion but may not be strong | Appropriate use of language and diction; tone is consistent with text; audience clearly defined; no individual voice | Same as 4 |
| 2 | Focus there but predictable; ideas not developed; no complexity | May lack either an introduction or conclusion; few or illogical use of transitions | Simple, clear diction; lacks a sense of voice, may use inappropriate tone for audience at times | A few mechanical errors |
| 1 | No clear focus; little or no development of ideas | Lacks introduction; series of unrelated paragraphs | May use inappropriate or incorrect language; no sense of audience | Numerous mechanical errors, which interfere with reading |

Created by Michele Woodward. Used with permission.

4. Take brief notes during the observation. Expand the notes on a record form as soon after the observation as possible.
5. Make additional observations if needed. The more observations, the more complete and accurate the information obtained. The disadvantage is the time involved and possible disruption caused by the visits.

For example, say two months after trainees complete a corporate training course on group leadership, the evaluator contacts them to identify times when they will be leading a group on the job. A prearranged visit is then coordinated with a given trainee, and permission is obtained to audio-record the session. The evaluator arrives at the meeting early and sits in the back of the room to be unobtrusive. The trainee introduces the evaluator to the group members at the beginning of the meeting and tells them her purposes for being there (and for audio-recording the meeting). The evaluator carefully observes the trainee's behavior during the meeting and takes notes, which she later expands. Following the meeting, she decides that the observation produced sufficient information, and that a second one with this trainee will not be needed. She decides, however, to observe several other trainees to compare the results.

Descriptive evaluation is time consuming and often impractical with large numbers of learners. As with rating scales, a degree of subjectivity can easily, and often unknowingly, find its way into an evaluation report. But when carefully prepared, with reference to a number of tasks over a period of time, an evaluator can gather valuable cumulative data on the performance of an individual. Similarly, by observing a sample of former trainees performing on the job, the evaluator can make more informed judgments about the adequacy of the instruction that the observed individuals received.

**Indirect Checklist/Rating Measures.**   In some instances, it is not feasible for the evaluator to observe behavior directly. Sometimes the reason is cost. For example, in a course designed to teach individuals how to make more effective presentations at conferences and meetings, it may prove too expensive for the evaluator to attend the presentations of enough former students to make valid judgments about their performances. Or it might prove too costly to observe teachers to determine how well they are applying classroom management skills taught in a recent workshop.

In other situations, direct observations are impractical. Common examples are courses designed to help people improve social interactions, interpersonal skills, employee relations, and the like. The difficulty is that, short of following an individual around during the day, the evaluator cannot be present when typical situations requiring such skills arise. And, if the evaluator were present, the situations would probably become unnatural or artificial as a direct result. For example, suppose you and your friend start arguing about whose turn it is to pay for lunch. Would you respond in a "natural" way if an evaluator were there specifically to observe your behavior? Probably not. If direct observations or assessments of behavior are not practical, the next best option might be to seek parallel information from individuals who are present when former students typically demonstrate the criterion skills. One source of data might be reactions from the former students themselves regarding the effectiveness of training for developing certain skills. Figure 12-5 displays items from such a survey. This instrument was administered to former students several months following their completion of a corporate training course on making effective presentations. Individuals were asked to rate the helpfulness of specific course features for improving the quality of presentations that they subsequently made. Instrument development essentially involves identifying, from the course objectives and materials, the criterion performance and the enabling (or component) skills involved. The skills/behaviors are then listed for evaluation by students using a conventional rating scale format.

Another indirect measure would be ratings or checklists submitted by individuals who work or interact with the former students in situations in which the target skills are likely to be exhibited. Figure 12-6 illustrates this type of instrument, as employed in the presentation skills evaluation referred to earlier. The instrument was developed by identifying component and criterion skills for the course. The skills

**FIGURE 12-5**
Job-based survey

| Skills | Degree of Use | | |
|---|---|---|---|
| | Not at all | Some | A great deal |
| Reducing nervousness before presenting | ☐ | ☐ | ☐ |
| Reducing nervousness while presenting | ☐ | ☐ | ☐ |
| Improving planning | ☐ | ☐ | ☐ |
| Improving organization | ☐ | ☐ | ☐ |
| Improving interruptions | ☐ | ☐ | ☐ |
| Maintaining proper pacing | ☐ | ☐ | ☐ |
| Using visual aids | ☐ | ☐ | ☐ |
| Responding to questions | ☐ | ☐ | ☐ |

were then listed with accompanying five-point rating scales for judging frequency of practice by the student, as observed by the respondent. In the actual evaluation (Morrison & Ross, 1991), respondents were managers, peers, and subordinates who worked with corporate trainees who completed the presentation skills course.

**Portfolio Assessments.** Performances frequently culminate, by design, in the creation of tangible products. Examples include paintings, essays, poems, musical compositions, and pottery. The nature of these products changes over time as a function of the students' experience and of the situation. Thus, examining only one sample (e.g., an essay on Thomas Jefferson written in a composition class) may provide a very limited view of the skills acquired from a composition class. Portfolios represent a form of "authentic testing," which, as described in Chapter 11, is an assessment of performance in realistic contexts (Mullin, 1998). Three primary characteristics of portfolios are (a) focus on *production* or *performance*, (b) emphasis on *higher-order learning*, such as critical thinking, and (c) necessity for *evaluative judgment* by a human as opposed to a computer (Osterlind, 2006).

As described by Arhar, Holly, and Kasten (2001), portfolios are "a carefully selected, constructed, and narrated collection of work pertaining to a special topic" (p. 21). As a result, the teacher and the student can examine actual work products together to determine effort, improvement, ability, and quality. In the same manner, portfolios can also be used to illuminate strengths and needs in the instruction itself.

*Procedure*

1. Involve students in selecting samples of their work for the portfolio.
2. Update the portfolios over time so that improvements or changes in the quality of the work may be noted.
3. Based on instructional objectives, identify criteria for judging the work. For example, for evaluating a portfolio of writing samples, such criteria might include organization, expression, use of a topic sentence, correct grammar, and spelling.

**FIGURE 12-6**
Job application survey

| Item | Always | Most of the time | Sometimes | Never | Does not apply |
|---|:---:|:---:|:---:|:---:|:---:|
| 1. This individual uses overhead transparencies or other visuals to communicate ideas. | ☐ | ☐ | ☐ | ☐ | ☐ |
| 2. This individual uses overhead transparencies to summarize main ideas. | ☐ | ☐ | ☐ | ☐ | ☐ |
| 3. It is evident that this individual has spent time preparing and rehearsing the presentation. | ☐ | ☐ | ☐ | ☐ | ☐ |
| 4. This individual uses graphs or pictures to emphasize the points he or she wishes to make. | ☐ | ☐ | ☐ | ☐ | ☐ |
| 5. This individual begins a talk with a statement of the purpose and expected outcome to focus the audience's attention. | ☐ | ☐ | ☐ | ☐ | ☐ |
| 6. This individual emphasizes the main points of the presentation | ☐ | ☐ | ☐ | ☐ | ☐ |
| 7. It is easy to follow the logic in this individual's presentations. | ☐ | ☐ | ☐ | ☐ | ☐ |
| 8. This individual uses personal examples or analogies to explain a point. | ☐ | ☐ | ☐ | ☐ | ☐ |
| 9. This individual identifies the benefits of implementing the presented idea | ☐ | ☐ | ☐ | ☐ | ☐ |
| 10. This individual arranges the room appropriately (e.g., seating, temperature, overhead projector) before the participants arrive | ☐ | ☐ | ☐ | ☐ | ☐ |
| 11. The presentations this individual makes have the appropriate level of detail needed for the audience. | ☐ | ☐ | ☐ | ☐ | ☐ |

Copyright 1991 The Dow Chemical Company. Used with permission.

4. Identify the evaluation mode. Possible modes, which may be used separately or in combination, include checklists (yes/no), rating scales (e.g., poor, average, superior), rubrics, and comments (e.g., "shows good effort, but lacks fundamentals").

By examining group results for different criteria at various times of the year, the designer can obtain useful information about how effectively skills are being applied. For example, it may be found that carpentry students' early work demonstrates very poor routing skills, but later products show high proficiency in this area. Just as there are different types of objective tests or rating scales, portfolios can take varied forms. Anderson (1994) described four formats she has used in working with elementary school children:

**Showcase:** Presents the student's "best" work while emphasizing self-assessment, reflection, and ownership

**Evaluation:** Presents representative work to be evaluated on the basis of showing movement toward a specific academic goal

**Process:** Asks students to reflect on work produced over time for the purpose of developing points of view on their long-term learning process and subject synthesis

**Documentation:** Presents work that represents academic accomplishment for presentation to parents, other students, or school administrators

Do portfolios provide accurate assessments of student performance? Research suggests inconsistency across studies regarding this issue (Herman & Winters, 1994). Suppose that you were evaluating a high school student's portfolio in a science class. What factors might compromise the validity of the score you assign? One could be the high subjectivity of judgments being made. A second could be how the student's products (also called artifacts) were selected (do they represent best or typical work?). A third might be the extent to which the student did the work independently. A fourth could be the limitations of using fairly restricted scales (see Figures 12-3 and 12-4) to judge quality of performance on complex tasks.

Compared with objective testing, portfolios provide a means of obtaining a richer, more meaningful impression of what students are able to achieve, but perhaps at the risk of some measurement precision. By using each type of test to its best advantage, evaluators and designers can increase the depth and range of information obtained about student learning.

**Exhibitions.**    For some types of instruction, the culminating products are best displayed in a special type of performance before an audience. These performances, commonly called exhibitions, are characterized by being public and requiring many hours of preparation.

*Examples*

Reciting poetry
Playing an instrument

Singing
Acting
Giving a speech
Performing a gymnastics routine

**Procedure**

Evaluating exhibitions requires using procedures comparable to those used for portfolios and shares similar advantages and disadvantages relative to objective testing. Typical procedures might include the following:

1. Identify skill behaviors and criteria based on instructional objectives.
2. Develop instruments such as checklists, rating scales, rubrics, or some combination thereof to evaluate the performance.
3. Use criterion-referenced measurement by focusing on how well the student has attained the desired level of competence for each skill.
4. Add comments to explain certain ratings, describe noteworthy events, and convey overall impressions of the performance.

## ATTITUDES

Just as it is a challenging task to write affective-domain objectives, much planning and thought are required to assess individuals' feelings and attitudes toward instruction. Feelings, values, and beliefs are very private matters that cannot be measured directly. Attitudes can be inferred only through a person's words and behaviors. The problem of evaluating attitudes is further compounded by two factors. First, a response expressed by a learner on an attitudinal survey may be stated so as to be socially acceptable, regardless of the individual's actual feelings. Therefore, true sentiments may not be conveyed. Second, outcomes of the most important objectives in a course may not become evident until quite some time after the course is completed, which makes it impossible to measure an attitude at the end of the study time. We sometimes hear students say something like, "I hated that course and old Dr. Brazle's lectures when I took it, but it really helped me in Algebra II."

Despite these limitations, there can be benefits from attempting to determine, at the conclusion of a unit or portions of an instructional program, whether it satisfied attitudinal objectives. At the same time, student attitudes provide formative evaluation data regarding how positively different aspects of the course instruction are perceived.

### Two Uses of Attitude Assessment

We commonly find two general categories of attitude assessments in formative, summative, and confirmative evaluations: evaluating instruction and evaluating affective outcomes. These approaches are similar in their basic methods and instruments employed (e.g., questionnaires, interviews, rating scales). What distinguishes them is their focus—the instruction itself or desired affective outcomes of the instruction.

**Evaluating the Instruction.**    In this approach, the interest is in determining how students or trainees react to the instruction they have received—what they like or do not like and their suggestions for improvement. The instruction, not the learner, is the focus. Exemplary evaluation questions are these:

- Was the course material well organized?
- Did you have sufficient time to learn the material?
- What suggestions do you have for improving the manual?

**Evaluating Affective Outcomes.**    In the second approach, the learners and their feelings toward certain ideas or behaviors are the focus. Of particular interest may be measuring how much attitude changes as a direct result of the instructional program (using a pretest-posttest design). For example, prior to a dental hygiene workshop, only 13% of the enrollees (who were practicing dentists) agreed that working with gloves is an important hygienic practice. Following the workshop, the agreement rate increased to 87%, which suggests that the workshop was successful in promoting that view. Other examples:

- Nurses' attitudes toward showing empathy to patients
- Employees' feelings about tardiness and absenteeism
- Police officers' attitudes toward using force in stopping crime
- Students' interest in visiting museums
- Home builders' attitudes toward using cypress wood as a siding

As we will see, regardless of whether the focus is on attitudes toward the instruction or attitudes toward behaviors and practices, a variety of data collection methods is available.

## Observation/Anecdotal Records

Just as observation is useful for evaluating performance, it can provide a valuable source of information about student attitudes. Observation is often carried out by the instructor while learners are at work in their normal study or activity area. The instrument for recording what is observed can be a simple questionnaire, a rating scale, or an open-ended form on which descriptions and comments are made as in an anecdotal record.

What you focus on during an observation will depend on the evaluation objectives. Normally, there will be interest in how students react to the instruction—what holds their interest, what loses it, and the like. Relevant attitudes will thus be conveyed in observable behaviors such as attentiveness, affect (e.g., smiling, nodding in agreement, laughing), and engagement (e.g., taking notes, answering questions, raising hands, etc.). Exemplary items that might be included in an observer rating scale are the following:

| *Student Attitude* | *Low* | *Some* | *High* |
|---|---|---|---|
| Interest in lesson | 1 | 2 | 3 |
| Attentiveness to lesson | 1 | 2 | 3 |
| Active engagement | 1 | 2 | 3 |
| Positive affect (smiles, laughter) | 1 | 2 | 3 |

## Assessment of Behavior

Students may smile frequently and be very enthusiastic about the instruction but not transfer their feelings about what is learned outside class. Consider, for example, a college-level art appreciation class that is intended to increase students' knowledge about and interest in music, art, and theater. Although students might like the class very much, few may increase their attendance at concerts, exhibitions, or plays as a result of it.

Positive attitudes toward instruction do not necessarily transfer to the subject, at least to the extent that behavior is changed. The most powerful type of instrument for assessing behavioral changes is direct observation of learner activities. For example, 60% of Ms. Leyton's Algebra I students may elect to take Algebra II, whereas only 10% of Mr. Petza's students make that choice. A clear implication (assuming classes have similar makeups) is that Ms. Leyton's course is more successful in producing positive attitudes toward algebra. Similarly, it may be found that 40% of the nurses in a particular health-care facility voluntarily attend a workshop on cardiopulmonary resuscitation (CPR) methods, whereas 10% of nurses in a neighboring facility do the same.

You could probably think of many examples for which such direct observation or measurement would be very impractical. After all, evaluators cannot easily follow students around to see what they do after class (e.g., how many visit the local art museum this month). In those cases, the best alternative is to construct a brief questionnaire that asks students to supply this information.

## Questionnaire/Survey

Probably the most common means of assessing attitudes is through questionnaires or surveys. Such instruments may include two types of items: (1) open-ended questions to which the learner writes answers and (2) closed-ended questions with a number of fixed responses from which learners choose the answer that best reflects their opinion. A variation of this latter type consists of a longer list of alternatives from which the learner checks interesting or important choices or rates the alternatives on a numerical scale. The decision to use open-ended or closed-ended items (or some combination of the two) may depend on the time available to tabulate the replies. The open-ended type provides data that are time consuming to analyze but may be more valuable in conveying learners' feelings and the reasons for them.

Closed-ended questions are quicker to process and more reliable (i.e., objective) but limit the depth and detail of expression. Examples of open-ended and closed-ended questionnaires are provided at the conclusion of this section.

A rating scale is a modification of the questionnaire in which the learner replies to a statement by selecting a point along a scale. The scale may be composed of two points (yes/no), three points (e.g., agree/no opinion/disagree), or up to five points (e.g., very often/quite often/sometimes/hardly ever/never). A commonly used scale is the five-point Likert-type scale consisting of "strongly agree," "agree," "undecided," "disagree," and "strongly disagree." Here are some guidelines for writing questionnaire and survey items:

1. Limit the number of rating scale points to a maximum of five or six. People usually have difficulty making finer discriminations. The younger the age group, the more restricted the choices should be. For example, in surveying first-grade students about their interest in reading, a simple yes/no scale should probably be used. A comparable survey for sixth-graders might use a three-point scale of "agree, uncertain, disagree." For high school students, a five-point scale would be an option. The more scale points, the greater the amount of information that will be obtained, but the greater the chances of confusing the respondent.

   **Poor:** Rate the organization of the course on a 10-point scale, where 1 = Very poor and 10 = Very good.

   **Better:** Rate the organization of the course on the following five-point scale, where 1 = Superior; 2 = Slightly above average; 3 = Average; 4 = Slightly below average; 5 = Inferior.

2. Use verbal descriptors to define numerical rating points. Examples are as follows:

   Rate the enthusiasm of clerical employees in the automotive division.

   | Low | | Average | | High |
   |---|---|---|---|---|
   | 1 | 2 | 3 | 4 | 5 |

   Rate the difficulty of the mechanical assembly for you.

   | Very easy | Somewhat easy | Average | Somewhat difficult | Difficult |
   |---|---|---|---|---|
   | 1 | 2 | 3 | 4 | 5 |

3. Use rating points that are clearly separable and nonoverlapping.

   **Poor:** How often do you play sports?

   | Never | Occasionally | Sometimes | Often | Frequently |
   |---|---|---|---|---|
   | 1 | 2 | 3 | 4 | 5 |

   **Better:** How often do you play sports?

   | Rarely/never | Sometimes | Frequently |
   |---|---|---|
   | 1 | 2 | 3 |

Note that, even in the last case, the meaning of "sometimes" and "frequently" may be ambiguous to students. Is twice a week "sometimes" or "frequently"? It would therefore be preferable to define these categories objectively, such as "Rarely (less than once a week)," "Sometimes (once or twice a week)," and "Frequently (more than twice a week)."

4. Use clear and concrete language to express the idea to be rated.
   **Poor:** There is adequate equipment in the office.
   **Better:** I have the equipment that I need to do my office work.
   **Poor:** The instructional strategy employed was beneficial.
   **Better:** The teaching method used was helpful to me in learning the material.
5. Express only a single idea in each item.
   **Poor:** I like working with my clients and my coworkers.
   **Better:** I like working with my clients.
   I like working with my coworkers.

## Interview

An interview allows learners to discuss their reactions toward instruction in more detail than can be done on a survey or questionnaire. The questions can be either structured or unstructured. A structured interview has the advantage of being more controllable with regard to time and content. An unstructured interview, on the other hand, may provide an opportunity to probe more deeply to clarify learners' responses as well as to follow up on unanticipated responses that may yield new insights. The disadvantages are loss of control and increases in time spent. It is generally valuable to audio-record interviews, but be sure that the interviewee approves of this. Also, for objectivity, the interviewer should be a person not affiliated with the instructional program.

Another important decision is whether to conduct interviews with individuals or with groups (sometimes called "focus groups"). We have found both to be valuable, but the choice of one over the other may depend on the respondents' comfort with each other and sensitivity about the issues. A question such as, "Is Ms. Hanley a good boss, in your opinion?" may create quite a bit of reticence in a group setting. It may also be difficult for the evaluator to capture the consensus of a response when several people offer diverse opinions (Creswell, 2002). On the other hand, focus groups may be much more lively and informative than individual interviews because of respondents' interactions with one another from diverse perspectives. For further descriptions of the various instruments, including their benefits and limitations, see the references for this chapter.

Examples of questionnaires, rating scales, and an interview guide appear in Figure 12-7.

**FIGURE 12-7**
Sample questionnaires, rating scales, and interview guide

---

**Questionnaire (Open-ended)**

(1) What is your general reaction to this topic? Comment specifically on the content treated, the way it was taught, your participation, and any other aspects that you feel are relevant.
(2) In your opinion, what was the greatest strength of the teaching approach used for learning the material on this unit?

**Questionnaire (Closed-ended)**
Select the response on each item that best reflects your reaction.

(1) Learner interest
   a. I feel this topic challenged me intellectually.
   b. I found the material interesting but not challenging.
   c. I was not stimulated very often.
   d. I do not feel the topic was worthwhile.
(2) Topic organization
   a. I could see how the concepts on this topic were interrelated.
   b. The instructor attempted to cover only the minimum amount of material.
   c. I didn't know where the instructor was heading most of the time.

**Rating Scale**

1. Did you have any difficulty or trouble operating the equipment?
   _____No  _____Yes  Comment:

2. How do you rate the self-study activity as a learning experience?
   0               1                2               3              4
   Waste of time  Slightly useful  Satisfactory   Good           Excellent

3. How demanding was the format used in the experimental unit compared with that in a conventional unit?
   _____More demanding  _____ About equal _____ Less demanding

4. Indicate your feeling about the value of wearing goggles for safety on your job:
   1             2          3          4          5
   No value                                       High value

**Interview Guide**

(1) What is your reaction to the value of the unit you have just completed?
(2) How would you rate the amount of assistance that the instructor and the assistants provided you outside the discussion sessions?
   _____None  _____Low  _____Some  _____Sufficient  _____Excellent
   Comments:
(3) Do you feel the criteria adopted by your instructor for assigning letter grades in this unit were fair to you? If not, why not?
(4) What suggestions do you have for improving the activities you completed for this topic?

---

## SUMMARY

1. The selection or development of evaluation instruments begins with a reexamination of the evaluation questions and the types of outcomes they assess: knowledge, skills and behavior, and/or attitudes.

2. Critical to the assessment of cognitive outcomes is the matching of test items to the level of learning specified by objectives.

3. Objective tests, such as multiple-choice, true/false, and matching, have the advantage of being easy to grade. Their disadvantage is their restriction to assessing recognition learning and relatively low levels of learning.

4. Fill-in-the-blank tests have the advantage over multiple-choice tests of assessing recall rather than simply recognition. Other constructed-response tests, such as short-answer, essay, and problem-solving, have the advantage of assessing higher levels of learning (e.g., application, analysis, and synthesis) but the disadvantage of being difficult to grade reliably.

5. Evaluations of performance frequently focus on both process (i.e., the behaviors that lead to an outcome) and product (i.e., the outcome).

6. Alternative means of assessing skills and behavior are direct testing, analysis of naturally occurring events, ratings of performance, anecdotal records, indirect checklist/rating measures, portfolio assessments, and exhibitions.

7. Attitudes cannot be directly measured but must be inferred on the bases of learners' verbal reports and behaviors. Common means for assessing attitudes are anecdotal records, observation of behavior, questionnaires, and interviews.

## THE ID PROCESS

The evaluator of instruction needs first and foremost to put the cart behind the horse by using course objectives (and associated evaluation questions) as the foundation for selecting evaluation instruments. Often, novices apply the reverse process by selecting attractive or convenient instruments first and then "force fitting" the evaluation questions to the resultant data. If the questions focus on knowledge, objective tests might be appropriate. If the focus is application or synthesis, then constructed-response or problem-solving tests might be the best choice. If the focus is on performance, then direct or indirect testing of actual skills might be preferred.

Second, in addition to the evaluation questions, practical constraints such as available resources, accessibility to trainees and testing contexts, and costs must be considered in developing evaluation instruments. A small design project with a limited budget may not be able to support on-the-job assessment of trainees by external evaluators. A third factor to consider is the type of evaluation to use. Formative evaluations tend to make greater use than summative or confirmative evaluations of measures that deal with attitudes and behaviors associated with receiving the instruction. The latter types of evaluation, in turn, place greater focus on measures of learner knowledge and skill. Whatever instruments are selected and developed, all must be properly validated and administered correctly. An old expression used by computer programmers is "garbage in, garbage out." The same applies to evaluation. Any weak link in the chain, such as a poorly constructed multiple-choice test or an unreliable performance-rating process, can result in incorrect decisions being made about the instruction.

Because learning and performance are complex processes, experienced evaluators avoid putting all their eggs in only one or two baskets. Multiple evaluation instruments provide a richer and more reliable (i.e., "triangulated") impression of instructional outcomes.

## APPLICATIONS

Given your known expertise in developing evaluation instruments, other designers frequently come to you with their questions. Here are several about which they would like your ideas today:

1. I am evaluating a training unit for Eagle Department Store employees on dealing with customer complaints. Most of the training involves simulated practice with instructor feedback. What type of testing approach (e.g., multiple-choice versus performance) should I emphasize and why?
2. I am evaluating a training unit that teaches automobile service technicians how to use new computer-based diagnostic equipment. Should I use portfolios as my primary evaluation instrument?
3. I am evaluating employee reactions to the "refresher training" courses at Airways Express, a large package-delivery company. The climate is fairly tense in this company because of downsizing. Should I use individual or group interviews?

## ANSWERS

You might have replied to each question as follows:

1. Given that the training mostly involves practicing skills, it doesn't seem as if using multiple-choice or other objective-type testing would be very appropriate. Rather, you would want to focus on setting up practice situations either in simulated or real contexts. In a simulated context, particular scenarios might be created by actors to rate trainees on their reactions. In a real context, trainees would be rated based on how they react to situations that naturally arise. Other possible measures would be analysis of naturally occurring events (e.g., customer commendations or complaints about the trainee) and indirect analysis by checklist or ratings by those who work with the trainees.
2. Portfolios would not appear a good choice as a primary measure. The service technicians are performing very specific functions using the computer equipment. It is unlikely that portfolios would provide a practical or reliable indicator of such skills. Direct or indirect performance testing would be preferable.
3. Individual interviews typically would be preferable because of the negative climate; that is, the employees may be reticent about expressing their feelings in front of their coworkers.

## INSTRUCTIONAL DESIGN: DECISIONS AND CHOICES

You began to think about test items during your initial meeting with the subject-matter expert. As the subject-matter expert articulated the instructional tasks, he also assisted in identifying appropriate criteria for each objective.

[Identifying the instructional content, specifying the objectives, and preparing the test items are often done simultaneously. Alternatively, a number of instructional designers begin the design process by asking the subject-matter expert to create the test items first—before developing the task analysis or writing the objectives. The designer then builds the task analysis and the objectives from the test items. This approach is advocated by experienced designers as one strategy to speed up the design process.]

Before writing the test items, however, you consider the purpose of the test. You want to use the test to ensure that the learner has demonstrated mastery of the objectives and to guide revisions to improve the effectiveness of the instruction. Thus, as reviewed in prior sections of this chapter, the designer must be knowledgeable about the course objectives and types of learning outcomes desired. The Human Resource Department, however, sees the purpose of the test as providing documentation to demonstrate that the organization has met state and federal requirements (i.e., OSHA regulations). [The point is that a single test often serves multiple purposes for different audiences.]

Next, you think about what type of test questions to develop. You want the test to be easy and quick to score, and you want one test that can be used for both the classroom and Web versions of the instruction. You decide on using mostly multiple-choice items and a few true/false questions. The one exception is that the classroom version will include a performance checklist for the hands-on activity involving the actual use of fire extinguishers. The checklist will provide the documentation to demonstrate compliance with government regulation for those employees for whom the training is mandatory (see the chapter on legal issues for more information).

Here are some test items that you have constructed.

### Objective 1

1. The three components necessary to start a fire are
   a. oxygen, heat, and an ignition source.
   b. oxygen, heat, and a fuel source.
   c. oxygen, a fuel source, and an ignition source.
   d. heat, a fuel source, and an ignition source.

### Objective 2

2. Paper, wood, cloth, and trash are examples of fire class
   A
   B
   C
   D

## Objective 2

3. An example of a ''Class B'' fire source is
   a. cardboard.
   b. paint thinner.
   c. a tungsten lamp.
   d. a foam pillow.

## Objective 3

4. A fire extinguisher that has a cone shaped nozzle is a _____ extinguisher
   A. water-type
   B. dry chemical
   C. carbon dioxide
   D. multipurpose

## Objective 4

5. An appropriate extinguisher to use for a grease fire is a _____ extinguisher
   A. water-type
   B. dry chemical
   C. wet chemical
   D. sulfur dioxide

## Objective 4

6. A water extinguisher may be used to fight an electrical fire.
   _____ True
   _____ False

## Objective 5

7. If a fire is small, but you are not sure what is burning, you should evacuate people from the building and
   A. do not attempt to fight the fire.
   B. use an ABC class extinguisher.
   C. use the fire hose.
   D. wet chemical extinguisher.

## Objective 6

8. A fire extinguisher should be aimed at the
   A. base of the fire.
   B. center of the flames.
   C. top of the fire.
   D. Any of the above would be equally effective.

## Objective 6

9. Aim the fire extinguisher at one spot.
   _____ True
   _____ False

## Example of Performance Checklist

_____ Simulates pulling fire alarm or calling 911
_____ Verbally identifies what is burning (simulated paper; simulated grease)
_____ Selects appropriate class of fire extinguisher from among water-type,
       dry chemical, and carbon dioxide
_____ Verbally identifies personal escape route
_____ Verbally states whether fire is spreading or remains localized
_____ Remains a safe distance from the fire
_____ Aims extinguisher at the base of the fire
_____ Sweeps discharge of extinguisher from side to side

## REFERENCES

Anderson, R. S. (1994). *Using portfolios in K–2 classrooms*. Unpublished manuscript, University of Memphis, TN.

Arhar, J. M., Holly, M. L., & Kasten, W. C. (2001). *Action research for teachers*. Columbus: Merrill-Prentice Hall.

Creswell, J. (2002). Educational research: Planning, conducting, and evaluating quantitative and qualitative research. Upper Saddle River, NJ: Merrill/Prentice Hall.

Herman, J. L., & Winters, L. (1994). Portfolio research: A slim collection. *Educational Leadership, 52*, 91–98.

Himelo-Silver, C. E., Duncan, R. G., & Chinn, C. A. (2007). Scaffolding and achievement in problem-based and inquiry learning: A response to Kirschner, Sweller, and Clark (2006). *Educational Psychologist, 42*(2), 99–107.

McBeath, R. J. (1992). *Instruction and evaluation in higher education: A guidebook for planning and learning*. Englewood Cliffs, NJ: Educational Technology Publications.

Meyer, C. A. (1993). What's the difference between authentic and performance assessment? *Educational Leadership, 51*, 39–40.

Morrison, G. R., & Ross, S. M. (1991, October). *Evaluation report for presentation skills: Final report for Dow Chemical USA*. Memphis, TN: Memphis State University.

Mullin, J. A. (1998). Portfolios: Purposeful collections of student work. In R. S. Anderson & B. W. Speck (Eds.), *Changing the way we grade student performance: Classroom assessment and the new learning paradigm* (pp. 79–88). San Francisco: Jossey-Bass.

Osterlind, S. (2006). *Modern measurement: Theory, principles, and applications of mental appraisal*. Upper Saddle River, NJ: Pearson Education.

Schmidt, H. G., Loyens, S. M. M., van Gog, T., & Paas, F. (2007). *Educational Psychologist, 41*(2), 91–97.

Shepard, L. A. (2001). The role of assessment in a learning culture. *Educational Researcher, 29*(7), 4–14.

Shrock, S. A., & Coscarelli, W. C. (2007). *Criterion-referenced test development: technical and legal guidelines for corporate training, 3rd edition*. San Franscisco: Pfeiffer Publishing.

# Using Evaluation to Enhance Programs: Conducting Formative and Summative Evaluations

## GETTING STARTED

You receive a contract from a software firm to evaluate a series of computer-based instructional units for teaching high school geometry. The units are still in draft stage, with the expectation that they can be revised based on the results of the evaluation. Using the eight-step model (see Figure 13-1), you determine the purposes of the evaluation, conduct an analysis of the audience, identify issues (questions and objectives), determine available resources, identify the evidence that will be needed, specify and implement data-gathering techniques, conduct the data analysis, and write and present reports of the findings. To address the main interests of the stakeholders (i.e., the software developers), you decide to employ small-group trials in which students work through the materials, give "think-aloud" reactions and other feedback, and take unit achievement tests. You also use two SMEs, three high school geometry teachers, and one CBI design expert to give impressions of the accuracy and quality of the content and user interface. Based on qualitative and quantitative analyses of the multiple data sources, you prepare a report detailing results and making specific recommendations for improving various parts of the units. One of the managers in the software firm criticizes your evaluation for "failing to prove whether the units actually increase learning." She further wants to know why you didn't use a control group. How would you respond to the manager's concern?

# QUESTIONS TO CONSIDER

"At what stage of instructional development does formative evaluation begin?"

"How can formative evaluation results be used to improve instruction?"

"How can an instructional designer provide evidence that systematic instructional planning does pay off?"

"What is the actual cost of an instructional program?"

"How can a training program be valuable if it doesn't directly produce income for the company?"

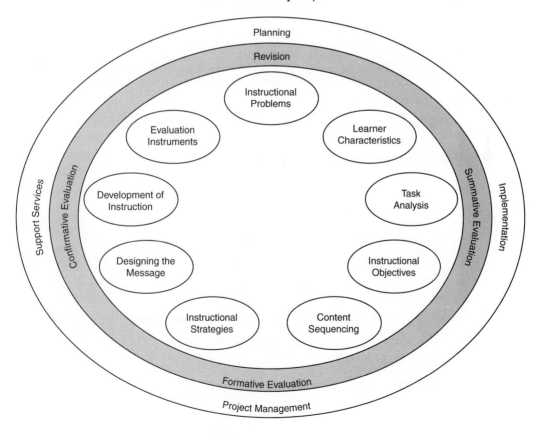

In Chapter 11, we differentiated between the three broad categories of evaluation—formative, summative, and confirmative—used by instructional designers. Now that you have a better understanding of the functions of evaluation as well as instrument construction, we turn to the procedures for conducting each type of evaluation.

## A BASIC MODEL FOR FORMATIVE EVALUATION

Formative evaluations are used to provide feedback to designers for making course improvements (Sterbinsky & Ross, 2005). These evaluations take place as instruction is "forming," and thus they precede the development of the final version of the instructional unit or course. As is true for the design of instructional material, formative evaluations must be carefully planned to be effective. To help structure the evaluation planning, Gooler (1980) suggests the eight-step approach summarized in Figure 13-1. Each of the steps is examined next.

### Purposes

The first step in conducting the evaluation is to determine its purposes: Are the purposes to improve the materials, determine time requirements, or satisfy administrative requirements of the corporation or institution? Perhaps the most important question is whether an evaluation is really needed. Suppose, for example, that you are asked to evaluate a multimedia unit on basic electricity. After questioning the

**FIGURE 13-1**
Steps in planning formative evaluations

- **Purpose**
  Why is the evaluation being conducted?
- **Audience**
  Who are the target recipients of the evaluation results?
- **Issues**
  What are the major questions/objectives of the evaluation?
- **Resources**
  What resources will be needed to conduct the evaluation?
- **Evidence**
  What type of data or information will be needed to answer the evaluation questions?
- **Data-gathering Techniques**
  What methods are needed to collect the evidence needed?
- **Analysis**
  How will the evidence collected be analyzed?
- **Reporting**
  How, to whom, and when will the results of the evaluation be reported?

Adapted from D. D. Gooler (1980), "Formative Evaluation Strategies for Major Instructional Development Projects," *Journal of Instructional Development, 3,* 7–11 course administrators, you discover that the unit cannot be changed without the software being rewritten. You further determine that there are no available funds to pay for new programming. Although there still may be good reasons for doing a formative evaluation, you certainly seem justified in questioning its purpose at the front end. That is, if the evaluation results cannot be used to make changes, is this really the best time for an evaluation?

The purposes of the evaluation are usually defined through consultation between the evaluator and the stakeholders of the course or program. As the name implies, stakeholders are individuals who have a "stake," or vested interest, in the instruction. They might include company or school administrators, course vendors, training professionals, and/or teachers or trainers.

## Audience

An additional part of the initial planning is to determine the intended audience(s) for the evaluation results. Will they be managers, teachers, course developers, or a combination of several groups? Depending on who the primary audience is, different types of information will probably be collected and reported. Clearly, instructors will be better able to use evaluation results dealing with the delivery of instructional material than results on the readability of the study guide; the study guide author, however, would have the opposite need. The key target audience(s) will usually be identified in the initial discussions with key stakeholders.

## Issues

As is the case for designing instruction, specifying objectives provides the foundation for the evaluation process. Now that you know the overall purposes of the evaluation (step 1) and the primary audience (step 2), what specific questions need to be answered? Is there an interest in student attitudes, learning gains, or the quality of certain materials? Once defined, the evaluation objectives determine what information sources (i.e., data collection instruments) and analyses are needed to answer the questions of interest. Evaluation objectives may be written as questions or statements. Examples using the question structure are as follows:

- After receiving the instruction, can students correctly enter the data into the spreadsheet?
- Which exercises in the recycling unit do students find most understandable and least understandable?
- Do students perceive the diagrams to be helpful?
- On average, how long does each practice unit take to complete?
- Do SMEs regard the instructional material as accurate and well designed?

If a statement format is preferred, the first two examples might be rewritten as follows:

- To determine students' accuracy, following the instructions, in entering the data into the spreadsheet

- To identify the exercises in the recycling unit that students find most understandable and least understandable

## Resources

Given the evaluation objectives (step 3), what resources are needed to address each? In the previous example, objective 1 implies the need for students to be tested, the need for computers and spreadsheets for the students to use during testing, and the need for keyboarding test(s) for measuring the degree of change from pre- to postinstruction. Objective 2 also involves gathering data from students, but this time using a survey or interview to determine the exercises they most and least prefer. The resources needed therefore differ from objective to objective. Common types of resources include these:

- Trainees/students
- SMEs
- Instructors
- Data collection and analysis instruments
- Copies of materials
- Physical facilities and equipment

## Evidence

In conjunction with identifying resources, careful consideration must be given to the types of evidence that will be acceptable for addressing the evaluation objectives. For objective 1 in our example, we obviously want to obtain keyboarding scores, but will scores from, say, five students on one test suffice, or will additional students and/or multiple testings be required? For objective 2, thought must be given to the type of student reporting (in reacting to the exercises) that will be most valid and informative. We might be skeptical, for example, about the validity of impressions conveyed in an interview immediately following a difficult final exam. In deciding what will constitute acceptable evidence, the evaluator and the stakeholders may want to consider these points:

- Sample size
- Objectivity of the information sources
- Realism of the testing context
- Degree of control in the testing context
- Need for formal statistical reporting
- Reliability/validity of SME reviews

## Data-Gathering Techniques

This step involves making final decisions about the instrumentation and data collection methods to be employed. Two key, and often opposing, factors need to be weighed: precise measurement versus feasible or practical measurement. For example, in planning a formative evaluation of a carpentry training program, the designer initially elects to rate actual projects that students complete on the job. But once the practical problems of identifying and validly assessing actual projects are considered, it is decided instead to employ a controlled assessment, specifically, a cabinet door of a specified design and size completed at the training site. Similarly, to reduce time and cost, planned interviews with 30 students may be reduced to include only 10 students. Or perhaps the designer may substitute an interview for a questionnaire when he or she considers that the former provides opportunities to probe for more in-depth explanations but is more time consuming.

The data-gathering techniques available were discussed in the two previous chapters. They include performance tests, written tests, observations, ratings, questionnaires, interviews, portfolios, and exhibitions. At this stage, the designer should consider the advantages and limitations of each type for addressing the evaluation objectives as well as the resources necessary for each. In Chapters 11 and 12, we recommended the use of multiple measures to increase validity (through the triangulation of findings across measures) and the provision of as much relevant information as feasible. Cognitive and constructivist paradigms have increased awareness about obtaining data regarding learning processes as well as products (Kay & Knaack, 2009; Ross & Morrison, 1995). By knowing about processes—how instructional material is used—designers are in a better position to interpret products (i.e., outcomes) and thereby improve the material.

## Analysis

Once the data are collected, the next step is analyzing the results. If the term *analysis* conjures up thoughts of complex statistics and formulas, reflect again on the main purpose of formative evaluation. It is to provide usable information for designers to improve instruction. Although the need for complex analyses should not be ruled out, the questions of interest are often best addressed by straightforward and fairly simple descriptive analyses. These types of analyses generally tell us how students performed on or reacted to a particular lesson. Typical analysis procedures include the following. Note that the first three are quantitative (i.e., involve numerical indices), and the fourth is qualitative (i.e., involves impressions); both types of analyses are discussed later.

- Frequency distributions
- Frequency graphs or histograms
- Descriptive statistics, such as percentages, means, and medians
- Listing of actual comments made by respondents

Figure 13-2 shows a frequency distribution and descriptive statistics for a class on a unit achievement test (maximum score = 100%). Note that the "bars" on the graph represent the number (i.e., frequency) of scores obtained within 10-point intervals (20–29, 30–39, etc.). From the distribution, it is clear that performances were quite spread out (range = 75) and also somewhat low for many students

**FIGURE 13-2**
Histogram of test score

| Mean: | Std. Dev: | Std. Error: |
|---|---|---|
| 68.077 | 22.765 | 4.465 |

| Minimum: | Maximum: | Range: |
|---|---|---|
| 23 | 98 | 75 |

(mean = 68.1). Although it is possible that these are desirable performances for this unit (i.e., it may be very difficult material), chances are, the designer will not be satisfied and will conclude that the instruction needs to be revised.

In many cases, an introductory-level knowledge of statistics will suffice for completing the data analysis. If more complex analyses are required, the designer can always seek assistance from a statistical consultant. Although traditional views of data analyses denote graphs, tables, numbers, and probability values, today's educational evaluators may find that they depend just as much (or more) on qualitative analyses. These types of analyses involve categorizing, interpreting, and, in general, "making sense" out of subjective data such as observations of instruction or student learning, interview responses, and open-ended survey responses. Qualitative researchers who are collecting data for scientific study and intended wide-scale dissemination of results will want to invest considerable effort into ensuring high reliability in their methods, inferences, and conclusions. Consequently, the thorough and systematic procedures for qualitative data analysis recommended by such authors as Miles and Huberman (1994) should be followed. The qualitative evaluator of instruction will also want to ensure valid conclusions, but may, because of time constraints and project needs, use a more practical, less rigorous approach. Key strategies should include the following:

- Reviewing notes and transcripts to extract major categories or themes (e.g., "The most common concerns about the training unit were inadequate length, poor readability of materials, and lack of relevance of the unit on reflective listening.")
- Providing a sense of the saliency or importance of the themes (e.g., "The inadequate length of the training was a critical weakness, as conveyed by the majority of trainees; only several, however, were concerned about the readability of materials.")
- Conducting "member checking" by having respondents review and validate, where feasible, your description and interpretation of what they said
- Providing tables that present typical responses or a complete listing so that stakeholders in the instructional design might review them
- Having more than one person participate in the data analysis so that reliability can be checked and increased by consensual agreement

## Reporting

The evaluation effort will generally be of little value unless the results are disseminated to individuals involved in the instructional unit or course (e.g., instructors, administrators, or designers). The most common means is the evaluation report. There is no single, standard reporting format; in fact, the best strategy is to adapt the report to the primary target audience with regard to content and style of writing. A "typical" report, however, is likely to include most or all of the following sections:

    I. Executive summary (abstract)
   II. Purposes of evaluation
      A. Evaluation objectives
      B. Description of target course/unit
  III. Methodology
      A. Participants
      B. Instruments
  IV. Results
      A. Analyses
      B. Findings
   V. Conclusions and recommendations

A second common dissemination approach is oral reporting. Depending on the context, such reports may be formal presentations, group meetings, or one-to-one discussions. Keep in mind that, whatever the form of reporting, the overall goal of formative evaluation is to recommend and make changes (as suggested by the results) to improve instruction. Formative evaluation results are unique to the particular project and thus will have limited generalizability to projects outside the same educational context or curriculum.

## TYPES OF FORMATIVE EVALUATION

As just described, the initial planning clarifies the purpose(s) of the evaluation and the target audience(s) for receiving the evaluation results (e.g., the design team, funders, potential clients, etc.). These decisions then dictate the evaluation approach that is most appropriate for the particular project. According to Flagg (1990), the most commonly used evaluation approaches can be classified into four categories: connoisseur-based, decision-oriented, objectives-based, and public-relations-inspired studies.

### Connoisseur-Based Studies

A connoisseur-based study employs SMEs and other appropriate consultants (e.g., media and design experts) to examine the instruction and give opinions regarding its accuracy and effectiveness. An important part of the expert's report is any recommendation for revising the instruction where improvements are needed. Expert review can be useful at all stages of the design process, from initial drafts of instructional material to the completed versions.

In using expert review, the experts are assumed to be competent and interested in the evaluation task. Important tasks for the designer are to determine the number and types of experts needed, the particular individuals who will fill these slots, and the best time(s) in the evaluation process to involve each. Expert review can provide valuable information for refining instruction. However, an important limitation of connoisseur-based studies is that so much depends on the biases and experiences of the selected experts. Remember, experts in a subject area are not necessarily knowledgeable about instruction and learning. Therefore, it is not advisable to blindly follow a recommendation that you question without seeking other opinions or data sources. In educational research, this type of verification process is called triangulation, the procedure of cross-validating a finding by using multiple information sources.

Consider this example: After reviewing a CBI lesson, a media expert suggests that children will not know which keys to press in selecting different branching options. A field test of the program reveals, however, that this problem does not occur—the children actually make very few errors. The implication: Keep the expert's concern in mind, but do not make changes in the screen design without further evidence.

It is also important that the expert is willing and able to provide accurate and objective feedback. In this regard, consider the situation described in the Expert's Edge section.

Expert's Edge

## Never Let a Fox Guard the Henhouse Even If He Claims to Be a Vegetarian

The workshop had been designed by a well-known training organization and followed a systematic product realization process. The process included several "gates," each of which specified a formative evaluation requirement. Early gates required reviews by SMEs, clients, and instructional designers, whereas the penultimate gate required a formal field trial. By all accounts, the workshop passed each gate with flying colors. The problem was, however, that participants' feedback on the workshop was not as positive as the client had hoped, and the work products participants created as a result of the workshop lacked the connection to business results the client had intended. Further investigation revealed that the formative evaluation process, although it had been followed to some extent, had been co-opted. In the interest of meeting the target dates in the project plan, "friendly" SMEs and client representatives had been selected for the reviews, and the instructional design review had been done by the project manager. Furthermore, the field trial was actually a run-through of workshop materials not before representative members of the target audience but before a small group of colleagues of the project manager. Conversations with those involved in the development of the workshop showed no malicious intent; as a matter of fact, there was no real conscious awareness that the process had been subverted. Eventually, the workshop was redesigned following a more stringent process. But considerable damage had been done, and because of the rework required, the financial cost was significant. Reputations were sullied, client trust was weakened, work was reassigned, and jobs were lost.

Formative evaluation can take many forms, and it can follow varying degrees of formality. Despite immediate pressures to the contrary, formative evaluation need not be incompatible with speed or staying within the budget. But formative evaluation is a *sine qua non* of our profession, and ultimately we bear the responsibility to our clients and to ourselves to conduct these activities with rigor and discipline. Here are some actions you might take in this regard:

- Build the time and cost of formative evaluation into your project plans. Make sure your clients and management understand in their own terms the value of formative evaluation.
- Design formative evaluations so that subversion is unlikely—use outside evaluators and employ audits or evaluation panels, for example.
- Develop and strive to maintain a set of personal standards by which your work can be known.
- Create an atmosphere where the truth can be told.
- Walk away from projects where your standards cannot be upheld.

Robert Bowman is an instructional development and evaluation manager in the Lucent Technologies Learning and Performance Center. His current assignment focuses on assessing the impact of leadership development programs and converting leadership development programs to technology-based systems. His work has included a broad range of needs assessment, instructional development, and evaluation assignments.

## Decision-Oriented Studies

Decision-oriented studies are designed to provide information related to particular questions about the instruction. Example concerns might include these:

- Does the lesson require too much time to complete?
- Is the amount of practice examples adequate?
- Are prerequisite math skills required?
- Should a student study guide be developed?

Given these questions, the evaluator then designs specific measures and procedures to address each. Decision-making evaluations are naturally most valuable when program changes are still feasible and economical. Good communication between the evaluator and the program stakeholders is essential to define the relevant questions around which the decision making will be based. The limitation of decision-making studies is that their results are usually descriptive, not prescriptive. That is, they tell us how the instruction is working but not what to do to make it better.

## Objectives-Based Studies

A third category of formative evaluation approaches involves investigating how well the instructional program is achieving its objectives. The basic methodology therefore resembles that employed in summative and confirmative evaluations (discussed later in this chapter) by assessing the amount of progress students have realized from completing the instruction. Summative and confirmative evaluations, however, use such information to judge the effectiveness of the program immediately (summative) and over time (confirmative). Objectives-based studies are an appropriate choice for evaluating a project such as a distance education course to determine whether it is effective. Formative evaluation uses them as a basis for improving the instruction where outcomes fall short of goals.

Objectives-based studies frequently employ pretest–posttest designs that measure gains on measures of achievement and attitude. Their main limitation is the same one noted earlier for decision-making studies: The findings by themselves provide limited direction for making improvements. For that reason, it may make sense to combine expert opinion (i.e., connoisseur-based study) with the objectives-based results.

## Public Relations-Inspired Studies

By making evaluation results known to targeted individuals, public-relations-inspired studies are used to solicit financial support or backing for a project. An example comes from one of the authors' recent experiences in trying to obtain funding from a private foundation to support an elementary school reading program. By conducting a formative evaluation of a pilot version of the program, he was able to present preliminary data that convinced the foundation representatives of the program's potential. The result was a foundation grant to expand both the program and the evaluation the next year.

These four categories should be viewed as complementary rather than exclusive. Most studies will employ combinations of two or more of these orientations, depending on the evaluation objectives. For example, in evaluating a new mathematics program for lower-achieving children, the designers might (1) employ experts to review the instructional materials (category 1), (2) administer surveys and use observation techniques to answer questions about the implementation (category 2), (3) administer achievement pretests and posttests to assess the level of reading improvement demonstrated by student participants (category 3), and (4) publicize the latter results to obtain additional funding for the program (category 4).

## Constructivist-Oriented Process

Are traditional formative evaluation approaches too limited and behaviorally oriented to assess contemporary Web-based instructional tools? Kay and Knaack (2009) raise this concern for evaluating what they generically label "leaning objects." Such support tools, which encompass help-systems prompting, hierarchical navigation aids, program-generated questions, graphics, and animations, are not designed to simply increase the amount of content remembered (Friesen & Anderson, 2004; Krauss & Ally, 2005; Nurmi & Jaakkola, 2006) but to engage students in higher-order learning and problem solving. The formative (and summative) evaluation model they propose uses a combination of the connoisseur-based and decision-oriented approaches to obtain *valid* triangulated data addressing the three factors of *learning construct* (e.g., interactivity, feedback, graphics, etc.), *quality* of the instruction (e.g., help supports, instructions, organization, etc.), and *engagement* (e.g., interest, motivational, enjoyment, etc.). Data sources are students participating in field trials who complete a survey, make open-ended comments, and complete pretests and posttests on the content of the instruction. Teachers, in turn, implement the field trial while answering questions on the degree of student learning, instructional quality, and student engagement.

This multifaceted model differs from traditional formative evaluation designs by examining broader, constructivist properties of the instruction. Depending on preferred theoretical and operational preferences of the designer, this approach may be considered as a useful paradigm for the increasing design work being performed to accommodate open-ended and Web-based learning environments (e.g., Clarebout & Elen, 2008; Saab, Gijlers, Van Joolingen, & van Hout-Wolters, 2008).

## STAGES OF FORMATIVE EVALUATION

At this point, we have presented general approaches and a specific procedural model (see Figure 13-1) for conducting formative evaluations. A remaining question may be how formative evaluation methods might vary at different stages of the design process. Dick and Carey (1991) addressed this issue in their three-stage model (see Table 13-1).

**TABLE 13-1**
Stages of formative evaluation

| Stage | Instruction Phase | Purpose | Learners | Main Measures |
|---|---|---|---|---|
| One-to-one trials | Development | Try-out impressions | Individuals | Observation, survey, interview |
| Small-group trials | Preliminary/draft version | Identify strengths/weaknesses | Small groups (8–20) | Observation, attitudes, performance |
| Field trials | Completed | Assess actual implementation | Regular classes | Performance, attitudes |

The first stage, occurring toward the beginning of the process and usually repeated several times, consists of one-to-one trials, or developmental testing (Thiagarjan, Semmel, & Semmel, 1974) in which the designer "tries out" the instruction with individual learners (Brenneman, 1989). The goal is to obtain descriptive information pertaining to the clarity, impact, and feasibility of initial versions of the instruction.

The second stage consists of small-group trials in which a more developed version of the instruction is used with a group of between 8 and 25 individuals. Through observational, attitudinal, and performance data, the evaluator attempts to identify strengths and weaknesses in the instruction before it is put into a "final" form.

The third stage is the field trial, which examines the use of the instruction with a full-sized learner group under realistic conditions. Based on the results from various outcome measures, the instructor would make final revisions and deliver the completed instruction to actual classes. But at this point, the need for evaluation is not over. Summative and confirmative evaluations are then required to determine whether the instructional program is achieving its goals.

## SUMMATIVE EVALUATION: DETERMINING PROGRAM OUTCOMES

Too often an instructional designer or an instructor may intuitively be convinced that what is being accomplished is worthwhile and successful. It is often assumed by persons in education and training that the merits of a program are obvious to other persons in the institution or organization. Unfortunately, rarely is either of these conclusions true.

A summative evaluation permits a designer or instructor to reach unbiased, objective answers to evaluation questions concerning expected program outcomes and then to decide whether the program is achieving those outcomes. With this evidence, the designer's intuition can be supported or rejected, and he or she has the facts for correctly informing others about the program results. The following important issues can be examined through summative evaluation procedures:

- Effectiveness of learner or trainee learning
- Efficiency of learner or trainee learning

- Cost of program development and continuing expenses in relation to effectiveness and efficiency
- Attitudes and reactions to the program by learners, faculty, and staff
- Long-term benefits of the instructional program

In this section, we examine methods for gathering data that can lead to a conclusion for each of the five issues stated earlier. Attention to these matters may be essential in proving the value of a new instructional program and then ensuring its continued support.

A summative evaluation of a course or program is more than a one-time activity. Immediately after each course or training program is concluded, the instructor should utilize some or all of the assessment methods described subsequently. By accumulating summative data, continuing positive trends in a program can be tracked over time, or deficiencies can be noted as they show up and corrections made immediately (Ross, 2005).

## Evaluation Versus Research

One way of measuring the value of a new program is to compare its results with those of a conventionally conducted course in the same subject. Most often this comparison cannot be made fairly because the two courses were planned to achieve entirely different objectives. It is very likely that there are no stated, measurable objectives for the conventional course that can be used as a basis for the comparison. Also, the subject matter treated in the two programs may be significantly different, with the content of the conventional course often being limited to a lower-level cognitive domain than that of the new program.

In some situations, evaluation is performed by using a formal research framework. This means that a carefully designed comparison study is based on control and experimental groups or classes. One or more hypotheses are stated as anticipated outcomes. Then, after instruction takes place, statistical methods are employed to gather data and report the evidence collected about learning outcomes. Conclusions are drawn that support or reject the initial hypotheses.

Such a methodology is usually more appropriate in basic or applied research studies that permit control over extraneous variables and allow for the establishment of reasonably equivalent experimental and control groups. Most instructional design projects are not planned to result in broadly applicable theories. Their purpose is to find out how well the needs that have been identified can be met. Growth in learner knowledge or skill activity, as measured by the difference between pretest and posttest results or by observing behavior before and after instruction, provides evidence of learning that can be directly attributable to the instructional program.

Sometimes the success in learning can be shown only in following up on-the-job work being done by individuals after instruction. For example, if after employees complete a safety course, accidents involving those employees are appreciably reduced (say, by more than 30%), then it can be inferred that the training was successful. Or, if company operating expenses decrease and revenues increase from the pretraining to the posttraining period, then one could infer that direct benefits are a result of the training. On the other hand, when results do not meet goals, the evaluation evidence would indicate the shortcomings. Steps can then be taken to improve the program before its next use.

Thus, for evaluating instructional design projects, it is not necessary to perform formal research involving control/experimental groups and a detailed statistical analysis. All that must be done is to gather evidence relative to accomplishments or change from preinstruction to postinstruction for as many of the five components (i.e., effectiveness, efficiency, costs, attitudes, and benefits) as are considered important for that course, then interpret the information to reach conclusions about the success or failure of the instructional program.

A special note: For some of the procedures considered here, it is advisable (or even essential) to start collecting data at the time the program is initially planned. By doing this, you will have the necessary information to determine costs, time, and other facts pertinent to the evaluation.

## PROGRAM EFFECTIVENESS

Effectiveness answers the question, "To what degree did students accomplish the learning objectives prescribed for each unit of the course?" Measurement of effectiveness can be ascertained from test scores, ratings of projects and performance, and records of observations of learners' behavior.

An analysis of scores can be prepared by hand or using a computer statistical package. The data may show the change from pretest to posttest results. Then, a summary may be presented in tabular form, as shown in Figure 13-3. The figure illustrates that the group, composed of six learners, accomplished 90% of the objectives. This figure is calculated by totaling the number of objectives satisfied (represented by the X marks in section c) and dividing by 6, which is the number of learners. The average number of objectives accomplished per learner is 4.5, which is 90% of the objectives. This result can be interpreted as a measure of the effectiveness of the instructional design plan for this group of learners. The percentage may be considered an effectiveness index representing the percentage of learners reaching a preset level of mastery (i.e., satisfying each objective) and the average percentage of objectives satisfied by all learners.

If all learners were to accomplish all objectives, the effectiveness of the program would be excellent. If 90% of the learners accomplish 90% of the objectives, can you report that the program has been effective? To answer this question, the instructor, along with the administrator or training director, must have previously decided the level at which the program would be accepted as effective. For a systematically planned academic course, attainment of the 80% level by at least 80% of the learners in a class could be acceptable as a highly effective program. In a vocational or skill area, 90–90 (90% of the trainees accomplishing 90% of the objectives) might be the accepted success level. Similar courses (e.g., in biology or electronics assembly) can be compared with respect to effectiveness indices and conclusions drawn for judging program effectiveness. Realistically, it is very likely

**FIGURE 13-3**
A sample analysis of test questions measuring cognitive objectives

a.

| Unit Objectives | Test Questions |
|---|---|
| A | 2, 4, 11 |
| B | 1, 7 |
| C | 3, 5, 12 |
| D | 8, 10 |
| E | 5, 9 |

b.

| Learner | Correct Answers to Questions |
|---|---|

| Learner | 1 | 2 | 3 | 4 | 5 | 6 | 7 | 8 | 9 | 10 | 11 | 12 |
|---|---|---|---|---|---|---|---|---|---|---|---|---|
| AJ | x | x | x | x |   | x | x | x | x | x | x |   |
| SF | x | x | x | x | x | x |   | x |   |   |   |   |
| TY | x | x | x | x | x | x | x | x | x | x | x |   |
| LM | x | x | x | x | x | x | x | x | x | x | x |   |
| RW | x | x | x | x | x | x | x | x | x | x | x |   |
| WB | x |   | x | x | x | x | x |   | x | x |   | x |

c.

| Learner | A | B | C | D | E |
|---|---|---|---|---|---|
| | Objectives Satisfied | | | | |
| AJ | x | x | x | x |   |
| SF |   | x | x | x | x |
| TY | x | x | x | x | x |
| LM | x | x | x | x | x |
| RW | x | x | x | x | x |
| WB |   | x | x | x | x |

that, because of individual differences among learners and a designer's inability to design ideal learning experiences, no one can hope to reach the absolute standard of mastery or competency—100%—in all instructional situations. (Some training programs for which life and safety are critical—medical or airline pilot training, for instance—may require a 100% level of mastery.)

Then another question must be asked. Assume that your own performance standard requires all learners to accomplish 85% of the objectives but that as a group they actually satisfy 82% of them. Is the effort to reach the 85% level worth the cost? If not, you may have to settle for a somewhat lower level of accomplishment until someone can design a revision of the program that will enable reaching the desired level of performance with reasonable effort and cost. When evaluating the effectiveness of an instructional program, a designer must recognize that there may be intangible outcomes (often expressed as affective objectives) and long-term consequences that would become apparent only after the program is concluded and learners are at work. Both of these matters are given attention in the following sections as part of other summative evaluation components. Here, the evaluation of effectiveness is limited to those learning objectives that can be immediately measured.

## Summative Evaluation Methods

The basic procedures for determining program effectiveness in summative evaluations are similar to those described earlier for formative evaluations (see Figure 13-1). Specifically, the major steps are these:

1. Specifying program objectives
2. Determining the evaluation design for each objective
   a. Pretest–posttest with one group
   b. One-group descriptive
   c. Experimental-control group
   d. Analysis of costs, resources, implementation
3. Developing data collection instruments and procedures for each objective
   a. Questionnaires
   b. Interviews
   c. Observations
   d. Achievement tests
4. Carrying out the evaluation
   a. Scheduling the data collection
   b. Collecting the data
5. Analyzing the results from each instrument
6. Interpreting the results
7. Disseminating the results and conclusions
   a. Evaluation report
   b. Group meetings
   c. Individual discussions

**Data Collection Instruments.**   As with formative evaluations, data collection addresses one or more of the three domains of skills/behavior, cognitive, and affective. The main difference in summative evaluation is judging a completed rather than developing program.

For assessing skills, key information sources (as in formative evaluations) are as follows:

- Direct testing
- Analysis of naturally occurring events
- Direct/indirect observations
- Portfolios
- Exhibitions

For assessing cognition, measurement options include objective tests (e.g., multiple choice, true/false, matching) and constructed-response tests (e.g., short answer, essay, and problem solving).

Assessments of affective outcomes entail gathering reactions from both learners and the instructional staff as they look back on the program just completed.

**FIGURE 13-4**
Types of questions for gathering subjective responses

---

**Checklist**
Check each word that tells how you feel about the group projects and oral presentations used in this course.

| | | |
|---|---|---|
| _____Interesting | _____Informative | _____Difficult |
| _____Dull | _____Practical | _____Important |
| _____Exciting | _____Worthless | _____Stimulating |
| _____Boring | _____Useful | _____Unpleasant |

**Rating Scale**
Compared with a typical lecture class, how useful was the format used in this experimental class for learning the course material? (Check one response.)

_____Better          _____About the same          _____Not as good

Now that you have completed the course, rate your feelings about history as a subject. (Circle the number that best reflects your reaction.)

| Dislike very much | Dislike somewhat | Neutral | Like somewhat | Like very much |
|---|---|---|---|---|
| 1 | 2 | 3 | 4 | 5 |

**Rating**
Please rank these topics as treated in the management course. Consider their value to you and your job. (Start with number 1 as the topic having the highest value.)

| | |
|---|---|
| _____Planning | _____Organization and management |
| _____Self-assessment | _____Development |
| _____Stress | _____Personnel management |
| _____Labor relations | _____Performance appraisal |
| _____Effective presentations | _____Internal affairs management |
| _____Budgeting | _____Media relations |
| _____State-of-the-art technology | |

**Open-Ended Questions**
What is your general reaction to this course: the objectives treated, the way it was conducted, your participation, its overall value to you, and so on?

---

Three categories of reactions may be given attention:

- **Opinions**: Judgments about the level of acceptance of course content, instructional methods, assistance from and relations with instructor and staff, study or work time required, grading procedure, and so forth
- **Interest**: Responses to the value of topics treated, learning activities preferred, and motivation for further study or work in the subject area
- **Attitude**: Reactions to the total program in terms of degree of its being pleasurable, worthwhile, and useful. Examples of types of questions for gathering subjective reactions are shown in Figure 13-4.

# PROGRAM EFFICIENCY

In evaluating efficiency, three aspects of a program require attention:

- Time required for learners to achieve unit objectives

- Number of instructors and support staff members required for instruction and the time they devote to the program
- Use of facilities assigned to the program

### Learner Time Required

Educational programs are designed typically in terms of available time periods—semesters, quarters, or other fixed time intervals (e.g., week, weekend, etc.). It is only when some flexibility is permitted that efficiency can be measured. If, for example, a conventional training program can be reduced from a period of possibly six to five weeks with the same or increased effectiveness in learning, the program can be considered efficient.

Efficiency can be used for measuring outcomes primarily of programs that give major emphasis to individualized or self-paced learning activities. From the learner's standpoint, the time required to satisfy unit or program objectives would be a measure of efficiency. Mathematically, this measurement is the ratio of the number of objectives a learner achieves compared with the time the learner takes to achieve them. Learners can be asked to keep records of time spent studying a unit or set of objectives (i.e., a time log). Or, in a more subjective fashion, an instructor can observe and make notations to indicate the number of learners at work in a study area during time periods.

For example, Mary satisfies seven objectives in 4.2 hours of study and work. Dividing the number of objectives Mary achieves by the amount of time it takes her to accomplish them yields her efficiency index, 1.7 (7/4.2). Bill achieves the seven objectives in 5.4 hours. His efficiency index is therefore 1.3. Thus, the higher the index, the more efficient the learning. Such an index can be calculated for each unit then averaged for each learner to give an efficiency index for the course. Keep in mind that many instructional programs will not yield such easily attainable and concrete measures of mastery over time. Also, efficiency indices may not be comparable across different units of instruction because of the nature of the material taught and the characteristics of the students. However, where feasible, an efficiency index or some other quantitative measure can provide highly useful information for evaluating allocations of time and resources. A clear advantage, especially in business contexts, is that quantitative measures often are expected and given more credibility by stakeholders than are subjective types of evidence.

### Faculty and Staff Required

The number of faculty and staff positions required for instruction, supervision, or support of an instructional program also relates to efficiency. The question is, "How many learners are being served by the staff?" If a course requires a half-time faculty position plus the equivalent of one full-time position in assistants and technicians to serve 48 learners, then the faculty-to-learner ratio would be 1:32 (i.e., 1.5:48. If the institution-wide ratio of faculty-to-student load is 1:20, then the lower ratio of 1:32 indicates a more efficient use of faculty and staff personnel. Greater efficiency, however, may not necessarily mean greater effectiveness.

The ratio of 1:32 may be reported on paper, but the actual working time of faculty and staff in the program can give another indication of efficiency. Let's assume that the same instructor and support staff (i.e., the 1.5 positions) are spending 60 hours a week on the program doing preparation, teaching, consulting with learners, evaluating performance, marking tests, providing resources, etc. If normal time devoted to a course is 45 hours per week for a staff of similar size, then the procedures may need some revision.

## Use of Facilities

Another factor of efficiency is the amount of time that learning facilities—classrooms, learning labs, and so forth—are available during a day, a week, or other time period. If a facility is used 12 hours a day, this may be considered an efficient use of space. By obtaining these data as a program is expanded, the need to increase use or to provide for additional training space can be evaluated.

A second component of efficient space utilization is the number of learners using the facility during a time period. When 110 learners are being served in a 15-station microcomputer lab on a weekly basis, this may be seen as an efficient use of space. Keep records so that the time learners and staff spend in the program and in the facility can be calculated and objectively related to this factor of efficiency.

## PROGRAM COSTS

Historically, a major concern in educational programs is the cost of instruction. Expense categories, such as personnel, equipment, and supplies, are established to aid the administration in controlling and reporting about programs. Standard bases that are frequently used for allocating funds in educational budgets are average daily attendance (ADA) in public schools, full-time equivalent (FTE) in higher education (i.e., the total number of courses being taken divided by the number of courses in a full course load), the number of faculty assigned in terms of FTE, and student credit hours or student-to-faculty contact hours. These bases for allocating funds are mainly accounting methods. They provide little information about the real costs of a single program.

Although a school or college is not the same as a business operation, for both, specific factors affecting costs can be identifed and controlled. The education and training literature contains numerous explanations and reports on how program costs can be derived. Formulas that consider many of the variables that affect costs are presented in detail, and their complexities are interpreted. Such terms as *cost effectiveness, cost efficiency,* and *cost benefits* are frequently used. Our concern here is simply to answer the question, "What does it cost to develop and operate a specific program for the number of learners served?" Once we have this essential information, we are able to relate costs to effectiveness, efficiency, and resulting benefits; thus, we are able to judge the acceptability of program costs. Any new course or a program being revised requires attention to the two major categories of costs: developmental and operational costs.

## Developmental Costs

As an instructional project is being planned and developed, some or all of the following costs, sometimes called start-up costs, may be incurred:

- Planning time: Amount of salary paid out for time spent by each member of the planning team on the project, calculated from the percentage of total work hours spent on it or the number of hours spent by each member multiplied by his or her hourly or monthly salary rate, plus fees for consultants
- Staff time: Amount of salary paid for time spent by each member engaged in planning, producing, and gathering materials, calculated from the percentage of total work hours spent on it or the number of hours spent by each person, multiplied by his or her hourly salary rate
- Supplies and materials for preparing print, media, and other materials
- Outside services for producing or purchasing materials
- Construction or renovation of facilities
- Equipment purchased for instructional uses
- Expenses for installing equipment
- Testing, redesign, and final reproduction of resources in sufficient quantity for operational uses (includes personnel time and costs of materials and services)
- Orientation and training of personnel who will conduct instruction
- Indirect costs: Personnel benefits such as retirement and insurance, related to time and salary charged to the project (this information is typically available from the personnel department)
- Overhead: Utilities, furniture, room and building costs or depreciation allowance, proportion of other institutional services charged to the project (this information is usually available from the business manager or the controller of the organization)
- Miscellaneous (e.g., office supplies, telephone, travel, etc.)

Here is an example of the developmental costs for a general education college-level course involving two instructors. It includes large-group presentations incorporating PowerPoint presentations, student self-directed learning with 10 interactive multimedia units, a study guide, and small discussion sessions.

*Design Time*

| | |
|---|---|
| 2 instructors, 1 month summer | $16,500 |
| Instructional designer, 1 month summer | $9,500 |
| Graduate assistant, 100 hours | $2,500 |
| | $28,500 |

*Development Time*

| | |
|---|---|
| 2 instructors, 0.25 time, 1 semester | $22,000 |
| Instructional designer, 0.25 time, 1 semester | $14,250 |
| Programming | $22,000 |
| Graphic artist, 80 hours | $3,500 |
| | $59,750 |

*Materials and Supplies*

| | |
|---|---|
| Office supplies | $250 |

*Equipment*

| | |
|---|---|
| 20 computers for lab | $24,000 |

*Renovative Facility*

| | |
|---|---|
| 20 learning stations | $16,000 |
| Electrical wiring | $9,000 |
| | $25,000 |

*Other Costs*

| | |
|---|---|
| Formative evaluation and revision costs | $12,000 |
| Staff benefits | $14,600 |
| | $26,600 |
| **Total Development Costs** | **$164,100** |

## Operational Costs

When the project is fully implemented and instruction is taking place, the recurring operational costs include the following:

- Administrative salaries (based on percentage of time devoted to project)
- Faculty salaries for time spent in the program (e.g., contact hours with groups and individual learners, planning activities, evaluating program, revising activities and materials, personnel benefits)
- Learner or trainee costs (applicable in business-oriented training programs: e.g., salary, travel and lodging, income for company reduced while trainee is not on job, or replacement cost of a person substituting for a trainee job)
- Salaries for assistants, maintenance technicians, and others
- Rental charges for classroom or other facilities if offered at an off-campus location

- Replacement of consumable and damaged materials
- Repair and maintenance of equipment
- Depreciation of equipment
- Overhead (e.g., utilities, facilities, furnishings, custodial services, etc.)
- Evaluation and update of materials (i.e., time and materials)

Here is an example of the operational costs for the college-level course shown in the previous example over a one-semester term:

| | |
|---|---:|
| *Salaries* | |
| 2 instructors, 0.25 time | $22,000 |
| Benefits | $5,000 |
| 2 graduate assistants | $22,000 |
| Subtotal | $48,000 |
| Replacements and repairs | $2,500 |
| **Total Operating Costs** | **$50,500** |

## Instructional Cost Index

We cannot attempt to judge whether the costs of an instructional program are acceptable by looking solely at the gross amount expended. If it costs a company $1,000 to manufacture pencils, this sum must be related to the number of pencils made. Then the price per pencil has meaning and can be compared with the price per unit manufactured by other companies. In an instructional program, costs should be related to the number of learners served in the program.

With data available on developmental and operational costs, we can calculate the cost per learner for a program. This is the important bottom-line amount that allows for comparison of costs between programs, leading to the acceptance of expense levels. Cost per learner or trainee may be labeled an instructional cost index. It is determined by the following procedure:

1. Spread the developmental costs over a series of time periods (e.g., 10 training sessions or 5 semesters). This would be the anticipated life of the program before it should require major revisions or cease to be useful. This procedure is known as amortizing the cost.
2. Add together the preceding prorated amount of the developmental costs (for 3 years) and the operational costs for one use period (either a complete training class or an academic semester).
3. Determine the average number of learners known or anticipated to be in the program with each use. Divide the total in step 2 by this number. The result is the cost per learner, or the instructional cost index.

An example of an instructional cost index calculated from the previous example of developmental and operational costs follows:

| | |
|---|---|
| Total operational costs | $50,500 |
| Portion of developmental cost (164,100/6) | $27,350 |
| Total cost per semester | $77,850 |
| Number of learners in program | 340 |
| Instructional cost index (77,850/340) | $228.97 |

(This is the total cost for each learner over one semester.)

If this program continues beyond five semesters (at which time all developmental costs will have been amortized) and the number of learners remains the same, the instructional cost index will then drop to 148.53 (50,500/340). During this period, limited funds are included for minor updates and revision of materials. At the end of five semesters, a reexamination of the program for this course may be advisable. The course then may be continued as is, or new developmental costs—hopefully lower than the original ones—would be required. These would affect the ongoing instructional cost index.

The index number itself has little meaning. Calculations could be made in the same way for traditional program costs in a comparable training or subject area. As previously stated, it is difficult (and usually unfair) to make a comparison between a new program with carefully structured objectives and a traditional program based on generalized objectives. It would seem more appropriate to compare two skill-type training programs, two math classes, or a biology and chemistry course if each one has been systematically planned and implemented. Once an instructional cost index has been calculated, the instructor or designer should ask these questions:

- Is the program cost-effective? This is a subjective decision, but useful information can be obtained by relating the instructional cost index to the level of learning outcomes (e.g., 90% of the learners accomplish 84% of the objectives). If a satisfactory learning level is reached and the instructional cost index seems to be within reason, the program would be considered cost-effective.
- Is the program cost-efficient? Relate the instructional cost index to efficiency factors (time required by learners to complete activities, staff time required for instruction and support, level of facilities' use). If the efficiency index seems acceptable, with a reasonable instructional cost index the program would be cost-efficient.
- Are the costs justified in terms of resulting benefits (cost–benefit analysis)? Relate the instructional cost index to the benefits that a company or other organization derives from personnel who complete the training program. (See the following section for details and discussion of potential benefits resulting from training.) If the benefits are high and costs acceptable, then the answer to this question is yes.

If the outcomes of a program prove to be acceptable but the instructional cost index remains higher than desired, certain steps might be taken to lower the operational cost portion of the index, as follows:

1. Consider the feasibility of including more learners in the program (as in a distance-learning course using television). Perhaps more individuals can be served without reducing the quality of the instruction.
2. Decide whether assistants might replace instructors for certain activities without lowering the effectiveness of the program. This would reduce higher-cost instructor time.
3. Plan to relieve instructors of some learner contact time by developing additional self-paced learning activities for learners.
4. As a last resort, reduce the training time or lower some of the required performance standards. Shorter instructional time would reduce instructor time and thus costs.

An alternative cost index measure is to calculate the index in terms of total contact hours. Thus, a weeklong course for 20 people has 800 total contact hours (40 hours × 20 people).

## CONFIRMATIVE EVALUATION: DETERMINING OUTCOMES OVER TIME

Instructional programs are most often offered for three general reasons:

- To "educate" individuals so that they may participate as informed, cultured, and productive citizens in society
- To prepare individuals for a gainful vocation
- To improve or upgrade competencies of individuals in a specific task or in certain aspects of a job

For each of these reasons, determining the success of an instructional program requires attention to important outcomes beyond the results of written and performance tests given at the end of a unit or a course. Often the accomplishment of major goals or terminal objectives stated for a program can be assessed only some time after instruction is concluded. As emphasized throughout this chapter and the preceding ones, the evaluation of instruction needs to be continuous. In our view, distinguishing between the constructs of formative, summative, and confirmative evaluations is mainly important in considering what the evaluation is likely to emphasize and when in the instructional design and implementation process the evaluation will be conducted. From an operational standpoint (e.g., planning, instrumentation, data collection, and analysis) the three evaluation types are much more similar than they are different. Confirmative evaluation represents a continuation of summative evaluation. Both approaches are designed to judge the effectiveness of instruction: summative soon after instruction is completed and confirmative after some time has passed.

Our practical view of both summative and confirmative evaluation is that rarely will either be used solely to pronounce an instructional program as "working" or "not working" and then conclude. In the real world, there will typically be opportunity to use the results of these evaluations to make improvements in future training. Thus, the important aspects of formative evaluation continue to be employed, and the instructional program regarded as never fully "completed."

Confirmative evaluation may encounter a few hurdles that earlier evaluations do not. After a course is completed, the learners or trainees move to other courses or work at different locations. Observations of them at work or communication with them may require an extra effort. Some important outcomes are in the affective domain. These may be difficult to identify and measure. Responses for evaluation may be needed from other persons (colleagues, supervisors, and others) who may not be understanding or cooperative. Regardless of these obstacles, attempts should be made to follow up on learners after an instructional program has ended. Evidence of follow-up benefits could be the most important summative results to measure.

## Approaches to Confirmative Evaluation

There are two basic types of situation that warrant conducting confirmative evaluation studies. One type is *learner oriented* and concerns the degree to which, as time passes, consumers of the instruction retain the skills and knowledge needed to perform at desired levels. A second type is *context oriented* and concerns the degree to which the instructional product remains effective as conditions (e.g., policies, politics, resources, technological advances) change over time.

**Learner-Oriented Approach.** Several years ago, two of us were hired by a large chemical corporation to evaluate its employee training courses in areas such as communication, public speaking, and interpersonal relations. Although the corporation routinely conducted follow-up evaluations of employee skills and attitudes soon after participants completed the courses, there was strong interest in assessing longer-term impacts. The corporation wondered whether, for example, although the employees might do well on an immediate performance or knowledge test after completing the course on making oral presentations, would they demonstrate the desired skills on the job a year later? If not, the need to strengthen the original course or offer refresher training would be implied. The confirmative evaluation that we conducted involved asking managers, peers, and subordinates to rate former trainees' on-the-job performance on target skills. A second measure was asking the trainees to rate retrospectively the helpfulness of various items of course content and activities for fulfilling their job requirements. From these data, the evaluation study identified course components that were successful for long-term achievement of objectives and those that were not.

Note that the measures employed in this example and in many confirmative evaluations were fairly low-cost and coarse-grained indicators of continued program success. Had the results indicated major weaknesses in these continuing training courses, refinements in the course designs accompanied by a more granular formative evaluation would have been implied.

**Context-Oriented Approach.** But what if the desired objectives of instruction or training change over time? Obviously, a course or unit that was formerly judged effective (in formative and summative evaluations) would no longer be optimum. The fact that learners might retain the skills taught over long periods of time would hardly matter if the skills mastered were no longer the ones desired. A second type of confirmative evaluation examines whether the instruction is achieving objectives following changes in conditions and policies as time passes.

For the most part, the context-oriented confirmative evaluation would use the methodology of summative evaluations. Although stakeholders in the instruction would hope for continued supportive results, the evaluation may uncover that the program's effectiveness has diminished due to changes in

- Learner characteristics
- Curriculum or performance expectations
- Technology
- Budgetary support for the program
- The training need
- Teacher support or preparation for using the program

## Educational Programs

Traditionally, the general, long-term benefits of educational programs are measured through statewide and national standardized tests given to students in public schools, undergraduate and graduate admission examinations for college students, and regional or national opinion surveys conducted at various times. Such tests measure broad, fairly general objectives. One limitation is that gains on these tests may not show up immediately after a new instructional program is implemented. The summative evaluation, therefore, may not indicate success, but a year later, a confirmative evaluation might. A second limitation, which affects both evaluation approaches, is that the objectives measured may be too broad to provide useful information on how well a particular course accomplished its specific instructional objectives. Concerns may also arise about the circumstances under which students prepare for or complete the standardized tests (Haladyna, Nolan, & Haas, 1991).

The long-term outcomes of the objectives of specific courses are frequently not examined or examined only casually. Within the framework of the goals and terminal objectives of a program, the following categories of outcomes might be considered:

- Capabilities in basic skills (e.g., reading, writing, verbal expression, and mathematics) required in following courses
- Knowledge and competencies in a subject as bases for study in subsequent courses
- Proficiencies to carry out job tasks and responsibilities in occupational employment
- Fulfillment of role as good citizen (e.g., law abiding, participating in democratic process, etc.)

As indicated at the beginning of this section, data concerning these outcomes are not easy to obtain. The following methods are commonly used in continuing (i.e., confirmative) evaluations to gather information:

- Completing questionnaires: Ask former students, present instructors, or employers to respond to a questionnaire designed to indicate learners' present proficiencies related to competencies derived from the course or program that is being evaluated (see Figure 12-2).
- Conducting interviews: Meet with former learners, present instructors, or employers to inquire about the present proficiencies of learners as related to competencies from the course or program being evaluated.
- Making observations: Observe learners in new learning or performance situations and judge their capabilities as a follow-up on competencies acquired in the course being evaluated.
- Examining records: Check grades and anecdotal records of students in school files to ascertain how they are now performing in their classes related to competencies gained in the course being evaluated. (Note: Because of privacy laws, this procedure may require permission from the former students before records can be retrieved.)

## Training Programs

A training program within a business concern, an industrial company, a health agency, or other organization usually has clearly defined outcomes to be accomplished. These planned results may have been identified initially when a needs assessment (see Chapter 2) was first made. The consequent benefits are expected to result in improved job performance and often can be translated into dollar savings or increased income for the company.

Three areas may need to be assessed in posttraining evaluation: appropriateness of the training, competencies of the employees, and benefits to the organization.

**Appropriateness of the Training.** Although the program was developed according to identified needs, changes in on-the-job operating procedures and the equipment used could necessitate job performance different from what was taught. Use confirmative evaluation to determine whether modifications are required before training is conducted the next time.

**Competencies of Employees.** It is one thing to pass written tests and perform satisfactorily in the controlled environment of a classroom or laboratory but, potentially, another to be successful in transferring the learning to a job situation. Determine how well the former trainees now perform the job or tasks they were trained to do.

**Benefits to the Organization.** The advantages need to be measured in terms of the payoff to the organization as well as to the individual. Some of the criteria that indicate that a training program has been beneficial to the organization are these:

- Reduced number of accidents through increased safety
- Increased service abilities, including both work quality and performance speed

- Improved quality of products being produced
- Increased rate of work or production
- Reduced problems with equipment due to malfunctions and breakdowns
- Increased sales of products and greater services, or more income being generated (referred to as "return on training investment")

With respect to affective-type outcomes, the following may be some of the expected results:

- Less employee tardiness and absenteeism
- Less employee turnover
- Greater job satisfaction
- Higher level of motivation and willingness to assume responsibilities
- Increased respect for the organization

The same methods for gathering information for educational programs would apply to measuring the follow-up benefits of a training program: questionnaires, interviews, observations, and examining records. In terms of actual performance levels, if careful records are kept, comparisons can be made between pretraining and posttraining competencies. A key method of follow-up evaluation can be related to measuring effects on company expenses or revenue. This approach requires a comparison of pretraining cost factors with the costs and income data determined at a reasonable time after training is completed. This evidence can be one of the best measures to relate training benefits to the bottom line, with which a company is most concerned. Keep in mind, though, that not all training courses will have a direct, measurable impact on the bottom line (e.g., courses in interpersonal relations, public speaking).

In summary, confirmative evaluations take up where summative evaluations leave off—once the instruction is completed, the application of learning begins and continues over time. A confirmative evaluation will tend to have the following characteristics:

- Continuous (i.e., repeated over time, where feasible)
- Occurs in realistic contexts (i.e., on the job, in practice)
- Emphasizes performance rather than simply knowledge
- Includes learner reactions as direction for improvement
- May address new evaluation questions as performance requirements or contexts change over time
- May use smaller samples (more case studies) due to attrition of original learner cohort
- May use indirect measures (e.g., colleague, supervisor, and self-ratings; data from naturally occurring events) because of the difficulty of collecting follow-up data in the field

# REPORTING RESULTS OF SUMMATIVE AND CONFIRMATIVE EVALUATIONS

The final step in creating evaluations of instruction is to prepare a report of the results for others to read and examine. Careful attention should be given to this activity. Future support for the program, as well as the assistance required for additional instructional design projects, can be influenced by the manner in which a summative or confirmative evaluation is reported. First, the evaluator must decide for whom the report is to be prepared—administrators/training managers, instructors, or another supporting agency. By considering those persons who are to receive the report, emphasis or special attention may have to be given to certain phases of the evaluation. For example, how and where funds have been spent may be of primary interest, or evidence of follow-up benefits may be of more value to the readers than are the efficiencies or effectiveness of instruction.

Second, the evaluator must decide on the format of the report. Should it be on paper for individual reading, or will it be presented to a group with the support of slides or overhead transparencies? In either case, plan to report results attractively. Not everyone will be as highly interested or as well informed about the project as the designer has been. Here are some suggestions:

- Give the report an interesting title.
- Summarize highlights so the key outcomes can be grasped quickly. Do this by setting them off on a page with white space or boxing each statement.
- Describe supporting data in visual ways with graphs rather than as detailed tables; use artwork as appropriate.
- If slides or PowerPoint will be prepared, limit the information displayed to only the key points. Prepare printed materials that correlate with the visuals and contain the details of information for the audience to retain.
- End by making appropriate recommendations for continuing, extending, modifying, or terminating the program.
- Where feasible, adapt the style and content of the report to the main target audiences. Different stakeholder groups will have different backgrounds, interests, and expectancies for what the report will convey.
- The reporting format for formative evaluations outlined in the section "Reporting" is generally appropriate as well for summative and confirmative evaluations.

## SUMMARY

1. Formative, summative, and confirmative evaluations serve the complementary purposes of assessing both developing and completed instructional programs.
2. A basic model for planning formative evaluations addresses eight areas: purposes, audience, issues, resources, evidence, data-gathering techniques, analyses, and reporting.

3. Common formative evaluation approaches can be classified as (1) connoisseur based, in which expert opinions are sought; (2) decision oriented, in which information related to particular questions is gathered; (3) objectives based, in which assessments are made of the degree to which particular objectives are obtained; and (4) public relations inspired, in which financial support or backing for a project is solicited based on the evaluation findings.

4. Recently proposed *constructivist-oriented* formative evaluation approaches focus on three factors related to learners' interactions with computer-based instructional support: *learning constructs* (interactivity, feedback, graphics), *quality of instruction* (help supports, instructions, organization), and *learner engagement* (interest, motivation, enjoyment).

5. Three major stages of formative evaluation consist of one-to-one trials, small-group trials, and field trials. Each successive stage focuses on a more developed version of the instructional program, using larger samples of students.

6. Summative evaluations, unlike experimental research, are designed to provide information about specific instructional programs. They are not used to test general theories and thus do not require rigorous research methods or control groups.

7. Program effectiveness is determined by analyzing test scores, rating projects and performance, and observing learner behavior.

8. Summative evaluations involve similar planning procedures and methodologies as do formative evaluations. The emphasis in summative studies, however, is on the full, completed program rather than on preliminary versions of the program.

9. A useful outcome measure for summative evaluations is program efficiency, computed as a ratio of the number of objectives achieved to the time taken to achieve them.

10. Program costs are evaluated by determining both developmental costs (the expense of designing the program) and operational costs (the expense of offering the program). The instructional cost index is the total cost per learner or trainee.

11. Confirmative (follow-up) evaluations should be conducted after the student leaves the program. In the case of educational programs, the important outcomes are basic skills, knowledge, competencies, and performance in occupational settings. For training programs, important outcomes include appropriateness of the training, competencies of employees, and benefits to the organization.

12. *Learner-oriented*, confirmative evaluations concern the degree to which, as time passes, consumers of the instruction retain the skills and knowledge needed to perform at desired levels. *Context-oriented* studies concern the degree to which the instructional product remains effective as conditions change over time.

13. The evaluation report should be carefully prepared and attractive in its appearance/presentation. Adaptation of content to stakeholder backgrounds and interests is highly important.

## THE ID PROCESS

Inexperienced designers sometimes view formative and summative evaluations as discrete strategies that respectively come at the "beginning" and at the "completion" of the design process. Our approach is to see them, along with confirmative evaluations, as overlapping processes having more similarities than differences. Although every design project is different in content, context, and goals, we offer the following as general guidelines based on our experiences.

Make continuous evaluation a primary component of the initial design plan. Once a project is launched, it seems to be human nature to want to devote more time and money to designing and implementing the instructional program. It is generally difficult to add "more" evaluation if it is not built in at the front end. In most contexts, being sensitive to the political aspects of a design project is critical to the project's success. Of the many stakeholders concerned (e.g., sponsors, learners, administrators, and instructors), there are likely to be both supporters and detractors. Evaluation, therefore, not only becomes a tool for refinement and judgment, it becomes a valuable means of communicating (with data) what is being accomplished. We have discovered many times that "data talk," particularly when there is disharmony among stakeholders on such matters as the need for the course, its content, how and when it is offered, the costs involved, or the delivery methods used.

Although the distinctions between the three types of evaluation is useful as a heuristic for evaluation timing, emphasis, and orientation, it seems most important to employ each as the evaluation objectives and conditions dictate at each point in time. There will be times when a formative evaluation that is conducted very early in the design process must produce preliminary data to satisfy the new training manager who wants some indication of the project's impact to support it. Such situations are not a matter of how the "book" says a pure formative evaluation must be done. Simply put, unless that particular manager receives some outcome data, there will be no project on which to conduct a pure formative evaluation! And there will be situations (probably many) when it makes perfect sense in a summative or confirmative evaluation to gather information for improving the design. Judging from our experiences, the art and science of instructional evaluation in the real world often necessitates developing well-constructed hybrid designs adapted to situational needs.

A final consideration in all phases of evaluation is to what degree outside experts should be employed. Different types of experts can be particularly valuable. The SME (e.g., a database administrator consulting on a course on database management) should be helpful in validating the content of the instruction. A media expert may be needed to help with instructional delivery using specialized technology (e.g., distance learning) with which the designer is less familiar. An external, professional evaluator may be needed to design the study, develop instruments, and analyze and interpret the data. When funding permits, we strongly recommend using experts. Not only is their knowledge important, but what they say adds objectivity and credibility to the project. Expert data usually "talk" very convincingly.

## APPLICATIONS

You are designing an instructional program to be used at kiosks in an art museum to acquaint visitors with the museum layout and exhibits. It is important to the philanthropic foundation that supported the stations that visitors (1) actually use the program and (2) find the information useful and interesting. Using examples, describe how each of the following types of formative evaluation might be used: connoisseur based, decision oriented, objectives based, and public relations inspired. Which of these orientations might you also apply in summative and confirmative evaluations?

## ANSWERS

Assuming that you are not highly knowledgeable about the particular art museum or art exhibits in general, connoisseur-based evaluation would be useful to confirm the accuracy of the content of the program, its organization, and its presentation. Decision-making evaluation might focus on questions such as, ''Is the program economical to update as new exhibits are featured?'' Answers to these questions will provide useful suggestions for refining the design. Objectives-based formative evaluation might focus on the criterion questions posed by the sponsoring foundation (as well as other relevant outcomes): ''What percentage of visitors use the program and for how long?'' and ''Do users find the program to be helpful and interesting?'' Given that this evaluation is formative, the results will be used less to judge its effectiveness than to provide directions for its improvement. For example, infrequent use of the program may lead to the decision to place the information stations in more visible locations in the museum lobby. Public-relations-inspired evaluation may involve providing the foundation with preliminary information showing that good progress is being made in the program design and implementation.

For summative and confirmative evaluations, the two most important orientations will probably be objectives based, to determine how effectively the completed program is achieving the desired outcomes, and public relations inspired, to keep the foundation satisfied and perhaps (assuming the program is successful) attract additional funding for related projects. With a completed program, connoisseur-based evaluation would probably not be needed. Assuming that the ''completed'' program can still be improved, decision-based evaluation, however, might be a helpful supplement providing data on how effectively different program components are working.

## INSTRUCTIONAL DESIGN: DECISIONS AND CHOICES

The draft materials for the unit on using a fire extinguisher have been completed and are ready for formative evaluation. You devise the following evaluation strategy:

1. SME review for content accuracy
2. Individual learner review of materials

3. Classroom instructor feedback
4. Classroom and Web test-item analysis

After the SME has signed off on accuracy of the content, you ask the client to provide three learners (ideally individuals from the primary audience such as mailroom clerks) to try out the instruction. You greet the first test subject and sit him down in front of a computer workstation. You tell the mailroom clerk, "We want to make sure that these instructional materials are effective, so your feedback is important to us. As you go through these materials on the Web (screen pages of instruction and practice activities), tell me what you are thinking, particularly if something you read is hard to understand or confusing, or if something works particularly well."

The learner then proceeds to go through the Web-based materials. [Some designers prefer to test the instruction before the actual Web pages are developed. In this case, a draft is prepared on paper, in the form of sketches of screen shots or as PowerPoint slides with links, and these are provided to the learner.] While the learner goes through the instruction, you observe, particularly noting where the learner pauses, returns to a previous screen, or rereads a section. You also look for a confused facial expression or other signs that the learner is stuck. After the learner completes the instruction, you interview him. Here are some sample questions:

1. What did you think of the instruction?
2. Was anything difficult to understand?
3. Could you relate to the examples?
4. How did you feel about the practice activities and feedback?
5. Are there any changes you would recommend?

[Notice how the first question is open-ended and is intended to obtain data about the learner's overall reaction to the instruction. The second question is specifically aimed at discovering weaknesses in the instruction. The third question will tell the designer whether the examples are good or need to be replaced. (The designer will want feedback from several test subjects before deciding to change any of the examples.) The fourth question, along with the posttest results, tells the designer whether the practice activities and feedback are effective.]

You revise the materials based on the feedback from the first test subject. These "fixes" may include revising sentences, changing the sequence of information, changing the practice activities, or correcting spelling. Sometimes, you may not be certain that a change suggested by the test subject is warranted. In this case, you hold off making that change until you receive feedback from a second or even third test subject.

You have also decided to sit in on the first classroom offering. You observe the learners taking notes, and you carefully attend to the questions that the learners ask the instructor. You also watch the learners practice using the fire extinguisher and note where the instructor provides new information or must review procedures. After the instruction you interview all the participants as a group for about 10 minutes (essentially a focus group). In addition to the questions used for the one-on-one tryouts, you add the following:

- How did you feel about the hands-on practice?
- How did you feel about the pacing of the instruction?
- Did you have enough time?

Next, you debrief the classroom instructor using a set of questions that you have prepared in advance. You ask questions such as:

- What is your overall impression of the instruction?
- Did the learners have any difficulty with the material?
- Were the in-class practice activities effective?
- Are there any changes that should be made to the performance checklist?
- Are there any other changes that we should consider?

Last, you examine the posttest results and prepare a summary chart:

| Question # | Objective # | % Correct/Accuracy |
|:---:|:---:|:---:|
| 1 | 1 | 40% |
| 2 | 2 | 85% |
| 3 | 2 | 80% |
| 4 | 3 | 100% |
| 5 | 4 | 95% |
| 6 | 4 | 100% |
| 7 | 5 | 95% |
| 8 | 6 | 100% |
| 9 | 6 | 100% |

Based on the posttest data, the introductory conceptual material appears to need revision. But, you also hypothesize that question 1, rather than the instruction, might need to be revised. After examining all the data, you conclude that both the instruction and the test item need revision.

## REFERENCES

Brenneman, J. (1989). When you can't use a crowd: Single subject testing. *Performance and Instruction, 28*, 22–25.

Clarebout, G., & Elen, J. M. (2008, March). *Help-seeking and advice: A complex relationship?* Paper presented at the annual meeting of the American Educational Research Association, New York, NY.

Dick, W., & Carey, L. (1991). *The systematic design of instruction* (2nd ed.). New York: Harper Collins.

Flagg, B. N. (Ed.). (1990). *Formative evaluation for educational technologies*. Hillsdale, NJ: Erlbaum.

Friesen, N., & Anderson, T. (2004). Interaction for lifelong learning. *British Journal of Educational Technology, 35*(6), 679–687.

Gooler, D. D. (1980). Formative evaluation strategies for major instructional development projects. *Journal of Instructional Development, 3*, 7–11.

Haladyna, T. M., Nolan, S. B., & Haas, N. S. (1991). Raising standardized achievement test scores and the analysis of test score pollution. *Educational Researcher, 20*, 2–7.

Kay, R. H., & Knaack, L. (2009). Assessing learning quality and engagement in learning objects: The Learning Object Evaluation Scale for Students (LOES-S). *Educational Technology Research and Development*, 57(2), 147–168.

Krauss, F., & Ally, M. (2005). A study of the design and evaluation of a learning object and implications for content development. *Interdisciplinary Journal of Knowledge and Learning Objects, 1*. Retrieved from http://ijklo.org/Volume1/v1p001-022Krauss.pdf

Miles, M. B., & Huberman, A. M. (1994). *Qualitative data analysis: An expanded sourcebook* (2nd ed.). Thousand Oaks, CA: Sage.

Nurmi, S., & Jaakkola, T. (2006). Effectiveness of learning objects in various instructional settings. *Learning, Media, and Technology*, 31(3), 233–247.

Ross, S. M. (2005). Assessment: Summative evaluation. In V. A. Anfara, Jr., G. Andrews, & S. Mertens (Eds.), *The encyclopedia of middle grades education* (pp. 126–128). Greenwich, CT: Information Age Publishing.

Ross, S. M., & Morrison, G. R. (1995). Evaluation as a tool for research and development. In R. D. Tennyson & A. Barron (Eds.), *Automating instructional design: Computer-based development and delivery tools* (pp. 491–522). Berlin: Springer-Verlag.

Saab, N., Gijlers, H., Van Joolingen, W. R., & van Hout-Wolters, W. R. (2008, March). *Using or not using the provided tool during collaborative inquiry learning*. Paper presented at the annual meeting of the American Educational Research Association, New York, NY.

Sterbinsky, A., & Ross, S. M. (2005). Assessment: Formative evaluation. In V. A. Anfara, Jr., G. Andrews, & S. Mertens (Eds.), *The encyclopedia of middle grades education* (pp. 122–126). Greenwich, CT: Information Age Publishing.

Thiagarjan, S., Semmel, D., & Semmel, M. (1974). *Instructional development for training teachers of exceptional children: A sourcebook*. Bloomington, IN: Center for Innovation in Teaching the Handicapped.

# Learning Theory and Instructional Theory

## GETTING STARTED

Because of your expertise in instructional design, you have been hired by a state university to assist in developing a series of online undergraduate courses. At your initial meeting with the group, the IT senior programmer is already well into the creation of the online version of Biology I and is quite pleased to demonstrate the beginning prototype. As you review the course structure and contents, you become a bit puzzled by some things that you see. For example, for the unit on mollusks, students are assigned to cooperative learning groups for a "course project" but told simply "to work together as effectively as possible through email exchanges and phone calls, because everyone will receive the group grade." You seriously question the "theory" for the latter policy, but decide to remain quiet for now. Another section of the course allows the student to "explore some aspect of 'biology in action' and describe it in an online journal." One of the faculty says she's always been a fan of "discovery learning and constructivision" (sic). She adds, "No grades will be given because extrinsic rewards might detract from the students' development of personal interests in science." But curiously, you later discover a course component in which students earn a participation point for each email posted on the course discussion board! You are told by one of the IT staff that some course units but not others will contain drill-and-practice tutorials, each containing a multiple-choice posttest. Posttest scores will not be made available until the next day based on a faculty member's belief that immediate feedback may "short-circuit" student interest in searching for the answers.

"What is learning theory and instructional theory?"

"What is the difference between a model and theory?"

"What are major paradigms of learning theory?"

"How is knowledge of learning theory useful to instructional designers?"

"What are major applications to instructional design of behavioral and cognitive theoretical approaches?"

"Should instructional design be purist or eclectic in drawing from different theoretical paradigms?"

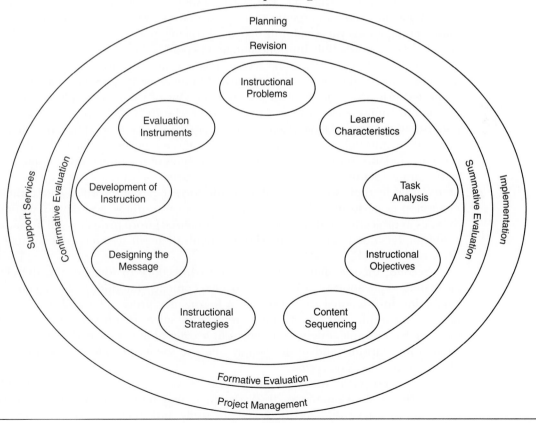

There is obviously much more planning and work to do on Biology I, and most of what you see looks quite good on the surface. But, disturbingly, the overall design appears to be an expanding patchwork of many different, and often dissonant, core assumptions about teaching and learning. The analogy occurs to you of a chef creating a meal by randomly mixing together ingredients from several favorite recipes. However, the queasiness you feel has less to do with this inedible hypothetical meal than with your anxiety over how to react to the present design at the formal planning meeting tomorrow. It's obvious that this course design is not being grounded systematically on theories of learning and instruction. How will you work with the team to try to establish that foundation?

## INTRODUCTION

The opening scenario described an instructional design project that was strong on surface appearance and designer intuitions but devoid of a theoretical base. The frustrated expert perceived the design process as analogous to that of a cook haphazardly combining many favorite ingredients to prepare a "potluck" dinner. The likely result in both contexts is a product (i.e., lessons or meal) that is indigestible and inexplicable. But, whereas we can easily toss a bad dinner into the disposal and make an urgent call for pizza delivery, we will have a much harder time redoing an instructional unit that was probably needed "yesterday" and has already taken considerable time and budget to create.

What the design team in the scenario lacks is an underlying theory to guide its actions. Such a theory, as will be discussed here, consists of a set of scientifically supported principles that explain phenomena. Few of us, for example, would be inclined to choose a family physician or dentist who treated symptoms but lacked understanding, derived from scientific theory, of the causes. Operating from theory rather than intuition accomplishes several important purposes. First, the theory provides guidance regarding how different strategies or manipulations are likely to work. An instructional designer might draw on behavioral theory, for example, to predict that learners who are reinforced for correct responses will increase their motivation to perform well. Another might draw on cognitive and developmental theories in projecting that concrete (i.e., personalized) word problems will be more readily understood by elementary school students than will abstract problems (e.g., "If $X$ is added to $Y$ . . . ").

Second, theories help give order and consistency to what we do, thereby facilitating replication of what works in new contexts. Randomly or subjectively combining instructional strategies into a lesson may prove successful in a given project, but results will be difficult to reproduce subsequently when the context changes, for example, due to differences in learner ability, subject difficulty, time allotted for learning, and so on. Simply put, the theory provides a road map or blueprint to keep us on course.

Third, especially today, in the era of "evidence-based practices" (Shavelson, Towne, & the Committee 2002), designers may find themselves increasingly in situations where they will be asked to justify and document the theoretical base supporting a new instruction. In K–12 contexts, many contemporary federal programs under the No Child Left Behind Act of 2001, such as in reading, supplementary educational services, and special education, require as a condition for funding that instructional practices and reform models be "scientifically based" (NCLB, 2002).

Do practicing instructional designers actually rely on learning theory in their work? In a recent study, experienced instructional designers were asked this very question across a series of interviews. Although deadlines, client demands, and the abstract nature of certain learning principles often made it difficult to apply theory, the designers acknowledged using theory in several important ways (Yanchar, South, Williams, Allen, & Wilson, in press). One way was for guiding decision making and suggesting ideas during the design process. Another was helping to make sense of complex design situations. A third was to defend decisions and justify certain decisions about pedagogy (e.g., why worked examples rather than incomplete ones were provided in early units). Given the importance of theory to effective instructional design, we will focus in this chapter on what learning theories are, how they differ from instructional theories and models, and their application in guiding the design process. We will further explore several influential learning theories and their applications to different design problems. The following ideas are emphasized throughout this chapter: (a) Learning theory provides the foundation for achieving consistency between it, instructional theory, and the design model. The selected instructional strategies, in turn, will be more likely to flow together, be explainable and supportable to project stakeholders, and most critically, achieve the instructional objectives and project goals. (b) There is no one "right theory" for every application and every designer. Which paradigms prove most useful will depend on project conditions, what learning needs are emphasized, and the preferences and skills of the designers. Most designers, including your textbook authors, find the multiple theories described following valuable for design planning.

## LEARNING THEORY

A learning theory is a set of laws and principles that broadly explain learning and behavior. Using theory, the prediction, observation, and interpretation of events becomes much more orderly rather than intuitive or subjective. A learning theory tends to be *descriptive*. It creates a "big picture" of what is likely to happen and why. For example, behavioral learning theory, as one might associate with B. F. Skinner's work (Skinner, 1954, 1965), emphasizes the effects of external conditions such as rewards and punishments in determining future behavior. In contrast, cognitive theory, as represented by the work of Jean Piaget (Piaget, 1952) and Jerome Bruner (Bruner, 1963, 1973), focuses on how individuals perceive, process, store, and retrieve information that they receive from the environment. A social-cognitive theory, such as that of Vygotsky (1962), might stress how students learn from others in cooperative settings.

As indicated earlier, most instructional designers draw from multiple theoretical paradigms, using the ideas and scientific principles that apply best to the design task at hand. Despite their importance as explanatory frameworks, learning theories don't tell the designer what to do specifically to achieve the goals of the particular task. For example, a designer hired to develop an advanced training unit on corporate tax law may consider, on the basis of learning theory, using small steps and frequent overt feedback (i.e., behavioral theory), including numerous examples and nonexamples to strengthen conceptual learning (i.e., cognitive theory), and practicing in small teams of students (i.e., social learning theory). These are sensible general thoughts, but will they fit the specific instructional goals and conditions of the learning context? Instructional theory can be invoked to shape these theoretical ideas into actual strategies of teaching.

## Instructional Theory

Whereas learning theories are descriptive and generic (see the section "Learning Theory," to follow), instructional theories should be *prescriptive* and situation specific (see Reigeluth, 1983, 1999). The instructional theory, in essence, applies the principles and assumptions of learning theory to the instructional design goal of interest. The focus, as explained in detail in Chapter 5, is the objectives of instructional material being designed. To return to the tax law example, suppose that one key objective from the training unit is that students could "accurately apply two approved state formulae for calculating exemptions from gross profits." Drawing from instructional theory, the designer would analyze the types of content and performance involved (e.g., facts, concepts, principles, knowledge or application) to determine (i.e., prescribe) the specific teaching strategy components to be used. Such components may involve, for example, rehearsing the definitions of important terminology, paraphrasing the concepts and principles, and engaging in guided practice on actual problems. Some instructional objectives for the lesson, as in this example, might rely predominantly on cognitive learning theory, whereas others (e.g., "work cooperatively with an accounting team on the audit to form a consensual recommendation") might be more sociocognitive or behavioral in nature.

## Instructional Design Model

At the risk of jargon overdose, again consider the different frameworks of knowledge that guide instructional design. *Instructional theory*, as informed by *learning theory*, defines the core teaching strategies to be incorporated in the lesson or training unit. These are the strategies identified by the instructional designer as likely to be most successful in achieving learning goals within the target context. However, developing, refining, and producing a completed product in real life requires the integration of many more elements that must operate interdependently. As you will learn later, these elements together compose the *instructional design model*, or plan. By following such a plan, the instructional designer can ensure that the design process is both comprehensive and systematic, thus leading to a quality product and, most critically, successful learner performance. So, in summary, the three frameworks provide the following hierarchical functions:

| | |
|---|---|
| Learning theory: | How you learn |
| Instructional theory: | How you ensure that the desired learning occurs |
| Instructional design model: | How you apply instructional theory to create an effective lesson or unit |

## Applications of Instructional Theories and Models

What influences the effects of instructional theories or models for predicting and producing achievement? According to Gropper (1983, p. 48), there are four factors. One factor is the capacity for a *differential analysis of learning requirements*. Some theories and models are highly specific and granular. Others are more general and holistic. For example, an instructional objective, such as "the learner solves two-step word problems in mathematics," can be approached simply and holistically as "problem solving." On the other hand, a more fine-grained analysis would attempt to identify the constituent skills, such as generalizations, discriminations, and connections, embedded in the particular task. The latter approach is clearly the more precise and descriptive. Some instructional designers, however, take the view that learning, unlike designing an automobile or an electrical system for a house, is not so predictable and mechanistic, due to the influences of many interactive factors (including the engagement, background, and "will" of the learners). These designers might prefer less-detailed differentiation of learning requirements.

A second factor is the capacity for *quantifying conditions and treatments*. Quantification as opposed to intuitive judgments allows for much more objectivity and accuracy in analyzing a task and designing conditions to achieve success. For example, a designer may use a validated scale to assess one set of math problems at difficulty level 8 (on a 10-point scale) and another set at level 5. The identified difficulty levels might then be used to determine the type and number of practice examples to be provided. Such quantification is more consistent with the behavioralistic theories of learning than with the cognitive and constructivist theories to be discussed in the following sections. However, regardless of theoretical preference, the designer can only benefit from knowing these quantitative difficulty ratings (e.g., providing additional instructional support on problems rated higher in difficulty). According to Gropper (1983), a third characteristic of effective instructional theories and models is *compatibility with a theory of learning*. This characteristic is the major theme of this chapter. That is, a theory of learning provides guidance and direction to the instructional designer by identifying (a) the types of learning requirements that describe objectives, (b) the parameters that affect how difficult or easy it will be to satisfy objectives, and (c) parameters that describe the conditions under which learning takes place (Gropper, 1983, p. 48). As will be seen later, behaviorist and cognitive theories define different types of learning requirements, conditions, and outcomes. Designers can potentially benefit from being knowledgeable about multiple theories and applying them in combination or independently depending on project needs.

The fourth characteristic is the *explicit linkage of the learning theory, instructional theory, and instructional model*. As a contrasting situation, recall the opening scenario, in which each designer tried to insert his or her pet instructional strategy into the course design based largely on personal intuitions and surface understanding of learning theory. Not surprisingly, a "collage approach" to instructional design ("throw it in and hope for the best") will have little face validity for impressing clients and, more critically, reduced potential to produce the desired learning outcomes. By linking learning theory, instructional theory, and the design model, a smoother, more effective bridge between theory and practice can be achieved. As Fox (2005) indicated in reference to contemporary practices in instructional design and technology (IDT):

> It has become increasingly rare to see an empirical demonstration of how the use of technology actually affected learning. This overemphasis on media development threatens to intellectually bankrupt the field as instructional technologists move further and further away from any kind of grounding in a science of learning. They are in danger of becoming mere technologists without a philosophy or science to guide, evaluate, distinguish, or advance their work. (p. 22).

Hopefully, readers of this textbook will eschew this pattern.

## Types of Learning Theory

For centuries, philosophers and great thinkers have questioned how we learn and remember things. It was only as recently as the late 1800s (Driscoll, 2005) that research methods were systematically applied to collect scientific evidence about learning. Subsequently, drawing from different epistemologies (e.g., rationalism, empiricism, and realism) of the philosophers and the research findings of experimental psychologists, several prominent theories of learning evolved. Describing any of these theories in detail would be well beyond the scope of this text. Rather, our intention is to provide exposure to several broad theoretical paradigms that are highly influential in contemporary educational psychology and instructional design.

**Behavioral Theory.**   Behavioral theory, or "behaviorism," is commonly associated with theorists such as B. F. Skinner, Ivan Pavlov, and E. L. Thorndike. It emphasizes maintaining desirable behaviors and eliminating undesirable behaviors by manipulating conditions in the environment. Such conditions essentially take the form of positive (i.e., reinforcement) or negative (i.e., punishment) consequences following a response. For example, a computer-based tutorial might be designed so a point is added to the student's total score for each question answered correctly or subtracted for each answered incorrectly. To ensure a good grade on the unit, students would therefore be motivated by the points system to learn the material covered. Conversely, behavioral theories avoid dealing with "mentalistic" constructs, such as thought, reasoning, processing, or memory. Because these are unobservable and subjective, they cannot be reliably controlled by a researcher, teacher, or instructional designer. However, as will be described later, cognitive and constructivist theories offer the complementary view that we can make many valid and useful *inferences* from research about how people think and acquire knowledge.

**Behavioral Principles and Applications.** The extensive research performed by behaviorists over the past 100 years has identified many principles of learning. Following are some examples that might provide guidance for a course or unit design.

**Principle:** Continuous reinforcement is superior to intermittent reinforcement for novice learners. Following acquisition learning, intermittent reinforcement is superior in increasing resistance to extinction.

**Application:** For teaching inexperienced or low-achieving learners, the designer decides to reinforce every correct response by providing the verbal feedback, "Correct." Once the learner demonstrates sufficient skills, the design strategy switches to intermittent reinforcement, whereby only some correct responses are reinforced.

**Principle:** Variable schedules of intermittent reinforcement produce more rapid and consistent responding than do fixed schedules.

**Application:** The designer is developing counseling courses for juvenile offenders. He structures the lessons so that points for good behavior are awarded following a random number of correct responses (e.g., 2, 5, 7, etc.) rather than after a set amount (e.g., every five responses).

**Principle:** An unconditioned stimulus, such as the aroma of food, naturally evokes an unconditioned response, such as salivating. When a previously neutral stimulus (e.g., a bell sound) is paired with the unconditioned stimulus (e.g., food), the neutral stimulus becomes a conditioned stimulus that will evoke a similar response (e.g., salivating).

**Application:** In applying these principles from Pavlov's classical conditioning experiment (see Figure 14-1), the designer decides to present some difficult math problems in humorous contexts in the hope of reducing learning anxiety and creating positive affect (e.g., smiling, relaxing, interest).

**Principle:** Performance in less-desirable activities can be increased by linking them with more-desirable activities.

**Application:** Using this principle (often called the "Premack Principle" or "Grandma's Rule"), the designer of a corporate training course in hazardous waste disposal builds in "free reading time" (a very desirable activity) when work stations have been properly cleaned (a less-desirable activity).

**Principle:** A small reinforcer given immediately has a stronger effect than a large reinforcer given later.

**Application:** The designer of an online military aviation fundamentals course included quizzes that are graded as soon as the students complete them, thus ensuring that reinforcement (in the form of feedback) will be immediate.

**Principle:** Immediate reinforcers for approximate (i.e., near, or close) responses are effective for developing complex skills.

**Application:** In requiring students to perform experiments in a chemistry course, the designer decides to reward students after they accomplish each of a series of *prerequisite* tasks. Those who are unsuccessful at prerequisite tasks are required to practice until they demonstrate mastery. This type of instructional strategy, which progressively builds complex skills in smaller steps, is often called "shaping."

**Implications of Behavioral Theory for Instructional Design.**   As just illustrated, the principles of learning derived from behavioral theories can potentially affect instructional design decisions in many ways. One important implication is arranging schedules and types of reinforcement to optimally enhance learner motivation and achievement. Note that, although "reinforcement" sometimes consists of extrinsic rewards such as gold stars, M&Ms, verbal praise, or points credited toward grades, it often takes the simple form of feedback about the correctness of the response.

A second broad implication of behavioral theory is the need for designers to perform a *task analysis* before developing instructional materials. As discussed in Chapter 4, a task analysis defines the content needed to address the key instructional problem, thereby guiding the identification of objectives and development of instructional strategies, lesson material, and test items. In accord with the principle of shaping just described, learning can be organized by objective, thus creating smaller steps and increased opportunities for reinforcement.

Third, behaviorism strongly supports the usage of instructional objectives, particularly (and hardly surprisingly) the behavioral type proposed by Robert Mager (1984) (see Chapter 5). Such objectives clearly identify the *overt responses* reflecting mastery of the content, the *level of achievement* indicating acceptable performance and the *conditions* under which the evaluation takes place. Using such objectives, the instructor can assess objectively and reliably the degree of learning attained for each lesson goal.

Fourth, behavioral theories have inspired the development of several influential and evidence-based instructional strategies and broader course designs. These include classic approaches such as Programmed Instruction (Skinner, 1954), Personalized System of Instruction (PSI; Keller, 1968), Mastery Learning (Bloom,

**FIGURE 14-1**
Classical conditioning

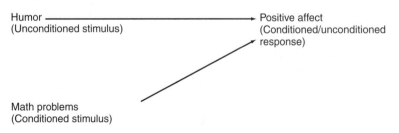

1976), and Direct Instruction (Englemann & Carnine, 1991). These models and their many derivatives incorporate task analysis, precise content objectives, highly sequenced instruction, active responding, and reinforcement linked directly to performance. Direct Instruction is a popular K–12 teacher-centered model incorporating lecture, questioning, and student responding, whereas the other examples (e.g., Mastery Learning and PSI) are student-centered approaches incorporating self-pacing and mastery assessments. Of note, in a recent meta-analysis of 24 comprehensive school reform models, Borman, Hewes, Overman, and Brown (2003) identified Direct Instruction as one of four models having the strongest evidence of yielding educational benefits. Behaviorism may not easily explain all types of learning, as will be described later, but it certainly is still alive and well in the contemporary instructional design field (see Fox, 2005; Fredrick & Hummel, 2004).

**Social Learning Theory.**    A derivative of behavioral learning theory is social learning theory, developed by Albert Bandura (1986). Social learning theory incorporates the major tenets of behaviorism, such as the influences of consequences on the frequency of behavior. However, it also views behavioristic explanations of learning as too limited to account for many types of learning. As a bridge between behavioral and cognitive approaches, social learning theory recognizes the role of internal mental processing and thought in influencing behavior. Behavior, in turn, influences thought. Social learning theory is best known for what its name implies—learning from others through observation and modeling. Bandura's theory provides a basis for our prescription for interpersonal skills in Chapter 7. Bandura proposed that observational learning consists of four phases:

- **Attention:** First learners pay attention to a model, usually someone they find important or attractive (e.g., a movie star, athletic hero, peer group leader).

- **Retention:** Having observed the model, the learner must repeat the behavior by mental rehearsal or practice to remember it.

- **Production:** Extending initial attempts to retain the behavior, the learner now tries to replicate the model's level of expertise. Extensive effort and practice may be required to ensure success.

- **Motivation:** Consonant with behavioral principles, reinforcement is needed to sustain motivation to repeat the behavior. The reinforcement may involve one or more of the following: feeling intrinsic satisfaction for emulating the model, receiving extrinsic rewards such as points or verbal praise, and/or obtaining vicarious pleasure through watching others being reinforced for the behavior.

Designers can draw on principles of social learning theory to improve instruction and learning. Some examples are as follows:

- **Principle:** People learn vicariously by seeing others receive positive or negative consequences for certain behaviors.
- **Application:** A designer includes, as a component of self-instructional units on hotel management, videos of successful managers performing desired

interactions with guests and being reinforced through the resolution of problems and positive feedback.

**Principle:** People learn by modeling their behavior on those of others.
**Application:** The designer begins each lesson in an automobile mechanics course with a demonstration by the instructor of the repair technique being taught.

**Principle:** Inhibitions for engaging in a particular task can be reduced by watching others perform the same task.
**Application:** In a swimming class designed for children with aquaphobia, the designer incorporates a coaching component in which children who are making the most progress formally serve as coaches and models for others.

**Implications of Social Learning Theories for Instructional Design.**   Social learning theories remind designers that the involvement of other people in the learning process can exert powerful influences on motivation and performance. One factor is the intrinsic reinforcement or satisfaction that we feel when emulating attractive models. Another is the desirability of being recognized by a respected peer or adult for performing well. A third is learning vicariously by observing a model demonstrate correct techniques. A fourth, to be developed further in the cognitive theories section, is reaching higher levels of understanding and mastery by solving problems in a group whose members possess differing levels of ability and expertise. Although there is probably no substitute for real-life (i.e., human) models, instructional designers today are increasingly exploring in computer-assisted learning environments the usage of intelligent tutors and, at a simpler level, "pedagogical agents as learning companions" (PALs) (Baylor, 2002). The latter are humanlike characters that appear during the lesson to motivate and model learning behaviors. Recent research has demonstrated that the characteristics (e.g., gender, ethnicity, expertise level) and personality of PALs may influence the degree to which learners are positively affected by their presence (Baylor & Kim, 2004).

## Cognitive Theory

Whereas behaviorists focus on what is directly observable and controllable, cognitive theorists are concerned with what occurs inside the mind—how we think, process information, remember and forget information, and acquire and use language to communicate. Similar to behaviorism, there is no single universally accepted "cognitive theory" but rather a collection of influential frameworks emphasizing different aspects of cognition. For example, the work of Piaget (1952) and other developmental cognitive theorists discourages the perception of children as "miniature grownups" who reason and think the same ways as adults but are simply less experienced. Rather, research has demonstrated that children think in qualitatively different ways as they mature, progressing from dependency on sensory and physical experience (e.g., feeling and touching) to being able to mentally manipulate concrete objects and, ultimately, to engaging in abstract and hypothetical thinking (e.g., "What would happen if...?").

Complementary perspectives dealing with the sociocultural nature of cognition were provided by Lev Vygotsky, a Russian psychologist. Vygotsky (1962) believed that cognitive growth is fostered when children operate in the "zone of proximal development," the area slightly above their present functioning but in which they can be successful with the assistance of adults and peers. Thus, an emphasis on social activities and cooperative learning is suggested. Drawing extensively on Piaget's (1952) and Vygotsky's (1962) work, constructivist theorists such as Bruner (1963, 1990) and Wittrock (1974, 1989) focused on the self-constructed (i.e., "generative" or discovered) nature of learning. Teaching methods supported by these perspectives include discovery learning and student-centered instruction. In contrast, other cognitive theorists such as David Ausubel (1963) believe that learning should take place deductively—from the general (i.e., the rule or principle) to the specific (i.e., the facts and details), rather than inductively—from the specific to the general (Slavin, 2008). Ausubel, in direct opposition to the constructivists, would much prefer to educate students via a well-organized lecture than an experiential learning activity.

Despite their differences, these alternative cognitive perspectives commonly support several important principles of learning. One is that students form personalized and unique knowledge structures, called "schema." This prior knowledge influences how new information, whether self-discovered or received, will be processed and understood. A second major principle is that, the more actively students process new material by relating it to prior knowledge and applying it to new tasks, the better it will be learned. Third, just as prior knowledge influences new learning, new learning experiences, in turn, change our knowledge structures. Piaget called these complementary processes assimilation and accommodation, respectively. As you read the present material, both processes should be happening simultaneously inside your mind. That is, you are interpreting (i.e., assimilating) this overview of cognitive theory uniquely, relative to your classmates, based on your current knowledge, interests, and frame of mind (hopefully, wakefulness is one of its characteristics). At the same time, the information is changing you (through accommodation), as you might consider, for example, how the various cognitive perspectives (e.g., those of Piaget, Vygotsky, Bruner, Ausubel) are similar to and different from one another. Maybe one of your present thoughts is that it's time to move from relatively abstract, general descriptions of cognitive theory to more specific applications that designers can use. That is also our plan.

**Cognitive Principles and Applications.**    Numerous principles of learning have been derived from cognitive learning theories. Following are some examples that instructional designers may find useful to consider.

> **Principle:** For information to be processed and transferred to memory, it must first be attended to.
> **Application:** In a computer-based unit on chemistry, the designer uses a bell sound as a signal for students to attend to each simulation about to occur in the program. Note that in using the bell sound the designer is also applying

a behavioral principle—classical conditioning to associate the sound with the instructional event.

**Principle:** Working memory is usually limited to holding from five to nine separate bits of information for a limited duration (e.g., 20 to 30 seconds).

**Application:** In presenting new terminology on the parts of the human brain, the instructor limits the number of terms presented together, while providing students with ample opportunity for rehearsal. The number of items presented *must* be less than working memory capacity in order to allow for the processing of all items (see Sweller, 2004). The instructor also assists the students in employing mnemonics, or memory aids, such as associating the image of a bell with the term *cerebell*um.

**Principle:** The more deeply information is processed, the greater the probability that it will be transferred to long-term memory and retrievable in the future.

**Application:** In developing an online course on geometric principles, the designer intersperses higher-order questions with definitions and problems. Examples include "Why is angle A smaller than angle B?" and "If the triangle were equilateral, how would that change side X?" The designer's goal is to engender meaningful processing of the material presented.

**Principle:** Children reason and view the world differently than do adults.

**Application:** In applying this classic principle of developmental cognitive theory, a designer who is creating an instructional unit on healthy foods for third-graders includes many pictures of food products and concrete examples in the content. She extensively edits or deletes text written by an expert who uses extensive jargon and abstract language. For example, the expert's definition, "Metabolism is the process by which the substance of plants and animals incidental to life is broken down or built up," is replaced by questions, such as, "What plants have you eaten lately?" "What happens to the plant when it is 'digested' by your body?"

**Principle:** Children can perform at cognitive levels higher than their present functioning through participating while learning in conversation and collaboration with peers or adults.

**Application:** In applying Vygotsky's notions of socially assisted learning, a designer developing mathematics lessons for children in primary grades incorporates intermittent cooperative learning activities in which children at different ability levels can interact with one another in solving problems.

**Principle:** Recall of previously learned information may decrease when new, similar information is learned.

**Application:** A designer is developing a technical manual to teach two related computer-based statistical analysis programs ("Stat Pak" and "Data Analysis 7.0") to the research staff at a large corporation. In considering the cognitive principle of "retroactive interference," she attempts to reduce potential interference as much as possible by (a) teaching Stat Pak thoroughly before beginning Data Analysis 7.0, and (b) using different teaching methods (e.g., workbook and teacher-led, respectively) for each.

**Principle:** When cognitive demands exceed processing capacity, degree of learning is reduced.

**Application:** In developing an online course in pre-algebra for middle school students, the designer includes adaptations in which students who perform poorly on pretests (i.e., low achievers) are presented first with completely worked examples to study, followed by incomplete examples to solve. In contrast, for high achievers, the incomplete examples are presented initially. The rationale is that, if prerequisite knowledge for a task is low, incomplete problems may exceed students' processing capacity and hinder understanding. Managing the information presented to the learner to account for working memory capacity is an application of cognitive load theory (Sweller, 2004).

**Principle:** When new information can be connected in memory to prior knowledge (or schema), the chances for meaningful learning as opposed to rote memorization to occur will increase.

**Application:** A designer is developing an instructional unit on Eastern religions for an adult education course. Realizing that the adult students may have little background in the content, he applies Ausubel's notion of "advance organizer" by developing a brief introductory unit that compares Christianity (i.e., the familiar) to Buddhism (i.e., the new). The organizer material provides background information to which students can relate the actual lesson content.

**Principle:** For meaningful learning to take place, learners must construct knowledge themselves through their actions, reflections, and experiences.

**Application:** In applying this constructivist view of learning, the designer orients the curriculum and teaching methods in a course for critical care nurses around simulations and cooperative learning. In particular, the nurses are grouped into teams of three members and assigned "patients" (role-played by other students) in simulated emergency situations. The team acts out its responses and then discusses with the instructor and class the rationale employed and perceived adequacy of its performance.

## Expert's Edge

### One Principle, Hold the Theory, and Add the Works
### First Principles of Instruction

Shortly after the appearance of the second "Green Book" (Reigeluth, 1999), I suggested to Charlie that I didn't think that the various theories described in this book were really that different. He challenged me to verify my statement. After a careful review of many instructional design theories, including many that were not represented in the Reigeluth anthology, I concluded that in one form or another most of these theories provided a common set of prescriptions that I came to call "first principles of instruction." In trying to be concise we suggested that these theories all agreed to five fundamental prescriptions for effective instruction (Merrill, 2002a, 2002b, 2007, in 2009, in 2008).

- Learning is promoted when learners engage in a task-centered instructional strategy.
- Learning is promoted when learners observe a demonstration.
- Learning is promoted when learners apply the new knowledge.
- Learning is promoted when learners activate prior knowledge or experience.
- Learning is promoted when learners integrate their new knowledge into their everyday world.

It should be noted that the theories reviewed included behaviorist, cognitive, and constructivist-oriented theories. It should also be noted that none of these theories included a contrary principle. The primary difference among theories is often in what is stressed and in secondary principles.

So, what is the point of being a purist? In my view a variety of scholars studying similar phenomena are likely to come to similar conclusions. When it comes down to prescriptions about what to do these prescriptions look very similar. When it comes to explaining why these prescriptions should be followed, there tends to be a considerable divergence of opinion. I have often stressed that what we should teach our designers are not theories (explanations of why) but rather empirically verified principles (prescriptions for practice). First, principles are one attempt to identify these commonly agreed to prescriptions for design. They are not grounded in any particular learning or instructional theory but can be found in most such theories. When we focus on prescriptions that can be derived from different theories, are we subscribing to multiple theories? Or are we ignoring theory and going for what works? You decide.

## References

Merrill, M. D. (2002a). First principles of instruction. *Educational Technology Research and Development 50*(3), 43−59.

Merrill, M. D. (2002b). A pebble-in-the-pond model for instructional design. *Performance Improvement 41*(7), 39−44.

Merrill, M. D. (2007). First principles of instruction: a synthesis. In R. A. Reiser & J. V. Dempsey (Eds.), Trends and Issues in Instructional Design and Technology, 2nd Edition (Vol. 2, pp. 62−71). Upper Saddle River, NJ: Merrill/Prentice Hall.

Merrill, M. D. (2009). First Principles of Instruction. In C. M. Reigeluth & A. Carr (Eds.), Instructional Design Theories and Models: Building a Common Knowledge Base (Vol. III) (pp 41−56). New York: Routledge Publishers. Merrill, M. D. (2008). Converting $e_3$ learning to $e^3$ learning: an alternative instructional design method. In S. Carliner & P. Shank (Eds.). (2008). The E-Learning Handbook: Past Promises, Present Challenges (pp. 359—400). San Francisco: Pfeiffer.

Reigeluth, C. M. (Ed.). (1999). *Instructional-design theories and models: A new paradigm of instructional theory.* Mahwah, NJ: Erlbaum.

M. David Merrill recently retired as a professor in the Department of Instructional Technology at Utah State University. He directed the $ID_2$ Research Group, a research group dedicated to the development of a Second Generation Instructional Design.

**Implications of Cognitive Theories for Instructional Design.**   The principles of learning derived from cognitive and constructivist theories can potentially affect instructional design decisions in many ways. One important implication is reminding the designer that learners at different stages of cognitive development do not think and process information in the same manner. Learning materials and activities need to be designed appropriately to fit developmental needs.

A second implication is that unless presented information is stored in long-term memory it will be quickly forgotten. Meaningful learning, which occurs when new information can be related (or connected) to existing knowledge, is much more resistant to forgetting than is rote memorization. Thus, by using examples, analogies, explanations, and advance organizers, designers can increase the chances for meaningful learning to occur.

A third implication, from Vygotsky's theory, is that social interactions can facilitate learners' progression to more advanced ways of thinking and problem solving. Instructional designers should therefore consider opportunities to incorporate into lesson designs cooperative learning or tutoring from peers or adults. Where real people cannot be so employed, usage of personalized agents for learning (PALs) might be explored in computer-assisted contexts (Mayer, Dow, & Mayer, 2001).

Fourth, constructivist theories emphasize the fundamental role of students as active participants in the learning process. By engaging in problem solving, cooperative tasks, and discovery learning, the individual learner experiences firsthand the meaning and application of rules and principles in the subject areas studied. Although constructivism appears to be in direct opposition to cognitive approaches that focus on "reception learning" (e.g., listening to lectures or reading text), both perspectives share a focus on the learner being an active participant in processing material, not simply memorizing it. As discussed later, successful designers typically learn how to draw from multiple theoretical perspectives to respond most effectively and with flexibility to project needs.

Fifth, while constructivist philosophy promotes the concept of learners "actively building coherent and organized knowledge" (Mayer, 2004), it also recognizes the strong influences of individual differences on learning processes. Thus, effective applications of constructivism do *not* necessarily call for placing students in pure "discovery learning" situations in which there is minimal guidance or instruction from teachers (Kirschner, Sweller, & Clark, 2006; Sweller, Kirschner, & Clark, 2007). Cognitive load theory (Sweller, 2004), as noted earlier, suggests that novice learners may become overwhelmed by the processing demands of such open learning environments. ''Active learning'' therefore should not be equated with ''independent learning'' or used with all students. Embedding guidance and support (e.g., worked examples, worksheets, cooperative learning, teacher presentations, etc.) in student-centered instruction should be considered where learners have limited background or low performance in the subject being taught.

---

#### ( Expert's Edge )

### Purely Theoretical or Theoretically Pure?

Should an instructional designer be a purist or take an eclectic point of view in regard to learning/instructional theory? I dislike either-or questions because they seem to imply that there are only two possible answers, like black and white, while I find the world to be full of shades of gray. On some fundamental level, designers probably are purists. This is because we have deeply held (and often unexamined) beliefs about the nature of knowledge and how learners come to know things. If you believe that knowledge is acquired from the outside in (the objectivist view), you cannot at the same time believe that knowledge is constructed from the inside out (the constructivist view). Because of this, I think it's likely that instructional designers approach problems from a particular point of view that is personal and unique to each of them, a kind of bias that affects their interpretation of the problem as well as candidate solutions they might consider.

I find it hard to imagine using the perspective of only one theory to inform instructional design decisions, even when there may be a good reason to do this. As an example, I wanted ID students to experience what it's like to be a learner in a constructivist environment. This meant allowing them to structure their own learning goals and select instructional strategies that would enable them to meet these goals, all with technology-based learning supports designed to help them make these decisions. But students didn't recognize the learning support that was available to them. They didn't make good decisions about what or how to learn, even when their peers in a collaborative learning group were depending on them. They ran out of time, despite my prompting them throughout the semester to plan their time and activities. So what happened? A purely constructivist environment didn't work very well partly because students were unprepared for it. But there were also institutional constraints such as the length of the semester that interfered.

It's a rare thing indeed for conditions to align in such a way that a pure application of learning theory is possible to implement or likely to succeed. Better to have lots of tools and be alert to their possibilities than to have a single hammer and treat everything like a nail.

Marcy P. Driscoll is dean of the College of Education at Florida State University. She is also Leslie J. Briggs Professor of Educational Research and a professor in the instructional systems and educational psychology programs within the Department of Educational Psychology and Learning Systems at Florida State University.

**Which Theory to Use?**    As the previous sections described, there are many potential applications of behavioral and cognitive theories in designing instruction. In summary, behavioral principles are most helpful in structuring the conditions of instruction to maintain student motivation, promote learning activity, and analyze tasks into objectively measurable component outcomes. Key decisions may involve how to administer feedback on performance, whether and when to provide external incentives (e.g., points, grades, privileges), and the amount of learner control over pacing and reinforcement to allow. Social learning principles provide frameworks for enhancing student learning through opportunities to observe and interact with others. Cognitive principles tend to be most helpful for making decisions involving how to design lesson content in accord with learners' prior knowledge and levels of development for reasoning, memory, and information processing. Clearly, behavioral, social, and cognitive learning theories have the potential to operate in a complementary, mutually supportive fashion in a given course.

How influential a given type of theory is in designing instruction will depend on a number of factors. One factor is the theoretical orientations of the individual designer. Which set of principles in the prior section most interested you—those derived from behavioral, social, or cognitive learning paradigms? As indicated by Marcy Driscoll in the Expert's Edge section, some designers tend to be "purists" favoring particular theories, whereas others are eclectic, considering multiple theoretical approaches depending on the project at hand.

Accordingly, a second factor affecting theory selection is the nature of the instructional design task—the conditions and requirements. For example, if the task is one with clearly defined performance objectives (e.g., "The learner must demonstrate ability to take patients' blood pressure with 95% or higher accuracy"), behavioral theory with its principles of practice and reinforcement schedules might seem most useful. Conversely, if the task emphasis was experiential in nature, such as traffic light technicians learning how to troubleshoot problems, a constructivist approach might be viewed as most compatible. Because the traffic light problems are unpredictable and open ended in nature, "hands-on" learning experiences could prove particularly valuable here as a learning mode. Earlier we considered applications of cognitive load theory promoting the usage of guided instruction (e.g. worked examples, teacher coaching, immediate feedback, etc.) for inexperienced or novice learners. On the other hand, if the primary goal of a unit in biology were to engage students in experiencing scientific inquiry, with little concern about their mastering particular content, a reasonable argument for designing a pure discovery activity might be made (Kuhn, 2007). By combining diverse theoretical perspectives, however, the designer might find even more appealing an inquiry-based learning activity with built-in support (e.g., peer mentoring) to guide students who become flustered due to inexperience or lack of prerequisite knowledge (Hmelo-Silver, Duncan, & Chinn, 2007).

A third factor is the preferences of the clients or project sponsors, who may not be learning theory scholars but often will have personal views of how students learn most effectively in the educational area of interest. Not surprising, the practicing designers interviewed by Yanchar et al. (in press) found "gate-keeping" by managers or other company employees to be a common barrier to basing decisions on theory as opposed to business considerations or subjective viewpoints. Specifically, the sponsors may make it clear that the type of learning they favor is, say, what's taught didactically by an instructor or reference manual rather than self-discovered or acquired through social interactions. The designers must then decide whether the "imposed" theoretical orientation is one with which they are comfortable and that they are willing to employ.

Is it *best* to be purist or eclectic? The answer, like that to questions concerning choice of political party or favorite TV show, depends on whom you ask. In general, the majority of designers (and university instructional design programs) favor taking an eclectic orientation where feasible (Yanchar et al., in press). Drawing from alternative theories increases the range of options for meeting project needs based on learner characteristics, type of task, client preferences, and the complementary strengths of varied perspectives. On the other hand, purist designers have the advantage of keeping within a paradigm that they most understand and value. Trying to "force-fit" into the design process theoretical ideas one doesn't believe in is unlikely to yield a quality product. However, as illustrated in the following scenario and advocated by Driscoll in the Expert's Edge, sometimes, clear advantages may result from collaboration between designers having different theoretical perspectives and expertise.

### Designers of a Different Feather Discover a Nest Egg

Veteran instructional designer Fred Santo is a staunch behaviorist, who views learning as the acquisition of knowledge and skills linked to clearly defined instructional objectives. Fred is highly skilled at working with subject-matter experts and instructors to define those objectives and then develop instructional units that teach the specific content, assess student performance, and adapt subsequent events accordingly (e.g., remediation, acceleration, variation of delivery mode). Sarah Tompkins, on the other hand, is a strong supporter of constructivist interpretations of learning. Her expertise is in developing open-ended learning environments in which students can explore solutions to problems under conditions that simulate real-life situations.

Fred is approached by the local school district to develop a series of units to prepare students for taking state-mandated achievement tests. Fred is delighted by this charge and has many ideas for using behavioral principles to develop effective and engaging tutorial units. However, in meeting with the district's curriculum committee, he is further informed that a part of the unit should be "learning how to learn" through students' self-assessments of their individual strengths, weaknesses, and needs. Fred feels his pulse rate beginning to increase; his personal self-assessment is sending vibrations that he is *not* adequately prepared to handle these expectations. But then he remembers that his colleague, Sarah Tompkins, specializes in cognitive learning applications. After a quick phone call, a partnership is formed that ultimately produces a highly effective instructional unit, grounded on eclectic learning principles, and which neither designer could have created as successfully alone. The next week, Sarah recalls that one of her clients keeps asking her to build into a lesson extrinsic incentives (group privileges) for students to stay on task. She decides to farm out that behavioral-sounding component to Fred.

## SUMMARY

1. Instructional design should be grounded on theories of learning and instruction.
2. A learning theory tends to be descriptive, explaining how learning takes place to achieve certain kinds of outcomes.
3. One major, influential theory of learning is behaviorism, which focuses on the influences of rewards and punishments in determining future behaviors. Another is social learning theory, which focuses on how people learn by observing and modeling the behavior of others. A third is cognitive theory, which focuses on receiving, processing, and remembering information through reception and discovery learning approaches.
4. Instructional theory, as informed by learning theory, defines the core teaching strategies (e.g., cooperative activities versus lecture, immediate versus delayed reinforcement, or worked examples versus incomplete examples) to be incorporated in a lesson. Instructional theories are prescriptive and situation specific.
5. The instructional design plan or model, as informed by both the learning and instructional theories, specifies how the core teaching strategies will be blended in the actual lesson (e.g., "Students will study two worked examples on their own, then solve three incomplete examples, each followed by immediate teacher feedback, in a cooperative learning group.").
6. According to Gropper (1983), four factors influence the effects of instructional theories or models on predicting and producing achievement: (a) the capacity for a highly differential analysis of learning requirements; (b) the capacity for quantifying conditions and treatments; (c) compatibility with a theory of learning; and (d) the explicit linkage of the learning theory, instructional theory, and instructional model.
7. The principles derived from theories of learning help the designer select and incorporate instructional strategies proven to be effective for achieving certain types of outcomes (e.g., frequent reinforcement or feedback for acquisition learning, distributed rather than massed practice for difficult material, or advance organizers for unfamiliar concepts).
8. Some designers take an eclectic approach in their work by drawing from alternative learning theories. Others tend to be more purist in nature, invoking one perspective only. The eclectic orientation increases the range of options for meeting project needs based on learner characteristics, type of task, client preferences, and the complementary strengths of varied perspectives. On the other hand, more purist designers have the advantage of keeping within a paradigm that they most understand and value.

## THE ID PROCESS

Learning theory provides the foundation for the instructional design process by explaining how learning takes place to achieve certain kinds of outcomes. Principles of learning (e.g., those involving reinforcement schedules, memory systems, and vicarious learning) derived from the broader theory can be translated into core teaching strategies that form the instructional theory for the particular design project. Most designers find it useful to be knowledgeable about alternative theories, such as behaviorism, social learning, cognitive theory, and constructivism. Applying this background to a given project, the designer is likely to benefit from asking the following types of questions:

- Which theoretical explanations and learning principles seem to best fit the instructional objectives of the lesson or unit?
- Which theoretical frameworks can best support an instructional theory and design model consonant with the conditions of the design project (e.g., resources, client choices, student characteristics)?
- Which theoretical framework best fits the interests and skills of the design team?
- How can learning theory be directly applied to developing, selecting, and supporting the specific instructional strategies that will compose the design model?

Recalling the opening scenario in this chapter, the design team essentially bypassed all these questions, preferring simply to pick and choose pet instructional strategies based on preferences and intuitions. Lacking a learning theory, an instructional theory, or a design model, that team can only hope that the strategies will operate fluently to achieve the desired outcomes. Unfortunately, in real-life situations, such hopes will rarely prevail over ineffective design processes.

## APPLICATION

Consider the types of learning outcomes described next. Which learning theory seems most relevant or useful to you as a framework for design solutions? (There are no correct answers, because all theories should have potential applicability, depending on conditions and designer inclinations.)

**Possible choices:**
Behaviorial
Social
Cognitive/sociocognitive
Constructivist

1. Instructional need: Reduce the amount of discipline suspensions of high school students in an urban school district.
2. Instructional need: Increase the skills of employees of a national food distributor in handling problems with customers' orders.
3. Instructional need: Increase the skills of school board members to work together rather than engage in divisive behavior.
4. Instructional need: Increase the ability of students to complete multiple-choice items, similar to those given on the state achievement tests, quickly and accurately.

## ANSWERS

Depending on the designer's preferences and the "instructional needs" identified, there is no one correct answer to any of the application items. By basing the development of the design model on learning theory and instructional theory (whatever ones are employed), the designer is much better positioned to develop a coherent instructional plan that is both grounded in and justified by scientific principles. Following are possible routes the designers may take in the sample situations.

1. To reduce the discipline problems, the designer views behavioral theory as offering many useful principles regarding behavior modification. The principles offer ideas about reinforcing students' appropriate behaviors and punishing inappropriate behaviors through providing and removing privileges, respectively. However, the designer also sees principles from social learning theory as suggesting there is value in students' observing desirable models demonstrating proper behaviors.

2. To increase the problem-solving skills of employees serving customers, the designer views constructivist principles as highly relevant. On that basis, the designer decides to build into the training course ample opportunities for experiential and cooperative learning, in which students attempt solutions to simulated problems. Sociocognitive principles also seem relevant here for creating situations in which less-advanced students can learn from more experienced ones.

3. As in the preceding example, the designer uses principles from constructivist and sociocognitive theories to engage students (i.e., the school board members) in simulations, cooperative learning, and discussions relative to the instructional goals. However, drawing from cognitive theory, she also develops a well-structured didactic presentation (written and lecture) on "rules and strategies for group interactions." The presentation includes numerous examples and prompts for students to relate concepts to their own experiences.

4. To increase students' preparation for standardized testing, the designer draws on behavioral theory to develop individually adaptive schedules of practice and feedback. However, based on cognitive theory, the designer also develops tutorials that explain how to use mnemonics and generative learning strategies to improve learning of the material.

## INSTRUCTIONAL DESIGN: DECISIONS AND CHOICES

Initially, as a designer, you were completely focused on establishing a relationship with the client, assembling your project team, and understanding the key goals. You gave no attention to instructional theory. However, as you began the task analysis and contemplated which instructional strategies to employ, the importance of instructional theory helped inform your design decisions.

As you conducted the task analysis, you considered whether the amount of conceptual content could result in exceeding the learner's cognitive capacity, or cognitive load. You were also concerned that the fire classes (A, B, C), types of extinguishers, and emergency procedures could create retroactive interference. You then intentionally applied cognitive learning theory and instructional theory principles as you designed the instruction. For example, you employed the following:

- Simple visuals to differentiate the types of fire extinguishers. You reduced cognitive load by eliminating nonessential information and focused the learner's attention by highlighting critical characteristics such as the presence of a pressure gauge and the shape of the nozzle.
- The acronym "PASS" (pull the pin, aim at the base of the fire, squeeze the handle, sweep from side to side) as a mnemonic to help the learner transfer the procedure to long-term memory.
- Repeated practice using fire extinguishers to strengthen the learner's formation of schemata. Another example of reinforcing the formation of appropriate schemata was the practice activity (i.e., generative strategy) that asked the learner to identify errors in carrying out emergency procedures.
- Authentic scenarios that were familiar to the learner. For example, you used office workplace examples rather than industrial workplace examples. The scenarios were challenging but not outside the learner's zone of proximal development. The introductory fire disaster story was used to gain attention and heighten interest and motivation.

From a behavioral perspective, repeated practice strengthened stimulus-response connections. The instructor's praise and corrective feedback reinforced the desired behavior. Students learned how to operate fire extinguishers through direct instruction as well as vicariously by observing the instructor (live or as a video stream in the Web version)—an application of social learning theory.

During the middle of the project, when the department manager asked you, "Is it really necessary to include all these practice activities?" you drew on your knowledge of learning and instructional theory to persuade him that the time necessary to include these "essential" activities would pay off in terms of learning gains.

[The application of instructional theory may be intuitive and automatic, tacit, and/or require conscious effort. Individual preferences also influence your choice of theory. The point is that skilled instructional designers use theory to guide their instructional decisions and to anticipate and resolve potential instructional difficulties. Last, consider how we have applied learning and instructional theory throughout this book and in the design vignettes in each chapter.]

## REFERENCES

Ausubel, D. (1963). *The psychology of meaningful verbal learning*. New York: Grune and Stratton.

Bandura, A. (1986). *Social foundations of thought and action: A social-cognitive theory*. Englewood Cliffs, NJ: Prentice Hall.

Baylor, A. L. (2002). Expanding preservice teachers' metacognitive awareness of instructional planning through pedagogical agents. *Educational Technology Research & Development*, *50*(2), 5–22.

Baylor, A. L., & Kim, Y. (2004). *Pedagogical agent design: The impact of agent realism, gender, ethnicity, and instructional role.* Paper presented at the Intelligent Tutoring Systems, Maceio, Alagoas, Brazil.

Bloom, B. (1976). *Human characteristics and school learning.* New York: McGraw-Hill.

Borman, G. D., Hewes, G., Overman, L. T., & Brown, S. (2003). Comprehensive school reform and achievement: A meta-analysis. *Review of Educational Research, 73*(2), 125–230.

Bruner, J. S. (1963). *The process of education.* New York: Vintage Books.

Bruner, J. S. (1973). *The relevance of education.* New York: W. W. Norton.

Bruner, J. S. (1990). *Acts of meaning.* Cambridge, MA: Harvard University Press.

Driscoll, M. (2005). *Psychology of learning for instruction* (3rd ed.). New York: Pearson Education.

Englemann, S., & Carnine, D. (1991). *Theory of instruction: Principles and applications* (Rev. ed.). Eugene, OR: ADI Press.

Fox, E. J. (2005). Constructing a pragmatic science of learning and instruction with functional contextualism. *Educational Technology Research and Development, 54*(1), 5–35.

Fredrick, L. D., & Hummel, J. H. (2004). Reviewing the outcomes and principles of effective instruction. In D. J. Moran & R. W. Mallot (Eds.), *Evidence-based educational methods* (pp. 210–221). San Diego, CA: Elsevier Academic Press.

Gropper, G. L. (1983). A metatheory of instruction: A framework for analyzing and evaluating instructional theories and models. In C. M. Reigeluth (Ed.), *Instructional-design theories and models: An overview of their current status* (pp. 37–53). Hillsdale, NJ: Erlbaum.

Hmelo-Silver, C. E., Duncan, R. G., & Chinn, C. A. (2007). Scaffolding and achievement in problem-based and inquiry learning: A response to Kirschner, Sweller, and Clark (2006). *Educational Psychologist, 42*(2), 99–107.

Keller, F. S. (1968). "Goodbye teacher . . . " *Journal of Applied Behavior Analysis, 1,* 79–89.

Kirschner, P. A., Sweller, J., & Clark, R. E. (2006). Why minimal guidance during instruction does not work: An analysis of the failure of constructivist. Discovery, problem-based, experiential, and inquiry-based teaching. *Educational Psychologist, 41*(2), 75–86.

Kuhn, D. (2007). Is direct instruction an answer to the right question? *Educational Psychologist, 42*(2), 109–113.

Mager, R. F. (1984). *Preparing instructional objectives* (2nd Ed.). Belmont, CA: Pitman.

Mayer, R. E. (2004). Should there be a three-strikes rule against pure discovery learning? The case for guided methods of instruction. *American Psychologist, 59*(1), 14–19.

Mayer, R. E., Dow, G. T., & Mayer, S. (2001). Multimedia learning in an interactive self-explaining environment: What works in the design of agent-based microworlds? *Journal of Educational Psychology, 95*(4), 806–812.

No Child Left Behind Act of 2001 (NCLB), Pub. L. No. 107-110, 115 Stat. 1425 (2002, January 8).

Piaget, J. (1952). *The origins of intelligence in children.* New York: Basic Books.

Reigeluth, C. M. (Ed.). (1983). *Instructional-design theories and models: An overview of their current status.* Hillsdale, NJ: Erlbaum.

Reigeluth, C. M. (Ed.). (1999). *Instructional-design theories and models: A new paradigm of instructional theory, Volume II.* Hillsdale, NJ: Erlbaum.

Shavelson, R. J., Towne, L., & the Committee on Scientific Principles for Education Research. (Eds.). (2002). *Scientific research in education.* Washington, DC: National Academy Press.

Skinner, B. F. (1954). The science of learning and the art of teaching. *Harvard Educational Review, 24,* 86–97.

Skinner, B. F. (1965). Reflections on a decade of teaching machines. In R. Glaser (Ed.), *Teaching machines and programmed instruction II.* Washington, DC: National Education Association.

Slavin, R. E. (2008). *Educational psychology. Theory and practice: International Edition* (9th ed.). New York: Allyn & Bacon.

Sweller, J. (2004). Instructional design consequences of an analogy between evolution by natural selection and human cognitive architecture. *Instructional Science, 32*, 9–31.

Sweller, J., Kirschner, P. A., & Clark, R. E. (2007). Why minimally guided teaching techniques do not work: A reply to commentaries. *Educational Psychologist, 42*(2), 115–121.

Vygotsky, L. S. (1962). *Thought and language* (E. Hanfmann & G. Vakar, Trans.). Cambridge, MA: MIT Press.

Wittrock, M. C. (1974). A generative model of mathematics learning. *Journal of Research in Mathematics Education, 5*, 181–197.

Wittrock, M. C. (1989). Generative processes of comprehension. *Educational Psychologist, 24*, 345–376.

Yanchar, S. C., South, J. B., Williams, D. D., Allen, S., & Wilson, B. G. (in press). Struggling with theory? A qualitative investigation of tool use in instructional design. *Educational Technology Research and Development*.

C H A P T E R $\;$ 15

# Planning for Instructional Implementation

### GETTING STARTED

You've just spent the last six months designing a new blended Web-based and classroom supervisor training program. The program was developed in response to the needs assessment. As part of the needs assessment, a human resource survey indicated that employees were dissatisfied with the quality of supervision, contributing to a rapid rise in employee attrition. The results from pilot testing the program with several supervisors demonstrates that the program is effective. Senior management has been highly supportive and delighted with the initial results. But, now that you have started to roll out the program, none of the senior managers, middle-level managers, or supervisors has enrolled in the course! You are completely surprised because you've heavily advertised the new program in the company newsletter, distributed emails to supervisors, and even sent personal invitations. And, there's no tuition charge for the course! In a water-cooler conversation, a senior manager tells you that she would be happy to write an endorsement memo to help with promotion but informs you that she and other senior managers ''know all this stuff already'' so they don't feel a need to take the course. You've spent many hours designing the program and wonder if the program will ever be used. Where did you go wrong? What can you do now? How can you convince managers and supervisors that they ''need'' to take the course?

You might start by considering how senior managers would be perceived by employees and peers after taking a course in which they should already have expert knowledge. Consider how taking the course would help or hinder fast-track promotion.

"What is planned change?"

"How do I develop a plan for implementing my project?"

"What resources can I use to implement a project?"

"What else must I consider when implementing a project?"

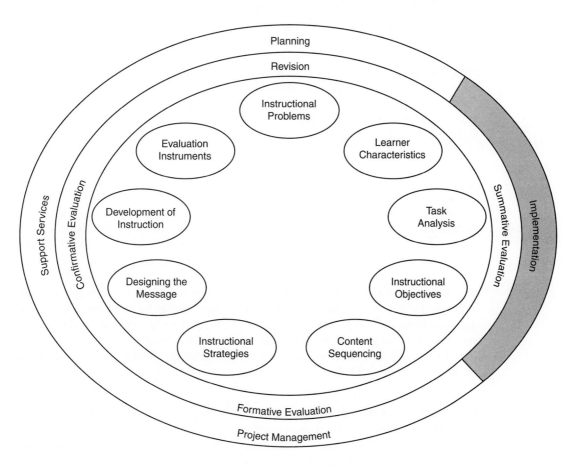

## PLANNED CHANGE

It would seem that if we have created the instruction necessary to solve a problem that would increase productivity, we could simply enroll students in the course or observe people accessing our Web-based instruction. The managers, instructors, and learners would see the advantage of learning the information and readily embrace the instruction. Sometimes, training programs, multimedia, Web-based instruction, and print units are readily adopted by our target audience. There are other times, however, when we have to sell the clients on our instructional product or intervention, that is, we try to change their perception and understanding so they will use the product. When working within a company, university, or school to implement an instructional product, the designer's effort is often focused on working with the individual in a collaborative manner. Bhola (1982) labeled this process *planned change*. Selling is an aspect of the implementation processes referred to as diffusion and adoption. Diffusion is the process of communicating information to a client and target audience about an innovation (i.e., an instructional intervention) (Rogers, 2003). Adoption is the decision to use the innovation. According to Rogers, there are four components of the diffusion process: the innovation, communication, time, and social system. The following paragraphs describe each of these components. The adoption of an innovation is one type of organizational change (King & Anderson, 2002).

### Innovation

An innovation is something new to an organization, manager, worker, teacher, or student who is considering using it. For example, we recall a radio advertisement that made an offer to the "last person on earth" who does not have caller ID. To those of us who have had caller ID for several years, it is an old idea; however, to the household that does not have it yet, caller ID is still an innovation. When we produce an instructional intervention, it is an innovation for our users. If you were to develop a course on conflict management, upgrading the interface system in a copy machine, or how to use a spreadsheet for sales forecasting, then the course would be an innovation. If and when the client or users decide to use the product is dependent on the five characteristics of the intervention discussed in the following paragraphs (Rogers, 2003).

**The Advantage of the Innovation.**    Each training product is judged on its relative merit. If the users perceive it as providing useful knowledge, then they are more likely to adopt it. Although the training program might have many advantages and make an employee more productive, leading to monetary or efficiency rewards, the user has to perceive it as being advantageous. For example, providing laptops and access to company databases to sales personnel on the road has the potential for making the sales force more productive. Computer-naive salespeople, however, might not see the advantage to the laptops and may resist using them.

**Compatibility with Values, Needs, and Experiences.**  Our users will evaluate a training program or instructional innovation to determine whether it is compatible with their values, matches their needs, and is compatible with what they have learned in the past. For example, in recent years there has been a push for professors and teachers to adopt a more student-centered approach to their teaching. This approach requires the professor or teacher to change his or her role from that of a lecturer to one of a facilitator. Some may perceive this role shift as incompatible with their values—teachers need to lecture to teach the student.

**Innovation Complexity.**  If the users perceive the innovation as complex or difficult to use, they are more likely to resist using it. This perception of complexity can become a major obstacle to adoption of the innovation. Consider the difficulty you might face implementing Web-based instruction for instructors who have limited experience with the Internet. If the software requires them to create pages using Hypertext Markup Language (HTML), participate in online chats, and create PowerPoint presentations with streaming video, they will probably view this innovation as too complex to adopt. Similarly, consider the problems you might have implementing a Web-based application for creating maintenance work orders in an organization in which most users have minimal, if any, computer skills. The complexity of such a system could cause the users to resist adopting it.

**Ability to Try the Innovation.**  Users often like to try an innovation on a small scale first. For example, a company introduces a new course for accountants on how to use an innovative software package for auditing clients' books. Some divisions in the organization might resist sending all their accountants to the training during the first offerings. Allowing a division to send one or two employees to the training allows them to sample or try it on a small scale and then determine whether they want to adopt it for everyone. Similarly, a school district might identify a need to use a wireless network in the schools where all the students have laptop computers. Rather than purchasing equipment for all the schools, the network administrator might install it in one or two classrooms to determine whether it will meet their needs. If it works, then the administrator may make the decision to install it in all the schools.

**Observability of Results.**  A training program is more likely to be adopted when the users can easily see the benefits. For example, if the managers and other accountants can see a benefit of the training for the new auditing software, they are more likely to send others to the training. However, if an accountant returns from the training and either refuses to use or seldom uses the new software, others will not see the benefits and may not attend the training. Also, if a critical mass of users is not trained, the training may become a wasted resource because those using the software will not have the support of management or other employees. As we plan an implementation strategy for a new instructional product, we must consider how to communicate the advantage of the product, its compatibility with existing ways, how the user can try it out with minimal risk, and how to make the results observable. We also must show that it is not a complex process.

## Communication

Communication is central to the diffusion process. We have to communicate information about the innovation to potential users so they can decide to use it. Although the instructional designer can prepare materials such as informative memos and presentations, the designer might not be the best individual to communicate the information or "advertise" the course. The most effective communication occurs between individuals who are similar, such as those belonging to the same peer group or having similar interests (Rogers, 2003). For example, a designer needs to consider who could best communicate information on a new course for plant electricians. Is it the instructional designer, or is it the master electrician who served as the SME for the project who should communicate information about the course? The master electrician is a member of the group of electricians and probably has more in common with group members than the instructional designer. Selecting the master electrician to sell the course may be more productive than having the instructional designer sell it, because the electrician has more in common with the target group.

## Time

Users make decisions to adopt an innovation at different times in the life of the innovation. You are probably familiar with an individual who is always the first to have the latest computer, television, or electronic gadget and also, on the other hand, an individual who still has a 13-inch black-and-white television. Rogers (1995) classified these adopters into five categories. The "first adopters" are the innovators who rush out to adopt innovations as soon as possible. Sometimes these first adopters are willing to accept prototypes or test versions of a product. The "early adopters" are the second group to adopt the innovation, often as soon as it is available in "commercial" form. The "early majority adopters" are the third group and comprise the first 50 percent to adopt the innovation. Fourth are the "late majority adopters" who adopt after it appears safe. The final group is the "laggards," who are the last to adopt an innovation or perhaps never adopt it.

The actual time frame for adoption varies depending on the nature of the instructional product. It is conceivable that the adoption cycle could be a week or less for a small project and upward of a year or more for a complex project.

## Social System

The social system describes the networks and relationships between the members of our target audience. Decisions to adopt a training program or instruction are typically influenced by the opinion leaders' views about the consequences of adopting the program. Identifying the opinion leaders and other stakeholders early in the implementation-planning process will identify one group to target with communications.

At the same time, we must identify the various networks in the social system that can help communicate information about the instructional intervention. These networks of people, however, may also resist the adoption process. Understanding the role of the innovation, communication, time, and the social system can help us develop a plan for implementing our product (Malopinsky & Osman, 2006). In the next section, we examine how to use this information to develop an implementation plan.

## THE CLER MODEL

The implementation strategy is a means of specifying how to communicate information about an instructional product and to whom. One strategy for preparing an implementation plan is Bhola's (1982, 1988–1989) CLER model. CLER is an acronym for configuration, linkages, environment, and resources, components that are used to facilitate the diffusion and adoption processes to implement an innovation.

The CLER model, or the configurational theory of innovation diffusion, defines diffusion or implementation of an innovation $(D)_i$ as a function of social configurations (C), linkages between the designer system and client system (L), the surrounding environment (E), and resources available to the designer and the client (R):

$$D_i = f(C, L, E, R)$$

The following paragraphs further explain each component of the CLER model.

### Configuration

Configuration represents the network of relationships of various social units in the organization and the individuals who play a variety of formal and informal roles in the "in" group. These relationships include the designer system and the client system. The designer system includes the instructional designer, the evaluator, and the manager of the instructional design department. The client system includes the target audience as well as the managers and other stakeholders. Identifying these configurational relationships and the roles of the various individuals helps us to develop a communication plan for the implementation strategy.

There are four types of configurational relationships: individuals, groups, institutions, and cultures. Groups are formal workgroups within an organization such as the accounting department or the electricians. Institutions are formal organizations such as businesses or schools. *Culture* describes subcultures or communities.

For example, there may be several accounting, marketing, finance, and engineering groups in a business (i.e., institution). One group might include individuals from engineering, finance, and marketing. Engineers from all these

**TABLE 15-1**

Configurational relationships

| Instructional Designer | Client | | | |
|---|---|---|---|---|
| | Individuals (I) | Groups (G) | Institutions (IS) | Cultures (CL) |
| Individuals (I) | I–I | I–G | I–IS | I–CL |
| Groups (G) | G–I | G–G | G–IS | G–CL |
| Institutions (IS) | IS–I | IS–G | IS–IS | IS–CL |
| Cultures (CL) | CL–I | CL–G | CL–IS | CL–CL |

various groups also belong to an engineering subculture that is open only to engineers. For preparing an implementation plan, the configuration includes both the instructional designer (e.g., innovator) and the client, or adopters. Using the four types of configurations, Bhola (1982) identifies 16 possible relationships (Table 15-1).

Table 15-1 lists the various configurational relationships for interactions between the instructional designer and the client. For example, the instructional designer could act as an individual on the various client relationships. Similarly, the instructional design group or department could act on the various client configurations.

Although Bhola (1982) identified 16 possible configurations, the most effective are those that are one-on-one. Although you might identify several different relationships such as managers "in" with the accounting managers (a group), the most effective way to communicate information about your instructional product would be by having your manager talk individually to each of the accounting managers.

## Linkages

Linkages represent networks or relationships between and within the instructional designer and client organizations. Formal linkages exist within the context of the group and institutional configurations as defined by the management structure. Informal linkages result from partnerships, friendships, and working relationships. These informal relationships often bypass traditional organizational structure. For example, consider a friendship between a vice president and a salesperson who happen to have children who take gymnastic lessons from the same coach. Although they both work for the same organization, the relationship is informal rather than formal. Identifying these different linkages can provide a rich source of communication links for the implementation plan.

## Environment

The environment represents the physical, social, and intellectual forces operating within a configuration. Environmental forces can provide a supportive, neutral, or inhibiting atmosphere for adopting an innovation. Consider, for example, a school that wants to provide students with their own laptop computers they can use in each classroom. A new school could create a supportive environment by providing training and readily available technical support for the teachers. An older school might have a more difficult time due to the physical environment. For example, a lack of electrical outlets placed around the room could make it difficult to charge the batteries during class. Similarly, the desks or tables may not be ergonomically correct or of the right size to hold the laptops. These environmental variables could hinder the plan's adoption.

## Resources

Resources are used to support the implementation process. There are six types of resources an instructional designer can use to support the implementation of a project (Bhola, 1982).

**Conceptual Resources.**   Technical skills and support are one type of conceptual resource that is often needed for implementing projects involving the use of technology. Consider the technical support needed to offer a database administrators' course at a hotel. The course needs computers, software, and access to the company's intranet. Successful implementation of this course requires networking and technical expertise from a variety of individuals. Other conceptual resources include management abilities and planning assistance.

**Influence Resources.**   Goodwill, brand names, incentives, shaming, and threatening are examples of influence resources one can use in the diffusion of an innovation. An instructional designer who has developed goodwill during the development phase will have a resource to act on with the client. Other types of influence resources include incentives such as bonuses or monetary incentives; for faculty, release time from teaching a course; and travel benefits. Negative-influence resources could include the withholding of monetary or promotional incentives.

**Material Resources.**   Financial backing is one type of resource that is often needed to implement a product. Other material resources include computers, software, books, DVD players, video projectors, and physical facilities that can support the implementation.

**Personnel Resources.**   Depending on the size of the project, worker resources can be a critical issue during the implementation phase. Having a number of individuals who can be available at the right time to provide essential training or facilitation is essential if the product implementation is on a short time frame.

**Institutional Resources.**   The infrastructure provided by the institution including both the technology/communication and personnel infrastructure is considered an institutional resource. Other resources can include institutional capabilities, such as printing and shipping instructional materials. For Web-based instruction, a server on either the Internet or intranet is considered an institutional resource necessary for implementation. Consider again the introduction of laptop computers. A new school could provide tables for using the laptops that have built-in electrical outlets and network connections. An older school's building could inhibit the use of laptops because the individual desks are too small to hold the laptops and there are only one or two electrical outlets in the room and a single network connection on the front wall.

## Expert's Edge

### Never Put the Cart After the Horse

From the beginning, the change team should include, besides engineering and IT, other stakeholders, such as manufacturing (a downstream customer of the CAD products), human resources, training, internal corporate communications, and finance. With this broadly representative team, implementation is a natural result of the team effort. There is no need to sell the change because the people being sold made the decision up front.

Traditional instructional design models tend to treat implementation as a phase, like design or development. As a phase, it's something you start when the preceding phase is done. I'm overstating the case, but that's the essential logic of phased approaches: First, we analyze; next, we design; and then we develop. And when the product is ready to go, we implement.

One important consequence of this approach is that there are lots of implementation horror stories. A session at an AECT (Association for Educational Communications and Technology) conference a couple of years ago described several implementation case studies, and most had one or more serious problems (Wilson, 1997). I have contributed my own to these field stories with a chapter in the *ID Casebook* (Spannaus, 1999).

Implementation seems to go much better when it is part of the project from the beginning. If we treat the whole project as a change management process, involving key decision makers and stakeholders from the beginning, implementation will be successful.

Let's consider a specific implementation problem. A company is considering moving to a new CAD/CAM (computer-aided design/computer-aided manufacturing) system. It goes without saying that training would be an important part of the plan. If the information technology (IT) people go to engineering and announce the change, they will encounter resistance. If, on the other hand, the IT people go to engineering and ask for a study, then the decision will be one supported by engineering and IT. There is, of course, a risk that engineering won't want to make the change. Given that they are major users of the CAD/CAM system, they should have a key role in the decision.

Implementation has switched from a top-down, expertise-driven approach to a bottom-up, consensus-driven approach. Such a change model is messy and unpredictable. It requires cooperation among several disciplines, meaning that many leaders will find themselves in a supporting role. But the result is change that works and remarkably reduced resistance to change (Spannaus, Binkert, & Lippit, 1998).

## References

Spannaus, T. W. (1999). Jim Huggins. In P. Ertmer & J. Quinn (Eds.), *ID casebook: Case studies in instructional design.* Upper Saddle River, NJ: Merrill.

Spannaus, T. W., Binkert, J., & Lippit, L. L. (1998, March). *Performance improvement team: An interdisciplinary approach.* Paper presented at the meeting of International Society for Performance Improvement, Chicago.

Wilson, B. (1997, February 23). "If you build it, will they come?" Panel discussion at AECT, Albuquerque.

Timothy W. Spannaus is program coordinator and senior lecturer with the instructional technology program at Wayne State University in Detroit. He has worked as an instructional designer, researcher, and teacher for over 30 years, mostly in technical areas, with technology-based training delivery. He is past president of ibstpi, the International Board of Standards for Training, Performance and Instruction, and ADCIS, the Association for Development of Computer-Based Instructional Systems.

**Time Resource.** It can take time for all the users to adopt a product. The time needed for the implementation must consider all the adopters, from the innovators to the laggards. Trying to implement the program in an unreasonably short time frame can result in poor results.

## PLANNING THE IMPLEMENTATION WITH THE CLER MODEL

An implementation plan identifies the various configurational relationships and then identifies ways to manipulate and capitalize on the configurations to facilitate the process. For this section we will use the following scenario to illustrate how the CLER model can be used to plan an implementation.

Your needs assessment of the network-engineering group found that it often selected a backup generator for clients that was much too large and costly. Your company was losing a fair number of contracts because of the price. The analysis indicated that the network engineers had very little knowledge of how to develop the specifications for a backup generator and tended to rely on the generator sales representative for the design and specifications. You worked with two senior engineers who are highly respected in the company to design a course on how to prepare the specifications for backup electrical generators. The pilot test results suggest the course is very effective—engineers completing the course were capable of developing specifications for a backup generator that were appropriate for the installation. You are concerned, however, that some of the 14 division managers do not believe their engineers need this type of training. "Any good network engineer should know how to develop the specifications for a generator, and all my engineers are good'' is a common response from the managers. Consider how will you convince these managers to send their employees to this course?

## Configuration

The key configurational relationships are the instructional designer (individual), the instructional design department (group), and the company (institution). There are several key relationships on the client side. First are the individuals, who include the chief network engineer, the vice president of the group of network engineers, the individual regional managers, and the 143 individual network engineers. The client group includes the 14 regional network-engineering departments. The institution is the same for the instructional designer and client. There is also a culture configuration. The individual engineers, their managers, and the chief engineer all belong to a subculture of those who share the same interest and expertise in network engineering.

## Linkages

Both the instructional design and client groups have the same formal management linkages. There are a number of valuable informal linkages. First is a strong rapport between the instructional designer and the two SMEs. The two SMEs have ownership of the course and respect the designer's efforts. Second is the informal linkage the SMEs have with the regional managers and engineers. Third is the linkage between the instructional design manager and the vice president and chief engineer. Fourth are the various informal relationships among the engineers, resulting from transfers, promotions, and collaborative efforts, that go across boundaries.

## Environment

The environment created by management is considered supportive of the project. The ''word'' has come down that the engineers will improve their design of the generators by relying less on the outside vendors.

## Resources

Management has indicated that they will provide the needed resources to complete the project. There is, however, a lack of technical resources to answer questions an engineer might have concerning the design of a generator package. Similarly, the vice president has indicated that he wants the training to be implemented as quickly as possible to avoid the loss of any additional bids. On the positive side is the goodwill toward the project generated by the association of the SMEs and the involvement of a number of engineers in the review of the instructional materials. There is also adequate support provided for delivery of the course.

## Analysis of the Situation

There is resistance by several of the regional managers to the course. They believe that their engineers know how to develop the specifications successfully (even though there is adequate evidence to the contrary). These managers are hesitant to enroll their staff in a three-day course.

## Implementation Plan

The following is the plan for the implementation of each component of the CLER model.

**Configuration and Linkages.**    We can create a one-on-one relationship by using the SMEs to communicate to each of the 14 regional managers. Our initial effort is to focus on this configurational relationship and linkage because it can provide a positive, supportive environment for the implementation. All the engineers are in the same subculture and speak a similar technical language. This homogeneous grouping should produce more effective communication than that between the instructional designer and the regional managers (Rogers, 2003). As a last resort, we can use the linkage between the instructional design manager and the vice president to offer incentives or some other inducement to implement the training.

**Environment.**    During the implementation by the adopters, the company has agreed to provide technical support that should result in fast resolution of any problems. The backing of upper management should help create a supportive environment for the adoption of the materials.

**Resources.**    The most important resource may be the goodwill the instructional designer has developed with the engineers and the ownership these two SMEs have of the project. Their support should provide a perception of low complexity for the project. The training materials are readily available as is a support staff to make arrangements for the course offerings. Financial support for the project will allow the instructional design department to pay for one to two engineers from the slow-adopting divisions to attend training. This will provide a regional manager with an opportunity to test the training on a trial basis before fully investing in the product.

**First Course Offering.**    We will work with the SMEs to identify one regional manager who is a respected innovator. The first course offering will be in this district. By implementing the course in a region that supports the innovation, we expect to see increased productivity. The observable benefits of the innovation will then reduce the risk and complexity perceptions of managers in other regions and increase the probability of adoption.

## DEVELOPMENTAL STAGES AND INFORMATION DECISION PROCESS MODELS

The Concerns-Based Adoption Model (CBAM) (Hall & Hord, 1987; Hord, Rutherford, Huling-Austin, & Hall, 1987; Newhouse, 2001) and information-decision process models (Dormant, 1986; Dormant, 1999; Rogers, 1995) describe sequential stages that an individual uses to investigate an innovation and decide whether to adopt or reject it. Table 15-2 synthesizes the stages of acceptance.

For CBAM, the individual is initially concerned with what the change is and how it will personally affect him or her. The concerns are informational and personal. The next stage is managerial: understanding the mechanics of the change, or "how to do it." The last stages of concern consider consequences and collaboration. In these later stages, the prospective adopter evaluates whether the change is effective and generates new ideas that refocus the innovation.

An individual must feel a sense of control; otherwise the change probably will be resisted (Conner, 1992; King & Anderson, 1995). Participation and involvement of supervisors and SMEs can increase a sense of control as well as reduce uncertainty (see Cummings & Worley, 2005).

**TABLE 15-2**

Synthesis of developmental/information decision-making models

| Stage | | |
|---|---|---|
| 1 | Awareness | The adopter has little information about the innovation and has formed no opinion about it. The prospective adopter is passive. Providing positive messages can increase interest. Brief messages, emails, and flyers heighten awareness. |
| 2 | Curiosity, Self-Concern, Information Seeking | The adopter expresses active interest, seeks information, and is concerned how the innovation would affect him/her. Providing specific information that responds to the individual's needs will reduce uncertainty. |
| 3 | Visualization | The adopter shifts from a personal focus to a job focus. The adopter perceives what will be involved in using the innovation and is concerned with how the innovation works. Demonstrating the innovation in a realistic setting enables the prospective adopter to visualize its use. |
| 4 | Tryout and Evaluation | The adopter tries the innovation, learns how it works, and forms an opinion to accept or reject the innovation. The adopter considers the impact of the innovation on him-/herself and others. Training and/or job aids can help build confidence and reinforce a positive opinion. |
| 5 | Use/Acceptance | The adopter accepts the innovation, actively uses it, and asks detailed questions to build expertise. Technical support ensures that the innovation is fully adopted. Rewards are useful to reinforce the new behavior. The adopter may also personalize the innovation or generate ideas that build on the innovation. |

Adapted from Dormant, 1986.

# IMPLEMENTATION DECISIONS

A training program in industry requires an infrastructure to implement and deliver instruction. The following sections describe the implementation decisions related to instructional delivery, instructional materials, scheduling, and instructors.

## Program Promotion

Often, the instructional designer is responsible for program promotion. This may involve preparing advertising for the employee newsletter, sending a promotional email announcement to supervisors, or posting flyers in the employee lunchroom. The instructional designer may also meet with the human resources department to ensure that the course is included for consideration in employee development plans. Once the course is implemented, the instructional designer might request that the communications department write a feature story for inclusion in internal publications describing how employees have benefited from the course and how the course has contributed toward organizational goals.

## Instructional Delivery

Some training departments have a support person or group that manages the delivery of the instruction. The complexity of this task grows with the number of different sites and the number of courses offered.

**Classroom Facilities.**   Training rooms at a company, university, or school are often booked months in advance. Once you have a schedule for a course offering, you'll need reservations for an appropriate room. Options for the room include one of the organization's conference and training rooms or a room at a hotel or conference center. Some rooms are flexible and can be arranged in various formats, whereas a conference room with one large table offers very little flexibility. Careful consideration must be given to the type of room arrangement needed for the course. Some courses require one large, lecture-style classroom with several breakout, or small-group meeting, rooms. A course such as the network-engineering course might require each student to review blueprints or other large documents. To accommodate these materials, you may need a room with a large table for every two students. Courses that use computers will require a different type of table and layout.

**Media Equipment.**   Arrangements for media equipment, such as DVD players and video projectors, must be made early in the planning process. Providing two-way audio and video facilities may require additional planning and scheduling at both the course location and the speaker's location. Visit the classroom before the first course offering and make note of existing projection screens, the need for additional screens, and other factors that may affect instruction and learning. This visit is also a good time to consider the layout of the room and position of the equipment. Employing computer labs presents a variety of problems especially if the learners need access to the Internet, intranet, or the organization's computing resources. Once this need is identified, the information technology and/or network support staff should become part of the planning team. They can help arrange for the installation of software and the necessary networking.

**Other Equipment.**   Technical training courses often require access to other equipment and labs for hands-on training. These needs can vary from cutaway engines to actual copy machines that repair technicians can practice repairing. Similarly, arrangements may be needed for tools and test equipment during the course.

**Transportation.**   There are two levels of transportation planning. First is transportation from the learner's home to the training site, which might require air transportation and either a shuttle service or rental car. This level also includes transportation for instructors and guest speakers. Second is group transportation for field trips during the course. Buses or vans from either the company car pool or from a private company are options for field-trip transportation.

**Housing.**   Some companies have training facilities resembling a small college campus that include not only classrooms but also dormitories and cafeterias. Other options include using a hotel that can also provide the training rooms. Again, these facilities must be scheduled in advance to obtain an adequate number of rooms at one location.

**Food.**   Hotels and many corporate training facilities provide a wide range of food services. Other food options include catering the lunch or allowing the learners to leave the "campus" for the noon meal. In addition to the regular meals, arrangements must be made for snacks and drinks during the day. The facility's food services manager or a dietician can help you select appropriate meals, snacks, and drinks. Breaks provide an opportunity for informal discussion, which often extends student learning.

## Materials

Coordinating the instructional materials for a course can require a substantial amount of time. The instructional designer is often responsible for the packaging, duplication, warehousing, and shipping of the materials. An organization may provide support staff to help with these tasks; however, the designer is usually responsible for initiating and monitoring the process. Be sure to allow enough time to follow the normal procedures of the support staff.

**Packaging.**   Most print materials need some form of binding, ranging from a single staple to three-ring binders to textbook-style binding. Three-ring notebooks, spiral binders, and comb binders are popular for when the number of copies is limited or the materials must lay flat while in use. Another feature of three-ring notebooks and some spiral and comb bindings is the option to add tabs to divide the different sections. An advantage of using three-ring binders is ease of updating them by changing materials as the course evolves over time. The print materials also need a cover, a cover design, and copyright information. A graphic artist or an individual in public relations or communications can provide information on printing standards and use of logos. Packaging nonprint materials such as CD-ROMs, DVDs, and USB drives requires some type of labeling and packaging. CD-ROM production houses will often print your design on the CD and provide jewel cases with printed inserts or simple cardboard mailers. For short runs of CDs, you can purchase labels at an office supply store or contract with a printer for a larger quantity. Another alternative is to make the materials accessible on the Internet or an intranet so learners can download the materials to their laptop or desktop.

**Duplication.**   The duplication of print materials can take just a few minutes at a copy machine to a week or more at an offset printer. Discussions with a representative of the group doing the duplication should start early. In an initial meeting you can receive helpful information on page and margin sizes for your layouts as well as schedule the duplication. You will need to coordinate the duplication of the materials so that they are ready for the initial (and subsequent) course offerings. It is prudent to check the final materials for accuracy of duplication, collation, and assembly prior to the beginning of a course. The same considerations must also be given to nonprint materials such as DVDs and CD-ROMs.

**Warehousing.**   It is easy to imagine an instructional designer ordering 1,000 copies of a training manual in a three-inch ring binder and then trying to find storage space for them when the printer's truck arrives! A training department located at the organization's headquarters is often faced with the problem of finding adequate office space. Finding a room to store the materials can be an almost impossible task. Consideration must be given to warehousing all training materials before they are ordered. An alternative is to order materials in smaller quantities as needed.

**Shipping.**   Some companies offer their courses all over the country and world. Special arrangements have to be made to box and ship the student materials prior to the course. If the materials are going to another country, special forms must be completed for customs and time must be allowed for the packages to pass through customs when leaving the country and on entering the destination country. Another option that also solves the warehousing issue is to upload or email electronic documents, such as word-processing or PDF files, to a commercial copy center near the training site. The copy center can duplicate, bind, and deliver the materials to the training center a day or two before the training begins.

## INSTRUCTORS

The last implementation decision concerns the instructors. The two primary issues of concern are the scheduling and training.

## Scheduling

Some companies have a group of professional instructors or rotate employee experts through the training department to serve as instructors. For example, expert company engineers might serve as instructors for the network-engineering course described earlier in this chapter. Regardless of the source of the instructors, careful planning is required to schedule their time. Using company experts as instructors assumes that their manager will allow them to leave their job several times a year to teach a course. Scheduling a course requires consideration of their workload to minimize the impact on their productivity.

## Instructor Training

There are three reasons to provide instructor training. First is to improve the instructors' teaching and presentation skills. In business, many of the individuals who serve as instructors have not had any formal training in teaching. One or more basic courses in presentation, facilitation, and teaching strategies can help them improve their skills. Second is to train instructors on how to teach a specific course. For example, the implementation plan for the network-engineering course example is to use the two SMEs as the instructors for the first six months. New instructors with the necessary technical knowledge and skills will be needed to conduct future courses. These new instructors may need to attend the course one or more times and receive tutoring or coaching to develop their technical expertise to teach the course. Last, instructor training ensures that all instructors consistently facilitate the course the same way.

## ROLE OF SUPERVISORS

Supervisors play an important role in preparing employees for training. Supervisor involvement increases the likelihood that the employee will learn what is expected. Ideally, the supervisor should meet with the employee prior to the training to discuss learning goals and after the training to review what was learned. During the meeting, the supervisor also makes clear what the employee is expected to do on the job (see Zenger, Folkman, & Sherman, 2006). Supervisor follow-up reinforces new behaviors. In some organizations, the instructional designer provides a briefing guide (or sends an email) to supervisors outlining their support role and a set of key points to discuss before and after the employee attends training.

## SUMMARY

1. The successful adoption of an instructional product is dependent on how the merits, compatibility, complexity, and visibility of results are perceived by the client system and on their ability to try it.
2. An implementation plan includes the analysis of the configuration, linkages, environment, and resources and how these elements can be optimized to provide

for effective communication between the instructional designer and the client. The CLER model provides a framework for developing the implementation plan.

3. When planning the implementation of a course, careful consideration must be paid to scheduling the facilities and arranging for equipment, transportation, housing, and food services.

4. The instructional designer is often responsible for the packaging, warehousing, and shipping of the various instructional materials. This planning often requires involving individuals such as a graphic designer early in the design process to develop a cost-effective layout for the duplication process.

5. Instructor scheduling and training is an important aspect of the course implementation process.

## THE ID PROCESS

Implementing a project begins during the problem identification process. A designer can use a needs assessment or goal analysis to generate interest and goodwill toward the project. During the design and development phases, individual buy-in may be developed by soliciting reviews and examples from various stakeholders. For example, we needed a sample diary page for an example in a training manual. We asked one of the regional engineers who was an opinion leader if he could provide us with a sample page from his diary. By using his example, we were able to give him both recognition and involvement in the project. Implementing a training product may require extensive traveling, meetings, and special training to gain adopters. For some courses that solve a real problem, the plan is as simple as informing managers and employees that the course or materials are available. Courses that conflict with existing values or methods typically require a more elaborate approach for convincing your clients of the value of the training.

## APPLICATIONS

You have just completed developing a major management training program for a national retail chain. Using existing classroom materials, your team has created a hybrid course that incorporates both Web-based instruction and traditional classroom instruction while significantly reducing the classroom time. This is your client's first experience with Web-based instruction. At the first implementation and instructor training meeting, you found resistance to the Web-based components by the instructors in the New England region. The regional training manager fully supports the concept, but the instructors refuse to use the materials. The course was well received by managers and instructors in the other two regions that have completed the instructor training and implementation. You have four remaining regions that need the implementation and instructor training. You now see a need to develop an implementation plan for the remaining regions plus the New England region. How would you develop the plan?

## ANSWERS

We would start first by identifying the different components of the CLER model. First are the configurations. The primary players include the design team, the regional managers, and the instructors. Most of these configurations will probably be the design team and managers and the design team and instructors. We would also want to identify individual-to-individual configurations where possible.

Second, we start searching for linkages that help us implement the project. The formal linkages, such as regional manager to instructors, are easy to identify with an organizational chart. But more important are the informal linkages that we might use. For example, we might identify an instructor who buys in to the course and who has worked with an instructor who is resistant to adopting the course design.

Third, we would need to identify the environment in each region and within the company. For example, the New England region might not have the ready and easy access to the intranet that the other regions have. Correcting this environmental constraint might increase the adoption of the course. We would also want to identify the climate created by the regional managers to identify other constraints to the implementation.

Fourth, we would need to identify the resources available to help the implementation. One example might be the use of an instructor from one region to offer a course in another region and serve as a model for the instructors. Finding informal linkages between instructors could help us identify instructors that would have the most potential for helping us implement the project. Using this information, we could develop an overall implementation plan as well as plans adapted to specific regions.

## INSTRUCTIONAL DESIGN: DECISIONS AND CHOICES

Although the fire extinguisher project is completed, its success depends on promoting it to employees and supervisors throughout the organization. Here are a number of issues to consider:

- Placing the electronic version of the material on the organization's internal Website
- Adding the instructional program to the course catalog (print and online versions)
- Announcing the availability of the course to the human resource department and to supervisors
- Adding the instruction to the new-hire orientation program
- Scheduling the classroom version (and coordinating with new employee hiring cycles)
- Preparing a senior management support memo to be distributed to supervisors

- Preparing a feature story about the program for the organization's monthly employee newsletter
- Monitoring employee enrollment data and generating appropriate statistics for demonstrating return on investment
- Planning for maintaining records for the program (particularly documentation of testing)
- Distributing the classroom program to remote locations (including international offices)

Some of these issues may involve coordinating with other individuals or departments such as human resources, internal communications, senior management, Website administrators, and the security/safety director.

[There are many stories of excellent instructional products that have rarely been used because the designer failed to consider promoting the finished product.]

## REFERENCES

Bhola, H. S. (1982). Planning change in education and development: The CLER model in the context of a mega model. *Viewpoints in Teaching and Learning, 58,* 1–35.

Bhola, H. S. (1988–1989). The CLER model of innovation diffusion, planned change, and development: A conceptual update and applications. *Knowledge in Society: The International Journal of Knowledge Transfer, 1,* 56–66.

Conner, D. R. (1992). *Managing at the speed of change: How resilient managers succeed and prosper where others fail.* New York: Villard Books.

Cummings, T. G., & Worley, C. G. (2005). *Organization development and change* (8th ed.). Mason, OH: South-Western.

Dormant, D. (1986). The ABCDs of managing change. In National Society for Performance and Instruction (Ed.), *Introduction to performance technology* (pp. 238–256). Washington DC: The National Society for Performance and Instruction.

Dormant, D. (1999). Implementing human performance technology in organizations. In H. D. Stolovitch & E. J. Keeps (Eds.), *Handbook of human performance technology* (2nd ed., pp. 237–259). San Francisco: Jossey-Bass Pfeiffer.

Hall, G. E., & Hord, S. M. (1987). *Change in schools: Facilitating the process.* Albany: State University of New York Press.

Hord, S. M., Rutherford, W. L., Huling-Austin, L., & Hall, G. E. (1987). *Taking charge of change.* Alexandria, VA: Association for Supervision and Curriculum Development.

King, N., & Anderson, N. (2002). *Managing innovation and changes: A critical guide for the organizations.* London: Thomson.

King, N., & Anderson, N. (1995). *Innovation and change in organizations.* London: Routledge.

Malopinsky, L. V., & Osman, G. (2006). Dimensions of organizational change. In J. A. Pershing (Ed.), *Handbook of human performance technology* (2nd ed., pp. 262–286). San Francisco, CA: Pfeiffer.

Newhouse, C. P. (2001). Applying the concerns-based adoption model to research on computers in classrooms. *Journal of Research on Computing Education, 33*(5), 1–21.

Rogers, E. M. (1995). *Diffusion of innovations* (4th ed.). New York: Free Press.

Rogers, E. M. (2003). *Diffusion of innovations* (5th ed.). New York: Free Press.

Zenger, J., Folkman, J., & Sherwin, B. (2006). Make learning stick. *Leadership Excellence, 23*(1), 10–11.

# Instructional Design Project Management

## GETTING STARTED

For the past two years, Green Energy, a company specializing in renewable technology, has been developing a new solar panel for residential application. Now that the product is ready to be launched nationwide, you have been asked to quickly prepare training for the sales force and installation technicians. The product manager tells you that the new product rollout will take place in about three months! The product manager promises to provide you unlimited access to SMEs and sales representatives as needed. The product manager also invites you to join the weekly product rollout meetings, which include about 25 engineers as well as representatives from marketing, sales, legal, information technology, and human resources. At the first weekly meeting you attend, a debate develops among the engineers concerning several technical changes being considered that will affect installation procedures.

## QUESTIONS TO CONSIDER

"What are the key tasks involved in planning an instructional design project?

How do I manage an instructional design project?"

"What are the components of a project agreement or proposal?"

"How can I reduce the time needed to carry out an instructional design project?"

"How are instructional design projects funded?"

"What responsibilities do the instructor and client share in the design process?"

"What are the legal responsibilities of the instructional designer?"

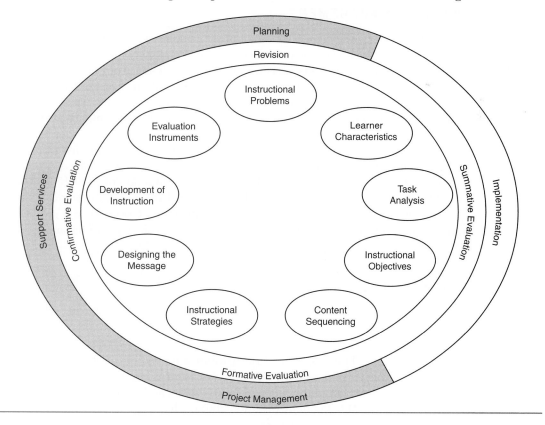

As you begin work on the task analysis, the SME informs you that he has just been placed on another project, so his time will be limited. Several other engineers provide assistance, but none of them has expert knowledge, and the product information they provide is inconsistent. The sales representatives are continuously preempted by sales calls, so they keep rescheduling meetings. After you create a draft prototype, you ask the lead design engineer, the sales manager, and a field installer to review the materials. At the review meeting, it's obvious that the sales manager has not reviewed the materials critically, and the lead design engineer and field installer disagree on the correctness of the technical installation procedures. The product design manager informs you that no budget is available to support a website and to develop a training video but suggests asking the sales manager for financial support. When you meet with the sales manager he tells you that the two-day training will have to be cut to four hours. At this point, you cannot determine whether the sales manager or product design manager is now in charge and which manager has the final authority to sign off on the training prototype. As you begin to discuss changes with your Web programmer, she reminds you that she will be on vacation for the next two weeks. You feel a perfect storm rising. Could you have taken some action early on to better manage this project?

## PROJECT MANAGEMENT

All projects are characterized as being unique in some way, finite in duration, and are intended to achieve a specific result (Project Management Institute, 2008). Instructional design projects vary in size and complexity from creating a simple job aid for making internal, local, and long-distance calls to developing a semester-long college chemistry course delivered asynchronously or 100 Web-based units on computer product design for your company's designers. Similarly, you might work on developing a course for network technicians that includes modules on cabling, network design, and network switches. Some instructional design projects involve only one designer; other projects may require a large team. A project or course that involves the design, development, and production of 15 or 100 different modules presents a unique problem: How does an instructional designer manage the process? We have divided the project management process into two major parts, applicable to both large and small projects: project planning and process management activities.

### Project Planning

The planning of an instructional design project requires a scope of work, scheduling and resource allocation, and budgeting.

**Scope of Work.**   The scope of work provides a definition of the boundaries of the project. This definition is used to gain a consensus among all the stakeholders concerning the purpose of the project, why it is done, and the expected outcomes or products (Project Management Institute, 2008). The scope of a project is affected by three constraints: the time available, the degree of quality required, and the budget (Lewis, 2007). The project's scope may also be modified during the life of the project to reflect unexpected changes.

**Scheduling and Resource Allocation.**   Developing a schedule for the design of a single unit is rather straightforward; however, developing a schedule for several units for a specific project is complex and requires careful attention to logistics and staffing. Scheduling begins by identifying all the specific tasks that need to be completed (called *work breakdown structure*). The project manager must then determine what tasks must be done first and assign individuals to each task, taking into account who is available when and how to make efficient use of employees' time.

The time required to complete each task is a function of the nature of the task. There are two types of tasks: fixed-duration and variable duration.

Fixed-duration tasks take a set amount of time. For example, viewing a 30-minute video recording will take 30 minutes. Other tasks have a variable duration; these are referred to as *resource-driven* tasks (Stevenson & Marmel, 1997). You can reduce the amount of time it takes to complete a resource-driven task by adding more resources. For example, it might take one graphic artist four days to complete 16 drawings, but the 16 drawings can be completed in one day by using four graphic artists. It still takes a total of four days of effort; it just happens that all "four days" of effort happen on the same day, and that shortens the project's timeline.

---

## Expert's Edge

### The Recipe for Success Requires the Right Mix

Managing an instructional design project in the context of higher education has become a new challenge, with new technologies and new paradigms converging and conflicting with established practice and interactive learning literacy. Within our unit at Deakin University, specifically where projects integrate online learning environments, we are developing a different approach to the management of instructional design projects by focusing on the long-term delivery of those environments and the dynamic nature of the educational content. This management approach integrates the essential features of instructional design while catering to the unique elements of online access (interactivity, collaboration, communication) and off-campus delivery (access, convenience, service) as well as the associated professional development and support (scaffolding) in online teaching and learning strategies for the academic staff. This brief synopsis highlights what we consider to be the six essential success factors for the management of our instructional design projects.

The first and most critical aspect of managing our instructional design projects is to ensure that we have established effective *liaison* with the "client," usually the course or program chair, who has overall responsibility for the effective delivery of the course of study. Until recently, it was assumed that our clients' familiarity with both educational design and online learning was sufficient to enable translation (instructional design) of the content material to the interactive medium without requiring additional professional development. What we have discovered, however, is that familiarity with these concepts is varied and that often extensive professional development is required to maximize the effectiveness of any instructional design and development projects. This situation is also consistent with evidence from other training and learning contexts that have manifested limited levels of competency in utilizing the online milieu effectively. In our situation, when professional development needs were identified, it was often during the development process, with the consequence that the output of content into the online environment became little more than a digitization process. Our revised approach, working closely with senior faculty, is to establish the necessary communication and understanding between client and designer and to delay formal instructional design work on the project *scope* until any necessary professional development and training have been completed.

The second factor relevant to the effective management of instructional design is to work with the client to confirm the project and the subsequent project specifications. In our context, the scope refers to the overall requirements for the project that focus on the educational rationale (what is going to be achieved by undertaking the work), the project deliverables (what we as a development team will produce for the client), the project responsibilities (the people who have been nominated to undertake specific tasks), the project plan (estimating when essential tasks will be completed), and the project resources (the people, equipment, and funds necessary to create the deliverables by a target date). While this model is consistent with accepted commercial practice, our experience has been that projects too often follow their own paths, becoming unwieldy, rather than conforming to an articulated plan. Once both the client and our development group have accepted and agreed to the project scope, more detailed specifications are generated. It is also important to note that this process assumes that the client is responsible for the provision of content and the statement of learning objectives, with strategies for teaching and learning being developed in consultation with educational designers from our development group.

Before embarking on the project, the third critical element for the manager is to ensure that the development team has the appropriate *skill mix*. Prior to the growth of online environments for off-campus delivery, our main mode of media production was print-based study guides and readers that were developed using a specific sequential process and clearly articulated roles. This linear process, however, is not suitable for online environments, and we are now emphasizing what skills are required to complete the instructional design project and the roles different people play in that process. The critical roles for the successful design and implementation of online resources include the educational designer, the teaching and learning innovator, and the visual/interactive designer. Rather than operating with a mind-set that we are creating text online, we must focus on providing engaging communication between learner and material presented. This requires project roles in which individuals can take on a wide range of skills relevant to the project—creating online material, integrating appropriate graphical or interactive objects, applying educational design to the course structure, and undertaking operational effectiveness (quality assurance) checks. This last role highlights the fourth success factor that must be included in our instructional design projects—*quality assurance*, which takes a number of different forms. In the first instance, quality checks are established to ensure the overall design is consistent with the original plan and, where necessary, to correct different design components such as screen layout or graphics. This process also provides feedback to team members who have expressed a need to better understand the impact of their work on the overall design effort. Subsequent quality checks are undertaken by independent experts to provide feedback to the team and the client on the overall impact of the product and any potential delivery issues. Through an iterative sequence of successive approximations, the instructional design effort is monitored for quality and educational effectiveness.

The fifth factor is to ensure that the *timelines* and *milestones* that are prescribed for the project are closely monitored and corrected to meet the objectives of the project. While this is clearly a standard component of any instructional development project, a major issue that we face is that traditional development has focused on completing the instructional design activities prior to delivery. Typically, this has been undertaken on a semester basis, with development in semester 1 for delivery in semester 2. However, this does not provide adequate time to ensure the ongoing effectiveness of teaching and learning resources in the context of higher education, and we are now conceptualizing the project as extending over a sequence of four or five delivery cycles, with each cycle implementing changes based on information from evaluation of the prior delivery cycle. The significant difference with this approach is that projects are conceptually always "under construction." This links to and highlights the sixth and final success factor, the ongoing *maintenance* of resources. Until recently, we had undertaken projects on a year-by-year basis and are now establishing a process by which a single project is scoped for development work over a number of years. Our projects are therefore conceptualized as the development of a series of resources that will be subject to ongoing change as a result of course evaluation and disciplinary developments. Moving from a mind-set that focuses on completion of these resources (and therefore the end of the project) to one in which resources will (theoretically) never be "complete" requires a new approach to the management of instructional design projects.

These success factors are critical in our current environment because we are moving rapidly to new ways of designing and delivering teaching and learning environments. Unless we change the way our clients think and our developers undertake projects, we will not be aligned to the appropriate methods for effective instructional design in the context of online teaching and learning in higher education.

Roderick C. Sims, PhD, is associate professor and director of the Teaching and Learning Support Unit at Deakin University, Australia. He is responsible for the educational design and quality assurance of online teaching and learning environments as well as the provision of academic professional development for the university faculties. Dr. Sims has over 20 years of experience with instructional design and educational computing, specializing in the learner–computer interface and visual communication.

A key term in scheduling is the critical path. The critical path is the series of tasks you must complete to keep a project on time. For example, if you are wallpapering your kitchen, you must first remove the old wallpaper before you can apply the new wallpaper. The critical path would include removing the old wallpaper and installing the new wallpaper. Returning the wallpaper-removal equipment is not critical to finishing the project on time.

Some tasks can be completed at various times before they cause a delay in the project. Selecting and purchasing the wallpaper can be done almost any time prior to the removal of the last strip of old paper. Selecting and purchasing the new wallpaper has slack time. That is, there is a time period for completing the task before it becomes part of the critical path. Thus, if we wait until after we have removed the old wallpaper to buy the new, then the selection and purchasing task becomes part of the critical path. Some tasks are also dependent on other tasks. Applying the new wallpaper is dependent on removing the old wallpaper and purchasing the new wallpaper. But removing the old paper and buying the new paper are not dependent on each other.

Milestones identify the completion of major accomplishments in a project. A milestone is actually a point in time. For example, one of our milestones is the purchase of the new wallpaper, a second is when the old wallpaper is removed, and a third is when the new wallpaper is applied. Each of these milestones indicates the completion of a phase or major task, not the time needed to complete the phase or task. In a design project, milestones might be the completion of the task analysis, learner analysis, statement of objectives, strategy design, approval of the design document, and first draft of the instruction.

Often, there is a deliverable associated with a milestone that you can give to a manager or client. The item might be a prototype of a screen design for a Webpage or a report, such as the results and recommendations of the formative evaluation. The scheduling process involves translating planned activities into the various tasks; determining the dependent tasks, milestones, deliverables; and then identifying the most efficient path for completing the project. Scheduling also involves determining who will carry out each task, either individually or as a team.

**Budgeting.**    Some organizations require that you prepare a detailed project budget, others require only that you track costs so they can be charged back, and others do not budget or track the costs. Once you have identified the tasks and their

**FIGURE 16-1**

Staffing budget estimate

| Dates | Task Description | Project Manager | Instructional Designer #1 | Instructional Designer #2 | Graphic Artist | Web Programmer | SME |
|---|---|---|---|---|---|---|---|
| | **Analysis** | | | | | | |
| 5/10-5/14 | Interview managers | 4 | 6 | 6 | | | |
| 5/18-5/24 | Administer survey | 2 | 12 | | | | |
| 5/15-5/17 | Word process raw interview data | | | 14 | | | |
| | **Design** | | | | | | |
| 5/19-5/27 | Conduct task analysis | 2 | 18 | 12 | | | 4 |
| 6/1-6/14 | Write instructional materials | | 40 | 40 | | | 4 |
| 6/12-6/30 | Produce graphics | 1 | 4 | | 20 | | |
| 6/20-6/28 | Create website pages | 2 | 4 | | | 20 | |
| | **Total Hours** | 11 | 84 | 72 | 20 | 20 | 8 |
| | x hourly rate | $200 | $100 | $75 | $75 | $100 | $100 |
| | **Total Cost** | $2,200 | $8,400 | $5,400 | $1,500 | $2,000 | $800 |

durations, you can determine how much effort is needed by the different team members and what resources are needed to complete the task (see Figure 16-1). Resources include people (e.g., instructional designers, SME consultants, graphic artists), facilities and equipment (e.g., offices, labs, video studios, computers), and materials (e.g., photographic film, burnable CDs, paper).

Business organizations and consulting firms often have a daily rate for their instructional designers that includes salary, benefits (e.g., health insurance, vacation, retirement), and overhead (e.g., for office space, computer support, telephone, etc.). In addition to labor costs, the project budget must also account for the rental of equipment and facilities (e.g., postproduction video editing) and the production of prototypes and master materials.

The output from preparing the scope of work, schedule, and budget is a project agreement or proposal, which we will discuss in greater detail later in this chapter.

## Management Activities

After the client approves the scope of work and the budget, the project begins. Throughout the project, the project manager monitors progress, resolves human relations issues among team members and stakeholders, and maintains communication with the client and other key stakeholders.

**Starting the Project.** For large projects, a project launch or kickoff meeting is held that includes all the stakeholders and key team members. The aim of the meeting is to ensure that everyone gains a common understanding of the scope, goals, and individual responsibilities. The project manager and team members can explain the project, the milestones, and deliverables to clarify any misconceptions. This meeting provides a means for the team to develop rapport with the stakeholders and to explain the instructional design process. It also provides the client with a forum to ask for explanations and to clarify their expectations.

Once the project is under way, the project manager is responsible for managing, tracking, and reporting the progress. Management involves coordinating the work of others, hiring consultants, facilitating cooperation, and managing resources.

**Managing Resources.**   The project manager is responsible for ensuring that adequate resources (human, material, and financial) are available to complete the tasks. A project manager must determine when the video production crew is needed and have it arrive at the appropriate time rather than a week early or a week late. When a project falls behind, the project manager may need to add additional resources to resource-driven tasks. For example, additional graphic artists could be hired to finish the graphic work, or additional programmers could be added to complete a multimedia project. Similarly, the project manager may ask the team to work six days a week or longer days to complete the project on time.

**Tracking.**   Tracking the completion of tasks and the budget are essential for completing the project on time and within budget. A project manager will need to establish processes and procedures (e.g., weekly status reports) for collecting information from the various team members to track the progress of the project. Similarly, weekly or scheduled team meetings are used to identify problems and successes so that personnel can be reassigned to keep the project on schedule. The project manager is also responsible for documenting client-requested changes and adjusting the schedule and budget as needed.

**Project Reporting.**   A project manager has the responsibility to keep management and the client informed of the project's progress. The type of reporting is dependent not only on the length and complexity of the project but also on what information management and the client want. Some organizations may want a weekly or monthly report, whereas the client may only want a final report. A project manager needs to determine the type of reporting at the beginning of the project and be willing to make changes as the project progresses. If management and the client do not want reports, we have always found it wise to maintain our own file of reports in case someone asks a question about the project. Similarly, it is always useful to keep logs of phone calls with the client and to document changes to the project.

Planning and managing a project may seem like an overwhelming task. The project management responsibilities often conflict with the instructional design responsibilities, leaving instructional designers in the position of determining which task to neglect to cause the least negative impact on the project. Project management software is a valuable tool that can help the instructional designer manage a project. These software tools can streamline the scheduling, budgeting, tracking, and reporting processes.

## Completing the Project

After the project is completed, the project manager meets with the client to turn over the deliverables, provide information for maintenance, and discuss any follow-up recommendations. The project manager may also arrange a debriefing meeting during which the project team and key stakeholders evaluate the project process by identifying what worked well, what could be improved next time, and other lessons learned. It should be noted that instructional projects are rarely ever "complete." They are often improved on an ongoing basis long after implementation. Last, the project manager rewards and recognizes the project team for their efforts. A project celebration can include a formal luncheon with speeches, a personalized gift such as a desk set, or a hand-written thank-you note.

## PROJECT AGREEMENT AND PROPOSAL PREPARATION

For some projects, a client or funding agency may request a proposal or bid. Such a request is often referred to as a request for proposals, or RFP. Some agencies (e.g., the National Science Foundation) provide a number of forms and specific instructions on how to prepare and submit a proposal. Internal proposals or project agreements prepared for corporate clients may not require a structure. Regardless of the client, a proposal should include the details of the project. A proposal should include six parts:

1. *Statement of purpose.* This section should describe the need or problem the project will address and a statement of goals. It should focus your reader's, the proposal evaluator's, or client's attention on the primary purpose of the proposal. Using signal words such as "The purpose of this proposal is" or headings such as "Project Purpose" or "Project Goals" helps direct the reader's attention.

2. *Plan of work.* This section might include a brief description of the instructional design process that you will use. The reader is probably unfamiliar with the instructional design process and the terminology, so the section should be written in terms a layperson can understand. Your reader should gain an understanding of what you will do if the project is funded.

3. *Milestones and deliverables.* Milestones are major accomplishments of the project (revisit "Project Planning" section). Typical milestones might include the completion of the needs assessment, completion of the design and prototypes, final version of print units, rough edits of video recordings, and completion of the field test. Deliverables are those objects such as units, videos, or reports that you will give to the client. Again, the design model can help identify the milestones and deliverables.

4. *Budget.* The fourth part of the proposal is the budget, which details all the costs associated with the project. One approach to preparing a budget is for the designer to complete a task analysis for each of the milestones to

identify the tasks associated with each. Then, the designer must determine the personnel, travel, and other costs associated with each task.

5. *Schedule.* This section includes a timeline or schedule describing the work on each milestone. The amount of detail in your schedule will vary depending on the requirements of the client or funding agency. Some proposals may require a schedule only for milestones and deliverables, whereas others may request only a date for completion of the total project.

6. *Staffing.* The final section describes the project personnel, perhaps in a brief biographical sketch of each individual or vitae or resumes. Often, clients and funding agencies want to know who will work on the project. This section needs to present each staff member in an honest and appropriate manner. When writing a proposal, the designer should always keep the readers' perspective in focus and write the proposal for the reader, not for other instructional designers. Many agencies place a page limit on the proposal (e.g., 25 pages of narrative).

A good proposal is concise and addresses the purpose. An unnecessarily long proposal may bring negative results. The following checklist will help you assess your own proposal:

1. Does the project title describe the purpose and nature of the project?
2. Are the goals or major objectives of the project clearly defined?
3. Is the procedure to develop the materials clearly defined?
4. Are the personnel, resources, facilities, and departments required for the project identified?
5. Does the budget clearly describe the costs of personnel, materials, travel, resources, design and production, reproduction of print and nonprint materials, evaluation, and assistance from other departments? These estimates should be based on the work effort required to complete the project.
6. Are the time frame, including completion, evaluation, and reporting points, and other requirements for carrying out the project included?
7. Are the client's approval and sign-off points identified?
8. Are the actual products, including instructional and learning resources, stated?
9. Is any subcontract work identified and explained?
10. Is the payment schedule described? (Payments are often requested at the completion of planning steps, design of materials, final preparation of materials, formative testing, or final completion.)
11. Are the qualifications of primary project personnel described?
12. Are other important matters (how to proceed with the project; project communications; change procedures; other personnel, resources, or departments you might call on for use, etc.) included in the proposal?

**FIGURE 16-2**
Sample project agreement

---

## Sample Project Agreement: Fire Extinguisher Training Program

### 1.0  Purpose and Overview

Our purpose is to improve emergency preparedness of office personnel in case of an office fire. Security personnel and employee fire marshals have been trained on procedures to evacuate the building and assist physically challenged employees but are unfamiliar with building fire equipment. This course will cover proper use of fire extinguishers.

### 2.0  Personnel

*2.1  Identification:*

The primary client is Keegan Coburn, Director of Security. A secondary funding sponsor is Mary Lou Rankin, Vice President of Human Resources. John Hernandez, a certified emergency responder, contracted from the county fire department, will serve as subject-matter expert. The corporate training department will oversee the project. Dee-Anne Gomes will serve as the project manager and Sherry Wise will be the lead instructional design specialist. Part-time support personnel will include Linda Campbell, Web programmer, and Cindy Mudge, graphic artist. Video production services (if needed) will be contracted with an external agency.

*2.2  Expectations:*

The client is responsible for signing off approval on all prototypes and final master deliverables. Budget and the associated charge code will be provided by the VP of Human Resources. The project manager has overall responsibility for the project and negotiating any extension of project timelines due to unplanned contingencies.

### 3.0  Project Communications

The project manager will update the client and sponsor weekly by providing a written status report. The report will identify accomplishments, changes and modifications, and budget expenditures. The project manager, client, and/or sponsor may arrange meetings anytime throughout the project to share problems and concerns about the design process, the deliverables, or the behavior of project personnel.

### 4.0  Project Goals

- Develop a two-hour workshop that enables participants to acquire fire safety knowledge, procedures, and practice using an office fire extinguisher
- Develop participant materials (including job aids)
- Develop a website (which will contain the workshop PowerPoint slides and/or podcast)
- Develop an instructor's/facilitator's guide for the workshop
- Pilot-test the workshop and revise the materials based on evaluative feedback
- Prepare advertising materials to promote the workshop

The instructional design team will also review existing commercial materials and determine whether they can be modified or adopted before creating custom materials.

*(continued)*

**FIGURE 16-2**
(*Continued*)

---

**5.0   Tentative Project Schedule**

The project must be completed in a short period of time: 6 weeks (by April 1). The plan for our work and milestones are shown in the following timeline:

| | |
|---|---|
| February 16 | Kick off communication meeting (client, sponsor, SME, and design team). |
| February 17–20 | Conduct learner and task analysis, prepare instructional objectives. |
| February 24 | Milestone: Review task analysis and objectives (client and project manager). |
| February 25–March 4 | Determine content sequencing and design the instructional strategies; develop first prototype of instructional materials and website layout. |
| March 5 | Milestone: Review first prototype of instructional materials and website design (client and design team). |
| March 6–11 | Revise prototype. Begin preparation of instructor's guide. |
| March 12 | Milestone: Review and approve final prototype instructional materials and website (client). |
| March 13–17 | Complete instructor's guide. Complete website and job aids. Prepare logistics for initial pilot test offering of workshop. Prepare evaluation materials. Run train-the-trainer session. |
| March 19 | Initial pilot-test offering (instructor, design team). |
| March 20 | Revise workshop materials based on pilot test (including participant materials, instructor/facilitator guide, supporting audio-visual materials). Revise and test website. |
| March 24 | Complete promotional materials. |
| March 27 | Milestone: Final sign-off and project hand-off (client and sponsor). |
| April 29 | Project Debriefing Meeting (client, sponsor, SME, instructional design team). |

**6.0   Resources**

The client will provide subject–matter experts as needed for assisting with task analysis and verifying the accuracy of the instructional materials, instructor's guide, website, and job aids. The in-house document services department will proofread the materials for grammar and mechanics and ensure the materials conform to the organization's document standards. The in-house general services department will provide photographic support and arrange for duplication of master print materials.

**7.0   Deliverables**

A number of products will be delivered:

(1)  Instructional design document (including a detailed task analysis and objectives)
(2)  Master instructional materials (including participant's guide, job aids, PowerPoint lecture slides)
(3)  Instructor's/Facilitator's Guide (including instructional and safety procedures for hands-on practice with fire extinguishers)

(*continued*)

**FIGURE 16-2**
(*Continued*)

---

(4) Website (containing PowerPoint lecture slides, self-test, and job aids)
(5) Evaluation Instrument (end-of-course)
(6) Promotional print materials
(7) Final project report (containing detail of project expenditures and future recommendations)

The project manager will hold a debriefing meeting with the client, sponsor, SME, and instructional design team approximately one month after completion of the project to review what was learned, identify opportunities to improve efficiency, and resolve any remaining project concerns.

**8.0  Evaluation**

A quasi-rapid prototyping approach will be used. Processes and materials will be reviewed throughout the project. Materials will be revised after pilot testing and before final production.

**9.0  Renegotiation**

Any part of this agreement may be revised at any time if all who are affected by such changes agree to them. The responsibility to engage in renegotiation rests with both the client and the project manager.

---

Modeled from Leitzman (1979).

The project agreement in Figure 16-2 would be used for internal projects. As an external consultant, you would include additional sections to address consulting fees, budget, use of subcontractors, ownership of the deliverables, and confidentiality.

## Expert's Edge

### Damn the Torpedoes . . . the Schedule, Full Speed Ahead

"Once you have the material reformatted and reorganized in a logical sequence, then I will read and approve the course." This was our first meeting with Ted. He was the new project lead manager for our client and had very definite ideas of how training should take place. He did not want the learning strategy or leader's guide format that his predecessor had *approved*.

**Changing project manager.**  The productivity workshop that we were designing for Kaptain Kidd Enterprises was the second in a series. The first workshop on time management was well received by the employees, and management saw the positive effect that the workshop had on production. They requested a second workshop and stipulated that it should follow the same format and learning strategy as the first.

We were a week away from our third meeting when one of the team members from Kaptain Kidd mentioned that the project manager for this workshop was being transferred to another location and a new project manager was being assigned. It was at the third meeting that we met Ted. According to our timeline, the third meeting is a paper walkthrough during which the revised course, workbook, and video scripts and/or audio scripts are reviewed to ensure continuity and accuracy in the course. The next phase is producing any video or audio and sending the drafts of the course and workbook to typesetting. Instead, Ted told us that we would receive samples of the new format in the morning. We should revise the course and reformat it accordingly. He did, however, expect that we would meet the deadline for delivery.

**Havoc on the timeline.**   The difference between the old format and the new format required more than 40 additional hours of work. These changes affected not only the writer but also the video production team, the desktop department, printing, and fulfillment. Video could not begin to shoot until the script was approved. The desktop design department could not produce the galleys for printing. And fulfillment had nothing to ship until all the material was printed. Everything from this point in the timeline was delayed, except for the deadline. In addition, there was a four-day holiday in this time frame. Everyone on the team worked longer hours and the weekend to shorten the delay time. The video costs were increased because the shoot was postponed. The printing and shipping costs were also higher because of the delay. Despite the time constraints and the cost overruns, the deadline was met.

**Future considerations.**   The event that led to this time crunch was not completely within our control. Project leaders can change in the middle of an assignment, and the new project leader may have his or her own standards. What we will do differently in the future is act immediately when we hear of a personnel change. If we had approached the new project leader before the third meeting to learn his expectations on the course, we might have learned about his views on the delivery of training material and his bias toward a certain layout of the material. We had the time *before* the third review, when we were incorporating the changes from the second review. Reworking the material at that time would have saved us the cost and frustration of trying to complete the project on time.

Linda M. Watson is a freelance instructional designer with over 10 years of experience. She has developed a variety of training products for the automotive and retail industries that were delivered as workshops, videotapes, interactive videodiscs, computer-based instruction, Web-based instruction, and interactive distance learning.

## INSTRUCTIONAL DESIGN SHORTCUTS

One criticism concerning the instructional design process is that the process "takes too long." Good project management, careful scheduling, and educating the client about the instructional design process can help ensure that time expectations are realistic.

Experienced designers often use rapid prototyping to reduce project time. "Prototypes are early and usually incomplete examples of what a final product may look like" (Nixon & Lee, 2001, p. 102). They enable the designer to create a tangible, somewhat concrete example that the client can react to (i.e., formatively evaluate) before the designer expends significant time developing the complete instructional unit. The prototype goes through several rapid design-evaluate-revise iterations, with each successive iteration becoming more refined and precise (Dorsey, Goodrum,

& Schwen, 1997). Rapid prototyping ensures that the overall design is "on track" with the client's expectations. The concrete prototype also helps a client express unarticulated needs.

Another strategy for reducing design time is to combine task analysis with the design of test items. Rather than conduct task analysis, the instructional designer asks the SME to develop test items first (see Thiagarajan, 2009). The test items are then used to construct the task analysis.

Designers may also omit phases. For example, if the designer is already familiar with the target audience, conducting a learner analysis is unnecessary. Other strategies to reduce project time include developing shorter instructional modules (or minimalist modules) that can be expanded or phased in over time and customizing existing materials. Lastly, you might develop job aids in place of instruction and then create instruction that teaches the learners how to use the job aids.

## FLEXIBILITY OF THE INSTRUCTIONAL DESIGN PROCESS

The instructional designer carefully follows an instructional design model to ensure that the instruction is designed, developed, and produced in a systematic manner that will consistently produce efficient and effective learning. However, a distinction is needed between rigidly following a model and adapting and modifying a model to solve an instructional problem. No single model is flexible enough to account for all conditions in all projects. Following a model in a rigid fashion will result in a misallocation of resources and lost time fulfilling the "needs" of the model rather than solving the instructional problem. The design model should serve as a flexible guide for designing the instruction. Those steps that are not relevant to the particular problem are skipped, so that effort can be concentrated on the parts of the model that are most applicable. Because every instructional project is unique, the designer must decide how much design is required. This decision is influenced by practical constraints including the time frame for addressing the problem, the nature of the delivery, and the resources available.

## INSTRUCTIONAL DESIGN IN ORGANIZATIONS

Instructional design services and activities are situated, managed, and funded in a number of ways across organizations. In this section we will examine how the role and purpose of instructional design is perceived in business and educational organizations, how placement within an organization affects service, and how instructional design groups are funded.

### Purposes and Role

In business organizations, instructional design and learning activities serve one purpose: to support improving employee performance. As a result of instructional design interventions, employees acquire new technical or interpersonal skills, knowledge, and/or attitudes. Instructional projects should contribute to helping the organization achieve its key goals (such as increasing sales or improving the quality of customer service.) Instructional projects are selected based on their potential to support revenue generation, reduce operational costs, ensure compliance with safety mandates, promote cultural transformation, or other similar criteria. The instructional intervention must produce valued results to ensure that executive-level decision makers recognize the contribution that instructional design work makes.

In education, instructional design groups provide service to faculty members and departments to improve student learning. Projects are undertaken based on faculty request, often to address a difficult learning problem. For both business and education, the application of instructional design is based on the assumption that performance and learning are improved through the application of a systematic planning process.

## Placement within the Organization

ISD services may be centralized at the organization's headquarters, or decentralized to serve a specific department or division such as sales or manufacturing. In large organizations, both centralized and decentralized structures may be used.

In higher education, instructional design groups benefit from centralized administrative placement as close as possible to the chief academic officer (e.g., academic vice president or provost). Services are readily available to any academic unit through simple requests. One popular location for instructional design groups is either in a faculty improvement or development center or in a distance education center. The type of services often varies; for example, distance-education designers tend to focus almost exclusively on the design and development of distance-education courses. Instructional designers in a faculty development or improvement center may also design and develop courses but will be involved in other activities, including evaluation, coaching, workshop planning and delivery, and facilitation.

The trend in business in recent years is to decentralize the training and instructional design groups. Some organizations place the instructional design group or staff in the human resources department. The mission of this group is often to provide management, administrative, and new employee training. Instructional design groups providing support for technical or sales training are often placed in the department they are supporting. For example, in an airline company there may be one instructional design group associated with the ground operations and another associated with flight training. In a manufacturing company, the design group may reside in the customer service department or field services department, depending on the clientele served. Similarly, a separate design group might work on only technical training for the sales staff. In all situations there is a direct working relationship among instructional design, reproduction, and media departments. If a separate testing or evaluation office exists, it should have close ties with instructional design. All these groups should report to the same senior-level manager or administrator so that project activities can be easily coordinated and to avoid duplication of effort.

## Budgetary Support

Instructional design groups are either a cost center or a profit center. As a cost center, the instructional design group provides service based on needs or requests. Clients are rarely turned away. In the cost center model, the cost of instructional design services is considered part of the organization's "overhead." As a profit center, the instructional design group is expected to generate income. As a result, instructional design services or courses are sold both inside and outside the company. The method of funding affects the selection of instructional design projects. Educational institutions are usually funded as a cost center; business organizations use either funding model.

**Business.**   In business organizations, an instructional design group's budget is usually influenced by its mission (e.g., cost center or profit center). There are four general types of funding. First, a department is given a fixed annual budget to complete a specific number of projects and to cover operational costs. Projects are selected based on need, number of individuals served, cost, alignment with organizational strategy, or to produce other benefits. Second, the group can work on a direct charge-back system, in which requesting departments contract for the instructional design work and pay for the effort out of their budgets. A market economy is used to select the projects, although management may provide additional funding for critical needs.

Third is an indirect charge-back system in which the costs of the instructional design department are included in the general overhead costs. Projects are often selected on a similar basis as a department working on a fixed budget. These three budgeting models are variations of a cost center. Fourth, a department with a mission to produce a profit may approach management and request funds in the terms of a loan to develop a project. Management views the instructional project as another product that the company can produce for profit, even though the customers are often members of the same company. With this type of funding approach, projects with the greatest potential to return a profit are most likely to receive funding.

**Education.**   There are four ways to provide financial support for instructional design activities in an educational environment. In the first, money is budgeted for the projects from the institution or organization. Allocations are made to fund personnel time and designate costs for projects that are commissioned, selected through a competition, or requested. Second, an academic department or a division can use its funds to contract for a specific project. Third, an administrator can provide funding to faculty as an incentive to create distance-education courses or to develop innovative uses of technology. Fourth, funding from outside the institution may be obtained as a grant or contract specifically to support a project. The last two methods usually require the submission of a written proposal that is evaluated according to specific criteria, often in competition with other proposals.

## WORKING WITH THE SUBJECT-MATTER EXPERT AND CONSULTANTS

Instructional design projects vary in size and scope and similarly vary in terms of the number of individuals involved with the project. The instructional designer's role often goes beyond the task of designing the instruction with a single SME.

Some projects might require working with several SMEs as well as video producers, graphic artists, Web programmers, and other consultants. This section discusses issues related to working with SMEs and other consultants/team members.

## The Subject-Matter Expert in Different Roles

Each design project has a client and an SME; however, these individuals are not always easily identifiable. The following section describes the participants of a design project in a business organization, in higher education, and in an instructional consulting firm that develops materials for other companies.

**Business Training Environment.**   In this business environment, all the project participants are usually employed by the same company; however, they may be separated geographically in different offices, buildings, states, or countries (Morrison, 1988). The client is typically the individual who "owns" the problem. The client/owner is usually a manager or supervisor of the target audience (i.e., the individuals with the problem). Transfer of real or paper money does not always point to the client. Another manager, a vice president, or even the training manager might "pay" for the instructional product. A client's primary responsibility in this environment is to provide access to the target population and to identify qualified SMEs.

The role of the SME is that of a consultant who often is not an employee of the training or instructional design group. The SME usually has some association with the target population (e.g., he or she worked at that level and was promoted) but is seldom the client. The primary responsibility of the SME is to provide accurate information during the task analysis and verify the accuracy of the instructional deliverables. This separation of roles between the SME and client allows the designer to contract with the client for the work and to assume the role of a proactive designer and leader.

**Higher Education Environment.**   The client in the higher education environment is usually the professor who approaches the instructional designer for assistance (Tessmer, 1988). Because the professor both owns the problem and is the SME, the professor typically maintains the leadership role. The SME is responsible for the accuracy of the content. The client/professor/SME may perceive the designer's role as limited to assisting with media production (such as producing graphics) or perceive the designer as a consulting partner who can provide suggestions and advice concerning instructional strategies. On projects requiring the development and use of multimedia technologies, the client/SME may request that the designer take a more proactive role.

The role of the instructional designer and SME often changes when the focus of the project is on the design of distance-education instruction. The client is often the university administration that contracts with a designer and professor. In this situation, the designer is often the project leader, yet both the designer and SME share overall responsibility for the project's success. In some cases, the professor may not serve as the distance-education instructor when the course is delivered.

**Developing Training for Third Parties.**   The final illustration is a business that develops instructional materials for other companies under a contract. There may actually be several clients (Foshay, 1988). First is the individual who signed the contract, but he or she may not have any further involvement in the project until the final product is delivered. A second client includes the individuals in the contracting company who will judge the technical accuracy of the instructional materials. Finally, the third client is the instructional designer's manager who may manage the contract. The designer has the responsibility of addressing the needs of each client and resolving conflicts between their needs. Correctly identifying all the clients is essential for a project of this nature.

When doing contract work, the SME can be an employee of the contracting organization, an employee of the designer's organization, or an independent consultant hired for the duration of the project. If the SME is an employee of either organization, the designer may face problems negotiating for the SME's time. If the SME, however, is hired specifically for the project, then access to the SME is seldom a problem.

Typically, in contract work the designer has the responsibility of assuming a proactive role for instructional design. This role is usually facilitated by the nature of the relationship between the clients and SME. Sometimes, the designer must also fulfill the role of the project manager. Although the project manager role can enhance the role of a proactive designer, the burden of administrative responsibilities can reduce the time a designer can spend on the design role. A designer fulfilling both roles will need to maintain a balance between the two roles.

## Working with Other Consultants and Team Members

**Performance Consultant.**   We described the larger field of performance consulting in Chapter 1. When you identify a problem for which an instructional intervention is not the appropriate solution (see "Performance Assessment" in Chapter 2), you may need to work with a performance consultant or other specialist to develop an appropriate solution. For example, if the problem requires the restructuring of the workstation, you may need to involve a human ergonomics specialist. For problems that require the implementation of incentives or restructuring of the job, you may need to involve a human resources specialist. Solutions for performance problems can involve a number of specialists, ranging from a manager who can coach a peer to an organizational development specialist who can help with conflict management problems.

**Graphic Artists, Video Producers, Photographers.**   Graphic artists, video producers, and photographers help with the creative aspects of instructional design projects. As a project manager, you will need to explain the vision of the project to these specialists. It is also critical that you discuss budget and time constraints. Because these individuals are often hired on a contract or hourly basis, you will need to carefully monitor progress. A video producer will usually arrange for a production crew, but you may be responsible for securing on-camera talent and scouting and arranging clearances for shooting locations. The video production crew is often assembled and managed (i.e., directed) by either a producer or director. The staff can include one or more camera operators, sound-recording specialists, lighting specialists, on- and off-camera talent, editors, and video or picture researchers.

**Programmers, Multimedia Designers, and Web Designers.**   It is important to discuss layout standards with multimedia designers, graphic artists, and Web programmers before work begins to ensure compliance with organizational requirements. Second, if you are contracting with external providers for Web services, be certain to coordinate the project with in-house information technology support, particularly since security firewalls could affect learner access.

## LEGAL CONSIDERATIONS IN ID PROJECT MANAGEMENT

As an instructional project manager, you must ensure that the training program you oversee is ethical and meets legal requirements to avoid liability claims and lawsuits. Therefore, you should become knowledgeable about contracts as well as state and federal regulations and statutes.

### Contracts

Occasionally, a need arises when some or all of the instructional design effort is contracted with outside consultants or vendors. Several situations could prompt such a need:

- Resources (e.g., time or personnel) are not available to complete the project.
- Current staff lack the necessary skills required for the project (e.g., producing a multimedia application, translating materials to a foreign language).
- A consultant is needed to fill a particular instructional design role—assessing needs, advising on instructional procedures, SME, or evaluating a completed project.

As project manager, you may have to draw up a proper legal contract when hiring a subcontractor to perform a task. You should check with the organization's legal department and personnel department for specific guidelines and policies before you make initial contact with any contractor. Any contract or letter of agreement should be either initiated or approved by the legal department. You will also want to ensure that the contract specifies who owns the copyright to any materials that the contractor produces.

### State and Federal Mandates

It is also important to become familiar with legislative enactments and local, state, and federal regulations that can affect education or training. For example, some major federal statutes that affect training include the following:

- Occupational Safety and Health Act (OSHA)
- Equal Employment Opportunity Commission (EEOC)

- Americans with Disabilities Act (ADA)
- Environmental Resources Act (ERA)
- Toxic Substance Control Act (TSCA)

In addition, other governmental agencies regulate work in different environments. Although some statutory provisions may specify topics or actions that require attention in training, planning, and implementation methods, others are left to local decision makers. You can ensure compliance by consulting with appropriate SMEs and the legal department and by keeping records of all evaluations that require students to demonstrate achievement of the objectives. If you are responsible for safety training, consulting with SMEs and the legal department is critically important.

## Common Legal Problems in Training

Eyres (1998) has identified a number of legal problems that affect those in the training field. The following paragraphs provide a brief description of these problems.

**Failure to Perform Training.**   Some industries are mandated by the federal government to train employees in specific areas. For example, the oil industry must provide training on hydrogen sulfide and carbon dioxide for employees who work in areas where those hazards are present. Companies that accept packages for shipping via air must train employees in the acceptance and rejection of hazardous goods. An employee can sue a company that fails to provide this training. A broader issue is that of providing a discrimination-free work environment. According to Eyres (1998), employers have an obligation to train employees on what constitutes unacceptable behaviors.

**Emotional Trauma or Physical Injury from Training.**   Nontraditional (e.g., new age) training programs that challenge an individual's comfort zone have provided the basis for legal action against the facilitators and company. Programs that include physical or wilderness activities have resulted in lawsuits from physical injury as well as charges of discrimination against disabled employees.

**Intellectual Property Infringement.**   It seems that at least once per week, we find one or two cartoons that would be great icebreakers for meetings, lectures, or even as additions to this book. Cartoons, quotes, exercises, and ideas conceived and developed by others have intellectual property right values that are protected by law.

Scanning a cartoon from the morning paper to include in your PowerPoint presentation may be a violation of the artist's intellectual property rights and probably of the copyright laws. Similarly, using an exercise that you have observed another person present at a workshop could also leave you liable. If you want to use ideas or materials developed by another individual, you need to obtain that person's permission or even pay a fee.

**Discriminatory Content.**   Most professionals would agree that one could be liable for including discriminatory (e.g., racial, ethnic, or sex-biased) materials in a training program. Eyres (1998) indicated that an activity designed to improve diversity could be used as evidence of discriminatory practices. For example, having supervisors list examples of statements that are discriminatory could be used as evidence against the company at a later time.

**Injury Due to Human Error.**   A mandate to provide training can lead to legal action if the appropriate and safe training is not provided. Individuals conducting the training must have adequate training and preparation. When the training involves the use of actual equipment, appropriate precautions must be taken to provide a safe environment for the trainee and trainer.

**Access to Training.**   Employees must have equal access to training within a company. Screening methods must be applied equally to all groups and be nondiscriminatory.

**Testing and Evaluation.**   Conducting criterion- or performance-based tests at the end of the training must not discriminate against any group of individuals. Any testing must be related to essential job tasks (see the Expert's Edge in Chapter 12).

**Failure to Perform.**   Individual consultants and companies that provide instructional design and training services to other companies typically do so under a contract for the service. Failure to perform as defined in the contract can lead to legal action. For example, a client may take legal action if you have delayed the delivery of a training product. Such actions are often avoided by keeping the client informed of your progress and any problems encountered. Another basis for legal action occurs when the qualifications of a member of the project have been overstated. For example, the qualifications of a consultant you plan to hire as the SME might be misleading (e.g., suggesting the individual has a doctorate in the field when she has only a master's degree) and could result in legal action.

**Inadequate Documentation.**   Many federal agencies require companies to maintain records of when employees are trained. Failure to maintain these records could result in fines or legal action in the case of an accident.

## SUMMARY

1. Each project involves a client who owns the problem, an SME who verifies content accuracy, and an instructional designer who is responsible for the design of the instruction. At the beginning of each project, a designer must identify the various roles, the number of clients, and other stakeholders so that each of their needs is addressed. Failure to identify these individuals and their needs can result in problems both with project development and implementation.
2. Preparing a detailed project agreement facilitates communication among the stakeholders, including the client, sponsor, instructional designer, and SME. The project agreement clearly describes the goals, deliverables, and expectations.

3. Project budgets are developed from a detailed list of project tasks and should account for personnel, facilities and equipment, materials, and overhead costs.

4. Following a systematic instructional design model increases the likelihood that the designed instruction will be effective and efficient. The model is flexibly modified for each specific situation to improve project efficiency.

5. Instructional design groups are either a cost center or a profit center. In business organizations, instructional design efforts should contribute to and support key organizational goals. The aim is to improve employee performance. In educational organizations, instructional design efforts focus on improving instruction and learning.

6. Instructional design projects are unique and vary in size and scope. A project manager plans the project before it begins and manages and monitors the activities throughout the duration. All projects are constrained by time, budget, and resources.

7. Keep persons within the organization informed by reporting progress and results in writing.

8. Be alert to legal liabilities and responsibilities relating to instructional program design and implementation.

## THE ID PROCESS

The success and life of an instructional design group or function is affected by its placement in an organization and by its funding process. A design group placed in the human relations department may have a different function, role, and impact on the organization than a group placed in a profit center, such as customer or warranty service. Similarly, a group whose charges and expenses are considered part of company or organizational overhead may select projects differently than a group that is considered a profit center and that must obtain funding for all projects. When you interview for a position, determine where the group is placed in the organization and how it is funded.

The way a group is funded and operates can also affect your approach to instructional design. A group that works on large projects or with funding from outside sources may require a greater emphasis on project management. Often, the project management responsibilities may conflict with the instructional design requirements, especially if you are the single instructional designer on a project and the project manager. Similarly, a consulting group or a group that must obtain funding for all projects will help you sharpen your proposal development skills.

## APPLICATIONS

Your organization has just received a request for a proposal (you are the sole source/bidder) to develop a basic store manager course for a new drugstore chain. The course can include no more than 40 hours of classroom instruction. The drugstore company will provide the instructors who will use the materials you have developed. The proposal has suggested that the instructional design company hire a number of SMEs with expertise in store management, pharmacy management, human resource development, and security. The company will provide you with access to six of its successful store managers during the proposal development. You will receive compensation (up to $10,000) only for the proposal and work associated with it if you are funded.

What personnel from your organization will you involve, and how will you proceed?

## ANSWERS

First, we would interview the six store managers to determine the scope of their work and responsibilities. This information would be used to define the scope of work. Second, we would identify a potential SME to define the initial goals for the course. Third, we would develop the project management plan to use as a resource to create the budget and schedule.

Individuals involved from our staff would be one or more instructional designers, an evaluator, support for developing the budget, and clerical support. Because we are hiring an outside consultant, we will need to use an existing contract or ask a company lawyer to prepare a contract.

## INSTRUCTIONAL DESIGN: DECISIONS AND CHOICES

Project management began the day the project was assigned to you. Establishing the project schedule and budget and assembling a skilled project team are essential. However, these tasks are insufficient to ensure that the project will proceed smoothly. Some other key project management tasks include the following:

**Client communication:** Early on, you ask the client how he wants to be kept informed of project progress. In addition, you ask the client to sign off at critical checkpoints. For example, you ask the client to sign off to approve the objectives and Website prototype. You also make an effort to keep other stakeholders, such as the security director, informed. [Maintaining ongoing communication with the client and key stakeholders is essential to catching problems early and avoiding surprises. Maintaining open communication increases the likelihood that the client will be satisfied with the work produced.]

**Project team communication:** This includes communicating a clear vision for the project as well as ensuring that each team member has the resources he or she needs for the project.

**Maintaining project momentum and team energy:** Sometimes, team energy attenuates after completion of the analysis or early design phase. To maintain momentum, you recognize and reward individual contributions during review meetings. [Ensuring that each team member feels his or her contribution is valued and appreciated can make all the difference. The appreciation must be honest and sincere. Insincere praise is usually quickly detected and will do more harm than good, eroding team morale and cooperation.]

**Obtaining legal clearances:** To speed up production time, you found pictures of fire extinguishers on the World Wide Web. Before you can use these images, however, you have to obtain copyright permission. [Obtaining legal clearances can be time consuming, so it's important to request clearances early. Although images on the Web can be easily downloaded, permission to use them is usually required. Fortunately, vendors who supply your company are often willing to provide pictures and graphics on request and free of charge for use in training materials.]

**Project closure:** This includes debriefing the project to reflect and identify "lessons learned." Project closure also includes celebrating completion, acknowledging and rewarding team members, and turning over the master materials to the client or the client's liaison. [This is similar to the wrap party at the end of a theater production. Creating a project celebration can be as simple as bringing in a decorated cake or as elaborate as offering a catered dinner.]

## REFERENCES

Dorsey, L., Goodrum, D., & Schwen, T. (1997). Rapid collaborative prototyping as an instructional development paradigm. In C. Dills & A. Romiszowski (Eds.), *Instructional development paradigms* (pp. 445–465). Englewood Cliffs, NJ: Educational Technology Publications.

Eyres, P. S. (1998). *The legal handbook of trainers, speakers, consultants: The essential guide to keeping your company and clients out of court.* New York: McGraw-Hill.

Foshay, R. (1988). I don't know is on third. *Performance and Instruction, 27*(8), 8–9.

Leitzman, D. F. (1979). Contracting for instructional development, *Journal of Instructional Development. 3*(2), 23–29).

Lewis, J. P. (2007). *Fundamentals of project management* (3rd ed.) New York: AMACOM.

Morrison, G. R. (1988). Who's on first. *Performance and Instruction, 27*, 5–6.

Nixon, E. K., & Lee, D. (2001). Rapid prototyping in the instructional design process. *Performance Improvement Quarterly, 14*(3), 95–116.

Project Management Institute. (2008). *A guide to the project management body of knowledge: PMBOK guide* (4th ed.) Newtown Square, PA: Author.

Stevenson, N., & Marmel, E. (1997). *Microsoft Project 98 bible.* Foster City, CA: IDG Books Worldwide.

Tessmer, M. (1988). What's on second. *Performance and Instruction, 27*, 6–8.

Thiagarajan, S. (2009). Rapid instructional design. Retrieved from http://www.thiagi.com /article-rid.html

# Sample Instructional Design Documentation

## PROPER BAGGING PRACTICE IN A SUPERSTORE ENVIRONMENT[1]

### PROBLEM IDENTIFICATION

Bagging customers' groceries and other purchases properly promotes customer satisfaction through personalized service and care for their purchases. It is important that the bag be presented to the customer based on solid principles of packing and handling. A poorly packed bag can lead directly to the ruin of the contents before customers can reach their destination. At busy times, many store team members are called on to assist register personnel so that the bagging process does not delay and inconvenience the customer being served or those waiting in line. High employee turnover and the involvement of personnel not normally involved in bagging, along with the importance of proper bagging, indicate the need for efficient training. The bagger has the last and most sustained customer contact. Based on the goals, the opportunities of training include the following:

- Better personal and efficient customer service, promoting repeat business
- Better utilization of bagging supplies and job performance
- Better protection of the customer's purchases

### Aim

Promote customer satisfaction and repeat business through improved bagging and service at time of checkout.

---

[1] Based on a project by Donald L. Boase

**Set Goals**

- Use the proper bag for the job.
- Be sure bags are properly stocked before beginning shift.
- Bag together items that belong together.
- Promote the protection of the customer's purchases.
- Promote customer satisfaction through courtesy.
- Work efficiently.
- Support the team effort of customer service.
- Help the register personnel ensure that all items are checked.
- Exhibit good hygiene.
- Run errands when necessary.
- Help customers even when away from the checkout lane.
- Use the principle of looking ahead.
- Know what is not bagged.
- Know which bag to use.
- Use principles of how items are grouped.
- Select items for "walls."
- Select items for "foundations."
- Select items for "fill."
- Use the principles of proper bag building.
- Place bags and items into the cart properly.
- Check supplies and stock bags.
- Place bags properly at the checkout lane.
- Put the proper number of each bag at the checkout lane.
- Get bags from the stockroom area.
- Hang the bags at the checkout lane.
- Stock additional bags.
- Use the principles of customer service opportunities.
- Use the area service rule—Within 10 feet, make positive contact.

**Refine Goals**

- Use the area service rule—Within 10 feet, make positive contact.
- Help customers even when away from the checkout lane.
- Use the proper bag for the job.
- Bag together items that belong together.
- Work efficiently by looking ahead.
- Know what is not bagged.
- Select proper items for "walls."
- Select proper items for "foundations."
- Select proper items for "fill."
- Place bags and items into the cart properly.

- Be sure bags are properly stocked before beginning shift.
- Put the proper number of each kind of bag at the checkout lane.
- Get bags from the stockroom area.
- Stock additional bags.
- Help the register personnel to be sure all items are checked.
- Run errands when necessary.

### Rank Goals

1. Be sure bags are properly stocked before beginning shift.
2. Put in the proper number of each kind of bag at the checkout lane.
3. Get bags from the stockroom area.
4. Stock additional bags.
5. Help the register personnel be sure all items are checked.
6. Bag together items that belong together.
7. Work efficiently by looking ahead.
8. Know what is not bagged.
9. Select proper items for "walls."
10. Select proper items for "foundations."
11. Select proper items for "fill."
12. Place bags and items into the cart properly.
13. Use the proper bag for the job.
14. Run errands when necessary.
15. Use the area service rule—Within 10 feet, make positive contact.
16. Help customers even when away from the checkout lane.

### Second Refinement

1. Demonstrate the job responsibilities, including maintenance and use of supplies, efficient work practices, and team member support.
2. Identify examples of "walls," "foundations," and "fill" for bagging.
3. Demonstrate how to use "walls," "foundations," and "fill" to complete a full bag.
4. State the customer service philosophy and practice including the "10-foot rule."

### Final Ranking

1. State the customer service philosophy and practice, including the "10-foot rule."
2. Demonstrate the job responsibilities, including maintenance and use of supplies, efficient work practices, and team member support.
3. Identify examples of "walls," "foundations," and "fill" for bagging.
4. Demonstrate how to use "walls," "foundations," and "fill" to complete a full bag.

## AUDIENCE DEFINITION

### General Characteristics

The primary audience is composed of both male and female team members in their midteens. Often this is their first job. This is a high-visibility position and requires a responsible individual with good grooming habits and a pleasant attitude. Although there is a high turnover in this position, many individuals who go on to a career in retail management start here. Retired people make up the next group. Often, these individuals have reentered the workplace as a means to stay active.

Other audiences include other store personnel, including the register operator in off-peak times. Although already understanding many of the store philosophies and people issues, this group still needs to know the best way to pack a bag.

### Specific Characteristics

**Four Distinct Audiences**
1. Both genders, 14- to 17-year-olds, may be first job (primary audience)
2. Retired or older people
3. Register personnel (handle checkout and bagging at off-peak times)
4. Other store personnel who may be called on at peak times

**Physical Requirements**
- Should be able to lift and manage a 20-pound bag
- Good hygiene and grooming characteristics

**Specific Educational or Training Requirements**
- Basic literacy consistent with a 14-year-old-student level
- Company orientation training

### Contextual Analysis

**Orienting Context.**   There are two factors to focus on regarding the orienting context. First, the designer needs to make sure the instruction is directly relevant to the learners' jobs so they perceive a high utility for the information. Second, the store supervisor or manager must stress the learners' accountability for bagging groceries properly and how this training will help them better perform their job tasks.

**Instructional Context.**   Each store has a training room that has two or more carrels where learners can access a CD-ROM to use the training materials or complete online instruction. There are also two more carrels for working on paper-based instructional materials. This room is available approximately 14 hours a day. It is supposed to be reserved strictly for training. Learners can obtain their training materials from the manager's office. However, company policy dictates that the materials must stay in the store. The training should be designed so that individual units can be completed in less than one hour. Each manager arranges times for the training of new employees that fit the schedules of the room and the new employee.

**Transfer Context.**    The training should be scheduled as close as possible to the employee's first day as a bagger to enhance the transfer of the training. In addition to scheduling the training, the employee's first day on the job should be coordinated with the head cashier to ensure that a coach is provided for the first hour or so on the job.

## TASK ANALYSIS

A. Check to see that supplies are sufficient, and if necessary, restock bags.
   1. A fully stocked lane will have 400 medium bags, 100 small bags, and 200 large bags.
   2. Bags are to be brought up from the storeroom.
B. Stand at the end of the checkout lane holding area so you can see the conveyor belt and have a view of the whole basket.
   1. The bag rack should be positioned directly in front of you.
C. The area of service is defined as a 10-foot radius around you wherever you are on store property.
   1. Whenever customers are in your area of service you should:
      a. Make eye contact.
      b. Greet them by smiling and saying hello.
      c. Offer to be of service.
   2. Always greet the customer when eye contact is made.
   3. Present an attitude of helpfulness.
D. As purchases are placed on the belt, begin looking at the nature of the items and think in terms of grouping and building the bag.
   1. Items similar in nature should be grouped together.
      a. Never mix food items with cleaning or toxic materials.
   2. The following six categories should be followed for grouping:
      a. Fresh produce, such as tomatoes and carrots.
      b. Packaged food—boxed and prepared items.
      c. Frozen food (wet items—condensation).
      d. Cleaning or toxic items.
      e. Other store items.
E. As the last items are placed on the belt, help the register personnel be sure all items have been accounted for.
   1. Double-check that nothing is missed underneath the basket.
      a. Think "IOU"—inside, outside, underneath.
      b. The places an item may be missed during checkout are inside another item, outside the basket, or underneath.
      c. The register personnel are very busy with the transaction and may miss something that is outside the basket.
      d. As a checkout team member, you are providing backup for the register personnel.
      e. Be sure all items are accounted for through the checkout.
         (1) Items may be inside larger products.

        (2) Although it is the primary responsibility of the register person-
nel to check, you are a team member and you should follow up
if an item was not checked.

  2. The customer may be absentmindedly holding an item, or the item may
be underneath the basket in the bottom of the cart.

  3. Some items are too big or awkward to be placed on the belt. Assist the
register personnel with the scanning if necessary.

F. As items are fed through the scanner and gather in the holding area, begin
bag building.

  1. Choose the right bag and build the bags following the principles for
solid construction.

    a. Plastic and paper bags are available for bagging.

    b. Plastic is the best based on cost, ecology issues, and ease of use.

    c. Paper is best if the customer asks for it.

    d. Paper bags are stored beneath the holding area, where they can be
easily retrieved for use without promoting their use through high
visibility.

  2. Choose from three sizes of bags or no bag at all.

    a. Match the size of the bag to the purchased item.

    b. The standard or medium-sized bag most commonly used for gro-
ceries is stocked in bales under the holding area.

      (1) A supply is hung on the bagging racks at the end of the lane,
ready to use.

      (2) These are prepared for use by placing the loops on each side
of the bags over the left and right arms of the rack, stretching
the bags across the back of the rack.

    c. What not to bag:

      (1) Oversized items, such as bagged dog food

      (2) Items with built-in handles, such as milk or bleach

      (3) Some things, such as goldfish, just should not be bagged and
need special handling. Find out from the customer how the
item should be handled.

G. Construction principles

  1. Build the walls

    a. Walls are built with items that can give structure and support to the
bag.

      (1) Boxes of cereal, crackers, or cake mix

      (2) Rigid items, such as carrots, celery, or even bananas

      (3) Packaged items, such as napkins, cookies, or plates

  2. Lay the floor

    a. After the walls are established, lay the floor.

      (1) Use heavy items first, such as canned goods.

      (2) Place heavy items between the walls to provide a solid base to
support continued filling.

    b. Examples:

      (1) Canned goods, such as green beans or soda pop

    (2)  Heavy packaged items, such as sugar or flour

    (3)  Glass jars, as used with jelly or mayonnaise

  3.  Fill the space

    a.  Now fill the rest of the bag with lighter or more fragile items, such as bread or chips.

      (1)  They will be protected within the walls and will not crush the items beneath. The bag is not built until it is full.

    b.  Examples

      (1)  Thinly packaged items, such as bread and chips

      (2)  Small items, such as pudding boxes, drink mixes, and cosmetics

      (3)  Fragile items, such as eggs and tomatoes

H.  As bags are built, place them back into the cart, keeping in mind the same principles apply to the cart as they did to the bag.

  I.  If customers appear to need assistance getting to their vehicles, offer to help.

    1.  Be insistant about helping.

## OBJECTIVES AND PRESENTATION STRATEGIES

## Objective 1

After completing this unit, the learner will correctly answer short-answer questions about individual responsibility, scope (10-foot rule), customer position, and importance of bagging to demonstrate a personal understanding of customer service. (*Fact–Recall*)

**Initial Presentation.**  An example will be used to demonstrate the company's philosophy, the principles of customer satisfaction, and the responsibility of the bagger to fulfill it.

**Generative Strategy.**  The bagger will provide an example of how he or she would demonstrate the philosophy, achieve customer satisfaction, and accomplish the bagger's responsibilities.

**Test Items.**

    We provide bagging to build customer _____.

    Your responsibility is to ensure our customers are _____.

    Your *area of service* is _____ ft. around you.

    The customer comes _____.

## Objective 2

After completing this unit, the learner will demonstrate how to restock bagging supplies with 100 percent accuracy. (*Procedure–Application*)

**Initial Presentation.**  Eg–Rule: The principles for bagging preparation and practice are presented and then are followed by examples of application.

**Generative Strategy.**   After the presentation, the learner will describe the process for restocking the bagging supplies. Using the demonstration area, practice stocking the bagging supplies.

**Checklist.**

| | | |
|---|---|---|
| Appropriate number of size of bags are stocked. | Yes | No |
| Bags are properly stacked or attached for use. | Yes | No |

## Objective 3

Given a display of 20 items, the learner will correctly select the appropriate bag to use for each item with 90 percent accuracy. (*Principle–Application*)

**Initial Presentation.**   Eg–Rule approach is used to illustrate the type of bag for various items and to illustrate the size of bag.

**Generative Strategy.**   The learner is shown four groupings of grocery items and is asked to explain the size and type of bag needed for each.

**Test Item.**   The learner is shown individual items and groups of items and selects the appropriate bag for each item or group.

## Objective 4

Given a grocery cart, the learner will demonstrate the procedure for ensuring all items have been scanned. (*Procedure–Application*)

**Initial Presentation.**   The learner will read a section with an illustration indicating the procedure to look inside, outside, and underneath the cart.

**Generative Strategy.**   A mnemonic device, IOU, will be given to the learner with instructions to rehearse it.
  Using the demonstration area, the learner will practice indicating how to check that all items have been scanned.

**Test Item.**   Using the drawing, indicate with arrows where you need to look for items that have not been scanned.

## Objective 5

Given a list of 40 products, the learner will correctly assign 90 percent to the correct category. (*Concept–Application*)

**Initial Presentation.**   For each of the six categories, learners are given a description and a best example of the concept.

**Generative Strategy.**    Provide the learner with a list of items for each category and have the learner match the item with the correct category.

**Test Item.**    Provide the learner with 40 products on a table with a number on each product. The learner writes the category beside the number of each item on the answer sheet.

## Objective 6

Given a picture of a group of grocery items on a table, the learner will correctly select two examples of "walls," "foundations," and "fill." (*Concept–Application*)

**Initial Presentation.**    For each of the three concepts, learners are given a description and a best example of the concept.

**Generative Strategy.**    Provide the learner with a list of items for each concept and have the learner match the item with the correct category.

**Test Item.**    Provide the learner with 20 products on a table with a number on each product. The learner classifies each item as use for a "foundation," "wall," or "fill."

## Objective 7

Given a group of 30 grocery items in a single line, the learner correctly bags the group following acceptable practice. (*Procedure–Application*)

**Initial Presentation.**    State each rule for bagging concerning grouping, walls, foundations, and fill, and then illustrate the rule.

**Generative Strategy.**    The learner will paraphrase the process for building a bag. Using the demonstration area, the learner will practice bagging three carts of groceries.

**Performance Checklist.**

| | | |
|---|---|---|
| 1. Most bags have walls, foundation, fill. | Yes | No |
| 2. Each bag has appropriate items. | Yes | No |
| 3. Heavy items are on the bottom. | Yes | No |
| 4. Fragile items are not broken. | Yes | No |

## PREINSTRUCTIONAL STRATEGY—ADVANCE ORGANIZER

The instruction will be built around the metaphor of building as in constructing a home. The learner will be introduced to the content in the opening copy and illustration through a building concept. The metaphor will be used to support the sequencing strategy. It will improve retention by providing a conceptual grid to hang the information on and by emphasizing the deliberateness and care that should be given the job of customer service through proper bagging and teamwork with imagery that an audience young or old would readily understand. Pretest as a strategy was not chosen because of the predominately entry-level job position. However, an argument could be made to use the pretest as a way of exposing preconceived attitudes, but then it would not lend itself well to support the balance of the cognitive objectives.

Behavioral objectives as a strategy was not chosen because of the predominately youthful audience. The "why" of the training needs to be established as well to provide meaning and context for the objectives. Although a clear statement of training purpose would leave no room for confusion for this first-time employee, the raw objectives could come across as too sterile and result in a negative response. Overview as a strategy was not chosen because of the lack of experience of a key target audience to build on. More is needed to establish the foundation and context of the workplace before presenting an overview.

## SEQUENCING CONTENT—TEMPORAL RELATION

Following through with the building metaphor, the content will be sequenced based on the chronological progression of the job: organizing the work site, planning, and working together to perform the tasks. The content will be presented, as the need to know is progressively established through the job/tasks sequence.

### SME Review

Based on research, interviews, and assumptions, a design document will be prepared for validation by project stakeholders. This review will be performed in a group meeting covering the objectives, content, and creative treatment through a guided reading of the design document. Comments, concerns, or new direction will be captured, noted on the designated master document, and agreed to by the group for implementation. A final design document will then be generated to facilitate development and report changes.

### Target Audience Review

Once the initial training materials are prepared in prototype form, usability testing on a representative small sampling of the target audiences will be performed with an opinion survey to capture additional information outside the inherent course testing and to document the results. For this evaluation, the participants will go through the course as designed. This will be a last check before publication. (See the "Formative Evaluation" survey.) Based on the results, modifications would be made and submitted for final SME approval.

# FORMATIVE EVALUATION

Date: _____

Course Title: _____

What is your current job title? _____

How long have you been at this job?
- ☐  1 year or less
- ☐  1–3 years
- ☐  3–5 years
- ☐  6–10 years
- ☐  11 years or longer

How did you find the course?
- ☐  Very interesting
- ☐  Somewhat interesting
- ☐  Fairly interesting
- ☐  Not very interesting
- ☐  Boring

Was the course challenging?
- ☐  Extremely easy
- ☐  Very easy
- ☐  Fairly easy
- ☐  Not too hard
- ☐  Very hard

Would you recommend the course to someone else?
- ☐  Yes
- ☐  No

What would you change?

What did you like?

Will the course help you do your job better?
- ☐  Significantly better
- ☐  Somewhat better
- ☐  About the same
- ☐  Worse
- ☐  Significantly worse

Was the course easy to follow?
- ☐  Extremely easy
- ☐  Very easy
- ☐  Fairly easy
- ☐  Not too hard
- ☐  Very hard

Did you always know what to do?
- ☐  Very clear
- ☐  Somewhat clear
- ☐  Fairly clear
- ☐  Not very clear
- ☐  Confusing

# A Sample Instructional Unit

## BUILDING BAGS[1]

## BUILDING CUSTOMER SATISFACTION

We are continually building our business, and we do it by filling one bag at a time. Customer service is the cornerstone. A cornerstone is the foundational stone in a building on which all the rest stands. It supports the weight and ensures the integrity of the structure. We are building on customer service every day through every opportunity we have. We are providing a special personal service to our customers through bagging.

As a bagger it is your responsibility to ensure our customers are served in a professional manner providing the best in attitude and practice. We build our bags better to build customer satisfaction.

Like building a house, you prepare, plan, and build with a purpose. And like a house, a properly built bag has walls and a floor protecting its contents. It sets upright on a solid foundation.

## BUILDING CUSTOMERS

### The Customer Comes First

Whether at the checkout lane or anywhere on store grounds, when you gain eye contact with customers greet them and present an attitude of helpfulness.

Also, whenever customers are in your area of service you should make eye contact and greet them. Your area of service is defined as a 10-foot radius (see Figure B-1) around you wherever you are on store property.

---

[1] Based on a project by Donald L. Boase

Area of Service

**10 Feet**

**FIGURE B-1**

## See the Opportunities

As you read the scenario (see most recent version in Trainee Manual) of a morning at the store, can you identify examples of baggers helping customers?

The following situations describe opportunities to build customer satisfaction.

- You are passing a customer who cannot reach an item on the top shelf, and you retrieve it for him.
- You are sent out to retrieve carts and while in the parking lot you pass a customer holding her bags while trying to get her keys from her purse. You offer to hold her bags.
- You pass a customer with his hands full and offer to get him a cart.
- A customer stops to ask you where the service desk is, and you show her where it is.
- You see a customer obviously looking for something and inquire whether you can help.

## NOW YOU CAN MAKE THE OPPORTUNITIES

Write in two situations you can think of where you could help.

1. _____
   _____
2. _____
   _____

## PREPARING TO BUILD

First check your supplies. When you come on shift, first check to see whether supplies are sufficient, and if necessary, restock the bags at your lane. A fully stocked lane will have 400 medium bags, 100 small bags, and 200 large bags (see Figure B-2).

The bags are packaged in bales of 200. Usually you will need to bring a fresh bale or two from the storeroom to the checkout lane at the beginning of your shift.

Your supervisor will show you the storeroom and show you how to hang the bags at the checkout.

**FIGURE B-2**

The bags are prepared for use by placing the bag handles over the left and right arms of the rack, stretching the bags across the back of the rack. The rest are stored under the holding area at the end of the lane.

## It Is Up to You

Describe what you should do at the beginning of your shift.

_____
_____

Using the demonstration area, practice stocking the bagging supplies.

## BAGS COME IN THREE SIZES

So, which bag to use? Just match the bag to the size of purchase. The most commonly used bag is the one you are probably most familiar with, the medium or standard-sized plastic bag used primarily for grocery purchases (see Figure B-3).

The large bag is used for other store items such as clothing.

The small bag is obviously used for small items or for food purchases that are very cold. Cold items develop condensation and could ruin other purchases if the water that condenses on them is allowed to be in contact with the other items.

**FIGURE B-3**

## NOT EVERYTHING IS BAGGED

Oversized items such as dog food or charcoal are in their own bag and do not need additional bagging. Items with built-in handles such as milk or bleach are bagged only if the customer requests it.

### Talk to Your Customer

Some things just should not be bagged and need special handling such as goldfish or a large plant. Talk to your customer and ask how he or she would like the item handled. The register personnel will ask the customer about single-item purchases. Quite often, single-item purchases are also not bagged with the customer's consent.

### Paper or Plastic?

Plastic or paper bags are available for bagging. Plastic is the preferred based on cost, ecology issues, and ease of use. Paper is best if the customer asks for it.

Paper bags are stored beneath the holding area where they can be easily retrieved for use without promoting their use through high visibility.

## The Right Tool for the Job

Select the appropriate bag for the items in Figure B-4.

Now that your supplies are checked and ready, stand at the end of the checkout lane holding area so you can see the conveyor belt and have a view of the whole basket. The bag rack should be positioned directly in front of you. You begin by greeting the customer with a smile and saying hello. Be ready to help.

As purchases are placed on the belt, begin looking at the nature of the items and think in terms of grouping the items and building the bags. Briefly use the holding area to help arrange the purchased items into groups. However, do not let too much accumulate before bagging.

Group together items similar in nature and never mix food items with cleaning or toxic materials. Later we will look at how within the groups there are best ways to build the bag based on weight, shape, and toughness. These are principles that can be applied to anything we sell.

## Types of Grocery Items

Grocery items are usually put away at home in the same way you should group them. Not only does this help you in bagging, but it also helps the customer in putting

**FIGURE B-4**

the items away. When our customers return home, they will appreciate the extra thought and consideration.

Take a look at the following five categories that should be followed for grouping your bag-building items and a representative product from each in Figure B-5:

1. Fresh produce
2. Packaged food
3. Frozen foods
4. Cleaning or toxic items
5. Other store items

**FIGURE B-5**

## Group Descriptions

Fresh produce includes food items that are not prepackaged, such as fruits and vegetables.

Packaged foods are those that are in a box or sealed package. Examples include cereals, boxed mixes, meats, and canned goods. Packaged foods also include some dry goods like paper plates and tissues.

Frozen foods are kept in a freezer and include ice cream, frozen vegetables, and frozen pizzas.

Cleaning or toxic items are used to clean or to kill pests such as ants or mice. They should always be kept separate from other purchased items. They include bar soaps, automotive fluids, ant killers, and window cleaners.

Clothing as well as other types of store purchases should have their own bag and should not be grouped with food items.

## Preparing to Build

Match the item on the left with an example from the group on the right in Figure B-6.

1. Fresh produce
2. Packaged food
3. Frozen foods
4. Cleaning or toxic items
5. Other store items

**FIGURE B-6**

## BAG BUILDING

### Construction Principles

**Build the Walls First.**   Bags do not have built-in support. Walls need to be built with items that can give structure and define the shape of the bag (see Figure B-7). Items that look like walls, such as a box of cereal or cookies, make good walls. Then, also look for items that are packaged like a wall such as napkins or even rolls of toilet paper. Finally, look for items that can give stiffness to the sides of the bag even if they are not square, such as celery, carrots, or paper plates.

Wall items are placed at both ends of the bag to square off the bag (left and right sides as you face the hanging bag) with the center open for other items. Walls are always built first and then you should not have to move them. Also, never place an item between a wall and the bag. The bag could be torn by it.

**Lay the Floor.**   After the walls are established, the floor is laid (Figure B-8). Heavy items placed between the walls provide a solid base to support continued filling.

Put items like canned goods, flour, sugar, and glass jars between the walls. And always plan ahead. Put aside any other good wall builders you may come across for the next bag or until that is all you have left.

When square off the sides and fill in the bottom, the bag stands up and holds the contents in during the ride home. A loosely packed or top-heavy bag tips over and spills.

**FIGURE B-7**                    **FIGURE B-8**

**Fill the Space.** Once you've got a solid, tight floor across the bottom, fill up the bag with items such as boxes of pudding, drink mixes, cosmetics, and other small, lightweight items (see Figure B-9). Never build more than one layer of heavy items. More than one layer of heavy items makes the bag too hard to carry and top heavy.

Fill the rest of the bag with lighter or more fragile items. They will be protected within the walls and will not crush the items beneath. But remember the bag is not built until it is full. Top off the bag with a small loaf of bread, a bag of cookies, or a bag of chips. But put only one or two crushable items on top. If you have more, put them all together in one bag. Keep in mind that the more bags that are used means more handling for our customers as well as wasted supplies.

**FIGURE B-9**

## The Building Parts

Label each of the following items as a wall, foundation, or fill (Figure B-10).

**FIGURE B-10**

## The Building

Describe the process for building a bag.

_____
_____
_____
_____
_____

Using the demonstration area, practice bagging groceries from three carts.

## BUILDING TEAMWORK

### Inside, Outside, Underneath

As the last items are placed on the belt, help the register personnel be sure all items have been accounted for. Double-check that nothing is missed underneath the basket. The places an item may be missed during checkout are inside another item, outside the basket, or underneath (see Figure B-11). The register personnel are very busy with the transaction and may miss something that is outside the basket. As a checkout team member, you are providing backup for the register personnel. Be sure all items are accounted for through the checkout.

Items may be inside larger products. Although it is the primary responsibility of the register personnel to check, you are a team member and should follow up if an item was not checked. The customer may be absentmindedly holding an item or the item may be underneath the basket in the bottom of the cart. Just tell the register person you owe them one. This lets the team member know what to look for without embarrassment to the customer.

Remember IOU to help your recall inside, outside, and underneath the cart. Practice saying this until you have memorized it. Now, use the demonstration area and practice checking two carts.

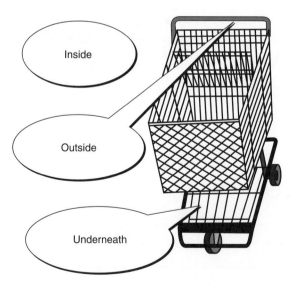

**FIGURE B-11**

# Glossary

**Affective domain**    That area of learning devoted to developing attitudes, values, or appreciations

**Application**    Performance requiring the learner to use or apply the information taught

**Assessment**    The systematic collection of data pertaining to programs or people

**Asynchronous learning networks**    A delivery system often used for distance instruction in which communication using tools such as e-mail and discussion boards does not occur in real time

**Authentic assessment**    Tasks that require the learner to demonstrate performance in a real-life context

**Behavioral objective**    Often referred to as a "Mager-style objective," this type of objective includes an observable verb, condition, and criteria written in a concise style. The typical format is condition (e.g., Given . . . , the learner will . . . at the level . . . )

**Behaviorism**    Learning theory in which subject content is divided into a series of small steps; the learner participates actively, receives feedback on effort, and is guided to success

**CD-ROM**    A compact disc containing a quantity of verbal and pictorial information, may also include a copy of one or more webpages for instructional purposes

**Client**    Person for whom instruction is being planned and who may serve as subject specialist when working with the instructional designer. May also be the individual who contracts for the training

**Cognitive domain**    That area of learning devoted to acquiring information, knowledge, and intellectual abilities relative to a subject or topic

**Cognitive load theory**    This theory focuses on the limitations of working memory and how designers can design instruction that effectively manages working memory for results

**Cognitive objective**    An objective used to describe learning intellectual skills that are not easily defined by a behavioral objective

**Cognitive strategies**    Highest level of cognitive learning, typified by problem solving

**Competency-based instruction**    Providing and evaluating instruction against a specific standard as indicated by the learning objectives for the topic or task

**Computer-based instruction (CBI)**    Uses a software program that displays information and instructions on a video screen, requiring learner participation and choices

**Concept**    Name or expression given to a class of facts, objects, or events, all of which have common features

**Confirmative evaluation**    A continuous form of evaluation that comes after summative evaluation used to determine whether a course is still effective

**Constructed-response test**    Consisting of questions requiring the learner to supply a short answer, write an essay, or solve a problem; allows for evaluation of higher-level cognitive objectives but is difficult to solve reliably

473

**Constructivism** An approach to instructional design based on the assumption that learners generate knowledge structures in their own minds

**Contextual analysis** A strategy for providing realistic information to provide rich instructional examples

**Cost center** Service provided within an organization for instructional development service with costs carried by the department

**Criterion-referenced instruction** *See* competency-based instruction

**Critical incident method** A type of task analysis for analyzing processes that is particularly well suited for applying to the analysis of interpersonal skills

**Culturally diverse learners** Students from various ethnic cultures

**Curriculum** List of courses and content framework for a subject

**Developmental costs** All personnel, resource, and service costs required to plan and develop an instructional program

**Diffusion** The process of communicating information to a client and target audience about an innovation

**Distance education** Instruction in which the instructor and student are separated in both physical location and time, requiring the instruction to be fully designed and developed prior to implementing the instruction

**Domains of learning** Cognitive, psychomotor, and affective categories

**Effectiveness** Measuring the degree to which learners accomplish objectives for each unit or a total course

**Efficiency** Measuring the amount of learner time, personnel services, and facilities use required to carry out an instructional program, and then deciding whether these amounts are acceptable or excessive

**E-learning** Learning from instruction offered via the Internet or intranet

**Evaluation** Using assessment or measurement to judge the worth or success of something

**Evaluator** Person responsible for assisting the instructor in designing tests to measure student learning, conduct formative, summative, and confirmative evaluations, and analyze results

**Fact** A statement associating one item to another

**Feedback** Providing the learner with answers to exercises and other information relative to progress in learning

**Flowchart** Visual description of the sequence necessary for performing a task, including decision points and alternate paths

**Formative evaluation** Testing a new instructional program with a sampling of learners during the development phase, and using the results to improve the program's front-end analysis

**Generative learning** An approach that helps the learner relate new information to prior information that results in new and/or revised schema

**Goal analysis** A process used to identify the initial outcomes or intents of an instructional intervention

**Goal statement** Broad statement describing what should take place in an instructional course or training program

**Human performance improvement** A strategy for improving productivity by considering various interventions in addition to training

**Individualized learning** Allowing learners to learn by providing each one with objectives and activities appropriate to his or her own characteristics, preparation, needs, and interests

**Instructional cost index** Mathematical calculation of the cost per learner or trainee to accomplish objectives for a topic or course, taking into account a portion of the developmental cost and implementation costs

**Instructional design** Systematic planning of instruction in which attention is given to nine related elements

**Instructional designer** Person responsible for carrying out and coordinating the systematic design procedure

**Instructional development** Managing the planning, development, and implementation procedure for instruction or training

**Instructional message design** The process of creating an effective message by manipulating words, pictures, and symbols

**Instructional need** A gap in performance between what is expected and actual performance that is best addressed through an instructional intervention

**Instructional objective** Statement describing what the learner is specifically required to learn or accomplish relative to a topic or task

**Instructional systems** A group of interdependent parts that work together to accomplish a goal such as a classroom or learning management system.

**Instructional technology** Resources (e.g., machines and materials) used for instruction and a process of systematic instructional planning

**Instructional theory** A prescriptive theory based on a learning theory that provides prescriptions for designing effective instruction

**Intellectual skills** Organizing and structuring facts for learning to form concepts, principles, rules, attitudes, and interactions

**Interactive technologies** Media forms that require frequent active participation by the student as learning takes place

**Interpersonal skills** Spoken and nonverbal (e.g., body language) interaction between two or more individuals

**Learner characteristics** Factors relating to personal and social traits of individuals and learner groups that need consideration during planning or learning

**Learning** A relatively permanent change in behavior that may or may not be the result of instruction

**Learning objective** This term is used in two ways. When the objective focuses on the product of the instruction, it is synonymous with a behavioral objective. A second use of this term is to describe the process of the instruction, which is quite different from the focus and purpose of a behavioral objective

**Learning styles** Various methods of learning that are preferred by individuals

**Learning systems design** Another expression for the instructional design concept

**Learning theory** A descriptive theory that explains and predicts how individuals learn

**Mastery-based instruction** *See* competency-based instruction

**Mastery learning** Indicating whether a learner successfully accomplishes the necessary level of learning for required objectives

**Module** A self-instructional package treating a single topic or unit of a course

**Multimedia** Computer program controlling display of verbal information along with still photographs, video, and audio sequences in various formats

**Needs assessment or analysis** Procedure of gathering information before deciding whether there is a substantive need for instruction or training

**Norm-referenced testing** Evaluating the results of instruction in a relative fashion by comparing test scores of each learner with those of other learners in the class

**Objective test** Consisting of questions for which a learner must select an answer from two or more alternatives; persons scoring the test can easily agree on the correct answer

**Operational costs** All costs of personnel resources and services incurred as an instructional program is being implemented

**Organization management** Management of an instructional development service that broadly includes all design and delivery functions

**Performance-based instruction** *See* competency-based instruction

**Performance gap** Where actual performance is not equal to or better than expected performance. A variety of interventions, including instruction, are used to improve performance

**Performance objective** A synonym for behavioral objectives (*see* behavioral objective)

**Posttest** Final examination given at the end of a course or training program (as opposed to pretest)

**Prerequisite test** Portion of a pretest that measures content or skill preparation a learner has for starting the course or unit

**Presentation teaching method** Technique used to disseminate information

**Pretest** Test administered prior to the start of instruction to determine the level of the learner's knowledge and the necessary preparation relative to a topic or task

**Principle** Expression of a relationship between concepts

**Procedural analysis** Used to identify the steps required to complete a task or series of tasks

**Procedure** Sequence of steps one follows to achieve a goal

**Profit center** Service provided within and outside an organization for instructional design services with costs charged to the client or sponsor

**Project management** Responsibilities for all functions that relate to the conduct of an instructional design project

**Psychomotor domain** That area of learning devoted to becoming proficient in performing a physical action involving muscles of the body

**Reinforcement learning** Receiving feedback on success in learning, thus being encouraged to continue learning

**Reliability** Ability of a test to produce consistent results when used with comparable learners

**Request for proposal (RFP)** Paper form with instructions to be completed when submitting a bid or proposal for a project to be funded

**Scope of work** The definition of the boundaries of a project that requires the consensus of the stakeholders

**Self-paced learning environment** Learning environment that allows the learner to satisfy required learning activities by accomplishing the objectives at his or her own speed or convenience

**Subject-matter expert (SME)** Person qualified to provide content, resources, and information relating to topics and tasks for which instruction is being designed

**Summative evaluation** Measuring how well the major outcomes of a course or program are attained at the conclusion of instruction (posttest) or thereafter on the job

**Support services** Matters such as budget, facilities, equipment, and materials that require attention for the successful preparation and implementation of a new instructional program

**Systems approach** An overall plan to problem solving that gives attention to all essential elements

**Task analysis** A collection of procedures for analyzing the information needed to achieve the objectives. *See also* topic analysis *and* procedural analysis

**Topic analysis** A task analysis procedure for identifying and describing the topics (including facts, concepts, and principles) related to a goal or need

**Validity** Direct relationship between test questions and the learning objectives

# Index